Valle
d'Aosta
Piemonte
Liguria
Trentino-
Alto Adige
Lombardia
Emilia-
Romagna
Marche
Friuli
Venezia
Giulia
Veneto

Adriatico

Sardegna

Donated
In Memory of

Michael d. Pane V

by:

Alexander and
Clarissa Pane
2018

a
Basilicata

Calabria

Osteria

Sicilia

Mediterraneo

1,000 GENEROUS AND SIMPLE RECIPES

SLOW FOOD EDITORE

Osteria

Translated by
Natalie Danford

FROM ITALY'S BEST LOCAL RESTAURANTS

RIZZOLI
NEW YORK

New York · Paris · London · Milan

TABLE OF CONTENTS

INTRODUCTION

In Italy, food is all. Cooking and eating run through almost every conversation. There is no event—from a multigenerational holiday gathering to an afternoon coffee break for a couple of friends—without food or drink served, passed around, dissected, and discussed.

Food is also highly local, a legacy of the days when Italy consisted of a series of distinct city-states, each with its own language, currency, ruler, and traditions. Local food products make Italy special. A Sicilia without cannoli or Parma without its beloved prosciutto is unimaginable. An Italian could be set down at a table in a restaurant almost anywhere in the country blindfolded, be served a meal, and instantly pinpoint the location (or perhaps be left befuddled by an entirely unfamiliar food, even within a fifty-mile radius of the place where that same person has lived his or her entire life).

Nowhere is this more true than at the type of restaurant known as an *osteria*. An *osteria* is the polar opposite of a tourist trap. These are home-away-from-home places frequented by locals, and many are situated in small towns and hamlets. They serve dishes that at an earlier time were known only to a handful of people, based on recipes passed down through generations by word-of-mouth. In short, the *osteria* is the kind of unpretentious Italian restaurant that for centuries has thrilled visitors and nourished Italians with simple, soulful regional cooking and local wines. The food eaten in an Italian *osteria* is a map, both atlas and guidebook. It is a history text and a mythology. An identity card and a photo album. But most of all, it is a source of joy.

Slow Food, which scoured the peninsula of Italy from top to bottom and out to its islands to gather the recipes in this book, celebrates Italian food, especially its highly local quality and its long and rich traditions. Slow Food was founded in 1989 to prevent the disappearance of local food cultures and traditions. Though the organization originated in Italy (in reaction to the announced opening of a McDonald's on Rome's Spanish Steps), it is now active in more than 160 countries and involves millions of participants. Among other activities, Slow Food has a program called the Ark of Taste that collects small-scale quality food products: fruits, vegetables, animal breeds, cheeses, breads, sweets, cured meats, and more. Many of those products are showcased in recipes in this book. A product that is at particular risk of extinction may be safeguarded through the creation of a specific Slow Food Presidium. At the time of this writing, there are 513 such presidia. Slow Food recognizes restaurants that adhere to its stringent guidelines and produce delicious food. For Italian restaurants, having a Slow Food snail sticker on the door is a big boon—the down-to-earth equivalent of a Michelin star.

Slow Food also has a publishing arm. The guidebook *Osterie d'Italia* was Slow Food's first book (the earliest edition dates to 1990) and is a beloved source for foodies traveling in Italy. Rather than focusing on slick, high-end eateries, the guidebook spotlights the singularly Italian phenomenon of the *osteria*. Though this is a cookbook and not a guidebook, it does contain a recipe index by location (and course) so that you can explore the food of a particular area. It might even inspire you to plan a pilgrimage to eat in some of the restaurants whose dishes you have relished, but in the meantime, I hope this book will afford you the experience of visiting those eateries in your own kitchen or dining room.

To create this book, Slow Food solicited recipes from chefs whose restaurants had been listed in *Osterie d'Italia* over the previous twenty years, with an emphasis on the dishes they offer to their customers every day and that are made with seasonal and available ingredients. Slow Food then diligently worked to transform those into recipes for home cooks rather than restaurant kitchens, and to translate instructions into terms that nonprofessionals could understand. Finally, they filled in obvious gaps—local recipes considered vital—with recipes from home cooks, some of them professionals in the food world, and others simply enthusiasts highly regarded in their home areas. In documenting these recipes, Slow Food was also documenting a way of life.

The original book contained even more recipes than this one—I worked with Slow Food to pare the number down to 1,000 or so essential local specialties. Each recipe is labeled with the original name (often in dialect rather than standard Italian), the English translation, the name of the contributing restaurant or individual, and the city, province (unless the city is the province capital), and region. Headnotes explain the origins of the dishes and offer serving tips, wine pairings, storage suggestions, variations, and the like. I have retained the unique colloquial voices of the cooks and all of their idiosyncratic techniques while supplying details that should help those of us who did not have the good fortune to learn and observe these techniques from a young age to use the recipes successfully.

The original Italian introduction to this book contains this sentence: *The kitchen, where the pleasure of food is born, should never be turned into a pharmacist's laboratory.* Indeed, the original recipes were sometimes casual by U.S. standards; pan sizes, ingredient amounts, and even yields were lacking. I have tried to clarify the recipes without making them into formulas, and with a few duly noted exceptions, they are incredibly flexible. There's a reason Italians have never adopted rigid recipe codification: cooking Italian food simply doesn't require it. For example, most recipes do not provide specific amounts of oil for sautéing or for drizzling on a finished dish. You can (within the obvious parameters) alter those measurements to your personal taste (and rest assured that an Italian would likely use twice as much oil as you instinctively would). Techniques such as kneading pasta dough and then rolling it out are rarely described in Italian recipes—that falls into the category of "everybody knows." I have included guidelines here where they seemed necessary.

I have also included substitutions for items (species of Mediterranean fish, for example) that may be hard to find outside of Italy, but don't be afraid to experiment. Using something similar that's fresh and available locally, possibly something from your own garden, may even get you closer in feel to the original than tracking down (and paying exorbitantly for) the specified Italian item. Though Italy's culinary heritage, as reflected on the tables of its *osterie*, is long and proud, it is not static or set in stone. It is a living thing affected by daily life, mood, curiosity, and interaction with others. If you abide by the basic rules of Italian cooking—using what's available, respecting those ingredients, and, most importantly, approaching food and cooking as a source of fun and an expression of love—you will always create something delicious.

Natalie Danford, *Translator*

Frittelle di Baccalà
Frega di Pomodoro
Frittelle di Zucca
Cracchè di Patate
Pizza con le Alici
Focaccia Ortolana
Pizza di Scarola
Subrich di Patate
Fettunta

ANTIPASTI

Farinata
Frisceu di Erbe
Frittata di Cipolle
Melanzane Ripiene
Insalata di Ovoli
Flan di Carciofi
Vitello Tonnato
Agliata di Polpo
& Many More

2

PIZZA DI SCAROLA
Escarole Pie
Trattoria La Chitarra, Naples, Campania

Pizza di scarola, as the name indicates, is a relative of the world's most famous flatbread, pizza, which is native to the Campania region in general and to Naples in particular. Salty capers and olives add punch to the filling and are balanced by the sweetness of the raisins.

SERVES 6 TO 8
DOUGH
- 2¼ teaspoons (one envelope) active dry yeast
- 2¾ cups unbleached all-purpose flour
- 7 tablespoons lard or vegetable shortening
- 1 pinch salt

FILLING
- 2 pounds escarole
- Salt to taste
- ½ cup extra-virgin olive oil
- 2 cloves garlic
- ¼ cup black Gaeta olives, pitted and coarsely chopped
- 2 tablespoons capers, rinsed and drained
- Crushed red chili pepper to taste (optional)
- 2 tablespoons black raisins, soaked in warm water and squeezed dry
- 1 tablespoon pine nuts
- 1 salted anchovy, rinsed, boned, and minced

To make the dough, dissolve the yeast in a small amount of warm water and set aside until bubbly, about 5 minutes. Combine the flour, yeast mixture, lard, and salt and knead until it forms a soft dough. When you slice the dough with a knife, the surface should be dotted with small holes and consistent. Set the dough aside at room temperature, covered, until doubled in size, 1 to 2 hours. You can also prepare the dough one day in advance and refrigerate it overnight. Just be sure to remove it from the refrigerator at least 2 hours before baking in order to allow it to come to room temperature.

For the filling, blanch the escarole in lightly salted water until just tender. Drain, cool, and then wrap in a flat-weave dish towel and squeeze very dry. Chop the greens. In a large skillet, heat the olive oil and sauté the garlic, stirring frequently so that it doesn't burn. Add the olives, capers, and the chili pepper if using.

Add the escarole, the raisins, the pine nuts, and the anchovy. Cook over medium heat, stirring occasionally, until the escarole is completely dry and not a trace of water remains. Taste and adjust salt. Then drain the filling of any excess oil and set aside.

When you are ready to bake the pie, preheat the oven to 425°F. Cut the dough in half. On a lightly floured wooden work surface, roll out half of the dough until thinner than ⅛ inch and use it to line a 12-inch pan with sides at least 1½ inches high. Poke holes all over the surface with a fork, then distribute the filling evenly over the bottom crust. Roll out the other half of the dough and place it on top of the pie. Crimp the edges to seal. Pierce the top crust in several places with a toothpick and bake in the preheated oven until lightly browned on top, 50 to 55 minutes.

Serve at room temperature or cold.

TORTA AL TESTO CON VERDURE 🌳
Griddle Cake with Greens
Taverna di Trimalcione, Perugia, Umbria

One of the signature dishes of the Umbria region, this flatbread is traditionally baked on a round baking stone, called a *testo*, that is placed on top of a burner (or heated in a wood-burning oven). A cast-iron pan or griddle makes a fine substitute.

SERVES 4

DOUGH
3½ cups unbleached all-purpose flour
2¼ teaspoons (one envelope) instant yeast
2 tablespoons whole milk
2 tablespoons extra-virgin olive oil
Salt to taste

FILLING
4 ounces spinach
4 ounces Swiss chard
4 ounces chicory
Salt to taste
1 clove garlic
Extra-virgin olive oil for sautéing

To make the dough, form a well on the work surface with the flour and place the other dough ingredients in the center of the well. Whisk together the milk and oil, slowly incorporating flour from the sides of the well until you have a crumbly mixture. Knead the dough until firm and soft. Shape the dough into a ball, cover with a damp towel, and set aside to rest for 30 minutes.

For the filling, blanch the greens in salted water. Drain, squeeze dry, chop, and then sauté the greens briefly with the garlic clove in a generous amount of olive oil. Set aside.

Roll out the dough to about ⅓ inch thick. Heat a testo or a cast-iron griddle or pan until a drop of water sizzles on it and then cook the bread directly on the surface, rotating it frequently with a fork and flipping it occasionally, until it is cooked through and the surface is mottled with brown spots.

Split the bread in half horizontally and spread the cooked greens on one half. Top with the other half and cut into wedges. Serve warm.

FOCACCIA ORTOLANA
Vegetable Focaccia
Giuliano Guidi, San Costanzo (Pesaro and Urbino), Marche

To make a double-crust focaccia large enough to serve 6, mince blanched asparagus, artichokes, potatoes, and wild greens and toss with olive oil to moisten. Taste and adjust salt. Make a dough of 3½ cups unbleached all-purpose flour, 1 envelope (2¼ teaspoons) yeast dissolved in a small amount of room temperature water, a pinch of salt, a pinch of sugar, and 1 tablespoon extra-virgin olive oil. Knead until smooth, then divide the dough into 2 equal pieces and roll both out to thin disks. Use one disk to line a cake or pie pan and scatter the vegetable mixture on top. Sprinkle on ½ cup grated Parmigiano Reggiano. Top with the second disk of dough and press edges together to seal. Brush the top with a little more oil and pierce with a fork in a few spots. Bake in a preheated 325°F oven until golden, about 30 minutes. Serve hot.

FUAZZA
Stuffed Spinach Roll
Osteria del Cacciatore, Torre di Castrofilippo
(Agrigento), Sicilia

Slices of this spinach roll form pretty pinwheels.

SERVES 4

DOUGH
- 2 cups unbleached all-purpose flour
- 2¼ teaspoons (one envelope) active dry yeast, dissolved in a small amount of room temperature water or milk
- Salt to taste

FILLING
- 2 pounds spinach
- Extra-virgin olive oil for moistening filling
- Salt and freshly ground black pepper to taste

To make the dough, form the flour into a well and pour the yeast mixture into the center. Add a pinch of salt and ½ cup room temperature water. Knead until you have a well combined and elastic dough. Set aside to rest for at least 20 minutes and up to 2 hours.

In the meantime, for the filling, blanch the spinach, drain, squeeze dry, and set aside to cool. Chop the cooked spinach and combine with enough olive oil to make a moist mixture and season with salt and pepper.

If you are using a pizza stone, place it in your oven. Preheat the oven as hot as it will go, probably 500°F. With a rolling pin, roll out the dough into a thin sheet. Arrange the cooked spinach on the dough and, working carefully, roll up the dough jelly-roll style. Pinch the edges to seal, place on a baking sheet (or directly on a pizza stone if you are using one) and bake until the outside is crisp, about 45 minutes. Allow to cool slightly before slicing.

PITTA DI PATATE
Potato Pizza
Trattoria Rua de li Travaj, Patù (Lecce), Puglia

What elsewhere in Italy is known as focaccia is called *pitta* (from the same root as "pizza") in the South. It is most typically a yeast-risen dough, baked in the oven, cut in half, and then stuffed with various fillings or simply topped with lashings of olive oil and salt and pepper. This is a variation on that traditional pitta made with a "dough" of cooked potatoes.

SERVES 8 TO 10
- 2 pounds (about 6 medium) yellow potatoes
- Salt to taste
- 4 large eggs
- ¼ cup tomato sauce
- 2 cups grated aged cheese
- 2 tablespoons extra-virgin olive oil plus more for oiling the pan and handling the dough
- Leaves of 1 sprig parsley, minced
- Freshly ground black pepper to taste
- 1 cup breadcrumbs

Boil the potatoes in lightly salted water until they are easily pierced with a knife. Set aside to cool, peel, and then crush with a potato ricer, letting them fall into a large bowl. Add the eggs, the tomato sauce (cold), the grated cheese, 2 tablespoons olive oil, and the minced parsley. Season with salt and pepper and mix by hand until well combined.

Preheat the oven to 400°F. Oil a cake or pie pan and arrange the dough on the pan. Generously oil your hands and use them to spread the dough out into the pan. Sprinkle the breadcrumbs over the surface. Pierce in several places with a fork and bake in the preheated oven until golden brown, about 30 minutes.

PIZZA RIPIENA DI BIETOLE 🐚
Swiss Chard Pies
Ristorante La Vecchia Quercia, Cerreto Sannita (Benevento), Campania

These individual pies never fail to impress, though they're not difficult to make. If you use sourdough starter, keep in mind that rising time can vary widely.

SERVES 6

DOUGH
2¼ teaspoons (one envelope) active dry yeast or 3 tablespoons active sourdough starter
5   cups unbleached all-purpose flour
Salt to taste
Extra-virgin olive oil for pans and drizzling

FILLING
1½ pounds tender Swiss chard
10 ounces prosciutto or dried sausage, diced
6   ounces aged sheep's cheese, grated
2 to 3 cloves garlic, minced
Salt to taste
Crushed red chili pepper to taste (optional)

To make the dough, dissolve the yeast or starter in a small amount of warm water and set aside until bubbly, about 5 minutes. Form a well with the flour on a work surface and add the yeast mixture and salt to the center of the well. Slowly incorporate flour from the sides of the well until you have a crumbly mixture. Knead the dough until soft. Divide the dough into 6 equal pieces, cover, and set aside to rest for 2 hours.

Meanwhile, for the filling, cut the chard into ribbons and combine with the prosciutto, cheese, garlic, salt, and chili pepper, if using. Mix to combine.

When you are ready to bake the pies, preheat the oven to 350°F. Oil six 8-inch pans and set aside. Divide one of the balls of dough in half and press out half into a circle about 8 inches in diameter and less than ¼ inch thick. Place in one of the prepared pans. Repeat with remaining balls of dough. Divide the filling among the pans, then roll out the remaining 6 pieces of dough and place those on top of the pies. Pinch the perimeter of the top and bottom crusts together to seal. Drizzle a little oil on each one and pierce the top crusts with a fork in several places.

Bake in the preheated oven until golden, 30 to 40 minutes.

PIZZA DE TURCO CON CICORIA ❦
Cornmeal Pizza with Chicory
Ristorante Belsito, Serrone (Frosinone), Lazio

Traditionally, the cornmeal mixture for the crust here is made using a special iron spatula, and ideally the mixture is cooked in a wood-burning oven. If you are lucky enough to have access to a wood-burning oven, pour the mixture directly onto a baking stone and cover it with a lid, then top the lid with hot ash.

SERVES 4

1 pound chicory greens, preferably wild
Salt to taste
2⅓ cups finely ground cornmeal
Extra-virgin olive oil for sautéing
2 cloves garlic
Finely ground red chili pepper to taste

Boil the greens in lightly salted water for 30 minutes. Drain, set aside to cool, then squeeze dry and chop.

Preheat the oven to 350°F. Bring 2 cups water to a boil and lightly salt the water. Mix together the water and the cornmeal and then spread the mixture in a 13-inch pan and bake in the preheated oven until firm to the touch.

Meanwhile, heat olive oil in a skillet and sauté the garlic cloves in the oil. Add the greens and chili pepper and sauté until the greens have absorbed the flavor, 3 to 5 minutes.

Remove the pizza from the oven, split it in half horizontally, and arrange the spinach mixture between the two halves (like a sandwich). Cut into pieces and serve.

PIZZALANDREA
Pizza with Tomatoes, Olives, and Sardines
Margherita Trucco, San Remo (Imperia), Liguria

This Ligurian flatbread probably takes its name from the Provençal specialty *pissaladière*. It goes by many other names, including *sardenaira*, *piscialà*, *pisciadela*, *machetusa*, *pasta cu a pumata*, and *machetaera*). Variations are myriad. This version highlights tomato and a strong garlic flavor, but others use onions, often flavored with thyme, bay leaf, and garlic and cooked low and slow until they dissolve into a puree. Still other versions include capers crushed with a mortar and pestle along with anchovies and black olives and then spread over the dough.

To make a small pizza to serve four, shape 2¾ cups all-purpose flour into a well on the work surface. Dissolve 1 envelope (2¼ teaspoons) yeast in 1 cup room temperature water and place in the center of the well with ½ cup extra-virgin olive oil and ¼ teaspoon salt. Knead into a soft dough, adding up to ½ cup whole milk if necessary. Shape into a ball, cover with a wool cloth, and set in a warm spot to rise for 1 hour. While the dough is rising, in a terra-cotta pan cook minced onion until translucent, then add peeled, seeded, and minced plum tomatoes, a bay leaf, a little salt, and a little sugar. Cook, stirring frequently, for 20 minutes, until it forms a sauce, but don't let it reduce so much that it sticks to the pan. Oil a 14-inch pizza pan and stretch the dough into the pan with your fingertips. Distribute the prepared sauce over the dough. Scatter on ¼ cup pitted Taggiasca olives, 12 whole cloves garlic, chopped sardine fillets, and dried oregano. Drizzle with additional olive oil and allow to rise for 1 additional hour, then bake in a 400°F oven until the crust is browned, 30 to 40 minutes.

ARVOLTO CON POMODORI PICCANTI 🍅
Fried Spicy Tomato Flatbreads
Locanda di Nonna Gelsa, Niccone di Umbertide (Perugia), Umbria

Arvolto (also known as *arvoltolo, bustrengo, tortuccia,* and *fregnaccia*) is a piece of fried dough that takes on a contorted look. It may be either sweet or savory.

SERVES 4 TO 6
Salt to taste
3½ cups unbleached all-purpose flour
Extra-virgin olive oil for frying and sautéing
2   cloves garlic
1½ pounds plum tomatoes, peeled, seeded, and roughly chopped
¼   teaspoon minced chili pepper

Add enough lightly salted water to the flour to create a soft, smooth dough. Divide the dough into equal-sized pieces by weight (5 to 6 ounces each), shape each piece into a ball, and set them aside on your work surface. Cover with a damp dish towel and allow to rest for 10 minutes.

Roll out the balls of dough one at a time. Their diameter should be just slightly smaller than the diameter of the pan you will use to fry them.

Line several baking sheets with paper towels. Fill a skillet with high sides with several inches of oil and heat until very hot but not smoking. Add one of the flatbreads. When it begins to puff, carefully turn it over using tongs. When both sides of the flatbread are brown, transfer to the prepared baking sheets. Repeat with the remaining circles of dough.

When the breads have all been cooked, sauté the garlic over medium heat. When the garlic has browned, add the tomatoes and cook until dissolving, about 10 minutes. Season with salt and the minced chili pepper.

To serve, arrange each flatbread on an individual serving plate, cut into quarters, and top with the tomato sauce.

FRICIEU ●
Savory Yeasted Fritters
Trattoria delle Langhe, Serole (Asti), Piemonte

Fricieu and *friciula* are Piemonte dialect words (in this dialect, "*eu*" is pronounced as it is in French) meaning "fritter." In some provinces these two words are synonymous and both refer to risen bread dough, rolled into a sheet, cut into lozenges, and fried. Today, these fritters are often served with cured meats. Fricieu may also be sweet, usually made with flour, yeast, white wine or Marsala, eggs, butter, sugar, lemon zest, and—for Carnival—raisins and apple slices. Another lovely seasonal variation incorporates zucchini blossoms into the batter for fricieu.

SERVES 6
2¼ teaspoons (one envelope) active dry yeast
2½ cups sparkling water at room temperature
4   large eggs, separated
2   cups unbleached all-purpose flour or 00 flour
2   cups whole milk at room temperature
Salt and freshly ground black pepper to taste
4   cups peanut oil

Dissolve the yeast in ½ cup sparkling water. Beat the egg whites to a stiff peak. In a bowl, combine the flour, egg yolks, the remaining 2 cups sparkling water, and the yeast mixture; season with salt and pepper. Whisk energetically until well combined and smooth. Set the mixture aside to rest for 45 minutes, then gently fold in the whipped egg whites.

Line a baking sheet with paper towels and set aside. Pour the oil into a deep pot and heat until very hot but not smoking. Drop the batter in by the spoonful. As the fritters brown, scoop them out with a skimmer or slotted spoon. Transfer to the prepared baking sheet to drain. Serve piping hot.

BARBAGIUAI ALLE ERBE ♣
Fried Dumplings Filled with Greens
Trattoria Armonia, Bajardo (Imperia), Liguria

Ristorante Terme di Pigna (also in the province of Imperia) makes a very different version of *barbagiuai*. In addition to greens and grated cheese, the filling incorporates pureed yellow squash and rice cooked in a mixture of milk and water. Still other versions use the fermented goat's milk ricotta known as *brusso* or *bruzzu* (a cousin to the bross cheese found in Piemonte).

SERVES 6

DOUGH
3½ cups unbleached all-purpose flour
Salt to taste
3 tablespoons extra-virgin olive oil

FILLING
1½ pounds chard
1½ pounds wild greens (borage, nettles, chicory)
Salt to taste
Leaves of 1 sprig parsley
Leaves of 1 sprig marjoram
6 ounces mortadella, diced
4 ounces prosciutto cotto, diced
2 large eggs, lightly beaten
1 cup grated Parmigiano Reggiano
Freshly ground black pepper to taste
Freshly grated nutmeg to taste
Extra-virgin olive oil for frying

To make the dough, place the flour and salt in a medium bowl and add the olive oil. Stir in enough warm (not hot) water to create a soft, malleable dough. Cover and refrigerate until chilled.

Meanwhile, for the filling, blanch the greens in lightly salted water. Transfer the cooked greens to a colander and when they are cool enough to handle, squeeze them dry, then mince them together with the parsley leaves, marjoram leaves, mortadella, and prosciutto cotto. Stir together with the eggs and grated cheese and season to taste with salt, pepper, and nutmeg. Knead the mixture until it forms a firm ball.

Remove the dough from the refrigerator. Cut off half of the dough, leaving the other half covered, and roll it out into a circle about 4 inches in diameter. Set aside and roll out the second half of the dough to the same size. As if making ravioli, arrange bits of the filling at regular intervals along one sheet of dough. Place the other sheet of dough on top of it and press between the portions of filling with your fingertips to make the two sheets of dough adhere. Using a pastry cutter, cut the dumplings between the portions of filling. Fry in olive oil until browned and serve hot.

CIACCIA AL FORMAGGIO ▦
Cheese Flatbread
Isabella Dalla Ragione, Città di Castello (Perugia), Umbria

To make a large flatbread that serves 8 to 12, dissolve 2 envelopes (1 tablespoon plus ½ teaspoon) yeast in room temperature water, then combine with ⅓ cup unbleached all-purpose flour to make a starter. Cover and set aside to rest for 1 hour. Make a well on the work surface with another 10 cups flour and place the starter, 12 eggs, 10 ounces leaf lard, 2 cups grated aged sheep's cheese, 2 cups diced young sheep's cheese, and salt and pepper to taste in the well. Knead into a soft, elastic dough. Pat into an oiled pan with high sides, cover, and let rest in a warm place until doubled in size. Bake in a preheated 400°F oven until lightly golden, about 50 minutes. Rub the surface generously with a pork rind and return to the oven until golden brown, about 10 additional minutes.

COCCOI PRENA 🦪
Small Sourdough Pies with Tomato and Garlic Filling
Gianni Serra, Carbonia, Sardegna

Traditionally, a piece of the dough would be held back and kept in a cool place to use as a starter for the next batch, but if you don't have a starter, make one by kneading together 1½ cups semolina flour and ⅔ cup all-purpose flour with 1 cup warm water (preferably bottled mineral water, not tap water). Cover and allow to ferment in a warm draft-free place for 2 to 3 days.

On the day you want to bake the pies, combine the starter with an additional 1 cup semolina flour and enough water to make a soft dough. Let the dough rest again for 2 hours. Finally, knead in ⅓ cup all-purpose flour and enough water to make a soft dough and let it rest again until doubled in size, about 1 hour. Divide the dough into 12 equal pieces and set aside to rest for 1 hour.

Seed about 1½ pounds ripe tomatoes, chop, salt lightly, and drain in a colander for 2 hours. Combine the tomatoes with torn basil leaves and minced garlic. Season with salt, pepper, and a drizzle of mastic oil or olive oil. (Don't go overboard if using mastic oil—it has a strong flavor.) Set aside to rest for at least 1 hour.

Lightly oil and flour pans large enough to hold the rolls with a few inches between them on all sides. Roll out the balls of dough with a rolling pin to about 5 inches in diameter, leaving the perimeters thicker (like a pizza crust). Place the dough on the pans and divide the filling among them evenly, about 1 tablespoon each. Fold the edges of the dough up so they don't quite meet in the middle, leaving a hole at the top of each pie. Folded pies should be about 3 inches in diameter. Brush with additional olive oil, then bake in a preheated 500°F oven until golden, about 30 minutes. Brush the pies with a little more olive oil when you remove them from the oven, then allow to cool and serve warm or at room temperature.

BORLENGHI ❗
Thin Flatbread
Agriturismo Tizzano, Monteombraro di Zocca (Modena), Emília-Romagna

Borlenghi are served in place of bread in the hills around Modena. These very thin unleavened breads look a little like Sardegna's famously thin carta da musica flatbreads, but they taste completely different. Borlenghi are traditionally served with pisté—diced pancetta and a little crumbled sausage sautéed with garlic and rosemary and sprinkled with grated Parmigiano Reggiano. Place a tablespoon or two of that mixture in the center of a flatbread, fold it in four, and eat with your hands. This is a great rustic appetizer before an informal meal with friends.

SERVES 6
- 1 large egg
- 2⅓ cups unbleached all-purpose flour or 0 flour
- Salt to taste
- 1 piece pork rind

Beat the egg with the flour and a pinch of salt. Gradually beat in 5 cups plus 3 tablespoons water until you have a thin batter. Set a pan (copper if you have one) that is at least 18 inches in diameter over low heat. Grease lightly by rubbing it with the pork rind, then pour in about ½ cup of the batter and quickly tilt the pan all around to cover the surface completely. When the bottom of the bread is set, flip and cook the other side. Repeat with the remaining batter. Each bread should cook for at least 10 minutes over low heat, and they will be very thin and crisp when cooked.

BACIOCCA CON I FUNGHI ◗
Mushroom and Potato Galette
Trattoria La Brinca, Ne (Genova), Liguria

Quarantina potatoes from the Genova area are an ancient variety of white potato that has been rescued from extinction. These potatoes have a dense texture and thin skin. They grow about 1,000 feet above sea level. They are, however, difficult if not impossible to track down outside of Liguria, so you will most likely have to substitute another type of white potato in this recipe. Note that no amount is given for the mushrooms in this recipe—aim for 3 to 4 cups once they are sliced. Always clean mushrooms very gently with a damp cloth, shaking them to remove any loose dirt or insects.

SERVES 6
1 pound Quarantina potatoes (see note)
Salt to taste
1 medium red onion, thinly sliced
Extra-virgin olive oil for sautéing
1½ cups plus 1 tablespoon unbleached all-purpose flour or 00 flour
Mixed wild mushrooms, such as porcini, russulas, chanterelles, black trumpets, and parasol mushrooms, sliced
1 clove garlic, minced
Leaves of 1 sprig parsley, minced

Boil the potatoes in lightly salted water until tender. Drain and peel the cooked potatoes, then slice them thinly. Transfer the potatoes to a medium bowl. Sauté the onion in a small amount of olive oil until just turning golden, then combine with the potatoes. Dissolve 1 tablespoon flour in a small amount of water with a pinch of salt and toss that mixture with the potatoes as well.

Sauté the mushrooms in a small amount of olive oil with the garlic and parsley just until wilted, about 3 minutes.

Preheat the oven to 350°F.

Combine the remaining 1½ cups flour with a pinch of salt and enough warm water to make

a soft dough. Roll out the dough to a circle or square (depending on which type of pan you're going to use) and place it on a pan. Leaving a 2-inch margin on all sides, arrange a layer of the potato mixture on top of the dough. Cover that with a layer of the mushroom mixture, then continue, alternating layers, and ending with a layer of potatoes on top. Fold the empty border of the dough over the filling. Bake in the preheated oven until golden, about 30 minutes, and serve hot.

CALZONE CON LE SPUNZALE ▬
Wild Onion Calzone
Grazia Galante, San Marco in Lamis (Foggia), Puglia

Spunzale are wild onions that appear in the spring. Your own local spring onions will make a fine substitute. This is best made in a very hot wood-burning oven, but instructions for using your home oven are provided below. Because this uses a sourdough starter, rising time can vary widely.

Combine 7 cups flour and 1 tablespoon starter and enough salted water to make a soft dough. Knead until elastic, then shape the dough into a ball, cover with a damp cloth, and set aside to rise. (It should look puffy and risen when ready.) While the dough is rising, sauté 2 pounds thinly sliced wild onions in a small amount of oil with a pinch of salt. Preheat your oven as high as it will go with a baking stone in it. Divide the dough into two equal portions and roll each one into a disk. Place one circle of dough on a peel, scatter the onion mixture, a dozen or so rinsed, boned, and chopped salted anchovies, and ¼ cup pitted black olives on top. Sprinkle with black pepper and drizzle with olive oil. Place the second circle of dough on top and pinch the edges together to seal. Brush the top with additional oil, sprinkle with a little salt, and sprinkle on a little additional pepper if desired. Bake in the preheated oven until golden brown and serve hot or cold.

CROSTATA DI CIPOLLE BIONDE 🧀
Savory Onion Bread Pudding
Ristorante Belvedere, Gremiasco (Alessandria), Piemonte

The same method used to make a sweet bread pudding can be used to create savory versions as well.

SERVES 4

- 6 tablespoons unsalted butter, plus more for buttering pan
- ½ cup extra-virgin olive oil
- 8 medium yellow onions, thinly sliced
- Salt and freshly ground black pepper to taste
- 2 tablespoons unbleached all-purpose flour
- 2 cups vegetable broth
- 20 slices rustic bread or sliced white sandwich bread, crusts removed
- ½ cup grated Parmigiano Reggiano
- ½ cup grated Emmental (Swiss) cheese

Preheat the oven to 350°F on the convection setting if your oven has this feature. Butter a casserole (just about the right size to hold the bread in one layer or overlapping slightly) and set aside.

Combine the 6 tablespoons butter and olive oil in a pot over medium-low heat. When the butter has melted, add the onions and cook until very soft but not browned, about 20 minutes. Season with salt and pepper. Stir in the flour with a wooden spoon and cook, stirring constantly so that the onions don't stick, for 2 minutes. Add the vegetable broth and cook for 5 additional minutes.

Line the bottom of the prepared pan with the slices of bread, overlapping if necessary. In a small bowl, mix the cheeses together. Spread half of the onion mixture over the bread. Scatter on half of the cheese. Spread the remaining onion mixture on top and sprinkle on the remaining cheese. Bake in the preheated oven until the top crust is golden, about 20 minutes.

CROSTATA DI CIPOLLINE 🌿
Onion Tart
Osteria del Cucco, Urbania (Pesaro and Urbino), Marche

Kamut is an ancient strain of wheat that has been rediscovered in Italy in recent years. It gives this tart a pleasantly hearty character. This tart is equally delicious when made with leeks, yellow bell peppers, celery root, or even chestnuts in place of the onions.

SERVES 6 TO 8

DOUGH
- 1½ cups kamut flour
- ¼ cup extra-virgin olive oil
- 2 large eggs, lightly beaten, or ½ cup water

FILLING
- 2 pounds (about 6 medium) yellow onions, diced
- Salt to taste
- ½ cup extra-virgin olive oil
- Leaves of 1 sprig rosemary, minced (optional)

To make the dough, combine the flour, oil, and eggs in a bowl and stir with a fork until the mixture has the texture of sand. Knead very briefly to combine, then shape into a ball, wrap in plastic, and set aside to rest for at least 2 hours, but 3 hours is preferable.

For the filling, steam the diced onions or cook them in a pan with 1 to 2 tablespoons water to keep them from sticking. They should be very soft. Season with salt and stir in the olive oil and the rosemary, if using. The mixture should be dry. If not, remove from the pan with a slotted spoon and transfer to a bowl, letting the excess liquid drain back into the pan.

Preheat the oven to 300°F. Divide the dough into two equal pieces and roll them out into thin disks. Use one disk to line a cake or pie pan. Spread the onion mixture on the crust, leaving a 1-inch border uncovered. Place the second disk of dough on top and press around the edges to seal. Pierce the top crust with a fork and bake until golden, about 30 minutes.

TORTA DI PORRI 🌿
Leek Tart

Ristorante Da Giusy, Pezzo di Ponte di Legno (Brescia), Lombardia

T his refined tart can be prepared in advance and served cold or at room temperature, making it a great choice for a buffet.

SERVES 12

DOUGH
2 cups unbleached all-purpose flour
Salt to taste
2 tablespoons extra-virgin olive oil

FILLING
9 ounces leeks, cut into julienne
Extra-virgin olive oil for sautéing
Salt to taste
7 ounces (1 medium) potato, peeled and thinly sliced
6 ounces fontina cheese, thinly sliced

4 ounces sliced prosciutto cotto, or smoked pancetta
3 large eggs, lightly beaten
¼ cup grated Parmigiano Reggiano
Leaves of 1 sprig chervil, minced

SAUCE
3 tablespoons unsalted butter
3½ cups unbleached all-purpose flour
2 cups beef broth
Salt to taste
Freshly ground black pepper to taste
Freshly grated nutmeg to taste

To make the dough, combine the flour with a pinch of salt and shape into a well. Add the olive oil and begin to gather flour from the sides of the well, adding water a little at a time and kneading until you have a firm dough. Shape into a ball, cover with a damp cloth, and set aside to rest for 1 hour.

Sauté the leeks in olive oil and season with salt; set aside.

To make the sauce, melt the butter in a small saucepan over low heat. Gradually sprinkle in the flour, stirring constantly, then whisk while adding the broth, salt and pepper, and a pinch of nutmeg. Bring to a boil while whisking constantly and cook for a few minutes until thickened, then remove from the heat. Add to the pan with the leeks and stir to combine.

Preheat the oven to 350°F. Divide the dough into two equal portions and roll both out quite thin with a rolling pin. Reserve scraps for decoration if desired. Use one of the rolled sheets of dough to line a pie or tart pan. Arrange about half of the potato slices on the crust and top with the leek mixture. Scatter on the fontina. Arrange the prosciutto on top of the cheese, and top with the remaining potato slices. Reserve about 1 tablespoon of the beaten eggs. Beat the remaining eggs with the Parmigiano Reggiano and the chervil and pour the mixture over the potatoes. Cover with the remaining sheet of dough and press firmly around the perimeter to seal the edges. Brush with the reserved egg and bake in the preheated oven until golden, about 40 minutes. Serve at room temperature or cold.

CROSTATA DI PISELLI 🌳
Green Pea Tart
Ristorante La Genzianella, Fabbrica Curone
(Alessandria), Piemonte

Since the peas are the star of this tart, you'll want to use freshly shelled peas. Pods generally account for about half of the weight of fresh peas, so purchase 2 to 2⅔ pounds of peas in the pods to get the amount of shelled peas required.

SERVES 4 TO 6

7 tablespoons unsalted butter, plus more for buttering pan
1 cup unbleached all-purpose flour, plus more for flouring pan
Salt to taste
1 to 1½ pounds (about 2 cups) shelled peas
1 medium yellow onion, minced
1 clove garlic
Extra-virgin olive oil for sautéing
3 large eggs
10 ounces (1¼ cups) ricotta
½ cup heavy cream
Freshly grated nutmeg to taste
Freshly ground black pepper to taste
2 tablespoons breadcrumbs

Melt 6 tablespoons butter. Place the 1 cup flour in a bowl with a pinch of salt. Pour the melted butter over the flour and stir with a fork to combine. Sprinkle on enough water just until the mixture looks like sand, then knead very briefly (2 or 3 times should do the trick), form the mixture into a ball, wrap in plastic, and set aside in a cool place to rest for 30 minutes.

Preheat the oven to 275°F. Butter a cake or pie pan, coat with flour, shaking to remove excess, and set aside. Meanwhile, blanch the peas in salted water until tender. Drain. Sauté the onion and the whole clove garlic in a small amount of olive oil. When the garlic browns, remove and discard. Add the cooked peas to the pan and sauté for 3 additional minutes, then remove from the heat.

In a medium bowl combine the eggs, ricotta, cream, and nutmeg until thoroughly combined. Fold in the pea mixture and adjust salt and pepper.

Divide the dough into two portions, one about two thirds of the whole and the remainder about one third. Roll out the larger piece of dough to fit the prepared pan as a bottom crust that comes up the sides and put it into place. Spread the pea mixture evenly in the crust. Sprinkle on the breadcrumbs. Dot the top with the remaining 1 tablespoon butter. Roll out the remaining dough and cut into strips. Use those strips to create a lattice top on the tart. Bake in the preheated oven until golden, about 40 minutes.

TORTA VERDE ⫷
Rice and Greens Tart
Francesca Ronco, Dusino San Michele (Asti), Piemonte

Nettles are a refreshing early spring green, but in their uncooked form they are covered with little prickles. Always wear gloves when handling raw nettles. Once cooked they are harmless (not to mention delicious).

Sauté thinly sliced leeks and onions in olive oil, then add a generous handful or two of rice and some minced lardo (cured fatback). Cook risotto style, first with some white wine, then with hot vegetable broth, until the rice is cooked al dente. Stir in minced blanched spinach, chard, and nettles and a generous amount of beaten egg and grated Parmigiano Reggiano. Season with salt and pepper. Pour into a buttered tart pan. Brush with egg wash, and sprinkle with breadcrumbs, more grated cheese, and minced fresh rosemary. Bake in a preheated 350°F oven until browned on top, about 1 hour. Serve hot or warm.

TORTA PASQUALINA 🌰
Easter Pie
Nina Colombo, Rapallo (Genova), Liguria

This is an ancient Ligurian recipe and appears on every table in the city of Genova at Easter without fail, alongside stuffed lettuce and roasted lamb or goat.

SERVES 6

DOUGH
- 2 cups unbleached all-purpose flour
- 2 tablespoons extra-virgin olive oil from Liguria
- Salt to taste

FILLING
- 2 pounds chard (or 10 small artichokes, trimmed), cut into narrow ribbons
- 3 bunches borage, cut into narrow ribbons
- Salt to taste
- ½ cup grated Parmigiano Reggiano
- 1 teaspoon minced fresh marjoram leaves
- 1 large yellow onion, thinly sliced
- Extra-virgin olive oil from Liguria for sautéing, oiling pan, brushing dough, and drizzling
- 2 cloves garlic
- Leaves of 3 sprigs parsley
- 8 large eggs
- 10 ounces (1¼ cups) ricotta
- 2½ tablespoons whipping cream
- 5 tablespoons unsalted butter
- Freshly ground black pepper to taste

To make the dough, form the flour into a well on a work surface and place the oil and a pinch of salt in the center. Knead in enough water to form a soft elastic dough. Knead for 10 minutes, then divide the dough into 6 pieces and form each piece into a ball. Lightly flour a tray, place the balls of dough on it, and cover with a damp towel. Set aside to rest for 1 hour.

For the filling, rinse the greens well and cook them just in the water that clings to the leaves. Season with salt, drain, and squeeze dry. Spread the cooked greens on a platter. Sprinkle with about ¼ cup grated Parmigiano Reggiano and marjoram and season with salt.

Sauté the onion in olive oil until transparent. Mince together the garlic and parsley. In a large bowl, beat 3 of the eggs with 1 tablespoon of the Parmigiano Reggiano and stir in the greens, the ricotta, the cream, the cooked onion, and the garlic and parsley mixture. Mix until well combined.

Preheat the oven to 375°F. Oil a cake or pie pan with high sides. Roll out one of the pieces of dough into a thin sheet. (It may be helpful to stretch the dough as you would a pizza in the air over your fists.) Place the sheet of dough in the pan. It should extend an inch or two over the side. Brush the surface of the dough with oil and repeat with another piece of dough. Top that second sheet of dough with a third piece, but do not oil the top of the third piece of dough. Spread the greens mixture on top of the dough and drizzle with a little oil. Cut about half of the butter into five pieces. Make 5 indentations in the filling. In each indentation place a piece of butter and then a whole egg, being careful not to break the yolks. Sprinkle the remaining grated cheese on top of the eggs and season with salt and pepper. Roll out one of the remaining pieces of dough and gently place it on top of the eggs. Brush with oil and dot the edges with a little butter. Roll out another piece of dough, place on top of the first and brush with oil and dot the edges with the remaining butter. Roll out the remaining piece of dough and place it on top. Fold the edges over to seal the tart. Brush the top with a little additional oil and pierce in a few places with a fork (being careful not to break the egg yolks). Bake in the preheated oven until the top crust is a deep golden color, about 1 hour. Serve warm or cold.

TORTINO DI BROCCOLI E GRANO SARACENO 🧁
Broccoli and Buckwheat Tartlets
Antica Osteria da Penacio, Arcugnano (Vicenza), Veneto

Silvana Valentini of Levico Terme (province of Trento) makes a tart using buckwheat and wheat flour that is filled with broccoli rabe, speck, and soft white tosela cheese.

SERVES 6

FILLING
- 10 ounces broccoli
- 1   shallot, minced
- ¼   cup minced pancetta
- 1   tablespoon extra-virgin olive oil
- 2   cups heavy cream
- 2   cups whole milk
- ⅓   cup buckwheat flour
- Salt and freshly ground black pepper to taste

DOUGH
- 2   cups unbleached all-purpose flour,
- ¼   cup buckwheat flour
- 10   tablespoons (1 stick plus 2 tablespoons) unsalted butter, softened, plus more for buttering pans

SAUCE
- 1¼ cups grated Grana Padano cheese
- ½   cup whole milk

To make the filling, cook the broccoli for 5 minutes in lightly salted boiling water. Drain and allow to cool. When cool enough to handle, mince the broccoli and set aside. Sauté the shallot and the pancetta in the oil. Add the broccoli and cook, stirring occasionally, for 10 minutes. Stir in the cream and milk, sprinkle in the flour, and season with salt and pepper.

Butter six 4-inch round baking dishes and set aside. Preheat the oven to 350°F.

For the crust, combine both flours with the butter to form a soft dough. Divide the dough into 6 equal pieces and shape them into balls.

If the dough is too soft to handle, chill to firm. Then roll out each portion of dough with a rolling pin and place each disk in one of the prepared dishes. Bake in the preheated oven for 10 minutes.

Divide the filling among the crusts and return to the oven to heat through, about 5 minutes. Meanwhile, in the top half of a double boiler, whisk the cheese and milk for the sauce until the cheese has melted. Spread a little sauce on each individual serving plate. Unmold the tarts, plate them on the sauce, and serve hot.

TORTA DI RADICCHIO 🌳
Radicchio Tart
Osteria Pironetomosca, Treville di Castelfranco
Veneto (Treviso), Veneto

Radicchio has a bitter edge when raw, but once it is sautéed its flavor softens and turns sweeter. The farro flour in the crust gives this an earthy taste.

SERVES 4

DOUGH
- ¾ cup plus 2 tablespoons unbleached all-purpose flour or 00 flour
- ¾ cup farro flour
- 1 large egg
- 2 egg yolks
- 7 tablespoons unsalted butter
- ½ cup grated Grana Padano cheese
- Salt to taste

FILLING
- 2 pounds Treviso radicchio, cut into ribbons
- 1 small yellow onion, minced
- Extra-virgin olive oil for sautéing
- 1 to 2 tablespoons red wine
- Salt to taste
- 9 ounces (1 cup plus 2 tablespoons) Cansiglio ricotta
- 2 egg yolks
- 2 tablespoons grated Grana Padano cheese
- ¼ cup heavy cream or whipping cream

To make the dough, combine the two types of flour, form them into a well on a work surface, and place the egg and yolks, butter, grated Grana Padano, and a pinch of salt in the center. Begin drawing in flour from the side of the well and mix until the mixture resembles sand. Knead briefly to combine, than wrap in plastic and refrigerate for 30 minutes.

For the filling, sauté the radicchio and onion in a small amount of olive oil, then add the wine and turn down to a simmer. Braise until the radicchio is soft and its liquid has evaporated, about 15 minutes. Adjust salt to taste. In a bowl combine the ricotta with the egg yolks, grated Grana Padano, and cream, then stir in the cooked radicchio to combine.

Preheat the oven to 350°F. Roll out the dough with a rolling pin and place it in a parchment-lined pan. Spread the radicchio mixture on top of the dough, level with a wooden spoon, and bake in the preheated oven until the crust is golden, about 30 minutes.

TORTA DI TROMBETTE 🌿
Trombetta Squash Tart
Marinella Badino Biancheri, Vallecrosia
(Imperia), Liguria

The filling for this delicious tart benefits from being made a day in advance so that the flavors have a chance to meld. Trombetta squash is a pale green crookneck squash with dry flesh that grows in Liguria. It is picked young and small from June to August, but it continues to grow—some trombetta squash get as long as 6½ feet!

Peel and seed about 1¾ pounds trombetta squash and grate it on the largest holes of a four-sided grater. Season with salt and set aside in a strainer to give off its liquid, about 20 minutes. Squeeze to get out as much liquid as possible, then sauté in olive oil with minced garlic and onion for 3 minutes. Once the squash has cooled, combine it with 2 eggs, ½ cup boiled rice, ½ cup grated Parmigiano Reggiano or aged sheep's cheese, and minced parsley and marjoram.

Knead 3½ cups all-purpose flour, 2 tablespoons olive oil, a pinch of salt, and ½ cup warm water into a soft and elastic dough. Set aside to rest for 30 minutes, then divide into 2 equal portions and roll them out. Arrange one sheet of dough in an oiled pan, spread the squash mixture on top, top with the second, and seal the edges. Brush the tart with a little oil and pierce with a fork. Bake at 325°F for 30 minutes, then raise the oven temperature to 350°F and bake for 10 minutes more.

TORTA DI RISO
Rice Tart
Trattoria Da Iolanda, Campomorone (Genova), Liguria

*f*our layers of crust provide a bit of extra texture to break up the creamy rice filling. This tart always wins raves.

SERVES 6 TO 8

DOUGH
3½ cups unbleached all-purpose flour
Salt to taste
1   tablespoon extra-virgin olive oil, plus more for oiling pan and brushing dough

FILLING
4   cups whole milk
1½ cups rice
1   medium yellow onion, minced
Leaves of 1 sprig parsley, minced
½   ounce dried mushrooms, soaked in warm water for 20 minutes, then drained and squeezed dry, chopped
2   tablespoons whipping cream
Freshly ground black pepper to taste
1   large egg, lightly beaten
¼   cup grated Grana Padano cheese
3   tablespoons extra-virgin olive oil

To make the dough, on a work surface knead together the flour, salt, and olive oil with enough water to make a soft dough. Divide the dough into 4 equal portions, cover, and set aside to rest for about 1 hour.

For the filling, place the milk in a saucepan over medium heat. When it begins to bubble, add the rice and cook over medium-low heat until the rice is cooked al dente, about 10 minutes. Drain and reserve.

In a skillet, sauté the onion, parsley, and chopped rehydrated mushrooms. Add the rice, cream, a pinch of pepper, and the beaten egg and sauté for 3 to 5 more minutes. Remove from the heat and stir in the grated cheese. Set aside to cool.

Preheat the oven to 350°F. Roll out the pieces of dough into thin sheets. Arrange one sheet of dough in an oiled pan and brush the top with

oil. Cover with a second sheet of dough. Spread the filling mixture on top of that dough. Place a third sheet of dough over the filling, brush the third sheet with oil, then top with the fourth sheet of dough. Brush with remaining oil. Pinch all around the perimeter to seal. Pierce the top of the tart with a fork and bake in the preheated oven until golden, 40 to 50 minutes.

CASADINAS
Cheese Tart
Ristorante Ispinigoli, Ispinigoli di Dorgali (Nuoro), Sardegna

*S*ardegna's famous *casadinas* can be either sweet or savory. In the Dorgali area this is also served at the close of a meal—something akin to a cheese course—with glasses of the local Vernaccia. Traditionally this is cooked in a wood-burning oven with a low fire.

SERVES 4
2   cups unbleached all-purpose flour
1   large egg
Salt to taste
10 ounces young sheep's cheese
Leaves of 1 sprig calamint
1   pinch saffron

Combine the flour, the egg, a pinch of salt, and enough water to make a soft and elastic dough. Knead briefly, then shape into a ball, wrap in a clean towel, and set aside to rest for 30 minutes.

Meanwhile, mince the cheese, calamint, and saffron together until fully broken down and thoroughly combined. (You can also use a food processor fitted with a metal blade.)

Preheat the oven to 350°F. Roll out the dough very thin (1.5 millimeters or 0.05 inch) and use it to line the bottom and sides of a cake or pie pan with high sides. Spread the filling evenly over the dough, then crimp the border of the dough.

Bake until the cheese is melted, keeping close watch on the dough to be sure it doesn't dry out or begin to burn in spots, about 20 minutes.

TORTA VERDE DELLA LUNIGIANA ❗
Lunigiana Tart with Chard and Borage
Ristorante Gavarini, Villafranca in Lunigiana (Massa-Carrara), Toscana

In the Lunigiana area, there are many different types of tarts made with greens. The greens for the filling may be braised and combined with ricotta, sheep's cheese, breadcrumbs, and nutmeg. Another version in Versilia features a combination of spinach, zucchini, and potatoes.

SERVES 4

FILLING
½ cup tightly packed borage
2 pounds chard
Salt to taste
½ cup extra-virgin olive oil
¾ cup grated Parmigiano Reggiano
2 potatoes, peeled, boiled, and crushed
   with a fork
2 leeks, minced
2 large eggs, lightly beaten
   (optional)

DOUGH
3½ cups unbleached all-purpose flour
½ cup extra-virgin olive oil, plus more
   for oiling the pan
Salt to taste

To make the filling, taste the borage, which can vary widely in terms of bitterness. If your borage is very bitter, you may want to use a little less. Mince together the borage and chard. Place in a fine-mesh sieve, salt lightly, and allow to sit for about 20 minutes to drain off liquid. Then squeeze the greens dry and transfer to a bowl. Add the olive oil, grated cheese, potatoes, and leeks and stir to combine. The mixture should form a paste. Adjust salt to taste. Stir in the eggs, if using. (They are helpful for binding the filling.)

Preheat the oven to 350°F. To make the dough, form the flour into a well on a work surface and place the ½ cup oil and a pinch of salt in the center. Knead into a crumbly dough, then add as much water as necessary to make it soft and elastic. Use a rolling pin to roll out the dough into a thin sheet, about twice the size of the pan you plan to use (or, alternatively, divide the dough into two equal pieces and roll out each one to a thin sheet.) Oil a cake or pie pan and place the dough in it. Spread the filling on the dough—it should be about 1 inch thick. Cover the filling with the other half of the dough by folding it over or placing the second sheet on top. Pinch the edges together to seal and bake until golden brown, about 40 minutes.

CROSTINI, BRUSCHETTE & TOASTS

FETTUNTA
Garlic Bread
Pia Lippi, Marina di Pisa (Pisa), Toscana

The variations on *fettunta* are endless. For example, the toasted bread may be topped with cannellini beans or other items. Fettunta is always a part of an antipasto platter of various types of cured meats. It was originally invented for practical reasons as a way to taste new olive oil that had just been pressed. Tuscan bread is traditionally made without salt. This is also a good way to use up slightly stale bread. Slice a loaf of Tuscan bread into 1-inch slices and toast on each side so that the interior remains soft but the outside is crisp. Rub a peeled garlic clove on one side of the bread and place garlic-side up on a platter. Season with salt and drizzle with a generous amount of olive oil. Serve warm.

FREGA DI POMODORO
Bruschetta
Luciano Bezzini, Donoratico di Castagneto Carducci (Livorno), Toscana

Bruschetta can be enhanced any number of ways: with pepper, herbs, and even beans. The tomatoes are key: they must be just-picked and perfectly ripe, but not over-ripe, and they should be the round, smooth-skinned variety. This is, of course, the perfect summertime snack, but in winter bruschetta may also be made using the dried tomatoes typically found in the South, especially along the Amalfi Coast and around Mount Vesuvius. Chop perfectly ripe tomatoes and toss with a generous amount of extra-virgin olive oil. Season with salt. Toast sliced Tuscan bread and rub with a garlic clove. Arrange the toasted bread on a platter and spoon the tomato mixture on top of it.

CROSTINI CON CAVOLFIORI
Cauliflower Crostini
Paola Braccioni, Urbania (Pesaro and Urbino), Marche

Toast thick slices of bread and rub them with garlic. Cook cauliflower in boiling salted water until tender but still crisp in the center. Remove cauliflower with a slotted spoon, reserving cooking water. Chop the cauliflower stalks finely, but leave the florets whole. Place the chopped cauliflower in a bowl, season with salt, and toss gently to combine. Dip the toasted bread in the cauliflower cooking water for a few seconds, then arrange in a single layer on a serving platter. Scatter the cooked cauliflower over the bread. Drizzle with a generous amount of oil, white wine vinegar, and freshly ground black pepper and serve immediately.

FETTA CON CAVOLO NERO
Toasted Bread with Black Kale
Osteria L'Acquolina, Terranuova Bracciolini (Arezzo), Toscana

This recipe can only be made with *cavolo nero*, or black kale, sometimes labeled Tuscan kale or lacinato kale, that has been through at least one frost. It has long, narrow leaves with an unusually bumpy surface. The other indispensable ingredient is newly pressed olive oil.

SERVES 4
Salt to taste
Extra-virgin olive oil for cooking water and drizzling
Freshly ground black pepper to taste
1   *bunch black kale*
4   *slices Tuscan (unsalted) bread*

Bring a pot of water to a boil, salt it lightly, and add some oil and a generous amount of black pepper. Add the kale leaves (discarding the tough leaves at the core).

Moisten the bread with the cooking water, either by arranging the bread on a platter and using a spoon to drizzle the cooking water over it, or by dipping each slice very briefly into the pot. Arrange the slices on a platter and drizzle on olive oil. Remove the cooked kale with a slotted spoon and arrange it on top of the bread. Drizzle on additional oil, a sprinkling of pepper, and a little more salt, if needed, and serve.

CROSTINI CON GAMBI DI CARCIOFI 🌳
Artichoke Stem Crostini
Osteria di Montecodruzzo, Roncofreddo (Forlì-Cesena) Emìlia-Romagna

The stems of artichokes are often discarded, but this recipe offers a chance to use them to make a tasty appetizer. *Raviggiolo* is a fresh (not aged) mild white cheese somewhat similar to farmer's cheese that can be made with either sheep's or cow's milk.

SERVES 4
- 8 artichokes with stems, hard outer leaves and choke trimmed and discarded and stems peeled
- Extra-virgin olive oil for sautéing
- 1 shallot, sliced
- 4 to 6 fresh mint leaves
- 4 to 6 fresh basil leaves
- Salt and freshly ground black pepper to taste
- 1 loaf rustic bread, cut into slices
- ½ cup diced raviggiolo cheese

Dice or cut into julienne the artichoke hearts and stems. Sauté them in a small amount of oil with the shallot. Tear in the mint and basil leaves and season with salt and pepper.

Toast the bread slices and top each slice with cubes of raviggiolo and cooked artichokes.

CROSTONE CON RATATOIA 🌿
Ratatouille Crostini
Agriturismo Da Elvira, Montegrosso d'Asti (Asti), Piemonte

For the bread, choose a long, oval loaf with a dense crumb, as it will be easier to slice. Avoid bread with large or small holes in the crumb, such as the Piemontese *biòva*, as the sauce will drip through it. The slices should be the size of the palm of your hand and about ½ inch thick.

SERVES 4
- ½ cup extra-virgin olive oil
- 1 tablespoon minced onion
- 1 tablespoon minced carrot
- 1 tablespoon minced celery
- 2 cloves garlic
- 1 small red bell pepper, diced
- 1 small yellow bell pepper, diced
- 1 medium eggplant, diced
- ½ cup whole peeled tomatoes and their juices, roughly chopped
- 1 pinch oregano
- Salt to taste
- 4 slices country-style bread

Place the olive oil in a skillet over low heat. Cook the minced onion, carrot, and celery until soft, stirring frequently. Add 1 clove garlic and the diced peppers. Cook, stirring frequently, until softened, about 5 minutes. Add the eggplant, tomatoes, oregano, and salt. Cover and cook for 15 additional minutes. The vegetables should be cooked through. Adjust salt.

Toast the bread.

Rub the toasted bread with the remaining clove garlic and arrange the slices on a platter. Top with the cooked vegetables and serve hot.

CROSTINI AL SALIGNON
Crostini with Spicy Ricotta and Fennel Seeds
Ristorante Capanna Carla, Gressoney-La-Trinità (Aosta), Valle d'Aosta

alignon is a spicy ricotta that hails from the Germanic Walser people of northern Italy who have lived in the Monte Rosa valleys for centuries. This dairy product is made from the whey left over after cheese is made, which is enriched with milk or cream. It is heated and then pressed, drained, and mixed with salt, pepper, chili pepper, and aromatic herbs. Finally, it is formed into balls that are lightly smoked. Salignon is not widely available, but you can use plain ricotta in this recipe and approximate the taste. Of course, if you can find salignon in your area, use that instead.

SERVES 4
- ½ cup ricotta
- 2 tablespoons fennel seeds
- 1 tablespoon crushed red chili pepper
- 1 tablespoon extra-virgin olive oil
- 8 slices day-old rye bread
- 3 tablespoons unsalted butter

In a bowl, thoroughly combine the cheese with the fennel seeds, chili pepper, and olive oil. Spread the mixture on the sliced bread. Cut the butter into small pieces and dot the crostini with butter.

CROSTINI NERI AL VIN SANTO
Chicken Liver-Vin Santo Crostini
L'Antico Borgo, Civitella in Val di Chiana (Arezzo), Toscana

weet Vin Santo wine bookends a classic Tuscan meal. It flavors an appetizer of chicken liver spread on crostini, as in this version, and cookies such as *cantucci* are dipped in Vin Santo for dessert.

SERVES 8
- 1 medium carrot, minced
- 1 rib celery, minced
- ½ medium yellow onion, minced
- Extra-virgin olive oil for sautéing
- 10 ounces chicken livers, cleaned and patted dry
- 1 tablespoon capers, rinsed and drained
- ½ cup Vin Santo
- Salt and freshly ground black pepper to taste
- 8 slices day-old Tuscan (unsalted) bread

Sauté the minced carrot, celery, and onion in olive oil until softened. Add the livers and cook over medium heat, stirring occasionally, for 10 minutes.

Add the capers and cook for 2 to 3 additional minutes, then add the Vin Santo, deglaze the pan, and allow the liquid to evaporate. Transfer the mixture to a food mill and process.

Cut the bread slices in half, toast, and spread each piece with a generous amount of the chicken-liver mixture.

CROSTONI DI FAVE E PERSICO
Fava Bean and Perch Crostini
Ristorante La Torre, Viterbo, Lazio

fava beans are available fresh in their pods in early spring. Fresh fava beans need to be removed from the fuzzy green pods, and then each bean needs to be liberated from the skin around it. This work is a little fussy, but the reward is worth it. When you shell 14 ounces of beans in the pods, you should obtain about 3½ ounces beans.

SERVES 4

- 14 ounces fresh fava beans in the pods
- ¼ cup extra-virgin olive oil, plus more for drizzling
- 1½ pounds perch fillets
- About ½ cup unbleached all-purpose flour for dredging
- Salt to taste
- 4 large slices bread
- 1 sprig chives, minced

Shell and peel the fava beans as described above. Mince finely and set aside.

Line a baking sheet with paper towels. Heat the olive oil in a skillet with high sides over medium-high heat. Dredge the perch fillets in the flour and fry them in the oil, turning once, until browned on both sides. Remove with a slotted spoon to the prepared towel-lined baking sheet to drain and season with salt.

Preheat the broiler. Place the bread slices in a single layer on a baking sheet and broil until toasted, turning once, about 1 minute per side. Sprinkle the minced fava beans on top. Drizzle with a little more oil and season with a pinch of salt. Arrange the perch fillets on top of the fava beans and run under the broiler just to heat through. Drizzle with a touch more olive oil and sprinkle on the chives.

FRITTATA DI CIPOLLE 🌳
Onion Frittata
Nara Nesi, Firenze, Toscana

Heat a generous amount of olive oil in a skillet over medium-low heat. Add a large amount of white onions cut into half-moons. Cook the onions, stirring occasionally, until transparent but not browned, at least 15 minutes. If the onions start to stick, add a small amount of water. Pour beaten eggs (seasoned with salt) into the skillet around the onions. With a spatula, push the cooked eggs from the edge into the center. At the same time, tilt the pan toward the edge that you are pushing in so that still-liquid egg mixture runs down and fills the now-empty space. Repeat several times. When the bottom of the frittata is firm but the top is still soft, cook over medium heat without moving until the bottom is browned and set, 2 to 3 minutes. Using a spatula, slide the frittata out of the pan onto a plate or pot cover, then flip it back into the pan so that the browned side is facing up. Cook until the bottom is browned and set, 2 to 3 additional minutes. Serve piping hot.

In the Roman variation on this dish, the onions are cooked in lard with a few strips of guanciale (cured pork jowl) and some tomatoes that have been seeded and drained and then diced. A small amount of butter is then added to the pan just before the eggs are poured in.

FRITTATA CON AGLIO ROSSO ⚫
Garlic Scape Frittata
Taverna de li Caldora, Pacentro (L'Aquila), Abruzzo

Garlic scapes are the stems of garlic flowers and are available fleetingly in spring. They are delicious in a frittata, and they can also be blanched and then dressed with a little lemon juice and salt and served as a side dish. They may also be preserved in jars to be eaten at a later date. Whole scapes look pretty in a frittata, but you can chop them if you'd prefer.

SERVES 4
- *10 ounces garlic scapes*
- *Salt to taste*
- *4 large eggs*
- *Extra-virgin olive oil for coating skillet*

Blanch the scapes in boiling salted water until just tender. Drain and set aside.

In a medium bowl beat the eggs with a pinch of salt. Stir in the scapes.

Place a small amount of olive oil in a skillet and place over low heat. Pour in the egg mixture. With a spatula, push the cooked eggs from the edge into the center. At the same time, tilt the pan toward the edge that you are pushing in so that still-liquid egg mixture runs down and fills the now-empty space. Repeat several times. When the bottom of the frittata is firm but the top is still soft, cook over medium heat without moving until the bottom is browned and set, 2 to 3 minutes. Using the spatula, slide the frittata out of the pan, then flip it back into the pan so that the browned side is facing up. Cook until the bottom is browned and set, 2 to 3 additional minutes. Serve hot, room temperature, or cold.

FRITTATA DI LAMPASCIONI 🌳
Hyacinth Bulb Frittata
Agriturismo La Fontana del Tasso, Francavilla in Sinni (Potenza), Basilicata

*L*ampascioni, or tassel hyacinth bulbs, are eaten (cooked) in the regions of Puglia and Basilicata and are often preserved. They can be messy to clean because the outer skin must be removed, and it is frankly a little oozy. Giuseppina Palmisano of Alberobello in the province of Bari makes an oven-baked version of this frittata. First she boils the bulbs and cuts them into small pieces. Then she mixes them in a bowl with day-old bread that has been softened in some water and squeezed dry, eggs, grated sheep's cheese, minced garlic and parsley, salt, and pepper. She bakes this mixture in a 350°F oven for 30 minutes.

SERVES 4
Extra-virgin olive oil for sautéing
14 ounces hyacinth bulbs (see note), thinly sliced
Salt to taste
4 large eggs
Freshly ground black pepper to taste

Place a small amount of olive oil over medium heat and cook the bulbs over medium heat, stirring occasionally, until golden. Season with salt. In a bowl, beat the eggs with some pepper. Pour the eggs into the skillet. With a spatula, push the cooked eggs from the edge into the center. At the same time, tilt the pan toward the edge that you are pushing in so that still-liquid egg mixture runs down and fills the now-empty space. Repeat several times. When the bottom of the frittata is firm but the top is still soft, cook over medium heat without moving until the bottom is browned and set, 2 to 3 minutes. Using the spatula, slide the frittata out of the pan onto a plate or pot cover, then flip it back into the pan so that the browned side is facing up. Cook until the bottom is browned and set, 2 to 3 additional minutes. Serve warm or at room temperature.

FRITTATA DI FIORI DI ZUCCA ▦
Zucchini Blossom Frittata
Trattoria Da Maria, Poggio Moiano (Rieti), Lazio

*T*o prepare zucchini blossoms for cooking, shake them over a sink to remove any loose soil or insects. Rinse very gently, pat dry, and pinch off and discard the pistils, which can be bitter.

SERVES 6
Extra-virgin olive oil for sautéing
¼ medium onion, minced
20 zucchini blossoms, cut into strips
Salt and freshly ground black pepper to taste
6 large eggs

Heat a small amount of olive oil in a pan and cook the onion over medium heat, stirring frequently, until golden. Add the zucchini blossoms, season with salt and pepper, and add about ½ cup water. Simmer the blossoms in the water for 10 minutes.

In a medium bowl, beat the eggs with a pinch of salt. Pour the eggs into the skillet. With a spatula, push the cooked eggs from the edge into the center. At the same time, tilt the pan toward the edge that you are pushing in so that still-liquid egg mixture runs down and fills the now-empty space. Repeat several times. When the bottom of the frittata is firm but the top is still soft, cook over medium heat without moving until the bottom is browned and set, 2 to 3 minutes. Using the spatula, slide the frittata out of the pan onto a plate or pot cover, then flip it back into the pan so that the browned side is facing up. Cook until the bottom is browned and set, 2 to 3 additional minutes.

FRITTATA DI PATATE E MELE 🍎
Potato and Apple Frittata
Letizia Palesi, Champorcher (Aosta), Valle d'Aosta

Northern Italy is crazy for apples and includes them in both savory and sweet dishes. Reinette apples are mildly flavored and firm. Cook peeled and thinly sliced potatoes in butter for 30 minutes. Add cored, peeled, and thinly sliced Reinette apples and cook for 20 additional minutes. Pour in eggs beaten with a pinch of salt. With a spatula, push the cooked eggs from the edge into the center. At the same time, tilt the pan toward the edge that you are pushing in so that still-liquid egg mixture runs down and fills the now-empty space. Repeat several times. When the bottom of the frittata is firm but the top is still soft, cook over medium heat without moving until the bottom is browned and set, 2 to 3 minutes. Using the spatula, slide the frittata out of the pan, then flip it back into the pan so that the browned side is facing up. Cook until the bottom is browned and set, 2 to 3 additional minutes. Blot on paper towels for a couple of minutes, then serve hot.

FRITTATA DI SPAGHETTI 🥚
Spaghetti Frittata
Pietro Grossolino, Molfetta (Bari), Puglia

Combine cooked spaghetti with beaten eggs, salt, and a generous amount of grated Pecorino Romano. Oil a skillet and place over medium heat, then add the egg mixture to the pan. Cook until the bottom is browned, about 5 minutes. Slide the frittata out of the pan onto a plate or pot cover, then flip it back into the pan so that the browned side is facing up. Cook until the bottom is browned and set, 2 to 3 additional minutes. Serve piping hot.

ERBAZZONE
Cheese Frittata with Greens 🌳
Alda Beltrami, Reggio Emilia, Emilia-Romagna

Erbazzone is a signature dish of the Reggio Emilia area. It can be cooked on the stovetop or baked in the oven, and there are also variations that incorporate rice. Caterina Gandino Mango in Modena treats her guests to a sweet version of erbazzone with chard, ricotta, sugar, eggs, and almonds, either baked in a short pastry crust or baked directly in a pan that has been buttered and floured.

For a savory erbazzone that will serve 4 as an appetizer, blanch about 2 pounds raw tender greens: Swiss chard, spinach, or another variety. In a medium bowl, whisk 2 eggs, then stir in ¼ cup flour, ¼ cup breadcrumbs, and 1½ cups grated Parmigiano Reggiano. Sauté minced blanched greens in 1 tablespoon butter, then stir the greens into the egg mixture. Season with salt, pepper, and nutmeg. Melt 1 tablespoons butter in a skillet and pour in the egg mixture. Cook as you would a frittata: At first, every few seconds tilt the pan while pushing the more solid eggs from the edge into the center so that the still-uncooked egg mixture fills the space around the perimeter. When the bottom is firm but the top is soft, let cook undisturbed for 2 to 3 minutes until the bottom is browned. Flip the frittata, return to the pan, and cook until both sides are browned, an additional 2 to 3 minutes. Serve hot, room temperature, or cold.

FLAN DI SPINACI CON FONDUTA
Spinach Flan with Fontina Sauce
Locanda Fontanabuona, Mombercelli (Asti), Piemonte

This flan is mildly flavored and tender and serves as the perfect foil for the rich cheese fonduta served over it.

SERVES 4

- 5 tablespoons unsalted butter, plus more for buttering pan
- ⅔ cup plus 3 tablespoons unbleached all-purpose flour
- 4 cups whole milk
- Freshly grated nutmeg to taste
- 1 pound spinach
- Salt to taste
- ½ cup grated Parmigiano Reggiano
- 6 large eggs
- ½ cup heavy cream
- 1 cup diced semi-aged fontina
- 2 egg yolks

Preheat the oven to 300°F. Butter a loaf pan, flour it with 2 tablespoons flour, shake it out, and set it aside. Place 2 cups of the milk in a small pot and heat without bringing to a boil. Melt 3 tablespoons unsalted butter in a small saucepan. Add ⅓ cup flour and cook, stirring constantly, for 1 minute. Whisk in the hot milk gradually and add a sprinkling of nutmeg. Continue to cook, stirring, until you have a very thick béchamel, then remove from the heat and set aside.

Blanch the spinach in boiling salted water, then squeeze dry. Mince very finely (a food processor works well) and combine the spinach with the béchamel, the grated Parmigiano Reggiano, and the eggs. Cut the remaining 2 tablespoons butter into small pieces. Adjust salt and add the cream, the remaining 2 tablespoons butter, and ⅓ cup flour to the spinach mixture. Stir until well combined.

Transfer the mixture to the prepared loaf pan and level the top. Cover the loaf pan with aluminum foil and set it in a large baking pan filled with hot water that reaches halfway up the sides of the loaf pan. Cook in the preheated oven for 2 hours.

When the flan is almost cooked, place the fontina in the top of a double boiler with the remaining tablespoon flour, the egg yolks, and the remaining 2 cups milk. Cook, whisking, until the cheese has melted and pour over the flan just before serving.

FLAN DI TOPINAMBUR
Jerusalem Artichoke Flan
Osteria Boccondivino, Bra (Cuneo), Piemonte

At the restaurant these individual flans are served with either a bagna caoda butter and anchovy sauce or a raschera cheese sauce.

SERVES 4

- Unsalted butter for buttering ramekins
- ½ gallon whole milk
- 1 pound Jerusalem artichokes, thinly sliced
- 3 large eggs
- Salt and freshly ground black pepper to taste

Preheat the oven to 325°F. Butter four individual ramekins and set aside.

Place the milk in a pot and bring to a simmer. Add the sliced Jerusalem artichokes and cook them at a lively simmer in the milk for 15 minutes. Drain and wait for the artichokes to cool.

In a bowl, beat the eggs with salt and pepper. Add the Jerusalem artichokes and stir to combine well.

Divide the mixture evenly among the prepared ramekins and arrange them in a large baking pan filled with hot water that reaches halfway up the sides of the ramekins. Bake in the preheated oven until set, about 30 minutes.

FLAN DI CARCIOFI 🌰
Artichoke Flan
Osteria I Santi, Capocastello di Mercogliano
(Avellino), Campania

Romanesco artichokes have been cultivated for hundreds of years. They are
round (rather than pointed) and often
tinged with purple.

SERVES 6
Juice of 1 lemon
5   Romanesco artichokes (see note)
Butter for buttering pan(s)
2   cloves garlic
Extra-virgin olive oil for sautéing
¼   cup grated Grana Padano cheese
8   large eggs, separated
Salt and freshly ground black pepper
    to taste

Prepare a bowl of cold water and add the lemon
juice to it. Remove and discard the outer leaves
and chokes of the artichokes, cut them into
wedges, and soak the wedges in the lemon juice
and water for 30 minutes.

Preheat the oven to 350°F. Butter six ramekins
or one loaf pan and set aside. Sauté the garlic
in olive oil. Drain the artichokes, pat them dry,
and add them to the pan. Cook over low heat,
stirring occasionally, until the artichokes are
tender. Puree in a blender or a food processor
fitted with the metal blade and allow to cool
slightly, then combine with the grated cheese,
egg yolks, salt, and pepper. Beat the egg whites
to a stiff peak and fold them into the mixture.
Transfer the mixture to the prepared pan or
pans and bake in the preheated oven until set,
about 45 minutes.

SFORMATO DI CARDI 🌱
Cardoon Custard
Ristorante Lou Chardoun, Luserna San Giovanni
(Torino), Piemonte

This custard can be served with a bagna
caoda sauce made with walnut oil or
with a cheese sauce.

SERVES 4
3   tablespoons unsalted butter, plus more
    for buttering pan
½   cup plus 1 tablespoon unbleached
    all-purpose flour, plus more for
    flouring pan
½   cup white wine vinegar
14 ounces cardoons
Salt to taste
1½ cups whole milk
Freshly ground white pepper to taste
Freshly grated nutmeg to taste
4   large eggs

Preheat the oven to 350°F. Butter and flour a
large rectangular baking dish or four individual
baking dishes and set aside.

In a bowl, combine the vinegar with cold
water. Peel the cardoons, removing any fibrous
strings, chop them roughly, and drop them
into the vinegar water. When all the cardoons
are prepared, bring a large pot of lightly salted
water to a boil and cook the cardoons until soft.
Drain, allow to cool, and then puree in a blender
or food processor with the milk.

Melt the butter in a medium pot over low
heat. Gradually add the flour, stirring constantly.
Do not allow the flour to brown or allow any
clumps to form. Whisk in the cardoon and milk
mixture. Bring the mixture to a boil while still
stirring constantly. When the mixture thickens,
remove it from the heat and season with salt,
pepper, and nutmeg. Allow the mixture to cool,
and when it has, whisk in the eggs.

Transfer the mixture to the pan or pans and
arrange them in a large baking pan filled with
hot water that reaches halfway up the sides of
the pan or pans. Bake in the preheated oven

until a golden crust forms on top. Remove from the oven and allow to cool before unmolding. Reheat before serving.

FLAN DI ZUCCHINE
Zucchini Flan
Ristorante La Locanda Alpina, Chiusa di Pesio (Cuneo), Piemonte

The zucchini for this simple flan must be extremely fresh and tender. If you prefer, you can sauté the zucchini in olive oil with a little minced onion rather than steaming it.

SERVES 4
Unsalted butter for buttering ramekins
1   *pound zucchini, roughly chopped*
4   *large eggs*
Salt to taste

Preheat the oven to 400°F. Butter four individual ramekins and set aside.

Steam the zucchini until soft, about 15 minutes. Allow the zucchini to cool, then puree with a blender or food processor.

In a bowl, beat the eggs, then whisk in the zucchini and beat until well combined. Season with salt.

Divide the mixture evenly among the prepared ramekins and arrange them in a large baking pan filled with hot water that reaches halfway up the sides of the ramekins. Bake in the preheated oven until the flans are set and the tip of a paring knife inserted into the center emerges clean, about 10 minutes.

SFORMATO DI ZUCCA E TARTUFO
Squash and Truffle Custard
Osteria Ardenga, Diolo di Soragna (Parma), Emîlia-Romagna

Tuber melanosporum, known in Italy as a Norcia truffle or a Spoleto truffle, is a hypogeal fungus that grows near the roots of oak, poplar, and hazelnut trees. This black truffle is less prized and less delicate than the white truffle (*Tuber magnatum*). While it would be a crime to cook a white truffle, the aroma and flavor of black truffle actually blossom during cooking.

SERVES 4
Unsalted butter for buttering pans and sautéing
1   *tablespoon breadcrumbs*
1   *pound peeled and seeded winter squash, diced*
2   *cloves garlic, minced*
4   *large eggs, lightly beaten*
About ¼ cup unbleached all-purpose flour or oo flour
¼   *cup grated Parmigiano Reggiano,*
1   *black truffle, shaved*
Salt to taste
Freshly grated nutmeg to taste

Preheat the oven to 350°F. Butter four individual baking dishes or ramekins, coat with the breadcrumbs, and set aside. Steam the squash. Process through a food mill and set aside. In a skillet, briefly sauté the garlic in butter over low heat until it begins to give off its aroma, then add the cooked squash puree and cook, stirring occasionally, until the squash begins to brown. Transfer the squash to a bowl and stir in the eggs and flour. (Add enough flour so that it is no longer runny, but not so much that it turns stiff. You may not need all of it.) Stir in the grated cheese, truffle shavings, salt, and a pinch of nutmeg. Transfer to the prepared pans and bake in the preheated oven until set, about 10 minutes.

SFORMATO DI BUCCE DI PISELLI 🎲
Pea Pod Custard
Leonardo Romanelli, Firenze, Toscana

Obviously, only the pods of organically grown peas cultivated far from any sources of pollution are suitable for this dish. For a custard to serve 6, make a very thick béchamel with 5 tablespoons butter, ½ cup plus 1 tablespoon all-purpose flour, 2 cups whole milk, salt, and nutmeg. Boil 2 pounds pea pods in lightly salted water until tender. Drain, pat dry, and puree through the smallest holes on a food mill. Combine the puree with 2 eggs, ½ cup grated Parmigiano Reggiano, and the béchamel. Butter and flour a ring pan and pour the mixture into the pan, then bake the custard in a water bath at 325°F until set. Allow to cool, then unmold to a serving platter.

NIDI DEL CACCIATORE 🌿
Polenta "Nests"
with Gorgonzola
Trattoria Cacciatore, Sulzano (Brescia), Lombardia

Loredana Bonetti says that these "nests" can also be topped with *sasaka*—a soft and creamy paste of pork lardo (fatback) and smoked goose breast—or with sliced mushrooms sautéed with garlic and parsley, or ragù, or one of myriad other delicious options. If you have a *paiolo*, a traditional polenta pot, use it to cook the polenta.

Make an extra-thick polenta by cooking polenta over low heat, stirring constantly, for 1 hour. To serve, scoop portions of the polenta, using an ice cream scoop if you have one. Place 2 to 3 scoops of polenta on each individual serving plate. With the back of a tablespoon, create small indents in the balls of polenta. Place creamy Gorgonzola in the indentations. Serve hot.

FONDUTA 🧀
Fontina Fondue
Ristorante Tre Galline, Torino, Piemonte

Traditionally, a recipe for fonduta calls for butter, egg yolks, and fontina cheese to be stirred over gentle heat (in a double boiler) with a wooden spoon or whisk. The problem with that method is that incorporating the egg yolks and milk with the cheese can be difficult, as they tend to seize up. If you don't remove the mixture from the heat at the exact moment when it begins to thicken, you can easily end up with a lumpy or over-melted mess. Marco Zurletti of Tre Galline recommends the method described below, which is the one most professional chefs use. If you prefer to go the traditional route and you run into difficulty, add a tablespoon of flour to the mixture. In season—and budget permitting—white truffle can be shaved atop the finished fonduta.

SERVES 6
- 1 pound fontina cheese, cut into cubes
- 4 cups whole milk
- 1 tablespoon unsalted butter
- 8 egg yolks
- Toasted bread cubes for serving

Place the fontina cubes in a bowl that can be used on top of a double boiler, pour the milk over it, and keep in a cool place for 12 hours. Add the butter to the bowl, place on top of a double boiler, and cook, whisking, until the cheese is completely melted. In a separate bowl, beat the egg yolks. Add the yolks to the cheese mixture. Whisk until completely incorporated, about 3 minutes. Serve piping hot with toasted bread for dipping.

❧{ P A N C A K E S & F R I T T E R S }☙

CECINA ▮
Chickpea Pancake
Fattoria del Grottaione, Castel del Piano
(Grosseto), Toscana

flavio Biserni says that you don't need
exact measurements to make a great
cecina—just a good eye. The amounts
provided below are merely meant as a guide
for those attempting to make cecina for the
first time. In the summer, you can scatter fried
zucchini blossoms on top of the cecina before
it finishes cooking, or serve it alongside grilled
vegetables and sliced buffalo mozzarella or
aged sheep's cheese.

SERVES 6

- 4 *cups chickpea flour*
- *Salt to taste*
- *Extra-virgin olive oil as needed*
- *Freshly ground black pepper to taste*

Preheat the oven to 350°F. Whisk together the
chickpea flour and 6 cups water to make a
fairly thin batter. Adjust salt. Pour a generous
amount of olive oil in a baking pan, add the
chickpea flour mixture, and stir to combine
well. The mixture should be a little less than
½ inch deep in the pan. Bake in the preheated
oven until a golden crust forms on top. Sprinkle with a generous amount of black pepper
and serve hot.

FARINATA ⫷
Crusty Chickpea and
Rosemary Pancake
Farinateria Da Puppo, Albenga (Savona), Liguria

keep in mind when making this that the
batter needs to rest for about 5 hours. The
resting time will vary depending on the
season—in summer, 2 to 3 hours will likely
be enough, but in winter you may want to let
the batter rest for as long as 6 hours. This thin,
crispy pancake is made in a copper pan 30
inches in diameter. Be sure your oven is large
enough before you begin, or try dividing it
between two smaller pans. If you like
your farinata extra-thin, about 1/10 inch, as
some people do, use about ¾ of the amounts
provided below.

SERVES 8
- 2 *tablespoons plus 1 teaspoon salt*
- 6 *cups chickpea flour, sifted*
- 1 *cup extra-virgin olive oil*
- *Leaves of 1 sprig rosemary or 1 chive*
  sprig, minced

In a large bowl combine 3 quarts water, the
salt, and the sifted chickpea flour. Mix with an
eggbeater until well combined, then set aside
to rest for 5 minutes. Skim any foam off the top
and discard, and then set aside to rest for about
5 hours. (See note.)

Preheat the oven to 475°F. It is best for heat
to be applied from all sides, so if your oven has
the option of a top and bottom heat source, use
both. Pour the oil into a (preferably copper) pan
at least 30 inches in diameter and swirl it to be
sure it covers the entire surface. Pour in the batter. Sprinkle on the minced rosemary. Briefly
mix the batter and then bake in the preheated
oven until the bottom is browned (use a spatula
to lift it carefully to check) and a crust has
formed on top, about 25 minutes. Serve hot.

FRICO CON PATATE 🌳
Cheese and Potato Pancake
Osteria dal Cjco, Oltrerugo di Castelnovo del Friuli
(Pordenone), Friuli Venezia Giulia

*f*rico is the signature dish of the Friuli mountains and parts of the region's plains as well. It seems that every valley lays claim to being the birthplace of frico, and each has one that's slightly different—soft or crisp, with polenta, with potatoes, with onions. The one thing that all share is the cheese, which is DOP (Protected Designation of Origin) cow's milk montasio. Mario Mancini, the chef at Vecchio Stallo in Udine, makes frico by peeling, boiling, and ricing two pounds of potatoes. In an 11-inch skillet, he then browns minced onion in oil and stirs in the potatoes, cooking the mixture until the flavors are combined. When it's nice and hot, he adds very thin slices of the cheese—both aged and fresh versions—and continues to cook patiently over low heat. At that point he turns up the heat and treats the mixture like a frittata, allowing it to form a nice browned crust on the bottom, and then flipping it to cook the other side. He cuts it into wedges and serves it with polenta.

SERVES 4
¾ cup diced smoked pancetta
1 medium yellow onion, thinly sliced
4 large potatoes, peeled and diced
Salt and freshly ground black pepper to taste
10 ounces 3-month aged montasio cheese, thinly sliced

In a pot, sauté the pancetta and the onion until the onion begins to color. Add the potatoes, season with salt and pepper, and add about ½ cup water. Cover and cook over low heat for 30 minutes.

Gradually stir in the cheese slices, allowing them to melt between additions. Skim off any fat and transfer the mixture to an 8-inch nonstick skillet. Cook the frico until golden on both sides, flipping it once using a spatula. Cut into 4 wedges and serve.

PANELLE ▦
Chickpea Flour Fritters
Antica Focacceria San Francesco, Palermo, Sicília

*T*o make these fritters, the cooked chickpea flour is usually placed in wood or aluminum molds. You can achieve a similar effect by spreading it on a sheet pan and then using a table knife to cut it into rectangles once it is cool. Professional panella makers like those at Antica Focacceria San Francesco fry their panelle in peanut oil, as they say olive oil imparts too strong a flavor.

SERVES 6 TO 8
4 cups finely ground chickpea flour
Salt and freshly ground black pepper to taste
¼ cup minced parsley or wild fennel fronds
Peanut oil for frying

In a pot, combine the chickpea flour with enough cold water to make a batter. Place over medium heat and bring to a boil, stirring constantly with a wooden spoon in the same direction, until the mixture is thick and well combined. Season with salt and pepper, stir in the parsley, and remove from the heat. While the mixture is still hot, use a spatula to spread it evenly in the appropriate aluminum or wood molds. (See note.)

Allow the mixture to cool somewhat, and when it is cool enough to handle, gently remove it from the molds using the tip of a knife. Set aside to cool completely.

When it is completely cool, bring a generous amount of peanut oil to high heat in a pot with high sides and fry the panelle until golden and crisp. Drain and serve.

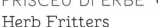

FRISCEU DI ERBE 🌿
Herb Fritters
Trattoria Chiapparino, Uscio (Genova), Liguria

risceu are a signature dish representative of the earthy side of Ligurian cuisine (as opposed to the region's many fish and seafood dishes). These fritters can be made with all kinds of greens, including chard, lettuce, radicchio, and nettles. In some places in the inland part of the Imperia area they are even made with beans. Liguria also has meat fritters and all kinds of sweet fritters made with rice, raisins, or fresh fruit. Apple fritters are a classic snack for Saint Joseph's Day here as they are in many areas of Italy.

SERVES 4
- 2 cups unbleached all-purpose flour
- 1 pinch active dry yeast
- 4 large eggs
- 1 bunch borage or chives
- Olive oil for frying
- Salt to taste

Mix the flour, yeast, and eggs to make a batter. Set aside to rest for 30 minutes.

Trim, wash, and dry the herbs, then mince and mix into the batter.

Line a baking sheet with paper towels. Place olive oil for frying in a pot with high sides and bring to high temperature. Drop the batter in by the spoonful. Fry the fritters, in batches if necessary, until puffed and golden, about 5 minutes. Remove with a skimmer and transfer to the prepared paper towels briefly to drain, then salt and serve.

CROCCHÈ DI PATATE ●
Potato-Cheese Croquettes
Ristorante Costantinopoli, Celso di Pollica (Salerno), Campania

rocchè, a dialect word for the Italian *crocchetta*, or croquette, indicates a rustic fritter cooked at home or available in the form of street food. Sicilia's *cazzilli* are potato croquettes, while in Napoli the most common fritter is made from risen dough. Cilento goat cheese is available fresh or aged. It has a mild flavor and a creamy consistency.

SERVES 4
- 2 pounds potatoes
- 3 large eggs, lightly beaten
- 2 ounces Cilento goat cheese (see note)
- 2 ounces provolone
- Salt and freshly ground black pepper to taste
- Extra-virgin olive oil for frying
- ¼ cup breadcrumbs

Boil the potatoes and peel and mash them while they are still warm. In a bowl combine them with the lightly beaten eggs. Crumble in the goat cheese (or grate if using a more aged type). Slice the provolone and add to the bowl. Season the mixture with salt and pepper. Knead until well combined and form the mixture into croquettes in your preferred shape (round or oval). Line a baking sheet with paper towels. Place olive oil for frying in a pot with high sides and bring to high temperature. Dredge the prepared croquettes in the breadcrumbs and fry until browned on the surface. Transfer to the prepared paper towels briefly to drain, then serve.

FRITTELLE DI BACCALÀ
Baccalà Fritters
Gino Zampolini, Magione (Perugia), Umbria

To serve 4 people, combine 1½ cups flour, ½ teaspoon baking soda, and a pinch of salt. Lightly beat together 3 tablespoons extra-virgin olive oil, 1 egg, and 1 egg yolk and stir into the dry ingredients, then add enough milk to make a batter with the consistency of sour cream. Place at least 2 cups olive oil for frying in a pot with high sides and bring to high temperature. Chop about 1½ pounds salt cod (soaked in several changes of water, skinned, and boned) and toss in the batter, then drop spoonfuls of the mixture in the oil and fry until golden. Serve hot or cold, accompanied by lemon slices if desired.

In Cupra Marittima, a town in the Ascoli Piceno province in the Marche, Eleonora Rossi makes baccalà fritters by boiling salt cod with an equal amount (by weight) of potatoes until soft, then pureeing them with a handful of parsley leaves and frying the resulting mixture.

FAVETTA
Fava Flour Puree
Licia Timossi, Genova, Liguria

Favetta is a relative of Sicilia's *maccu* and Puglia's *'n capriata*, which incorporate chicory or broccoli rabe with the fava flour puree. You can also make a very good soup by using half the amount of fava flour.

To make enough to serve 4, combine 2½ cups fava flour and 4 cups salted water in a pot and cook over low heat, stirring constantly, for 1 hour. When the mixture is very dense, pour it onto a plate, spread evenly with a spatula, and allow it to cool. Cut the cooked and cooled puree into ½-inch slices. Serve the favetta one of two ways: drizzle on olive oil and sprinkle with black pepper and serve at room temperature; or sauté thinly sliced spring onions

in olive oil, then add the favetta slices to the skillet and heat through, and, finally, sprinkle with sliced scallions and serve warm.

PANISSA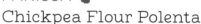
Chickpea Flour Polenta
Trattoria La Brinca, Ne (Genova), Liguria

This recipe provides instructions for serving panissa at room temperature, which is absolutely delicious, but you can also pan-fry slices of panissa or warm them quickly on a griddle.

SERVES 6
2½ cups chickpea flour
Salt to taste
Extra-virgin olive oil for drizzling
Freshly ground black pepper to taste
    (optional)
1   small yellow onion, thinly sliced

In a pot, whisk the chickpea flour with about 4 cups warm water until there are no lumps. Season with salt and place over low heat. Cook, stirring constantly, until thickened, about 40 minutes. Pour the mixture onto a plate, spread evenly with a spatula, and allow to cool.

Cut the cooled panissa into slices and place them on a platter. Drizzle with olive oil, season with a little salt and pepper, if desired, scatter on the onion, and serve.

BELECAUDA
Chickpea Flour Pancake with Rosemary
Luigi Morando, Nizza Monferrato (Asti), Piemonte

Belecauda is local dialect for "good and hot," and it is the name given to a chickpea flour pancake in southern Piemonte (Nizza Monferrato, Ovada, Novi Ligure, the provinces of Asti and Alessandria). This recipe comes from Luigi "Gigi" Morando, who was the chef and the creative force behind Pro Loco in Nizza Monferrato for years. He strongly recommends using spring water in this dish and baking it in a copper pan in a wood-burning oven, and he cautions that results may otherwise be less than satisfactory. Below we provide instructions for making belecauda in a home oven at high heat. Just keep a close watch on it to be sure it doesn't burn. If a 16-inch pan won't fit in your oven, make a smaller belecauda in a pan 14 inches in diameter, but leave about 1 cup of the batter aside or the belecauda will be too thick.

SERVES 4 TO 5
4 cups spring water or bottled mineral water (still, not sparkling) at room temperature
2½ cups chickpea flour
About 1 teaspoon salt
1½ cups whole milk
½ cup extra-virgin olive oil
Leaves of 1 sprig rosemary
Freshly ground black pepper to taste

Place the water in a large bowl and very gradually sprinkle in the chickpea flour, whisking constantly to keep lumps from forming. Season with salt to taste, but keep in mind that the mixture always tastes flat. Whisk in the milk. Set the mixture aside to rest for 2 hours. After 2 hours, skim any foam from the batter, then stir in ¼ cup olive oil. Preheat the oven to 500°F.

Use the remaining ¼ cup olive oil to grease a copper pan 16 inches in diameter and pour the batter into it. The batter should be no more than ⅓ inch thick. Scatter the rosemary leaves on top. Bake in the preheated oven until it has a dark golden crust on top. Serve hot with a sprinkling of salt and black pepper.

FRITTELLE DI ALGHE MARINE
Seaweed Fritters
Ristorante La Guardiola, Diamante (Cosenza), Calabria

Ulva lactuca, or sea lettuce, can be purchased in some fish stores, but in their restaurant Claudio and Pino Perrone use seaweed that they harvest just outside their establishment, which sits right on the coast. Seaweed can be fried either in its natural state or, as it is here, in a batter, and it can also be eaten raw dressed with a little oil, garlic, lemon juice, and a pinch of pepper. These fritters can also be made with an eggless batter—simply make a batter of flour, water, and salt and add the seaweed. Drop into the oil with a tablespoon.

SERVES 4
¼ cup unbleached all-purpose flour
Salt to taste
2 egg whites
Extra-virgin olive oil for frying
16 (4 by 4-inch) leaves of sea lettuce, cut into strips

Place the flour in a bowl and whisk in ½ cup water. Whisk smooth. Add a pinch of salt. Beat the egg whites to stiff peaks and fold into the mixture. Line a baking sheet with paper towels. Place olive oil for frying in a pot with high sides and bring to high temperature. Dredge the strips of sea lettuce in the batter and fry in the oil until puffed and golden, working in batches if necessary to keep from crowding the pot. Remove with a skimmer and transfer briefly to the prepared paper towels to drain, then season with a little salt. Serve hot and crispy.

❧ {VEGETABLE DISHES} ☙

INSALATA DI FARRO E VERDURE 🍃
Farro and Vegetable Salad
Locanda dell'Arte, Città Sant'Angelo (Pescara), Abruzzo

A room temperature rice salad with vegetables is an Italian summertime classic. Farro stands in for the rice with wonderful results not only in terms of flavor, but also in terms of nutrition.

SERVES 4 TO 6

1   tablespoon white wine vinegar
¼   cup fresh corn kernels
1   red bell pepper, seeded and cut into julienne
1   yellow bell pepper, seeded and cut into julienne
¼   cup shelled peas
¼   cup sliced mushrooms
2   carrots, cut into julienne
3   artichokes, trimmed and cut into wedges
1   rib celery, cut into julienne
8   cups vegetable broth
1   medium yellow onion, minced
1   clove garlic, minced
Extra-virgin olive oil for sautéing and dressing
1   cup pearled farro
½   cup dry white wine
½   cup pitted black and green olives
¼   cup capers, rinsed and drained
⅓   cup canned tuna in olive oil, drained
2   tomatoes, cut into wedges
1   cucumber, cut into julienne
Leaves of 1 sprig basil
Salt to taste

Bring a large pot of water to a boil. Add the vinegar. Cook separately (because each will have a different cooking time) until tender the corn, peppers, peas, mushrooms, carrots, artichokes, and celery. Drain and set aside.

Place the broth in a pot, bring to a boil, then turn down to a simmer. In a skillet, cook the onion and garlic in olive oil over low heat. When they begin to color, add the farro and cook, stirring frequently, until it begins to toast. Add the wine and continue to cook until the liquid has evaporated. Begin to add the broth, about ½ cup at a time, stirring until incorporated between additions, until the farro is cooked al dente. You may not need all of the broth.

Allow the farro mixture to cool and when it has cooled, transfer it to a large bowl and combine with the cooked vegetables. Dress with additional olive oil. Toss with the olives and capers and flake in the tuna, then add the tomatoes and cucumber and the basil leaves. Season with salt and serve.

BAGNÉ 'NT L'EULI
Raw Vegetables Dipped in Olive Oil
Anna Maria Montersino, Lequio Tanaro (Cuneo), Piemonte

This simple dish highlights the incredible aroma and flavor of traditionally produced olive oil (made from Ligurian olives) and the equally amazing produce cultivated on the plain between Alba, Bra, and Carmagnola. To this day farmers in the Langhe, Roero, and Monferrato areas begin their days with a hearty breakfast of *bagné 'nt l'euli* (Piemonte dialect for "dip in oil"). Needless to say, all vegetables here should be fresh and young so that they are tender, and the olive oil should be of the highest quality.

Use these vegetables in any combination: tomatoes cut into wedges; artichokes trimmed, chokes removed, and quartered; fennel bulbs cut into wedges; bell peppers seeded and cut into strips; whole small radishes; ribs of celery; whole young leeks; whole spring onions. Place the vegetables on a large platter in the center of the table. Give each diner a small bowl of oil and a small dish of salt and allow everyone to serve themselves, dip in the oil, sprinkle with salt, and enjoy.

CONDIGGION
Ligurian Salad with Tomatoes and Olives
Lucia Parodi, Latte di Ventimiglia (Imperia), Liguria

This rustic summer dish is redolent with the flavors of the garden, the sea, and Liguria's famed local olive oil. Rub a wooden salad bowl all over with a garlic clove. Add slightly under-ripe oxheart tomatoes cut into wedges; long green peppers cut into strips; spring onions cut into strips; cucumber peeled and cut into strips. Add torn basil leaves, pitted Taggiasca olives, and either

rinsed, boned, and chopped salted anchovies or thinly sliced *mosciame* (salt-cured tuna). Make a dressing of extra-virgin olive oil, white wine vinegar, and a pinch of salt, then pour over the vegetables and toss. You can also add sliced hard-boiled egg if you like. Allow to rest at room temperature 10 to 20 minutes.

INSALATA DI FAVE COTTOIA
Fava Bean Salad
Trattoria La Rusticana, Modica (Ragusa), Sicilia

Mattea Magistri of Messina boils fresh, tender fava beans in salted water with an onion and then drains the beans, retaining a bit of their cooking liquid. She slices off the bump on the top of each bean, then dresses them with extra-virgin olive oil, a pinch of oregano, and a few mint leaves.

SERVES 4
1 pound dried fava beans
Salt to taste
Extra-virgin olive oil for dressing
White wine vinegar for dressing
1 rib celery, diced
1 clove garlic, minced
1 small piece chili pepper, minced
Leaves of 1 sprig parsley, minced

Soak the fava beans in warm water until softened, about 3 hours. Use the tip of a paring knife to cut away the black spot on the tip of each. Place the beans in a pot with a generous amount of cold water. Bring to a boil and cook for about 20 minutes from the time the water comes to a boil. Drain the water and add boiling water to the pot. Salt and cook the fava beans until they are floury, about 45 minutes. Drain the beans, retaining enough of their cooking liquid to keep them moist.

Dress the beans with oil and vinegar and toss with the celery, garlic, chili pepper, and parsley. Allow to rest at room temperature until the flavors meld, about 10 minutes, and serve.

INSALATA DI OVOLI
Ovolo Mushroom Salad
*Trattoria Antica Filanda, Capri Leone
(Messina), Sicilia*

Ovolo mushrooms are found in the hills of Sicilia and they resemble eggs. Always rely on an expert's advice when foraging for mushrooms, especially when picking ovolo mushrooms, which bear a close resemblance to several poisonous varieties.

SERVES 4

4 *ovolo mushrooms (about 2 ounces each)*
Salt to taste
Lemon juice to taste
¼ *cup light and fruity extra-virgin olive oil*
Freshly ground black pepper to taste

Thinly slice the mushrooms and toss them with a little salt. They will begin to give off their liquid in a very short time, and after they do they will absorb the other flavors better.

Whisk together a small amount of lemon juice, the olive oil, and a pinch of pepper to use as a dressing. Be sure not to overdress the mushrooms, as that will cover up their delicate flavor. Toss to combine. Adjust salt if necessary and serve.

POMODORI SECCHI RIPIENI
Stuffed Dried Tomatoes
Giuseppe Carollo, Castelbuono (Palermo), Sicilia

There is no shortage of recipes for stuffed tomatoes, whether the tomatoes in question are left raw or roasted. This recipe is a little out-of-the-ordinary in its use of sun-dried tomatoes, which are made by cutting ripe tomatoes in half, salting them, and leaving them in the sun until they shrivel. The tomatoes are then pressed and typically are dressed with a little chili pepper and basil or with capers, oregano, and wild fennel and preserved in oil. You will need good-quality, meaty sun-dried tomatoes for this dish, though they needn't have been soaked in oil as they will be boiled to soften.

Soak sun-dried tomato halves overnight in cold water. The next day, drain and boil until soft. Drain well. Make a filling of beaten eggs, minced parsley, minced mint, a small amount of grated aged sheep's cheese, and crumbled stale bread (moistened with water to soften and squeezed dry). Season with salt and pepper. Make a batter by whisking together flour, a pinch of baking soda, lemon juice, and a drizzle of olive oil. Sandwich a pinch of the filling between 2 tomato halves, dredge in the batter, then fry in a generous amount of hot olive oil. Repeat with remaining tomato halves, filling, and batter. Drain briefly on paper towels and serve hot.

INSALATA DI ZUCCHINE E PINOLI
Zucchini Pine Nut Salad
Trattoria Antica Cereria, Parma, Emilia-Romagna

If you prefer not to eat your zucchini raw, you can steam the zucchini for a few minutes to soften them. Either way, this salad is delicious.

SERVES 4

1 *pound baby zucchini, thinly sliced into rounds*
¾ *cup pine nuts*
1 *cup Parmigiano Reggiano shavings*
2 *tablespoons balsamic vinegar*
½ *cup extra-virgin olive oil*
Salt to taste

In a bowl, combine the zucchini, pine nuts, and Parmigiano Reggiano. Gently mix to combine.

With a fork, whisk together the vinegar, olive oil, and a pinch of salt until amalgamated. Use that mixture to dress the salad, then let it sit for about 15 minutes before serving.

FRIGGIONE DI VERDURE
Sautéed Vegetables
Trattoria E' Parlaminté, Imola (Bologna), Emília-Romagna

This quick sauté highlights the flavor of spring vegetables. Feel free to vary the proportions if you like.

SERVES 6

1   medium eggplant, cut into 2-inch julienne
Salt to taste
2   zucchini, cut into 2-inch julienne
Extra-virgin olive oil for frying and sautéing
1   red bell pepper, seeded and cut into ¾-inch dice
14 ounces (about 3 medium) onions, thinly sliced
3   tomatoes, diced
2   cloves garlic, minced
Leaves of 1 sprig rosemary, minced
Freshly ground black pepper to taste

Salt the eggplant and let it drain in a colander for at least 1 hour. Do the same for the zucchini in a separate colander. Place an inch or two of oil in a skillet with high sides and fry the eggplant, zucchini, and pepper pieces separately. Drain and keep warm.

In a clean skillet, sauté the onions in a small amount of oil and when they begin to color, add the tomatoes. When the tomatoes have broken down, add the eggplant, zucchini, and peppers and the minced garlic and rosemary. Adjust salt and pepper, sauté for a few minutes to combine the flavors, and serve.

PANZANELLA
Tomato and Bread Salad
Ristorante Il Carlino d'Oro, Gaiole in Chianti (Siena), Toscana

In addition to the ingredients provided here by Marisa Azzurrini of the Ristorante Il Carlino d'Oro, a Chianti restaurant that has been in the able hands of the Fabbri family for half a century, other garden vegetables can be added to this dish. A panzanella on the heartier side makes an excellent light supper when the weather is too warm to turn on the stove.

SERVES 8

2   pounds (1 large loaf or about 8 cups large cubes) stale bread
5   tomatoes, peeled and diced
2   medium onions, minced
Leaves of 1 sprig basil
Extra-virgin olive oil for dressing
Wine vinegar for dressing
Salt to taste

Soak the bread in water for about 20 minutes. Squeeze very dry and tear it into pieces by hand, letting the pieces fall into a salad bowl. Add the tomatoes and the onions to the bowl, then tear the basil leaves into small pieces and add those as well. Make a dressing of olive oil, a small amount of vinegar, and salt and toss. Refrigerate for at least 1 hour before serving.

INSALATA RUSSA 🥕
"Russian" Salad
Osteria La Salita, Monforte d'Alba (Cuneo), Piemonte

What Italians call "Russian salad" actually hails from the Piemonte region (and, oddly, in Russia is known as "Italian salad"). It probably came from Paris during the Belle Époque, at a time when wealthy Russian nobles were moving to Paris in droves. The original recipe was elaborate and costly—it often included cubes of truffle, cow's tongue, lobster, and caviar. Today's version is lighter. Ornella Scarzello of Osteria La Salita in Monforte d'Alba says that the secret is to use only the freshest vegetables from your garden and, of course, always make your own mayonnaise.

SERVES 8

- 8   potatoes, peeled and diced
- 4   carrots, diced
- 4   ribs celery, diced
- 1   red bell pepper, diced
- 1   yellow bell pepper, diced
- ¼   cup shelled peas
- Salt to taste
- 3 to 4 whole cloves
- 2   tablespoons white wine vinegar
- 2   tablespoons sugar
- 4   zucchini, diced
- ¼   cup chopped green beans
- 3   egg yolks
- Juice of 1 lemon
- 2   cups extra-virgin olive oil
- ⅔   cup canned tuna in olive oil, drained
- 1   tomato, diced
- ¼   cup Taggiasca olives
- ¼   cup minced parsley

Cook the potatoes, carrots, celery, bell peppers, and peas separately in lightly salted boiling water until just tender. Add the cloves, the vinegar, and the sugar to the boiling water and cook the zucchini and the green beans. Drain vegetables and set aside to cool.

In a large bowl, make a mayonnaise by beating the egg yolks with a pinch of salt and the lemon juice and slowly drizzling in the oil while whisking constantly. Flake in the tuna and stir until evenly distributed. Fold the cooked and cooled vegetables into the mayonnaise and stir until evenly distributed. Transfer the mixture to a serving platter and garnish with diced tomato, olives, and parsley.

INSALATA DI SEDANO RAPA E MELE 🍎
Celery Root and Apple Salad
Ristorante Baita Ermitage, Ermitage di Courmayeur (Aosta), Valle d'Aosta

Celery root is widely appreciated in northeastern Italy, where many recipes highlight its unusual flavor. The edible portion of this vegetable is its root, which is round and wrinkled and has tender off-white flesh. It should be peeled.

SERVES 4

- 1   tablespoon white vinegar
- Salt to taste
- 7   ounces celery root (see note), cut into julienne
- 2   large eggs
- Juice of ½ lemon
- 1½   cups extra-virgin olive oil
- 2   Delizia Valdostana apples or other crisp apples
- ½   cup walnuts, chopped

Bring a pot of water to a boil and add the vinegar and salt lightly. Boil the celery root until just tender but still crisp in the center. Set aside to cool for at least 1 hour.

In the meantime, make a mayonnaise by beating the eggs with a pinch of salt and the lemon juice and slowly drizzling in the oil while whisking constantly.

Peel and core the apples and thinly slice them. In a bowl, toss the apple slices, the celery root, and the mayonnaise and stir to combine. Garnish the salad with chopped walnuts.

TOMATICHE AL BAGNET VERD 🌿
Tomatoes with Parsley Stuffing
Agriturismo Ca' del Re, Verduno (Cuneo), Piemonte

I t's best to prepare the stuffing a couple of hours in advance to give the flavors a chance to meld.

SERVES 6

1   (2- to 3-inch) square piece of crustless stale bread
1   tablespoon wine vinegar
2   cups tightly packed flat-leaf parsley leaves
1   clove garlic
4   salted anchovies, rinsed and boned
2   large eggs, hard-boiled
Extra-virgin olive oil for drizzling
Salt to taste
6   tomatoes

Soak the bread in the vinegar, then squeeze dry. Mince the parsley, garlic, anchovies, and bread together. Transfer the mixture to a bowl and force the yolks of the hard-boiled eggs through a sieve and into the bowl. (Reserve the egg whites for another use.) Stir the yolks while drizzling in olive oil—add enough oil to make a thick mixture. Taste and adjust salt. Halve and seed the tomatoes and stuff them with the parsley mixture.

FRITTO DI VERDURE LIGURE 🍅
Ligurian Fried Vegetables
Ristorante Dâ Casetta, Borgio Verezzi (Savona), Liguria

A selection of fried vegetables in Liguria is usually served with some cubes of fried *latte brusco* as well. To make latte brusco, clarify some butter in a large-diameter pot with low sides, then add chopped onion and

parsley. Whisk in flour and milk, stirring constantly to avoid allowing lumps to form. Cook over low heat for 15 minutes, stirring constantly, until the mixture has become a dense cream. Remove from the heat, add egg yolks one at a time, whisking to combine between additions, then season with salt and spread evenly on a large serving platter, leveling the top with a spatula. Once the mixture has cooled, it solidifies and can be cut into cubes that are then dredged in breadcrumbs and fried along with the vegetables.

SERVES 4

1   bulb fennel, cut into julienne
1   black salsify root, cut into julienne
1   bunch asparagus, tips only
¾   cup unbleached all-purpose flour
Salt to taste
Extra-virgin olive oil for frying
1   eggplant, cut into julienne
3   tomatoes, seeded and cut into wedges
2   zucchini, cut into julienne
1   medium yellow onion, sliced into rings
3 to 4 rosemary leaves
¼   cup loosely packed sage leaves
2   sprigs marjoram

Bring a large pot of water to a boil and boil the fennel and salsify until tender, about 3 minutes. Boil the asparagus until tender, about 1 minute.

Place the flour in a soup bowl and whisk in enough water to make a batter that is a little runnier than sour cream. Make sure no lumps form. Season with salt. Fill a pot with high sides with a generous amount of olive oil for frying and place over medium-high heat. Working with a few pieces at a time and without crowding the pan, dredge the vegetables in the batter and then fry until crisp and golden. As they are finished, remove from the oil with a skimmer. Fry the rosemary leaves, sage leaves, and marjoram as well.

SCHIBBECI 🖤
Vegetables in Escabeche
Tea Bucafusca, Mîlazzo (Messina), Sicîlia

Cut round eggplant, yellow onion, bell peppers, peeled potatoes, and seeded tomatoes into pieces roughly the same size and shape. Fry the vegetables separately in olive oil. Combine fried vegetables in a clean pot and stir gently to combine. Add a generous amount of white wine vinegar and enough tomato sauce to coat and cook over low heat for 10 minutes. Tear mint leaves into the pot and scatter in caciocavallo cheese cut into small dice. Adjust salt to taste, stir to combine, and remove from the heat. Allow to cool before serving.

ASPARAGI CON SALSA AL BASILICO 🍃
Asparagus with Basil Sauce
Osteria Boccondivino, Bra (Cuneo), Piemonte

It is a truism of Italian cooking that items that share a growing season always go well together. Case in point: the combination of asparagus and basil.

SERVES 4
Salt to taste
1 bunch asparagus, stalks peeled if tough
1 large egg
2 basil leaves
½ teaspoon white wine vinegar
½ cup extra-virgin olive oil

Bring a pot of salted water to a boil and cook the asparagus briefly, until just tender and still crisp in the center. Drain. Place the egg, basil leaves, vinegar, and salt in the bowl of a food processor fitted with the metal blade. With the processor running, pour the olive oil through the tube in a thin stream to make a green sauce. Serve the asparagus with sauce on the side.

ASPARAGI E UOVA BASOCCHE 🎲
Asparagus with Soft-Boiled Eggs
Vecia Osteria del Moro, Pordenone, Friuli Venezia Giulia

The Veneto dialect term *basocche* means "soft-boiled" and refers to the eggs in this dish, which have a firm white but a soft and creamy yolk.

SERVES 4
8 large eggs
24 stalks asparagus, stalks peeled
Salt to taste
Juice of ½ lemon
1 tablespoon white wine vinegar
Extra-virgin olive oil for drizzling
Freshly ground black pepper to taste

Bring a pot of water to a boil and add the eggs. Boil for 4 minutes, then set aside to cool.

Cook the asparagus, standing up with their tips facing upward, in a pot of boiling lightly salted water with the lemon juice and vinegar added to it for 10 minutes.

Peel the eggs, taking care not to break them. Arrange the warm asparagus on a platter and drizzle with olive oil. Season with salt and pepper and place the whole eggs on top.

CARCIOFI ALLA ROMANA
Roman Artichokes
Osteria Tram Tram, Roma, Lazio

The Roman or Romanesco artichoke is a variety with a large round top that is used throughout central Italy and is informally known as a *mamma* or *mammola*. The most common artichoke of this type takes its name from the Medieval city of Campagnano, located north of Roma, but the methods used to prepare it indicate that it originated in the south, in the land of the Volsci people along the Appian Way, which for 1,500 years was heavily populated by Jews. Indeed, the mammola is the artichoke used in perhaps the most famous traditional Jewish recipe in Italy, carciofi alla giudìa, made by trimming away all of the hard leaves and chokes, boiling the artichokes, and then deep-frying them just before serving so that they resemble crispy golden flowers.

SERVES 4
8   Romanesco artichokes
1   lemon
2 to 3 cloves garlic, minced
Leaves of 1 sprig calamint, minced
Leaves of 1 sprig parsley, minced
Salt and freshly ground black pepper
    to taste
Extra-virgin olive oil for drizzling

Remove and discard the hard outer leaves of the artichokes. Trim the tops and use a spoon to scoop out the chokes. Drop into acidulated water (a bowl of water with the juice of the lemon added) for 10 minutes or rub all over with the cut side of the lemon.

Combine the garlic, calamint, and parsley, season with salt and pepper, and stuff each artichoke with some of this mixture. Fill a pot taller than the artichokes about one third of the way up the side with water and arrange the artichokes so that they are standing vertically, face-down. Drizzle with a generous amount of oil and cook over low heat for 50 minutes. Serve hot.

CARCIOFI ARROSTITI
Roasted Artichokes
Ristorante Fenesta Verde, Giugliano in Campania (Napoli), Campania

This dish is simplicity itself, but it does require a fireplace or a charcoal grill. If you don't have access to one of those, move on to a different recipe.

SERVES 4
4   medium artichokes
2   cloves garlic
Leaves of 1 sprig parsley
Salt and freshly ground black pepper to taste
Extra-virgin olive oil for drizzling

Trim the artichokes, removing and discarding the stems, and pat dry. Mince together the garlic and parsley, season with salt and pepper, and use this mixture to stuff the artichokes.

Build a fire in a fireplace with a grate or a charcoal grill. Drizzle the artichokes with olive oil and cook in the prepared fire for 20 minutes. Let the artichokes cool, then pull off and discard their tough outer leaves and arrange them on a serving platter. Drizzle with additional oil before serving.

CARCIOFI E UOVA IN SALSA RAVIGOTTA 🌳
Artichokes and Eggs in Herb Sauce
Osteria Burligo, Burligo di Palazzago (Bergamo), Lombardia

*R*avigotta sauce is made by crushing herbs, capers, onions, vinegar, and oil in a mortar and pestle. In this recipe, two anchovy fillets are added to perk up the flavor further.

SERVES 4

1   medium yellow onion
¼   cup salted capers, soaked and drained
Leaves of aromatic herbs such as parsley, chervil, chives, and tarragon, chopped, to taste
Salt and freshly ground black pepper to taste
2 to 3 tablespoons white wine vinegar
½   cup extra-virgin olive oil
4 to 5 artichokes
½   cup dry white wine
Juice of 1 lemon
2   bay leaves
4   large eggs, hard-boiled
1   tablespoon minced flat-leaf parsley for garnish

Mince the onion and rinse it with cold water, then squeeze dry and process in a mortar and pestle with the capers, a generous amount of herbs, and salt and pepper. Process while slowly adding the vinegar and the oil in a thin stream. The result should be a thick sauce. Taste and adjust seasoning.

Trim the hard outer leaves and the chokes, but leave the artichokes whole. Bring a pot of salted water to a boil and add the wine, the lemon juice, and the bay leaves. Blanch the artichokes until tender, then drain and cool.

Gently open up the artichokes so they look like flowers. Cut the hard-boiled eggs into wedges. Arrange the artichokes and eggs on a serving platter. Pour the sauce over the eggs and artichokes, sprinkle with parsley, and serve.

INSALATA DI CASTRAURE 🌿
Baby Artichoke Salad
Trattoria Cortevecchia, Polesella (Rovigo), Veneto

*F*or five centuries, special violet-colored artichokes have grown on the island of Sant'Erasmo in the Venetian lagoon, where the island's salty soil, rich with seashells, gives them a unique flavor. They now have their own Slow Food Presidium. *Castraure* are not a special variety of artichoke, but the first apical buds of the artichoke, harvested in late April, at the start of artichoke season. They are tender enough to be eaten raw as a salad. Indeed, though this salad is delicious, they can also be dressed only with extra-virgin olive oil, salt, and pepper.

SERVES 4

8   Sant'Erasmo castraure or other baby artichokes (see note)
Juice of ¼ lemon
Extra-virgin olive oil for dressing
2   cloves garlic, minced
1   tablespoon minced flat-leaf parsley
Salt and freshly ground black pepper to taste
Grana Padano cheese shavings for garnish
Leaves of 1 sprig parsley for garnish

Trim the artichokes and cut them into julienne. Whisk together the lemon juice, a small amount of olive oil, the garlic, and the minced parsley. Season with salt and pepper and toss with the artichokes until well combined. Arrange on a serving platter and garnish with the cheese and parsley leaves.

CARCIOFI RITTI
Stuffed Artichokes
Ristorante Il Mecenate, Lucca, Toscana

At the Osteria dell'Acquasanta in Mele (province of Genova), they make a stuffing out of the artichoke hearts and stems, garlic, parsley, marjoram, a drop of extra-virgin olive oil, salt, and pepper. In Catania, Alfonso La Rosa makes a stuffing of grated aged sheep's cheese, bread-crumbs, anchovies, garlic, and parsley and a drizzle of extra-virgin olive oil. Another Sicilian version replaces the anchovy with crumbled pork sausage.

SERVES 6

10 ounces top-quality ground beef

¼ cup plus 2 tablespoons grated Parmigiano Reggiano

Leaves of 1 sprig parsley, minced

1 (2- to 3-inch) square piece of crustless stale bread, soaked in water and squeezed dry

Salt and freshly ground black pepper to taste

Juice of 2 lemons

18 artichokes

Extra-virgin olive oil for sautéing

1 cup diced smoked pancetta

2 cups whole peeled tomatoes

Combine the beef, grated cheese, and parsley. Tear the bread into the mixture and season with salt and pepper. Stir to combine.

In a bowl, combine the lemon juice with cold water. Remove and peel the stems of the artichokes. Remove and discard the hard outer leaves and chokes. Carve out the hearts of the artichokes, leaving the rest intact. Drop the artichokes, their hearts, and their stems into the water as you prepare them. Drain artichoke stems and hearts and chop roughly.

Place a generous amount of oil in a pot over medium heat and add the pancetta. Add the chopped artichoke stems and hearts, peeled tomatoes, and salt and pepper. Cook until tender and combined.

Stuff the artichoke bodies with the beef mixture and arrange them in a pot so that they are supporting each other and standing up vertically. Gently pour the pancetta mixture over them. Cook over medium heat, occasionally basting them with the cooking liquid that forms in the bottom of the pot. If the pot appears to be drying out, add a little water. Cook until the bases of the artichokes are tender and easily pierced with a knife, about 40 minutes. Place 3 artichokes standing vertically on each of 6 individual serving plates and drizzle with cooking liquid.

CASTRAURE IN TECIA 🌰
Braised Baby Artichokes
Ofelia Facco, Cavallino Treporti (Venezia), Veneto

Trim Venetian castraure (or other baby artichokes) and gently open them like flowers. Arrange them standing up in a pot with a tight-fitting lid. Drizzle on a little oil and season with salt and pepper, then add enough cold water to cover the artichokes. Cover the pot and cook over low heat until the liquid has evaporated, about 20 minutes, shaking the pot occasionally to be sure the artichokes don't stick.

PARMIGIANA DI CARCIOFI 🌿
Artichoke Parmigiana
Pietro Grossolino, Molfetta (Bari), Puglia

Trim and slice artichokes and pat dry. Dredge in flour, then beaten egg, and fry in hot oil until golden. Make a tomato sauce (not too thick) with garlic, tomato puree, salt, and a couple leaves of basil. Spread some of the tomato sauce in the bottom of a baking dish and top with a layer of artichokes. Top with a layer of sliced hard-boiled eggs, and then scatter on diced soppressata from Calabria and diced provola cheese. Sprinkle with grated Parmigiano Reggiano. Repeat layers in this order, ending with a layer of tomato sauce on top. Scatter on torn basil leaves. Bake in a preheated 350°F oven until the top is golden and the cheese is melted, 30 to 45 minutes. Serve warm.

SFOGLIA DI CARCIOFI E PROVOLONE 🥖
Artichoke and Provolone Pies
Maria Orlandi, Vedano Olona (Varese), Lombardia

You can use store-bought puff pastry for this dish or make your own. You will need 7 ounces pastry. Roll out the puff pastry to about 1/5 inch to form a 12 by 8-inch rectangle, then cut the rectangle into six 4-inch squares. Arrange the squares on a baking sheet, brush with egg yolk, and bake at 400°F until golden, about 15 minutes. Remove and allow to cool, but leave the oven on. Boil trimmed artichokes in lightly salted water with a spoonful of lemon juice in it until tender. Drain, chop, and sauté in a small amount of extra-virgin olive oil until they begin to color, about 10 minutes. Cook 1/4 cup all-purpose flour in 1 tablespoon butter for 1 minute, then whisk in about 2/3 cup diced provolone. Add 1 cup milk in a thin stream while whisking constantly. When the cheese has melted, add 1 additional cup milk. Season with a pinch of pepper, and cook, whisking constantly, until it has formed a fluid and well combined sauce. Cut the squares of puff pastry in half horizontally. Set the tops aside and divide the artichoke mixture among the bottoms. Drizzle on the provolone sauce and top with the top halves of the puff pastry squares. Return to the oven to heat through, about 2 minutes, and serve immediately.

TOPINAMBUR CON CREMA DI BAGNA CAODA 🐟
Jerusalem Artichokes in Bagna Caoda Sauce
Osteria del Boccondivino, Bra (Cuneo), Piemonte

Jerusalem artichokes are pale purple tubers that brighten any garden with their large yellow flowers. They are traditionally eaten raw in bagna caoda. Beppe Barbero of the Osteria del Boccondivino offers this innovative twist on that classic.

SERVES 4
6   salted anchovy fillets, rinsed and boned
3   cloves garlic, crushed
3   tablespoons extra-virgin olive oil
3   tablespoons heavy cream
¼   teaspoon potato starch
14 ounces Jerusalem artichokes
4   cups whole milk
Juice of ½ lemon
Salt to taste

Roughly chop the anchovies and place the anchovies, the garlic, and the olive oil in a small pot. Cook over low heat, stirring occasionally, until the garlic just begins to color. Add the cream and the potato starch and stir to combine. Remove from the heat and puree. (An immersion blender works well.)

Slice the Jerusalem artichokes very thin using a truffle slicer (or a mandoline). In a pot combine the milk, Jerusalem artichokes, lemon juice, and a little salt. Cook over medium heat until the artichokes are tender, 6 to 7 minutes. Drain the artichokes and arrange them in a baking pan. Pour the anchovy sauce over the Jerusalem artichokes and run the pan under the broiler until the top turns golden, 1 to 2 minutes.

TORTINO DI TOPINAMBUR 🥕
Jerusalem Artichoke Flans
Ristorante Garibaldi, Cisterna d'Asti (Asti), Piemonte

At their restaurant in Cisterna d'Asti, the Vaudano family serves these individual flans with a cheese sauce that combines raschera and bra cheeses.

SERVES 6
1   small onion, thinly sliced
Extra-virgin olive oil for sautéing
1   small carrot, thinly sliced
1   rib celery, thinly sliced
1   clove garlic, thinly sliced
1½ pounds Jerusalem artichokes, thinly sliced
2   tablespoons unsalted butter
2   tablespoons unbleached all-purpose flour
1   cup whole milk
Salt and freshly ground black pepper to taste
6   large eggs
¼   cup grated Parmigiano Reggiano

Preheat the oven to 275°F. Sauté the onion in a little olive oil in a large skillet until golden. Add the carrot, celery, garlic, and Jerusalem artichokes and cook over low heat for 40 minutes, until very soft. Set aside to cool.

For the béchamel, melt the butter in a small pot. Whisk in the flour and cook over low heat, whisking constantly, for 1 minute. Pour in the milk in a thin stream, whisking constantly. Continue to cook, whisking constantly, until the mixture has thickened to a consistency slightly thinner than sour cream. Season with salt and pepper and set aside. In a bowl, beat the eggs. Force the vegetable mixture through a sieve into the bowl. Whisk in the béchamel and the grated cheese and adjust salt and pepper. Divide the mixture among 6 individual ramekins or other baking dishes. Arrange the ramekins in a larger baking pan, pour in hot water to come halfway up the sides of the ramekins, and bake in the preheated oven until set, about 40 minutes. Allow to rest for 10 minutes before unmolding.

CARDI GOBBI IN SALSA
Gobbo Cardoons in Garlic Sauce
Francesca Ronco, Dusino San Michele (Asti), Piemonte

Gobbo cardoons are literally "hunchback" cardoons, so named because early on the plants are curved and redirected back underneath the soil. The resulting vegetables are especially tender. A cardoon tastes like a less bitter artichoke. Like artichokes, cardoons should be dropped into acidulated water as they are chopped so that they don't discolor. To make enough to serve 4, boil 1½ to 2 pounds roughly chopped gobbo cardoons until tender, about 1 hour. Meanwhile, place the cloves of 2 heads garlic in a small pot with milk to cover and simmer until soft, about 20 minutes. Drain the garlic, transfer to an earthenware pot, and crush with a fork. Mash in a couple of rinsed, boned, and minced salted anchovies and mash again with the fork. If the mixture is still chunky, purée it until smooth using an immersion blender. Cook over medium heat, stirring with a wooden spoon, for 10 minutes. Drain cooked cardoons and transfer to a serving platter. Pour the sauce over the top and serve.

CARDI INSABBIATI AL DRAGONCELLO
"Sandy" Cardoons with Tarragon
Ristorante Letizia, Nuxis (Carbonia-Iglesias), Sardegna

If you can find wild cardoons, they are preferable for this recipe, but if all you can find are the cultivated kind, those will do fine. Boiling the cardoons with a sprinkling of bran in the water strips them of their bitter skin.

SERVES 4

Salt to taste
10 ounces cardoons, chopped
¼ cup bran
½ cup white wine vinegar
2 fresh tomatoes, roughly chopped
4 dried tomatoes, roughly chopped
Extra-virgin olive oil for making sauce and sautéing
1⅓ cups breadcrumbs
4 salted anchovies, rinsed, boned, and chopped
Leaves of 1 sprig tarragon, minced
Freshly ground black pepper to taste

Bring a large pot of salted water to a boil and cook the cardoons with the bran and the vinegar until soft and easily pierced with a fork, about 20 minutes. Drain and set aside to cool.

Make a sauce by combining the fresh tomatoes and the dried tomatoes in the bowl of a food processor fitted with the metal blade. Process the tomatoes while drizzling olive oil through the tube in a thin stream until the mixture forms a thin sauce. Set aside.

Heat a small amount of olive oil in a skillet and add the breadcrumbs and the anchovies. Cook, stirring frequently, over low heat until the breadcrumbs have toasted. Add the cardoons and the tarragon and a pinch of pepper. Cook over high heat, stirring, until the breadcrumbs coat all sides of the cardoons. Transfer the cardoons to a serving platter and drizzle on the tomato sauce.

CAPONATA DI MELANZANE
Eggplant Caponata
Ristorante Villa Rainò, Gangi (Palermo), Sicilia

Caponata is one of Sicilia's most famous dishes. Pantelleria capers are large and meaty. They hail from the island of that name south of Sicilia.

SERVES 8

4 eggplant, diced
Extra-virgin olive oil for frying and sautéing
Salt to taste
3 medium yellow onions, thinly sliced
3 carrots, diced
1 celery heart, diced
Freshly ground black pepper to taste
1 pinch chili pepper flakes
1 tablespoon Pantelleria capers (see note), rinsed and drained
¼ cup white wine vinegar
1 tablespoon sugar
⅔ cup tomato sauce

Line a baking sheet with paper towels. Fry the eggplant in a generous amount of olive oil until golden. Transfer to the prepared baking sheet and sprinkle with salt.

Sauté the onions, carrots, and celery heart in olive oil over low heat. Season with salt, pepper, and chili pepper. Stir in the capers and cook, stirring occasionally, until soft, about 25 minutes. Add the vinegar and the sugar. Stir in the fried eggplant cubes and the tomato sauce and cook until the liquid has reduced slightly, 5 to 6 minutes.

Remove from the heat and allow to rest for about 2 hours. Serve cold.

CANNOLI DI MELANZANE
Eggplant Rolls
Antico Frantoio Oleario Bardari, Curinga (Catanzaro), Calabria

In this savory version of cannoli, fried eggplant stands in for the pastry shells.

SERVES 4

2 long eggplant, peeled and cut the long way into ½-inch thick slices
Salt to taste
Extra-virgin olive oil for frying
½ cup unbleached all-purpose flour
4 ounces thinly sliced prosciutto cotto
⅔ cup diced provola cheese
1 cup tomato sauce
¼ cup grated Parmigiano Reggiano

Place the eggplant in a colander, sprinkle with salt, and let drain for about 20 minutes. Line a baking sheet with paper towels. Preheat the oven to 350°F. Heat oil for frying in a skillet with high sides. Rinse the eggplant slices, dry them, dredge them in the flour, then fry them until golden. Remove and transfer to the prepared baking sheet to drain.

Place a slice of eggplant on a work surface. Arrange a slice of prosciutto cotto on top of the eggplant and place a cube of cheese at one end. Roll up the eggplant slice and place in a baking pan, seam-side down. Repeat with remaining eggplant, prosciutto cotto, and provola. Distribute the tomato sauce over the eggplant. Sprinkle the grated cheese on top, and bake in the preheated oven until top is browned and cheese has melted, about 20 minutes.

MELANZANE IN SAOR 🍃
Eggplant in Saor
Trattoria al Forno, Refrontolo (Treviso), Veneto

Saor is a delicious sweet-and-sour preparation that predates refrigeration—the vinegar acted as a preservative.

SERVES 4

2 medium round eggplant
Salt to taste
Extra-virgin olive oil for drizzling and
    sautéing
4 medium yellow onions, halved and
    sliced
½ cup white wine vinegar or *dry
    white wine*
2 bay leaves
2 whole cloves
Freshly ground black pepper to taste
¼ cup plus 1 tablespoon black raisins
⅓ cup pine nuts

Preheat the oven to 350°F. Cut the eggplant into slices about ½ inch thick. Arrange the slices in a single layer on a baking sheet, salt lightly, and drizzle with a little olive oil. Bake in the preheated oven until golden, about 15 minutes. Allow to cool.

While the eggplant is cooking, prepare the marinade. Sauté the onions in olive oil. Add the vinegar, the bay leaves, and the cloves. Season with salt and pepper and cook for about 20 minutes over medium heat. Remove from the heat and stir in the raisins and pine nuts. Remove bay leaves and cloves.

Arrange a layer of eggplant slices in a glass container with a tight-fitting lid. Drizzle on some of the marinade and a drizzle of oil. Continue alternating layers until you have used up all of the eggplant and marinade, ending with a layer of marinade on top. Cover and refrigerate at least 24 hours before serving.

MELANZANE RIPIENE 🍅
Stuffed Eggplant
Osteria delle Travi, Bari, Puglia

Look for firm eggplant that are not too heavy for this recipe. (Weighty eggplant often contain an unappetizingly large number of seeds.) Round eggplant do not need to be salted and drained.

SERVES 4

2 round eggplant
Extra-virgin olive oil for sautéing
10 ounces ground beef
2 large eggs, lightly beaten
1¾ cups diced mozzarella
⅓ cup diced prosciutto crudo
¾ cup grated Parmigiano Reggiano
Salt and freshly ground black pepper
    to taste
1 cup tomato sauce

Preheat the oven to 375°F. Halve the eggplant the long way and carve out the flesh, leaving the outer shells intact. Cut the eggplant flesh into cubes and sauté in extra-virgin olive oil until golden. Add the ground beef and cook, stirring occasionally, until the meat is cooked through. Transfer the mixture to a bowl and add the eggs, the mozzarella, the prosciutto, and about half of the grated Parmigiano Reggiano. Season with salt and pepper and mix until thoroughly combined.

Spread about half of the tomato sauce in the bottom of a baking dish. Arrange the eggplant shells on top of the sauce. Stuff the eggplant shells with the meat mixture. Spread the remaining tomato sauce on top of the eggplant and sprinkle on the remaining Parmigiano Reggiano. Bake in the preheated oven until the filling is set, about 30 minutes, then broil for a minute or two to brown the tops.

MELANZANE IN SCAPECE
Eggplant in Escabeche
Ristorante Letizia, Nuxis (Carbonia-Iglesias), Sardegna

Like *saor*, escabeche provided a method for preserving foods by frying them and then marinating them in a vinegar-based liquid. These methods are both used largely for fish and for various vegetables, including eggplant, zucchini, and carrots. Camona tomatoes hail from Sardegna and are very sweet. *Pane carasau* is the island's famous crisp flatbread.

SERVES 4

- 1 rib celery, minced
- 1 medium carrot, minced
- 1 medium yellow onion, minced
- 1 clove garlic, minced
- Extra-virgin olive oil for sautéing and frying
- 1 tablespoon capers, rinsed and drained and chopped
- 8 anchovy fillets in oil, drained
- 2 bell peppers, seeded and diced
- 14 ounces (2 to 3) Camona tomatoes or other very sweet tomatoes, peeled, seeded, and chopped
- 6 dried tomatoes, minced
- ¼ cup white wine vinegar
- 4 medium eggplant
- Salt to taste
- 1 piece pane carasau (see note)
- Freshly ground black pepper to taste
- Extra-virgin olive oil flavored with mint

Sauté the celery, carrot, onion, and garlic in olive oil. When the onion begins to color, add the capers, anchovies, and peppers. Then add the tomatoes and dried tomatoes. Add the vinegar and continue to cook, stirring frequently, until the sauce has reduced and the pan is largely dry, about 45 minutes. Remove from the heat.

Line a baking sheet with paper towels. Peel the eggplant with a vegetable peeler and cut the peel into very thin strips. Fry the eggplant peel in oil and remove to the prepared baking sheet to drain.

Cut the eggplant flesh into ⅓-inch cubes. Fry in olive oil, then with a skimmer remove to the paper towel–lined baking sheet, salt, and let drain. Place some of the eggplant cubes in a terrine dish. Top with some of the tomato mixture. Continue to alternate layers of eggplant cubes and tomato mixture until you have used up the ingredients. Allow to rest for about 2 hours to firm up.

Just before serving, fry the pane carasau and season it with salt and pepper. Place it on a serving platter and invert the terrine dish on top of it. Carefully remove the dish. Garnish with fried eggplant peel. Drizzle on a little mint-flavored olive oil and serve.

POLPETTE DI MELANZANE
Eggplant "Meatballs"
Rosa Lazzaro, Sant'Andrea Apostolo dello Ionio (Catanzaro), Calabria

You can make these more substantial by adding some stale bread soaked in water or milk and then squeezed dry, smoked Scamorza cheese or any other cheese that melts nicely, eggs, or even ground beef. You can also use parsley in place of the basil or substitute zucchini for the eggplant and bake the "meatballs" in the oven.

Salt eggplant and drain bitter liquid, then squeeze dry and boil in salted water until soft, about 3 minutes. Drain and cool, then squeeze dry again and mince with basil and garlic. Combine with grated aged sheep's cheese and season with salt and pepper. Form the mixture into balls, adding breadcrumbs or flour if the mixture is too loose. Dredge the balls in breadcrumbs and fry in a generous amount of extra-virgin olive oil, turning, until browned on all sides.

FRITTELLE DI MELANZANE
Eggplant Fritters
Mattea Magistri, Messina, Sicilia

Round eggplants are recommended here because they do not need to be salted. To serve 6 to 8, slice 2 pounds round eggplants and blanch, then drain, squeeze dry, and mince. Combine with 3 egg yolks, ½ cup grated long-aged sheep's cheese, oregano, nutmeg, salt, and pepper. Stir in ½ cup golden raisins (rehydrated if dry). Form eggplant mixture into small balls and dredge in beaten egg, flour, and breadcrumbs (separately) and fry in hot oil until golden. Avoid crowding pan. Drain briefly and serve hot.

SCARPONI DI MELANZANE
Baked Eggplant Boats
Mario Carpentieri, Napoli, Campania

The name of this recipe indicates the type of eggplant to be used: the long thin ones. This is an ancient recipe, though the inclusion of cheese is a modern development. Cut long eggplant in half the long way and scoop out the flesh. Mince garlic, parsley, rinsed and boned salted anchovies, mozzarella or provolone, and a couple of tomatoes with the eggplant flesh. Add enough breadcrumbs and extra-virgin olive oil to make a moist but dense mixture. Season with salt. Stuff the eggplant shells with this mixture and arrange in a baking pan. Tear basil leaves and scatter them over the eggplant. Bake in a preheated 400°F oven until golden on top, about 30 minutes. Serve hot or cold.

PEPERONI CON BAGNA CAODA
Peppers in Bagna Caoda
Trattoria Nonna Genia, Grinzane Cavour (Cuneo), Piemonte

In the mountains near Cuneo, Pier Antonio Cucchietti blanches peppers in boiling water with a little vinegar in it, then serves them with a sauce of tuna, capers, and tomato paste. *Corno di bue*, or ox horn, peppers are long and thin and brightly colored. They hail from Carmagnola, Italy's pepper capital.

SERVES 4
- 4 *red and yellow corno di bue peppers (see note)*
- 3 *heads garlic, peeled*
- 4 *cups whole milk*
- 2 *cups extra-virgin olive oil*
- 16 *salted anchovies, rinsed, boned, and minced*

Preheat the oven to 250°F. Roast, peel, and seed the peppers and cut each one into 3 strips. Arrange the strips on a baking sheet.

Boil the (whole) garlic cloves in the milk until soft, about 10 minutes. Drain the garlic, crush the cloves, and place them in a pot with the oil and the anchovies. Place over low heat and cook, stirring constantly, until the mixture has broken down to form a creamy sauce.

Pour the sauce over the peppers and bake in the preheated oven until heated through, about 5 minutes. Serve very hot.

DIAVOLICCHI IN GUAZZETTO 🌶
Charred Hot Peppers
Osteria di Salvatore Cucco, Gravina in Puglia
(Bari), Puglia

The heat in this tasty appetizer comes from a dried diavolicchio pepper. These bright red chili peppers are usually sold in bunches of about one dozen.

SERVES 4

- 10 ounces sweet dried peppers
- 5 cherry tomatoes, diced
- 2 to 3 cloves garlic, crushed
- 1 spicy diavolicchio chili pepper (see note), ground
- Extra-virgin olive oil for dressing
- Salt to taste
- Leaves of 1 sprig parsley, minced

Use tongs to char the sweet dried peppers over a burner very briefly, then crush them in a mortar and pestle. Combine the crushed roasted peppers with the tomatoes, garlic, chili pepper, olive oil, and salt. Garnish with the parsley.

FRIARELLI RIPIENI 🌿
Stuffed Friarelli Peppers
Antonietta Gorga, Montecorvino Rovella
(Salerno), Campania

Friarelli, also known as *friggitelli*, are small mild green peppers perfect for frying. Tear a roll into small pieces and moisten it with water. Combine with minced cherry tomatoes, minced garlic, capers, and rinsed, boned, and minced salted anchovies. Mix by hand until the mixture is well combined and soft. Cut off the stems of friarelli peppers, leaving the peppers whole, and stuff with the bread mixture. Fry the peppers in hot olive oil until golden.

FRIGGITELLI ALLA VERZA 🌿
Peppers Stuffed with Cabbage
Ristorante Pietrino e Renata, Genzano di Roma
(Roma), Lazio

Friarelli or friggitelli peppers are often fried, but these narrow, mild green peppers can also be stuffed and baked. This cabbage stuffing adds an interesting twist.

SERVES 4

- 12 friarelli peppers
- ½ head Savoy cabbage
- Salt to taste
- 1 (2- to 3-inch) square piece of crustless stale bread
- 1 large egg, lightly beaten
- ¼ cup grated Parmigiano Reggiano
- Leaves of 1 sprig thyme, minced
- 1 medium yellow onion, minced
- 2 cloves garlic, minced
- Freshly ground black pepper to taste
- Extra-virgin olive oil for moistening
- ¾ cup tomato puree
- Breadcrumbs for topping

Preheat the oven to 350°F. Stem and seed the peppers, but leave them whole. Cut the cabbage into ribbons. Bring a pot of lightly salted water to a boil and cook the cabbage until soft, then drain and place in a bowl. Moisten the bread with water and tear it into the bowl with the cabbage. Add the egg, grated cheese, thyme leaves, onion, and garlic. Season with salt and pepper.

Moisten the mixture with a little olive oil and mix until well combined. Stuff the peppers with the mixture and arrange them in a baking pan. Top each pepper with 1 tablespoon tomato puree. Carefully add about ½ cup water to the bottom of the pan, slowly pouring it in at the side of the pan so that you don't douse the peppers. Sprinkle on the breadcrumbs and bake in the preheated oven until heated through, about 20 minutes. Serve warm.

PEPERONI AL FORNO 🌶
Roasted Bell Peppers
Angela Carrisi, Foggia, Puglia

Preheat the oven to 350°F. Sauté rinsed, boned, and minced salted anchovies, capers, pitted black olives, minced parsley, and minced garlic in extra-virgin olive oil until soft and well combined. Taste and adjust salt. (You may not need any.) Place strips of seeded bell peppers in a single layer in a baking dish. Drizzle extra-virgin olive oil on the peppers and scatter on the anchovy mixture. Sprinkle on a little vinegar, if you like. Bake in a preheated 350°F oven until heated through, 10 to 15 minutes.

PEPERONI CON OLIVE E CAPPERI 🍂
Peppers with Olives and Capers
Ristorante Il Sebeto, Volla (Napoli), Campania

Use bell peppers of different colors to make this dish look as good as it tastes.

SERVES 4
2/3 cup extra-virgin olive oil
1   clove garlic
1½ pounds bell peppers, seeded and cut into julienne
2   tablespoons capers, rinsed and drained
½   cup green and black olives, pitted
Salt to taste
¼   cup minced flat-leaf parsley

Heat the olive oil in a large skillet and add the garlic. When the garlic begins to color, add the peppers, capers, and olives. Season with salt and cook over medium heat, stirring constantly with a wooden spoon, until softened, 30 minutes. If the mixture starts to stick, add a small amount of water to the pan. Transfer to a serving dish, garnish with parsley, and serve.

PEPERONI E UOVA 🎛
Peppers and Eggs
Osteria del Leone, Penne (Pescara), Abruzzo

Vittoria Del Prete of Francavilla al Mare in the province of Chieti makes a similar dish without adding any cheese so that the flavor of the peppers really takes center stage. If at all possible, it is suggested that you use organic peppers for this dish, and the chef recommends that they not be too large and meaty.

SERVES 4
½   cup extra-virgin olive oil
1½ pounds red and green bell peppers, seeded and cut into thin strips
Salt to taste
4   large eggs
Grated Parmigiano Reggiano or aged sheep's cheese to taste

Heat the oil in a large cast-iron skillet over high heat and as soon as it begins to sizzle, add the peppers. Cook over high heat, stirring frequently, but don't allow them to poach in the oil, as that will cause their skins to come off. When they begin to color, season with salt.

In a bowl, beat the eggs with a pinch of salt and add a small amount of grated cheese. Beat the egg mixture with a fork. Add the eggs to the skillet with the peppers and stir gently until the eggs begin to set. Remove from the heat but continue cooking until soft with the heat retained by the pan.

PEPERONI RIPIENI
Stuffed Peppers
Trattoria La Chitarra, Napoli, Campania

Don't overcook the eggplant when frying it, as it will cook a little further in the oven.

SERVES 4

- 4 eggplant, cut into strips
- ⅔ cup extra-virgin olive oil
- 4 large bell peppers, roasted and peeled
- ½ cup Gaeta olives, pitted
- 1 heaping tablespoon capers, rinsed and drained
- 4 salted anchovy fillets, rinsed
- 2 tablespoons breadcrumbs
- Salt to taste
- ¼ cup minced parsley

Preheat the oven to 350°F. Fry the eggplant in the oil until just golden. Remove with a slotted spoon or skimmer and reserve the oil. Carefully cut the peppers down one side and open them flat, leaving them whole. Sprinkle each pepper with some of the eggplant, the olives, and the capers. Arrange one anchovy fillet on each pepper and sprinkle with the breadcrumbs. Roll up the peppers jellyroll style and arrange them in a baking pan (it's best if they fit snugly) seam side down. Pour the cooking oil over the peppers. Sprinkle some salt on top of the peppers and bake in the preheated oven until browned, 30 to 40 minutes, basting occasionally with the oil so that they remain moist. Serve warm, and garnish with the parsley just before serving.

PEPERONI RIPIENI FRITTI
Fried Stuffed Peppers
Osteria del Pescatore, Tropea (Vibo Valentia), Calabria

These peppers are a little labor-intensive, but they are well worth the effort. Use high-quality Italian tuna canned in olive oil.

SERVES 4

- 1 (2- to 3-inch) square piece of crustless stale bread
- 2 cloves garlic, crushed
- Leaves of 1 sprig parsley, minced
- 1 tablespoon capers, rinsed and drained
- ¼ cup black olives, pitted and chopped
- 1 pinch oregano
- ¼ cup plus 2 tablespoons grated Parmigiano Reggiano
- 1⅓ cups tuna in olive oil, drained
- Salt to taste
- Extra-virgin olive oil for moistening stuffing and frying peppers
- 4 small round peppers, seeded but left whole
- ¼ cup tomato sauce

Preheat the oven to 350°F. Crumble the bread and combine with the garlic, parsley, capers, olives, oregano, and a little more than half of the grated cheese, and the tuna. Season with salt and stir the mixture, drizzling in a little olive oil to moisten it. Stuff the peppers with the bread mixture. In a large skillet, heat a generous amount of olive oil and fry the peppers in the oil, turning them carefully with tongs, until their skins are wrinkled and they are quite soft, about 10 minutes.

Transfer the peppers to a baking pan. Top each pepper with 1 tablespoon of the tomato sauce and sprinkle on the remaining grated Parmigiano Reggiano. Bake until the cheese has browned and the peppers are heated through, about 30 minutes. Serve hot.

CARPIONE DI ZUCCHINE E UOVA ▦
Zucchini and Eggs in Carpione
Trattoria Nonna Genia, Grinzane Cavour (Cuneo), Piemonte

*C*arpione is another preparation invented to preserve foods before the advent of refrigeration. This dish needs to rest for a full day before being served, so plan accordingly. It's handy to prepare it in a glass container with a tight-fitting lid.

SERVES 6
Olive oil for frying
6   *zucchini, cut into julienne*
6   *large eggs*
1   *tablespoon unbleached all-purpose flour*
Leaves of 1 sprig sage, minced
4   *cloves garlic, minced*
Extra-virgin olive oil for sautéing
1¼ *cups red wine vinegar*
Salt to taste

Line a baking sheet with paper towels. Heat a generous amount of olive oil and fry the zucchini, working in batches if necessary to keep from crowding the pan. Remove with a slotted spoon or skimmer to the prepared pan to drain. Fry the eggs over easy in the oil. Transfer the eggs and zucchini to a nonreactive bowl or container.

To make the carpione, whisk the flour with 2 tablespoons water to make a paste. Sauté the sage and garlic in a small amount of extra-virgin olive oil. Add the red wine vinegar and 2½ cups water, stir to combine, and bring to a boil. Stir in the flour mixture. Simmer briskly for 5 minutes, stirring frequently. Remove from the heat and season with salt.

Drizzle the carpione all over the zucchini and eggs and allow to rest for 1 day before serving.

ZUCCHINE GRIGLIATE 🌳
Grilled Zucchini
Filippo Leone, Alliste (Lecce), Puglia

*T*he zucchini for this dish should not be too small so that when you slice them you have lovely long strips of zucchini to grill. Make a dressing of white wine vinegar, extra-virgin olive oil, and salt. Whisk energetically to emulsify. The amount of dressing you'll need will vary depending on the size of your zucchini and how thickly you slice them. If you run out, it only takes a moment to make more. Grill zucchini slices (cut lengthwise) on both sides until tender. Brush the bottom of a flat-bottomed non-reactive container or bowl with the dressing. Arrange a layer of grilled zucchini on top and brush with a little more dressing, then sprinkle with minced garlic and minced calamint. Continue placing grilled zucchini in the container, brushing each layer and sprinkling with garlic and calamint until you have used up the zucchini. Check whether the zucchini are completely submerged in dressing; if not, make a little more and pour it in at the side of the container. Allow to rest in a cool, dry place for at least 2 days before serving.

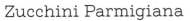

PARMIGIANA DI ZUCCHINE

Zucchini Parmigiana

Trattoria La Bottegaccia, Simeri Crichi
(Catanzaro), Calabria

ucchini parmigiana also makes a very satisfying vegetarian main course if you omit the soppressata, and it can be prepared in advance and then baked just before serving. Tropea onions are elongated sweet red onions from Calabria.

SERVES 4

2 pounds (about 6 medium) zucchini
Salt to taste
1 small Tropea onion (see note), minced
½ cup plus 1 tablespoon extra-virgin olive oil
4 cups tomato puree
½ cup unbleached all-purpose flour
5 to 6 basil leaves
3 hard-boiled eggs, sliced
6 ounces soppressata, preferably from Calabria, diced
7 ounces provola cheese, preferably from Calabria, diced
1 scant cup grated Parmigiano Reggiano

Preheat the oven to 350°F. Cut the zucchini into strips the long way, salt, and set in a colander to drain for about 1 hour.

Sauté the onion in 1 tablespoon extra-virgin olive oil. When it begins to turn golden, add the tomato puree and season with salt. Cook over low heat until reduced, about 40 minutes.

Place the flour in a soup bowl. Fill a pot with high sides with the remaining ½ cup olive oil for frying and set over medium-high heat. Line a baking sheet with paper towels and set aside. Dredge the zucchini slices in flour and fry on both sides until golden. Remove and transfer to the prepared baking sheet.

Tear the basil leaves into the tomato sauce. Cover the bottom of a baking dish with a little of the tomato sauce. Arrange some of the zucchini on top. Place a layer of hard-boiled eggs on top of the zucchini and top the eggs with soppressata and provola. Sprinkle on some of the grated cheese. Repeat layers in this order until all ingredients have been used up, ending with a layer of tomato sauce on top. Tear remaining basil leaves and scatter on top.

Bake in the preheated oven until the top is golden and the cheese is melted, 30 to 45 minutes. Serve warm.

POLPETTE DI ZUCCHINE

Zucchini "Meatballs"

La Tradizione Cucina Casalinga, Minervino Murge
(Bari), Puglia

n winter, these can be made with grated butternut squash in place of the zucchini.

SERVES 4

1 pound (about 3 medium) zucchini
2 large eggs, lightly beaten
¼ cup unbleached all-purpose flour
¼ cup breadcrumbs
Salt to taste
½ cup extra-virgin olive oil

Grate the zucchini on the largest holes of a four-sided grater, letting it drop into a bowl. Add the eggs, flour, breadcrumbs, and a pinch of salt. Stir to combine thoroughly. The mixture should not be dry, but firm enough that you will be able to form a ball by squeezing some together in the palm of your hand. Set aside to rest for 1 hour.

Line a baking sheet with paper towels and set aside. Form the mixture into small balls and set aside. Heat the olive oil in a skillet and cook the zucchini balls, working in batches if necessary to keep from crowding the pan, until browned on all sides. Drain briefly on the prepared baking sheet before serving.

ZUCCHINE 'MBUTTUNATE 🌰
Stuffed Zucchini
Trattoria La Collinetta, Martone
(Reggio Calabria), Calabria

Look for zucchini on the smaller side. The round varieties are particularly easy to leave whole and stuff. This same stuffing can be used with eggplant, but you'll need to halve eggplant the long way and then cut them into two to four more manageable pieces. These may also be served with tomato sauce.

SERVES 6

- 1 pound (about 6) small zucchini
- 1 (2- to 3-inch) square piece of crustless bread
- 2 to 3 large eggs, lightly beaten
- 2 cloves garlic, minced
- Leaves of 1 sprig parsley, minced
- ¼ cup grated Parmigiano Reggiano
- ¼ cup grated aged sheep's cheese
- Salt to taste
- 4 ounces sausage, casing removed (optional)
- Olive oil for frying

Steam the whole zucchini (ends trimmed and discarded) until just tender, about 5 minutes. Allow to cool. If necessary, halve the long way. Carefully scoop out the zucchini flesh, leaving the shells intact. Crush the flesh with a fork.

If the bread you are using is a day or two old, grate it; if it is still very fresh, moisten it with a little water and crumble it. Mix the zucchini flesh with the bread, the eggs, the garlic, the parsley, the two grated cheeses, salt, and the sausage, if using. Stir (or mix by hand) until compact and well combined.

Stuff the zucchini with this mixture. Line a baking sheet with paper towels. Fill a pot with high sides with a generous amount of olive oil and place it over high heat. Fry the stuffed zucchini in the oil on all sides (including the "open" sides with the stuffing in the case of halved zucchini) until browned. Drain briefly on the prepared pan, then serve hot.

TURBANTI DI ZUCCHINE CON MISTICANZA 🍃
Zucchini "Turbans" with Mesclun
Lidia Autero, Udine, Friuli Venezia Giulia

Line ramekins with grilled zucchini slices, winding them in a spiral so they resemble turbans. Mince together baked eggplant flesh; rinsed, boned, and minced salted anchovies; capers; and marjoram and combine with grated Parmigiano Reggiano, breadcrumbs, salt, and pepper to make a firm, moist filling. Fill the zucchini-lined ramekins with the mixture and bake at 350°F for 15 minutes. Toss mixed greens with a dressing of extra-virgin olive oil, grated lemon zest, lemon juice, and salt and serve alongside the turbans. Use a mix of your own local greens for this recipe. Chervil, valerian, endive, chicory, dandelion, and monk's beard are all good candidates. In spring, wild greens abound, but at other times of the year you can replace them with puntarelle, radicchio, endive, and other cultivated greens. Arugula—whether the wild or cultivated type—adds an aromatic note.

FIORI DI ZUCCA FRITTI 🌳
Fried Zucchini Blossoms
Francesca Ronco, Dusino San Michele (Asti), Piemonte

This simple preparation really lets the flavor of the blossoms shine through. They make a lovely appetizer on their own, or they can be served as part of a larger array of fried items. Remove and discard the pistils from zucchini blossoms, as well as stems and leaves. Make a thin batter by whisking water into unbleached all-purpose flour. Dredge the blossoms in the batter and fry in hot olive oil until golden. Season with salt and serve hot.

CAPONET •
Stuffed Zucchini Blossoms
Osteria dell'Unione, Treiso (Cuneo), Piemonte

This dish is from the Langhe region of Piemonte. A more traditional stuffing uses leftover boiled or roasted meat, salami, parsley, garlic, eggs, and grated cheese. At the 'L Bunet restaurant in Bergolo (also in the province of Cuneo), zucchini blossoms are stuffed with a puree of peas and basil. Rinse and pat dry zucchini blossoms very gently before using.

SERVES 4

- 3 tablespoons extra-virgin olive oil, plus more for frying
- 1 pound (about 6) small tender zucchini, cut into julienne
- Salt to taste
- ¼ cup crumbled amaretti cookies
- 1 tablespoon unsweetened cocoa powder
- 1 teaspoon sugar
- 2 egg yolks, lightly beaten
- 12 zucchini blossoms

Line a baking sheet with paper towels and set aside. Heat 3 tablespoons oil in a skillet over medium heat and cook the zucchini, stirring frequently, for 15 minutes. The zucchini should be golden and cooked, but not completely soft. Remove from the pan with a skimmer or slotted spoon and drain briefly on the prepared pan. Season with salt.

Chop the cooked zucchini with a mezzaluna, then combine in a bowl with the amaretti, cocoa powder, sugar, and egg yolks. Gently mix until well combined. Stuff the zucchini blossoms with this mixture. Fill a skillet with high sides with a generous amount of oil, bring to medium-high heat, and fry blossoms until golden, about 10 minutes. Season with salt and serve piping hot.

FRITTELLE DI ZUCCA
Squash Fritters
Trattoria Zio Salvatore, Siderno Superiore (Reggio Calabria), Calabria

Winter squash can be used to make savory fritters such as these, but it is also used in sweet fritters in Venezia. Those pair the squash with golden raisins and lemon zest, and after frying the fritters are dusted with confectioners' sugar.

SERVES 6

- Salt to taste
- 1 pound peeled and seeded winter squash, such as butternut squash
- 2 large eggs
- ¼ cup unbleached all-purpose flour
- Leaves of 1 sprig parsley, minced
- ¼ cup grated aged sheep's cheese
- 1 clove garlic, minced (optional)
- Olive oil for frying

Bring a pot of lightly salted water to a boil and boil the squash until tender and easily pierced with a fork. Drain and crush with a fork.

In a bowl, beat the eggs. Whisk in the flour and parsley, the grated cheese, and the garlic, if using. The mixture should be creamy and fairly fluid. Whisk in the crushed cooked squash.

Line a baking sheet with paper towels. Fill a pot with high sides with a generous amount of oil and fry tablespoons of the mixture until browned on all sides, working in batches if necessary. Remove the fritters with a slotted spoon or a skimmer, drain briefly on the prepared pan, and serve hot.

FIORI DI TROMBETTA RIPIENI

Trombetta Squash Blossoms Stuffed with Potatoes and Beans

Marinella Badino Biancheri, Vallecrosia (Imperia), Liguria

The blossoms of crookneck trombetta squash are short-lived and should only be harvested just before cooking. As soon as you have picked them, open their petals slightly and place them top-down on a clean cloth to keep them from closing up and to give any insects inside them a chance to exit. If you can find fresh white beans, simply shell them and continue with the recipe, but if you are using dried white beans, soak them overnight in water to cover, then rinse them before cooking. If you prefer not to fry the blossoms, they can be baked in a preheated 350°F oven for 15 to 20 minutes.

SERVES 4

- 4 medium potatoes
- ¼ cup white beans, such as cannellini beans
- 2 large eggs, lightly beaten
- Grated Parmigiano Reggiano or aged sheep's cheese to taste
- 1 clove garlic, minced
- Leaves of 1 sprig parsley, minced
- Leaves of 1 sprig marjoram, minced
- 1 slice prosciutto cotto, minced (optional)
- 8 trombetta squash blossoms
- Olive oil for frying
- Salt to taste

Place the potatoes in a small pot with cold water to cover and boil until tender enough to pierce easily with a fork. Separately, boil the white beans until tender enough that you can easily crush one between your tongue and palate. Drain the beans.

Peel the cooked potatoes and in a bowl crush the potatoes and beans with a fork (or use a potato ricer). Add the eggs, grated cheese,

garlic, parsley, marjoram, and the prosciutto cotto, if using. Mix until well combined. Stuff the blossoms with this mixture, then fold over the petals to close them. Line a baking sheet with paper towels. Heat a generous amount of olive oil in a skillet with high sides and fry the blossoms until golden. Drain briefly on the prepared pan, salt, then serve.

ZUCCA IN SAOR

Squash in Saor

Trattoria al Forno, Refrontolo (Treviso), Veneto

At the restaurant, the squash is cooked in a steam oven, but at home you can simply cook it in a steamer basket set over boiling water.

SERVES 4

- 7 ounces peeled and seeded winter squash, such as butternut squash, cubed
- Salt and freshly ground black pepper to taste
- 4 medium yellow onions, cut into julienne
- Extra-virgin olive oil for sautéing and for topping off jar, if necessary
- White wine vinegar (or dry white wine)
- 2 bay leaves
- 2 to 3 whole cloves
- ¼ cup plus 1 tablespoon black raisins
- ⅓ cup pine nuts

Season the squash with salt and pepper and steam until soft, about 15 minutes. Set aside to cool.

Meanwhile, sauté the onions in olive oil until soft. Add the vinegar, bay leaves, and cloves. Season with salt and pepper and cook, stirring frequently, for 20 minutes. Remove from the heat and add the raisins and pine nuts.

Mix the cooked squash with the onion mixture and transfer to a glass jar with a tight-fitting lid. If there is empty space at the top of the jar, fill with additional olive oil. Seal the jar and refrigerate for at least 24 hours before serving.

MOUSSE DI CAROTE
Carrot Mousse
Gelateria Io Tu e i Dolci, Alba (Cuneo), Piemonte

Carrots make a sweet and surprisingly delicate mousse.

SERVES 4
- 3 tablespoons unsalted butter
- 1½ pounds (about 9 medium) carrots, grated
- 1 teaspoon unflavored gelatin
- 2 large eggs, separated
- Salt to taste
- 1 cup heavy cream
- Freshly ground black pepper to taste

Melt the butter in a pot over low heat. Add the grated carrots and ½ cup warm water and bring to a boil. Simmer briskly for 15 to 20 minutes. Set aside to cool. When the carrot mixture is cool, dissolve the gelatin in ¾ cup plus 1 table-spoon water and whisk the egg yolks and the gelatin into the carrot mixture.

Whip the egg whites with a pinch of salt to a stiff peak. Separately, whip the cream to a stiff peak. Fold the whipped cream and whipped egg whites into the carrot mixture. Season with salt and pepper.

Brush four molds with water. Transfer the mixture to the molds and smooth the tops. Refrigerate until set, about 2 hours. Unmold and serve.

PATÉ DI FAGIOLINI
Green Bean Terrine
Osteria della Scièa, Pelago (Firenze), Toscana

The time required to cook the green beans will depend on how large they are, but since they are going to be pureed in any case, overcooking isn't really an issue.

SERVES 4
- Oil for molds
- Salt to taste
- ½ pound green beans, trimmed
- ⅓ cup heavy cream
- 1 teaspoon unflavored gelatin
- ⅓ cup canned tuna in olive oil, drained
- ½ tablespoon salted capers, rinsed and drained
- Juice of ½ lemon

Brush 1 large mold or 4 individual molds with oil and set aside.

Bring a large pot of lightly salted water to a boil and cook the green beans until soft. Scald the cream without bringing it to a boil and whisk in the gelatin until dissolved. In a food processor fitted with the metal blade, combine the green beans, tuna, capers, lemon juice, cream, and a pinch of salt and process until smooth and well combined. Transfer to the pre-pared mold or molds and refrigerate overnight. Unmold before serving.

POLPETTONE DI FAGIOLINI, CAROTE E PATATE
Green Bean, Carrot, and Potato "Meatloaf"
Ludovica Sasso, Genova, Liguria

To make enough to serve 4, bring three pots of lightly salted water to a boil and separately cook 1 pound trimmed green beans, 1 pound (about 6 medium) carrots, and 1 pound (about 3 medium) potatoes until tender. Drain and mince cooked green beans, cut cooked carrots into dice, and peel the cooked potatoes and crush with a fork or potato ricer. Sauté minced rehydrated dried porcini mushrooms in 1 tablespoon butter and 1 tablespoon extra-virgin olive oil. Add green beans, carrots, 1 minced yellow onion, and 1 clove minced garlic and sauté over low heat until they begin to color. Combine with crushed potatoes, then stir in 6 eggs, 1 cup grated Parmigiano Reggiano, and minced marjoram. Salt and season with pepper if desired.

Transfer the mixture to a loaf pan oiled and coated with breadcrumbs. Use a fork to draw a grid on the top. Drizzle on a little more oil and sprinkle with additional breadcrumbs. Bake in a preheated 350°F oven until a golden crust forms on top, about 30 minutes. Unmold and slice.

FINOCCHI ALLA GIUDIA
Jewish-Style Braised Fennel
Giuseppina Gagliardi, Roma, Lazio

This is the most common use of fennel in traditional Italian Jewish cuisine. Look for small, tender fennel bulbs when preparing this dish. Sauté a clove of garlic in a generous amount of oil in a large deep skillet or a pot with a tight-fitting lid. When the garlic begins to turn dark, remove and discard it and add wedges of fennel bulb to the pan. Cook, stirring frequently, for 15 minutes. Season with salt and add about ¼ cup water to the pan.

Bring to a boil, then turn down to a simmer and cook, covered, over low heat until the fennel is very tender and most of the water has evaporated.

RADICCHIO MARINATO
Marinated Radicchio
Osteria alla Pasina, Dosson di Casier (Treviso), Veneto

In Treviso, Marina Righetti prepares a similar dish that uses ten or so bay leaves in place of the pepper. She tops her radicchio with a sauce made by mincing hard-boiled eggs and mixing them with lemon juice and a few drops of vinegar, as well as oil and minced parsley. To serve, she alternates layers of radicchio with the hard-boiled egg mixture, then lets the dish sit for a few hours before serving. La Ragnatela di Mirano in Venezia chars radicchio on a griddle and then serves it in a *saor* (sweet and sour) sauce of onions, vinegar, raisins, and pine nuts like those on pages 50 and 60.

SERVES 4 TO 6
1¼ cups white wine vinegar
5 or 6 juniper berries
2 teaspoons whole black peppercorns
2 tablespoons sugar
4 heads Treviso radicchio
½ cup extra-virgin olive oil
Salt to taste

Combine 2 quarts water and the vinegar in a large pot and bring to a boil. Add half the juniper berries, 1 teaspoon black peppercorns, the sugar, and the radicchio and cook at a brisk simmer for 10 minutes. Drain the radicchio in a colander and as soon as the heads are cool enough to handle, cut them in half the long way and arrange them in a non-reactive container. Coarsely grind the remaining 1 teaspoon black peppercorns and combine with the oil, the remaining juniper berries, and salt to taste. Pour this mixture over the radicchio and marinate in a cool place for about 10 hours.

FINOCCHI GRATINATI
Baked Fennel
Ristorante La Lanterna, Somma Vesuviana
(Napoli), Campania

ora Torrini of Fiesole, outside of Firenze, makes a similar dish that's a bit quicker to prepare: she cooks the fennel, then cuts it into slices and arranges it in a buttered baking dish. Then she simply sprinkles on grated Parmigiano Reggiano, dots it with butter, and bakes it in a 325°F oven until the top is browned, which takes 4 or 5 minutes.

SERVES 4
- 4   bulbs fennel, sliced
- 3   tablespoons unsalted butter
- ⅓   cup unbleached all-purpose flour
- Salt and freshly ground black pepper
- Freshly grated nutmeg (optional)
- 4   ounces provola cheese, sliced
- ½   cup grated Parmigiano Reggiano
- ¼   cup fresh breadcrumbs
- Extra-virgin olive oil for drizzling

Preheat the oven to 350°F. Bring a pot of water to a boil, cook the fennel until tender, then remove the fennel to a colander with a slotted spoon or skimmer and allow it to drain. Reserve cooking water.

In a small pot, melt the butter over medium heat. Whisk in the flour, then whisk in 2 cups of the fennel cooking water. Continue whisking over medium heat until the sauce has thickened, then season with salt and pepper. Add the nutmeg, if desired.

Arrange a layer of the cooked fennel in a baking dish. Spread a few tablespoons of the prepared sauce on top of the fennel. Layer some of the provola slices on top of the sauce and sprinkle on some of the grated cheese. Continue to make layers in that order. When you have used up all of the ingredients, sprinkle on the breadcrumbs. Drizzle on a small amount of oil and bake in the preheated oven until the top is browned and the cheese is melted, about 20 minutes.

INVOLTINI AL RADICCHIO 🐟
Pancetta-Wrapped Radicchio
Trattoria alla Cima, Valdobbiadene (Treviso), Veneto

At another restaurant in Treviso, El Patio di Preganziol, radicchio is baked or cooked on a griddle and then wrapped in a slice of speck and a thin slice of turkey breast along with provola cheese and tomatoes. The rolls are browned in oil on the stovetop for a few minutes, then finished in the oven.

SERVES 4
- 4   heads late-season Treviso radicchio
- ¾   cup Valdobbiadene prosecco
- Extra-virgin olive oil for braising
- Salt to taste
- 8   slices pancetta
- 8   slices montasio cheese (not aged)

Preheat the oven to 350°F. Cut the radicchio the long way into ribbons. Reserve a few pieces of radicchio for garnish and place the rest in a pot. Add the prosecco and a small amount of oil. Season with salt, cover, and cook over low heat for 5 minutes.

Arrange the slices of pancetta on the work surface. Cover the surface of each slice of pancetta with cheese and then the cooked radicchio. Roll up the slices and place them seam side down in a baking dish. Bake in the preheated oven until heated through, about 5 minutes. Transfer the bundles to individual serving plates and garnish with reserved radicchio.

SCIATT CON LA CICORIA ❗
Buckwheat Cheese Dumplings with Chicory
Trattoria Altavilla, Bianzone (Sondrio), Lombardia

cimud and its smaller relative *scimudin* are creamy cheeses made in the mountain pastures of northern Valtellina and aged very briefly. Once made with sheep's milk, today they are almost exclusively made with cow's milk. The word *sciatt* is dialect for "frog," a reference to the bumpy and irregular shape of these delicious dumplings.

SERVES 4
1¼ cups buckwheat flour
¾   cup plus 2 tablespoons unbleached
     all-purpose flour
Salt to taste
½   cup beer
1   tablespoon grappa
Olive oil for frying
4   ounces soft scimud cheese (see note),
     cubed
1   head chicory

In a bowl, combine the flours with a pinch of salt, the beer, and the grappa. Stir in water in a thin stream, adding as much as you need to make a batter with a consistency a little thinner than sour cream. Cover and refrigerate for 2 to 3 hours.

Line a baking sheet with paper towels. Fill a skillet with high sides with a generous amount of oil and bring to medium-high temperature. Dredge the cubes of cheese in the prepared batter, then fry them in the oil until browned. Remove to the prepared pan with a slotted spoon or skimmer and allow to drain briefly.

Cut the chicory into thin ribbons and arrange on a serving platter. Place the dumplings on top of the greens and serve immediately.

POLPETTE DI CICORIA
Chicory "Meatballs"
Trattoria La Piazza, Poggiardo (Lecce), Puglia

f you'd like to serve these with a sauce, combine cream and grated aged sheep's cheese in the top of a double boiler and cook, whisking frequently, until reduced, about 25 minutes.

SERVES 4
Salt to taste
1   pound wild chicory
1   large egg, lightly beaten
1½ tablespoons grated aged sheep's cheese
2   tablespoons breadcrumbs
Freshly ground black pepper to taste
Extra-virgin olive oil for frying

Bring a large pot of salted water to a boil and cook the chicory leaves for 5 minutes. Drain and squeeze dry, then mince and transfer to a bowl. Add the egg, cheese, and breadcrumbs and season with salt and pepper.

In a skillet with high sides, bring a generous amount of olive oil to medium-high temperature. Form the chicory mixture into small balls and fry in the olive oil until browned on all sides, working in batches if necessary to keep from crowding the pan.

INVOLTINI DI FAGIOLINI
Green Beans with Pancetta
Trattoria Da Luciana, San Piero Patti
(Messina), Sicîlia

These little bundles are a tasty start to any meal.

SERVES 6
Salt to taste
1 *pound tender green beans*
¼ *cup plus 2 tablespoons grated Grana Padano cheese*
12 *slices pancetta*

Preheat the oven to 350°F. Bring a large pot of lightly salted water to a boil and blanch the string beans until tender, about 8 minutes. Drain in a colander, then mix with the grated cheese. Place the slices of pancetta on a work surface, divide the green beans among them (lining them up so that they are perpendicular to the slices) and roll up each slice of pancetta around the string beans. Arrange in a baking pan, seam side down, and bake in the preheated oven until heated through, about 15 minutes.

SEDANO NERO RIPIENO
Stuffed Black Celery
Orazio Falchi, Trevi (Perugia), Umbria

Black celery is an IGP (Protected Geographic Origin) product that grows only in Trevi and the surrounding area and is celebrated with its own annual festival. It is actually a very dark green in color. It is tender and flavorful and does not contain any of the fibers that can make common celery less palatable. Its ribs are very long.

Blanch black celery until tender, about 15 minutes, then stuff with crumbled pork sausage (casing removed and discarded) and set aside. In a skillet, make a spicy tomato sauce

by sautéing crumbled chili pepper, minced onion, minced carrot, and minced common celery with a pinch of salt in extra-virgin olive oil until the onion begins to color. Add some red wine and cook stirring frequently, until evaporated, then add canned peeled tomatoes and their juices and a little black pepper and simmer. Make a thin batter by whisking together flour, eggs, milk, and salt. Dredge the stuffed celery in the batter, then fry in a generous amount of hot extra-virgin olive oil until golden. Transfer to a baking pan and top with the tomato sauce. Sprinkle on grated Parmigiano Reggiano and caciotta di Colfiorito and bake in a preheated 350°F oven until lightly browned, about 30 minutes.

PUNTARELLE IN SALSA DI ALICI
Puntarelle with Anchovy Sauce
Osteria Tram Tram, Roma, Lazio

Puntarelle are a variety of chicory. They are quite bitter and are therefore soaked in cold water for an hour before being eaten in salad to soften their edge.

SERVES 4
14 *ounces (about 2 heads) puntarelle*
6 to 8 *anchovy fillets in oil, drained*
1 *clove garlic*
Salt to taste
1 *tablespoon white wine vinegar*
Extra-virgin olive oil for dressing

Prepare a large bowl of ice water and soak the puntarelle for 1 hour. They should curl up.

In a mortar and pestle or a food processor fitted with the metal blade, crush the anchovy fillets, garlic, salt, and vinegar. Add enough oil to make a creamy mixture.

Drain the puntarelle and transfer to a salad bowl. Spoon the anchovy mixture on top and serve.

SEDANI RIPIENI
Stuffed Celery
Trattoria La Vecchia Cucina di Soldano,
Prato, Toscana

Celery is the neglected resident of the vegetable crisper. Here it takes center stage and its subtle flavor is highlighted.

SERVES 4

- 4 large ribs celery
- Salt to taste
- 7 ounces ground veal
- 7 ounces chicken livers
- Extra-virgin olive oil for sautéing and frying
- Freshly ground black pepper to taste
- ½ cup dry white wine
- ¼ cup unbleached all-purpose flour
- ½ cup meat ragù (page 211)

Preheat the oven to 350°F. Cut the celery into 6-inch pieces. Bring a large pot of lightly salted water to a boil and cook the celery until tender, about 15 minutes. Drain and cool and remove any threads with a paring knife.

Chop the veal and chicken livers together and sauté in a skillet with oil. Season with salt and pepper. When the mixture begins to color, add the wine and sauté, stirring frequently, until the meat is cooked and the liquid has evaporated. Fill the concave sides of the pieces of celery with the veal mixture. If necessary, tie with kitchen twine to keep the filling in place. Place the flour in a soup bowl and fill a pan with high sides with a generous amount of oil for frying and bring to medium-high heat. Dredge the stuffed celery in the flour and fry in the oil. Remove with a skimmer and transfer to a baking pan. (Cut and remove twine, if necessary.) Spoon the ragù over the celery and bake in the preheated oven for 30 minutes.

CAPPELLE DI MORECCI IN GRATELLA
Grilled Porcini Mushrooms
Osteria Bagnoli, Castagneto Carducci
(Livorno), Toscana

Morecci, or porcini, mushrooms are highly sought after in Toscana and elsewhere, and grilling highlights their unique and wonderful flavor and aroma. There are plenty of variations on this recipe: some don't marinate the mushrooms, but simply brush them with oil; others dot them with butter after they're cooked. Just be sure not to use excess oil when cooking them, as it will drip onto the grill and create smoke that covers up the flavor of the mushrooms.

SERVES 4

- 1 bunch calamint or flat-leaf parsley
- ½ cup extra-virgin olive oil
- 2 cups white wine vinegar
- Salt and freshly ground black pepper to taste
- 4 large porcini mushroom caps

Reserve 1 sprig calamint and strip the remaining sprigs of their leaves and mince them. Combine the oil, vinegar, and calamint in a bowl. Season with salt and pepper and marinate the mushroom caps in the mixture for 30 minutes.

Preheat a grill until very hot. Remove the mushrooms from the marinade, reserving the marinade, and place them gill-side down on the grill. Grill, turning them once and basting them with the marinade occasionally using the reserved calamint sprig as a brush, until just soft, about 6 to 8 minutes per side (though less if they are particularly small).

INVOLTINI DI PORRI E PROSCIUTTO 🌳
Leek and Prosciutto Bundles
Trattoria Nonna Genia, Borzone di Grinzane Cavour (Cuneo), Piemonte

Cervere leeks are long and thin. Leeks are used liberally in all kinds of dishes in Piemonte, and the town of Cervere—where these special leeks originated—holds a festival dedicated to them in the second week of November.

SERVES 4
- 4 Cervere leeks, sliced into rounds
- ¼ cup béchamel (page 217)
- ¼ cup grated Parmigiano Reggiano
- Freshly grated nutmeg to taste
- Salt to taste
- 12 thin slices prosciutto cotto

Preheat the oven to 275°F. Steam the leeks until soft, about 10 minutes. Combine the leeks with the béchamel and half of the grated cheese and flavor with a pinch of nutmeg. Season with salt, if needed. Place the prosciutto slices on a work surface. Top with the leek mixture and roll up jelly-roll style. Place the rolled up prosciutto in a baking dish, seam side down. Sprinkle with the remaining cheese and bake in the preheated oven until browned on top, about 15 minutes.

CIPOLLE FARCITE DI ZUCCA E MOSTARDA 🌱
Onions Stuffed with Squash and Mostarda
Luigia Bevione, Monteu da Po (Torino), Piemonte

Mostarda is a preserve made with wine must and fruit. The cognà variety (page 416) from the Langhe area of Piemonte is especially prized. Boil large onions (peeled but left whole) until tender. Remove the onions with a slotted spoon, reserving cooking water, and add peeled, seeded, and roughly chopped butternut squash to the pot. When the squash is tender enough to pierce with a paring knife, drain it and force it through a sieve into a bowl. Stir in mostarda, beaten egg, crumbled amaretti cookies, and nutmeg. Cut the cooked onions in half and scoop out the centers. Stuff with the squash mixture and arrange cut side up in a buttered pan. Dot the tops of the onions with butter and bake in a preheated 400°F oven until golden, about 45 minutes. Serve either hot or warm.

CIPOLLINE IN AGRODOLCE 🌶
Sweet-and-Sour Cipollini Onions
Giuliana Ascoli, Venezia, Veneto

Soak golden raisins in Marsala to cover. Meanwhile, sauté whole cipollini onions in extra-virgin olive oil over medium heat, stirring occasionally. When the onions begin to color, season with salt. Add a generous spoonful of sugar and another spoonful of red wine vinegar and cook over low heat, stirring occasionally, for 30 minutes. Remove the raisins from the Marsala (reserve Marsala) and add to the onions. Add a spoonful of the Marsala used to soak the raisins and a tablespoon or two of water and cook until the onions are golden and the liquid has caramelized, at least 30 additional minutes. Serve cold.

LAMPASCIONI IN PURGATORIO

Hyacinth Bulbs in Purgatory
La Tradizione Cucina Casalinga, Minervino Murge (Bari), Puglia

Boiled hyacinth bulbs make an excellent salad when dressed with oil and vinegar. They can also be dredged in flour and beaten egg and fried crisp. These make a delicious and unusual appetizer, but they can also be served as a side dish for lamb, goat, or pork sausage. In this recipe, the bulbs are soaked overnight in cold water to make them less bitter. Cook these over very low heat—as low as your burner will go; traditionally the pot was not placed directly over the fire, but rested next to it for many hours.

SERVES 4

2   pounds hyacinth bulbs
Salt to taste
Extra-virgin olive oil for oiling pan
¼   cup diced pancetta or lardo (fatback)
10   small tomatoes, seeded and diced
¼   cup grated aged sheep's cheese

Peel the bulbs and cut an X into the bottom of each one. Bring a large pot of salted water to a boil and parboil the bulbs, about 20 minutes. Prepare a bowl of cold water. Drain and place in the cold water and leave them there 8 to 10 hours, changing the water once about halfway through.

Lightly oil an earthenware pot large enough to hold the bulbs. Drain the bulbs, dry them, and place half of them in the pot. Scatter on the pancetta, the tomatoes, the grated cheese, and a little salt. Add the remaining bulbs. Pour in a little water and cook over very low heat for 1 hour. If the pot seems to be getting dry, add water in small amounts to keep the bulbs from sticking.

SPONSALI GRIGLIATI

Grilled Sponsali Onions in Pancetta
La Tradizione Cucina Casalinga, Minervino Murge (Bari), Puglia

Sponsali are long, thin spring onions that resemble leeks. They are used widely in the cuisine of Puglia in the spring. Any tender spring onion will work in this recipe.

SERVES 4

8   sponsali onions (see note), cut in half
Salt to taste
16   slices pancetta
Extra-virgin olive oil for drizzling

Preheat a grill to medium-low temperature and grill the onions for about 10 minutes. Season with salt and remove from the heat to cool. Keep grill lit.

When the onions have cooled, wrap each half in a slice of pancetta. Return the pancetta-wrapped onions to the grill and cook until the pancetta begins to melt, about 3 minutes. Transfer to individual serving plates and drizzle with olive oil before serving.

FRITTELLE DI CIPOLLE 🧅
Onion Fritters
Antico Frantoio Oleario Bardari, Curinga
(Catanzaro), Calabria

If you are working with onions on the larger side, slice them into half-moons, but if they are small, you can leave the rings whole.

SERVES 4
- 4   *yellow onions, thinly sliced*
- 2   *large eggs, lightly beaten*
- 1   *cup unbleached all-purpose flour*
- *Grated Parmigiano Reggiano to taste (optional)*
- *Leaves of 1 sprig parsley, minced (optional)*
- *Extra-virgin olive oil for frying*
- *Salt to taste*

Fill a large bowl with cold water and soak the onion slices for 30 minutes. Meanwhile, whisk the eggs and the flour in a bowl large enough to hold the onions, and then whisk in enough water to make a fairly thick batter. Stir in the grated cheese and/or parsley, if using.

Drain the onion slices, pat them dry, and toss the onion slices with the batter.

Line a baking sheet with paper towels. Fill a skillet or pot with high sides with a generous amount of oil for frying and bring to medium-high temperature. Drop spoonfuls of the onion mixture into the oil, working in batches if necessary to keep from crowding, and fry until golden. Remove with a slotted spoon or skimmer to the prepared pan, salt lightly, and drain briefly before serving.

FOGLIE DI AGLIO ORSINO FRITTE 🌿
Fried Ramps
Trattoria Al Sasso, Castelnuovo di Teolo (Padua), Veneto

Ramps can also be used to make fantastic gnocchi, as the owners of the Real Castello restaurant in Verduno do.

SERVES 4
- 2   *egg whites*
- *Extra-virgin olive oil for frying*
- 8   *ramps*
- *Unbleached all-purpose flour for dredging*
- *Salt to taste*

Line a baking sheet with paper towels. In a bowl, whip the egg whites to a stiff peak. Place olive oil for frying in a pot with high sides and bring to a high temperature. Dry the ramps thoroughly and dip them first in the egg whites then in the flour and add them to the oil. Fry until golden brown. Remove with a skimmer or slotted spoon to the prepared pan to drain briefly, salt, and serve hot.

FRITTELLE DI SANT'ANTONIO 🐷
Fried Cauliflower
Laura Romanò, Tuscania (Viterbo), Lazio

Fried cauliflower is prepared to celebrate the Feast of Saint Anthony the Abbot on January 17, and may be savory or sweet. The sweet cauliflower is dusted with a generous amount of sugar rather than salt after frying. Bring a large pot of lightly salted water to a boil and boil cauliflower until tender enough to pierce with the tip of a paring knife. Drain in a colander. Combine all-purpose flour with a little ground cinnamon. Toss the florets with the flour mixture, then shake off any excess flour and fry in a generous amount of olive oil until golden. Sprinkle with salt, and serve hot.

CAPUNEIT VALSESIANI 🥕
Stuffed Cabbage with Vegetables
Ristorante Il Ghiottone, Chiesa di Vocca (Vercelli), Piemonte

Stuffed cabbage is eaten in many places in Italy. In Milan, cabbage leaves are stuffed with leftover roasted meat, salami, Parmigiano Reggiano, breadcrumbs, eggs, and garlic. At Ristorante Il Ghiottone, Marco Veziaga includes lardo (cured fatback) and the liver mortadella known as *fidighìn* (made on the shores of Lake Orta and other parts of northeastern Piemonte) and *salam dla doja* (a pork salami preserved in lard that is a specialty of southern Valsesia).

SERVES 4

- 7 ounces (about 2 small) potatoes
- 4 ounces liver mortadella
- 4 ounces salam dla doja (see note) or other pork salami, casing removed
- 2 ounces streaky lardo (fatback)
- 2 carrots, chopped
- 1 rib celery, chopped
- 1 large yellow onion, chopped
- 2 cloves garlic, chopped
- 1 (3-inch) square piece of crustless stale bread
- Whole milk for moistening
- Salt and freshly ground black pepper to taste
- 8 large Savoy cabbage leaves, blanched
- 1 tablespoon unsalted butter
- 1 tablespoon extra-virgin olive oil
- ½ cup red wine
- 2 cups beef broth

Boil the potatoes until tender enough to be pierced with a fork. Drain and peel. Process the potatoes, mortadella, salami, lardo, carrots, celery, onion, and garlic through a grinder fitted with medium-sized holes. Crumble in the stale bread (moisten it with a little water if necessary) and knead the mixture with your hands until it is well combined. Moisten the mixture with a little milk, just until it is soft enough that it clumps together when you grasp some in your hand. Season with salt and pepper.

Spread the blanched cabbage leaves on a work surface and place a heaping tablespoon of the stuffing in the center of each. Fold the cabbage leaves. Place the butter and olive oil in a pot or skillet with high sides large enough to hold the stuffed cabbage in a single layer and place over medium heat to melt the butter. Place the stuffed cabbage in the pot, seams down, and cook until the leaves begin to brown. Add the wine and cook over low heat until the liquid has evaporated. Add enough broth just to cover the cabbage leaves (you may not need all of it depending on the size of the pot). Cook over low heat for 20 minutes. Serve warm or cold.

SALVIA FRITTA 🌿
Fried Sage Leaves
Ristorante Da Delfina, Antimino di Carmignano (Prato), Toscana

This excellent antipasto is usually made in early spring, when sage leaves are young, tender, and wide. It's a little labor-intensive, but definitely worth the effort.

SERVES 6
- 50 *fresh sage leaves*
- 6 *salted anchovies, rinsed and boned*
- ¼ *cup unbleached all-purpose flour*
- *Salt to taste*
- *Extra-virgin olive oil for frying*

Wash the sage leaves and dry thoroughly on a clean kitchen towel or paper towels. Chop the salted anchovies into pieces about ⅓ inch long—you should have twice as many sage leaves as pieces of anchovy. (In other words, chop the largest anchovy into 5 pieces and the others into 4 pieces each.)

Whisk the flour with a pinch of salt, then whisk while adding water in a thin stream until you have a fairly thin batter.

Line a baking sheet with paper towels. Place olive oil for frying in a pot with high sides and bring to a high temperature. Pinch one piece of anchovy between two sage leaves and press them firmly to make them stick. Dredge in the prepared batter and fry in the oil until golden. Remove with a slotted spoon or skimmer to the prepared baking sheet to drain briefly and repeat with remaining leaves and anchovy pieces. (Work in batches if necessary to avoid crowding the pan.) Serve hot.

TORTINO DI ORZO IN FOGLIA DI VERZA 🥄
Baked Barley and Cheese in a Cabbage Crust
Letizia Palesi, Champorcher (Aosta), Valle d'Aosta

This recipe offers a creative take on items that have been staples for hardworking people in the mountains for centuries: barley, toma cheese, and cabbage. To serve 4 people, boil ⅔ cup barley in salted water until tender on the outside but still brittle in the center and drain. Sauté a minced leek in olive oil and add the barley and about 1 cup warm beef broth. Simmer until the broth has been absorbed and taste. If the barley is tender, remove from the heat. If it's still brittle, continue to cook, adding additional broth in small amounts. Allow to cool, then combine with ¾ cup cubed toma cheese. Butter four ramekins and line each with a blanched cabbage leaf. Scatter in an additional ¾ cup cubed toma cheese, dividing it evenly among the ramekins. Fill with the barley mixture, season with salt and pepper, and fold the cabbage leaves over to seal. Bake in a preheated 350°F oven until the cheese is melted and the mixture is set, 10 to 15 minutes. Unmold and serve with a fonduta (page 30) flavored with chervil.

SUBRICH DI PATATE 🥔
Potato Pancakes
Livia Borgata, Montegrosso d'Asti (Asti), Piemonte

In Magione (in the province of Perugia), Gino Zampolini makes potato pancakes by grating raw potatoes. He lets the grated potatoes sit on a clean dish towel for a couple of hours to drain them of their liquid. Then he mixes the grated potato with beaten egg and fries the mixture by spoonfuls. You can also use minced parsley in the recipe that follows, or make *subrich* with cauliflower, leeks, or other vegetables in place of the potatoes.

Boil yellow potatoes (about 1 per person) in lightly salted water until tender but not falling apart, about 30 minutes. Peel and crush with a potato ricer, then mix with egg (about 1 egg for every 2 potatoes) and season with salt and pepper. Drop tablespoons of the potato mixture in an inch or two of hot extra-virgin olive oil until golden, turning once, about 5 minutes per side. (Work in batches to avoid crowding the pan.) Serve hot.

CAZZILLI
Potato Croquettes
Antica Focacceria San Francesco, Palermo, Sicilia

In Palermo, potato croquettes are often small in size—about as thick as a pencil and no longer than a middle finger. In Catania, such croquettes incorporate garlic and parsley and are dredged in beaten egg whites and breadcrumbs before they are fried.

SERVES 6

2 pounds (about 6 medium) potatoes
Leaves of 1 sprig parsley, minced
3 to 4 mint leaves, minced
Salt and freshly ground black pepper
    to taste
Peanut oil for frying
Extra-virgin olive oil for moistening hands

Boil the potatoes until they are easily pierced with the tip of a paring knife. As soon as the potatoes are cool enough to handle, peel them, then crush the potatoes through a food mill and mix them with the parsley and mint and season with salt and pepper.

Fill a pot with a generous amount of peanut oil for frying and heat until the oil reaches 350°F on a deep-fry thermometer. Moisten your hands with olive oil and shape the potato mixture into small oval croquettes. Fry the croquettes in the oil, working in batches if necessary to keep from crowding the pot, until they are dark brown. Serve hot.

TORTINO DI PEPERONI E PATATE
Baked Potato and Bell Pepper Cakes
Trattoria Da Luciana, San Piero Patti (Messina), Sicilia

These little cakes elevate humble ingredients to a special dish.

SERVES 6

Extra-virgin olive oil for brushing molds
    and sautéing
Breadcrumbs for coating molds
½ medium yellow onion, thinly sliced
14 ounces (about 3 medium) red bell
    peppers, seeded and diced
1½ pounds (about 4 medium) potatoes
Salt to taste
4 tablespoons unsalted butter, cut
    into pieces
½ cup whole milk, scalded
2 large eggs, lightly beaten
¼ cup grated Parmigiano Reggiano

Preheat the oven to 350°F. Brush six individual metal molds with oil and coat with breadcrumbs. Sauté the onion in a small amount of olive oil. When the onion begins to color, add the peppers and cook over low heat until soft. Puree the pepper mixture and set aside.

Meanwhile, boil the potatoes in lightly salted water until tender enough to be pierced with the tip of a paring knife. Drain, peel, and pass through a potato ricer, letting them drop into a pot with the butter. Place the pot over low heat and cook, stirring constantly with a whisk or wooden spoon, until the butter is melted. Remove from the heat, season with salt, and stir in the milk until the mixture is smooth. (You may not need all of it.) Stir in the pureed pepper mixture, eggs, and grated cheese. Fill the prepared molds with this mixture and bake in the preheated oven until set, about 20 minutes. Unmold and serve.

GAGGETTE PINN-E
Stuffed Savoy Cabbage Heads
Antica Trattoria dei Mosto, Conscenti di Ne (Genova), Liguria

This stuffed cabbage dish is unusual because the leaves are not detached, but are left connected to the core of the cabbage for stuffing and cooking. The cabbage is then sliced before serving. The result is quite impressive.

SERVES 4

1   (2-inch) square piece of stale bread
½   cup whole milk
8   large eggs
¾   cup plus 1 tablespoon grated
     Parmigiano Reggiano
Leaves of 1 sprig marjoram, minced
Salt to taste

2   heads Savoy cabbage
1   (2-ounce) chunk lardo (fatback)
1   small yellow onion, minced
1   shallot, minced
1   leek, minced
Extra-virgin olive oil for sautéing
2   pounds plum tomatoes, chopped

Soak the bread in some of the milk until soft. Beat the eggs with the grated cheese, the marjoram, and a pinch of salt. Crumble in the bread and add a little additional milk (you may not need all of it) until the mixture is a spreadable consistency.

Trim off the ends of the cabbage heads but leave the leaves attached to the core. Carefully spread the leaves out from each other. Beginning at the center of one head, stuff the leaves with filling and fold them. Leave the outer 2 or 3 leaves empty. Repeat with second head of cabbage. Tie the heads of cabbage with kitchen twine. Bring a pot of water to a boil, then turn down to a gentle simmer, add the lardo to the water and carefully lower in the heads of cabbage. Cook for 1 hour.

In the meantime, make a tomato sauce by sautéing the onion, shallot, and leek in a small amount of oil. Add the tomatoes and season with salt. Cook until tomatoes have given up their liquid and collapsed, then process through a food mill.

When the cabbage heads are cooked, remove and place between two plates. Place a weight, such as a couple of cans, on top of the plates to press out as much liquid as possible. Allow to sit for 15 to 20 minutes, tilting the plates every once in a while to drain off any excess water that accumulates. Cut the cabbage into slices about ½-inch thick and serve with the tomato sauce (reheated briefly to warm it, if necessary).

OLIVE ASCOLANE FARCITE E FRITTE 🫒
Stuffed and Fried Olives
Trattoria L'Arco, Maltignano (Ascoli Piceno), Marche

Tender Ascolana olives are a must for this recipe—they are large, green, and sweet. Even the ancient Romans loved these olives and imported them from the territory inhabited by the Picentes along Via Salaria. This dish works as an appetizer, but also as a snack or side dish. It has its roots in recipes from the Renaissance and also echoes some French haute cuisine dishes, but it is absolutely the signature dish of Ascoli Piceno. If you are unsure of your ability to pit olives—and few can rival Maria Cesira of Trattoria L'Arco in Maltignano—you can use an olive pitter for this recipe.

SERVES 8
1 pound veal
10 ounces pork
7 ounces turkey breast
2 carrots, minced
1 rib celery, minced
1 medium yellow onion, minced
Grated zest of 1 lemon
Freshly grated nutmeg to taste
Salt to taste
2 cups dry white wine
2 pounds green tender Ascolana olives (see note)
5 large eggs
¼ cup grated Parmigiano Reggiano
Unbleached all-purpose flour for dredging
Breadcrumbs for dredging
2 cups extra-virgin olive oil

Chop the veal, pork, and turkey breast. Combine with the carrots, celery, onion, zest, and nutmeg. Season with salt and cook, without browning, in a large skillet. Add the wine and cook until the liquid has evaporated.

While the meat is cooking, pit the olives using a spiral motion so that the olives remain whole.

Once the meat is cooked, allow it to cool and then mince or grind it, reserving any fat that has collected in the skillet. Add 3 eggs and the Parmigiano Reggiano to the meat mixture and combine. Add any reserved fat back into the meat mixture as well. Stuff the olives with the meat mixture, squeezing them gently to keep them closed around the stuffing. Beat the 2 remaining eggs in a shallow bowl. Arrange two additional shallow bowls, one with the flour and one with the breadcrumbs. Dredge the olives first in flour, then in beaten egg, and lastly in breadcrumbs, working in batches if necessary.

Line a baking sheet with paper towels. Place the olive oil in a pot with high sides and heat until a deep-fry thermometer registers 350°F. Fry the olives in small batches until golden, about 10 minutes. Remove with a skimmer and transfer to the prepared paper towels briefly to drain, then serve piping hot.

NOCCIOLINE DI PATATE
Fried Potato Nuggets
Giuliana Verni, Poppi (Arezzo), Toscana

Like Piemonte's *subrich* (page 71) and other vegetable fritters, these *noccioline* (literally "hazelnuts") are an everyday home-style preparation. These are served with tomato sauce, which is unique. In Toscana, potato fritters known as *polpette pelliccia* may also incorporate boiled beef (a canny way to use a small amount of leftovers).

Boil the potatoes in lightly salted water, peel them, and pass them through a potato ricer while still hot. Mix the hot potatoes with butter, eggs, salt, pepper, and nutmeg. Form the potato mixture into small balls the size of hazelnuts. Dredge the balls first in flour and then in beaten egg and fry in a generous amount of hot olive oil until golden. Serve with tomato sauce.

FRITTELLE DI PESCE PERSICO 🌿
Perch Fritters
Giuseppina Rigoli, Tolentino (Macerata), Marche

Make a marinade of dry white wine, lemon juice, marjoram, and pepper. Marinate perch fillets in this mixture for 1 hour. In a bowl combine all-purpose flour with a pinch of salt and with a fork whisk in milk and extra-virgin olive oil in equal amounts until the batter reaches the consistency of sour cream. Set aside to rest for a few minutes, then fold in stiffly beaten egg white. Drain the fillets, chop them, and dredge them in the batter, then fry in hot olive oil until golden. Serve hot.

BORICCHE DI NASELLO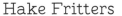
Hake Fritters
Elvira Menegon, Orgiano (Vicenza), Veneto

Boricche are one of the many *cicheti*, or snacks, served in Veneto as an accompaniment to the traditional *ombra*, a small glass of wine. Other seafood cicheti include boiled mantis shrimp, baby octopus, or sea snails, masanete—female crabs eaten while fertile—boiled and fried baccalà and creamy baccalà spread, sardines in saor, gray shrimp, fried skate, roasted cuttlefish, cuttlefish eggs, and more.

Clean a large hake and boil in salted water. Drain, cool, then skin and bone and extract as much flesh as possible, shredding it as you do. Sauté minced garlic and onion in olive oil and add the hake flesh. Combine the hake mixture with beaten egg to make a thick mixture that holds together when you pinch some in your hand. Form the hake mixture into small balls, then dredge the balls in breadcrumbs and fry them in a generous amount of extra-virgin olive oil until golden brown. Salt and serve hot.

ACCIUGHE AU ZEMÌN 🐟
Stewed Anchovies
Osteria Magiargè, Bordighera (Imperia), Liguria

Zimino or *inzimino*—zemìn in Ligurian dialect—indicates a method for stewing several types of foods, including legumes, organ meats, and seafood, such as cuttlefish, calamari, baccalà, and oily fish. Zimino dishes, common in both Liguria and Toscana, always incorporate beet greens, though sometimes spinach is used as a substitute.

SERVES 4
- 24 fresh anchovies
- Extra-virgin olive oil for sautéing
- 1 clove garlic
- 2 teaspoons pine nuts
- Salt to taste
- 2 cups fennel fronds or dill, chopped
- ½ cup Vermentino wine
- 5 Pachino cherry tomatoes
- 1 cup tightly packed beet greens or chard, blanched and cut into ribbons
- Leaves of 1 sprig parsley, minced

Clean and bone the anchovies without cutting the fillets apart. In a nonstick pan large enough to hold the anchovies in a single layer, heat a small amount of olive oil with the garlic. Fold the anchovies closed and place in the pan. Add the pine nuts, salt, and fennel. Cook until lightly browned, about 2 minutes, then add the Vermentino and let it evaporate. When the wine has evaporated, add the tomatoes and the beet greens. Transfer to a platter, sprinkle with parsley, and serve.

ACCIUGHE AL VERDE 🌿
Anchovies with Parsley Sauce
La Cantina del Rondò, Neive (Cuneo), Piemonte

Emanuela Merli makes a classic version of this dish, which is one of the most simple and delicious in Piemonte's cuisine and is often eaten for *merende sinòire* (a summertime snack eaten at 6 p.m., after which work- ers returned to the fields to work at night). A word about *povrón sotto raspa*, local dialect for peppers preserved in vinegar, which can be replaced with fresh bell peppers: in the Langhe area of Piemonte, as in many other areas of Italy (the Ciociaria area of Lazio, for example), peppers were preserved in vinegar by placing them in jugs with grape dregs that had not been pressed, meaning they were the leftovers from winemaking, consisting of stalks, skins, seeds, and some must. At the Boccondivino osteria in Bra, the kitchen prepares anchovies in *bagnet ross*: they make a tomato sauce and when it is almost cooked add a little sugar and vinegar to give it a sweet-and-sour dimension. Then they let it cool and place the fish on a platter and cover it with the sauce, along with minced garlic, parsley, and bay leaf mixed with extra-virgin olive oil. After resting for a couple of hours, the anchovies are then served with curls of butter and toasted bread.

SERVES 4
9   salted anchovies
Dry white wine for rinsing
White wine vinegar for rinsing and
    moistening
Extra-virgin olive oil for marinating and
    for sauce

1   small piece (about 2 by 2 inches)
    crustless bread
1   clove garlic
¼   cup flat-leaf parsley leaves
¼   bell pepper, fresh in season or preserved
    out of season
Salt to taste

Carefully clean the anchovies under running water to rinse off the salt, then cut them open and remove and discard the heads, guts, and bones. Then rinse them again with a mixture of white wine and vinegar. Dry the anchovy fillets with a dish towel or paper towels and place them in a container. Add enough olive oil to cover.

Moisten the bread with a little vinegar, then squeeze dry (it will crumble) and set aside. With a knife or mezzaluna, mince together one of the anchovies (drained of its oil), the garlic clove, the parsley, and the pepper. If you are skilled enough to do so, mince all the ingredi- ents together. If you are less skilled, mince them separately, then combine. In any case, do not use a food processor or other equipment. Com- bine the minced ingredients with the bread and add as much olive oil as the mixture can absorb. Adjust salt to taste. Drain the remaining anchovies, arrange them in a single layer on a platter, and cover with the parsley sauce just before serving.

BAGNUN DE ANCIUE 🏮
Anchovies and Onions
Osteria dell'Acquasanta, Mele (Genova), Liguria

This is a light soup of fresh anchovies cooked in a "bath" (the *bagnun* in the name) of tomatoes and sautéed garlic, oil, and onions, all served over toasted bread. This dish is popular along the Ligurian coastline where since the 1950s it has been served in Sestri Levante and Riva Trigoso (in the province of Genova). It is often spooned over *gallette del marinaio*, or sailor's bread, long-lasting flat round rusks that were used by both the military naval forces and others on board ships. These rusks are made with a dough of soft wheat flour, sourdough starter, water, salt, extra-virgin olive oil, and malt that is allowed to rise only slightly. This dish may be served as an appetizer or a first course.

SERVES 8
- 2 pounds fresh anchovies
- ¼ cup flat-leaf parsley
- 1 medium yellow onion
- 2 cloves garlic
- 1 carrot
- *Extra-virgin olive oil for sautéing*
- ½ cup dry white wine
- 2 pounds plum tomatoes, peeled and minced
- 6⅓ cups fish broth (optional)
- 1 pinch dried oregano
- *Salt to taste*
- *Toasted bread rubbed with garlic for serving*

Clean the anchovies. Remove and discard the heads, scale the fish, bone them, and rinse them thoroughly. Mince the parsley, onion, garlic, and carrot together. In a pot (use a terra-cotta pot if you have one) sauté the minced mixture in extra-virgin olive oil until soft. Add the wine and when it has evaporated add the tomatoes. Cook over medium heat until reduced, about 20 minutes, then add the fish broth or 6⅓ cups water and cook for 15 minutes. Add the anchovies and cook for an additional 10 minutes.

Sprinkle on the oregano and season with salt. Serve over the toasted bread.

ACCIUGHE IN SCABECCIO ⫷
Anchovies in Escabeche
Osteria Vicolo Intherno, La Spezia, Liguria

To prepare *scabeccio*, the Ligurian word for *scapece* or what the Spanish call escabeche, first the item being prepared is fried, and then it is marinated in an acidic liquid. Scabeccio is similar to the *carpione* of Italy's northwest or what those in the Veneto region term *saor*.

SERVES 4
- 2 pounds fresh anchovies
- *Oil for frying*
- ½ cup unbleached all-purpose flour or 00 flour
- 1 medium onion, thinly sliced
- 1 sprig rosemary
- 2 cups wine vinegar
- *Salt to taste*

Wash the anchovies, gut them, and remove and discard the heads, but do not bone them. Place the oil for frying in a pot with high sides and bring to high temperature. Dredge the anchovies in the flour and fry them in the oil. Remove with a skimmer and reserve the oil.

In a separate pot, combine the onion, rosemary, and vinegar. Season with salt and bring to a boil. When the mixture has reduced somewhat, remove from the heat and combine with the frying oil.

Arrange the anchovies in a single layer in a nonreactive container and pour the vinegar mixture over them. Marinate for at least 24 hours before serving.

AGLIATA DI POLPO
Garlic Octopus
Osteria Macchiavello, Alghero (Sassari), Sardegna

Octopus that is cooked long and slow will be beautifully tender, so don't rush the process.

SERVES 8
- 4½ pounds octopus, gutted and eyes and beak removed
- 1 head garlic, cloves separated and peeled
- 10 sun-dried tomatoes
- 2 tablespoons extra-virgin olive oil
- ¼ cup wine vinegar
- 4 pounds 6 ounces plum tomatoes, peeled, seeded, and processed through a food mill
- Salt to taste
- Crushed red pepper flakes to taste
- Leaves of 1 sprig parsley, minced

Place the octopus in a pot full of water, bring to a boil, then simmer over medium heat for 1½ hours. Let the octopus cool in the cooking water. While the octopus is cooking, mince the garlic and sun-dried tomatoes together and then sauté in a pot with the olive oil for 10 minutes. Add the vinegar and bring to a boil, then let the mixture simmer briskly until the vinegar has evaporated. Add the plum tomatoes and cook over low heat, stirring occasionally, for 1½ hours.

Drain the octopus and cut it into rings. Transfer the rings to a bowl. Add the tomato sauce and toss. Adjust salt to taste. Sprinkle on pepper flakes and minced parsley. Serve at room temperature, or refrigerate for 3 hours and serve cold.

ALICI IN TORTIERA
Baked Anchovies
Agriturismo Sant'Agata, Palinuro di Centola (Salerno), Campania

This is a simple version of a very common dish from the South. This dish also often incorporates grated sheep's cheese. Tradition dictates that the ingredients be arranged in layers. In this case the anchovies alternate with the breadcrumb mixture, but in other versions they alternate with layers of tomatoes, onions, or potatoes; naturally, those versions need to cook a little longer.

SERVES 4
- 10 ounces fresh anchovies
- Extra-virgin olive oil for drizzling
- Salt to taste
- 2 cloves garlic
- Leaves of 1 sprig parsley
- 3 to 4 leaves fresh mint
- 1 small piece (about 2 by 2 inches) day-old crustless bread

Preheat the oven to 350°F. Clean the anchovies, bone them, and arrange them in a baking pan in a single layer. Drizzle with oil and sprinkle with salt. Mince the garlic and parsley and sprinkle them over the anchovies. Tear the mint leaves and sprinkle them over the anchovies. Crumble the bread over them. Sprinkle with a few drops of water. Bake in the preheated oven until cooked through, 15 to 20 minutes.

INVOLTINI DI ACCIUGHE CON ZUCCHINE ❦
Anchovies Stuffed with Zucchini
Locanda del Centro, Pagno (Cuneo), Piemonte

Passito wine is made from grapes that have been dried on straw mats. It is usually sweet and has a very intense flavor.

SERVES 4

4 large anchovy fillets
Salt and freshly ground black pepper to taste
1 clove garlic
Leaves of 1 sprig rosemary
4 to 5 capers, rinsed and drained
3 light green zucchini
Extra-virgin olive oil for sautéing and drizzling
½ cup passito wine (see note)

Clean the fillets, being sure to remove all the bones. Season with salt and pepper. Mince the garlic, rosemary, and capers and set aside in a bowl.

Slice the zucchini into thin rounds and sauté in a small amount of oil until browned. Divide the zucchini roughly in half. Combine one half with the minced garlic mixture and keep the other half warm. Spread the zucchini mixed with the garlic on top of the fillets and then roll up each fillet and close with a toothpick.

Heat a small amount of oil in a skillet and brown the anchovy rolls, turning to brown both sides. Add the wine and once it has evaporated remove the skillet from the heat.

Spread the remaining zucchini rounds on a serving platter and arrange the anchovies on top. Drizzle with a little more extra-virgin olive oil.

POLPETTE DI ALICI
Anchovy "Meatballs"
Agriturismo Sant'Agata, Palinuro di Centola (Salerno), Campania

Is there anything the humble anchovy can't improve? Here it combines with all the traditional ingredients for meatballs (even grated cheese, unusually paired with fish) for very tasty results.

SERVES 4

1 day-old roll, crusts removed
½ cup whole milk
10 ounces fresh anchovies
1 large egg, lightly beaten
¼ cup grated aged goat cheese
2 cloves garlic
Leaves of 1 sprig flat-leaf parsley, minced
Salt to taste
Extra-virgin olive oil for frying and sautéing
10 cherry tomatoes, lightly crushed

Soak the roll in the milk until soft. Clean and bone the anchovies. Rinse under running water and dry. Mince with a mezzaluna and place in a bowl. Add the egg and the cheese, then crumble the softened bread into the mixture. Mince 1 clove garlic and add, along with about half of the minced parsley. Season with salt and stir or knead to combine. The mixture should form a ball when you grip it in the palm of your hand. Use a teaspoon to shape the mixture into small "meatballs."

Line a baking sheet with paper towels. Place the oil for frying in a pot with high sides and bring to high temperature. Fry the meatballs until browned and remove with a skimmer. Drain briefly on the prepared pan.

In a large skillet, heat a small amount of oil and add the remaining clove garlic. Sauté over medium heat until browned, then add the cherry tomatoes, the meatballs, salt, and a small amount of water. Cook for a few minutes to combine flavors. Sprinkle with the remaining minced parsley and serve.

TORTINO DI INDIVIA E ALICIOTTI ⚘
Baked Escarole and Anchovies
Osteria del Velodromo Vecchio, Roma, Lazio

Escarole and anchovies bake into a kind of cake that should slice neatly into individual portions. Let it rest in the pan for a few minutes before serving.

SERVES 4

- 2 pounds escarole
- 14 ounces fresh anchovies, heads removed, butterflied, and boned
- 6 to 8 tablespoons (½ cup) extra-virgin olive oil
- 1 clove garlic, minced
- Salt and freshly ground black pepper to taste
- Leaves of 1 sprig parsley, minced

Preheat the oven to 400°F. Clean the escarole, discarding the outside leaves and any browned stems. Cut into medium-sized ribbons and soak in cold water for about 10 minutes. Drain the escarole.

In a medium baking pan with sides at least 2 inches high, arrange about one third of the escarole in a layer. Arrange a layer of about half of the anchovies on top. Drizzle with oil and sprinkle on about half of the garlic, then season with salt and pepper. Create another layer of escarole, then a layer of anchovies, seasoning as above. Finish with a layer of escarole and bake in the preheated oven, checking frequently and turning the pan from front to back and side to side, until anchovies are cooked through, about 1 hour. Allow to cool slightly, then cut into 4 portions, sprinkle with the parsley, and serve.

'MPANATA CON LE ALICI 🏮
Stuffed Anchovy Focaccia
Trattoria del Crocifisso da Baglieri, Noto (Siracusa), Sicilia

'Mpanata is a kind of focaccia that is folded over a filling. The dialect word has its roots in the Spanish word empanada. Sicilia has long been home to various savory pastries filled with meat, cheese, or other items. Other names include scaccia, 'nfigghiulata, pastizzu, cudduruni, and sfinciuni.

SERVES 4

FILLING
- 1 pound fresh anchovies
- Leaves of 1 bunch flat-leaf parsley
- ¼ cup capers, rinsed and drained
- 1 small yellow onion, minced
- 2 cloves garlic, minced
- Salt and freshly ground black pepper to taste
- Extra-virgin olive oil for drizzling and oiling pan

DOUGH
- 2¼ teaspoons (one envelope) active dry yeast
- 3½ cups semolina flour
- 2 tablespoons olive oil
- Salt to taste

Clean and fillet the anchovies and rinse them under running water until very clean, then dry thoroughly and set aside.

To make the dough, dissolve the yeast in a small amount of lukewarm water. Make a well with the flour on a work surface and add the oil, salt, and the yeast mixture. Gradually incorporate the flour from the sides of the well, incorporating as much water as needed to make a soft dough. Cover and set aside to rise for 1 hour.

Preheat the oven to 375°F. Lightly oil a baking sheet and set aside. Roll out the dough into a circle. Sprinkle the parsley over one half of the circle. Top with a layer of the anchovies, then the capers, the onion, the garlic, a pinch of salt, black pepper, and a drizzle of oil. Fold the empty half of the dough circle over the filled half and press and crimp the border to seal. Transfer to the prepared pan and bake in the preheated oven until browned, about 30 minutes.

MACHETTO
Anchovy Spread
Trattoria Aütedo, Marola (La Spezia), Liguria

This anchovy paste can be used to top *sardenaira*, also known as *pizzalandrea* (page 7). It can also be served over bread or stirred into the oil for *pinzimonio* or incorporated into *condiglione*, a salad made with firm tomatoes, bell peppers, cucumbers, and young onions. *Machetto* is a dialect word that means grinding, pressing, or crushing—the action required to produce it. You will need very young anchovies for this recipe—small enough that they don't need to be boned.

SERVES 10
12 ounces very small fresh anchovies
1½ pounds rock salt
2 tablespoons ground cayenne pepper, plus more for seasoning
Dry white wine for rinsing
Extra-virgin olive oil for drizzling

Remove the heads from the anchovies and gut them without boning them. Arrange them in a bowl or a steel container. Cover with the rock salt. Sprinkle on the cayenne pepper. Set aside to rest for about 20 days.

Rinse the anchovies in wine to remove excess salt. Grind or crush into a paste. Drizzle on some olive oil, season with a little more pepper, and serve as an appetizer.

PIZZA CON LE ALICI
Anchovy Pizza
Orazio Falchi, Foligno (Perugia), Umbria

Anchovies have been used in Italy since ancient times. The Romans made liberal use of a condiment called *garum* made from fermented salted anchovies. You will need 2 baseball-sized pieces of bread dough for this recipe. Roll each into a circle. Oil a baking sheet or pizza pan and set one piece of dough on it. Arrange a few beet greens or chard leaves on it in a single layer, just to line the dough. Brush with extra-virgin olive oil, sprinkle with black pepper, and place brined anchovy fillets on top. Top with the second disk of dough, pinch around the border to seal, and brush the top with more oil. Bake in a preheated 350°F oven until golden brown, 30 to 45 minutes.

POMODORI RIPIENI
Tuna-Stuffed Tomatoes
Salvatore Grieco, Firenze, Toscana

This is a very simple dish, perfect for a casual summer dinner. Hollow out 1 beefsteak tomato per person using a teaspoon or melon baller. Combine drained canned tuna in olive oil, flaked with a fork, with capers, minced cipollini onion, minced garlic, and chopped parsley. Moisten with a little olive oil and add enough mayonnaise to make the mixture smooth. Taste and adjust salt. Stuff the tomatoes with the tuna mixture and top each with a basil leaf and a stuffed olive. Feel free to vary this by using chives or marjoram in place of the basil. The tomatoes can also be stuffed with a mixture of anchovies, olives, parsley, and chopped hard-boiled eggs, or plain rice, parsley, basil, and a few leaves of calamint.

INVOLTINI DI PEPERONI ALLA LIGURE 🍎
Bell Peppers with Tuna Stuffing
Ristorante Quintîlio, Altare (Savona), Liguria

Choose the wine vinegar for soaking the bread thoughtfully—it will impact the taste of the finished dish.

SERVES 4

- 2 yellow bell peppers
- 2 red bell peppers
- 1 (3 by 3-inch) square piece of bread
- Wine vinegar for soaking bread (see note)
- 1 cup canned tuna in olive oil, drained
- 1 hard-boiled egg, minced
- 2 tablespoons plus 1 teaspoon salted capers, rinsed and drained
- Salt to taste
- ½ cup mixed baby salad greens
- Extra-virgin olive oil for dressing
- Apple cider vinegar for dressing

Preheat the oven to 350°F. Roast the peppers in the oven for 15 minutes. When the peppers are cool enough to handle, peel and seed them and cut each pepper into 8 strips along the ribs. Soak the bread in wine vinegar to soften.

Flake the tuna into a bowl and combine with the egg and 2 tablespoons capers. Remove the bread from the vinegar, letting it drain slightly, then crumble it into the tuna mixture. Mix gently to combine without crushing the ingredients. Taste and adjust salt.

Divide this mixture in equal amounts on each strip of pepper and roll them up. Cut the baby lettuce into julienne. Puree the remaining 1 teaspoon capers with olive oil and apple cider vinegar to make a sauce. Make a bed of salad on each serving plate, then top with the prepared pepper rolls and serve with the caper sauce on the side.

SARDE IN SAOR 🧅
Sardines in Sweet-and-Sour Vinegar Sauce
Ristorante La Ragnatela, Scaltenigo di Mirano (Venezia), Veneto

This traditional recipe predates refrigeration—the large amount of vinegar in the sauce preserved the fish. It can also be prepared with mackerel, anchovies, eel, or goby fish.

SERVES 4

- Extra-virgin olive oil for sautéing and frying
- 2 pounds (about 6) white Chioggia onions, thinly sliced
- ½ cup dry white wine
- ½ cup white wine vinegar
- Salt and freshly ground black pepper to taste
- 2 pounds fresh sardines
- Unbleached all-purpose flour for dredging

Place a small amount of oil for sautéing in a skillet and set over low heat. Add the onions, then the wine, the vinegar, salt, and pepper and cook until the wine evaporates.

Meanwhile, clean and fillet the sardines. Rinse them and dry them, then dredge them in flour and fry them in hot oil until cooked through but soft. Drain on paper towels and salt.

Arrange one layer of the sardines in a glass container and cover with a layer of the onion mixture. Continue to create alternating layers of sardines and onion mixture. Allow to rest for 2 days in a cool place before serving.

SARDONCINI ALLA MENTA
Anchovies with Mint
Ristoro della Cooperativa Coomarpesca, Fano (Pesaro and Urbino), Marche

This restaurant in Fano also prepares anchovies in vinegar. If you'd like to try that variation, clean and bone 1 pound anchovies and arrange the fillets in a stainless steel or ceramic dish. Dilute 1 cup white wine vinegar with ¼ cup water and mix with a few minced fresh bay leaves and some whole black peppercorns. Refrigerate for 24 hours, then drain the sardines and immerse them in ½ cup extra-virgin olive oil. Let them sit for another day before serving.

SERVES 4
- 1 pound fresh anchovies
- Olive oil for shallow-frying
- ⅓ cup unbleached all-purpose flour
- 1 large egg, lightly beaten
- ¼ cup extra-virgin olive oil
- 1 tablespoon vinegar
- 1 clove garlic, minced
- 3 to 4 mint leaves
- ½ cup toasted breadcrumbs

Clean and fillet the anchovies. Fill a pot with a small amount of oil for shallow-frying and bring to high heat. Dredge the anchovy fillets in the flour and then in the egg and brown. Remove with a skimmer and transfer to a serving platter.

In a pot, combine the extra-virgin olive oil with the vinegar and place over high heat. When the mixture begins to bubble, remove it from the heat and pour over the fish. Scatter on the garlic, tear the mint leaves and scatter them over the fish, and scatter on the breadcrumbs. Refrigerate for several hours before serving.

SURI IN UMIDO
Stewed Jack Mackerel
Ristorante Al Pesce Azzurro, Fano (Pesaro and Urbino), Marche

Jack mackerel is a fish in the *Carangidae* family that goes by many names in Italy. It has firm and flavorful flesh, and it is suitable for all kinds of preparations, including stewing, grilling, baking, and frying. In Toscana, mackerel fillets are braised in the oven. Layer the fillets in a baking pan with minced garlic, parsley, and fennel fronds. Season with salt and pepper and pour tomato puree over them. Drizzle with oil and white wine and bake at 350°F for about 20 minutes.

SERVES 4
- 4 jack mackerel (about 6 ounces each)
- ½ cup extra-virgin olive oil
- 4 cloves garlic
- 1½ cups chopped tomatoes
- ½ cup dry white wine
- Salt and freshly ground black pepper to taste

Fillet the fish and skin the fillets. Place the oil in a skillet and place over medium heat. When the oil is hot, add the garlic cloves and cook until golden. Remove the garlic with a slotted spoon and add the chopped tomatoes. Cook for a few minutes until reduced slightly, then add the mackerel fillets. Add the wine and cook until evaporated. Season with salt and pepper, then turn the heat to low and simmer gently until the fish is cooked through, about 15 minutes.

CARPIONE BOLLITO
Carpione Fish in White Wine
Natalina Favaro, Peschiera del Garda (Verona), Veneto

Carpione (*Salmo carpio*) is a salmonid fish that lives only in Lake Garda. It is often simply grilled and drizzled with olive oil these days, but in earlier times its delicate and highly prized flesh was preserved in a marinade of vinegar and herbs—that is why carpione is also the name of a traditional method for preparing all kinds of fish and vegetables. (See the recipe for Zucchini and Eggs in Carpione on page 56.)

Fill a pot with equal amounts of water and dry white wine. Add 1 onion, 1 carrot, and 1 rib celery and a few parsley stalks to the pot (reserve the leaves.) Add bay leaves, a quartered lemon, and salt. Bring the mixture to a boil and boil for 15 minutes. Remove from the heat and allow to cool. Add scaled, gutted carpione fish (heads and tails attached) to the pot and bring to a simmer without allowing the liquid to reach a full boil. When the fish is cooked through, remove it and cut off the heads and tails and fillet it, cutting each fish into 2 fillets. Arrange on a serving platter and drizzle with a little olive oil. Season with salt. Mince the reserved parsley leaves and sprinkle them over the fish.

CARPIONATA ALLA PIEMONTESE
Rosemary Marinated Freshwater Fish
Pier Antonio Cucchietti, Stroppo (Cuneo), Piemonte

This dish actually improves with time—the longer it rests in the refrigerator, the tastier it will be. Sauté thinly sliced onion and whole garlic cloves in extra-virgin olive oil. When they begin to brown, add white wine vinegar and a little red wine and allow them to evaporate. Add sage leaves and a little water and cook for a few additional minutes.

Place a sprig of rosemary and a whole clove of garlic in the center of each small scaled and gutted freshwater fish you are using. Dredge the fish in the flour, then fry in hot olive oil until golden, turning to cook both sides. Salt lightly and transfer to a nonreactive container. Pour the vinegar mixture over the fish, cover, and refrigerate for at least 24 hours.

You can also make carpionata by sautéing sliced onion and the herbs, then adding the fish and browning it on both sides, and finally adding the vinegar to the pan and cooking for a few minutes. Let the dish cool and transfer it to an earthenware container, ensuring that the marinade completely covers the fish. Another version calls for cooking the fish in the marinade without frying it first. If you prefer a slightly less pungent marinade, use white wine in place of the vinegar.

TARTARA DI SALMERINO
Brook Trout Tartare
Ristorante Boivin, Levico Terme (Trento), Trentino-Alto Adige

Riccardo Bosco, the chef at Ristorante Boivin, uses a large amount of ginger to give Italian raw fish dishes like this one zing. If you are not a fan of a strong ginger flavor, scale it back.

SERVES 6
- ½ clove garlic
- 3½ ounces ginger, grated
- Juice of ½ lemon
- 2 tablespoons sour cream
- 1 pound brook trout
- Salt to taste

Crush the garlic with a mortar and pestle and mix in the ginger, lemon juice, and sour cream until well combined. Clean and fillet the trout and remove the skin, then cut into ¼-inch cubes. Toss the fish with salt and the prepared sauce and chill in the refrigerator at least 1 hour before serving.

INSALATA DI FAGIOLI E FILETTI DI ARINGA ≪≪
Herring and Bean Salad
Osteria La Piazzetta del Sole, Farnese (Viterbo), Lazio

agioli del purgatorio, literally "purgatory beans," are small white beans similar to cannellini beans with a very tender skin. They are so small that they do not need to be soaked. If you cannot locate these delicate beans in your area, substitute another white bean, but do soak them in water overnight. Since 1600, fagioli del purgatorio have been eaten in Gradoli on Ash Wednesday as part of a "purgatory lunch."

SERVES 4
1¾ cups dried fagioli del purgatorio beans
1 clove garlic
2 bay leaves
Salt and freshly ground black pepper to taste
Extra-virgin olive oil for drizzling
White wine vinegar for drizzling
2 to 3 stalks wild fennel
4 smoked herring fillets
2 spring onions

Cook the beans in a generous amount of water with the garlic and the bay leaves until they are soft, about 1 hour. Season with salt, then drain. Discard garlic and bay leaf. Arrange the cooked beans on individual serving dishes and season with a little more salt, a generous amount of pepper, plenty of olive oil, and a few drops of vinegar.

Mince the wild fennel fronds and sprinkle them over the beans. Chop the herring fillets and arrange them in a circle on each plate, then thinly slice the onions and place them in the center. Drizzle on a little more oil and sprinkle with a little more pepper just before serving.

MISSOLTINI CON POLENTA 🍃
Marinated Lake Fish with Grilled Polenta
Osteria Sali e Tabacchi, Mandello del Lario (Lecco), Lombardia

o make *missoltini*, agone, a small lake fish in the shad family, are first salted and set in the sun and wind to dry, then transferred to containers, where they are layered with bay leaves—a natural preservative. They are pressed and allowed to rest for at least two months to extrude their naturally occurring oil. They will stay good for several months.

SERVES 4
Extra-virgin olive oil for sauce
Bay leaf–infused rosé wine vinegar for sauce
4 missoltini (shad preserved in salt)
4 to 8 slices cooked and cooled polenta

In a container large enough to hold the fish in a single layer, make an emulsion of two parts oil to one part vinegar. Heat the missoltini on a griddle until very hot and submerge them in the oil mixture and set aside to marinate. Just before serving, briefly grill the polenta slices.

AGLIATA DI SURI 🐚
Fried Jack Mackerel in Garlic Sauce
Marco Lombardo, Milazzo (Messina), Sicîlia

alve small jack mackerel (leave on the bone), dredge in flour, and fry in hot olive oil until golden. Drain, then transfer to a platter. Brown 4 cloves garlic in a little oil. (Strain and reuse the oil you used to fry the fish if you like.) As soon as the garlic begins to color, add white wine vinegar (enough to cover the fish) and cook until it has reduced. Season with salt and pepper and pour it, still hot, over the fried fish. Let sit at room temperature at least 4 hours before serving.

ARANCINI DI PESCE ●
Rice Balls with Fish
Carmela Scapaci, Caltanissetta, Sicília

These are the perfect bites with an apéritif.

SERVES 4

RICE
1½ cups superfino rice
Salt to taste
1 pinch saffron
½ cup grated aged sheep's cheese
3 large eggs
Freshly ground black pepper to taste
   (optional)
Extra-virgin olive oil for frying
Unbleached all-purpose flour for dredging
Breadcrumbs for dredging

FILLING
1 clove garlic
Extra-virgin olive oil for sautéing
1 small yellow onion, thinly sliced
4 plum tomatoes, peeled, seeded, and diced
10 ounces baby cuttlefish, cut into thin strips
2 slices swordfish, diced
Unbleached all-purpose flour for dredging
7 ounces small shrimp, peeled and deveined
¼ cup dry white wine

Boil the rice in salted water until tender and drain.

Dissolve the saffron in 1 tablespoon lukewarm water and stir it into the rice along with the grated cheese. Lightly beat 2 eggs and add. Season with pepper if using. Combine thoroughly.

Set aside the rice mixture to cool and prepare the filling. Crush the garlic clove and brown it in a small amount of oil, then remove and discard. Add the onion, then the tomatoes. Cook for a few minutes, then add the cuttlefish. Lightly dredge the swordfish in flour and add it to the pan. Finally, add the shrimp. Add the wine and let it evaporate, then continue cooking until the fish is cooked through. If the sauce seems too dry—it should be creamy—add a small amount of water.

To make a rice ball, take about 1 teaspoon of the filling and surround it with enough rice to enclose it completely and make a ball the size of a walnut. Repeat with remaining rice and filling. Line a baking sheet with paper towels. Place the olive oil for frying in a pot with high sides and bring to high temperature. Whisk the remaining egg in a shallow bowl and prepare another shallow bowl with flour for dredging and a third with the breadcrumbs. Dredge the rice balls first in flour, then in beaten egg, and lastly in breadcrumbs and fry until golden. Work in batches if necessary.

Remove with a skimmer to the prepared pan briefly to drain, then serve hot.

ZEPPOLE DI ROSSETTI
Whitebait Fritters
Ristorante Crescenzo, Chiaiolella, Isola di Procida (Napoli), Campania

Rossetti (also known as *gianchetti*) are the whitebait (very small young fish) of Mediterranean fish, most commonly anchovies and sardines. They are translucent with a red tinge (hence the name). This should be made with the tiniest of fish, which can be eaten whole—heads, bones, and all.

SERVES 4

- 10 ounces very small whitebait (see note)
- 1 large piece (about 9 by 9 inches) crustless day-old bread, roughly chopped
- ½ cup fish fumet or broth
- ¼ cup grated Parmigiano Reggiano
- ¼ cup grated young Pecorino Romano cheese
- 1 egg yolk
- Leaves of 1 sprig parsley, minced
- Salt and freshly ground black pepper to taste
- Olive oil for frying

Soak the whitebait in a generous amount of cold water and let any debris sink to the bottom. Then rinse well in running water, drain, and dry.

Soak the bread in the fish fumet. When it is soft, squeeze dry and crumble into a bowl. Add the cheeses, the egg yolk, the parsley, and the whitebait, season with salt and pepper, and mix well to combine. The mixture should be soft. Shape the mixture into balls the size of a walnut, arrange them in a single layer, and refrigerate for at least 2 hours.

Place the olive oil for frying in a pot with high sides and bring to high temperature. Fry the prepared balls until golden and serve immediately.

FRITTATA DI MOLECHE
Soft-Shell Crab Frittata
Armanda Vianello, Venezia, Veneto

Venezia's *moleche*, particularly delicate soft-shell crabs, have a Slow Food Presidium. Dredge soft-shell crabs in flour, then fry in hot oil until browned, 3 to 4 minutes per side. Roughly chop the crabs and toss them with beaten eggs seasoned with salt and pepper. Heat extra-virgin olive oil or butter in a skillet. When it begins to sizzle, pour in the egg mixture and cook, shaking the pan frequently. When the bottom is firm and there is a narrow margin of cooked egg around the perimeter, flip the frittata and cook until the other side is firm as well.

MOLECHE FRITTE
Fried Soft-Shell Crabs
Luigino Bissaco, Chioggia (Venezia), Veneto

With kitchen shears, cut soft-shell crab claws to about ⅓ inch, but leave the pincer claws intact. Press gently with your fingers to eliminate some of the water the crabs contain, then place them in a colander and let them dry completely. Bring oil for frying to 350°F. Dredge the crabs in flour very lightly, shaking off any excess, then, working in batches if necessary to avoid crowding the pan, use a fry basket to fry them until crisp. Lift the basket and let them drain over the pot. Salt and serve immediately.

A variation of this recipe calls for placing about 1½ pounds of crabs in a bowl of eggs (3 large eggs for about 1½ pounds of crabs) beaten with a little salt and leaving them there for a couple of hours. They will absorb all of the egg.

PATÉ DI PESCE DI LAGO
Lake Fish Terrine
Trattoria Santo Stefano, Lenno (Como), Lombardia

Iandlocked Lombardia has numerous lakes that are home to a wide variety of fish.

SERVES 8 TO 10

1 medium yellow onion, thinly sliced
Extra-virgin olive oil for sautéing
1 to 2 fresh bay leaves
Leaves of 1 sprig fresh rosemary
Leaves of 1 sprig wild thyme
1 to 2 fresh sage leaves
2 pounds lake fish fillets, such as whitefish, chub, or perch
2 tablespoons brandy
1 cup dry Marsala
Salt to taste
2½ teaspoons (1 envelope) unflavored gelatin
1 pound (4 sticks) unsalted butter

Sauté the onion in a small amount of oil. Add the herbs and the fish fillets and cook over medium heat until cooked though. Add the brandy and ¼ cup Marsala and season with salt. Remove from the heat and allow to cool.

Make a gelatin with the remaining ¾ cup Marsala with 2¼ cups water and the gelatin. Pour about 1 inch of this mixture into the bottoms of four individual serving dishes and cool to firm.

Melt the butter. Grind the fish mixture finely in a food processor fitted with the metal blade or a grinder. Pass the mixture through a drum sieve or tamis, scraping with a scraper or knife blade. With a spatula, gradually fold the melted butter into the fish mixture. Whip with a whisk until very fluffy and cool on the lowest shelf in the refrigerator for 15 minutes.

Fill a pastry bag fitted with a French tip with the mixture and pipe it on top of the gelatin in the serving dishes. Refrigerate for 30 minutes. When the remaining gelatin mixture is cool (but not completely thickened) brush it on top of the pâté. Chill until firm.

TORTINO DI CICENIELLI
Whitebait with a Breadcrumb Crust
Taverna Portosalvo, Villammare di Vibonati (Salerno), Campania

This dish can also be baked in a 400°F oven until the whitebait is cooked through.

SERVES 4

1½ pounds whitebait
Juice of 1 lemon
Extra-virgin olive oil for dressing and drizzling
Salt to taste
Leaves of 2 sprigs flat-leaf parsley, minced
½ clove garlic, minced
1 tablespoon unsalted butter
¼ cup breadcrumbs
1 pinch dried oregano

Place the whitebait in a colander and rinse under running water. Drain and transfer to a bowl. In a small bowl, whisk the lemon juice with enough extra-virgin olive oil to make a dressing that will coat the whitebait and season with salt. Whisk in half of the parsley and all of the garlic. Pour the dressing over the whitebait and mix thoroughly with your hands.

Use the butter to butter a skillet, then pour in the whitebait mixture and sprinkle the top with the breadcrumbs, the oregano, and the remaining parsley. Drizzle on a little more olive oil, cover the pan, and cook over low heat until the whitebait is bright white on top, about 5 minutes.

MUGGINI ARROSTO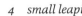
Grilled Mullet
Ristorante Il Caminetto, Cabras (Oristano), Sardegna

One variation of this dish calls for coating the fish in an herbaceous mixture of wild fennel, shallot, thyme, myrtle leaves, bay leaves, black peppercorns, and myrtle berries and letting it sit for a couple of hours to absorb the flavor. The cooked fish is then served with a sauce of minced anchovies, capers, and lemon juice. If you are absolutely certain that your mullet is exquisitely fresh, it can be cooked without being scaled or gutted.

SERVES 4

4   small leaping mullet (7 to 10 ounces each)
1   clove garlic, crushed
Salt to taste

Prepare a grill with a low fire. The ideal fuel for the grill is reeds, which will get a lively fire going and scent the fish with a pleasant aroma. You can also use charcoal, however. Set the fish on the grill and cook for 40 minutes, turning occasionally. Meanwhile, make a brine with the garlic clove, salt, and water. When the fish are cooked, dip them in the brine, then remove, drain, and serve.

BACCALÀ MANTECATO 🐚
Dried Cod Spread
Ristorante La Ragnatela, Mirano (Venezia), Veneto

Baccalà mantecato is one of Venezia's signature dishes. The Jewish community in Venezia—which was substantial in size at one time—prepares this dish with oil and milk or cream. However, the name is misleading: Venetians tend to call dried cod, or stockfish, *baccalà*, though baccalà is technically salted dried cod. The two are very similar, in any case, though you probably won't need to salt the finished dish if you use true baccalà, as it is heavily salted for the sake of preservation. Be sure to start well in advance to leave time for soaking.

SERVES 4

1   pound dried whole cod
Rock salt to taste
2   cloves garlic, minced
Extra-virgin olive oil for whipping
Freshly ground black pepper to taste
Salt to taste

Place the dried cod on a wooden work surface and beat energetically with a hammer until it is flexible, then soak in a generous amount of water for 2 to 3 days.

Drain the fish, dry it, cut it open, and fillet it and skin it. Mince the skinned rehydrated fillet and place it in a pot with cold water to cover and rock salt to taste. Bring to a boil, then remove from the heat and allow the cod to rest in the water in the pot for 20 minutes.

Drain the fish and place it in a bowl with the garlic. Beat with a whisk while slowly drizzling in a generous amount of olive oil in a thin stream, as if making a mayonnaise. Continue drizzling and beating until the mixture is fluffy like a mousse. Season with black pepper and adjust salt to taste.

STOPETA
Marinated Baccalà
Trattoria Aütedo, Marola (La Spezia), Liguria

This is almost like a marinated carpaccio. It's ironic that this hails from a coastal area, where presumably fresh fish is widely available. The area in and around Genova has many recipes for salt cod and stockfish, which became popular due to brisk maritime trade with northern Europe.

SERVES 10
1 pound salt cod
¼ cup white wine
2 cups extra-virgin olive oil
1 teaspoon ground cayenne pepper
Leaves of 1 sprig thyme, minced
2 spring onions, thinly sliced
Slices of country-style bread

Wipe the salt cod with a cloth dipped in the white wine in order to remove the salt on the surface. Remove any bones and skin and mince finely by hand. Place the fish in a bowl and add the oil, cayenne pepper, thyme, and onions. Set aside to rest for 3 to 4 days. Lightly toast or grill bread just before serving and top the bread with the marinated baccalà.

ARSELLE ALLA MARINARA
Clams Marinara
Carlotta Olivieri, Sarzana (La Spezia), Liguria

Rinse clams under running water and scrub the shells. Place them in a large skillet and place them over medium heat, covered, until they open. Discard the empty half-shells and filter the clam cooking liquid and reserve. Mince garlic and parsley together. In a large skillet, sauté the garlic and parsley in extra-virgin olive oil, then add the clams in their half-shells. Add diced plum tomatoes and a little of the clam cooking liquid. Cook

for a few minutes to combine the flavors. Season with pepper and adjust salt to taste.

Neapolitan-style clams are made with the same ingredients, but using a slightly different technique: the clams are cleaned thoroughly and then cooked in the tomatoes directly.

INSALATA DI STUCCO
Stockfish Salad
Ristorante Al Duomo, Taormina (Messina), Sicília

To make a similar salad with salt cod, soak in several changes of water over several days, then boil the salt cod, let it cool in the cooking water, drain, and flake the fish. Then mix with minced garlic and parsley, salt, pepper, and extra-virgin olive oil. You can also incorporate minced salted anchovies that have been rinsed and boned, capers, and/or pitted black olives.

SERVES 4
1½ pounds dried cod, beaten and soaked
10 Pachino cherry tomatoes
1 celery heart, sliced
2 shallots, sliced
Extra-virgin olive oil for drizzling
Juice of 2 lemons
Salt and freshly ground black pepper
    to taste

Boil the dried cod in salted water for a few minutes until soft. When it is just warm enough to handle, skin and fillet it. Flake the fish and toss in a bowl with the cherry tomatoes, the celery heart, and the shallots. Drizzle with oil and the juice of the lemons. Season with salt and pepper.

FRITTATA CON I SALTARELLI
Shrimp Frittata
Ristorante Ancilla, Pozzolo di Marmirolo
(Mantua), Lombardia

Serve this delicately flavored frittata with some baby lettuce or other greens in season.

SERVES 4
Oil for frying
7   ounces freshwater shrimp, shelled and
    deveined
6   large eggs
2   tablespoons grated Grana Padano cheese
Salt to taste
1   tablespoon extra-virgin olive oil

Line a baking sheet with paper towels. Place the oil for frying in a pot with high sides and bring to high heat. Fry the shrimp in the oil, then use a skimmer to transfer them to the prepared pan to drain. Beat the eggs until frothy. Whisk in the grated cheese and season with salt.

Heat the extra-virgin olive oil in a nonstick skillet. Arrange the shrimp in a layer in the skillet, then pour the egg mixture over them. When the bottom is browned and there is a narrow margin of cooked egg around the perimeter, flip the frittata and cook until the other side is browned as well.

COZZE, COCOZZE E OVE
Mussels, Cucuzza Squash, and Eggs
Ristorante Bufi, Molfetta (Bari), Puglia

Long green cucuzza squash, mussels, and eggs are three of Puglia's signature ingredients. Another similar dish incorporates cucuzza squash, mussels, rice, and potatoes.

SERVES 4
1   small white onion, cut into julienne
3   tablespoons extra-virgin olive oil
10 ounces cucuzza squash (see note),
    sliced into rounds
2   pounds mussels
3   large eggs
2   tablespoons grated aged sheep's cheese
Salt and freshly ground black pepper to taste

In a skillet, sauté the onion in the oil and once it begins to color add the squash. Add 1 tablespoon water and cook over low heat until softened. Add the mussels and cook, uncovered, until their shells have opened. Remove the mussels from their shells and return them to the pan.

In a bowl, beat the eggs with the grated cheese and season with salt and pepper. Pour the egg mixture over the mussels and stir until well combined. Serve immediately.

MOSCARDINI IN CASSUOLA

Braised Baby Octopus

Ristorante A Ridosso, Bacoli (Napoli), Campania

This dish can also be served as a main course.

SERVES 4

1¾ pounds baby octopus
2 cloves garlic
1 piece hot pepper
½ cup extra-virgin olive oil
About ½ cup broth
12 cherry tomatoes, halved
Leaves of 1 sprig flat-leaf parsley
Salt to taste
Toasted bread for serving

Clean the octopus and mince the garlic and hot pepper together. Heat about half of the oil in a saucepan and sauté the garlic and hot pepper until golden. Add the octopus and enough broth to keep the garlic from sticking. Cook for about 7 minutes, then add the tomatoes. Sprinkle on the parsley and season with salt. Drizzle on the remaining oil. Cook until the liquid is creamy and the octopus are cooked through, about an additional 7 minutes. If the octopus is not tender, add a little more broth and continue cooking for a few more minutes.

Arrange the bread in a single layer on a serving dish and ladle the octopus and the cooking liquid over it.

OSTRICHE TARANTINE IN TIELLA

Taranto-Style Baked Oysters

Sofia Sorvino, Taranto, Puglia

Open oysters with a knife. Rinse briefly in salted water to get rid of any sand and little shards of shell that broke off while you were opening them. Discard the empty half-shells and put the half-shells with oysters in a baking pan in a single layer. Sprinkle on parsley and breadcrumbs. Season with pepper and drizzle with olive oil. Bake at 400°F for 10 minutes and serve immediately.

IMPEPATA DI COZZE

Peppery Mussels in White Wine

Trattoria Pantagruele, Brindisi, Puglia

This dish can also be served as a main course.

SERVES 4

3⅓ pounds mussels
½ cup extra-virgin olive oil
1 clove garlic, minced
½ cup dry white wine
Freshly ground black pepper to taste
2 tomatoes, peeled and diced (optional)
Leaves of 1 sprig parsley

Clean and scrub the mussels. Place in a pot with the oil and garlic. Place over high heat. Add the wine and allow it to evaporate, then cover the pot and cook over high heat until the shells open.

Remove the mussels from the shells (filter and reserve cooking liquid) and transfer them to a clean pot. Season generously with black pepper. Drizzle with some of their cooking liquid. Add the tomatoes if using.

Cook for an additional 5 minutes and sprinkle with parsley just before serving.

SAUTÉ DI COZZE
Sautéed Mussels
Ristorante La Brace, Praiano (Salerno), Campania

This simple and delicious dish can also be made with clams or a mix of shellfish. The amount of spiciness is up to you. If you leave out the hot pepper completely, use a generous grinding of black pepper.

SERVES 4

- 2 cloves garlic, minced
- Extra-virgin olive oil for sautéing
- Leaves of 1 sprig flat-leaf parsley, minced
- 2 pounds mussels
- 1 piece hot pepper to taste (optional)

In a skillet or sauté pan, sauté the garlic in a generous amount of olive oil. As soon as it begins to color, add the parsley, the mussels, ½ cup water, and the hot pepper, if using. Cover and cook over high heat until the mussels have opened. (Discard any unopened mussels.) Transfer the mussels to a bowl with a slotted spoon, then filter the cooking liquid and drizzle it over the mussels.

INSALATA DI MARE
Seafood Salad
Ines Diodori, Maratea (Potenza), Basilicata

Boil octopus and calamari separately in salted water until tender. Drain and dice the octopus and cut the calamari into rings. Boil shrimp in water with vinegar added to keep them from discoloring. Cook mussels and clams in a skillet until they open. Filter and reserve their cooking liquid. Shell and set aside. For the dressing, whisk lemon juice with extra-virgin olive oil and season with salt and pepper and a few tablespoons

of the filtered shellfish cooking liquid. Place the cooked seafood on a platter and top with this dressing. Sprinkle on minced parsley, minced garlic, and minced celery. Allow to cool before serving.

'NTUPPATEDDI A 'MBRIACA
Snails in Red Wine
Trattoria Cava Grande, Avola (Siracusa), Sicilia

Paola and Luigia of the Trattoria Cava Grande have contributed this recipe, which calls for land snails with opercula. An operculum (singular) is a white membrane that works like a trapdoor to close off the shell. These are cooked with plenty of red wine—hence the name, which means "drunken snails."

SERVES 5

- 2 pounds snails with opercula
- 1 medium yellow onion, thinly sliced
- Extra-virgin olive oil for sautéing
- 2 teaspoons freshly ground black pepper
- 1½ teaspoons freshly grated nutmeg
- Leaves of 1 sprig oregano
- Salt to taste
- 1 cup red wine

Blanch the snails in boiling water until any impurities have emerged. Sauté the onion in a little olive oil in a large pot. Drain the snails and add them to the pot. Add the pepper, nutmeg, oregano, salt, and wine and stir to combine. Cover and cook over medium heat until almost all of the liquid has evaporated. Serve hot.

POULTRY & MEAT DISHES

BISTECCHINE DI POLLO IN CARPIONE

Chicken in Vinegar and Onion Sauce

Osteria dell'Unione, Treiso (Cuneo), Piemonte

This is a summer dish that's perfect for picnics. You can also use turkey in place of the chicken. This dish has its roots in nineteenth-century cuisine, which had many similar poultry preparations that used white wine and lemon juice in place of the vinegar more common nowadays.

SERVES 4

- 1 boneless chicken breast
- 2 large eggs
- ¾ cup breadcrumbs
- ¾ cup extra-virgin olive oil
- Salt to taste
- 1 medium yellow onion
- 1 rib celery
- 2 cloves garlic
- 20 fresh sage leaves
- Leaves of 1 sprig fresh rosemary
- ½ cup white wine vinegar

Cut the chicken breast into thin strips. Beat the eggs in a shallow bowl and place the breadcrumbs in another bowl. Place ½ cup oil in a pot with high sides and bring to high heat. Dredge the chicken strips first in the eggs and then in the breadcrumbs, then fry until browned. Season with salt. Place in a nonreactive heatproof container. Mince the onion, celery, garlic, sage, and rosemary. Sauté in the remaining ¼ cup olive oil until softened. Season with salt and add the vinegar and ½ cup water. Bring to a boil and then pour the hot liquid over the chicken. Allow to cool completely before serving.

CARNE CRUDA

Steak Tartare

Osteria dell'Arco, Alba (Cuneo), Piemonte

One of Piemonte's signature dishes is this tartare made with local Fassone beef, chopped by hand, dressed with olive oil, garlic, salt, pepper, and lemon juice. Sometimes the dish is embellished with slices of white truffle or hard-to-find ovolo mushrooms, shavings of Parmigiano Reggiano, or thin slices of celery. In the 1960s, restaurants in Alba began serving a similar dish with the meat thinly shaved rather than chopped, labeling it *carne cruda all'albese*, or Alba-style raw beef. Fassone beef from *Razza Piemontese* (literally Piemonte breed) cattle has less fat and less connective tissue than standard beef, making it perfect for this dish. Trim and discard any fat or membrane with a sharp knife.

SERVES 6

- 1 pound Fassone (Razza Piemontese) top round beef (see note)
- 6 cloves garlic
- ½ cup plus 2 tablespoons extra-virgin olive oil
- Salt and freshly ground white pepper to taste
- Juice of 2 lemons

Chop the beef very finely, preferably by hand using a heavy butcher's knife. If you must, use a meat grinder, but never a mixer or food processor. You can also ask the butcher to chop the meat for you by hand, as long as you dress the beef immediately afterward.

Place the chopped beef on a plate. Crush the garlic cloves, leaving them whole, and mix them into the chopped beef. Add the oil 1 tablespoon at a time, mixing to combine between additions. Season with salt and white pepper. Lastly, mix in the lemon juice. Mix one more time, then remove and discard the garlic cloves and serve immediately.

FRECACHA
Stovetop Meat and Vegetable Pie
La Brasserie du Bon Bec, Cogne (Aosta), Valle d'Aosta

This simple and delicious crustless meat and vegetable pie was invented as a way to use boiled meat left over from Sunday supper, along with a few potatoes and onions, which were always available in the mountains, even in the most impoverished areas. (If you have leftover meat, feel free to substitute it for the veal shoulder here.) The chefs at La Brasserie du Bon Bec, a lovely restaurant in beautiful Cogne, make their *frecacha* with veal cuts from the shoulder that are not overly lean.

SERVES 8

- 3½ pounds veal shoulder
- 2 bay leaves
- 1 sprig sage
- 2 carrots, roughly chopped
- 1 rib celery, roughly chopped
- 1¾ pounds potatoes
- 4 medium yellow onions
- 2 tablespoons unsalted butter
- 1 clove garlic, minced
- Grated nutmeg to taste
- Ground cinnamon to taste
- Salt and freshly ground black pepper to taste
- ½ cup beef broth

Place the meat in a pot with the bay leaves, sage, carrots, and celery. Bring to a boil, then turn down to a simmer and simmer for 2½ hours. In a separate pot, boil the potatoes until easily pierced with a fork, then drain and as soon as they are cool enough to handle, peel them and slice them. Slice the onions as well. When the meat is extremely tender, cut into slices and set aside.

Melt the butter in a skillet and sauté the onions. When they are golden, mix in the minced garlic. Add the meat and the potatoes and stir to combine. Season with nutmeg, cinnamon, salt, and pepper and stir to combine. Add the beef broth. Cover the skillet and cook over low heat for 30 minutes. When all the broth has been absorbed, remove the cover and turn up the heat to medium. Cook until a golden crust has formed on the bottom. Serve hot.

FRITTATA CON GLI ZOCCOLI
Cured Pork Belly Frittata
Nara Nesi, Firenze, Toscana

This inexpensive dish is made using pancetta, or cured pork belly. Pancetta is often compared to bacon, but pancetta is simply salted for preservation and not smoked. In Italy, it is generally available in two forms: rolled or in a slab. This recipe calls for the slab-type pancetta, but you can also use the rolled form—just omit the olive oil, as rolled pancetta has plenty of fat.

Place cubes of pancetta and a generous amount of extra-virgin olive oil in a skillet and cook over medium heat until transparent. Don't let the pancetta dry out too much. Add beaten eggs. With a spatula, push the cooked eggs from the edge into the center. At the same time, tilt the pan toward the edge that you are pushing in so that still-liquid egg mixture runs down and fills the now-empty space. Repeat several times. When the bottom of the frittata is firm but the top is still soft, cook over medium heat without moving until the bottom is browned and set, 2 to 3 minutes. Using the spatula, slide the frittata out of the pan, then flip it back into the pan so that the browned side is facing up. Cook until the bottom is browned and set, 2 to 3 additional minutes.

ARANCINI AL SUGO ⬚⬚
Rice Balls with Meat Sauce
Sabina Zuccaro, Siracusa, Sicîlia

There are dozens if not hundreds of variations of this recipe. They can be made with boiled chicken in place of the pork and rice cooked in chicken broth. Peas are often part of the filling, mixed with leftover ragù. Other frequent players are prosciutto and cheese, spinach and cheese, eggplant, artichokes, and mushrooms. *Strattu* is a very thick and concentrated form of tomato paste found in Sicilia. Use only high-quality tomato paste, as its flavor will be evident.

SERVES 6
- 1 small onion, thinly sliced
- 2 tablespoons extra-virgin olive oil, plus more for frying
- 1 (14-ounce) piece lean pork
- Salt to taste
- ¼ cup red wine
- Freshly grated nutmeg to taste
- ¾ cup strattu or tomato paste
- 4 cups (2 pounds) rice for risotto
- ¼ teaspoon saffron
- ¾ cup grated aged caciocavallo cheese
- 12 ounces young caciocavallo cheese from Ragusa
- 5 large eggs
- 2 cups breadcrumbs

In a large (preferably earthenware) pot, sauté the onion in 2 tablespoons oil. Add the pork and salt and raise the heat to high. Cook, turning frequently, until browned on both sides. Add the wine and let it evaporate over high heat. Season with nutmeg and remove the meat from the pot. Combine the strattu with about ½ cup lukewarm water and add it to the pot. Return the pork to the pot and add enough water to cover. Cover the pot and cook over the lowest possible heat until the sauce has reduced and grown very dense, about 3 hours. You may want to cook it uncovered for the last 30 minutes or so in order to keep it from reducing too quickly and to be able to keep an eye on it.

In the meantime, cook the rice in about 8 cups salted water, aiming to have the rice absorb the water during cooking. When the rice is cooked al dente, fold in the saffron and the grated aged caciocavallo cheese. Spread onto a wooden board to cool.

Cut the pork into thin slices, then into cubes. Cut the young caciocavallo cheese into small dice. Beat the eggs with a little salt in a low bowl such as a soup bowl. Spread the breadcrumbs out on a large work surface. Place a golf ball–sized amount of rice in the cupped palm of one hand and press it to make an indentation in the center. Fill the indentation with a generous spoonful of sauce, a few pieces of pork, a few pieces of cheese, and another spoonful of sauce. Place a bit more rice on top and shape into a pyramid, working with your hands as you would to shape a meatball. Dredge in the eggs and the breadcrumbs, pressing lightly on the base of the pyramid so that it can stand flat. Set aside and repeat with remaining rice, sauce, cheese, and pork.

Line a baking sheet with paper towels or a brown paper bag. Place oil for frying in a pot with high sides or a deep fryer and bring to high temperature. Place the arancini on their bases in a fry basket and fry them in the oil, working in batches if necessary. Transfer them to the prepared pan to drain and serve hot.

GUANCIA DI MANZO CON PATATE E FINFERLI 🌰
Beef Cheek with Potatoes and Chanterelle Mushrooms
Ristorante Rifugio Fuchiade, Soraga (Trento), Trentino-Alto Adige

At this restaurant on the Trento side of the Marmolada mountain, this dish is listed on the menu as "beef jowl." We've corrected it to beef cheek here, both to avoid confusion with pork jowl (cows don't have jowls) and the cured meat known as guanciale and to emphasize the inclusion of this tasty cut, which is too often overlooked.

SERVES 4
- 1   medium yellow onion, roughly chopped
- 1   carrot, roughly chopped
- 1   rib celery, roughly chopped
- Salt to taste
- Whole black peppercorns to taste
- 2   beef cheeks
- 5   potatoes
- Freshly ground black pepper to taste
- Balsamic vinegar for dressing and drizzling
- Extra-virgin olive oil for dressing and drizzling
- 1   tablespoon unsalted butter
- 1   clove garlic
- 7   ounces chanterelle mushrooms, sliced
- 1   chive

Fill a pot with water. Add the onion, carrot, celery, salt, and peppercorns. Cook the beef cheeks in this water until tender. Meanwhile, boil the potatoes, slice them into rounds, and toss gently with salt, ground pepper, balsamic vinegar, and olive oil. Melt the butter in a skillet. Crush the garlic clove and add. Briefly sauté the mushrooms. Season with salt. Remove and discard garlic.

Thinly slice the beef cheeks. Arrange the potatoes on a serving platter and arrange the beef cheeks on top of the potatoes. Mince the chive and sprinkle it on top. Drizzle the platter with

a little more oil and balsamic vinegar (using a light hand). Arrange the mushrooms on top of the meat and serve.

CIPOLLE RIPIENE
Onions Stuffed with Meat
Osteria dell'Unione, Treiso (Cuneo), Piemonte

In the Langhe area, leftover roasted meat (a classic Sunday lunch) and other bits of cooked meat have long been set aside for two purposes: to make the filling for the area's signature pasta, agnolotti (pages 194 and 200), and to make this dish. Some variations incorporate salami as well.

SERVES 4
- 4   medium onions
- 6   ounces roasted veal
- 6   ounces roasted pork
- ¼   cup flat-leaf parsley leaves
- 2   tablespoons grated Parmigiano Reggiano
- 2   large eggs, lightly beaten
- Salt and freshly ground black pepper to taste
- 2   tablespoons extra-virgin olive oil
- 2   tablespoons unsalted butter
- 2   tablespoons breadcrumbs

Preheat the oven to 325°F. Peel the onions and boil them until they are about three quarters cooked: the cores should still be hard when they are pierced with a knife and they should hold their shape. Cut in half horizontally just above the middle. Scoop out the center of each half with a spoon and reserve scooped onion flesh.

With a mezzaluna, chop the roasted meats, the parsley, and the scooped onion flesh. Mix in the Parmigiano Reggiano and the eggs. Knead until well combined. Season with salt and pepper.

Oil a baking pan with the olive oil. Fill the onion halves with the mixture and arrange in the baking pan. Cut the butter into small pieces and dot the onions with it. Sprinkle on the breadcrumbs. Bake in the preheated oven until golden, about 10 minutes. Serve hot.

VITELLO TONNATO 🌿
Veal in Tuna Sauce
Vineria della Signora in Rosso, Nizza Monferrato (Asti), Piemonte

Marco Cantamessa, the chef at the winery attached to the Bottega del Vino in Nizza Monferrato that contributed this recipe, calls this by a different name, but anyone from Piemonte or anywhere else will recognize it as the region's famous vitello tonnato. Vitello tonnato as we know it today—with a sauce made of mayonnaise and tuna canned in oil—is less than a century old, while recipes for veal with a sauce of anchovies and capers date back to the eighteenth century. Cantamessa's updated version calls for roasting the meat in salt and then letting it rest overnight so that it remains soft and pink when sliced. It's best to roast the veal the day before serving.

SERVES 8

- 4   pounds 8 ounces rock salt
- 2   pounds fine salt, plus more for seasoning
- 1   (2- to 3-pound) Fassone (Razza Piemontese) veal top round, trimmed and trussed
- 2   large eggs
- 2   egg yolks
- 2¾ cups sunflower oil
- 1¾ cups extra-virgin olive oil
- ⅓   cup white wine vinegar
- 3 or 4 drops Worcestershire sauce
- 2½ cups tuna in olive oil, drained
- ¼   cup salted Pantelleria capers, rinsed and drained
- 4 to 5 anchovy fillets, rinsed and drained

Preheat the oven to 400°F. Place all of the rock salt and the 2 pounds of fine salt in a bowl. Add enough cold water to make a soft paste, but do not dissolve the salt.

Cover the bottom of a baking pan large enough to hold the veal with the salt mixture about ¼ inch deep. Rest the meat on top of the salt and cover it with the rest of the salt, pressing to adhere. Roast in the preheated oven for 1½ hours.

Remove the meat from the oven and break the crust. Cut the veal in half and allow to drain, cut-sides down, in the refrigerator overnight. The next day the meat should be compact, velvety, and pink.

For the sauce, make a mayonnaise by whisking (or blending in a blender or food processor) the eggs and egg yolks, sunflower and olive oil, vinegar, Worcestershire sauce, and a pinch of salt.

Drain the tuna and mince with the capers and anchovies until the mixture forms a paste. Whisk the tuna mixture into the mayonnaise.

Thinly slice the veal (preferably with a meat slicer) and arrange the slices on a serving platter, overlapping slightly. Cover about half of the surface of the veal with the sauce and serve.

CRAUTI ROSTIDI 🌳
Sauerkraut and Beans
Nereo Pederzolli, Cavedine di Stravino (Trento), Trentino–Alto Adige

Farmers in northeastern Italy once ate sauerkraut almost daily, especially in winter; it was even served at breakfast. It gave them the strength to face long and exhausting days in the fields. Anyone over the age of fifty who grew up in the countryside in Trentino can't help but wax nostalgic when talking about this rustic and filling food. Serve with warm bread right out of the oven. A surprising pairing for this extremely simple dish is a classic sparkling wine from the Trento DOC region.

Boil fresh shelled borlotti beans or dried borlotti beans soaked in water to cover for at least 12 hours until tender, about 40 minutes for fresh beans and 2 hours for dried beans. When soft, drain them. Melt a spoonful of leaf lard in a large cast-iron skillet and sauté a generous amount of sauerkraut over high heat, stirring, for 5 minutes. Add the beans and cook until the mixture is browned and crusty and beginning to char in spots. Season with salt and pepper and serve.

CAPUSS DE VERZA ●
Stuffed Cabbage with Sausage
Anita Aldrighetti, Trento, Trentino-Alto Adige

This is a variation on the stuffed grape leaves that are also served in the Giudicarie area. The dish calls for a hearty companion—corn polenta, buckwheat polenta, or potatoes.

SERVES 6

- 1 medium head Savoy cabbage
- Salt to taste
- Extra-virgin olive oil for sautéing
- 14 ounces chard ribs or spinach
- 2 cloves garlic
- 3 large eggs, lightly beaten
- 6 ounces fresh lucanica sausage, casing removed and crumbled
- ⅓ cup diced smoked pancetta
- 1½ cups grated cheese, such as spressa, vezzena, or Trentingrana
- ⅔ cup breadcrumbs
- Freshly ground black pepper to taste
- ½ cup whole milk
- 1 tablespoon unsalted butter
- 1 medium yellow onion, sliced
- ½ cup dry white wine
- Tomato sauce or tomato paste diluted in water for sauce

Remove about a dozen of the largest outer leaves from the cabbage and boil them in lightly salted water for 2 minutes. Transfer to a colander, then spread out on a kitchen towel to dry. Slice the remaining cabbage, discarding the core. Sauté the sliced cabbage in olive oil for a few minutes. Boil the chard ribs in salted water until very tender, about 10 minutes, then drain, squeeze dry, and chop. In a mortar and pestle, crush the garlic into a paste.

In a bowl, combine the sautéed cabbage, the cooked chard, the eggs, the sausage, the pancetta, the grated cheese, the breadcrumbs, the garlic, pepper, and salt. Stir in the milk a little at a time to make a firm mixture. (You may not need all of the milk.) Set aside to rest for 30 minutes.

Place one cabbage leaf on the work surface and place a couple teaspoons of the stuffing in the center. Fold the bottom of the cabbage up, then fold in the two sides, and then roll up the leaf. Tie with kitchen twine and repeat with remaining cabbage and filling.

Melt the butter in a tin-lined copper pot and sauté the onion until browned. Arrange the cabbage bundles in the pot and cook over low heat, turning occasionally, until browned. Add the wine to the pot, allow it to reduce almost completely, and add enough water to come halfway up the cabbage rolls. Cook over low heat for 30 minutes. Add the tomato sauce and cook until it reduces to coat the cabbage rolls. Remove twine before serving.

AGNELLO SAMBUCANO IN SALSA TONNATA ANTICA

Sambucano Lamb in Tuna Sauce

Ristorante della Pace, Sambuco (Cuneo), Piemonte

This is excellent as an appetizer or as a main course. Bartolo Bruna's recipe uses a sauce inspired by a historic recipe that marries perfectly with tender Sambucano lamb. This breed, protected by a Slow Food Presidium, is raised in the Occitan Stura Valley and provides very lean and flavorful meat.

SERVES 10

1 boneless rack of Sambucano lamb (10 to 12 ounces)
Extra-virgin olive oil for sautéing
4 ounces lamb trimmings
1 boneless chicken breast
¾ cup plus 2 tablespoons heavy cream or whipping cream
Leaves of 1 sprig thyme
Leaves of 1 sprig rosemary
Salt and freshly ground black pepper to taste
⅔ cup canned tuna in olive oil, drained
4 cups dry white wine
2 salted anchovy fillets, rinsed, drained, and chopped
10 capers, rinsed and drained
1 hard-boiled egg
4 slices day-old bread

Brown the lamb rack on all sides in olive oil, then set aside to cool. Preheat the oven to 300°F. Mince together the lamb trimmings and chicken breast. In a blender or food processor fitted with the metal blade, process this minced meat with the cream, thyme leaves, and rosemary leaves. Season with salt and pepper, then spread this mixture in an even layer on a piece of commercial-grade plastic wrap. Place the browned rack on top of the mixture and then wrap the filling and plastic around the rack. Wrap two additional layers of plastic wrap around the lamb, then immerse the wrapped lamb in a pot with water to cover and bake in the preheated oven for 30 to 35 minutes.

Meanwhile, prepare the sauce. Combine the tuna, wine, anchovies, and capers in a saucepan and cook over medium heat, stirring occasionally, until the anchovies have dissolved and the liquid has reduced, 15 to 20 minutes. Use a slotted spoon to transfer the solids to a food processor fitted with the metal blade, reserving liquid. Process with the egg and bread. Gradually add back in the reserved liquid until you have a runny sauce. Remove the baked lamb from the water bath and allow it to rest in the refrigerator for 2 to 3 hours. Unwrap, slice finely, and serve slices topped with the sauce.

CALZONE DI CARNE E CIPOLLE

Boar and Onion Calzone

Lucia Coscia, Toritto (Bari), Puglia

To serve a hungry crowd, build a fire in a wood-burning oven or preheat a regular oven to the highest temperature possible (probably 500°F) with a pizza stone set on the lowest rack. Mix 8 cups all-purpose flour with about ¼ cup sourdough starter. Add enough salted lukewarm water to make a soft dough. Knead until smooth and set aside to rise. Meanwhile, sauté 2 pounds thinly sliced spring onions in extra-virgin olive oil with a pinch of salt. When the onions are golden, add about 14 ounces ground boar meat (purchase from a specialty butcher) and cook over low heat until about halfway cooked but not completely browned.

Divide the risen dough into 2 equal portions and roll them out into 2 disks with a rolling pin. Cover one disk with the onions and the meat, a sprinkling of pepper, and a drizzle of extra-virgin olive oil. Cover with the other disk of dough and crimp the borders, pinching with your fingers, to seal. Brush a little oil on the top and season with salt and additional pepper, if desired. Bake in the preheated oven until browned on the top and the bottom. Serve warm or cold.

FLAN DI GRANA CON CARNE SALADA ♣
Grana Cheese Flan with Corned Beef
Ristorante Nerina, Malgolo di Romeno (Trento), Trentino–Alto Adige

Trentingrana is an aged cheese with a deep yellow color and an especially grassy flavor. The milk used to make it comes from animals that graze in mountain pastures. These flans can also be drizzled with a balsamic vinegar reduction. Puff pastry breadsticks make a nice accompaniment.

SERVES 4
2½ cups grated Trentingrana cheese from Castelfondo (see note)
1¾ cups heavy cream or whipping cream
3 large eggs, lightly beaten
1 tablespoon minced flat-leaf parsley
Salt to taste
1 tablespoon unsalted butter
4 slices corned beef
About 2 cups mixed salad greens, cut into julienne

Whisk the grated cheese into the cream. Beat in the eggs, parsley, and a pinch of salt. Butter four ramekins, divide the mixture among them, filling the ramekins three quarters of the way up the sides, and steam over boiling water for 40 minutes.

Arrange one of the slices of corned beef on a work surface. Set about one quarter of the julienne greens on top and fold or roll the corned beef around the greens. Repeat with remaining corned beef and greens. On each individual serving plate, unmold one of the flans and place the corned beef bundle next to it.

FARINATA CON LE LEGHE 🌿
Cornmeal with Cabbage and Beans
Trattoria dell'Abbondanza, Pistoia, Toscana

This provides a hearty start to a large rustic meal. It can also serve as a main course.

SERVES 4
1 cup dried borlotti beans, soaked in water to cover overnight
⅔ cup diced prosciutto
1 medium yellow onion, minced
½ rib celery, minced
2 carrots, minced
Extra-virgin olive oil for sautéing
2 tablespoons tomato puree
2 zucchini, sliced into thin rounds
14 ounces kale, cut into ribbons
¼ head Savoy cabbage, cut into ribbons
Salt and freshly ground black pepper to taste
1½ cups cornmeal

Drain the beans of their soaking water and place them in a pot of salted cold water. Bring to a boil, then simmer until soft, about 1 hour after the water in the pot returns to a boil. Remove from the heat. Drain and reserve cooking water. Puree the beans and set aside.

In a large pot, sauté the prosciutto, onion, celery, and carrot in olive oil. Add the tomato puree, the zucchini, the kale, and the cabbage. Season with salt and pepper and cook for 1 hour. Add the bean puree and enough of the reserved liquid to make the mixture fairly soupy. Stir with a wooden spoon for a few minutes, then very gradually sprinkle in the cornmeal and cook, stirring constantly with a wooden spoon, over medium heat for 30 minutes, until the cornmeal is cooked through. The mixture should be pourable, but not soupy. If it gets too dry and stiff before it is cooked, add small amounts of the reserved cooking liquid to loosen it.

Ribollita
Tortellini in Brodo
Pasta e Fagioli
Zuppa di Dormienti
Pasta alla Norma
Risotto al Barolo
Gnocchi alla Romana
Pasticcio di Carciofi
Risi e bisi
Tortelli
di Zucca
Polenta
e Baccalà
Risotto con
Cavolo
Nero
Bomba
di Riso
Orecchiette con
le Brasciole
Pasta alla
Scarpariella
Lasagne di Verdure
Amatriciana
Gnocchetti al Pesce
Timballo di Anellini
& Many More

PRIMI
PIATTI

ACQUACOTTA MAREMMANA 🍅
Maremma Bread Soup
Trattoria La Pergola da Ghigo, Suvereto
(Livorno), Toscana

*A*cquacotta literally means "cooked water."
This name can indicate many different
dishes, but it is always a soup that incorporates humble ingredients.

SERVES 6
8   red onions, preferably Tropea onions,
      thinly sliced
Extra-virgin olive oil for sautéing
½   rib celery, strings removed, stalk diced,
      and leaves reserved
Leaves of 1 bunch basil
1   chili pepper, minced
Salt to taste
2 to 3 ripe tomatoes, processed through a
food mill (about ½ cup)
6   large eggs
12   slices dry (stale but not too stale) bread,
      lightly grilled

In a large soup pot, sauté the onions in a generous amount of oil until all of their water has
evaporated but they do not turn golden. Add
the celery and any celery leaves to the onions.
Tear the basil leaves by hand and drop them
into the pot, and then add the chili pepper and
cook for 2 to 3 minutes. Add 1 quart water, salt
to taste, and the tomato puree. Cook over low
heat for 1 hour. Just before serving, add the
eggs and let them poach in the soup. To serve,
place 2 slices bread in an individual soup bowl.
Ladle some soup over them, then gently place
1 poached egg on top. Repeat with remaining
bread, soup, and eggs.

BAZZOFFIA
Bread Soup with Vegetables
Antica Osteria Fanti, Priverno (Latina), Lazio

*B*azzoffia was once prepared for men
who were working in the fields. While
different versions may include or omit
peas, fava beans, zucchini, chard, and spinach, bazzoffia always includes artichokes.
Romanesco artichokes that grow on the upper
portion of the plant are best, even better if
they are the IGP (Protected Geographic Origin)
artichokes from the Latina province.

SERVES 4
4   artichokes, preferably Romanesco
      artichokes
1   pound chard, chopped
1   cup shelled peas
3 to 4 ounces fava beans in the shells, shelled
      and peeled (about ¼ cup)
2   spring onions, chopped
Extra-virgin olive oil for cooking and
      drizzling
Salt to taste
Thin slices country-style bread
4   large eggs
Grated aged sheep's cheese for finishing

Trim the artichokes, removing hard outer leaves
and sharp tips; remove and discard the chokes.
Cut into wedges and drop into a large pot of
cold water. Add the chard, peas, fava beans, and
onions. Drizzle in some oil, season with salt,
bring to a boil, then simmer for 1 hour.

While the vegetables are cooking, line the
bottom of a fairly deep ceramic dish with two
layers of thinly sliced bread. As soon as the
vegetables are done cooking, slip the eggs into
the pot with the vegetables, where they should
poach. Transfer the contents of the pot over
the bread in the dish, taking care not to break
the egg yolks. Cover with a dish towel and set
aside to allow the bread to soak. Sprinkle with a
generous amount of grated cheese, drizzle on a
little more oil, and serve.

PANCOTTO ALLE ERBE MURGIANE 🌱
Bread Soup with Greens
IPSSAR of Molfetta (Bari), Puglia

An IPSSAR is a culinary and hospitality school for those training to work in hotels and restaurants. *Canestrato* means "basket cheese," and a form of canestrato is always marked with the ridges of the basket in which it aged. Canestrato di Corato is a dense, flaky DOP sheep's cheese from Puglia.

SERVES 6

Salt to taste
2   pounds broccoli rabe
1   tablespoon extra-virgin olive oil, plus more for broth and toasting bread
2   cloves garlic
1   small piece chili pepper
1   potato, peeled and diced
8   cherry tomatoes, lightly crushed
½   leek, sliced
8   cups loosely packed mixed wild greens, such as dandelion, sow thistle, borage, mustard greens
3   thick slices stale Altamura or Pugliese bread
6   quail eggs
4 to 5 ounces DOP canestrato di Corato or other aged sheep's cheese, shaved
½ bunch arugula, sliced into ribbons

Bring a pot of salted water to a boil and cook the broccoli rabe. Remove with a skimmer or slotted spoon and transfer to an ice-water bath, then drain and puree with 1 tablespoon olive oil and 1 to 2 tablespoons of the cooking water. Keep warm. In a pot of water combine more oil, salt, the garlic, chili pepper, potato, tomatoes, and leek. Bring to a boil, then add the wild greens and simmer for 20 minutes.

Meanwhile, cut the bread into cubes, reserving any crumbs and scraps. Toss the bread cubes with some oil and toast in the oven until lightly browned. Brown the breadcrumbs and scraps in a skillet with a little more oil. When the greens are cooked, add the quail eggs to the pot to poach. Remove from the heat and keep warm. Add the toasted bread cubes to the warm broth.

To serve, place 2 to 3 tablespoons of the broccoli rabe puree in the base of each dish. Sprinkle on the cheese shavings. Place 1 quail egg in each dish. Remove the bread cubes and vegetables from the broth with a slotted spoon or skimmer and distribute among the plates. Scatter on the toasted breadcrumbs and scraps. Garnish with the arugula and serve warm.

CECAMARITI CON CIME DI RAPA E PISELLI 🌶
Frise with Broccoli Rabe and Peas
Osteria del Pozzo Vecchio, Cavallino (Lecce), Puglia

Frise are rather hard rusks that keep for a long time. To serve 4 people, soak 2 cups fresh shelled peas in water for 2 to 3 hours, then cook in a small amount of lightly salted water until they have broken down into a puree. Blanch about 1 pound broccoli rabe in lightly salted water, drain, cool, and chop. Crumble a generous amount of frise (if you have broken leftover rusks, this is a good way to use them up) and toast them in extra-virgin olive oil with some ground chili pepper. Divide the frise among individual soup bowls and arrange the broccoli rabe and pea puree on top. This soup can also be made in winter using dried split peas.

PANE FRATTAU ▦
Sardinian Music Bread with Tomato and Eggs
Ristorante Ck, Oliena (Nuoro), Sardegna

In southern Sardegna, this dish is sometimes called *mazzamurru* and is made without eggs. Sardinian music bread is a large, thin, crisp sheet of bread. Needless to say, any leftover broth and boiled meat should be reserved for another use.

SERVES 4
- 2 pounds mutton
- Salt to taste
- ¼ cup wild herbs, such as wild horseradish, fennel, and garlic
- 4 to 5 ripe tomatoes, peeled, seeded, and chopped
- 4 sheets pane carasau (Sardinian music bread)
- 2 cups grated aged sheep's cheese
- 4 large eggs

To make the broth, in a large pot combine the mutton, 3 to 4 quarts cold water, salt, and the wild herbs. Bring to a boil, then simmer for 2 hours, skimming the foam from the surface. Meanwhile, in a skillet cook the tomatoes with a little warm water and a pinch of salt until they have broken down into a loose sauce.

Strain the broth through a fine sieve. Break each piece of pane carasau into rough quarters and dip them in the hot broth just until softened. Place one of the 16 pieces of bread in an individual serving dish. Smear on a little of the tomato sauce, sprinkle on a little of the grated cheese, and top with a second quarter piece of bread. Continue making layers in this manner, using 2 more bread quarters and ending with tomato sauce on top. Set aside a little of the tomato sauce and cheese for finishing. Then repeat with the remaining bread, tomato sauce, and cheese so that you have 4 servings consisting of 4 quarters of bread each.

Lightly poach the eggs in boiling salted water one at a time. Place a poached egg on each portion of bread. Top with the reserved tomato sauce and cheese and serve.

BRÖ BRÜSÀ 🐄
Thickened Broth
Locanda delle Tre Chiavi, Isera (Trento), Trentino-Alto Adige

This simple soup obviously was invented as a way to stretch broth to fill more bellies. Be sure not to let the flour get too dark. You can use lard in place of the butter if you prefer. This can be further enriched with sautéed thinly sliced mushrooms, cooked borlotti beans, cubes or strips of pancetta, handmade tagliolini noodles, or leftover scraps of pasta dough.

SERVES 6
- ¾ cup unbleached all-purpose flour
- 6 tablespoons unsalted butter
- 1½ quarts beef broth, warm
- Salt to taste

Preheat the oven to 350°F. Spread the flour on a baking sheet and toast the flour until it is very lightly golden. (Don't let it get too dark or the finished soup will taste burnt.) Melt the butter in the top of a double boiler. As soon as it melts, whisk in the toasted flour, then immediately add the broth, season with salt, and whisk over the heat until combined and thickened, 10 to 15 minutes.

CARDONE IN BRODO
Cardoon Soup
Ristorante Mastro Micchele, L'Aquîla, Abruzzo

Cardoon soup is traditionally served as the first course of the Christmas meal in Abruzzo, followed by capon or turkey. You can make the broth with any kind of meat you like.

SERVES 4 TO 6

1   *pound veal stew meat*
½   *chicken*
1   *potato, peeled and chopped*
1   *rib celery, chopped*
1   *medium yellow onion, chopped*
1   *carrot, chopped*
Rock salt to taste
½   *cup plus 1 tablespoon unbleached all-purpose flour*
1   *tablespoon beer or white wine*
Extra-virgin olive oil for batter and frying
Salt to taste
1   *egg white, whipped to a stiff peak*
3   *ribs cardoons*
2   *slices bread*
1   *cup whole milk*
3 to 4 ounces ground veal
1   *large egg, lightly beaten*
Grated Parmigiano Reggiano to taste
2   *pounds escarole*
1   *ball fresh mozzarella, diced, for serving*

To make the broth, combine the veal stew meat, ½ chicken, potato, celery, onion, carrot, and rock salt to taste with 4 quarts water in a stock pot. Cook over low heat for 2½ hours. Meanwhile, combine the flour, ¼ cup water, beer, a little olive oil, a pinch of salt, and the whipped egg white. Set aside to rest for 30 minutes. Boil the cardoons until tender, then drain. Toss the cardoons with the batter. Pan-fry in a generous amount of hot oil, pressing them into the pan with a fork. When the cardoons are golden, remove and chop. To make meatballs, soak the bread in the milk until crumbly. Combine the crumbled bread with the ground veal, egg, and grated cheese. Season to taste with salt. Form the mixture into small meatballs and brown in a generous amount of oil. Set aside. Blanch the escarole, drain, and mince.

Strain the broth. Puree the potato, celery, onion, and carrot together, then stir that puree back into the broth. Add the cooked escarole, cooked cardoons, and meatballs to the broth. Return to medium heat for a few minutes to warm through. Taste and adjust salt. Serve very hot in individual bowls with the diced mozzarella sprinkled on top. You can also top with additional grated Parmigiano Reggiano if you like.

CICORIELLE A'ZISE
Chicory Soup
Ristorante L'Antica Locanda, Noci (Bari), Puglia

The word *a'zise* in the name of this dish is local dialect for "sitting down," which is what the chicory is meant to do in the pot before the broth is added. Sometimes small meatballs are added to this soup.

SERVES 4

2   *pounds wild chicory*
½   *cup extra-virgin olive oil*
3   *cloves garlic, minced*
2   *bay leaves*
8   *cherry tomatoes, diced*
2   *quarts chicken broth*
1   *cup grated aged sheep's cheese*
Salt to taste

Boil the chicory for 30 minutes. Drain and set aside. Meanwhile, heat the oil in a pot, then add the garlic and the bay leaves. When the garlic begins to brown, add the tomatoes and the chicory. Cook briefly without stirring, then add the broth and grated cheese and simmer for 15 minutes. Remove and discard the bay leaves. Taste and adjust salt and serve hot.

RIBOLLITA 🌿
Bean and Kale Stew
Ristorante Boscaglia, Radicondoli (Siena), Toscana

As the name indicates, true *ribollita*, literally "reboiled," is reheated and eaten the day after it is cooked, though you can serve it when freshly made, of course. Tuscan kale, sometimes called lacinato kale, has long, narrow leaves with a bumpy surface. Tuscan bread is always made without salt. At the restaurant, they bake this soup in the oven, but you can also cook it on the stovetop—you may need to add a little more broth or water, and be sure to keep a close eye on it so the bottom doesn't scorch.

SERVES 8

- 4 cups dried cannellini beans, soaked for 12 hours
- 2 sprigs parsley
- 3 ribs celery
- 2 carrots
- Extra-virgin olive oil for sautéing and drizzling
- 2 large red onions, sliced
- 1 leek, sliced
- 1 pound (about 8) plum tomatoes, peeled, seeded, and diced
- 1 pound (about 3 medium) potatoes, peeled and diced
- 1 bunch Tuscan kale, chopped
- ½ head Savoy cabbage, chopped
- 2 pounds chard, chopped
- Salt and freshly ground black pepper to taste
- 1 loaf stale Tuscan (saltless) bread, sliced
- 2 cipollini onions, minced

Drain the beans and cook them in water to cover with 1 sprig parsley and 1 rib celery until tender. Remove and discard celery and parsley. Reserve the beans in their cooking water. Mince the remaining 2 ribs celery, the carrots, and the leaves of the remaining sprig parsley. In a soup pot, heat a generous amount of oil and add the red onions and leek. As soon as they begin to turn golden, add the minced celery, carrots, and parsley and the tomatoes and cook, stirring frequently, for 2 to 3 minutes. Add the potatoes, Tuscan kale, cabbage, and chard. Cook, stirring frequently, to combine, then add water to cover. Season with salt and pepper and cook over medium-low heat for 1½ hours.

Puree about half of the cooked cannellini beans through a food mill and add the pureed beans, the whole beans, and the cooking liquid to the pot. Stir to combine, bring to a boil, and cook over very low heat for 30 minutes.

In a soup tureen or other large bowl, alternate layers of the bread slices with the soup, then set aside to rest. To make true ribollita, the following day transfer the contents of the tureen to a terra-cotta pot. Add a little water. Drizzle with oil, season with freshly ground pepper, and sprinkle on some of the minced onions. Bake in the oven without stirring until most of the liquid has evaporated and a crust has formed on top. Drizzle with additional oil and the minced cipollini and serve.

CIPOLLATA SENESE
Pork and Onion Soup
Ede Bossini, Ponte d'Arbia (Siena), Toscana

This soup is made with pork ribs, but if you have a prosciutto bone that has almost been picked clean but has some meat clinging to it, you can use that in their stead. Ede Bossini uses beef broth in her soup, as she finds the result less fatty, but if you prefer, you can strain the broth created from cooking the ribs and use that instead. To make enough to serve 4, place about 1 pound pork ribs (on the bone) in a pot with 1 rib celery, ½ onion, 1 carrot chopped into 2 pieces, and 1½ quarts water. Season with salt and bring to a boil, then simmer until the meat is falling off the bones. Strip the meat from the bones, cut it into strips, and set aside in a warm place. While the ribs are cooking, thinly slice 1¾ pounds to 2 pounds white onions. Place them in a bowl and set under running water for 15 minutes. (This will make their flavor milder.)

In a soup pot, heat about ½ cup extra-virgin olive oil and add about ¼ cup diced pancetta and ¼ cup crumbled pork sausage, casing removed and discarded. Sauté for a few minutes, then drain the onions well and add them to the pot. Cook until onions are dry and just beginning to turn golden. Add about ½ cup beef broth or the broth from cooking the ribs. Cook over medium heat, uncovered, for 1 hour or more, adding broth a little at a time, about 2 cups total. Add the meat to the pot and cook for 15 additional minutes. Cut some slices of rustic bread (better if a little stale) and toast them in the oven, then rub with a garlic clove. Place the toasted bread in individual soup bowls and top with the onion soup. Allow to rest for a few minutes before serving.

TAGLIERINI NEI FAGIOLI
Bean Soup with Egg Noodles
Locanda Apuana, Colonnata di Carrara (Massa-Carrara), Toscana

Lamon beans are a speckled borlotti variety that grow at a high elevation in the Belluno province. The best lardo, the cured layer of fat from a pig's back, hails from Colonnata, where it is aged in vessels made of marble from the Apuan Alps following an age-old procedure.

SERVES 4
- 1 medium yellow onion, minced
- 1 carrot, minced
- 1 rib celery, minced
- 1 clove garlic, minced
- Minced rosemary to taste
- 2 to 3 tablespoons lardo (fatback)
- Extra-virgin olive oil for sautéing and drizzling
- 4 cups dried Lamon borlotti beans, soaked overnight
- 1 potato, peeled and diced
- 1 small piece pork rind
- 1 small piece chili pepper
- Salt to taste
- 2½ cups unbleached all-purpose flour
- 1 large egg

In a pot, sauté the onion, carrot, celery, garlic, rosemary, and lardo in a small amount of oil. Drain the beans and add them to the pot, along with the potato, pork rind, and chili pepper. Season with salt and add water to cover. Bring to a boil, then simmer for 1½ hours.

Meanwhile, on a work surface shape the flour into a well. Add the egg and a little water to the center of the well and mix, gradually pulling in the flour from the sides of the well to make a crumbly dough, then knead until smooth, adding more flour if the dough feels too sticky and more water if it feels dry. Let the dough rest, then roll into a very thin sheet. Cut into thin noodles (less than 1/10 inch wide) and set aside to dry slightly while the soup is cooking.

When the soup is cooked, remove about one third of the beans and process through a food mill into a puree. Remove the pork rind and dice, then return to the pot along with the pureed beans. Cook the noodles in boiling water (they will cook very quickly), then remove with a slotted spoon or skimmer and transfer to the soup. Drizzle with additional oil and serve.

MINESTRA DEI PRATI
Foraged Greens and Herbs Soup
Renato Imberti, Parre (Bergamo), Lombardia

Ramps, maidenstears, pellitory-of-the-wall nettles, primrose, violets, meadow clary, tender linden leaves, good king Henry, purple salsify, baby lettuce, sorrel, shepherd's purse, wild cardoon shoots, thyme, oregano: these are just some of the wild greens and herbs that can be foraged in the area in and around Bergamo. To make enough to serve 4, bring about 2 quarts broth (preferably a light beef broth) to a boil. Add 2 pounds (or more) foraged wild greens. Cook for 20 minutes after the broth has returned to a boil. The soup should be brothy and the greens should not disintegrate. Taste and adjust salt, then remove from the heat. Place a tablespoon of cooked polenta or a slice of toasted bread (on the stale side works best) in each soup bowl and ladle soup over it. Stir a beaten egg into each serving and sprinkle on a generous amount of grated *formai de mut* (a local raw cow's milk cheese). If you prefer rice to polenta or bread, throw a handful of rice into the broth with the greens and let it cook along with them, stirring occasionally to keep it from sticking.

MINESTRONE ALLA PIEMONTESE
Piemontese Minestrone with Tagliatelle
Trattoria Razmataz, Alessandria, Piemonte

This is a winter version of minestrone that you can vary using whatever is available. As spring arrives, feel free to swap out the winter vegetables for young zucchini with their blossoms, eggplant, onion, chard, lettuce, shelled peas, tomatoes, and aromatic herbs. In the country, cooks often add leftovers from hog butchering to this soup, or perhaps a spare prosciutto bone or chicken carcass for extra flavor. The beans do not need to be soaked overnight.

SERVES 4

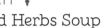

- 2 carrots
- Extra-virgin olive oil for sautéing and drizzling
- 1 bay leaf
- 3 ribs celery, minced
- 1 leek, minced
- ¼ cup dried cannellini beans
- ¼ cup dried black-eyed peas
- 1 bulb fennel, diced
- ½ cardoon, diced
- 1 potato, peeled and diced
- 1 piece winter squash, peeled and diced
- 2 Savoy cabbage leaves, chopped
- 2 Jerusalem artichokes, peeled and diced
- Salt and freshly ground black pepper to taste
- 2 to 3 ounces fresh handmade tagliatelle, chopped

Mince 1 carrot and place in a pot with olive oil, the bay leaf, the celery, and the leek. Cook over low heat until broken down, about 1 hour. Dice the remaining carrot. After 1 hour, add the beans, fennel, cardoon, potato, squash, cabbage, Jerusalem artichokes, and diced carrot to the pot. Stir to combine, then add 2 quarts water to cover and cook over medium-low heat for 5 to 6 hours, adding more hot water if the pot appears to be drying out. Remove the soup from the heat, season with salt and a pinch of pepper, and immediately stir in the chopped tagliatelle, which should cook quickly. Be sure to bring the bottle of extra-virgin olive oil to the table so that diners can add a little drizzle to their bowls.

MINESTRONE 🍃
Vegetable Soup with Filatieddi
Serafina Magro, Monterosso Calabro
(Vîbo Valentia), Calabria

This thick soup—more of a vegetable stew—is made with *filatieddi*, a semolina flour and water pasta from Calabria that resembles fusilli. If you're not up for making your own pasta, use store-bought penne instead. Filatieddi may also be served with tomato sauce or ragù. To make filatieddi for 4 to 6 people, shape about 2½ cups semolina flour into a well on a work surface. Gradually add about 1 cup water to the center of the well, drawing in the flour from the sides of the well in between additions until you have a crumbly dough. Knead the dough until it is very smooth and well combined, at least 15 minutes, then shape into ropes the diameter of your pinkie finger. Cut the ropes into 4-inch lengths and wrap them around a thin dowel or skewer to curl them. Blanch about 2 pounds chopped chard, 2 diced zucchini, 3 peeled and diced potatoes, and 10 ounces trimmed green beans. Sauté a thinly sliced onion and 1 heaping cup peas in olive oil in a soup pot until they begin to brown. Add 5 or 6 chopped cherry or plum tomatoes and cook, covered, for 10 minutes, then add the blanched vegetables and cook until well combined. Meanwhile, cook the pasta very al dente, then drain and add to the pot with the vegetables and cook until the pasta is tender. Taste and adjust salt. Serve with lots of grated aged sheep's cheese.

UOV' A SCIUSCIELLU ●
Poached Egg and Sausage Soup
Ristorante La Caveja, Pietravairano
(Caserta), Campania

Researcher Giuseppe Colitti reports that in Polla (and also in Campania) a soup by the same name omits the sausage and incorporates legumes—and is particularly well suited to being eaten during a snowfall.

SERVES 4
3   medium yellow onions, cut into julienne
Extra-virgin olive oil for sautéing
3   ounces sausage, sliced into rounds
1   piece Grana Padano rind
16   cherry tomatoes, peeled and halved
4   large eggs
Salt to taste
4 to 8 slices of day-old bread

Sauté the onions in extra-virgin olive oil over very low heat, then add the sausage and then ¼ cup water and the Grana Padano rind. Cook briefly, then add 1 to 2 cups water and cook for 15 additional minutes. Add the cherry tomatoes and cook 2 to 3 minutes, then slide in the eggs, salt, and cook for 10 additional minutes without stirring. To serve, place a slice or two of day-old bread in each individual soup bowl. Gently remove the poached eggs with a skimmer and place on the bread slices, then ladle the soup around the eggs and bread.

RINDFLEISCHSUPPE 🍃
Beef and Potato Soup
Huber Kaser, Luson (Bolzano), Trentino-Alto Adige

Rindfleischsuppe is German for "beef soup" and is just one of the many soups in the Bolzano-Bozen area (which has a strong Austrian influence) made with a generous amount of butter and potatoes. To serve 4 to 6 people, sauté 2 minced onions and about

1 pound beef cubes in a few tablespoons of butter in a soup pot. Add 3 to 4 tablespoons water when it begins to stick. When the beef is nicely browned on all sides, pour in about 1 cup dry white wine. Add about 3 medium peeled and diced potatoes and when they begin to brown, sprinkle in 1 tablespoon flour. Pour in 1½ quarts hot water and a couple cloves of garlic. Cover and cook over low heat for about 1 hour. Adjust salt and pepper and serve very hot, preferably in earthenware bowls.

PIOVANA
Kale and Winter Squash Soup
Osteria Picciarello, La Spezia, Liguria

This soup is called "rain" in reference to the light sprinkling action used to add the cornmeal to the dish.

SERVES 8
- Stale bread, cut into cubes
- Unsalted butter for toasting bread
- 1 medium yellow onion, minced
- 1 carrot, minced
- 1 rib celery, minced
- Extra-virgin olive oil for sautéing
- 1 sprig rosemary
- Leaves of 1 sprig sage, minced
- 2 heads Tuscan kale (about 1 pound each), cut into ribbons
- Salt to taste
- 14 ounces peeled and seeded winter squash, diced
- ½ cup cooked borlotti beans
- 2 tablespoons cornmeal
- Grated aged sheep's cheese or Parmigiano Reggiano to taste

Toast the bread cubes in butter and set aside. In a soup pot, sauté the onion, carrot, and celery in oil with the rosemary sprig and sage leaves. When they begin to brown, add the Tuscan kale and cook, stirring frequently, until wilted. Add 2 quarts water, season with salt, and cook until

tender, 30 to 40 minutes. Add the squash and cook for an additional 20 minutes. Remove the rosemary sprig. Add the beans and then slowly drizzle in the cornmeal in a very thin stream while stirring constantly with a wooden spoon or a spatula. Continue to cook, stirring constantly, until the mixture begins to thicken. Serve immediately with the toasted bread cubes and a sprinkling of grated cheese.

PREBUGIUN DI PATATE E CAVOLO NERO
Potato Puree with Kale
Trattoria La Brinca, Ne (Genova), Liguria

Quarantina potatoes are white and yellow potatoes grown on the slopes of the Ligurian Apennines. They have a short growing cycle of only forty days. You can substitute fine-grained, non-starchy white potatoes.

SERVES 4
- 1 pound Quarantina potatoes (see note)
- 1 bunch Tuscan kale, about 1 pound, cut into ribbons
- 2 cloves garlic
- Rock salt to taste
- Extra-virgin olive oil for whipping and drizzling
- 2 red onions or a few spring onions, sliced

Place the potatoes in a pot with cold water to cover and boil until tender. Blanch the kale and drain. In a mortar and pestle, crush the garlic with a pinch of rock salt.

When the potatoes are tender, drain and peel them while still hot and pass them through a ricer fitted with the disk with the largest holes. Mix together the kale with the crushed garlic. Place the potatoes in a pot and place over low heat. Add the kale mixture a little at a time, stirring to combine between additions. Whisk in a generous amount of olive oil to make a creamy puree. Serve warm drizzled with additional olive oil and garnished with the sliced onions.

PAPPA AL POMODORO 🍅
Tomato Soup
Enoteca La Torre di Gnicche, Arezzo, Toscana

Tuscan bread is white bread made without salt. This is best made with slightly stale (at least one day old) bread. This recipe makes a substantial amount, but you can easily halve it.

SERVES 8 TO 10

- 2 to 3 cloves garlic
- 1 cup tightly packed basil leaves
- Vegetables for broth (carrot, celery, onion)
- 2 red onions, thinly sliced
- Extra-virgin olive oil for sautéing and drizzling
- Salt to taste
- Ground chili pepper to taste
- 12 ounces very ripe plum tomatoes
- 8 ounces day-old Tuscan bread, cut into cubes

Make about 12 cups vegetable broth with the garlic, basil, and any other vegetables. Remove the other vegetables once they have given up their flavor and reserve for another use.

In a wide pot at least 4 inches high, sauté the sliced onions in olive oil with a pinch of salt and a pinch of chili pepper. When the onion is nicely browned, crush the tomatoes by hand and let them fall into the pot. (If you prefer you can peel and puree them with a food mill.) Cook until the tomatoes form a thick sauce and begin to change color, 7 to 8 minutes.

Add the bread, and about half of the vegetable broth along with the garlic and basil. Stir until the bread absorbs the broth and breaks down. Add the remaining broth (it will look like a lot) and smooth the surface. The solids should be covered by the liquid. Cook without stirring until the first of the "seven veils" has formed on the surface. When a light veil forms, break it up, stir the soup, and repeat six additional times, about 30 minutes total. Drizzle with additional olive oil and serve.

SCAFATA 🌿
Light Spring Vegetable Soup
Trattoria da Checco, Cori (Latina), Lazio

This soup has seasonal variations and sometimes a little diced guanciale or pork rind is sautéed with the onion at the beginning. If the fava beans are young enough, they don't need to be peeled.

SERVES 6

- 3 small yellow onions
- ¼ cup extra-virgin olive oil, plus more for drizzling
- 1 cup shelled and peeled fresh fava beans
- 2 ribs celery, cut into small dice
- 10 ounces chard, finely chopped
- 4 baby artichokes, trimmed and cut into small dice
- About 6 cherry tomatoes, cut into small dice
- Salt to taste
- 1 to 2 medium potatoes, peeled and cut into small dice
- 14 ounces stale bread, cut or torn into chunks

Chop 1 onion and sauté in a soup pot in the oil until just turning golden, then add the fava beans and celery, the chard, the artichokes, and the cherry tomatoes. Sauté for 5 minutes, then add 12 cups water. Bring to a boil, then simmer for 30 minutes, adjusting salt. Add the potatoes and cook for an additional 40 minutes, adding water in small amounts if the pot begins to look dry or the soup seems too thick.

Meanwhile, place the bread in an earthenware serving dish. Pour the cooked soup over the bread and set aside to rest for 10 minutes. Then drizzle with a little additional olive oil. Thinly slice the remaining 2 onions and sprinkle on top of the soup, then serve.

GENOVESE 🌿
Genovese Minestrone with Pesto
Osteria dell'Acquasanta, Mele (Genova), Liguria

The cooks on fishing boats traditionally served this soup—which is delicious hot or cold—to sailors in small earthenware bowls as they pulled into the port of Genova. If you cannot find *brichetti*, which are narrow tubes, substitute ditaloni rigati or broken spaghettoni.

SERVES 4

SOUP
- 1¾ cups dried borlotti beans, soaked overnight
- 1½ pounds (4 to 5 medium) potatoes, peeled and diced
- 7 ounces peeled and seeded winter squash, diced
- 1 small yellow onion, diced
- 10 ounces zucchini, diced
- 7 ounces green beans, chopped
- 2 ribs celery, diced
- 7 ounces chard, chopped
- Extra-virgin olive oil for cooking
- Salt to taste
- 5 ounces dried semolina pasta, preferably brichetti, ditaloni rigati, or broken spaghettoni

PESTO
- 1 clove garlic
- 3 tablespoons pine nuts
- Leaves of 1 bunch basil
- Salt to taste
- ½ cup grated Parmigiano Reggiano and aged sheep's cheese
- Extra-virgin olive oil for drizzling

Drain the beans of their soaking water and in a large pot combine the beans, potatoes, squash, onion, zucchini, green beans, celery, and chard with 12 cups water. Add a little oil, season with salt, and cook until beans and vegetables are very soft, about 1½ hours.

Meanwhile, prepare the pesto. Mince the garlic, pine nuts, and basil and combine in a small bowl. Season with salt. Stirring constantly, sprinkle in the grated cheese, then add olive oil in a thin stream until the sauce is a somewhat loose paste.

Crush the vegetables in the pot with a fork and cook the pasta in the soup. Stir in a couple spoonfuls of the pesto and serve any leftover pesto on the side.

VIRTÙ 🍃
Vegetable and Pasta Soup with Meatballs
Associazione Big Match, Teramo, Abruzzo

This substantial dish—traditionally served at a communal meal at the Associazione Big Match on May 1—contains a little bit of everything and combines winter leftovers with the new arrivals for spring. To make enough to serve 30, soak 5 cups dried chickpeas, 5 cups dried borlotti beans, 5 cups dried tondini beans, and 5 cups dried cannellini beans separately overnight. In a separate bowl, soak 4 pieces of pork rind with a chopped prosciutto bone in warm water.

The next day, drain and chop the pork rind. Drain the beans and cook separately with some of the pork rind in each pot. Reserve cooked beans and cooking liquid. Make small meatballs out of 1¾ pounds ground beef mixed with salt, pepper, and grated nutmeg and brown them in oil. Dredge 3 trimmed baby artichokes and julienne of 2 zucchini in beaten egg and fry until golden. In a large pot melt a generous amount of butter with extra-virgin olive oil. Add about 4 ounces diced prosciutto crudo (about ½ cup) and 2 ounces lardo or fatback (beaten with a fork until smooth) and cook over medium heat. When the prosciutto begins to brown, add 1 minced clove garlic, 2 minced onions, 5 peeled and diced potatoes, 4 diced carrots, 2 diced zucchini, the meatballs, 1 diced rib celery, 1 diced bulb fennel, 1 trimmed and diced baby artichoke, 2 cups shelled young fava beans, and 2 cups shelled peas. Season with a few cloves (in a sachet for easy retrieval, or ground), grated nutmeg, and chopped dill, parsley, marjoram, sage, and thyme.

Cook over low heat, adding a scant cup of hot water when the mixture starts to stick to the pot and additional water in small amounts if the liquid reduces before the vegetables have absorbed all the flavor from the herbs. When the vegetables are cooked and well combined, add a few blanched turnips, the blanched leaves of 1 head escarole and 1 head lettuce, some blanched spinach, the blanched leaves of 1 bunch chicory and 1 bunch chard, the blanched leaves of 1 head cabbage, and the blanched florets of 1 small head cauliflower and cook for an additional 15 minutes over low heat. Add ½ bottle tomato puree and simmer for 10 minutes. Add the cooked beans and some of their cooking liquid and cook for 10 minutes.

In a separate pot, cook egg pasta cut into various shapes, some of which is colored red with tomato and some green with spinach, in boiling salted water just until it rises to the surface. If you want to include dried semolina pasta, cook that in a separate pot. Drain the pasta and rinse in cold water, then add to the pot with the vegetables. Stir to combine and remove from the heat. Sprinkle on a generous amount of grated aged sheep's cheese and add the fried artichokes and zucchini. Allow to rest before serving.

SPATATATA 🌶
Vegetable Soup with Calamint and Hot Pepper
Trattoria La Tana dell'Orso… Bruno, Bolsena (Viterbo), Lazio

In a soup pot, sauté thinly sliced onion in extra-virgin olive oil until golden. Add a few peeled, seeded, chopped tomatoes and sauté for a few more minutes. Add peeled potato slices (about ¾ inch thick) and a generous amount of calamint leaves. Season with salt and either black pepper or chili pepper and add warm water to cover. Bring to a boil, then simmer over medium heat for 30 to 45 minutes. Meanwhile, toast some slices of bread (better if slightly stale) and rub them with the cut side of a garlic clove. When the soup is cooked, whisk eggs (1 per person) into the soup and cook for a few more minutes. Arrange the garlic-rubbed bread in individual soup bowls and pour the soup over it. Sprinkle with grated Parmigiano Reggiano, drizzle with additional extra-virgin olive oil, and serve hot.

SCIUSCIELLO 🌰
Wild Asparagus and Guanciale Soup
Osteria Lo Vottaro, Trentinara (Salerno), Campania

If you can't get wild asparagus where you live, feel free to substitute the cultivated type, but do seek out the thinner stalks.

SERVES 4

1   pound wild asparagus
1   spring onion, minced
¼   cup diced guanciale (cured pork jowl)
Extra-virgin olive oil for sautéing
2   large eggs
2   tablespoons grated aged cheese
Salt and freshly ground black pepper
     to taste
4   slices bread, toasted

Break off the woody stems of the asparagus and reserve the tips. Boil the stems in 2 cups water for about 10 minutes to make a broth.

In a soup pot, sauté the onion and guanciale in oil until golden. Add the asparagus tips and sauté over high heat for 1 minute, then add the prepared broth (strain out and discard the asparagus stems) and cook until the tips are tender. In a small bowl, beat the eggs with the cheese, then add to the soup in a thin stream, whisking constantly. Taste and adjust salt and pepper. As soon as the egg firms up, remove from the heat. Place the bread in soup bowls and ladle the soup over it.

ZUPPA FRANTOIANA 🌿
Olive Oil and Vegetable Soup
Osteria del Carcere, San Gimignano (Siena), Toscana

The name of this chunky soup means "from the olive mill," indicating that it should be made with fresh just-pressed oil. While cannellini beans are by far the most commonly used bean in Toscana, this soup uses borlotti beans for a thicker and more colorful result.

SERVES 8

1   cup dried borlotti beans, soaked
     overnight and drained
3 to 4 cloves garlic
Bouquet garni (1 sprig sage, 1 sprig
     rosemary, and 1 sprig bay leaves)
2   ribs celery, minced
1   carrot, minced
1   medium yellow onion, minced
Extra-virgin olive oil for sautéing, brushing
     bread, and drizzling
Rock salt to taste
¼   cup tomato puree
2   pounds assorted potatoes, carrots,
     zucchini, green beans, and other
     seasonal vegetables, peeled if necessary
     and chopped
1   pound spinach or chard, chopped
½   cup wild herbs
Slices of day-old bread
Freshly ground black pepper to taste

Cook the beans in salted water with 2 cloves garlic and the bouquet garni. When the beans are tender, remove and discard herbs and puree about two thirds of the beans by forcing them through a sieve. Sauté the minced celery, carrot, and onion in oil in a pot and season with rock salt. Add the tomato puree and cook until thickened, 15 to 20 minutes. Add the pureed beans, the chopped vegetables, the spinach, and the wild herbs. Add enough water to make the soup brothy and cook until vegetables are tender but not falling apart. Add the whole beans and cook briefly, then remove from the heat. Toast the bread, rub with the cut side of a garlic clove, and brush with oil. Place the bread slices in individual serving bowls and top with the soup. Season with black pepper, drizzle on a little more oil, and serve.

ZUPPA DI VERDURE MAGGENGHE 🌱
Month of May Vegetable Soup
Luigino Bruni, Alessandria, Piemonte

As the name indicates, this is a soup to be made in spring with fresh seasonal vegetables, young onions, and green garlic. To serve 6 people, make a vegetable broth with about 3 quarts salted water, 2 peeled and sliced potatoes, 1 quartered yellow onion, 4 generous cups shelled peas, and 1 bunch of asparagus. Cook for 30 minutes, puree the vegetables in their cooking liquid, and set aside. Melt a slice of lardo (cured fatback) in a terra-cotta soup pot and sauté minced spring onions and green garlic (you can't have too much) until softened. Add a few tablespoons beef broth and cook for 10 minutes. Add 4 cups diced zucchini, cook briefly, then gradually add the pureed asparagus mixture, whisking it in to combine. Cook for 15 minutes.

Just before serving time, energetically whisk together 3 egg yolks, ½ cup grated Parmigiano Reggiano, a few tablespoons of beef broth (or whole milk or cream, if you prefer), some minced parsley, salt, and pepper. When the soup is cooked, remove it from the heat and energetically whisk in the egg yolk mixture. Allow to rest for a few minutes, then serve with toasted bread.

LATTUGHE RIPIENE IN BRODO 🌱
Stuffed Lettuce Rolls in Broth
Trattoria La Brinca, Campo di Ne (Genova), Liguria

An Easter Monday classic, this dish sometimes includes a touch of aromatic meat and tomato sauce that tinges the broth red.

SERVES 4
20 lettuce leaves
7 ounces lean veal, chopped
Extra-virgin olive oil for sautéing
¼ cup pine nuts
1 medium yellow onion, chopped
1 carrot, chopped
Rosemary to taste
Marjoram to taste
2 cloves garlic
Salt to taste
1 egg yolk, lightly beaten
1 quart chicken and beef broth
2 tablespoons grated Parmigiano Reggiano

Preheat the oven to 350°F. Steam or blanch the lettuce leaves, then spread them in a single layer on a kitchen towel to dry. In a pot, sauté the veal in a small amount of oil with the pine nuts, onion, carrot, and rosemary. Brown for 10 minutes, then mince the mixture, incorporating marjoram and garlic and mincing them as well. Season with salt and stir in the egg yolk.

Use a spoon to place a ball of the filling in the center of each lettuce leaf. Fold the leaves up into round packets, arrange them in a baking dish, and bake in the preheated oven for 15 minutes. Meanwhile, heat the broth. Arrange the stuffed lettuce leaves in a soup tureen and gently ladle the hot broth over them. Sprinkle on the Parmigiano and serve.

ZUPPA DI DORMIENTI
March Mushroom Soup
Ristorante Silvio, Cutigliano (Pistoia), Toscana

March mushrooms (*Hygrophorus marzuolus*) grow from February to April in the Apennine woods, especially around fir trees and other conifers. They are light gray and grow almost completely underground and under snow's cover, making them particularly difficult to find. You can make this soup with any wild mushrooms you like.

SERVES 8
- 1 medium white onion, minced
- 2 tablespoons extra-virgin olive oil, plus more for drizzling
- 2 pounds March mushrooms, sliced
- Vegetable broth (optional)
- Salt to taste
- 1 clove garlic, minced
- Leaves of 1 sprig parsley, minced
- Slices day-old bread, toasted
- Freshly ground black pepper to taste

In a pot, sauté the onion in the olive oil. Add the mushrooms and cook until they have given up all of their liquid, about 20 minutes. Add enough vegetable broth, if using, or water so that the volume of the pot's contents doubles. (In other words, if there are 2 inches of mushrooms in the pot, the liquid should cover them by 2 inches.) Simmer for 10 minutes, season with salt, then turn the heat to high and add the minced garlic and parsley. Cook for a few minutes, then serve with toasted bread. Drizzle with olive oil and sprinkle with a generous grinding of pepper.

MINESTRA DI SCAROLA E POLPETTINE
Escarole and Meatball Soup
Osteria U' Parlatorio, Vallo della Lucania (Salerno), Campania

Escarole is a plant in the chicory family with leaves that are lighter at the center of the head and darker at the outside. There are several different varieties, but all are tasty, with a slight bitterness.

SERVES 4
- 1 pound escarole
- 1 medium potato, peeled
- 1 zucchini
- 1 rib celery
- 4 to 5 cherry tomatoes
- Salt to taste
- 1 to 1⅓ pounds mixed ground meat, such as beef, turkey, and pork
- 2 large eggs, lightly beaten
- 2 cups grated aged sheep's cheese or Parmigiano Reggiano, or a combination of the two
- ¼ cup minced flat-leaf parsley
- 7 to 8 pine nuts, minced
- 7 to 8 raisins, minced

Place the escarole, potato, zucchini, celery, and tomatoes (left whole) in a pot with 1 quart water and salt to taste. Simmer over medium heat until the vegetables are tender and have given up their flavor, about 30 minutes. While the vegetable broth is cooking, prepare the meatballs by combining the ground meat, eggs, grated cheese, a pinch of salt, parsley, pine nuts, and raisins and form into very small balls.

When the vegetable broth is ready, remove the vegetables with a slotted spoon or skimmer, cut into small dice, and add them back to the broth along with the meatballs. Bring the broth to a boil. Taste and adjust salt. As soon as the meatballs rise to the surface, remove from the heat and serve.

PASTA E FAGIOLI
Pasta and Bean Soup
Osteria Mangiando Mangiando, Greve in Chianti
(Firenze), Toscana

Beef broth gives this soup a more intense flavor, but you can use a vegetable broth if you prefer.

SERVES 4
2⅓ cups dried cannellini beans, soaked
    overnight
Salt to taste
6   sage leaves
2   cloves garlic
¼ cup plus 1 tablespoon extra-virgin olive
    oil, plus more for drizzling
1   sprig rosemary
1   medium yellow onion, minced
1   carrot, minced
1   rib celery, minced
1   quart broth, preferably beef broth, hot
1   tablespoon tomato paste
8   ounces (about 3 cups) small dried
    semolina pasta suitable for soup
Freshly ground black pepper to taste

Drain the beans and boil them in salted water with 2 sage leaves, 1 clove garlic, and 1 tablespoon olive oil until very soft, about 2 hours. In a soup pot, sauté the remaining clove garlic in ¼ cup olive oil with the rosemary and remaining 4 sage leaves. When the garlic browns, remove the garlic and the herbs and discard. Sauté the minced onion, carrot, and celery in the oil until soft, then drain the cooked beans and add to the soup pot. When the flavors are combined, add the broth. Stir in the tomato paste and cook for 30 minutes.

    With a slotted spoon or skimmer, remove about half of the beans and puree through a food mill, then return the pureed beans to the pot, stir to combine, bring to a boil, and cook the pasta in the soup. Serve with plenty of freshly ground black pepper and a drizzle of additional oil.

CUCINA
Bean, Wild Greens and Herbs, and Cabbage Soup
Ristorante Il Passeggero, Massa, Toscana

This recipe uses various greens and herbs that grow wild in late winter in the hills of Toscana. In the town of Massa, they are sold in large bunches at the market. There are at least twenty-five different herbs that grow in the area—some scholars have listed as many as forty-seven. Most are harvested just before they blossom. Be sure to clean the herbs and greens in several changes of water and to use the appropriate parts—for some you'll want the leaves, for others the bulbs.

SERVES 4 TO 6
2   cups dried borlotti beans, soaked
    overnight
3⅓ pounds wild greens and herbs, such as
    dandelion, wild fennel, wild leek,
    borage, milk thistle, rampion, pimpi
    nella, primrose, violets, and more,
    trimmed and chopped
½ head Savoy cabbage, cut into ribbons
Salt to taste
Toasted slices of day-old bread
Extra-virgin olive oil for drizzling
Freshly ground black pepper to taste

Drain the beans, boil them until soft, and puree through a food mill. Place the pureed beans in a soup pot. Thin the puree with water, then stir in the wild greens and herbs and the cabbage. Add more water to make a brothy mixture, bring to a boil, and simmer for about 1 hour. Taste and adjust salt. Serve with the toasted bread, a generous drizzle of olive oil, and some black pepper.

PERBUREIRA 🦪
Garlicky Pasta and Beans
Trattoria Alla Rocca, Rocca Grimalda (Alessandria), Piemonte

Rocca Grimalda is a small town on one of the old salt roads that on the last Sunday in August holds a festival celebrating *perbureira*. Each family has its own closely guarded recipe for this soup, but a large amount of garlic is a must. The garlic is cooked over very low heat and then sits in the oil for days. If you are in a real hurry, you can cook the garlic the same day you use it, but the flavor will never be the same.

SERVES 8 TO 10

13 *cloves garlic*
½ *cup extra-virgin olive oil*
3½ *cups dried borlotti beans*
1¾ *cups dried cannellini beans*
3 *medium yellow onions*
2 *carrots*
2 *ribs celery*
4 *cups unbleached all-purpose flour*

Salt to taste
5 *egg yolks*
5 *ounces lardo (cured fatback)*
Leaves of 1 sprig rosemary
1 *bay leaf*
2 *large potatoes, peeled and diced*
Freshly ground black pepper to taste
1 *tablespoon tomato paste*
¼ *cup grated Parmigiano Reggiano*

Three to four days before you intend to serve the soup, slice 10 cloves garlic, place them in the oil (cold) in a small saucepan, and cook over lowest possible heat for 30 minutes. Transfer the garlic and the oil to a bowl, cover, and store in a cool place. The night before you intend to serve the soup, soak the borlotti beans and cannellini beans in a generous amount of water. The next morning, make 4 to 5 quarts of broth by simmering 1 onion, 1 carrot, and 1 rib celery in a generous amount of water in a stockpot until soft and straining out the vegetables once cooked.

While the broth is cooking, make the pasta. Arrange the flour in a well on the work surface. Add a pinch of salt and the egg yolks to the center of the well, and make a dough by gradually pulling in flour from the side of the well. Knead the dough and roll to medium thickness, then cut into rectangles about 1½ by 3 inches. You should have 56 to 64 noodles.

Mince together the remaining 2 onions, remaining carrot, remaining rib celery, and the lardo. Crush the 3 remaining cloves garlic and sauté the garlic, rosemary, bay leaf, and lardo mixture in a soup pot, then drain the beans and add them to the pot. Add the potatoes as well. Cook, stirring, until combined, then add most of the prepared vegetable broth, holding back a little bit. Season with salt and pepper, stir in the tomato paste, and cook until the beans are soft and the soup is thick, about 2½ hours. If the pot begins to look dry, add the reserved broth in small amounts. After about 2 hours, stir in the grated Parmigiano. Bring a pot of salted water to a boil and cook the pasta, then drain and add to the soup. Ladle the soup into individual bowls and top each serving with a generous amount of the prepared garlic and oil mixture. The mixture should form a layer on top. You can also serve the garlic and oil mixture on the side and let diners help themselves, but perbureira always has a very generous amount of garlic on top.

PETT' E FASULL
Bean Soup with Flour and Water Pasta
Ristorante La Magnatora, Fondi (Latina), Lazio

The beans for this soup are not soaked, as their skins break if they are. This is traditionally cooked in a *pignata*, a kind of earthenware jug that is set in a fireplace or wood-burning stove. If you are using this system, the beans will need about 4 hours to cook rather than 2 hours.

SERVES 4 TO 6

1   cup dried beans
2   tablespoons extra-virgin olive oil
1   clove garlic
2   tablespoons trimmed and diced
    prosciutto crudo
2   ribs celery, chopped
Salt to taste
½   cup tomato sauce or ragù
2½ cups unbleached all-purpose flour

Place the dried beans in a pignata or other pot and add water to cover by several inches. Add the olive oil, garlic, prosciutto, celery, and salt to taste. Simmer on a stovetop until the beans are cooked, about 2 hours. (See note for other instructions.) Check the beans occasionally while cooking and add a little more water if the pot appears to be drying out. When the beans are about 10 minutes from being fully cooked, stir in about half of the tomato sauce.

While the beans are cooking, make the pasta. Combine the flour with a little salt and enough water to make a soft dough. Knead briefly, then set aside, covered with a kitchen towel, for about 1 hour. Roll out the rested dough with a rolling pin to a sheet about ⅒ inch thick, then roll into a cylinder and cut into fettuccine (⅒ to ⅕ inch wide). Leave the noodles on the work surface to dry slightly.

Bring a large pot of salted water to a boil for cooking the pasta. Add the pasta, stir, and cook until halfway cooked—still very firm in the center—then drain the pasta and add it to the

pignata or soup pot with the beans. Add the remaining tomato sauce and thin with a little water if the soup seems excessively thick, but keep in mind that this is not a brothy soup. Serve immediately.

STRACCIATELLA
Stracciatella Egg Broth
Luisa Gargiulo, Marino (Roma), Lazio

Stracciatella is Roman, but similar soups are made elsewhere. In the Marche, Giuliano Guidi of San Costanzo adds a few tablespoons of breadcrumbs and flour and the grated zest of a lemon. In Bologna, Palmira Giovannini makes a soup with twice as much Parmigiano. To serve 4 people, in a bowl beat 4 eggs with about ½ cup grated Parmigiano Reggiano, a pinch of salt, and a pinch of freshly grated nutmeg. Bring 1 quart broth to a boil over medium heat, then off the heat drizzle in the egg and cheese mixture while whisking energetically so that the egg mixture firms up into shreds of various sizes. Return to a boil and simmer for 2 minutes, then serve.

SELINKA
Bean Soup with Potatoes and Leaf Celery
Gostîlna Devetak, Savogna d'Isonzo (Gorizia), Friuli-Venezia Giulia

Cut up a prosciutto bone and to soften the flavor place it in a pot with water to cover, bring to a boil, and simmer for about 30 minutes after it comes to a boil. In a soup pot, place these items in this order in layers: peeled and diced potatoes, chopped leaf celery, borlotti beans that have been soaked overnight and drained, chili peppers, a piece of rind from hard cheese suitable for grating, such as Parmigiano Reggiano or Grana Padano, and the drained prosciutto bone, and salt to taste. Add water to cover. Place in a wood-burning oven (preferable) or over very low heat and cook for 6 hours without stirring. When the soup is cooked, crush any pieces of potato that have not broken down.

JOTA TRIESTINA ●
Bean and Potato Soup
Trattoria Suban, Trieste, Friuli-Venezia Giulia

The sharp sauerkraut in this classic dish cuts through the fattiness of the pork for a perfect pairing. Like many soups, this benefits from resting after it is cooked.

SERVES 4
- 1¾ cups dried Lamon beans, soaked overnight
- 2 bay leaves
- 7 ounces smoked pork shank
- 5 cloves garlic
- Extra-virgin olive oil for sautéing
- 1 pound sauerkraut, rinsed and drained
- 1 pinch caraway seed
- Salt and freshly ground black pepper
- 2 potatoes, peeled and diced

Drain the beans, rinse them, and in a soup pot cook them in a generous amount of water with the bay leaves and pork shank.

In a separate pot, brown the garlic cloves in olive oil. Add the sauerkraut and caraway seed, season with salt and pepper, and simmer for at least 1 hour, preferably a little longer, occasion-ally adding some of the cooking liquid from the beans.

When the beans are about halfway cooked, add the potatoes to the pot with the beans. When both the beans and potatoes are soft, transfer about half of the beans and potatoes (be sure not to scoop up the bay leaves) and puree them by forcing them through a sieve. Return the puree to the pot with the beans, and transfer the sauerkraut mixture to the pot with the beans.

Cook over low heat until thickened and well combined, about 2 hours. Let the soup rest for a few hours, then reheat just before serving.

MES-CIUA RICCA ◄◄◄
Bean Soup with Farro
Antica Trattoria Cerretti, Riccò del Golfo (La Spezia), Liguria

This same soup can be made with wheat berries (instead of farro), which will take a little longer to cook.

SERVES 6
- 1 cup dried black-eyed peas
- 1 cup dried cannellini beans
- 1 cup dried chickpeas
- ¼ cup lentils
- ¼ cup farro
- Salt to taste
- 1½ to 2 quarts beef broth
- 2 small yellow onions
- 1 carrot
- 1 rib celery
- 1 sprig rosemary
- 1 sprig sage
- Whole black peppercorns to taste
- Leaves of 1 sprig parsley, minced
- Leaves of 1 sprig basil, minced
- Extra-virgin olive oil for sautéing
- 2 tablespoons dry white wine
- 1 teaspoon tomato paste

Rinse the legumes and soak the legumes and the farro in lightly salted lukewarm water to cover by several inches for 12 hours. Drain the legumes and farro and place in a soup pot with broth to cover by several inches. Wrap 1 onion, the carrot, the celery, the rosemary, the sage, and a few peppercorns in cheesecloth, tie into a sachet, and place in the pot with the legumes. Bring to a boil and simmer until the legumes and farro are soft. Remove the sachet and puree about one quarter of the legumes and farro by forcing them through a sieve.

Meanwhile, mince the other onion and sauté with the parsley and basil in a little olive oil. Add the wine and cook until evaporated, then remove from the heat. Add this mixture and the tomato paste to the broth, return the soup to a boil and simmer for a few minutes, then adjust salt and serve.

ZUPPA DELLE FARFALLE
Bean, Chestnut, and Borage Soup
Marinella Badino Biancheri, Vallecrosia (Imperia), Liguria

This soup is made along the border between Liguria and Piemonte. In Piemonte it is traditionally made for Easter with wild spinach and served with stewed rabbit, while in Liguria it is made with borage and served with rabbit cooked with aromatic herbs, white wine, and Taggiasca olives. It also marries well with stockfish, braised meat, or grilled sardines. The soup straddles two seasons, meaning it uses the winter stores of dried chestnuts and dried beans, but also the earliest spring leaves of borage and wild spinach. Soak either dried red beans or chickpeas and dried chestnuts in cold water (separately) the night before. Cook the dried chestnuts in their soaking water until tender. Reserve both chestnuts and cooking water. Cook the beans in fresh water until tender. In a soup pot, sauté minced garlic, onion, rosemary, thyme, and bay leaf in extra-virgin olive oil until golden. Add the chestnuts and some of their cooking water. Season with salt and puree through a food mill, then return to the pot along with the cooked beans and bring to a boil. Stir in a generous amount of borage or wild spinach. Serve warm with a sprinkling of grated Parmigiano Reggiano and a drizzle of additional oil on top.

SEUPA A LA UECA
Gratinéed Barley Soup
Ristorante Capanna Carla, Gressoney-La-Trinità (Aosta), Valle d'Aosta

If you prefer, you can use pork ribs in place of the lardo in this hearty soup. It has been served at the restaurant in one form or another since the 1970s.

SERVES 4

- ¾ cup pearl barley, soaked overnight in water to cover
- 2 ounces lardo (cured fatback) in one piece
- ¼ cup diced pancetta
- 2 tablespoons extra-virgin olive oil
- 1 potato, peeled and diced
- 1 zucchini, diced
- 1 carrot, diced
- 1 rib celery, diced
- ½ medium yellow onion, diced
- Salt to taste
- 8 slices whole-wheat bread, toasted
- 7 ounces fontina cheese, thinly sliced
- 3 tablespoons unsalted butter
- Leaves of 1 sprig parsley, minced

Drain the barley and cook in boiling water with the lardo until tender, about 40 minutes.

In a separate soup pot, sauté the pancetta in the oil and then add the potato, zucchini, carrot, celery, and onion. Season with salt, add water to cover, and cook at a low simmer for 1 hour.

When the barley is tender, drain and add it to the soup pot and stir to combine. Transfer the mixture to a baking pan. Arrange the toasted bread in a layer on top. Arrange the fontina slices on top of the bread, dot with the butter, and broil until nicely browned on top. Garnish with parsley and serve hot.

VIGNAROLA 🌳
Farro and Barley Vineyard Soup
Ristorante La Mula, Ferentino (Frosinone), Lazio

This soup does not contain grapes, but instead is made with ingredients that grow amid the grapevines. In spring, it may also include wild asparagus, new potatoes, hops, or wild garlic. As the weather turns cold, dried cicerchia beans are often soaked and cooked separately and then added in place of the peas and fava beans. Blanching the fava beans briefly makes them easier to peel. Cacioricotta is a cheese made with a method that combines the techniques used to make ricotta (meaning the milk is heated) with those used to make other cheese (meaning rennet is added). It is typically made with sheep's or goat's milk, and it can be eaten fresh or aged.

SERVES 8

- 3 spring onions
- Extra-virgin olive oil for sautéing and drizzling
- 2 tablespoons diced speck
- 1⅓ cups shelled and peeled fava beans
- 1⅓ cups shelled peas
- 3 cloves garlic, unpeeled and crushed
- 3 to 4 small artichokes, trimmed and quartered
- Vegetable broth for braising
- ¾ cup pearl barley
- ¾ cup farro
- 1 rib celery, minced
- 1 carrot, minced
- Leaves of 1 sprig parsley, minced
- Salt and freshly ground black pepper to taste
- Ground chili pepper to taste
- 4 ounces sausage, casing removed and minced
- Grated aged cacioricotta or other aged cheese to taste (see note)
- 1 fresh bay leaf, minced

Thinly slice 1 onion and sauté in a few spoonfuls of olive oil in a pot. Add the speck and the fava beans. Cook, covered, over medium heat. Meanwhile, thinly slice the second onion and sauté briefly just until softened in oil a separate pot, then add the peas and cook, covered, until tender. Add a little water if the vegetables appear to be browning. In a third pot, first sauté a crushed clove of unpeeled garlic, then remove the garlic and add the artichokes. Add vegetable broth or water to cover and bring to a brisk simmer, then cover and cook over low heat. In separate pots, cook the barley and the farro in boiling water until al dente. Drain and set aside.

Mince the remaining onion. In a large soup pot, sauté the remaining 2 cloves garlic, then remove and discard them and add the minced onion with the celery, carrot, and parsley. Season with salt, pepper, and ground chili pepper. When the vegetables begin to brown, add the sausage. When the sausage has browned, add vegetable broth to cover and cook until very soft. Puree the mixture and return to the pot (or puree in the pot with an immersion blender), then place over medium heat and stir in the farro and barley. Cook, adding small amounts of broth as needed, until the grains are very tender.

Stir in the fava beans, peas, and artichokes and stir to combine. Simmer for a few minutes, then drizzle with olive oil and sprinkle on the grated cheese and the bay leaf. Allow to rest 10 minutes before serving either hot or warm.

TOFEJA

Spiced Bean Soup Cooked in a Terra-Cotta Pot

Trattoria Ramo Verde, Carema (Torino), Piemonte

A *tofeja* is a terra-cotta pot from Castellamonte, a city famed for its ceramics. This is a very old recipe dating back to at least the seventeenth century, when it was served to the poor by the confraternities of Corpus Domini for lunch the day before the Pentecost. Saluggia beans come from the tiny town of that name in the province of Vercelli. *La saporita* is a spice mixture consisting of ground coriander, cinnamon, nutmeg, cloves, star anise, and caraway seeds.

SERVES 8

4½ cups dried Saluggia beans, soaked for at least 8 hours and preferably overnight
Salt to taste
2   cloves garlic, minced
1   medium yellow onion, minced
1   rib celery, minced
1   carrot, minced
1   sprig rosemary
2   sage leaves
3 to 4 whole cloves
1   cinnamon stick
½   teaspoon la saporita spice mixture
2   rolled pork rinds
1   pig trotter, chopped into 8 pieces
8   small pork ribs, halved
2   fresh salami for cooking

Preheat the oven to 325°F to 350°F. Drain the beans and place them in an earthenware pot, preferably a tofeja. Add 2 quarts cold water, some salt, and the garlic, onion, celery, carrot, rosemary sprig, sage leaves, cloves, cinnamon stick, spice mixture, pork rinds, trotter, and ribs. Bake in the preheated oven until beans are soft and pork is tender, 4 to 5 hours. (You can also cook the soup on the stovetop, but be sure to use a flame tamer to prevent the ingredients from sticking to the bottom of the pot and to keep the earthenware pot from cracking; this will take about 2 hours and 30 minutes.)

Meanwhile, in a separate pot, cook the salami in boiling water for 30 minutes. Cut into 8 slices, remove and discard casing, and add the salami to the pot with the soup for the last 30 minutes or so of cooking.

ZUCCA E CANNELLINI

Squash and Cannellini Bean Milk Soup

Osteria Terranima, Bari, Puglia

Most Italian soups are brothy—creamy soups enriched with dairy are a little unusual. Serve this one with slices of toasted bread.

SERVES 4

1¾ cups dried cannellini beans, soaked overnight
1   rib celery
1   carrot
1   clove garlic
2   cups skim milk, hot
1½ cups diced peeled winter squash
Salt to taste
1   medium yellow onion, sliced
2   tablespoons extra-virgin olive oil

Drain the beans and transfer to a pot with the celery, carrot, and garlic. Add cold water to cover by a couple of inches and cook at a gentle simmer until the beans are just tender. Remove garlic, carrot, and celery and about half of the cooking liquid. Add the milk and squash and cook until the squash and beans are soft. Season with salt.

In a skillet, brown the onion slices in the olive oil. Divide the soup among individual serving bowls and top with the browned onion.

ZUPPA DI CANNELLINI CON ERBA PAZZA ❦
Cannellini Bean and Wild Herb Soup
Enoteca Saint Patrick, Terracina (Latina), Lazio

Enoteca Saint Patrick makes this soup with a mixture of wild herbs and greens known as "crazy herbs." This can include borage, balsam herb, broccoli rabe, chicory, fennel, salad burnet, cardoons, and milk thistle. Rinse them thoroughly in several changes of cold water.

SERVES 4

- 2 cups dried cannellini beans, soaked overnight
- 3½ pounds mixed wild herbs and greens (see note)
- 1 clove garlic, unpeeled
- ¼ cup extra-virgin olive oil
- 1 rib celery, cut into small dice
- 1 carrot, cut into small dice
- ½ medium yellow onion, cut into small dice
- Leaves of 1 sprig rosemary, minced
- 1 slice smoked pancetta, cut into small dice
- 2 very ripe tomatoes, peeled, seeded, and crushed
- Salt and freshly ground black pepper to taste
- Slices day-old country-style bread, either grilled or torn into cubes and toasted

Drain the beans, cover with water, and simmer over medium heat until tender, about 1 hour. Reserve both beans and cooking liquid. Blanch the herbs and greens and set aside. In a soup pot, sauté the garlic in 3 tablespoons olive oil until browned, then remove and discard. Add the celery, carrot, onion, rosemary, and pancetta and cook for a few minutes until softened, then add the tomatoes and cook for a few minutes. Add the beans and their cooking liquid and the blanched herbs and greens and cook over lowest heat until very soft and broken down, about 2 hours.

Season with salt, drizzle on the remaining tablespoon of oil and a grinding of black pepper, and serve with the grilled or toasted bread.

CACCIUCCO DI CECI ❦
Chickpea Bread Soup
Ada Nencioni, Cascina (Pisa), Toscana

In Livorno, *cacciucco* is a fish soup, but elsewhere it is a bean soup like this one, or sometimes a chicken stew. Soak dried chickpeas for at least 24 hours and for 48 hours if they have been in the cupboard for more than one year. In a terra-cotta pot, sauté sliced onion and whole garlic cloves in extra-virgin olive oil. Add anchovy fillets, crushing them with a fork until they break down. Drain and add the chickpeas, blanched chard or spinach, and a small amount of tomato puree or tomato paste dissolved in a little water. Add water to cover, cover the pot, bring to a boil, then cook over low heat for at least 3 hours. Season with salt and freshly ground black pepper. Serve with toasted slices of unsalted bread and a handful of grated aged sheep's cheese.

MILLECOSEDDE ❦
Mixed Bean and Porcini Mushroom Soup
Antonina De Marco, Castrovillari (Cosenza), Calabria

Soak equal amounts cannellini beans, chickpeas, cicerchia beans, dried fava beans, and lentils overnight. In the morning, drain the legumes and rinse in cold running water. Place the legumes in a soup pot with chopped celery, chopped onions, chopped Savoy cabbage, and sliced porcini mushrooms (or rehydrated dried porcini mushrooms). Add water to cover by a couple inches. Bring to a boil, then simmer for 2 hours. Add short dried semolina pasta (about ¾ cup per person), adjust salt, and cook until pasta is soft, about 10 additional minutes. Sprinkle with grated aged sheep's cheese and black pepper, drizzle on a little olive oil, and serve.

CICERI E TRIA 🌶
Chili Pepper Chickpea Soup with Pasta
Osteria A Casa tu Martinu, Taviano (Lecce), Puglia

This is one of the best-known dishes in southern Puglia's Salento region. On March 19, for the feast of Saint Joseph, broccoli sautéed in olive oil with lots of garlic is added to the soup.

SERVES 4
- 3½ cups dried chickpeas, soaked overnight
- Salt to taste
- 2½ cups unbleached all-purpose flour
- 1 clove garlic
- Extra-virgin olive oil for sautéing
- Ground chili pepper to taste

Drain the chickpeas, place them in a pot with water to cover by several inches, bring to a boil, then season with salt and simmer until tender, about 2 hours. Meanwhile, make the pasta. Shape the flour into a well on a work surface and add a pinch of salt, then place enough warm water in the well to make a soft dough as you gradually pull in flour from the sides of the well. Knead until combined, then set aside to rest for at least 10 minutes. With a rolling pin, on a lightly floured surface roll into a thin sheet, then cut into strips 1 to 1½ inches wide. Spread pasta in a single layer on a kitchen towel (flour lightly if necessary) and set aside to dry.

When the chickpeas are almost cooked, bring a large pot of salted water to a boil and cook all but a few pieces of the pasta until al dente. Drain the pasta and add to the chickpeas. In a skillet, sauté the garlic in olive oil, season with a little chili pepper, then brown the reserved (uncooked) pieces of pasta in the oil. Add the browned pasta and the oil to the soup, stir to combine, and serve.

ZUPPA DI CECI ED ERBE DI CAMPO 🌳
Greens, Chickpea, Cherry Tomato, and Foraged Greens Soup
Trattoria La Tavernetta, Gerace (Reggio Calabria), Calabria

Frittole is a specialty of Calabria. It is made during the period when hogs are butchered using the organs, snout, ears, and rind, which are flavored with chili pepper and cooked in their own fat in a copper pot. It is then preserved in lard.

SERVES 4
- 2⅓ cups dried chickpeas, soaked in lukewarm water for 24 hours
- Salt to taste
- 7 ounces (about 16) cherry tomatoes, quartered
- 1 sprig wild fennel, chopped
- 1 pound young wild chicory
- 12 ounces wild broccoli rabe
- 4 to 5 cloves garlic
- Extra-virgin olive oil for sautéing and drizzling
- 1 chili pepper, minced
- 7 ounces frittole or diced cooked pork rind (optional)
- 8 slices country-style bread

Drain the chickpeas, then cook them in salted water until tender. When the beans are almost cooked, add the tomatoes and the wild fennel. In a separate pot, blanch the chicory and broccoli rabe. Mince 3 to 4 cloves garlic. Drain the greens, chop, and sauté in olive oil with the chopped garlic and chili pepper. Add the greens to the chickpeas. Stir in the frittole, if using, and cook for about 10 minutes, adding a little more water if the soup seems to be getting too thick. Meanwhile, toast the bread and rub with the cut side of the remaining garlic clove. Serve the soup in earthenware bowls with a drizzle of oil on top and the garlic toast on the side.

ZEMIN 🍃
Sage Leaf Chickpea Soup
Trattoria Alla Rocca, Rocca Grimalda
(Alessandria), Piemonte

This can easily be made into a one-pot meal by browning eight pork ribs in the oil before adding the chard. You may need to add a little of the chickpea cooking liquid to keep the ribs from sticking.

SERVES 8
- 4½ cups dried chickpeas, soaked in room temperature water for 12 hours
- 7 ounces pork rind
- 1 medium yellow onion, minced
- 1 rib celery, minced
- 2 cloves garlic, crushed
- 3 sage leaves
- Extra-virgin olive oil for sautéing
- 1 bunch (12 to 14 ounces) chard
- 2 tablespoons tomato paste
- ½ cup dried porcini mushrooms, rehydrated, squeezed dry, and chopped
- 1 tablespoon unbleached all-purpose flour
- Salt and freshly ground black pepper to taste
- Grated Parmigiano Reggiano for serving

Drain the chickpeas and place in a pot with fresh water. Bring to a boil, then turn down to a simmer and cook over medium-low heat for 1 hour. Add the pork rind and continue cooking until the beans are tender but not falling apart, about 2 hours total.

In a soup pot, sauté the onion, celery, garlic, and sage leaves in olive oil. When they begin to brown, tear the chard by hand and add it to the pot. Dissolve the tomato paste in ¼ cup of the cooking water from the chickpeas and add that as well, along with the porcini mushrooms. Cook, stirring for a few minutes, then remove the cooked chickpeas from their cooking liquid with a slotted spoon or skimmer (reserve liquid) and transfer to a colander. Sprinkle the flour over the chickpeas and toss to coat the chickpeas with the flour, then add the chickpeas to the pot. Season with salt and pepper and cook, stirring with a wooden spoon, over medium heat for 10 minutes. If the soup is beginning to look dry, add some of the cooking liquid from the chickpeas. Cook for an additional 10 minutes, then serve with grated Parmigiano on the side.

MENESTRA DE FREGOLOTI ❟
Milk Soup
Maso Cantanghel Trattoria da Lucia, Civezzano
(Trento), Trentino–Alto Adige

Though it has very few ingredients, this milk soup is surprisingly complex. To elevate it further, sprinkle on some grated Trentingrana cheese and, in truffle season, garnish with a few thin slices of black truffle.

SERVES 6
- 2½ cups unbleached all-purpose flour
- 1 quart whole milk
- 2 tablespoons unsalted butter
- Salt to taste

Place the flour in a bowl. In a very thin stream, pour in 2 cups of the milk and 2 cups cold water. Mix by hand in the bowl until you have a sandy mixture with clumps the size of corn kernels. Place the remaining 2 cups milk in a saucepan with 2 cups water, bring to a boil, then very gradually drizzle the flour mixture into the milk mixture, whisking constantly. Simmer gently over low heat for 30 minutes, whisking very frequently. Stir in the butter and a pinch of salt and remove from the heat.

MARICONDE

Bread Dumplings in Broth
Marialuisa Monesi, Brescia, Lombardia

Tear a few stale rolls (at least 1 per person) into large chunks and soak them in warm milk to cover until they are thoroughly moistened, then crumble them into a pot with a little melted butter. Cook over low heat, stirring with a wooden spoon, until the mixture is dry and creamy looking. Remove from the heat and transfer to a bowl, and when the mixture has cooled, beat in eggs (about 1 egg for every 2 rolls used) one at a time, a handful of grated Parmigiano Reggiano, a pinch of salt, and a dusting of freshly grated nutmeg. The mixture should clump if you squeeze some in a fist. If not, add some breadcrumbs. Let the mixture rest for 30 minutes, then shape into balls (the size is up to you—they can be as small as a ping-pong ball or almost as large as a tennis ball). Bring beef broth to a boil and add the dumplings. As soon as they rise to the surface, they are cooked. Serve the dumplings in broth. You can vary this by cooking chicken livers in the broth with the dumplings or even adding minced leftover roasted or boiled chicken or other meat to the dumpling mixture. These dumplings can also be cooked like pasta in boiling salted water and topped with tomato sauce or butter and sage.

MLINCI CON LA SUPETA

Chicken Stew with Roasted Herb Pasta
Gostîlna Devetak, Savogna d'Isonzo (Gorizia), Friuli-Venezia Giulia

In a pot, brown a quartered chicken in a generous amount of extra-virgin olive oil, then add some white wine and a generous amount of minced onion, salt, pepper, and minced marjoram. Add broth to cover and simmer gently for 3 hours. Meanwhile, on a work surface make an egg pasta dough with about 1 egg per person, ¾ cup unbleached all-purpose flour or 00 flour per egg, 1 tablespoon olive oil per egg, a pinch of salt, and a generous dose of minced aromatic herbs. Roll into a thin sheet, then place on a floured baking sheet and bake at 400°F for 10 minutes so that it is toasted and browned. Strip the chicken meat from the bones and chop. Discard bones and return chicken to the pot. Stir in a little tomato paste dissolved in water and a handful of breadcrumbs. Break the toasted pasta dough sheet into irregular pieces and boil the pieces in salted water for 5 minutes. Drain and toss with melted butter, then serve with the chicken stew.

MINESTRA DI PASTA REALE

Popover-Style Dumplings in Broth
Alessandra Magnani, Parma, Emília-Romagna

To serve 4 to 6 as a first course, combine 8 tablespoons (1 stick) butter with ½ cup water in a saucepan and melt over medium heat. As soon as it comes to a boil, add a pinch of salt and ⅔ cup flour and continue to cook, stirring constantly, until the mixture pulls away from the sides of the pan. Let the mixture cool, then add 2 eggs, beating to combine between additions. The mixture should be very smooth. Transfer to a pastry bag fitted with a smooth tip about ¼ inch wide or slightly less, pipe small balls of the dough onto a buttered and floured baking sheet with a little room in between them. Bake at 400°F until puffed and golden. (It should only take a few minutes.) Set the dumplings on a clean dish towel (not touching each other) to cool. When the dumplings have cooled, place them in a soup tureen and bring about 1½ quarts beef broth to a boil, then pour the hot broth over the dumplings and serve. The dumplings will keep for a couple of days in a tightly sealed container once baked.

INCAPRIATA
Fava Beans and Chicory
Ristorante Cîbus, Ceglie Messapica (Brindisi), Puglia

The combination of fava beans and chicory is a popular one in all the areas of Italy that were once under Greek rule, such as Sicilia and Puglia. Indeed, the Pugliese name *incapriata* likely is derived from *kapyridia*, ancient Greek for porridge. Use dried light-colored fava beans.

SERVES 4
2   cups small dried fava beans
7   ounces (1 to 2 medium) potato
Salt to taste
Extra-virgin olive oil for drizzling
14 ounces wild chicory

Place the beans in an earthenware pot, cover with water by several inches, and soak for 2 hours. Peel the potato and add to the pot with the beans, then cover and bake in a wood-burning oven for 3 hours. Uncover, season with salt, and continue cooking until very soft. Using a wooden spoon, crush the beans and potato against the sides of the pot until the mixture is chunky. Drizzle on a generous amount of olive oil.

Blanch the chicory in salted water, squeeze dry, and add to the fava beans. Stir to combine and drizzle with additional oil.

SCRIPPELL 'MBUSSE
Crepes in Broth
Trattoria La Tacchinella, Canzano (Teramo), Abruzzo

In Abruzzo, crespelle are served in broth, in timbales, and layered with sauce (frequently mushroom sauce) and mozzarella.

SERVES 4
2   pounds mixed meat for broth, such as beef, chicken, turkey, and pork
1   carrot
1   rib celery
1   potato
1   tomato
1   sprig parsley
Salt to taste
6   large eggs
¼   cup plus 2 tablespoons unbleached all-purpose flour
Extra-virgin olive oil or lardo (fatback) for greasing pan
Grated Parmigiano Reggiano to taste

To make the broth, place the meat, carrot, celery, potato, tomato, and parsley in a stockpot with 12 cups water. Salt, bring to a boil, then simmer for 3 hours.

Meanwhile, to make the crespelle, in a bowl beat the eggs with a little salt and gradually sprinkle in the flour while whisking. Make sure no lumps remain. Drizzle in a small amount of water to make a liquid batter, then beat gently with a whisk. With oil or lardo, lightly grease a nonstick pan and heat it until quite hot. Add about ¼ cup of the batter, turning the pan to distribute it in a thin layer. Cook on one side, then flip and cook for 1 minute on the other side. Repeat with remaining batter, greasing the pan again as needed.

To serve, sprinkle the crespelle with grated Parmigiano, roll them up, and arrange them in soup bowls. Strain the broth and stir grated Parmigiano into it, then ladle the hot broth over the crespelle and serve.

TORTELLINI IN BRODO
Tortellini in Broth
Osteria Bottega, Bologna, Emília-Romagna

This recipe is based on the official recipe registered with the Bologna Chamber of Commerce on December 7, 1974, by the Scholarly Confraternity of the Tortellino. If you want a truly spectacular presentation, prepare twice as much broth and cook the pasta in half of it, then reheat the clean broth—sometimes the broth used to cook the tortellini gets a little cloudy from the flour and any filling that leaks out of the pasta—and serve the cooked tortellini in it. Tradition dictates that there should be one spoonful of broth for every tortellino.

SERVES 6

BROTH
2   pounds rib eye
1   pound capon
½   chicken
5   beef bones
1   medium yellow onion
Salt to taste

PASTA
8   ounces mortadella
6   ounces prosciutto crudo
4   ounces veal loin
1½ cups grated Parmigiano Reggiano, plus more for serving
7   large eggs
Salt and freshly ground black pepper to taste
Freshly grated nutmeg to taste
4   cups unbleached all-purpose flour

To make the broth, which should be on the rich side, in a stockpot, combine the ingredients with 4 quarts cold water. Bring to a boil, then simmer for 3 hours. Allow to rest for at least 30 minutes, then strain.

To make the filling for the pasta, mince the mortadella, prosciutto, and veal loin together. In a bowl, combine the minced meat with the 1½ cups grated Parmigiano, 1 egg, salt, pepper, and nutmeg and mix by hand until well combined. The mixture should form a clump if you pinch off a bit of it.

On a work surface, shape the flour into a well. Place the 6 remaining eggs and a pinch of salt in the center and begin pulling in flour from the sides of the well and kneading until the mixture forms a compact dough. On a lightly floured surface, with a rolling pin roll out the dough to less than ¹⁄₁₀ inch thick. Cut into squares with 3-inch sides. Place a small amount of the filling in the center of each square, then fold a square in half to form a triangle. Wrap the triangle around your finger so that two points of the triangle meet and press to seal. Repeat with remaining squares.

Reheat the strained broth to a boil, then turn down to a simmer and drop in the tortellini. Cook the pasta until it rises to the surface, which should take only a few minutes. Serve with additional grated Parmigiano.

PASTA CO MACCU 🐚
Broken Spaghetti in Fava Bean Puree
Filippa Gatì, Palermo, Sicìlia

Roman soldiers subsisted on grain and bean porridges centuries ago. *Maccu* gets very thick as it sits, so while it's a soup when freshly made, you can use it as you would cooked polenta the day after and pan-fry pieces of it (or simply thin with water and reheat). Soak dried fava beans in room temperature water for at least 12 hours. Drain, peel, and place in a pot with extra-virgin olive oil and minced onion and wild fennel. Add water to cover, season with salt, and cook, covered, over low heat for 2 hours. When the beans have broken down, bring a pot of salted water to a boil and break spaghetti by hand over the pot and drop into the water. Cook until al dente, then drain and add to the fava beans. Crush any fava beans that have remained intact with the back of a wooden spoon. Cook for a few additional minutes, then serve with grated aged sheep's cheese or a healthy sprinkling of freshly ground black pepper on top.

MACCU DI SAN GIUSEPPE 🌰
Bean and Lentil Puree
Rosalia Battaglia, Siracusa, Sicìlia

This more complex version of maccu includes a variety of beans; it is eaten in rural areas throughout Sicilia to celebrate Saint Joseph, Mary's husband and the patron saint of carpenters, on March 19. Soak dried fava beans along with dried chickpeas, dried peas, and dried borlotti beans (each about half the amount of the fava beans) overnight in cold salted water, changing the water several times. The next day, drain the beans and combine with lentils (equal to the amount of chickpeas) in a terra-cotta pot with water to cover. Cook over low heat until the beans are broken down, at least 3 hours. About halfway through the cooking time, add borage, wild fennel, minced onion, and a couple of minced sun-dried tomatoes. When the soup is cooked, season with salt and pepper and drizzle with a little olive oil. If you like, cook some corallina pasta in the soup or add some cubes of bread that you have quickly browned in olive oil.

SBROSCIA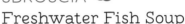
Freshwater Fish Soup
Trattoria La Tana dell'Orso, Bruno, Bolsena (Viterbo), Lazio

This soup can also be made with smelts, rudd, and freshwater crabs and shrimp and can be flavored with garlic, parsley, and basil.

SERVES 10
- 1 large yellow onion, sliced
- 1 chili pepper, minced
- Leaves of 1 bunch calamint
- Extra-virgin olive oil for sautéing and drizzling
- 6½ pounds mixed freshwater fish, such as tench, whitefish, eel, perch, and pike, gutted, boned, and chopped
- 4 large plum tomatoes, chopped
- Salt and freshly ground black pepper to taste
- 20 slices day-old bread
- 2 cloves garlic

Place the onion, chili pepper, and calamint leaves in oil in a pot and place over medium heat. When the oil is hot, add the fish and brown over medium heat. Add hot water to cover, raise the heat, and then add the tomatoes. Season with salt and pepper and simmer, uncovered, for 30 minutes.

Meanwhile, toast the bread and rub the toast with the garlic. To serve, place 2 slices garlic toast in each individual bowl and top with 2 or 3 piece of fish and some of the broth. Drizzle with olive oil and serve.

ACQUAPAZZA
"Crazy Water" Fish Soup
Augusto Manfredi, Massa, Toscana

Acquapazza is a method for cooking fish with olive oil, garlic, tomatoes, and water (at one time seawater was used, which may explain the origin of the name, as sailors who drank seawater lost their minds). This is a rather unusual version—it is more commonly made with fresh fish. In a large terra-cotta pot, sauté thinly sliced onion in olive oil, then crumble in some sausage (remove and discard casing) and cook until it has lost its raw red color. Add seeded tomatoes that have been squeezed dry and then diced, a piece of baccalà that was previously soaked in water for at least 36 hours with several changes of water, and some chopped herring. Cook 10 to 15 minutes, then season with salt and pepper and add water to cover by a couple of inches. Bring to a boil, then simmer for 20 minutes. If the fish hasn't broken up, break it into rough chunks in the pot with a wooden spoon. Toast slices of stale bread, rub with a cut garlic clove, and place in the bottom of soup bowls, then ladle the hot soup over the bread and serve.

CIUPPIN DEL LEVANTE
Fish Soup from the Coast of Liguria
Rosanna Orlandini, Genova, Liguria

Ciuppin (the forebear to San Francisco's cioppino) was invented as a way for the fishermen of Liguria to use the less popular types of fish that weren't worth much in commercial terms, but at least could be eaten at home. Mince together onion, parsley, and garlic and sauté in extra-virgin olive oil in a terra-cotta pot. As soon as it begins to turn golden, add some white wine and cook until evaporated. Add seeded peeled tomatoes cut into strips and cook for 15 minutes, stirring

frequently. Add hot water and a little salt, then gently place fish fillets that you have cut into wide strips in the pot. Good choices include gurnard and scorpionfish. Cook, covered, over low heat for 30 minutes without stirring. When the fish is cooked, pull out a few pieces of fillet per person and set aside, then puree the rest through a sieve. If the resulting puree is too stiff, add hot water in small amounts until it reaches a more pleasant consistency. Taste and adjust salt and return the puree to the pot to cook for a few more minutes. To serve, divide the puree among individual bowls and top with the reserved whole pieces of fish. Serve with toasted bread rubbed with a cut clove of garlic.

GNOCHES DE GRIES IN BRODO
Semolina Dumplings in Broth
Giuliana Fantin, Polcenigo (Pordenone), Friuli-Venezia Giulia

*S*emolina flour is used all over Italy to make pasta, porridge, strudel-like rolls, and dumplings. To make dumplings for 4 people, beat about 3 tablespoons butter with a wooden spoon or spatula. Add 4 egg yolks (reserve the whites) one at a time, beating between additions. Gradually beat in 1½ cups semolina flour, a little salt, and a pinch of freshly grated nutmeg. Whip the 4 egg whites to stiff peaks and fold them into the mixture. Form into small balls and cook them in beef broth for about 10 minutes. Serve with grated Grana Padano cheese.

PASSATELLI IN BRODO
Breadcrumb Pasta in Broth
Trattoria Marianaza, Faenza (Ravenna), Emîlia-Romagna

Passatelli dough must be kneaded on a hard work surface—don't try to knead it in the bowl. Though passatelli are traditionally served in broth, in recent years it's become trendy to serve them in tomato sauce or with a light ragù or fish sauce, in which case the lemon zest is omitted. There is a special tool for making passatelli, but a potato ricer fitted with a disk with large holes will work as well.

SERVES 4 TO 6

- ½ chicken for broth
- 1 pound beef for broth
- 1 rib celery
- 1 carrot
- 1 medium yellow onion

- ⅔ cup grated Parmigiano Reggiano
- ⅔ cup breadcrumbs
- Grated zest of ¼ organic lemon
- 2 large eggs, lightly beaten
- Salt and freshly ground black pepper to taste
- Freshly grated nutmeg to taste

To make the broth, combine the chicken, beef, celery, carrot, and onion in a stockpot and add cold water to cover by several inches. Bring to a boil, then reduce the heat to a simmer and simmer over low heat for 2 to 3 hours. Strain and set aside.

To make the passatelli, combine the grated cheese, breadcrumbs, and the lemon zest and shape the mixture into a well on a work surface. Add the eggs to the center of the well and season with salt, pepper, and nutmeg. Knead, gradually pulling in the dry mixture from the sides of the well, until you have a soft and compact dough.

If the dough feels too wet, add breadcrumbs and Parmigiano, but always in equal amounts.

Bring the broth to a boil in a soup pot and then force the dough through the passatelli maker or a potato ricer fitted with the disk with large holes to make thick spaghetti noodles an inch or two long and let them drop directly into the pot where the broth is boiling. Turn the broth down to a simmer and cook just until the pasta rises to the surface (a couple of minutes). Serve very hot. Any leftovers can be reheated and they will still be excellent.

CAPPELLETTI IN BRODO ALLA REGGIANA 🍲
Cappelletti in Broth
Osteria in Scandiano, Scandiano (Reggio Emilia), Emilia-Romagna

In the southern part of the region, a dash of local Lambrusco is often added to the broth.

SERVES 8

- 7 tablespoons unsalted butter or lardo (cured fatback)
- 1 medium yellow onion, thinly sliced
- 2 cloves garlic, crushed
- 7 ounces lean veal or beef, cut into cubes
- 5 ounces pork loin, cut into cubes
- Salt to taste
- 3 to 4 whole cloves
- 1 piece cinnamon stick

- Beef broth for braising and serving
- 5 cups unbleached all-purpose flour
- 9 large eggs
- 4 ounces mortadella
- 2 ounces prosciutto crudo
- 1 dried sausage, casing removed
- ¼ cup grated Parmigiano Reggiano, plus more for serving
- 1 pinch freshly grated nutmeg
- Breadcrumbs, if needed

For the filling, in a pot, melt the butter or lardo and sauté the onion and garlic. When the garlic browns, remove and discard and add the veal and pork. Season with a pinch of salt. Wrap the cloves and cinnamon stick in cheesecloth and add to the skillet. Add broth to cover, cover the pot, and braise over low heat until very tender, 1 to 1½ hours. Allow to cool.

While the meat is cooking, form the flour into a well on a work surface. Add 6 eggs to the center of the well, beat lightly with a fork, and pull in flour from the sides of the well, then knead into a compact dough. Wrap in a kitchen towel and set aside for 30 minutes.

Chop the cooked meat with the mortadella, prosciutto, and dried sausage. Combine with the 3 remaining eggs, ¼ cup grated Parmigiano, and a pinch of nutmeg. Mix to combine. If the mixture seems too soft, add breadcrumbs a little at a time until it is stiff enough to clump if you pinch off a bit. Season with salt.

Roll out the pasta dough with a rolling pin until it is extremely thin—no thicker than 1 millimeter. With a serrated pastry wheel, cut it into squares with 1- to 1½-inch sides and cover them so they don't dry out. Working with just a few squares at a time, place a ball of filling the size of a walnut in the center of each. Fold one square into a triangle, pressing to seal. Then, fold it around your left index finger (assuming you are right-handed), overlapping the two corners slightly. Press to seal and flip up the "tail." Repeat with remaining pasta and filling.

To serve, place the broth in a pot and bring to a boil, then cook the pasta directly in the broth. Serve with additional grated Parmigiano on the side.

MINESTRA DI ACCIO E BACCALÀ
Leaf Celery and Baccalà Soup
Trattoria Valleverde, Atripalda (Avellino), Campania

There are two versions of this dried salt cod soup: one for summer, and the other for winter. Leaf celery, as the name indicates, consists mostly of leaves rather than ribs. Uncooked, the leaves can be bitter, but their flavor softens with cooking. Look for small, deep green leaves with an intense aroma. Always be sure to check baccalà carefully for bones and remove any skin.

SERVES 4

SUMMER VERSION
- 1 pound (about 30 stalks) leaf celery
- 2 cloves garlic
- Extra-virgin olive oil for sautéing
- 7 ounces (about 16) cherry tomatoes
- 2 pounds (about 6) potatoes, peeled and diced
- Salt to taste
- 1½ pounds baccalà, soaked in several changes of water until pliable and chopped

WINTER VERSION
- 1 pound (about 30 stalks) leaf celery
- Extra-virgin olive oil for sautéing
- ¼ cup walnuts, ground
- ¼ cup hazelnuts, ground
- 2 cups tomato puree
- Salt to taste
- 1½ pounds baccalà, soaked in several changes of water until pliable and chopped
- 4 peppers preserved in vinegar, drained and diced

For the summer version, blanch the leaf celery. In a pot, sauté the garlic in some oil, then add the tomatoes. Cook, stirring frequently, until the tomatoes collapse, then add the potatoes. Add water to cover by a couple of inches, season with salt, bring to a boil, and simmer until the potatoes are beginning to soften but still firm. Add the leaf celery, stir to combine, and place the baccalà on top. Continue cooking until the potatoes are tender and baccalà is soft.

For the winter version, briefly sauté the leaf celery in oil until wilted. In a separate pot, sauté the walnuts and hazelnuts in oil until browned. Add the tomato puree and cook for a few minutes, then add the leaf celery. Add enough water to cover by a couple of inches and season with salt and simmer until well combined. Arrange the baccalà on top and cook until the baccalà is soft. Sprinkle on diced peppers and serve.

ZUPPA DI COCCETTI
Red Mullet Soup
Trattoria Fraschetta del Mare, Anzio (Roma), Lazio

Use small mullet for this soup. They are cooked on the bone for extra tenderness.

SERVES 4
- 1 clove garlic
- Extra-virgin olive oil for sautéing and drizzling
- Ground chili pepper (optional)
- 1¾ pounds red mullet, gutted
- 1 cup dry white wine
- 10 cherry tomatoes, quartered
- Salt to taste
- Leaves of 1 sprig parsley
- Day-old bread, toasted and cut into cubes

In a soup pot, brown the garlic in oil with the ground chili pepper, if using. When the oil is quite hot, add the mullet and cook, turning gently to brown on all sides. Add the wine and let it evaporate, then add the tomatoes and cook for 10 minutes. Add about 1 cup water, season with salt, add most of the parsley, reserving a little for garnish, and cook for 10 additional minutes. Divide the soup among individual serving bowls and garnish with the toasted bread. Drizzle with oil and garnish with the reserved parsley.

PASTA E BROCCOLI IN BRODO D'ARZILLA 🐟
Pasta and Broccoli in Skate Broth
Osteria del Velodromo Vecchio, Roma, Lazio

This is the "lean" version of this dish; the more filling version uses lardo, prosciutto, lard, or pork rind. This was often served on Good Friday. The cooked skate—steamed to reheat and seasoned with parsley, lemon juice, and a drizzle of olive oil—can be served as a second course.

SERVES 4

1   carrot
2   ribs celery
½   medium yellow onion
2 to 3 sprigs parsley
1   tablespoon rock salt
2   pounds skate, gutted and skinned
1   pound Romanesco broccoli, heads quartered
2 to 3 cloves garlic, minced
1   small piece chili pepper, minced
¼   cup plus 2 tablespoons extra-virgin olive oil
2 to 3 ripe plum tomatoes, chopped
½   cup dry white wine
6   ounces vermicelli or other long pasta

Combine the carrot, celery, onion, parsley, rock salt, and the skate in a soup pot and add 12 cups water. Cover and bring to a boil over medium heat. As soon as the water boils, uncover the pot. Skim any foam from the top, then strain the broth and transfer to a clean pot. Bring to a boil again and add the broccoli. When the broccoli is tender, remove to a bowl and let it cool. (Strain and reserve broth.) When the broccoli is cool, cut off the florets. Mince the core and any leaves.

In another pot, sauté minced garlic and chili pepper in ¼ cup of the oil. When the garlic begins to brown, add the minced broccoli and the tomatoes and cook until it begins to stick to the bottom of the pot. Add the wine and once

it has evaporated add the broth. Bring back to a boil and cook for 10 minutes, then add the florets, bring to a boil, and boil 5 to 6 minutes.

Break the pasta by hand and drop it into the pot. Cook until al dente, then let rest for a few minutes and drizzle with the remaining 2 tablespoons oil before serving.

MACCHERONI DI NATALE ALLA GENOVESE 🐄
Meat-Filled Christmas Macaroni in Broth
Antica Osteria dei Mosto, Ne (Genova), Liguria

Christmas macaroni are small dried semolina pasta with a hole through the center. Their diameter is about that of a thumb and they are about 10 inches long. For Christmas they are stuffed and cooked in broth.

SERVES 4

2   tablespoons unsalted butter
1   carrot, minced
1   small yellow onion, thinly sliced
7   ounces lean veal, cut into cubes
7   ounces veal brain, marrow, and sweetbreads, cleaned, blanched, and diced
¼   cup pine nuts
Salt to taste
2   large eggs, lightly beaten
2   tablespoons grated Parmigiano Reggiano, plus more for serving
Freshly grated nutmeg to taste
Leaves of 1 sprig marjoram, minced
1   roll, crusts removed, soaked in milk to soften
7   ounces Christmas macaroni or similar pasta (see note)
1   quart mixed chicken and beef broth
Freshly ground black pepper to taste (optional)

In a skillet melt the butter, then add the carrot and onion. Add the meat and the organ meats and the pine nuts. Cook, stirring frequently, until browned, about 20 minutes. Season with salt. When the mixture has cooled slightly, grind it to medium grind, then combine with the eggs and 2 tablespoons Parmigiano, a little nutmeg, and the marjoram. Add enough of the soaked bread so that the mixture is soft but not runny.

Use a pastry bag to fill the macaroni with the meat mixture. Work from each end of each piece of pasta, leaving about ¾ inch empty on each side. Place the broth in a large pot, bring to a boil, then add the macaroni and cook until the pasta is al dente. Break the pasta into shorter pieces and transfer to soup bowls with the broth. Sprinkle with a little pepper, if using, and serve with additional grated cheese.

CAPPELLETTI DI MAGRO IN BRODO
Cheese Cappelletti in Broth
Antica Osteria del Teatro, Lugo di Romagna (Ravenna), Emília-Romagna

The meatless filling in these cappelletti lets the flavor of the cheese shine through. The restaurant recommends straining the broth so that it is limpid.

SERVES 6

1   carrot
1   rib celery
1   medium yellow onion
4 to 5 cherry tomatoes
10 to 14 ounces beef
½   beef tongue
½   chicken
Salt to taste
4   cups unbleached all-purpose flour
7   large eggs
6   cups grated Parmigiano Reggiano
Freshly grated nutmeg to taste

To make the broth, combine the carrot, celery, onion, and tomatoes in a pot. Add the beef, tongue, and chicken and 5 quarts cold water. Season with salt and simmer over low heat for about 5 hours.

To make the pasta, form the flour into a well on a work surface. Place 5 eggs in the center and lightly beat with a fork, then begin pulling in the flour from the sides of the well. When you have a crumbly mixture, knead into a smooth and elastic dough. Set aside to rest for 30 minutes.

To make the filling, in a bowl combine the grated Parmigiano with the remaining 2 eggs and beat with a pinch of salt and a generous sprinkling of nutmeg. With a rolling pin, roll out the dough to a very thin sheet, less than 1/10 inch thick, and cut into squares with 1-inch sides. Place a small spoonful of the filling in the center of each square. Fold one square into a triangle, then seal two opposite ends of the triangle so that they overlap slightly, flipping up the "tail" so that it looks like a three-cornered hat. Repeat with remaining squares of dough.

Strain the broth through a fine sieve or a cheesecloth-lined colander, taste and adjust salt, and bring to a boil. Lower the heat slightly so that it is simmering briskly but not at a rolling boil and add the cappelletti. Cook until they rise to the surface, which should take only a few minutes. Remove from the heat, cover the pot, and allow to rest for a few minutes before serving.

RAVIOLINI IN BRODO DI PESCE 🐟
Raviolini in Fish Broth
Lidia Angelini, Imperia, Liguria

To make enough to serve 6, place a 2-pound whole fish (scorpionfish, gurnard) in a soup pot along with about 1 pound fish and fish scraps for broth, 1 rib celery, 1 small carrot, 1 small onion, 1 clove garlic, a few sprigs parsley, salt, ½ cup white wine, 1 seeded and chopped ripe tomato, and a few sprigs of wild fennel. Add water to cover, bring to a boil, and simmer for 15 minutes after it returns to a boil. Remove the whole fish, which will be used for the filling, and continue to cook the remaining ingredients until they have given up all of their flavor. This will be the broth.

Bone and skin the whole fish and chop the flesh. Combine with a little blanched and minced borage and cook in a skillet in 2 tablespoons oil. Season with salt and pepper and when the mixture has cooled, mix in 4 egg whites. (Reserve the yolks for the pasta.) If the stuffing mixture seems too loose, add breadcrumbs a little a time until it is stiff enough.

Make a pasta dough with 4 cups flour, the 4 reserved egg yolks, a pinch of salt, and as much water as required. Knead until smooth and set aside to rest for 30 minutes, then roll the dough into a thin sheet and make small ravioli, about 1 inch per side, filled with the fish and borage mixture. Strain the broth, bring to a boil, and cook the ravioli in the broth until they float to the surface, which should take just a few minutes. Taste and adjust salt and serve piping hot.

GNOCCHI DI LUCCIO IN BRODO 🐟
Pike Dumplings in Broth
Agriturismo Oasi degli Angeli, Cupra Marittima (Ascoli Piceno), Marche

These gnocchi can be made with other types of fish, including saltwater fish: mackerel, dorade, and sea bream would all be delicious. Crumble the bread by hand—breadcrumbs will be a little too fine.

SERVES 4
- 1 whole pike, about 2 pounds, gutted and scaled
- 1 carrot
- 1 rib celery
- 1 medium yellow onion
- 1 leek
- 2 sprigs thyme
- Whole black peppercorns to taste
- 3 cups crumbled fresh (not stale) unsalted bread, crusts removed
- ¼ cup extra-virgin olive oil
- Salt to taste

Fillet and skin the fish. Use the fish head and bones to make a fish fumet by placing them in a stockpot with 1½ quarts water, the carrot, the celery, the onion, the leek, 1 sprig thyme, and black peppercorns. Bring to a boil and simmer for 1 to 1½ hours.

Meanwhile, thinly slice the fish fillets. Pound them to break them down, then place them in a bowl and combine with the crumbled bread and olive oil. Mince a few thyme leaves and add to the mixture. Season with salt and ground pepper. Mix by hand until well combined. Form the mixture into balls about ¾ inch in diameter and refrigerate for 30 minutes.

Strain the broth through a cheesecloth-lined sieve, then place in a pot and bring to a boil. Taste and adjust seasoning if necessary. Distribute the fish dumplings among individual serving plates, then ladle the hot broth over them. Allow to cool somewhat before serving.

SEMOLINA PASTA & OTHER DRIED PASTA

CARBONARA

Pasta alla Carbonara

Ristorante L'Arcangelo, Roma, Lazio

This is one of the best-known dishes in Italy. It is simple, but you must work quickly and vigorously to avoid having the spaghetti stick together. Guanciale is cured pork jowl from the Lazio region.

SERVES 4

3 to 4 whole black peppercorns
3   ounces guanciale (see note), cut into strips
4   egg yolks
¾   cup grated Pecorino Romano
Salt to taste
14 ounces spaghetti

Toast the peppercorns in a cast-iron pan over medium heat, shaking the pan frequently, until they give off their aroma. Set aside to cool, then crush with a mortar and pestle. Cook the guanciale in the cast-iron pan for a few minutes, just until it begins to brown and renders its fat. Remove with a slotted spoon or spatula and set aside, reserving the fat.

In a large heatproof bowl, beat the egg yolks with about half of the grated cheese. Whisk in some of the fat from the guanciale and the crushed black pepper. Season with salt.

Bring a large pot of salted water to a boil and cook the spaghetti al dente, reserving about 1 cup of the cooking water. Drain the spaghetti and transfer to the bowl with the egg yolk mixture. Add about 1 tablespoon of the pasta cooking water and mix vigorously to coat the strands of pasta. If the pasta looks very dry, add a little more cooking water, but 1 tablespoon is usually the right amount. Mix in the cooked guanciale and the remaining grated cheese. Again, if the pasta looks dry, mix in a little more of the cooking water. Serve immediately.

AMATRICIANA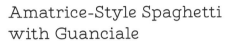

Amatrice-Style Spaghetti with Guanciale

Ristorante Lo Scoiattolo, Amatrice (Rieti), Lazio

Use authentic guanciale from Amatrice if you can. It is slightly spicy and smoked. If you can't find spicy guanciale, add one-half minced chili pepper along with the tomatoes.

SERVES 4

6 to 7 San Marzano tomatoes, peeled and seeded, or 2 cups canned peeled tomatoes
4   ounces guanciale (see note), cut into thick strips
Extra-virgin olive oil for sautéing
¼   cup dry white wine
Salt to taste
1   pound spaghetti
Grated Pecorino Romano to taste, plus more for serving

If you are using fresh tomatoes, puree them through a food mill. If you are using canned tomatoes, crush them with a fork or by hand. In a large skillet, sauté the guanciale in a small amount of olive oil. Splash with the white wine, then cook until liquid has evaporated. Add the tomatoes, season with salt, and cook until reduced, about 12 minutes with fresh tomatoes and 10 minutes with canned tomatoes. Remove about half of the sauce to a bowl and leave the remainder in the skillet.

Meanwhile, bring a large pot of salted water to a boil and cook the pasta al dente. Drain and add to the skillet and toss to coat with the sauce. Sprinkle on a generous amount of grated cheese and toss to combine, then transfer to a serving bowl, top with the rest of the sauce, and serve with additional grated cheese on the side.

AMATRICIANA DE PRESCIA 🌿
Quick Spaghetti with Umbrian Barbozzo
Osteria Molenda, Città di Castello (Perugia), Umbria

This sauce comes together very quickly—you can make it in the time it takes to cook the pasta. That said, the ingredients are key. This dish must be made with high-quality dried semolina pasta. At the restaurant they use pasta made with the Senatore Cappelli variety of durum wheat. Barbozzo is cured pork jowl from Umbria. It is sprinkled with minced garlic, salt, and pepper and then aged for two to three months in a cool, damp environment. Formaggio di fossa is cheese aged in pits dug into rock. You could replace barbozzo with guanciale and formaggio di fossa with another aged, sharp cheese if you wish, but at that point you might as well turn back to the previous page and make *Amatriciana* instead, which incorporates those ingredients.

SERVES 4
Salt to taste
14 ounces spaghetti
1   shallot, minced
Extra-virgin olive oil for sautéing and
    drizzling
½   cup dry white wine
7   ounces barbozzo (see note)
1   pound tomatoes, cut into wedges and
    seeded
Ground chili pepper to taste
Grated formaggio di fossa to taste
3 to 4 basil leaves

Bring a large pot of salted water to a boil and add the spaghetti.

While the pasta is cooking, in a large skillet sauté the shallot in olive oil, then add the white wine and allow it to evaporate. Slice the barbozzo very thin, less than 1/10 inch, then cut into strips. Add the barbozzo to the pan and cook for 2 minutes without allowing it to brown. Add the tomatoes and turn the heat up as high as possible and cook, stirring constantly but gently so the tomatoes keep their shape, for 2 minutes. Add the chili pepper, season with salt, and remove from the heat.

When the pasta is cooked al dente, add it to the skillet and toss with the sauce. Transfer to a serving bowl, top with a drizzle of olive oil, a sprinkling of grated cheese, and a few basil leaves and serve.

SPAGHETTI AGLIO, OLIO E PEPERONCINO 🌶
Spaghetti with Garlic and Hot Pepper
Trattoria L'Oste della Bon'Ora, Grottaferrata (Roma), Lazio

Lazio, Abruzzo, Campania, and Calabria all lay claim to this dish, but it is eaten all over Italy. Use a generous number of garlic cloves (1 per person) and, depending on how pronounced you would like the garlic flavor to be, either leave them whole, cut them into halves or thirds, mince them, or crush them. Brown the garlic and a generous amount of chili pepper torn into pieces by hand in a large skillet in a generous amount of oil. When the garlic has browned, remove and discard both garlic and hot pepper. Cook spaghetti in a generous amount of boiling salted water until al dente, then add to the skillet with the oil and toss over medium heat until coated. Garnish with minced parsley. If you prefer less spice, you can simply pour the hot oil mixture over the drained spaghetti in the serving bowl. You can also make a raw version by rubbing the bottom and sides of a bowl with a cut clove of garlic, adding pasta and oil, and tossing them, and then adding minced parsley and chili pepper.

SPAGHETTI CON IL FRIGGIONE 🍅

Handmade Spaghetti in Long-Cooked Tomato and Onion Sauce

Trattoria Giampi e Ciccio, Bologna, Emília-Romagna

This dish is not difficult, but the sauce requires a long cooking time to reach the correct creamy consistency. This used to be made with lard, but these days most cooks use olive oil. The pasta can be shaped using a potato ricer.

SERVES 4

- 1¾ pounds ripe tomatoes, peeled, seeded, and chopped
- 1½ pounds (4 to 5 medium) white onions, diced
- Extra-virgin olive oil for sautéing and drizzling
- Salt to taste
- 1¾ cups semolina flour
- Parmigiano Reggiano for grating (optional)

In a large pot, cook the tomatoes and onions in olive oil over very low heat, uncovered, stirring occasionally and adding water in small amounts if they begin to stick to the bottom, until completely broken down and soft, 4 to 6 hours. Season with salt and keep warm.

On a work surface, make a well of the flour and add a pinch of salt and some lukewarm water to the center. Knead into a compact dough, adding more water as needed. Cover with a kitchen towel and set aside to rest for 30 minutes. Force the dough through a potato ricer, cutting off the noodles every 10 to 12 inches. Spread out the noodles and dry briefly.

When you are ready to serve the dish, bring a large pot of salted water to a boil and cook the pasta until soft, 6 to 7 minutes, then drain and toss with the sauce. Drizzle with a little olive oil and, if desired, pass a piece of Parmigiano Reggiano and a grater so that diners can top their servings with grated cheese.

SPAGHETTI ALLA CUCUNCIATA 🌶

Spaghetti with Eggplant, Peppers, Caperberries, and Olives

Ristorante 'A Cannata, Santa Marina Salina (Isole Eolie, Messina), Sicília

Oval caperberries are the fruit of the caper bush. (Capers are small buds.) A special variety of round capers is grown on Salina, one of the Aeolian Islands.

SERVES 4

- 2 eggplant, diced
- Salt to taste
- 2 cloves garlic, crushed
- Extra-virgin olive oil for sautéing
- 14 ounces (about 1 pint) cherry tomatoes, chopped
- 2 bell peppers, roasted, peeled, seeded, and cut into julienne
- ¼ cup black olives, pitted
- 8 to 10 salted caperberries, rinsed, dried and minced
- 2 salted anchovies, rinsed, boned, and minced
- 4 to 5 basil leaves
- Freshly ground black pepper to taste
- 14 ounces spaghetti
- Grated aged Pecorino Siciliano to taste

Toss the eggplant with salt and let it sit at room temperature for 1 hour to drain any bitterness, then rinse and dry it. In a skillet sauté the garlic in olive oil until browned, then remove the garlic and add the eggplant. Sauté for a few minutes over medium heat, then add the tomatoes and cook, stirring frequently, until the vegetables are soft, about 10 minutes. Add the peppers, olives, caperberries, and anchovies. Remove from the heat and tear in the basil leaves. Stir to combine, then taste and adjust salt and pepper.

Bring a large pot of salted water to a boil and cook spaghetti al dente. Drain and toss with the prepared sauce. Sprinkle with cheese and serve.

'O SICCHIO D'A MUNNEZZA 🫒
Spaghetti with Nuts, Raisins, Capers, and Olives
Osteria 'E Curti, Sant'Anastasia (Napoli), Campania

The name of this dish is dialect for "garbage pail," not the most appetizing name, but one meant to indicate that this is made with leftovers from the traditional Christmas lunch in this part of Campania. Ingredients should be locally sourced: walnuts from Sorrento, hazelnuts from Giffoni, spaghetti from Gragnano. At one time they would have been found even closer to home: not long ago, pine nuts were picked by hand out of pine cones, and raisins were obtained by drying grapes grown right outside the family home.

SERVES 8
Salt to taste
1   clove garlic, lightly crushed
Extra-virgin olive oil for sautéing
¾   cup walnuts, chopped
½   cup hazelnuts, chopped
16 pine nuts
10 raisins, soaked in warm water and drained
18 capers, rinsed and drained
9   ounces (about 20) piénnolo cherry tomatoes, seeded and chopped
8   black olives, pitted
1   pinch dried oregano
¼   cup minced parsley
1¾ pounds spaghetti

Boil a large pot of salted water for the pasta. Meanwhile, for the sauce, in a skillet quickly sauté the garlic in olive oil until golden. Add the nuts, raisins, and capers and sauté for 2 minutes. Add the tomatoes to the pan, season with a little salt (keep in mind the olives and capers), and cook over medium heat until combined, 4 to 5 minutes. Add the olives, a pinch of oregano, and the parsley. Cook, stirring, to combine, then cover, and set aside. Cook the pasta in the boiling water until al dente, then drain and toss with the prepared sauce.

SPAGHETTI CON LE NOCCIOLE 🌰
Spaghetti with Hazelnuts
Ristorante Il Brigante, Giffoni Sei Casali (Salerno), Campania

Giffoni hazelnuts are easy to peel and stand up especially well to cooking. Bring a pot of salted water to a boil and cook the spaghetti in it. Meanwhile, toast hazelnuts (about ¼ cup per person or a little less) lightly, then peel and mince them. Brown minced garlic and some crumbled chili pepper in a generous amount of olive oil in a skillet large enough to hold the amount of pasta you are making. Add the hazelnuts to the skillet and sauté briefly, then add a few spoonfuls of the pasta cooking water. Sprinkle in minced parsley and adjust salt to taste. When the spaghetti is cooked al dente, drain it and add it to the skillet and toss briefly over medium heat to combine.

SPAGHETTI CON LE ALICI DI MENAICA 🌿
Spaghetti with Menaica Anchovies
Menaica Anchovies Presidium, Pisciotta (Salerno), Campania

Menaica anchovies are caught using an ancient fishing technique that today is utilized in just a few places in Italy. Fishermen go out at night and spread out nets to catch large, meaty anchovies. (Smaller specimens swim through the holes in the net.) Some of the catch is sold fresh, and the rest is layered with salt in terra-cotta jars and aged for at least three months. The Menaica Anchovies Presidium provided this recipe, which calls for both fresh and salted anchovies, with about 3 times as much fresh as salted fish. Sauté halved piénnolo cherry tomatoes in olive oil in a skillet with minced garlic and white onion. In a separate skillet, sauté more minced white onion, minced parsley, and a couple of rinsed, boned, and chopped salted anchovies. When the onion begins to brown, add boned and chopped fresh anchovies. Deglaze with some Fiano del Cilento wine and add the tomato mixture from the other skillet. Cook spaghetti in salted boiling water until al dente, then drain and add to the skillet. Sprinkle with additional minced parsley and a little minced fresh wild oregano and serve.

SPAGHETTI AL SUGO DI LUPO

Spaghetti with Wolffish

Trattoria del Pesce Fresco, Marina di Caulonia (Reggio Calabria), Calabria

Wolffish is related to cod. It is very tasty but does not keep well, so you will find it only in places where it is fished. Wolffish can also be fried, cooked in soup, stewed, or baked in parchment. Substitute cod or another firm-fleshed white fish if necessary.

SERVES 4

1 clove garlic, minced
Leaves of 1 sprig parsley, minced
Extra-virgin olive oil for sautéing
2 cups tomato puree
1½ pounds wolfish (see note), gutted, boned, and cut into strips
Salt to taste
14 ounces spaghetti

In a skillet, sauté the garlic and parsley in olive oil. Add the tomato puree and cook until reduced, about 10 minutes. Add the fish and season with salt. Cook over medium heat until the fish is opaque, 10 to 12 minutes.

Meanwhile, bring a large pot of salted water to a boil and cook the pasta al dente. Drain the pasta, transfer to a serving bowl, and top with the fish and sauce.

SPAGHETTI CON LA MATALOTTA

Spaghetti with Mahi Mahi

Trattoria La Gazza Ladra, Siracusa, Sicilia

This is one of the few traditional Italian dishes that combines fish with cheese.

SERVES 4

1 medium yellow onion, sliced
Extra-virgin olive oil for sautéing
1 tablespoon tomato paste
½ cup dry white wine
2 pounds mahi mahi, filleted and skinned
½ green chili pepper
10 black olives, pitted
1 tablespoon capers, rinsed and drained
1 bay leaf
Salt to taste
14 ounces spaghetti
Grated aged sheep's cheese to taste

In a skillet, sauté the onion in olive oil. Add the tomato paste and the wine, then the fish, the pepper (left whole), the olives, the capers, and the bay leaf. Add water to cover and cook, uncovered, over high heat until reduced, about 15 minutes. Season with salt.

Meanwhile, bring a large pot of salted water to a boil and cook the pasta al dente. When the sauce is ready, remove and discard the bay leaf and pepper. Drain the pasta, transfer to a serving bowl, and toss with the sauce and fillets. Sprinkle with cheese and serve.

PIATTU DE SOS ISPOSOS 🐚
Spaghetti with Tiny Meatballs
Ristorante Barbagia, Olbia, Sardegna

The meatballs here should be quite small, the size of marbles.

SERVES 4

2 cloves garlic
4 ounces ground pork
4 ounces ground beef
1 large egg
2 tablespoons breadcrumbs, plus more for dredging
½ cup grated Pecorino Sardo, plus more for serving
Leaves of 1 sprig parsley, minced
¼ cup dry white wine
Salt to taste
Freshly ground black pepper to taste
Extra-virgin olive oil for browning (optional) and sautéing
½ medium yellow onion, minced
1 small carrot, minced
½ chili pepper (optional)
5 to 6 ripe tomatoes, peeled, seeded, and pureed
14 ounces spaghetti

Mince 1 clove garlic. In a bowl combine the ground pork and beef and combine with the egg, 2 tablespoons breadcrumbs, ½ cup grated pecorino, parsley, minced garlic, and the wine. Season with salt and pepper and mix by hand until well combined, then form the mixture into small meatballs the size of marbles, dredge them in breadcrumbs, and set aside. Briefly brown the meatballs in oil in a large skillet in a single layer, or bake them in a low-temperature oven, turning frequently, until they are crisp on all sides. They will cook further in the sauce.

In a skillet, sauté the onion and carrot with the remaining clove garlic in olive oil. Add chili pepper if using. As soon as the onion starts to brown, add the tomatoes, season with salt, and cook over medium heat for 10 minutes. Then add the meatballs and cook, covered, until the sauce is reduced and meatballs are cooked through, 10 to 12 additional minutes. Meanwhile, bring a large pot of salted water to a boil, cook the pasta al dente, drain and add to the skillet. Toss to combine, sprinkling in additional grated pecorino as you do.

VERMICELLI CU' 'O PESCE FUJUTO 🍅
Vermicelli Pasta with Fish-That-Got-Away Tomato Sauce
Antonio Rizzo, Napoli, Campania

As the name indicates, this dish is meant to taste like a fish dish without the fish. The chef uses piénnolo tomatoes, cherry tomatoes that grow along the shore in the shadow of Mount Vesuvius. They absorb the flavor of iodine and salt from both the breezes off the water and the rich volcanic soil. Clusters of the tomatoes are allowed to dry slowly—you will often see them hanging from archways in people's homes in the area. Once dry, their flavor is even more intense and they last through the winter and up to the following spring. To start, pull piénnolo tomatoes from the vine and seed them. Crush a few cloves of garlic and fry them in extra-virgin olive oil until golden. Add the tomatoes and a pinch of salt and cook for a few minutes. Meanwhile, cook vermicelli (very thin spaghetti) in boiling salted water. Drain the pasta, toss with the tomato sauce, and garnish with a few whole or torn basil leaves.

LINGUINE CON CAPETROCCOLE E OLIVE 🌶

Linguine with Baby Octopus and Olives

Ristorante Il Gatto & la Volpe, Formia (Latina), Lazio

This is a typical meat-free dish served on Fridays and other holidays when Catholics are forbidden from eating meat.

SERVES 4

1   cup Gaeta olives in brine, pitted
1   clove garlic, lightly crushed
Extra-virgin olive oil for sautéing
1   chili pepper
1   pound baby octopus, cleaned, eyes removed, and drained
½   cup dry white wine
10   ounces (about 24) cherry tomatoes, quartered and seeded
Salt to taste
14   ounces linguine
Leaves of 1 sprig parsley, minced

In a saucepan sauté the olives and garlic in a little oil for a few minutes. Add the chili pepper and octopus and cook, stirring frequently, over medium heat until the octopus begin to brown, 5 to 6 minutes. Add the wine and let it evaporate, then add the tomatoes and season with salt. Cook until the liquid has evaporated and the octopus is tender enough to pierce with a fork, 5 to 10 minutes. Remove from the heat and keep warm.

Bring a large pot of salted water to a boil and cook the linguine al dente, which will probably take 8 to 10 minutes. Drain the pasta and toss with the octopus mixture. Sprinkle with parsley and serve.

LINGUINE ALLO SCAMMARO 🌿

Linguine with Anchovies, Olives, and Capers

Osteria-Gastronomia Timpani e Tempura, Napoli, Campania

Gragnano is a small town in the Napoli metropolitan area that is famous for its dried pasta. Legend has it that a gentle breeze blows in this town—positioned between the mountains and the sea—that is particularly suited to drying pasta.

SERVES 4

Salt to taste
1   pound Gragnano linguine
2   cloves garlic
Extra-virgin olive oil for sautéing
1½   cups green olives, pitted
2   salted anchovy fillets, rinsed and chopped
¾   cup capers, rinsed and drained
Leaves of 1 sprig parsley, minced
1½   cups Gaeta olives, pitted
1½   cups grated Pecorino Romano

Bring a large pot of salted water to a boil for cooking the pasta. While the linguine are cooking, sauté the garlic in olive oil in a skillet until browned, then remove and discard. Add the green olives and the anchovy fillets. Sauté for a minute or two, then add the capers. Sauté for 1 additional minute and add about ¼ cup of the pasta cooking water. Cook, stirring, for 2 minutes, then add the parsley and Gaeta olives. Toss to combine. When the pasta is cooked al dente, drain and add to the skillet. Toss the pasta with the olive mixture. Sprinkle on the grated cheese, toss again, and serve.

BAVETTE CON RAGÙ DI LAGO E BOTTARGA D'ACQUA DOLCE

Bavette Pasta with Freshwater Fish and Bottarga

Ristorante Collina, Almenno San Bartolomeo (Bergamo), Lombardia

Bottarga is salted and aged fish roe, in this case the roe of fish from Lake Como. It can be found either grated or in a block.

SERVES 4

- 4   perch
- 2   whitefish
- 1½ medium yellow onions
- 1   carrot
- 1   rib celery
- Salt to taste
- Extra-virgin olive oil for sautéing
- 1   tomato, crushed
- Leaves of 1 sprig thyme
- Leaves of 1 sprig marjoram
- 12 ounces bavette
- 1   tablespoon plus 1 teaspoon grated freshwater fish bottarga

Fillet the fish and use the bones and heads to make a fish fumet by combining them in a stockpot with ½ onion, the carrot, and the celery and adding cold water to cover by a couple of inches. Salt, then simmer for 20 minutes. Strain the fumet and set aside.

Cut the whitefish fillets into cubes and cut each perch fillet in half the long way. Mince the remaining onion. In a nonstick skillet, sauté the minced onion in oil, then add the tomato, thyme, marjoram, and a pinch of salt. Stir to combine and place the fish on top. Cook until the fish is opaque, 2 to 3 minutes. Transfer the fish to a platter. Add about ¼ cup of the strained fumet to the nonstick skillet with the sauce.

Bring a large pot of salted water to a boil and cook the pasta very al dente. Drain and add to the sauce and cook, tossing, over medium heat until the pasta is tender, adding small amounts of the fish fumet if the pan begins to get dry. When the pasta is cooked, add the fish to the skillet. Mix gently and divide among individual bowls. Top each portion with 1 teaspoon bottarga and serve.

LINGUINE DI FARRO CON CICORIETTA

Farro Linguine with Chicory

Ristorante Taverna 58, Pescara, Abruzzo

Farro is an ancient grain that has been grown in Italy since the earliest days of agriculture. Roman soldiers were nourished with a porridge made of farro. In Abruzzo, farro is still grown all over, and its flour is used to make all kinds of delicious pasta. Here, the sweetness of the farro contrasts beautifully with the bitterness of the chicory.

SERVES 4

- 7   ounces (1 bunch) wild chicory
- 1   clove garlic
- 1   pinch wild fennel seed
- 3   tablespoons extra-virgin olive oil
- Salt to taste
- 1   pound farro linguine

Rinse the chicory and with the water clinging to its leaves place it in a large pot with the garlic, fennel seed, and olive oil. Season with a little salt, cover the pan, and place over low heat for 10 minutes to cook the greens. Let the greens rest for a few minutes, then remove and discard the garlic and puree the greens with any cooking liquid in the pan. Return the puree to the pot.

Bring a large pot of salted water to a boil and cook the pasta al dente. Drain and add to the sauce. Toss to combine thoroughly.

BUCATINI CON BROCCOLI ARRIMINATI 🌿

Bucatini with Cauliflower, Anchovies, and Raisins

Trattoria Don Ciccio, Bagheria (Palermo), Sicîlia

Bucatini are like thick spaghetti with a round hole down the middle. They pair well with vegetables, as well as butter-based sauces.

SERVES 4

1 small yellow onion, diced
Extra-virgin olive oil for sautéing
4 salted anchovies, rinsed and boned
2 tablespoons golden raisins, softened in water and squeezed dry
3 tablespoons pine nuts
½ cup double-concentrate tomato paste
½ chili pepper, minced
2 pounds (1 large or 2 small heads) cauliflower, broken into florets
Salt to taste
1 pound bucatini
¼ cup toasted breadcrumbs

In a skillet, sauté the onion in olive oil. Add the anchovies, the raisins, the pine nuts, the tomato paste, and the chili pepper and cook, stirring frequently, until the anchovies have broken down. In a pot, boil the cauliflower in salted water until tender. Drain off any excess water, leaving a few tablespoons, and add the onion mixture to the pot with the cauliflower. Cook over medium heat for 3 minutes.

Bring a large pot of salted water to a boil for cooking the pasta. Cook until al dente, about 8 minutes. Drain and place in a pot with about ½ cup of the cauliflower mixture. Cook, tossing, over medium heat for 2 minutes, then transfer to a serving bowl and top with the remaining cauliflower mixture. Sprinkle on breadcrumbs and serve.

MEZZANIELLI AL PESTO CILENTANO 🌱

Pasta with Tomatoes, Herbs, and Two Kinds of Ricotta

Ristorante La Pergola, Capaccio (Salerno), Campania

Mezzanielli, sometimes labeled "perciatelli," are long tubes of pasta similar to bucatini.

SERVES 4

10 ounces (about 24) cherry tomatoes, diced
Salt to taste
½ cup plus 2 tablespoons extra-virgin olive oil
1 small piece chili pepper
Leaves of 1 sprig oregano
1 clove garlic, minced
3 sprigs basil with large leaves
⅓ cup grated aged smoked ricotta di bufala
7 ounces (about ¾ cup) fresh ricotta di bufala
14 ounces mezzanielli (see note)

In a bowl combine the tomatoes with salt, 2 tablespoons oil, chili pepper, oregano, and garlic. Set aside. Pick the leaves off of the basil and puree with the remaining ½ cup oil, a pinch of salt, and the grated aged ricotta. Add to the bowl with the tomatoes, stir to combine, and puree all together. Transfer this puree to a large skillet and heat for a few minutes. Remove from the heat and stir in the fresh ricotta.

Meanwhile, bring a large pot of salted water to a boil and cook the pasta. Drain and add to the skillet and toss off the heat. Serve immediately.

LAGANE E CECI ✺
Pasta with Chickpeas
Osteria Nunzia, Benevento, Campania

agane are rectangular eggless noodles, a little more than an inch wide. They are often served with legumes, including chickpeas, lentils, and cicerchia beans.

SERVES 4

- 1 cup dried chickpeas, soaked overnight
- 1 pinch baking soda
- Salt to taste
- 14 ounces lagane or other eggless noodles
- 1 clove garlic, minced
- Leaves of 1 sprig rosemary, minced
- ½ cup diced prosciutto crudo
- 7 to 8 cherry tomatoes, chopped
- Extra-virgin olive oil for sautéing
- Leaves of 1 sprig parsley, minced
- Ground chili pepper to taste (optional)

Drain the chickpeas and sprinkle them with the baking soda. Bring a large pot of salted water to a boil, rinse the chickpeas, then add them to the pot and cook until tender. Add the pasta to the pot and cook until both chickpeas and pasta are tender.

Meanwhile, sauté the garlic, rosemary, prosciutto, and tomatoes in oil. When the tomatoes have broken down and their liquid has evaporated, remove the chickpeas and pasta with a slotted spoon and add to the tomato mixture. Toss to combine, then stir in the parsley and chili pepper, if using.

PENNE AL COCCIO ❗
Penne with Porcini, Peas, and White Truffle Cooked in an Earthenware Pot
Hosteria del Bricco, Firenze, Toscana

his should be cooked in an earthenware pot and served in earthenware dishes for maximum effect.

SERVES 4

- 2 ounces pancetta, diced
- ¼ cup extra-virgin olive oil
- 4 ounces porcini mushrooms, sliced (about 2 cups)
- ⅔ cup shelled peas
- Salt and freshly ground black pepper to taste
- ¼ cup dry white wine
- 12 ounces penne
- ¾ ounce white truffle

In an earthenware pot large enough to hold the pasta, sauté the pancetta in the olive oil. When the pancetta is golden, add the mushrooms and peas and cook, stirring frequently, for 5 minutes. Season with salt and pepper and add the wine, then cook until evaporated. Set aside to cool.

Bring a large pot of salted water to a boil and cook the pasta al dente. Drain and add to the pot with the mushrooms. Cook, tossing, over high heat to combine. Divide among earthenware serving dishes and shave the truffle over the top.

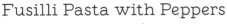

FUSILLI A CIAMBOTTELLA

Fusilli Pasta with Peppers

Antica Trattoria Di Pietro, Melito Irpino
(Avellino), Campania

iambottella is a sauté of summer vegetables (peppers, eggplant, potatoes, garlic, onion, zucchini) with a little tomato sauce. Here it is used as a topping for homemade fusilli.

SERVES 4

- 3   cups semolina flour
- 4   large eggs
- Salt to taste
- 4   cloves garlic
- Extra-virgin olive oil for sautéing
- 2   red bell peppers, cut into julienne
- 2   yellow bell peppers, cut into julienne
- 1   chili pepper, minced
- 2   pounds plum tomatoes, chopped
- 2   basil leaves

To make the pasta, sift the flour onto a work surface and shape into a well. Place the eggs in the center of the well with a pinch of salt and enough water to make a compact but soft dough. Bring in the flour from the sides of the well, then knead the dough until very well combined. Pinch off a piece of dough and roll into a thin rope, then cut into 1-inch lengths. Repeat with remaining dough. Curl fusilli by wrapping around a knitting needle and rolling lightly across the work surface. They should form a coiled shape. As they are shaped, slip them from the knitting needle and transfer to a kitchen towel.

For the sauce, in a skillet sauté the garlic in oil and then add the bell peppers. Cook for a few minutes, then add the chili pepper and the tomatoes. Cook over medium heat for 20 minutes, then season with salt and tear in basil leaves.

Bring a large pot of salted water to a boil and cook the pasta al dente, then drain and add to the skillet with the pepper mixture. Toss over medium heat to combine and serve.

PENNE AL POLLO SCAPPATO

Penne with Chicken-That-Got-Away Sauce

Trattoria da Burde, Firenze, Toscana

*n Italy there is a long tradition of dishes like this one that simulate the presence of more expensive ingredients (namely meat) without actually including them. (These days, the copious amount of olive oil used may be as expensive as chicken.) If you like, you can whisk a little butter into the finished sauce until it melts or serve this over egg noodles rather than dried semolina pasta.

SERVES 8

- 2   medium yellow onions, minced
- 2   carrots, minced
- 2   ribs celery, minced
- 2   cloves garlic, minced
- 1   cup extra-virgin olive oil
- ¼   cup red wine
- 2   tablespoons tomato paste
- Salt and freshly ground black pepper to taste
- 1½ pounds penne rigate
- Grated cheese for serving (optional)

Sauté the onions, carrots, celery, and garlic in the olive oil. When they are nicely browned, add the wine and cook until evaporated, then stir in the tomato paste. Season with salt and pepper and cook over very low heat until very dense, 40 to 50 minutes. If the contents of the pan begin to stick and scorch, add water in very small amounts.

Bring a large pot of salted water to a boil and cook the pasta, then toss with the sauce. Serve grated cheese on the side, if using.

ZITI AL RAGÙ NAPOLETANO 🐖
Ziti with Neapolitan Meat Sauce
Antonio Tubelli, Napoli, Campania

In another era, the air of Napoli was filled with the scent of this long-cooking sauce on Saturday evenings. The sauce cooks achingly slowly so that the meat contributes all of its tasty juices. The most important ingredients are time and patience. To make the sauce, in a pot with high sides, heat ¼ cup extra-virgin olive oil and add 10 ounces each of roughly chopped pork leg (the meaty muscle from the lower portion), roughly chopped veal leg (same), and pork ribs and brown for a few minutes. Gradually add 1 cup red wine, allowing the liquid to evaporate between additions. Dissolve 1 tablespoon pepper paste (sweet, not spicy) in a little water and add to the pot. Cook for a few more minutes, then add 5½ quarts San Marzano tomato puree. Season with salt and pepper and cook, uncovered, over medium heat for 2 hours, keeping a close watch on the pot. After 2 hours, remove the ribs (they should be tender but not falling apart), turn the heat down as low as possible, and cook with the lid on the pot but ajar (place a wooden spoon under the lid on one side to prop it up a bit). The sauce should be at the barest simmer—there is a special verb for this in local dialect, *peppiare*, which references the almost imperceptible bubbling sound that a pipe makes when you draw on it. In other words, a bubble should break the surface of your sauce only very occasionally. Cook this way for 4 additional hours, keeping a close eye on it to be sure the bottom of the pot doesn't begin to scorch. When the sauce is cooked, remove the meat. Cook ziti pasta al dente in boiling salted water and top with some of the sauce. Serve each portion with a piece or two of meat and some grated Parmigiano Reggiano.

CANDELE CON LA GENOVESE 🧅
Candele with Long-Cooked Onion and Meat Sauce
Trattoria da Rispoli, Amalfi (Salerno), Campania

No one knows why this meat sauce from the Campania region is called "Genovese," after a city far to the north. One theory is that it was invented by a chef from Geneva, not Genova. *Candele* are tubes of dried semolina pasta similar to ziti but longer. (If you can't track down candele, you can use ziti as a substitute.) The traditional cut of beef to use for this is the meaty muscle from the leg.

SERVES 6 TO 7
- 2 pounds yellow onions, thinly sliced
- 10 ounces beef, diced
- 1 cup extra-virgin olive oil
- Salt to taste
- ½ cup dry white wine
- 1½ pounds Gragnano candele (see note)
- Grated Parmigiano Reggiano for serving

Combine the onions, beef, and oil in a large pot and place over medium heat. Brown the meat on all sides, season with salt, then cook for 1 hour 30 minutes, adding the wine and then water in small amounts and letting each addition evaporate before you add the next one. When the onions have broken down into a puree and the mixture is a deep, rich brown, it is ready.

Mark the candele into halves or thirds using the tip of a paring knife, then break along the lines you marked. (That way they won't splinter.) Bring a large pot of salted water to a boil, cook the pasta al dente, drain, and toss with the sauce. Serve hot with grated Parmigiano on the side.

FAVÒ
Short Pasta with Fava Beans
Bar à Fromage, Cogne (Aosta), Valle d'Aosta

This is one of the few pasta dishes native to the Valle d'Aosta region, and it comes from Ozein, a tiny town up in Aymavilles. This area's cuisine borrows heavily from that of the Piemonte region, which is connected to it via numerous mountain passes. Make the tomato sauce for this recipe by sautéing minced onion, carrot, celery, garlic, and sage in a little olive oil, then adding fresh tomatoes pureed with a food mill and simmering until thickened.

SERVES 4
- 3   cups fresh shelled fava beans, peeled
- 1   piece (about 2 inches by 3 inches) whole-wheat bread, cut into cubes
- 3   tablespoons unsalted butter
- Salt to taste
- 7   ounces ditali or other short pasta
- ¼   cup tomato sauce
- 4   ounces fontina cheese, diced or thinly sliced

In a large pot, boil the fava beans in (unsalted) water to cover until tender. There should be very little water left in the pot. Set aside fava beans and cooking water in the pot. In a small skillet, toast the bread cubes in the butter until lightly browned. Bring a large pot of salted water to a boil and cook the pasta al dente. Drain pasta and add to the pot with the fava beans. Over medium heat, stir in the tomato sauce and the fontina. Cook, stirring, for 1 additional minute, then serve with the toasted bread scattered on top.

PACCHERI CON PANCETTA E PISTACCHI
Paccheri with Pancetta and Pistachios
Ristorante Il Vecchio Castagno, Serrastretta (Catanzaro), Calabria

Paccheri are short tubes of dried semolina pasta that are used throughout southern Italy. The pistachios from Bronte, a town on the slopes of Mount Etna, are particularly flavorful, with grassy and mineral undertones.

SERVES 4
- ¾   cup Bronte pistachios (see note), ground
- Extra-virgin olive oil for sautéing
- ⅓   cup rice flour
- 4   ounces thinly sliced pancetta
- Salt to taste
- 1   pound paccheri (see note)
- ½   cup grated aged sheep's cheese

Place the pistachios in a skillet with a little oil and the rice flour and toast over low heat, stirring constantly with a wooden spoon, for 5 minutes. Add the pancetta and cook for 1 additional minute.

Bring a large pot of salted water to a boil and cook the pasta al dente. Drain the pasta but not completely and add it to the skillet with the pistachios. Toss over medium heat to combine, then sprinkle with cheese and serve.

CALAMARATA CON TOTANI E ZUCCHINI
Pasta with Calamari and Zucchini
Hostaria Il Brigante, Salerno, Campania

alamarata are dried semolina pasta rings that look like the sliced tubes of calamari bodies, hence the name. They are often paired with calamari for a verbal and visual pun.

SERVES 6

- 2 pounds calamari
- Salt to taste
- ¼ cup extra-virgin olive oil
- 2 cloves garlic
- ½ cup dry white wine
- 4 cherry tomatoes, lightly crushed
- 1½ pounds (4 to 6) zucchini
- ½ medium yellow onion, thinly sliced
- Freshly ground black pepper to taste
- Leaves of 1 sprig parsley, minced
- 1 pound calamarata

Remove the ink sacs and eyes from the calamari if they haven't already been removed. Rinse and dry thoroughly, then use kitchen shears to cut the bodies into rings. Cut any large heads into strips and place the heads in a pot with water to cover by a couple of inches. Season with salt and simmer to make a broth. Reserve both broth and cooked heads.

In a pot with high sides and two handles, cook the calamari rings over high heat until they give up their liquid. Add 2 tablespoons olive oil and the garlic and cook until the garlic browns, then remove and discard the garlic. Add the wine and cook until evaporated, then add the tomatoes and cook, covered, over medium heat. While the calamari are cooking, slice the zucchini into rounds, removing a little of the center. Place the zucchini and onion in a saucepan and cook over medium heat. When they have given up their liquid, add the remaining 2 tablespoons olive oil and brown over medium heat.

Add the zucchini and onions to the calamari mixture. Cook over medium heat, moistening with a little of the prepared broth if the pot looks dry. When the mixture is heated through, add the heads, season with salt and pepper, and sprinkle with about half of the parsley.

Bring a large pot of salted water to a boil for the pasta and cook it al dente. Drain the pasta and add to the pot with the calamari. Toss to combine, then garnish with remaining parsley and serve.

VERMICELLONI ESTIVI
Summer Vermicelloni with Eggplant, Peppers, Tomatoes, and Basil
Marco Lombardo, Milazzo (Messina), Sicîlia

*B*rown crushed garlic cloves in extra-virgin olive oil, then remove and discard garlic and add cubes of eggplant (salted and drained of their bitter liquid). Cook briefly, then add peeled and seeded tomatoes that you have forced through a sieve. Season with salt and pepper and add strips of roasted bell peppers, chopped black olives, minced anchovy fillets, and a couple spoonfuls of capers. Cook, stirring frequently, until vegetables are soft, then stir in torn basil leaves and remove from the heat. Cook vermicelloni (a slightly thicker spaghetti) in boiling salted water until al dente, then drain and transfer to a bowl. Spoon the vegetables over the pasta, toss to combine, sprinkle with grated aged sheep's cheese, and serve.

PACCHERI CON PATATE E COZZE 🦪
Paccheri with Potatoes and Mussels
Ristorante La Torre, Massa Lubrense (Napoli), Campania

Be sure to clean the mussels thoroughly before beginning to cook the dish.

SERVES 4

7   ounces (1 to 2 medium) potatoes
1   pound mussels
Salt to taste
14 ounces paccheri
2   cloves garlic
Extra-virgin olive oil for sautéing
Freshly ground black pepper to taste
½   cup minced parsley

Boil the potatoes in salted water until tender enough to pierce with a paring knife. When cool enough to handle, peel and dice. Place the mussels in a pot with a small amount of water and cook over medium heat until opened. (Discard any mussels that refuse to open.) Remove the meat from the shells and set aside. Strain any cooking liquid and reserve.

Bring a large pot of salted water to a boil to cook the pasta. Meanwhile, make a sauce. In a skillet large enough to hold the pasta, brown the garlic in oil. Add the mussel meat and the diced potatoes. Add about ¼ cup of the cooking liquid from the mussels. Season to taste with salt and pepper. (You may not need salt as the mussels are naturally salty.) Sprinkle with some of the parsley and cook for a few minutes to combine.

When the pasta is cooked al dente, drain it and add it to the skillet. Toss over medium heat to combine, but don't let the pan dry out. Sprinkle with the remaining parsley and serve.

MANICHE DI FRATE CON SALSICCIA E CAVOLFIORI 🐖
Monk's Sleeves Pasta with Sausage and Cauliflower
Ristorante La Briciola di Adriana, Grottaferrata (Roma), Lazio

Maniche di frate are "monks' sleeves," wide tubes of dried semolina pasta very similar to paccheri.

SERVES 4

1   pound (1 small head) cauliflower, chopped
1   clove garlic
Ground chili pepper to taste
¼   cup extra-virgin olive oil
2   pork sausages, casings removed and crumbled
Salt to taste
½   cup dry white wine
10 ounces maniche di frate
3   tablespoons grated Parmigiano Reggiano and grated aged sheep's cheese

In a large skillet, brown the cauliflower with the garlic and chili pepper in 2 tablespoons of the oil. In another skillet, cook the sausage in the remaining oil until browned, then add to the cauliflower. Season with salt to taste and add the wine, then cook over low heat, covered, for about 20 minutes. Check to be sure the ingredients don't stick to the pan.

Blend the contents of the skillet into a puree. If it seems too thick, add water a little at a time until it is the correct consistency. Keep warm.

Bring a large pot of salted water to a boil for the pasta. Cook the pasta until al dente, then drain and add to the skillet with the puree. Toss over medium heat for a few minutes. Sprinkle on the cheese, mix to combine, and serve.

PASTA ALLA NORMA

Pasta with Eggplant, Tomatoes, and Ricotta

Ristorante Metrò, Catania, Sicîlia

Composer Vincenzo Bellini, a native of Catania, wrote his wildly successful opera *Norma* in 1831. In his book *Il libro d'oro della cucina e dei vini di Sicilia* (The Golden Book of Sicily's Food and Wine), Pino Correnti recounts that it became a great compliment in Catania to say that something was a "Norma," meaning it was a masterpiece. He goes on to recount that in the fall of 1920, writer and producer Nino Martoglio was served a dish of pasta and eggplant cooked by Saridda D'Urso at a lunch attended by journalists and performers, and after one taste he declared, "This is a real Norma." The name stuck.

SERVES 5

- 2 eggplant
- Salt to taste
- 3⅓ pounds plum tomatoes, peeled and chopped
- 2 cloves garlic
- Extra-virgin olive oil for drizzling and pan-frying
- 4 to 6 leaves basil
- 1 pound spaghetti or penne
- 2 cups grated ricotta salata

Peel the eggplant, slice them, and soak them in salted water for at least 1 hour to purge them of their bitter liquid.

In an earthenware pot, combine the tomatoes and garlic and cook over very low heat until they have thickened. Remove from the heat, then drizzle in olive oil and tear in half of the basil leaves. Pan fry the eggplant in several inches of oil until golden brown and drain on paper towels.

Bring a large pot of salted water to a boil and cook the pasta al dente. Transfer to a serving bowl. Add the tomato sauce and mix. Divide the pasta among individual serving bowls and top each with some of the eggplant, a portion

of the grated cheese, and the remaining basil leaves, torn if large.

PASTA ALLO SCARPARIELLO

Shoemaker's Pasta with Fresh Tomatoes

Ristorante Arcara, Cava de' Tirreni (Salerno), Campania

This quick and easy dish is eaten all over Campania. Legend has it that shoemakers prepared it for a quick lunch before getting back to work.

SERVES 4

- 2 cloves garlic
- 1 piece chili pepper
- Leaves of 1 sprig basil
- ¼ cup extra-virgin olive oil
- 1 pound 5 ounces (about 1½ pints) grape or cherry tomatoes, seeded and chopped
- Salt to taste
- 14 ounces short Gragnano pasta
- ½ cup grated aged sheep's cheese
- ¾ cup grated Parmigiano Reggiano

In a skillet large enough to hold the pasta, sauté the garlic, chili pepper, and 4 basil leaves in the olive oil over low heat. Add the tomatoes, season with salt, and cook until soft, 12 to 15 minutes.

Meanwhile, bring a large pot of salted water to a boil and cook the pasta al dente. Drain and add to the skillet with the tomatoes. Sprinkle on the cheese and toss over the heat to combine. Garnish with a few more basil leaves and serve.

ORECCHIETTE CON LE BRASCIOLE 🐄
Orecchiette with Veal Rolls
Ristorante Peppe Zullo, Orsara di Puglia (Foggia), Puglia

Puglia's famous orecchiette are traditionally made by hand. You can make your own fairly easily: combine 1⅔ cups unbleached all-purpose flour and ⅔ cup semolina flour. Shape into a well and add enough warm salted water to make a firm dough. Pull off pieces of the dough and roll into ropes about ¾ inch thick, then slice those (a few at a time) and drag them one by one across a floured work surface with your thumb. They should form into a cup shape with an indentation in the middle and a thicker rim around the outside. Let them rest for a couple of hours before cooking.

SERVES 4
- 14 ounces veal fillet
- 20 mint leaves
- 1½ cups grated Pecorino Pugliese
- 1 clove garlic, minced
- Extra-virgin olive oil for drizzling and sautéing
- ¼ cup red wine
- 1⅓ cups tomato puree
- Salt to taste
- 12 ounces orecchiette (or a batch made following instructions in note)

Slice the veal into 8 thin slices and top each with a mint leaf, a little of the grated cheese, and a few drops of oil. Roll them up and seal with toothpicks.

In a skillet, sauté the minced garlic in olive oil. Add the veal rolls. Brown on both sides, then add the wine and let it evaporate. Add the tomato puree and cook over medium heat for 30 minutes. Season with salt.

Meanwhile, bring a large pot of salted water to a boil and cook the pasta al dente. Drain the pasta and transfer to a serving dish. Top the pasta with the sauce and veal rolls, sprinkle on the remaining grated cheese, and serve hot.

TUBETTI CACIO E UOVA 🌿
Tubetti Pasta with Cheese and Egg
Antonio Tubelli, Napoli, Campania

Melt some lard in a skillet and add al dente tubetti pasta. Sprinkle in grated aged sheep's cheese, lemon juice, minced parsley, beaten eggs, and a generous dose of freshly ground black pepper and toss over low heat until the eggs firm up. Serve immediately.

PASTA CON I TENERUMI 🌿
Broken Spaghetti with Tenerumi Greens
Filippa Gatì, Palermo, Sicilia

Tenerumi greens are the leaves of cucuzza squash plants. Cucuzza is a long, pale green squash native to Sicilia. Boil a generous amount of tenerumi greens for 20 minutes, then remove with a skimmer or slotted spoon, chop, and set aside, reserving cooking water. In a large skillet, sauté garlic and a crumbled dry chili pepper. Add the cooked greens and some diced sun-dried tomato and cook for about 10 minutes. Meanwhile, break spaghetti in half or thirds and cook in boiling salted water until al dente. Drain the pasta and add to the skillet. Toss over medium heat for a few minutes. The mixture should be fairly loose, not stiff. Add some of the cooking water from the greens to thin if necessary. Sprinkle on shavings of caciocavallo or aged sheep's cheese and serve hot.

PASTA C'ANCIOVA E MUDDICA ATTURRATA 🌿
Pasta with Anchovies and Breadcrumbs
Trattoria Ai Cascinari, Palermo, Sicîlia

*S*trattu is a preserve that is made by drying salted cooked tomatoes in the sun and then forcing them through a sieve.

SERVES 4

- 1 tablespoon strattu (see note)
- ¼ cup tomato paste
- 2 cloves garlic, minced
- ¼ cup plus 1 tablespoon extra-virgin olive oil
- 2 teaspoons anchovy paste
- 4 salted anchovies, rinsed, boned, and chopped
- 3 tablespoons raisins
- 3 tablespoons pine nuts
- Salt and freshly ground black pepper to taste
- 1 pinch sugar or to taste
- ¼ cup plus 1 tablespoon breadcrumbs
- 1 fresh bay leaf, minced
- 12 ounces tripolini

Dissolve the strattu and the tomato paste in about 1 cup water in a small saucepan. Bring to a boil and simmer briskly for 20 minutes.

In a large skillet, sauté the garlic in ¼ cup olive oil. Add the anchovy paste and the anchovies and cook over low heat until the anchovies have dissolved. Add the tomato paste mixture, the raisins, and the pine nuts. Season very lightly with salt (the anchovies are salty) and season with pepper. Stir in 1 pinch sugar.

In a small skillet, toast the breadcrumbs and minced bay leaf in the remaining 1 tablespoon oil, stirring frequently so that they brown without burning. Bring a large pot of salted water to a boil and cook the pasta al dente. Drain the pasta and add to the skillet. Sprinkle on the toasted breadcrumbs and toss briefly to combine, then serve.

PASTA CON LE SARDE 🌿
Pasta with Sardines and Fennel
Osteria Paradiso, Palermo, Sicîlia

*L*ike many dishes from western Sicily, this one evokes its Arab roots with a combination of savory and sweet ingredients. This dish is made with wild fennel, sometimes labeled "mountain fennel" in Sicily, which is all stem and no bulb.

SERVES 6

- 1 pound wild fennel stalks
- Salt to taste
- 1 medium yellow onion, diced
- ½ cup raisins
- ¼ cup pine nuts
- 6 small salted anchovies, rinsed, boned, and chopped
- Extra-virgin olive oil for sautéing and drizzling
- Freshly ground black pepper to taste
- 2 to 3 threads saffron
- 1 pound small fresh sardines, filleted
- 1 pound bucatini
- ¼ cup breadcrumbs toasted in olive oil (optional)
- 1 teaspoon sugar (optional)

Blanch the fennel in salted water until tender and drain, reserving cooking water. In a skillet, sauté the onion, raisins, pine nuts, and anchovies in olive oil. Chop the blanched fennel stalks and add to the skillet with a little of the fennel cooking water. Season with pepper and crumble in the saffron. Cook over medium heat, stirring frequently, for 10 minutes, then add the sardines. Cook, stirring frequently, for an additional 15 minutes, then drizzle with additional olive oil.

Bring a large pot of salted water to a boil and cook the pasta very al dente, then drain the pasta and add to the pot. Cook, tossing, over medium heat for a few minutes, incorporating the breadcrumbs and sugar, if using.

PASTA PATATE E PROVOLA 🍅
Simmered Pasta with Potatoes and Provolone
Ristorante L'Europeo di Mattozzi, Napoli, Campania

This is one of the rare recipes that does not call for boiling pasta in salted water or broth, but instead cooks it right in the skillet, where the starch from the pasta contributes to a silky sauce. It is also a good way to use up odds and ends of pasta, though it's best to stick to those that share similar cooking times.

SERVES 4 OR 5

- 2 ounces lardo (cured fatback)
- 1 large yellow onion
- 1 small carrot
- 1 rib celery
- ¼ cup extra-virgin olive oil
- 8 piénnolo or other cherry tomatoes, lightly crushed
- 1 pound (about 3) potatoes, peeled and diced
- Salt to taste
- 14 ounces mixed short dried semolina pasta
- Freshly ground black pepper to taste
- 3 tablespoons grated Parmigiano Reggiano
- 2 cups smoked provolone cubes
- 4 to 6 leaves basil

Mince together the lardo, onion, carrot, and celery and in a pot brown in the olive oil. Add the tomatoes and the potatoes and simmer, adding small amounts of water if necessary to keep the pan from drying out. When the potatoes are about halfway cooked, add 1 cup warm water and salt. When it boils, add the pasta and stir. Cook as you would risotto, stirring constantly and adding warm salted water in small amounts as the previous addition is absorbed. Remove from the heat when the pasta is almost cooked but still fairly al dente.

Transfer the potato and pasta mixture to a sauteuse or any other skillet with high sides that you don't mind serving at the table. Place over medium heat and continue to cook while

stirring in black pepper, grated Parmigiano, and provolone. Tear in the basil and once the provolone has melted, serve immediately.

PASTA LORDA
Pasta with Meat and Eggplant
Ristorante Nangalarruni, Castelbuono (Palermo), Sicilia

In Sicilia, ragù is made with a mix of pork and beef and sometimes incorporates small meatballs and/or sausage. Basil is a must, as is a high-quality flour-and-water pasta.

SERVES 4

- 1 medium yellow onion, thinly sliced
- Extra-virgin olive oil for sautéing and frying
- 7 ounces beef, cut into cubes
- 7 ounces pork, cut into cubes
- ½ cup red wine
- ¼ cup tomato puree
- Salt to taste
- 2 eggplant, sliced
- 14 ounces pasta
- Leaves of 1 sprig basil
- Grated ricotta salata to taste

In a pot, sauté the onion in oil with the meat. Add the wine and cook until evaporated, then stir in the tomato puree and cook over low heat until the meat is very tender and falls apart easily at the touch of a fork. Season with salt.

While the meat is cooking, fry the eggplant slices and drain on paper towels.

Bring a large pot of salted water to a boil for the pasta and cook the pasta al dente. Drain and transfer to a serving bowl. Top with the sauce and the meat, shredding the meat slightly if it's not already broken down. Add the fried eggplant and sprinkle on the basil and grated ricotta salata.

CORSETTI AL POLPO
Figure Eight Corsetti Pasta with Octopus
Trattoria Barisone, Genova, Liguria

There are three different types of pasta that in Liguria go by the name *corsetti* (sometimes rendered as *corzetti, crosetti,* or *croxetti*). The type used here are little ovals of pasta that are dragged along the work surface (similar to orecchiette) and then squeezed into a figure eight. Though they are tiny—no larger than a fingernail—and small pasta is almost exclusively eaten in soup in Italy, these are eaten in a sauce.

SERVES 6

- 2 cloves garlic, minced
- ⅓ cup pine nuts
- 3 bay leaves
- ¼ cup Taggiasca olives, pitted
- Extra-virgin olive oil for sautéing and drizzling
- ½ cup dry white wine
- 1 octopus, chopped
- 1 pound tomatoes, diced
- Salt to taste
- 2 teaspoons sugar
- Leaves of 1 sprig parsley, minced
- 3 tablespoons unsalted butter
- 1 pound corsetti (see note)
- Freshly ground black pepper to taste

In a pot, sauté the garlic, pine nuts, bay leaves, and olives in olive oil. Add the wine and cook, stirring frequently, until evaporated. Add the octopus and tomatoes and 2 cups water. Cook, covered, over low heat until tender, about 1 hour. If the pan is dry but the octopus is not yet tender, add a small amount of water. Season with salt, sprinkle in the sugar, and sprinkle on the parsley. Add the butter and stir until melted.

Bring a large pot of salted water to a boil and cook the pasta al dente. Drain and add to the pot with the octopus. Cook, tossing, until well combined, then divide among individual serving bowls. Top with a drizzle of olive oil and a generous amount of black pepper.

SAGNE CON SALSICCIA E PANCETTA
Sagne Pasta with Sausage and Pancetta
Clarice Natelli, Castiglione Messer Marino (Chieti), Abruzzo

Sagne are diamonds of homemade pasta made by cutting wide ribbons of pasta at an angle. To serve 6 people, combine 2¾ cups 00 flour or unbleached all-purpose flour with 1¾ cups semolina flour and a pinch of salt. Shape into a well and knead in enough water (1½ to 2 cups) to make a pasta dough. Knead at length and divide into 3 equal logs of dough. Wrap 2 of the logs with plastic wrap and refrigerate, then immediately use a dowel-type rolling pin to roll 1 log of dough into a thin sheet the length of the rolling pin. When the dough is thin, leave it wrapped around the rolling pin in a cylinder and with a long knife make two cuts all the way through the dough along the length of the rolling pin. Sprinkle the resulting strips of dough with a tablespoon or so of semolina flour, stack them, then cut them at an angle to make diamonds about 1 inch long. Repeat with remaining logs of dough. To serve, place about 1 cup diced pancetta in a skillet with a little water and heat, then add 2 tablespoons extra-virgin olive oil and about 14 ounces dried sausage slices (casing removed) and sauté for a few minutes to heat through. Cook the sagne in boiling salted water one at a time or in small batches so that they don't stick, and remove with a slotted spoon or skimmer. Drain the pasta al dente, top with the pancetta and sausage mixture, toss to combine, and sprinkle with a little paprika before serving.

BUDELLETTI 🌿
Yeast-Risen Pasta with Guanciale or Tuna
La Cittadella dei Sibillini, Montemonaco (Ascoli Piceno), Marche

Budelletti are flour-and-water pasta with a twist: they contain a little yeast, which gives them an unusual texture. It's likely that at one time they were made with leftover bread dough. They are good with the guanciale sauce below and just as good with a sauce made by sautéing 1 clove garlic in about ¼ cup olive oil until browned, then removing the garlic and flaking in 8 ounces of canned tuna in olive oil (drained), ½ cup chopped black olives, 7 or 8 chopped anchovy fillets, and minced parsley.

SERVES 4
1   *cake compressed yeast or 3 teaspoons active dry yeast*
5½ cups unbleached all-purpose flour
Salt to taste
1   *cup diced guanciale (cured pork jowl)*
Freshly ground black pepper to taste
⅓   *cup grated aged pecorino cheese*
Leaves of 1 sprig parsley, minced

Dissolve the yeast in a little warm water until foamy. Shape the flour into a well on the work surface. Add a pinch of salt and the yeasted water to the well and begin pulling in flour from the sides of the well. Add as much water as needed to make a soft dough, then knead until compact and elastic. Shape the dough into a ball, cover with a damp kitchen towel (you don't want a skin to form on the top), and set aside to rise for about 1 hour. Roll the dough into a sheet about ¹/₁₀ inch thick and cut into strips 3 to 4 inches wide. Cut these crosswise into thin noodles. Set aside to rest on a floured work surface.

Bring a large pot of salted water to a boil and cook the pasta until it rises to the surface. Meanwhile, sauté the guanciale in a large skillet. When it begins to color, drain the pasta and add to the skillet. Toss vigorously over high heat. Transfer to a serving bowl and top with pepper, grated cheese, and parsley.

CORZETTI AVVANTAGGIATI 🎲
Enriched Corzetti with Green Beans
Ristorante Terme, Pigna (Imperia), Liguria

These corzetti are shaped like small butterflies or bowties. *Avvantaggiati* means "enriched," in this case with whole-wheat flour.

SERVES 6
2   *cups unbleached all-purpose flour or 0 flour*
2   *cups whole-wheat flour*
3   *large eggs, lightly beaten*
Salt to taste
7   *ounces green beans, trimmed and chopped*
3   *ripe tomatoes, diced*
Extra-virgin olive oil for drizzling
½   *cup grated Parmigiano Reggiano*

Combine the flours and shape into a well on the work surface. Place the eggs in the center with enough salted warm water to make a soft dough. Knead, pulling in flour from the sides of the well, until the dough is compact and well combined. With a rolling pin, on the work surface roll the dough out to a thin sheet and cut the sheet into pieces about 2½ inches by 1¼ inches. Pinch the long sides of each rectangle together to make a butterfly or bowtie shape.

Bring a large pot of salted water to a boil and add the green beans. Cook for 6 minutes, then add the pasta and cook, stirring frequently, until both beans and pasta are tender, 4 to 5 minutes. Drain the beans and pasta and transfer to a serving bowl. Scatter the tomatoes on top and drizzle with a little oil. Taste and adjust salt, then mix well. Sprinkle with Parmigiano, mix again, and serve.

CICATIELLI COL PULIEIO
Semolina Pasta with Tomatoes and Pennyroyal
Antica Trattoria Di Pietro, Melito Irpino (Avellino), Campania

Pennyroyal is an aromatic herb with small oval leaves. *Cicatielli* are also known as *cavatelli*. They are a classic homemade flour-and-water pasta of the South.

SERVES 4

- 2½ cups semolina flour
- Salt to taste
- 4 cloves garlic
- 5 ounces (5 to 6 packed cups) pennyroyal
- ¼ cup extra-virgin olive oil
- 2 large plum tomatoes, peeled, seeded, and cut into julienne
- 14 ounces (about 1 pint) cherry tomatoes
- 1 chili pepper

Form the flour into a well. Place 1 pinch salt in the center, then gradually add warm water to the center, pulling in flour from the sides of the well, until you have a soft, elastic dough. You will probably need ½ cup to 1 cup water, but the amount can vary. Knead until soft and well combined. Pull off a small piece of the dough and use your palms to roll it into a rope about ½ inch in diameter, then cut into ¾-inch lengths. Place a piece of dough horizontally in front of you on the work surface. Using your index finger and your middle finger, press the dough against the surface to thin it while also rolling it toward you. The dough should flatten out and then curl up: it will look like a hot dog bun. Repeat with remaining dough, transferring the pasta to a floured kitchen towel as you work.

To make the sauce, in a mortar and pestle crush the garlic and about two thirds of the pennyroyal. Transfer to a saucepan with ¼ cup olive oil and cook, stirring frequently, over low heat. Add the plum tomatoes and the cherry tomatoes and cook for 8 minutes. Add the chili pepper and the remaining pennyroyal leaves, season with salt, and cook for an additional 8 minutes.

Bring a large pot of salted water to a boil for the pasta and cook al dente. Drain pasta and toss with prepared sauce, then serve.

TRENETTE AL PESTO
Trenette Pasta with Pesto
Lorenza Costa, Camogli (Genova), Liguria

Pesto is probably Liguria's most famous contribution to cuisine. It is traditionally served over trenette pasta, thin flat noodles similar to linguine. Genovese basil, a DOP (Protected Designation of Origin) product, is best here. To serve 4 people, pluck the leaves from 4 bunches of basil, very gently so as not to crush them, and rinse and dry them. Place 1 to 2 cloves garlic in a mortar with a pinch of rock salt and grind with the pestle. Add the basil leaves and grind. Gradually add ¼ cup pine nuts, ¼ cup grated Parmigiano Reggiano, 2 tablespoons grated aged sheep's cheese, and 1 tablespoon butter, grinding to combine between additions. When the mixture has turned into a paste, taste and add a little fine salt if necessary, then transfer the mixture to a bowl and gently stir in extra-virgin olive oil in a thin stream until it has reached the proper consistency. You can do all of this in a blender, but the results will never be quite as good. If you do go that route, use the blender on low speed and stop frequently during the process so that the sauce does not heat up. This recipe gives you enough pesto to use with 14 ounces fresh trenette. Cook the pasta until al dente, drain, and transfer to a serving bowl. Thin the pesto with a tablespoon or so of the pasta cooking water, then toss with the pasta and serve immediately.

CARRATI AL RAGÙ DI PECORA 🌶
Semolina Pasta with Mutton Rolls and Walnut Sauce
Trattoria Masella, Cerreto Sannita (Benevento), Campania

This is an all-in-one dish, meaning that it makes both a pasta first course and then delicious rolls for a second course. Naturally, you can serve them together if you prefer. This recipe makes more pasta than you need. You will use 14 ounces, a little less than half. You can freeze the extra for longer storage. No need to thaw it out before cooking—just drop frozen pasta directly into boiling water.

SERVES 4

- 4¾ cups semolina flour, plus more for dusting surface
- 1 large egg
- ¼ cup extra-virgin olive oil, plus a drizzle for the dough
- Salt to taste
- 7 ounces sliced leg of mutton
- 2 cloves garlic, minced
- Leaves of 1 sprig parsley, minced
- 1 chili pepper, minced
- Freshly ground black pepper to taste
- 4 cups tomato puree
- 1 small yellow onion, peeled but left whole
- 12 walnuts, shelled
- 1 cup grated aged sheep's cheese

Make a dough with the semolina flour, the egg, a drizzle of oil, a pinch of salt, and as much water as you need to make the dough a good consistency. Pass pieces of the dough through the rollers of a pasta machine until you have rectangular sheets of pasta a little less than 1/10 inch thick. Cut into rectangles ¾ inch by 2 inches. One by one, wrap the noodles around a knitting needle and then decisively pull out the needle to make them into tubes. Spread on a flour-dusted surface and allow to dry.

While the pasta is drying, make mutton rolls. Spread the slices of mutton in a single layer on the work surface. Combine the garlic, parsley, and chili pepper and sprinkle this mixture evenly on the slices of mutton. Season with salt and pepper, roll up, and tie with kitchen twine. Arrange the rolls in the ¼ cup oil in an earthenware pot and brown on all sides. Season with salt and add the tomato puree and the onion. Cook over very low heat, barely simmering and stirring occasionally, for 2 hours. Grind the walnuts with a mortar and pestle.

Bring a large pot of salted water to a boil. Add 14 ounces of the pasta and cook, stirring occasionally, for 5 minutes. Place about ½ cup of the sauce in a large skillet over medium heat. Drain the pasta and add to the skillet. Stir in about half of the grated cheese and 1 tablespoon of the ground walnuts. Divide the pasta among individual serving bowls and top with the remaining sauce, walnuts, and grated cheese.

MALLOREDDUS ALLA CAMPIDANESE 🍅
Malloredus with Sausage
Ristorante Sa Domu Sarda, Cagliari, Sardegna

There is a special instrument for making *malloredus* called a *ciuliri*: it is a flat-bottomed basket hand-woven of thin reeds. The malloredus are pressed against it so that ridges form on the outside. You can use a ridged wooden board, a bamboo mat, or anything else you have on hand that will imprint lines into the dough, but do use something: those lines are more than just decoration; they serve to capture the sauce and help it cling to the pasta. This is traditionally served in a *scivedda*, an earthenware bowl with a flat bottom.

SERVES 4
- 2½ cups semolina flour
- 1 teaspoon salt, plus more to taste
- ¼ teaspoon ground saffron threads, plus 1 pinch
- 1 clove garlic
- 1 small yellow onion, minced
- Extra-virgin olive oil for sautéing
- 9 ounces fennel sausage, diced
- 1 cup Cannonau or other red wine
- 14 ounces ripe tomatoes, peeled, seeded, and chopped
- Grated Pecorino Sardo for serving

On a work surface, shape the flour into a well. Dissolve 1 teaspoon salt in about ½ cup lukewarm water and add to the center of the well. Begin to knead, pulling in flour from the sides of the well, and continue until you have a compact, smooth dough. Add a little more water if it feels dry. Divide the dough in half. Dissolve half of the saffron in 1 tablespoon water and sprinkle that on one of the pieces of dough, then knead briskly to work it in. The dough should be a uniform color. Shape each piece of dough into a ball, wrap in a kitchen towel, and set aside to rest for 1 hour.

In a skillet, sauté the garlic and onion in oil until golden. Add the sausage and brown over medium heat. Add the wine and cook until evaporated, then add the tomatoes. Season with salt, lower the heat, and cook, uncovered, for 20 minutes. Stir in a pinch of saffron and remove from the heat.

Roll pieces of the pasta dough into ropes about ⅕ inch in diameter and cut into ¾-inch lengths. Place one piece of dough on a ridged surface and press with your thumb, rotating it quickly so that the piece of dough both stretches into an oval and curls up on itself. Transfer to a platter or kitchen towel (lightly floured if necessary) and repeat with remaining pieces of dough.

Bring a large pot of salted water to a boil and cook the pasta al dente. Drain and transfer to a serving bowl. Toss with the prepared sausage mixture and sprinkle with grated cheese.

PICI ALLA NANA
Traditional Flour-and-Water Pici with Duck, Pork, and Beef
Trattoria La Solita Zuppa, Chiusi (Siena), Toscana

Pici are thick spaghetti made from flour, water, and salt. (If you are feeding a crowd, say more than 10, you may want to add an egg to the mix.) The dough must be kneaded very energetically and then shaped into a ball, oiled on the surface so it doesn't dry out, and allowed to rest for at least 1 hour. Roll the dough out to about ½ inch and cut into strips about ½ inch wide, then roll the strips under your palms to make thin cylindrical strands.

SERVES 4
- 1 carrot, minced
- 1 medium yellow onion, minced
- 1 rib celery, minced
- Extra-virgin olive oil for sautéing
- 5 ounces coarsely ground lean pork
- 5 ounces coarsely ground beef
- Meat of ¼ Muscovy duck, chopped
- 1 duck liver, rinsed in water and white wine vinegar, then chopped
- Salt and freshly ground black pepper to taste
- ½ cup dry white wine
- 1 tablespoon tomato paste dissolved in ½ cup warm water
- 9 ounces ripe tomatoes, peeled, or 1¼ cups canned peeled tomatoes
- Light broth for thinning sauce
- 12 ounces pici (see note)

In a pot, sauté the carrot, onion, and celery in a little olive oil until just softened and not browned. Add the pork, beef, duck, and liver. Season with salt and pepper (use a light hand) and brown. Over high heat, add the wine and cook until completely evaporated. Add the tomato paste and the tomatoes. Simmer over low heat until meat is cooked, adding broth in small amounts if the pot begins to look dry.

Bring a large pot of salted water to a boil and cook the pasta al dente. Drain, toss with the sauce, and serve.

STRASCINATE ALLA PEZZENTE
Strascinate with Sausage
Ristorante Le Botteghe, Matera, Basilicata

Strascinate are very similar to orecchiette but a little larger. (See page 155 for instructions for making orecchiette.) Pezzente is a kind of salami or dried sausage from Matera that has its own Slow Food Presidium. It is made using pork muscles, neck, nerves, and stomach, flavored with Senise pepper, chili pepper, fennel seed, and garlic. It's aged for fifteen to twenty days.

SERVES 4
- Extra-virgin olive oil for sautéing
- 1 small yellow onion, minced
- 1 cup diced pezzente salami (see note)
- 1 bay leaf
- 1 cup tomato puree
- Salt and freshly ground black pepper to taste
- 12 ounces fresh strascinate (see note)
- Aged sheep's cheese for grating

In an earthenware pot, heat a small amount of oil and sauté the onion until golden. Add the pezzente and the bay leaf and cook for 5 minutes, stirring frequently. Remove the bay leaf and add the tomato puree, season with salt and pepper, and cook over low heat for 8 minutes. The mixture should remain fairly loose.

Bring a large pot of salted water to a boil to cook the pasta. Cook for just a few minutes and drain when still quite al dente. Drain the pasta partially but not completely and add it to the pot. Cook, stirring, for a few more minutes until the flavors are combined and the pasta is fully cooked. Top with a generous amount of grated cheese and serve.

CUSCUS DI PESCE
Fish Couscous
Osteria Cantina Siciliana, Trapani, Sicilia

Though couscous is often mistaken for a grain, it is a type of semolina pasta, a staple in the western part of Sicilia, which displays a strong Arab influence. A couscoussier has two parts: a bottom pot for boiling water, and a steamer basket that sits on top and holds the couscous. The best type of bowl for finishing and serving the couscous is a *mafaradda*, an earthenware bowl with sloping sides and a flat bottom (a sort of inverted cone with a flat top). This is a complex one-pot meal, well worth the effort.

SERVES 6

3½ cups medium-grind semolina flour
Salt to taste
Ground cinnamon to taste
Leaves of 1 sprig parsley, minced
2 fresh bay leaves, minced
Extra-virgin olive oil for drizzling and
    sautéing
6½ pounds fish for soup, such as scorpionfish,
    Saint Peter's fish, hammerhead, grouper,
    carp, weever, and sea bream
1 medium yellow onion, thinly sliced
2 tablespoons tomato paste
2 to 3 cloves garlic, crushed with a mortar
    and pestle
Freshly ground black pepper to taste
3 to 4 basil leaves, torn
¼ cup ground almonds

Spread the semolina flour on a work surface. Fill a bowl with water and moisten your fingertips, then begin moving your hands counterclockwise in a spiral in the flour, frequently dipping your fingertips in the water to keep them damp. The flour should begin to clump into small balls. Transfer the clumped flour to a large earthenware bowl and sprinkle with a pinch of salt, a pinch of ground cinnamon, the parsley, the bay leaves, and a generous drizzle of olive oil. Mix by hand to coat and rub between your fingers to break up any large clumps and make the couscous consistent. Fill the bottom of a couscoussier with water and bring to a boil. Place the couscous in the top of the couscoussier. Roll up a damp kitchen towel and use it to seal the rim between the two parts of the couscoussier to keep steam from escaping. Place the top of the couscoussier in position and steam the couscous, uncovered, for 1½ hours.

Meanwhile, gut and fillet the fish. With the bones and other discards make a fish broth. In a pot, sauté the onion in a little olive oil until it begins to brown, then add the tomato paste, stir, and cook over low heat for 2 minutes. Add the garlic, salt, a pinch of ground cinnamon, pepper, and basil. Finally, add 12 cups water and stir to combine. Bring to a boil and add first the smaller fish and then the larger ones. Turn down the heat as low as possible and cook, covered, for 1 hour and 15 minutes. Remove the larger fish fillets and puree the smaller fish and the contents of the pot through a food mill. If the resulting puree feels overly thick, dilute with a small amount of water. It should be rather brothy.

When the couscous is cooked, transfer it to an earthenware bowl. Drizzle on ¾ cup to 1 cup of the fish broth, rake gently with a fork to distribute, cover with a dishtowel, and set aside to rest in a warm place for 40 minutes. Slice or chop the whole fish fillets and serve with the couscous. Sprinkle on the ground almonds, but serve the fish puree on the side and let diners help themselves.

PICI ALL'AGLIONE 🐚
Pici Egg Pasta with Garlic Sauce
Osteria Le Panzanelle, Radda in Chianti (Siena), Toscana

This recipe is a more "modern" take on pici, which traditionally, as noted in the recipe on page 163, do not include egg.

SERVES 4
- 6 cups unbleached all-purpose flour
- 2 large eggs, lightly beaten
- Salt to taste
- 2 tablespoons extra-virgin olive oil, plus more for oiling the work surface
- 8 to 10 cloves garlic, minced
- 1 tablespoon unsalted butter
- 2 cups grated aged pecorino cheese
- Freshly ground black pepper to taste

Shape the flour into a well on the work surface. Place the eggs in the center with a pinch of salt. Gradually add warm water, pulling in flour from the sides of the well, until you have a soft dough. Knead until compact. Shape into a ball, cover with a linen kitchen towel, and set aside to rest for 30 minutes. With a rolling pin, roll out the dough to a thin sheet (but not paper-thin), then cut the sheet of dough into thin strips. Lightly brush the work surface with a little oil, then roll the strips of dough on the surface into thin strings about as thick as spaghetti. Flour them lightly as you finish them to keep them from sticking.

Bring a large pot of salted water to a boil and cook the pasta. While the pasta is cooking, in a skillet sauté the garlic over very low heat in the butter and 2 tablespoons oil. When the garlic begins to turn golden, add about ¼ cup of the pasta cooking water to stop it from cooking.

Drain the pasta partly but not completely and add to the skillet. Sprinkle on the grated cheese and toss over medium heat until the pasta is coated in a creamy sauce. Sprinkle with black pepper and serve.

CAVATELLI CON RAGÙ DI POLPETTINE 🥕
Cavatelli Pasta with Small Meatballs
Trattoria L'Aquîla d'Oro, Cirò (Crotone), Calabria

This recipe breaks with tradition by incorporating egg into cavatelli dough. Leave plenty of time for the noodles to dry. If you don't have access to boar, use pork.

SERVES 6
- 6 cups semolina flour
- 4 large eggs
- Salt to taste
- 1 rib celery, minced
- 1 carrot, minced
- 1 medium yellow onion, minced
- Extra-virgin olive oil for sautéing
- 7 ounces ground boar meat (see note)
- 7 ounces ripe tomatoes, peeled and chopped, or ¾ cup tomato puree
- 7 ounces ground veal
- ¼ cup breadcrumbs
- 1 clove garlic, minced
- Leaves of 1 sprig parsley, minced
- Freshly ground black pepper to taste
- Grated aged ricotta or aged sheep's cheese (optional)

Make a dough with almost all of the flour, 2 of the eggs, a little water, and 1 pinch salt. Knead until compact and elastic. Cut off a piece of dough, roll it into a small cylinder, and cut into slices about ¾ inch thick. One by one, drag the pieces of dough across the work surface and let them curl up around your thumb, as for orecchiette. As the cavatelli are finished, sprinkle them with the remaining flour so they don't stick to each other and transfer them to a platter to dry for an entire day or overnight.

For the sauce sauté the celery, carrot, and onion in a little olive oil, then add the boar meat and tomatoes and cook over low heat until the meat is tender and sauce is thick, 1½ to 2 hours.

In a bowl combine the veal, the remaining 2 eggs, the breadcrumbs, the garlic, and the parsley. Season with salt and pepper. Shape into small meatballs and simmer them in the tomato sauce.

Bring a large pot of salted water to a boil and cook the pasta until the pieces begin to open up and are tender. Drain and add to the pot with the sauce. Sprinkle on cheese, if using, and serve.

CAVATELLINI CON FAGIOLI E COZZE 🌿
Small Cavatelli with Beans and Mussels
Osteria L'Antica Locanda, Noci (Bari), Puglia

You can purchase cavatelli or make your own following the recipe on page 160.

SERVES 4

1¾ cups dried beans, soaked for 12 hours
Salt to taste
2 pounds mussels
2 cloves garlic, minced
7 ounces plum tomatoes, peeled, seeded, and diced
Extra-virgin olive oil for sautéing
Freshly ground black pepper to taste
10 ounces small cavatelli
Leaves of 1 sprig basil, torn
Leaves of 1 sprig parsley, minced

Drain the beans and boil them in salted water until tender. Drain and set aside.

Cook the mussels, covered, over medium heat (or in the oven) until the shells open. (Discard any unopened mussels.) Shell the mussels. In a skillet, sauté the garlic and tomatoes in a little olive oil for 10 minutes, then add the shelled mussels. Season with salt and pepper. As soon as the mixture starts to boil, remove from the heat. Stir in the beans.

Bring a large pot of salted water to a boil and cook the pasta al dente. Drain and add to the pan with the mussels and beans. Sprinkle on basil and parsley and serve.

PILAU 🐟
Fregola Cooked Pilaf-Style with Seafood
Trattoria da Pasqualino, Calasetta (Carbonia-Iglesias), Sardegna

Fregola is like couscous with a very bumpy and irregular surface. Purchase readymade fregola or make your own as follows: Place 1¾ cups semolina flour in a large earthenware bowl with a flat bottom, spread thinly enough that you see the bottom of the bowl. Crumble a few threads of saffron into a bowl of lukewarm water. Moisten your fingertips in the saffron water and move them in a circular motion through the flour, spiraling from the outside to the center and dipping your fingers frequently in the water until the flour clumps into small balls. Let the fregola rest for a few hours before using.

SERVES 4

1 quart fish broth
1 medium yellow onion, thinly sliced
Extra-virgin olive oil for sautéing
2 cloves garlic, minced
¼ cup minced parsley
1 pound plum tomatoes, chopped, or 2 cups canned peeled tomatoes
1 pound clams, soaked in cold salted water for 2 hours to clean
1 pound mussels
1 pound large shrimp
12 ounces fregola (see note)
Salt to taste
Ground chili pepper to taste

Place the fish broth in a small saucepan and keep warm. In a large skillet, sauté the onion in a small amount of oil. When it turns golden, add the garlic and parsley, then the tomatoes and cook over medium heat for 10 minutes. Add the clams, mussels, shrimp, and fregola. Cook as you would a risotto, stirring constantly and adding small amounts of warm broth, then waiting until it has been absorbed before adding more. Season with salt and ground chili pepper.

MACARRONES FURRIAOS ❗
Semolina Pasta with Sage and Sheep's Cheese
Ristorante Ispinigoli, Ispinigoli di Dorgali (Nuoro), Sardegna

accarones are one of several types of semolina pasta on Sardegna. In the Nuoro area, they are made to look like little fists.

SERVES 6
- 2½ cups fine semolina flour, plus more for flouring towel
- Salt to taste
- 2 large eggs
- 11 ounces (about 2 cups) diced fresh sheep's cheese
- 3 to 4 threads saffron
- 5 sage leaves, minced
- 1 tablespoon unsalted butter

Form the semolina flour into a well on the work surface. Place a pinch of salt and the eggs in the center of the well and begin to knead, gradually pulling in flour from the sides of the well and adding enough water to make a soft but somewhat dry dough. Pinch off a piece of dough the size of a kidney bean and roll into a ball, then place on a ridged surface (you can use a flat-bottomed wicker basket) and press down with your thumb, pushing at the same time so that the pasta stretches and curls up. (It will resemble a hot dog bun.) As you shape the pieces, transfer them to a floured kitchen towel to rest.

Bring a large pot of salted water to a boil and cook the pasta al dente, 3 to 4 minutes. Drain thoroughly and return to the pot. Place the pot over low heat and stir in the cheese, the saffron, the sage, and the butter. Cook, stirring constantly, over low heat until the butter and cheese have melted and the ingredients are well combined. This should only take a minute or two. Serve piping hot in the pot.

ANDARINOS CON PURPUZZA E FIORE SARDO 🐖
Andarinos with Pork and Cheese
Trattoria Il Rifugio, Nuoro, Sardegna

piral andarinos are made with a special tool, but you can also use a ridged board or a wicker basket.

SERVES 4
- 8 ounces ground pork
- Salt to taste
- Freshly ground black pepper to taste
- ¼ cup minced wild fennel
- 1 clove garlic, minced
- 1 cup dry white wine
- ½ cup wine vinegar
- 1¾ cups semolina flour
- 1 spring onion, thinly sliced
- Extra-virgin olive oil for sautéing
- ¼ cup aromatic herbs such as wild thyme, rosemary, and bay leaf, minced
- 1½ cups grated Pecorino Sardo

In a bowl combine the pork, 2 pinches of salt, a pinch of pepper, the fennel, and the garlic. Mix to combine, then add ½ cup wine and vinegar. Mix by hand and refrigerate, covered, for 2 days, mixing occasionally.

On a work surface combine the semolina flour, a pinch of salt, and enough water to make a smooth and elastic dough. Knead until well combined. Pull off a small piece of dough and roll it into a thin rope, then cut into short pieces. Roll each piece on a ridged board, turning it into a spiral as you do. Set aside the pasta and allow to dry briefly.

In a skillet, brown the onion in a little oil. Add the meat (let any excess marinade drain away) and the remaining ½ cup wine and cook, stirring occasionally, until meat is cooked through.

Bring a large pot of salted water to a boil and cook the pasta al dente. Drain and add to the skillet. Stir in the herbs and grated cheese and toss over high heat for a few minutes.

EGG PASTA & OTHER HANDMADE PASTA

Come Fare La Pasta Fresca
How to Make Fresh Pasta

To make pasta dough, form the flour (or other dry ingredients) into a well on a work surface. Crack the eggs and/or any liquid ingredients into the well and whisk with a finger or small fork. Gradually draw in flour from the sides of the well until you have a crumbly dough surrounded by dry ingredients. Knead to combine. Clean your hands and work surface, then return the dough to the surface and knead it until it is compact and smooth, adding water or flour, respectively, about a tablespoon at a time, if it feels too dry or too wet. Knead the dough until it is consistent and smooth, about 10 minutes. Shape the dough into a ball, cover with an overturned bowl, and let it rest for at least 30 minutes.

To roll a sheet of pasta by hand, shape the dough into a rough circle on a lightly floured work surface. With a dowel rolling pin, start in the center and roll away from you to the outer edge. Turn the circle of dough a quarter-turn and repeat. When you have done this four times, continue rolling, turning the dough about one-eighth of the way around, until the sheet of dough is ⅛ inch thick or less. Scatter a small amount of flour on the dough if it sticks. Finish thinning the sheet of dough by wrapping three-quarters of the sheet around the rolling pin toward you, then unrolling it while running your hands across the sheet of dough, from the center of the rolling pin to the ends. Continue to do this, turning the dough between rolls, until the sheet is so thin it is somewhat transparent.

To cut a hand-rolled sheet of pasta dough into noodles, roll the sheet loosely into a flat cylinder. Cut the roll of dough into strips of the desired width, then gently lift them in the air and let them drop to separate them.

PAGLIA E FIENO ALLO SCALOGNO DI ROMAGNA
Green and Yellow Egg Pasta with Shallots

Osteria La Campanara, Galeata (Forlì-Cesena), Emîlia-Romagna

Romagna shallots have been grown in the area since the early 1900s and are an IGP (Protected Geographic Origin) product. The shallots are eaten fresh, but they are also dried in braids. Some are preserved in olive oil. Traditionally they were harvested on the night of June 23 (the eve of the feast of Saint John) and left to dry in the fields.

SERVES 4

7 ounces spinach
Salt to taste
2½ cups unbleached all-purpose flour
3 large eggs
1½ ounces lardo (fatback) or ¼ cup plus 1 tablespoon extra-virgin olive oil
4 cups thinly sliced Romagna shallots
6 ripe tomatoes, peeled, seeded, and diced
Freshly ground black pepper to taste

Blanch the spinach in salted water, drain, squeeze dry, and mince very finely. On the work surface, shape the flour into a well. Place the eggs in the center with a pinch of salt. Use a fork to beat the eggs and then gradually to pull in flour from the sides of the well. Knead by hand into a soft and well-combined dough. Divide the dough in half and knead the minced spinach into one piece until the color is uniform. Cover the dough and set aside to rest for 1 hour.

While the dough is resting, make the sauce. Mince the lardo until creamy, then sauté in a skillet and when it melts add the shallots. Turn the heat down as low as possible, cover, and cook for 30 minutes, adding water in small amounts to keep the mixture soft. It should not brown. Add the tomatoes and cook, uncovered, stirring occasionally, for 15 minutes. Season with salt and pepper.

Roll out the two pieces of dough into thin sheets. Place one on top of the other and without pressing too hard (you don't want to seal them, so sprinkle a small amount of flour in between if necessary to keep them from sticking), roll them into a cylinder. Cut them into thin noodles, about 1/10 inch wide or a little wider.

Bring a large pot of salted water to a boil and cook the pasta until it rises to the surface. Drain and transfer to the skillet with the shallots. Toss over low heat to combine and serve.

FOIADE CON FONDUTA DI STRACCHINO E ASPARAGI ●
Egg Noodles with Stracchino Cheese and Asparagus
Trattoria Dentella, Bracca (Bergamo), Lombardia

foiade are egg noodles, but every family in the Bergamo and Mantova areas seems to make them in a slightly different size and shape. In some areas, a portion of the wheat flour is replaced with cornmeal. They can be topped with everything from pork ribs to porcini mushrooms. Stracchino is a soft cow's milk cheese.

SERVES 6

7   ounces stracchino cheese (see note), diced
Whole milk to cover cheese
2¾ cups unbleached all-purpose flour or
      00 flour
⅔   cup semolina flour
2   large eggs, lightly beaten
2   tablespoons extra-virgin olive oil
Salt to taste
1   egg yolk
1   pound asparagus, stems peeled
Unsalted butter for sautéing
1   clove garlic, minced
Diced pancetta or pancetta strips crisped
      in butter (optional)

Place the stracchino in the top of a double boiler and add milk to cover. Set aside for 1 hour.

Combine the flours and shape into a well on the work surface. Place the eggs, olive oil, and a pinch of salt in the middle of the well and begin gradually pulling in flour from the sides of the well. Add enough water to make a soft dough that is on the dry side, then wrap it in a kitchen towel and set aside to rest for 30 minutes. Roll out the dough to 1/10 inch thick or a little thinner, then cut into squares, rectangles, or irregular shapes.

Place the saucepan with the cheese and milk over a double boiler filled with boiling water. Whisk in the egg yolk and cook, stirring constantly with a wooden spoon or whisk, over low heat until thickened. Take care that no lumps form—if they do, you can eliminate them using an immersion blender. Keep warm.

Tie the asparagus with kitchen twine and cook vertically (tips up) in a narrow, tall pot of boiling salted water until tender. Remove the kitchen twine and cut the stems into thin rounds, keeping the tips whole. Sauté the asparagus stems in butter with the garlic until golden. Season with salt.

Bring a large pot of salted water to a boil for the pasta. Cook al dente, then drain, reserving the cooking water. Toss the noodles with the cheese mixture and the asparagus stems, stirring in a little of the cooking water to coat the pasta smoothly. Divide among individual serving plates and garnish with the asparagus tips and the pancetta cubes or strips, if using.

TONNARELLI CACIO E PEPE 🍴
Tonnarelli with Cheese and Black Pepper
Enoteca Vino e Camino, Bracciano (Roma), Lazio

tonnarelli are egg noodles that look like square spaghetti. You can also make this dish using spaghetti. This preparation sounds simple, but it is greater than the sum of its parts. Bring a large pot of salted water to a boil and cook the pasta until very al dente. Meanwhile, in a skillet large enough to hold the pasta, sauté an unpeeled clove of garlic in a generous amount of olive oil. Discard garlic and add a generous amount of freshly ground black pepper. Add a good amount of the pasta cooking water and the drained pasta and toss over high heat until the pasta has absorbed all of the liquid. Remove from the heat and add a generous amount of grated Pecorino Romano cheese—about ½ cup for each serving of pasta—and toss vigorously. The cheese should melt and turn into a creamy sauce. Return to high heat for 1 minute, then divide among individual serving bowls and top with more pepper and cheese.

CANNEROZZI ALLO ZAFARANO
Semolina Egg Pasta with Saffron and Ricotta
Federico Valicenti, Terranova di Pollino (Potenza), Basilicata

In the fall of 2009, the Chamber of Commerce in Matera, Basilicata, held an event celebrating pasta and selected four types of local pastas to serve, including cannerozzi, which are short tubes of semolina egg pasta. Here they are paired with saffron and ricotta, but they are also delicious with chopped raw tomatoes, garlic, and basil; beans, guanciale (cured pork jowl), and hot pepper; mussels in tomato sauce; or baby octopus. To serve 4, make a pasta dough with 2 cups semolina flour, 3 eggs, and a pinch of salt. Roll into a thin sheet and cut into small squares, then shape the squares into tubes by wrapping them one by one around a knitting needle or skewer (or the special tool made for this purpose if you have one). Set aside to rest on a clean dishtowel floured with semolina flour. When you are ready to serve the dish, cook the pasta in a generous amount of boiling salted

water until al dente. (You can add a spoon-ful of olive oil to the water if you are afraid the pasta might stick together.) Heat a little extra-virgin olive oil in a skillet. Add 1 teaspoon saffron and stir until dissolved. Add 1¼ cups ricotta and stir with a wooden spatula to loosen and combine. If the ricotta is stiff, add a few tablespoons of the pasta cooking water to thin it a little. Drain the cooked pasta and add it to the skillet, season with a generous amount of freshly ground black pepper, and serve immediately.

FETTUCCINE CON REGA JE DI POLLO
Fettuccine with Chicken Livers
Taverna Mari, Marino (Roma), Lazio

Organ meats and the like have gone from the food of the poor to gourmet delicacies, in part due to delicious dishes like this one.

SERVES 4
- 1 spring onion, thinly sliced
- Extra-virgin olive oil for sautéing
- 10 ounces chicken livers, hearts, and gizzards, cleaned and diced
- ½ cup white wine
- 6 peeled tomatoes
- Salt and freshly ground black pepper to taste
- 14 ounces fettuccine
- 1 cup grated sheep's cheese
- 1 cup grated Parmigiano Reggiano

In a pot, sauté the onion in olive oil until golden. Add the livers, hearts, and gizzards and cook, stirring frequently, until browned. Add the wine and cook until evaporated, then add the tomatoes and season with salt and pepper. Cook over low heat for 1 hour.

Bring a large pot of salted water to a boil and cook the fettuccine. Drain, transfer to a serving bowl, and toss with the prepared sauce. Sprinkle with the grated cheese and serve.

TAJARIN ALLE 22 ERBE CON SUGO D'ANATRA ❦
Tajarin Noodles with 22 Herbs, Spices, and Greens and Duck Sauce
Ristorante Garibaldi, Cisterna d'Asti (Asti), Piemonte

Herbs and spices are the unsung heroes of the kitchen, and this dish places wild and cultivated herbs, spices, and greens center stage by incorporating them into pasta dough. The resulting noodles are beautiful. The chef recommends using no more than ⅓ ounce of each type by weight so that no one flavor or aroma will dominate the others. *Tajarin* are thin egg noodles.

SERVES 4

PASTA
2¾ cups stoneground unbleached all-purpose flour or 00 flour
4 large eggs, lightly beaten
1 tablespoon extra-virgin olive oil
Salt to taste
⅓ ounce each rosemary, bay leaf, sage, mint, thyme, marjoram, lemon verbena, oregano, fennel fronds, leaf celery, spinach, nettles, hops, borage, chard, fumitory, chives, parsley, and basil, minced together
Freshly ground black pepper to taste
Ground chili pepper to taste
Freshly grated nutmeg to taste

SAUCE
1 carrot, minced
1 medium yellow onion, minced
Leaves of 1 sprig rosemary, minced
1 rib celery, minced
¼ cup minced parsley
3 to 4 sage leaves, minced
Extra-virgin olive oil for sautéing
10 ounces boned duck leg, chopped
1 cup Marsala
Salt to taste
Minced fresh thyme to taste
Freshly grated nutmeg to taste
Freshly ground black pepper to taste

For the pasta, knead together the flour, the eggs, the olive oil, a pinch of salt, and the herbs, greens, and spices. Knead until well combined and then roll into a thin sheet. Allow to dry, then dust lightly with flour, roll into a cylinder, and cut into thin noodles.

For the sauce, in a skillet sauté the carrot, onion, rosemary, celery, parsley, and sage leaves in a small amount of oil until soft. Add the duck meat and when it begins to brown add the Marsala. Cook over medium heat until tender, at least 1½ hours. Season with salt, thyme, nutmeg, and pepper.

To serve, bring a large pot of salted water to a boil and cook the pasta. It should cook in just a few minutes. Drain the pasta and toss with the sauce in the skillet to combine.

STRANGOZZI CON ZUCCHINE, RICOTTA E TARTUFO ▼

Handmade Pasta with Zucchini, Squash Blossoms, Ricotta, and Black Truffle

Ristorante L'UmbriaCo, Acquasparta (Perugia), Umbria

This dish showcases some of the earthy ingredients that are the pillars of Umbria's cuisine: truffle and the slightly dry aged sheep's milk ricotta from Norcia. This cheese is aged with a coating of bran, and it looks like a humble potato but has a fantastically complex flavor. Truffle is never cooked but always added just before serving, and even the tender zucchini blossoms that appear here should not be exposed to heat for too long.

SERVES 4

PASTA

2½ cups semolina flour, plus more for dusting
1 large egg
2 teaspoons salt

SAUCE

1 cup white wine
1 shallot, minced
Extra-virgin olive oil for sautéing

½ cup vegetable broth
2 zucchini, seeded and cut into julienne
Minced chili pepper to taste
Salt to taste
1 cup grated Grana Padano cheese
12 zucchini blossoms, stems and pistils removed
Aged Norcia ricotta shavings for garnish
1½ ounces black summer truffle

For the pasta, knead together the semolina flour, about ¼ cup water, the egg, and the salt until you have a compact but elastic dough. Divide into 2 or 3 equal parts and on a work surface roll each into a sheet, then roll into a loose cylinder and cut into noodles a little more than ¹⁄₁₀ inch wide. Spread the noodles out on the work surface, dust with semolina flour, and set aside to dry for a couple of hours.

For the sauce, place the wine in a small saucepan and bring to a boil, then (very carefully) light the surface to burn off the alcohol. In a skillet, sauté the shallot in a small amount of oil until it just begins to sizzle, then add the wine

and cook until evaporated. Add the vegetable broth, the zucchini, and the chili pepper. Season with salt and cook until the zucchini are tender but still a little crisp, about 5 minutes.

Bring a large pot of salted water to a boil and cook the pasta until tender, 4 to 5 minutes, then drain and add to the skillet with the zucchini. Toss over medium heat while stirring in the grated cheese. Tear the zucchini blossoms in and stir to combine, then cook for just a few seconds more. Transfer to a serving bowl, garnish with the Norcia ricotta shavings, grate the black truffle on top, and serve immediately.

TALLARINUS BIANCHI E NERI AI FRUTTI DI MARE 🏮
Black and White Noodles with Seafood
Ristorante Sa Pischedda, Bosa (Oristano), Sardegna

This recipe feeds a crowd. If you are throwing a more intimate gathering, you can freeze fresh pasta and use it at a later date. No need to thaw it before cooking. The shrimp and scampi are cleaned but left in their shells. The cockles should be soaked in salted cold water for 2 hours to purge them of sand. Scrub the mussels thoroughly as well and remove their beards.

SERVES 10

PASTA
3   cups semolina flour
4   cups unbleached all-purpose flour
5   large eggs, lightly beaten
10 egg yolks
1   pinch salt
1½ teaspoons cuttlefish ink

SAUCE
14 ounces scampi
10 ounces Mediterranean shrimp
Extra-virgin olive oil for sautéing
4   cloves garlic
10 ounces mussels
7   ounces cockles or other small clams
10 ounces ripe San Marzano tomatoes,
     peeled and pureed
Salt to taste

For the pasta, combine the flours and form them into a well on the work surface. Place the eggs and yolks in the center with a pinch of salt. Begin to pull in the flour from the sides of the well and when you have a crumbly dough, knead until it is smooth and compact. If it feels dry, add a little water. Divide the dough into two equal pieces. Knead the cuttlefish ink into one piece of dough until evenly distributed. Wrap both pieces of dough in plastic wrap and set aside to rest.

In separate pots, cook the scampi and shrimp in a little oil with 1 clove garlic in each for 5 minutes. In a separate pot, uncovered, cook the mussels and cockles in a little oil with another clove of garlic over high heat until they open. Remove cockles and mussels from their shells and strain their cooking liquid.

In a large skillet, brown the remaining clove garlic in olive oil and add the pureed tomatoes and the cooking liquid from the shellfish and cook over medium heat for 5 minutes. Turn the heat as low as possible and add the shrimp and scampi, then the mussels and clams. Cook, stirring, until combined and the shrimp and scampi are cooked, 3 to 4 minutes. Taste and adjust salt.

Roll out the two pieces of pasta dough into thin sheets. Place one sheet on the work surface, brush with a little water, and place the other sheet on top. Roll over them with the rolling pin to seal. Cut into noodles about ⅕ inch wide. Bring a large pot of salted water to a boil and cook the pasta al dente. Drain and toss in the skillet with the sauce.

PASTA ARROSTITA 🐖
Blistered Pasta with Onion and Boccolaio
Ristorante Liviù, Tessano di Dipignano (Cosenza), Calabria

Make egg pasta dough and roll into a thin sheet. Cut the dough into triangles with 1½-inch sides. Cook the pieces of dough between 2 cast-iron griddles, one with ridges and one smooth (you may be able to find a hinged pan like a waffle iron; if so, use it), until speckled with burnt spots. Bring a large pot of salted water to a boil and cook the pasta triangles al dente, 4 to 5 minutes. Meanwhile, sauté thinly sliced onion in olive oil and add diced boccolaio to the skillet and cook until crisp. (*Boccolaio* is spicy cured pork jowl. If you can't find it where you live, use pancetta instead.) Drain the pasta and add to the skillet. Sprinkle with grated Parmigiano Reggiano and serve.

173

GARGANELLI ALLA RUSTICA
Garganelli with Sausage and Beans
Osteria di Piazza Nuova, Bagnacavallo (Ravenna), Emilia-Romagna

Garganelli are tubes of egg pasta that look like quills. They are always ridged. Mora Romagnola sausage is a pork sausage made from this heirloom breed of pigs.

SERVES 4

SAUCE
1   medium yellow onion, minced
1   carrot, minced
1   rib celery, minced
Extra-virgin olive oil for sautéing
3   Mora Romagnola sausages, casing removed and crumbled
1   tablespoon tomato paste
4   cloves garlic, chopped
Leaves of 3 sprigs rosemary, minced, plus more for garnish

⅔   cup dried borlotti beans, soaked overnight, soaking water reserved
½   cup Sangiovese wine (optional)
Salt to taste
1   tablespoon unsalted butter

PASTA
2   cups unbleached all-purpose flour or 0 flour
½   cup semolina flour
3   large eggs
1   pinch salt

To make the sauce, in a pot sauté the minced onion, carrot, and celery in olive oil until they being to brown. Add about ¼ cup lukewarm water and add the sausages. Brown for 2 minutes, then stir in the tomato paste and cook, covered, over the lowest possible heat until thickened, 1 to 2 hours. If the ingredients are sticking to the bottom of the skillet, add small amounts of water. Remove from the heat and keep warm. Meanwhile, sauté the garlic and the minced rosemary in a separate pot. Use a skimmer or slotted spoon to remove about half of the beans from their soaking water and add to the pot. Add about ½ cup of the soaking water from the beans as well. Cover and cook over low heat for 1½ hours, adding more of the soaking water as it evaporates. Add the remaining beans and continue cooking in the same way, adding small amounts of the soaking water, for an additional 1½ hours. Some of the beans should be so soft that they have broken down to form a puree, while the rest will be tender.

To make the pasta, on a work surface knead the flours with the eggs and a pinch of salt until compact and smooth. Cover with a kitchen towel and set aside to rest for 15 minutes. Roll out with a rolling pin very thin, less than 1/10 inch, and cut into squares with 1½-inch sides. Place a pasta square on the work surface so that one corner points toward you (a diamond). Place a thin dowel or skewer perpendicular to you so that it lines up with the top and bottom corners of the pasta. Wrap the square around the dowel or skewer, overlapping two corners at the center to seal. Roll the pasta on a ridged wooden board to make ridges in the outer surface. Slip off of the dowel or skewer and repeat with the remaining squares.

Add the cooked beans to the skillet with the sausage. Add the wine, if using, and stir to combine. Season with salt and cook, stirring occasionally, over low heat for 30 minutes so the flavors combine. Meanwhile, bring a large pot of salted water to a boil and cook the pasta al dente. Drain and add to the pot with the sauce. Toss over medium heat to combine for 2 to 3 minutes then stir in butter until melted. Garnish with fresh rosemary.

UMBRICELLI AL TARTUFO NERO
Umbricelli with Black Truffle
Trattoria La Palomba, Orvieto (Terni), Umbria

*U*mbricelli are thick spaghetti that pair beautifully with mushrooms and truffles. If you can't locate fresh porcini mushrooms, you can substitute a few button mushrooms. They won't be as flavorful or meaty, but the dish will still taste great.

SERVES 4

2¾ cups unbleached all-purpose flour or 00 flour
4 egg whites
1 pinch salt
2 cloves garlic, crushed
2 salted anchovies, rinsed, boned, and chopped
Extra-virgin olive oil for sautéing
2 porcini mushrooms, chopped
3 ounces black truffle
Leaves of 1 sprig parsley, minced
Salt to taste

On a work surface, shape the flour into a well. Place the egg whites and a pinch of salt in the center and begin to knead, incorporating enough water to make a compact and elastic dough. Shape the dough into a ball, place it in a bowl, cover with a kitchen towel, and set aside to rest for about 20 minutes.

In a skillet, sauté the garlic and anchovies in olive oil until the anchovies break down. Add the porcini and cook until they have given up their liquid and it has evaporated. Remove from the heat. Grate a little of the truffle on top and sprinkle on minced parsley, adjust salt to taste, and allow to cool.

Divide the pasta dough into 2 or 3 equal parts and roll each one out to a sheet a little less than ½ inch thick. Cut into strips about 1/10 inch wide and roll each one under your palms on the work surface so that they are round.

Bring a large pot of salted water to a boil, add the pasta, and cook until al dente, 7 to 8 minutes.

Drain. While the pasta is cooking, puree the mushroom mixture to a creamy consistency and return it to the skillet. Add the cooked pasta, toss to combine, then grate on the remaining truffle and serve.

FILEJA AL RAGÙ DI MAIALE
Long Egg Noodles with Pork Sauce
Ristorante Il Vecchio Castagno, Serrastretta (Catanzaro), Calabria

*F*ileja are long twisted noodles. To shape them, you wrap them around a thin wooden dowel or skewer. In summer they are served with fresh tomatoes, basil, and grated sheep's cheese. In winter they are more likely to appear in a meat sauce like the one below, served at this restaurant on the southeastern slope of the Sila Piccola mountain.

SERVES 4

1 cup semolina flour
1 cup unbleached all-purpose flour or 00 flour
1 large egg
Salt to taste
1 medium Tropea red onion, thinly sliced
Extra-virgin olive oil for sautéing
10 ounces pork, such as ribs, rind, and jowl, chopped
4 cups tomato puree
Freshly grated nutmeg to taste

Knead together both types of flour with the egg, a pinch of salt, and enough water to make a medium-soft dough. Roll into a sheet about 1/10 inch thick and cut into strips 1 to 1½ inches wide. Wrap each strip around a thin wooden dowel or skewer to make a tight spiral, pressing lightly with your hands to help it keep its shape.

Let the pasta rest while you prepare the sauce. In a saucepan, sauté the onion in a small amount of oil until it begins to turn golden, then add the pork and cook until tender, which will take quite a long time. Add the tomato puree and cook until it has thickened, then season with salt and add a pinch of freshly grated nutmeg.

Bring a large pot of salted water to a boil and cook the pasta, then drain it, transfer to a serving bowl, top with the sauce, and serve.

SCIALATIELLI AI FRUTTI DI MARE AMMOLLICATI 🐚
Scialatielli Pasta with Seafood
Ristorante Perbacco, Pisciotta (Salerno), Campania

cialatielli are noodles similar to fettuccine but a little thicker and shorter. Always clean shellfish thoroughly by soaking it in cold salted water.

SERVES 4

1½ cups semolina flour
1½ cups unbleached all-purpose flour or 0 flour
1 large egg, lightly beaten
½ cup grated aged goat's milk cacioricotta cheese
2 tablespoons extra-virgin olive oil, plus more for pasta dough and breadcrumbs
Salt to taste
3 cups torn day-old bread
Leaves of 1 sprig parsley, minced
2 cloves garlic, minced
2 pounds assorted shellfish, such as cockles, clams, mussels, and razor clams

To make the pasta dough, combine the two flours and shape into a well on the work surface. Place the egg and grated cheese in the center of the well with a drizzle of olive oil and a pinch of salt. Begin to pull in flour from the sides of the well and then knead, adding as much water as necessary to make a compact dough. Knead for at least 15 minutes. Form the dough into a ball, cover with a kitchen towel, and set aside for at least 30 minutes.

Meanwhile, toast the torn bread until crisp,

then crumble and combine with the parsley. Add 1 clove garlic to the breadcrumbs and season with salt. Toss with a little oil.

Roll out the pasta dough with a rolling pin to about 1/10 inch thick and allow to rest for about 10 minutes. Then roll up the sheet into a cylinder and cut into noodles 1/10 inch thick or a little thicker and about 4¾ inches long.

In a large skillet, heat 2 tablespoons olive oil. Sauté the remaining clove garlic, then add the shellfish. Cook over high heat until the shellfish have opened. (Remove and discard any that refuse to open.) Bring a large pot of salted water to a boil and cook the scialatielli, then drain and add to the skillet. Toss to combine, then sprinkle on the breadcrumbs.

TROCCOLI ALLO SCOGLIO 🍴
Troccoli Pasta with Shellfish
Ristorante da Pompeo, Foggia, Puglia

roccoli are similar to spaghetti but square. They are made by rolling out a sheet of egg pasta dough and then rolling over it with a ridged rolling pin. Spaghetti alla chitarra are made in the opposite way (they are rolled with a smooth rolling pin on top of a box with wires strung across it like a guitar) but are very similar. Troccoli are often paired with fish, meat sauces, or sausage and porcini mushrooms. Soak the cockles and mussels in salted water to clean them.

SERVES 4

1 clove garlic, crushed
Extra-virgin olive oil for sautéing
8 scampi
4 cuttlefish
14 ounces mussels
14 ounces cockles
8 cherry tomatoes, seeded
Salt to taste
11 ounces troccoli pasta (see note)
Leaves of 1 sprig parsley, minced
Freshly ground black pepper to taste

In a large pot, sauté the garlic in oil. When it begins to brown, add the scampi, cuttlefish, mussels, and cockles. When the mussels and cockles open, add the tomatoes and cook for about 10 minutes.

Meanwhile, bring a large pot of salted water to a boil and cook the pasta al dente. Drain and add to the pot with the shellfish and toss gently. Sprinkle on the parsley, season with pepper, and serve.

MACARON DEL FRET AL RAGÙ DI SALSICCIA 🍅
Handmade Macaroni with Sausage
Ristorante 'L Bunet, Bergolo (Cuneo), Piemonte

Macaron del fret are made by wrapping rectangles of egg pasta dough around a knitting needle, a fairly common technique in southern Italy, but more unusual in the North. These are delicious with sausage and also pair beautifully with chanterelle mushrooms. In Piemonte, egg pasta is often made with a mix of whole eggs and yolks, which results in an extra-rich, bright yellow dough.

SERVES 8 TO 10
1   medium yellow onion, thinly sliced
2   tablespoons extra-virgin olive oil
1   pound pork sausage, casing removed and crumbled
1   pound tomatoes, peeled, seeded, crushed, and drained
Salt to taste
4   cups unbleached all-purpose flour
3   large eggs
12 egg yolks
Grated Parmigiano Reggiano (optional)

For the sauce, in a saucepan, sauté the onion in the oil until just turning golden. Add the sausage and brown for a couple of minutes. Add the tomatoes, season with salt, and cook over low heat until thickened.

For the pasta, shape the flour into a well on the work surface and place the eggs, yolks, and a pinch of salt in the middle. Pull in flour from the side of the well until you have a crumbly dough, then knead, adding water as necessary, until you have an elastic, soft dough. Roll out the dough with a rolling pin or a pasta machine. With a serrated pastry wheel, cut into rectangles 4 inches by 1 inch. Wrap a rectangle around a knitting needle (or a thick wooden skewer) pressing firmly as you roll it on the work surface with the palm of your hand. Repeat with remaining rectangles.

Bring a large pot of salted water to a boil and cook the pasta al dente. Drain, transfer to a serving bowl, and toss with the sauce. Sprinkle on the Parmigiano, if using.

CAMPOFILONI CON SCAMPI E CANOCCHIE 🌿
Thin Noodles with Scampi and Mantis Shrimp
Ristorante Chalet Galîleo, Civitanova Marche (Macerata), Marche

Campofiloni are very thin egg noodles, only slightly thicker than angel hair pasta.

SERVES 4
1   pound small mantis shrimp
1   clove garlic
Extra-virgin olive oil for sautéing
1   pound scampi
½   cup dry white wine
Salt to taste
Grated zest of 1 lemon
12 ounces campofiloni or other very thin egg noodles
Leaves of 1 sprig parsley, minced

Clip off the antennas and pincers of the mantis shrimp and cut a slit in the belly of each the long way. In a large skillet, sauté the garlic in oil. When the garlic browns, remove and discard it. Add the scampi and cook for 1 minute, then add the mantis shrimp. Brown over medium heat. Add the wine and let it evaporate. Season with salt and add the lemon zest. Stir to combine, then cook for a few minutes more over medium heat, stirring frequently. Remove from the heat and set aside. Bring a large pot of salted water to a boil and cook the pasta al dente. Drain the pasta and add it to the skillet. Toss to combine and sprinkle with parsley.

PASTA CON LE FAVE NOVELLE ⚜
Pasta with Young Fava Beans
Osteria U Locale, Buccheri (Siracusa), Sicilia

This is a springtime recipe, as it calls for the tiniest fava beans that have not yet developed a tough outer skin. In many regions, these beans are eaten raw with salami and sheep's cheese, though here they are briefly cooked. Tagliolini are thin fresh egg noodles.

SERVES 4

- 3   cups shelled young fava beans
- 1   clove garlic, sliced
- 1   small yellow onion, sliced
- 3   tablespoons extra-virgin olive oil, plus more for sautéing
- Leaves of 1 sprig marjoram, minced
- Salt to taste
- ⅓   cup diced pancetta
- 12 ounces fresh tagliolini
- 1   pinch ground chili pepper

Blanch the fava beans for 5 minutes. In a skillet, sauté the garlic and onion in 3 tablespoons olive oil. Add the blanched fava beans and the marjoram and season with salt. When the mixture is soft, puree it through a food mill.

In a skillet large enough to hold the pasta, sauté the pancetta in a little oil, then add the fava puree. Bring a large pot of salted water to a boil and cook the pasta al dente, then drain and add to the skillet. Toss to combine and sprinkle with a pinch of ground chili pepper.

MALTAGLIATI CON IL GULASCH ⚜
Noodles with Goulash
Trattoria Vecia Gorizia, Gorizia, Friuli-Venezia Giulia

Maltagliati are literally "poorly cut," and these egg noodles can take various sizes and shapes—that's part of their charm. A touch of whole-wheat flour gives these a hearty taste and texture. You will probably need to add water in addition to the eggs, as whole-wheat flour is quite "thirsty."

SERVES 4

SAUCE
- 1¾ pounds (5 to 6) medium yellow onions, thinly sliced
- 3   tablespoons extra-virgin olive oil
- Salt to taste
- 1¾ pounds beef cheek, diced
- Leaves of 1 sprig rosemary, minced
- Leaves of 1 sprig marjoram, minced
- 1   fresh bay leaf, minced
- 1   tablespoon sweet paprika
- 1   tablespoon tomato paste, diluted in 1 cup warm water
- Freshly ground black pepper to taste

PASTA DOUGH
- 2½ cups unbleached all-purpose flour or 00 flour
- ⅔   cup whole wheat flour
- 1   pinch salt
- 4   large eggs

In a pot, sauté the onions in the oil over low heat, uncovered. Add a little water at a time so that the onions do not brown. After 15 minutes, season with salt, then continue cooking until the onions break down completely, about 1 hour total.

Meanwhile, for the pasta, combine both types of flour with the salt. Work in the eggs and knead for 10 minutes, adding a little warm water if needed to make a soft dough. Roll out the dough into a sheet less than ¹⁄₁₀ inch thick and allow to dry for about 15 minutes, then cut into

3 parts. Roll up each sheet and slice into many strips, then cut crosswise and lift up the noodles and let them fall onto the work surface so that they separate.

Add the beef cheek to the pot with the onions and cook over high heat for 5 minutes, stirring frequently. Add the rosemary, marjoram, bay leaf, paprika, and tomato paste mixture. Cook, covered, over low heat for 2 hours, adding warm water in small amounts if the pot seems to be drying out. Season with salt and pepper.

When the sauce is cooked, bring a large pot of salted water to a boil to cook the pasta al dente. Drain the noodles and combine with the goulash, then serve.

BIGOLI CON LE SARDE
Bigoli with Sardines
Trattoria dell'Alba, Vho di Piadena (Cremona), Lombardia

To serve 6 people, make a pasta dough with 4 cups all-purpose flour and 5 large eggs. The dough should be on the stiff side—if it is too soft, add a little extra flour. Use a bigoli-maker (an extruder) to make thick spaghetti. Let the pasta rest while you make the sauce. In a large skillet, sauté 2 very thinly sliced onions in a little olive oil, over low heat until soft (do not brown). Rinse and bone 6 to 7 salted sardines, chop, and add to the onions. Cook, stirring constantly, until the sardines break down. Bring a large pot of salted water to a boil and cook the pasta, then drain the pasta and toss in the skillet with the sardine mixture. In summer, this dish is sometimes topped with diced tomatoes and/or zucchini. In the Veneto, salted anchovies are used in place of the sardines.

SPÄTZLE CON RAGÙ DI SELVAGGINA
Spaetzle with Venison Sauce
Pretzhof, Tulve-Tulfer di Val di Vizze-Pfitsch (Bolzano-Bozen), Trentino-Alto Adige

Spaetzle are made with a special tool similar to a grater. They are little nubby pasta dumplings with all kinds of nooks and crannies that capture sauce. The Trentino–Alto Adige region was once part of Austria-Hungary, and its cuisine reflects that heritage.

SERVES 4

SAUCE
Extra-virgin olive oil for sautéing
1   medium yellow onion, minced
1   carrot, diced
½   rib celery, diced
10 ounces venison or mountain goat shoulder, trimmed and diced
2   cups red wine
Sweet paprika to taste
Bouquet garni (1 sprig rosemary, 1 sprig thyme, 1 sprig sage, 3 juniper berries)
1   cup beef broth, warm
Salt and freshly ground black pepper to taste

PASTA
1¼ cups buckwheat flour
⅓   cup unbleached all-purpose flour
3   large eggs
1   pinch salt

Heat a little olive oil in a pot and sauté the onion until golden. Add the carrot, celery, and meat and brown over high heat until the meat begins to stick to the pot. Add the wine a little at a time and cook over medium heat until it has all been added and has evaporated. Season with a pinch of paprika, add the bouquet garni and the broth, then turn the heat to low and cook over low heat until reduced. When the sauce is cooked, taste and season with salt and pepper, then remove from the heat. Remove the bouquet garni.

Meanwhile, for the pasta combine the two types of flour and make a dough with the flour, eggs, a pinch of salt, and as much water as needed (probably about ¼ cup) to make a soft and elastic dough. Shape into a ball, cover, and set aside to rest.

Use a spaetzle maker to make small spaetzle. Bring a large pot of salted water to a boil and cook the pasta, stirring frequently so it doesn't stick. As soon as the pasta floats to the surface, remove with a slotted spoon or skimmer and dunk briefly in cold water to stop the pieces from cooking further and keep them separate. Drain and add to the sauce. Toss over medium heat to combine and serve.

BIGOI CO' L'ARNA
Bigoli with Duck
Ristorante Ai Monti da Zamboni, Arcugnano (Vicenza), Veneto

Bigoli are thick strands of pasta made with a press extruder. If you don't have the specific tool, however, you can make a decent facsimile using a crank pasta machine and rolling the dough a little thicker than usual so that the noodles are as wide as they are thick. Bigoli are sometimes made with whole-wheat flour. Vezzena is an herbaceous medium-fat Alpine cheese.

SERVES 4
- 1   shallot
- 1   rib celery
- Extra-virgin olive oil for sautéing
- 2   sage leaves
- 1   bay leaf
- 1   sprig thyme
- 1   clove garlic
- 6   ounces Muscovy duck meat, chopped
- About ½ cup duck broth
- Salt and freshly ground black pepper to taste
- 2½ cups unbleached all-purpose flour
- Vezzena cheese (see note) for grating

Crush the shallot and celery in a mortar and pestle, then in a skillet sauté them in olive oil with the sage, bay leaf, and thyme and the garlic until they begin to color. Add the duck meat and cook over low heat for 1½ hours, adding small amounts of duck broth to keep the skillet from drying out. Season with salt and pepper.

Meanwhile, for the pasta combine the flour with a pinch of salt and as much warm water as you need to make a compact dough. Pull off a small piece of the dough and insert it in the center cylinder of a bigoli maker (called a *bigolaro*) and turn the press. Thick spaghetti with a rough surface will be extruded. Spread them out on a kitchen towel to dry.

When the sauce is cooked, remove and discard the herbs and the garlic. Bring a large pot of salted water to a boil and cook the pasta, then drain and toss in the skillet with the sauce, sprinkling in the grated cheese as you do.

BIGOLI CON BROCCOLI DI TORBOLE
Bigoli with Torbole Broccoli
Ristorante La Terrazza, Torbole di Nago-Torbole (Trento), Trentino-Alto Adige

Torbole broccoli is a kind of small cauliflower (because broccoli and cauliflower hail from the same family, both are called broccoli in many parts of Italy) that has an especially delicate flavor; the leaves as well as the florets are eaten. It grows on the Trentino side of Lake Garda, which is warmed to a slightly higher temperature than the rest of the area by the northeastern winds. That, in turn, prevents the formation of frost. It is harvested from November to January. Molche olive paste is the pulp that stays behind after pitted olives have been pressed to make olive oil. You can use olive paste made with black olives in its stead. The preceding recipe includes instructions for making bigoli.

SERVES 4

1 head Torbole broccoli (see note)
Salt to taste
1 clove garlic
2 tablespoons molche olive paste (see note)
Extra-virgin olive oil for sautéing
12 ounces bigoli (see previous recipe)
Leaves of 1 sprig parsley, minced
Grated Grana Padano cheese to taste

Blanch the broccoli leaves in boiling salted water, then cut into ribbons. Break up the head into florets and blanch those as well. In a skillet, sauté the garlic and the molche olive paste in a little oil. Add the broccoli leaves and sauté, stirring frequently, for a few minutes. Add the florets and continue cooking over medium heat, stirring frequently, until the flavors are combined.

Bring a large pot of salted water to a boil and cook the pasta. When the bigoli are cooked, drain them and add them to the skillet with the broccoli. Remove from the heat, sprinkle with the parsley and cheese, and serve.

PIZZOCHERI ●
Buckwheat Noodles with Potatoes and Cabbage
Trattoria Altavîlla, Bianzone (Sondrio), Lombardia

izzoccheri are small noodles made with a mix of buckwheat and wheat flour. Their size and shape varies according to where in the region you find them, and sometimes they even appear as small dumplings. They are typically paired with potatoes and cabbage (chard sometimes replaces the cabbage when available) and cheese and drizzled with a large amount of buttery browned onions. Valtellina casera is a DOP cheese made with the milk of brown cows that graze on the Alpine slopes.

SERVES 4 TO 5

3⅓ cups buckwheat flour
1 cup unbleached all-purpose flour
Salt to taste
7 ounces (about 1 large or 2 small) potatoes, peeled and diced
7 ounces Savoy cabbage, finely chopped
1 cup grated Parmigiano Reggiano
9 ounces Valtellina casera cheese (see note), shaved
14 tablespoons (1 stick plus 6 tablespoons) unsalted butter
2 tablespoons minced onion
Freshly ground black pepper to taste

Combine the two types of flour with 1 pinch salt and knead in enough water to make a firm but elastic dough. With a rolling pin, roll it into a sheet about 1/10 inch thick and cut into strips 2 ¾ inches wide. Stack the strips together and cut them horizontally so that you have rectangular noodles a little less than ½ inch wide and 2¾ inches long.

Bring a large pot of salted water to a boil and add the potatoes and the cabbage. When the water returns to a boil, gradually add the noodles, a handful at a time, stirring to keep them from sticking. Cook until the pasta is cooked al dente and potatoes are tender, about 10 minutes after the water returns to a boil.

When the pasta is cooked, remove some of the pasta, potatoes, and cabbage with a skimmer or slotted spoon and transfer to a warm serving pan. Top with some of the grated Parmigiano and the casera shavings and continue to alternate layers of pasta and vegetables with cheese until you have used up both.

Melt the butter in a skillet and brown the onion, then drizzle the butter and onions on top of the pasta. Do not mix. Season with freshly ground black pepper and serve immediately.

PENCIANELLE AL POMODORO
Yeast-Risen Pasta with Tomatoes and Pancetta
Giardino degli Ulivi, Castelraimondo (Macerata), Marche

Like the flour-and-water pasta on page 159, this pasta incorporates yeast. It, too, was probably once made with bread dough. This recipe serves six rather generously and can be stretched to feed more, especially if it is part of a multi-course meal.

SERVES 6

- ½ cake compressed yeast or 1½ teaspoons active dry yeast
- 8 cups unbleached all-purpose flour or 00 flour, plus 1 to 2 cups for dusting
- 2 egg whites, lightly beaten
- Salt to taste

- 1 medium yellow onion, thinly sliced
- ¼ cup plus 2 tablespoons extra-virgin olive oil
- ⅔ cup diced pancetta
- Ground chili pepper to taste (optional)
- 3 cups tomato puree
- ½ cup grated aged pecorino cheese

Dissolve the yeast in 1 cup warm (not hot) water until foamy. Shape the flour into a well on the work surface and place the yeast and water, the egg whites, and a pinch of salt in the center of the well. Begin drawing in flour from the sides of the well, and when you have a crumbly mixture knead until you have a soft, elastic, compact dough, about 15 minutes. If the dough feels too sticky, add a little flour; if the dough feels too dry, add a little water. Shape into a ball and set aside to rest in a cool, dry place.

When you are ready to shape the pasta, heavily dust a baking sheet or tray with 1 to 2 cups flour. Pinch off a piece of dough and hold it over the floured baking sheet. Rub it between your palms to elongate it and let it drop onto the floured baking sheet. Repeat with the remaining dough. Don't worry about making the pieces of pasta consistent—they are supposed to be irregular in size and shape.

Let the pasta rest and make the sauce. In a skillet, saute the onion in ¼ cup olive oil until golden, then add the pancetta, a pinch of chili pepper, if using, and the tomato puree. Simmer to thicken, then taste and adjust salt.

Bring a large pot of salted water to a boil for the pasta. Stir in the remaining 2 tablespoons olive oil. Lift the pasta from the baking sheet and shake off excess flour (a sieve is helpful for this), then drop in the boiling water and cook al dente. The pasta should cook in just a few minutes. Remove with a slotted spoon or skimmer, reserving cooking water, and transfer to the pot with the sauce. Toss over medium heat to combine, stirring in the grated cheese as you do. If the dish looks dry, add a tablespoon or two of the pasta cooking water. Serve immediately.

BISCIOLONI CON SUGO FINTO 🌱
Yeast-Risen "Snake" Pasta with Meatless Ragù
Osteria Perbacco, Cannara (Perugia), Umbria

This pasta was once made from leftover bread dough. The yeast gives it an interesting texture. Please note that while this sauce is "meatless" in the Italian sense—it does not contain large pieces of meat—if you are serving it to vegetarians you should leave out the guanciale as well.

SERVES 4

PASTA
- ⅔ cake compressed yeast or 2 teaspoons active dry yeast
- 4 cups unbleached all-purpose flour
- 1 tablespoon extra-virgin olive oil
- 1 pinch salt

SAUCE
- 2 cups canned peeled tomatoes, roughly chopped
- 1 medium white onion, thinly sliced
- 1 small carrot, sliced into rounds
- 1 rib celery, diced
- 1 thick slice guanciale (cured pork jowl), diced
- 3 tablespoons extra-virgin olive oil
- 1 tablespoon unsalted butter
- Ground chili pepper to taste
- Salt to taste
- Grated Parmigiano Reggiano to taste

For the pasta, dissolve the yeast in a little warm water until foamy. Shape the flour into a well on the work surface. Place the dissolved yeast, the olive oil, and 1 pinch salt in the center of the well and knead, drawing in flour from the sides of the well. Knead until well combined. The dough should be a little firmer than typical bread dough. Shape into a ball and set aside to rest for 30 minutes.

For the sauce, in a pot combine the tomatoes, onion, carrot, celery, guanciale, oil, butter, and chili pepper and simmer until reduced.

Meanwhile, remove a small piece of the dough and roll it on a lightly floured work surface under the palms of your hands into a long, thin rope, like a thick piece of spaghetti. Repeat with the remaining dough and allow to rest for 15 minutes. The dough should puff slightly. Then bring a large pot of salted water to a boil and cook the pasta until it rises to the surface. Puree the solids in the sauce and stir them back into the pot, then drain the pasta and toss with the sauce. Sprinkle with a generous amount of grated Parmigiano and serve.

TAGLIOLINI DI GRANO SARACENO CON PORRI ●
Buckwheat Noodles with Creamy Leek Sauce
Trattoria del Regolo, Garessio (Cuneo), Piemonte

This leek sauce is a classic in and around Garessio. It uses ingredients that have long been widely available in this agricultural region, namely leeks from the kitchen garden, mushrooms from the woods, and milk and cream from cows on the many dairy farms in the area. Cervere leeks are thinner and sweeter than standard leeks. Chop them with a mezzaluna or use a food processor. They should dissolve into a puree without browning during the long, slow cooking.

SERVES 4

2½ cups unbleached all-purpose flour
¾ cup buckwheat flour
5 large eggs
Salt to taste
1½ pounds Cervere leeks, chopped
3 tablespoons unsalted butter
About 2 cups whole milk
¾ cup dried porcini, rehydrated in warm water, squeezed dry, and chopped
2 cups heavy cream or whipping cream

On a work surface, combine the flours. Beat the eggs with a pinch of salt and then knead the eggs and flour into a well-combined dough. Roll into a thin sheet (according to your taste in these matters), then roll into a cylinder and cut into long noodles about 4 inches wide or into tagliatelle if you prefer.

Place the leeks and butter in a skillet and cook over low heat for 30 minutes, stirring frequently. Once the leeks have given up all their liquid, gradually add the 2 cups milk, waiting for each addition to bubble before you add the next. Cook for an additional 30 minutes. Add the mushrooms and the cream, season with salt, and cook until reduced to a thick sauce, another 30 minutes. If the sauce is thickening too quickly, thin with a little more milk.

When the sauce is ready, bring a large pot of salted water to a boil and cook the pasta al dente. Drain the pasta, transfer to the skillet with the sauce, and cook, stirring, for a few minutes to combine.

TAGLIATELLE PICCANTI DI CASTAGNE 🌶
Spicy Chestnut-Flour Tagliatelle
Trattoria La Pergola, Gesualdo (Avellino), Campania

Plain button mushrooms would be overwhelmed by the taste of chili pepper, but porcini mushrooms have a robust flavor and hold their own in this dish. Both the chili and porcini play beautifully off of the nutty chestnut-flour pasta.

SERVES 4

1⅔ cups chestnut flour
1 cup semolina flour
Salt to taste
1 clove garlic, minced
1 chili pepper, minced
4 ounces porcini mushrooms, sliced
Extra-virgin olive oil for sautéing
3 ounces (about 6) cherry tomatoes
Leaves of 1 sprig parsley, minced

Combine the flours with a pinch of salt and enough water to make a smooth and elastic dough. Wrap the dough in plastic wrap and set aside to rest for 30 minutes.

Roll out the dough into a thin sheet and cut into noodles about ⅕ inch wide. Spread out and allow to dry slightly before bringing a large pot of salted water to a boil for cooking the pasta al dente.

Meanwhile, in a nonstick skillet, brown the garlic, chili pepper, and mushrooms in oil until the mushrooms have given up all of their liquid. Add the cherry tomatoes, season with salt, and cook until well combined, about 10 minutes, incorporating small amounts of pasta cooking water (about ¼ cup total) to keep the pan moist. When the pasta is cooked al dente, drain and add to the skillet. Toss over medium heat to combine, then sprinkle with the minced parsley and serve.

TAGLIOLINI RUSTICI AL RAGÙ DI VERDURE
Chestnut, Whole-Wheat, and Farro Tagliolini with Vegetables
Trattoria Conca Verde, Trescore Balneario (Bergamo), Lombardia

The combination of three types of flour makes these noodles especially hearty and flavorful. Be sure to knead the dough at length. When you cut it in half, it should be perfectly consistent all the way through with no streaks or marbling.

SERVES 4 TO 6

PASTA
- 3⅓ cups chestnut flour
- ¾ cup whole-wheat flour
- ¾ cup farro flour
- 4 large eggs, lightly beaten
- Salt to taste

SAUCE
- 2 carrots, cut into small dice
- 2 tablespoons extra-virgin olive oil
- 2 zucchini, cut into small dice
- 2 leeks, cut into small dice
- Salt to taste
- ¼ cup heavy cream
- 1 cup grated Parmigiano Reggiano

For the pasta, combine the three types of flour and knead with the eggs, a pinch of salt, and enough lukewarm water to make an elastic dough, about ½ cup. Knead at length, then roll out on a work surface and cut into noodles a little less than ½ inch wide and about 4 inches

long. Set the noodles aside to dry while you prepare the sauce.

In a skillet, sauté the carrots in the olive oil for a few minutes. Add the zucchini and leeks and sauté until golden. Season with salt. Then bring a large pot of salted water to a boil and cook the pasta al dente. Drain the pasta and add to the skillet with the vegetables. Stir in the cream and grated cheese and toss over medium heat to combine.

TAGLIOLINI DI CASTAGNE CON NOCI E CACAO
Chestnut-Flour Noodles with Walnuts and Cocoa Powder
Ristorante Il Vecchio Castagno, Serrastretta (Catanzaro), Calabria

Cocoa powder is, of course, most frequently used in desserts, but in its unsweetened form it can add an interesting bitter edge to savory dishes as well. It pops up most frequently in Italy in regions that at one time or another were under Spanish rule—Calabria is one of those regions.

SERVES 4

- 1¾ cups semolina flour
- 2¼ cups chestnut flour
- 2 large eggs, lightly beaten
- ¼ cup unsweetened cocoa powder
- Salt to taste
- 9 ounces (1 cup) sheep's milk ricotta
- About 3 tablespoons milk
- Extra-virgin olive oil for sautéing
- Freshly grated nutmeg to taste
- 1 cup walnuts, ground
- Grated smoked ricotta to taste (optional)

Combine the semolina flour and chestnut flour and knead with the eggs, the cocoa powder, a pinch of salt, and enough water to make a compact but soft dough. Roll into a sheet of medium thickness for pasta, dust lightly with flour, then roll up and cut into thin noodles with a knife. (You can also do this with a pasta machine.) Set aside to rest on the work surface.

Combine the ricotta with enough milk to loosen it to the consistency of sour cream. In a skillet, sauté the ricotta mixture in a little oil. Season with grated nutmeg and cook, stirring frequently, for 10 minutes.

Bring a large pot of salted water to a boil and cook the pasta al dente. When the pasta is cooked, drain and add to the skillet. Toss to combine for a minute or two, then sprinkle on the walnuts and the smoked ricotta, if using.

MACCHERONI DOLCI
Sweet Macaroni with Cocoa Powder
Osteria Perbacco, Cannara (Perugia), Umbria

At one time, flour and water pasta tossed with honey was eaten as a first course on major religious holidays, such as Christmas and All Saints' Day. As spices became more widely available, they were incorporated into sweet pasta dishes, and after Europeans discovered the cocoa bean in the Americas, cocoa powder was added to the mix as well. This dish is a riff on those early sweet dishes, and we're including it in this chapter, but you can also serve it as a rather unusual dessert, accompanied by a glass of Vernaccia di Cannara.

SERVES 4

- 2½ cups unbleached all-purpose flour
- 1 egg white
- ⅔ cup breadcrumbs
- 2¾ cups walnuts, finely chopped
- ¾ cup sugar
- 1½ teaspoons ground cinnamon
- Grated zest of 1 lemon
- ¼ cup plus 3 tablespoons unsweetened cocoa powder
- Salt to taste

Combine the flour, the egg white, and enough water to make a soft, elastic dough. Shape into a ball, cover, and set aside to rest, then roll into a sheet. Let the sheet dry for a few minutes, roll into a loose cylinder, and cut into strips about ⅕ inch wide.

In a bowl combine the breadcrumbs, walnuts, sugar, cinnamon, lemon zest, and cocoa powder. Stir to combine and set aside.

Bring a lightly salted pot of water to a boil for the pasta and cook the pasta until it rises to the surface. Remove with a slotted spoon or skimmer when cooked al dente, and don't drain it completely dry. In a serving platter, alternate layers of the pasta with the prepared breadcrumb mixture, ending with the breadcrumb mixture on top. Allow to cool completely before serving.

TESTAROLI PONTREMOLESI 🌿
Griddle-Cooked Pasta
Trattoria da Bussè, Pontremoli (Massa-Carrara), Toscana

Obtaining the proper type of covered griddle is the first step to making *testaroli*, but you also need to have an open fire in order to cook them properly. This pasta is made from a batter that is cooked into thin pancakes, then cut into triangles and boiled in salted water. In the Lunigiana area (which falls partly in Toscana and partly in Liguria), many people cook over the fire in a *gradile*, which is a small stone structure where chestnuts are dried over a constantly burning fire (see the next recipe for more about Calizzano and Murialdo chestnuts). Artisanal Pontremoli testaroli have their own Slow Food Presidium.

To make testaroli, heat both the bottom and top of the traditional cast-iron covered griddle on an open fire. Meanwhile, make a batter of all-purpose or oo flour, a pinch of salt, and enough water to make a batter thin enough to be pourable but not watery (similar to pancake batter). Whisk smooth. Pour a little of the batter on the bottom of the griddle and tilt to distribute evenly. Cover and place on the fire. After 5 minutes, lift the lid and see how it is doing—it should form a thin pancake dotted with small holes all over the surface where the water has evaporated. Remove and wrap in a cotton towel. Repeat with remaining batter.

While the pancakes are cooling, make pesto: in a mortar and pestle, pound basil, grated Parmigiano Reggiano and a touch of grated aged sheep's cheese, and garlic (any green shoots removed). When the mixture is finely ground, transfer to a small bowl and whisk in a drizzle of not-overly-fruity Ligurian extra-virgin olive oil. Bring a large pot of salted water to a boil and cut the pancakes into diamonds with 2¾-inch sides. When the water in the pot is just about to boil, add the pasta and leave it for only a couple of minutes. (If the pasta is very freshly made, it may cook in as little as 60 seconds.) When the pasta is cooked, drain in a colander than divide among individual serving dishes in alternating layers with the pesto and a little additional grated cheese, if desired.

PICAGGE DI CASTAGNE CON BACCALÀ E OLIVE 🫒
Chestnut-Flour Egg Noodles with Baccalà and Olives
Ristorante La Lanterna, Mallare (Savona), Liguria

In the towns of Calizzano and Murialdo, chestnuts are dried in special one-room stone buildings with shingled roofs, where they are arranged on wooden racks hung from the ceiling. A small fire burns constantly below the chestnuts, infusing them with a pleasantly smoky taste. The chestnuts, ground into flour, and also preserved or used in desserts, have their own Slow Food Presidium. Fewer than two dozen chestnut pickers still use this technique.

SERVES 6

PASTA
- 2¾ cups unbleached all-purpose flour or 00 flour
- 2¼ cups coarsely ground Calizzano and Murialdo chestnut flour
- 5 large eggs, lightly beaten
- 1 tablespoon extra-virgin olive oil

SAUCE
- 1 clove garlic
- ¼ cup minced parsley
- 1 tablespoon extra-virgin olive oil
- 14 ounces baccalà, soaked in several changes of water until pliable, drained, skinned, boned, and chopped
- 7 ounces tomatoes, chopped
- Ground chili pepper to taste
- ¼ cup Taggiasca olives, pitted
- ¼ cup pine nuts
- Salt to taste

For the pasta, combine the two types of flour and shape them into a well on the work surface. Place the eggs and olive oil in the center of the well and knead, drawing in flour from the sides of the well until you have a crumbly dough. Knead until well combined and elastic. Roll the dough into a thin sheet and cut into noodles a little less than ½ inch wide.

For the sauce, in a skillet, saute the garlic and parsley in the olive oil. Add the baccalà, tomatoes, a pinch of chili pepper, the olives, and the pine nuts. Cook, stirring frequently, for 10 minutes. Taste and season with salt if needed.

Bring a large pot of salted water to a boil for the pasta and cook al dente. (The pasta will cook quickly.) Drain the pasta and add it to the skillet. Toss to combine, then serve.

FREGNACCE CON VERDURE

Buckwheat Noodles with Herbs and Vegetables
Ristorante Enoteca Il Bistrot, Rieti, Lazio

fregnacce are irregularly shaped noodles (similar to maltagliati) eaten throughout central Italy. *Puntarelle* is a kind of chicory and adds a delicious, faintly bitter edge to the sweetness of the other spring vegetables used here.

SERVES 4

2½ cups unbleached all-purpose flour

⅓ cup semolina flour

⅓ cup buckwheat flour

Salt to taste

2 tablespoons extra-virgin olive oil, plus a drizzle for pasta dough

Minced aromatic herbs, such as rosemary, parsley, marjoram, basil, chives, and oregano, to taste

1 clove garlic

Freshly ground black pepper to taste

11 ounces of a combination of asparagus tips, trimmed and thinly sliced baby artichokes, chiodini mushrooms, shelled peas, shelled and peeled fava beans, and puntarelle (see note) cut into strips and soaked in cold water to curl

About ½ cup vegetable broth

Grated ricotta salata to taste

Combine the three types of flour and knead with 1 pinch salt, a drizzle of olive oil, and enough water to make a compact but elastic dough. Roll the dough into a thin sheet and cut into irregular pieces.

In a skillet, heat the 2 tablespoons olive oil and add the aromatic herbs and the garlic. Cook over low heat until the garlic browns, then remove and discard it. Season with salt and pepper. Add the vegetables. Cook until tender, adding the broth in small amounts to keep the mixture from sticking to the pan, about 10 minutes. Stir in grated ricotta salata.

Bring a large pot of salted water to a boil and cook the pasta al dente. Drain and toss over low heat in the skillet with the vegetables to combine.

CENCIONI AL RAGÙ

Fava-Flour Pasta with Meat Sauce
Lucia Savelli, Pergola (Pesaro and Urbino), Marche

o make *cencioni*, roughly textured "rags" of pasta, combine equal amounts all-purpose flour and fava bean flour with 1 egg for every ½ cup (combined) of flour to make a pasta dough. Knead until tender, then roll out a little less than ¼ inch thick and set aside to rest. To make a sauce, sauté minced onion, celery, and carrot in a little extra-virgin olive oil and add ground veal and pork sausage with the casing removed. (You can also include sliced mushrooms if you like.) When the meat browns, add tomato puree. Simmer for about 1 hour and adjust salt and pepper. To cut the pasta, roll the sheet of dough into a cylinder and cut into strips a little wider than ¹⁄₁₀ inch, and then cut those into lengths about equal to the palm of your hand. Cook the pasta in salted boiling water, drain, and toss with sauce.

CAJONCIE DI SPINACI
Rye Ravioli with Lambsquarters
Ristorante Tyrol, Moena (Trento), Trentino-Alto Adige

The Ladin people of the Dolomites speak a Rhaeto-Romance language and have a unique culinary tradition that includes these meatless ravioli. These ravioli are sometimes fried rather than boiled. Lambsquarters are wild spinach.

SERVES 6

½ medium yellow onion, minced
1 tablespoon unsalted butter
1 pound lambsquarters
⅔ cup mascarpone or other fresh, creamy cheese
Salt and freshly ground black pepper to taste
Freshly grated nutmeg to taste
3½ cups rye flour
1¾ cups unbleached all-purpose flour, plus more for dusting
4 large eggs
4 egg yolks
2 tablespoons extra-virgin olive oil (optional)
Warm melted butter for finishing
Grated smoked ricotta for finishing
Poppy seeds for finishing

For the filling, sauté the onion in the butter until soft and golden. Add the lambsquarters and cook until reduced, 2 to 3 minutes. Remove from the heat, mince the mixture, and set aside to cool. When the mixture is cool, combine with the mascarpone, season with salt, pepper, and nutmeg, and refrigerate until using.

For the pasta, combine the rye flour and all-purpose flour and shape into a well on the work surface. Lightly beat the eggs and yolks together and add to the center of the well. Add the olive oil, if using. (It makes the dough easier to work, but results in a pasta with less bite.) Roll into a thin sheet and let it rest briefly, then dust lightly with flour and cut into squares with 2½-inch sides using a wheel cutter.

Remove the filling from the refrigerator and knead for a few seconds, then use the tip of a teaspoon to place a little bit of the filling in the center of each square of pasta. Fold the squares into triangles, taking care not to trap any air in the pockets with the filling. Press to seal. Bring a large pot of salted water to a boil and cook until the pasta rises to the surface, a few minutes at most. Remove with a slotted spoon or skimmer and toss with melted butter, grated smoked ricotta, and poppy seeds.

RAVIOLI DI BORRAGINE
Borage Ravioli
Osteria d'Angî, Alassio (Savona), Liguria

Borage grows all over Italy, but it is highly prized in Liguria, where it appears in stuffed pasta fillings like this one, as well as in soups and savory pies. It is also a key ingredient in *preboggion*, the region's famed mix of herbs and greens.

SERVES 8

2 pounds borage
1 pound chard
Salt to taste
1 large yellow onion, chopped
Extra-virgin olive oil for sautéing
Leaves of 1 bunch marjoram
7 large eggs
1 cup grated Parmigiano Reggiano
Freshly grated nutmeg to taste
About ¼ cup breadcrumbs, if needed
1 clove garlic, crushed
2 pounds ripe tomatoes, roughly chopped
Leaves of 2 bunches basil
¼ cup pine nuts, crushed with a mortar and pestle
4 cups unbleached all-purpose flour or 00 flour

For the filling, cook the borage and chard in boiling salted water until tender, drain, and squeeze dry. In a skillet, sauté the onion in olive oil. Add the borage and chard and cook, stirring frequently, 2 to 3 minutes, then season with salt and add the marjoram. Puree the mixture through a food mill, then combine with 3 eggs, Parmigiano, and nutmeg. If the filling is too loose, add some breadcrumbs.

For the sauce, in a medium pot, brown the crushed garlic in olive oil, then remove and discard and add the tomatoes. Cook over high heat, stirring frequently, until softened, 3 to 4 minutes. Remove from the heat, stir in the basil leaves, then puree through a food mill. Stir the pine nuts into the tomato sauce.

For the pasta, shape the flour into a well and place the remaining 4 eggs in the well with a pinch of salt and a little water. Begin drawing in flour from the sides of the well, then knead into a smooth and elastic dough, adding more water as needed. Divide the dough into 2 equal pieces and roll each piece into a thin sheet the same size and shape. Dot 1 sheet of pasta with small amounts of the filling (about 1 teaspoon) spaced evenly in rows. Place the second sheet of pasta over the first (avoid trapping air), then cut into equal-size squares. Seal the edges of each piece of pasta by pressing firmly with your fingertips. Bring a large pot of salted water to a boil and cook the pasta for 5 minutes. Drain and top with tomato sauce.

PULINGIONI CON POMODORO E PECORINO 🍅
Ravioli with Sweet Ricotta Filling in Tomato Sauce
Ristorante Il Tirabusciò, Calangianus (Olbia-Tempio), Sardegna

These ravioli hail from the Gallura area of northeastern Sardegna. They can be served with a tomato sauce, as here, or with braised mutton.

SERVES 6

PASTA

4 cups unbleached all-purpose flour
1 pinch salt
2 egg yolks

FILLING

14 ounces (1⅔ cups) ricotta
3 tablespoons sugar
Leaves of 1 sprig parsley, minced
Grated zest of 1 lemon

SAUCE

1 clove garlic
1 medium yellow onion, minced
1 carrot, minced
Extra-virgin olive oil for sautéing
5 to 6 ripe tomatoes, chopped
Salt to taste
4 to 5 basil leaves
Grated Pecorino Sardo to taste

For the pasta, make the flour into a well on a work surface. Place 1 pinch salt and the egg yolks in the center and knead into a soft and elastic dough, adding water as needed. Cover and set aside to rest for 30 minutes. In the meantime, for the filling, in a bowl combine the ricotta, the sugar, the parsley, and the lemon zest.

Roll out the pasta into a thin sheet, no more than 1/20 inch thick. Cut into 4-inch-wide strips. Use 2 teaspoons to form small amounts of the ricotta mixture into little balls and arrange them along half of the strips, regularly spaced. Place the other strips of pasta on top of the filling and press all around the filling to seal. With a wheel cutter, cut into ravioli and set aside.

For the sauce, in a skillet sauté the garlic clove with the onion and carrot in a little oil. Add the tomatoes, season with salt, and cook, stirring frequently, until reduced, about 20 minutes. Meanwhile, bring a large pot of salted water to a boil and cook the pasta. As soon as it rises to the surface, remove gently with a skimmer and transfer to a serving bowl. Toss the pasta with the tomato sauce. Tear the basil leaves onto the pasta, sprinkle with grated cheese, and serve.

ROFIOI
Large Cheese Ravioli with Sage Butter
Circolo Pensionati, Montagne (Trento), Trentino-Alto Adige

When a crowd gathers to celebrate a baptism or wedding in the mountains of Trentino, these large square ravioli are almost always on the menu. These can either be boiled in water and served as they are here, with lots of melted sage butter and grated Trentingrana or spressa cheese, or they can be cooked in beef broth, drained, and topped with a sauce made with ground veal. Trentingrana is the aged cheese most commonly sprinkled on pasta in the Trento area.

SERVES 6

FILLING
- 3   cups grated day-old bread
- 3   cups grated Trentingrana cheese
- 1   tablespoon raisins, soaked in warm water to soften
- 1   large egg, lightly beaten
- Salt and freshly ground black pepper to taste
- 3   tablespoons unsalted butter
- Leaves of 1 sprig sage

PASTA
- 4   cups unbleached all-purpose flour or oo flour
- 4   large eggs, lightly beaten
- 1   pinch salt

SAUCE
- Melted butter
- Sage leaves
- Grated Trentingrana or aged spressa cheese

For the filling, combine the grated bread and grated Trentingrana. They should be equal in volume. Stir in the raisins and the egg. Season with salt and pepper. In a small skillet, melt the butter with the sage leaves (if you are planning to serve the cooked ravioli in sage butter, you can make extra and set it aside) and toast until the butter has taken on the aroma of the sage. Remove and discard leaves and let the butter cool slightly, then add it to the mixture for the filling. The filling should be firm but moist. If it feels dry, add a little water. Mix to combine, then set aside to rest.

For the pasta, combine the flour with the eggs and a pinch of salt. Knead to a soft, compact dough, incorporating water in small amounts if necessary. Roll into a thin sheet and cut into squares with 4-inch sides. Place about 1 teaspoon of the filling in the center of half of the squares. Cover each with another square and press around the perimeter with your fingertips to seal tightly.

Bring a large pot of salted water to a boil and cook the pasta just until it rises to the surface. Remove gently with a slotted spoon or skimmer and transfer to a serving bowl. Melt butter with sage, then pour over the cooked pasta. Sprinkle on grated cheese and serve.

TORTELLI DI ZUCCA
Tortelli Stuffed with Squash
Hostaria Viola, Fontane di Castiglione delle Stiviere (Mantova), Lombardia

A sage butter is the traditional topping for these and many other types of stuffed pasta, but at the restaurant they sometimes serve these tortelli in a tomato sauce with some chopped sausage. The apple mostarda here helps the filling achieve a good balance of sweet, savory, and spicy. If you want to try your hand at making your own mostarda, see the recipe on page 415.

SERVES 6 TO 8

FILLING
- 1 Mantova squash or other winter squash, about 4½ pounds, peeled, seeded, and chopped
- 1 shallot, minced
- 11 tablespoons unsalted butter
- 5 amaretto cookies, crumbled
- ⅓ cup apple mostarda, minced
- 2 cups grated Parmigiano Reggiano
- Breadcrumbs for firming filling
- Freshly grated nutmeg to taste
- Salt and freshly ground black pepper to taste
- Grated orange or lemon zest or grated ginger (optional)

PASTA
- 5 cups unbleached all-purpose flour
- 6 large eggs, lightly beaten
- 1 pinch salt

FINISHING
- Unsalted butter to taste
- 3 to 4 sage leaves
- Salt to taste

For the filling, preheat the oven to 400°F. Place the squash, shallot, and a couple of tablespoons of water in a baking pan and roast in the preheated oven until soft, about 30 minutes.

Meanwhile, for the pasta, shape the flour into a well on the work surface. Place the eggs and salt in the center of the well. Begin to draw in flour from the sides of the well, then knead into a compact and elastic dough. Set aside to rest for at least 30 minutes.

Crush the cooked squash through a potato ricer and place in a medium pot. Beat in the butter, crumbled amaretto cookies, mostarda, and grated Parmigiano. Add as many breadcrumbs as you need to make a firm filling. Season with nutmeg, salt, and pepper, and stir in the zest or ginger, if using. Cook, stirring, over medium heat until the mixture is compact and firm and almost feels like a dough.

Use a crank pasta machine to roll out the pasta dough into a thin sheet, then cut into 2-inch squares with a wheel cutter. Place a small amount of the prepared filling on each square then fold in half, pressing firmly with your fingertips around the edge to seal.

Melt butter for serving with sage leaves. Bring a large pot of salted water to a boil and cook the pasta until it rises to the surface, which should take only a couple of minutes. Remove with a skimmer, transfer to a serving bowl, drizzle with the butter and sage, and serve immediately.

KLOTZNNUDLN ●
Dried Pear Ravioli
Antica Trattoria da Giusi, Malborghetto-Valbruna
(Udine), Friuli-Venezia Giulia

The dried pears in these ravioli are clearly a crossover from southern Austrian cuisine, which often overlaps with that of Friuli-Venezia Giulia. The ricotta can be replaced with the same amount (in volume) of cooked polenta.

SERVES 4
1   pound dried pears
2   cups unbleached all-purpose flour
2   large eggs
Salt to taste
½   medium yellow onion, minced
Unsalted butter for sautéing and topping
7   ounces (¾ cup) ricotta

Place the pears in a heatproof bowl and add boiling water to cover. Set aside to soften for 1 hour. Make the pasta dough by kneading together the flour, the eggs, and a pinch of salt dissolved in a little warm water. Add enough water to make a smooth, compact dough.

Drain the softened pears and mince them. In a skillet, sauté the onion in a little butter. In a bowl, combine the ricotta, sautéed onion, and minced pears and beat until well combined. Taste and adjust salt.

With a rolling pin, roll out the pasta dough into a very thin sheet and cut it into disks 2¾ inches to 3 inches in diameter. Reroll scraps. Place a small spoonful of the ricotta mixture in the center of each disk. Fold the pasta in half to make half-moons and seal the edges firmly by pressing with your fingertips.

Melt butter for topping pasta. Bring a large pot of salted water to a boil and cook the pasta until it rises to the surface. Gently remove with a skimmer and transfer to a serving bowl. Drizzle pasta with melted butter and serve.

RAVIOLI DI CAVEDANO
Ravioli with Chub Filling in Cucumber Puree
Antica Trattoria Alle Rose, Salò (Brescia), Lombardia

European chub is a freshwater fish with sweet white flesh that responds well to grilling. Because its flavor is pleasant and mild, it is also good chopped up and used to make dumplings and fillings for pastas such as these delicate and delicious ravioli.

SERVES 4
2½ cups unbleached all-purpose flour
3   large eggs
1   tablespoon extra-virgin olive oil, plus
      more for drizzling
Salt to taste
1   (1½- to 1¾-pound) chub, gutted and scaled
1   cup white vinegar
3 to 4 bay leaves
3 to 4 potatoes
Freshly ground black pepper to taste
2   cucumbers, peeled and seeded

For the dough, knead the flour with the eggs, 1 tablespoon extra-virgin olive oil, and a pinch of salt. Set aside to rest for a few hours.

In a stockpot over medium heat, bring the chub, vinegar, 2 quarts cold water, and bay leaves to a boil, then cook for 10 minutes. Let the fish cool in the pot in its cooking liquid. Meanwhile, cook the potatoes in boiling salted water until tender, then drain, peel, and mash with a potato ricer.

Clean the flesh from the fish (discarding skin and bones) and chop. For the filling, combine the mashed potatoes, the chopped chub, a drizzle of oil, and salt and pepper to taste.

Roll the dough into a thin sheet and use the prepared filling to make square ravioli with 2-inch sides. Puree the cucumbers with a little oil, salt, and pepper and place in a large skillet. Bring a large pot of salted water to a boil and cook the pasta. (It will cook in just a few minutes.) Remove with a skimmer and transfer to the skillet with the cucumber puree, then toss over low heat for a minute or two to combine.

AGNOLOTTI VERDI
Green Agnolotti
Ristorante del Mercato da Maurizio, Cravanzana (Cuneo), Piemonte

Though technically Cravanzana is located in Piemonte, it is close enough to Liguria to feel that region's sea breeze. This proximity is also reflected in the cuisine—these vegetarian *agnolotti* (small, crescent-shaped stuffed pasta) are filled with greens, including borage, a great favorite in Liguria.

SERVES 6

FILLING

1   cup rice
Salt to taste
3   tablespoons unsalted butter
½   cup grated Parmigiano Reggiano
2   leeks
¼   head Savoy cabbage
1   bunch escarole
10 ounces chard
½   cup chopped borage

PASTA

7   ounces chard, blanched
4   cups unbleached all-purpose flour or
    00 flour
3   large eggs
1   tablespoon extra-virgin olive oil
Salt to taste

FINISHING

Salt to taste
Unsalted butter to taste
Leaves of 1 sprig sage
Grated Parmigiano Reggiano to taste

For the filling, cook the rice in boiling salted water as you would pasta, stirring frequently. Drain and while still warm mix with the butter and grated Parmigiano. Set aside to cool. Blanch the leeks, cabbage, escarole, chard, and borage until just tender, then drain. (It's convenient to blanch the chard for the pasta dough at the same time.) Mince the greens for the filling as finely as possible and stir into the rice mixture.

For the pasta dough, mince the blanched chard very finely and combine it with the flour, eggs, olive oil, and a pinch of salt into an elastic dough. Roll into a thin sheet with a rolling pin.

To make the agnolotti, arrange small amounts of the filling in a row down the side of the sheet of pasta, spacing them a little less than ½ inch from each other and leaving a clear border a little less than ½ inch wide. Fold the border of the dough over and press around each clump of dough to seal with your fingertips. Use a wheel cutter to cut off the strip from the empty sheet of dough the long way, and then to cut in between the filling portions to cut into squares. Repeat with the remaining dough and filling. Let the filled pasta rest for a couple of hours.

When you are ready to cook the pasta, bring a large pot of salted water to a boil and cook the pasta until al dente, just a couple of minutes. Meanwhile, in a skillet, melt butter with sage. When the pasta is cooked, use a skimmer to remove and transfer to a serving bowl, then toss with the melted butter and sage and grated cheese and serve.

TULTRES DI CRAUTI
Fried Rye Ravioli Filled with Sauerkraut and Speck
Trattoria Garsun, Marebbe-Enneberg
(Bolzano-Bozen), Trentino-Alto Adige

Pasta dishes are an anomaly in the German-speaking Val Pusteria area. When filled with sauerkraut, tultres are always fried, but similar rye ravioli filled with spinach, cabbage, or a mix of ricotta and chives are boiled in salted water and then tossed with melted butter and breadcrumbs.

SERVES 4

FILLING AND FINISHING
1 *bay leaf*
2 *juniper berries*
1 *pinch cumin seed*
1 *tablespoon unsalted butter*
4 *cups sauerkraut, minced*
½ *medium yellow onion, minced*
1 *clove garlic, minced*
1 *tablespoon unbleached all-purpose flour*
½ *cup vegetable broth*
¼ *cup minced speck*
Extra-virgin olive oil for frying

PASTA
2 *cups rye flour*
1½ *cups semolina flour*
1 *large egg*
2 *tablespoons extra-virgin olive oil*
½ *cup milk*
Salt to taste

For the filling, in a skillet sauté the bay leaf, juniper berries, and cumin in the butter until aromatic, then remove and discard the bay leaf, berries, and seeds. Add the sauerkraut, onion, and garlic and sauté until golden. Sprinkle on the 1 tablespoon flour, add the vegetable broth, and stir to combine, then simmer until sauerkraut is very soft. Stir in the speck.

For the dough, combine the flours, then mix with the egg, olive oil, milk, and a pinch of salt until it forms an elastic dough. Roll into a thin sheet. Dot half of the sheet with pieces of the filling (about 1 teaspoon) leaving enough space between them to make large ravioli. Fold the empty side of the sheet over the filling, press between the clumps of filling to seal, and cut into ravioli. Fry the ravioli in olive oil, drain briefly, and serve.

RAVIOLI DI CARDO GOBBO
Gobbo Cardoon Ravioli with Black Truffle
Livia Borgata, Montegrosso d'Asti (Asti), Piemonte

For the filling, place cubes of fontina cheese in a bowl, add whole milk to cover, and keep covered in a cool place for 3 or 4 hours. Then cook in the top of a double boiler with a small amount of butter, whisking constantly, until the cheese has melted and the mixture is thoroughly combined. Whisk in beaten egg yolks until thick and creamy. Boil gobbo cardoons in water with lemon juice, then puree. Mix with the prepared fontina mixture and stir in a little grated Parmigiano Reggiano. Taste and adjust salt, then refrigerate filling for a few hours. Make a pasta dough with all-purpose flour, egg yolks, and milk. Roll into a sheet a little thicker than normal and cut into strips 4 inches wide. Place small amounts of the filling down one side of the strips, leaving 1 inch in between the filling portions, and fold the empty side of the strip over to cover the filling. Seal carefully by pressing on all sides of the filling and cut with a pastry wheel or ravioli cutter. Repeat with the remaining strips and filling. Cook the ravioli in boiling salted water with a few bay leaves in it. Drain and top with melted butter, a generous amount of grated Parmigiano Reggiano, and shavings of black Piemontese truffle.

AGNOLOTTI DAL PLIN
Pinched Veal Agnolotti
Trattoria Madonna della Neve, Cessole (Asti), Piemonte

This is the most famous pasta dish from the northern Langhe region. These are served plain with no topping whatsoever to allow their flavor to shine.

SERVES 4

FILLING

7 *ounces escarole*
1 *medium yellow onion, minced*
1 *rib celery, minced*
1 *carrot, minced*
Extra-virgin olive oil for sautéing
1 *clove garlic, chopped*
Leaves of 1 sprig rosemary, chopped
3 to 4 bay leaves, chopped
4 *ounces veal breast, chopped*
4 *ounces pork leg, chopped*
4 *ounces rabbit, chopped*
Salt and freshly ground black pepper
   to taste
1 *large egg*
½ *cup grated Parmigiano Reggiano*

PASTA

1¾ *cups unbleached all-purpose flour or*
    00 flour
2 *large eggs, lightly beaten*
1 *egg yolk*

To make the filling, blanch the escarole, then drain, cool, and mince. In a pot, sauté the onion, celery, and carrot in a little olive oil with the garlic, rosemary, and bay leaves. Add the meat and brown, then season with salt and pepper. Cook over very low heat until tender, about 2 hours, adding a little water (or beef broth, if you prefer) to the pot to keep it from drying out. Let the mixture cool, then grind through a meat grinder. Mix with the egg and grated Parmigiano. Adjust salt and pepper.

For the pasta dough, make the flour into a well on a work surface and add the eggs and yolk to the center of the well along with ¼ cup

water. Knead until you have a soft and elastic dough (add more water if needed) and roll into the thinnest sheet possible. It should be almost transparent. Immediately position small pieces of the filling, each about the size of a hazelnut, in a row on the sheet of pasta, spacing them a little less than ½ inch apart and leaving a border a little less than ½ inch wide at the edge. Fold the border over the filling to cover, press with your fingertips to seal, and with a serrated wheel cutter cut the strip of pasta the long way to separate it from the unused dough. Pinch with your thumb and index finger between each portion of filling. With a serrated wheel cutter, cut in between each portion of filling to make small individual pieces of filled pasta. They will fold into their characteristic shape as you cut them. Repeat with remaining filling and dough.

Bring a large pot of salted water to a boil and cook the pasta until it rises to the surface, 3 to 4 minutes, then remove with a skimmer. Serve plain in individual bowls lined with cloth napkins.

TORTELLI DI PROVOLONE
Tortelli Stuffed with Provolone
Osteria de l'Umbrelèer, Cicognolo (Cremona), Lombardia

Provolone cheese has long been made in southern Italy, but since the late nineteenth century it has made inroads in the North as well. Today, both mild and sharp versions are made in Lombardia, Trentino, Veneto, and Emilia-Romagna. Provolone comes in many shapes and may resemble a salami, a melon, a mandarin orange, a flask, or a cone, but the most common shape is like a pear with a little round head on top. Use DOP provolone from the Po Valley if you can find it. Make an egg pasta dough and set aside to rest, then roll into a thin sheet. Make a filling of equal amounts grated mild provolone and grated sharp provolone, a little less sheep's milk ricotta, eggs, salt, pepper, and grated nutmeg. Cut out circles or squares of the pasta, fill with the filling, and seal. Cook the tortelli in boiling salted water. Quickly sauté some chopped shallot and sage leaves in butter, then remove the pasta when it rises to the surface of the cooking water and transfer to a serving bowl. Pour the butter, shallot, and sage over it. Sprinkle with grated Parmigiano, if desired, and serve.

RAVIOLI DI CODA DI BUE CON TARTUFO NERO 🥕

Oxtail Ravioli with Black Truffle

Osteria dell'Arco, Magliano di Tenna (Fermo), Marche

Rich braised oxtail and sliced black truffle are a match made in heaven. Though this recipe requires an investment of time, if you read it through you'll see that it's not terribly complex or difficult.

SERVES 8 TO 10

FILLING
1 rib celery, chopped
1 carrot, chopped
1 medium yellow onion, chopped
Extra-virgin olive oil for sautéing
1 oxtail
1 cup dry white wine
2 large eggs, lightly beaten
½ cup grated Parmigiano Reggiano
Freshly grated nutmeg to taste
Salt and freshly ground black pepper to taste

PASTA
4 cups unbleached all-purpose flour
5 large eggs
1 pinch salt

FINISHING
1 tablespoon unsalted butter
Thinly sliced black truffle to taste
Salt to taste
Grated Parmigiano Reggiano to taste

For the filling, in a pot sauté the celery, carrot, and onion in olive oil until browned, then add the oxtail and cook, covered, over very low heat for 1 hour, adding water to the pot in small amounts so that there is always a little liquid in the bottom of the pot. Add the wine and cook for 1 additional hour. Again, add water in small amounts as the meat cooks.

Meanwhile, for the dough, on a work surface knead the flour with the eggs and 1 pinch salt until you have smooth and elastic dough. Cover and set aside to rest.

Clean the oxtail meat from the bone and puree it smooth along with the vegetables. Strain and reserve any cooking liquid left in the pot. In a bowl, combine the pureed meat mixture with the 2 eggs and ½ cup Parmigiano. Season with nutmeg, salt, and pepper and mix by hand until well combined.

Roll the dough into a thin sheet about 1 millimeter (³⁄₁₀₀ inch) thick and cut into squares with 1½- to 2-inch sides. Use the tip of a teaspoon to distribute the filling on half of the squares. Top with the remaining squares and seal the edges with the tines of a fork.

Transfer the strained cooking liquid from the oxtail to a saucepan. Place over medium heat and whisk in the 1 tablespoon butter to thicken. Shave truffle on top and remove from the heat.

Bring a large pot of salted water to a boil for the pasta. As soon as the pasta rises to the surface, remove with a skimmer and transfer to a serving platter. Top with the prepared sauce, sprinkle with additional grated cheese, and serve immediately.

TULTEI
Griddle-Cooked Ravioli
Trattoria Il Borgo, Ormea (Cuneo), Piemonte

*T*ultei were once cooked on a griddle set atop a wood-burning stove and later eaten cold on a break from work, or they were fried, coated with sugar, and served to children for a sweet snack. Serve with bruzza, made of soured ricotta.

SERVES 4

8   cups unbleached all-purpose flour or oo flour
1½ cups heavy cream or whipping cream
Salt to taste
3   tablespoons extra-virgin olive oil
2   leeks, minced
1   tablespoon unsalted butter
1   quart whole milk
Freshly ground black pepper to taste
2   pounds (about 6) potatoes, peeled
7   ounces wild greens and herbs, such as nettles and lambsquarter

On the work surface, shape the flour into a well. Place ½ cup cream, a pinch of salt, and 3 tablespoons olive oil in the center. Knead into a well-combined and elastic dough. Shape into a ball, cover with a towel, and set aside to rest.

In a saucepan, sauté the leeks in the butter. Add the milk and cook over very low heat until greatly reduced, about 1 hour. Add the remaining 1 cup cream and season to taste with salt and pepper.

For the filling, cook the potatoes in lightly salted water until very soft, about 1 hour, then puree through a food mill. Blanch the greens and herbs, drain, and mince. Combine the potatoes, greens and herbs, and leek mixture and stir to combine.

Use a crank pasta machine to roll the dough into thin strips. Dot half of the pasta strips with small amounts of the filling, then top with the remaining strips of pasta. Seal around the filling and cut into large ravioli. Cook on a griddle and serve warm.

TORTELLI CON LA CODA
Braided Ricotta and Spinach Filled Tortelli
Ristorante Antica Locanda del Falco, Gazzola (Piacenza), Emîlia-Romagna

*T*ortelli con la coda, literally "tortelli with a tail," are little braided packets of egg dough with a spinach and ricotta filling. They are as pretty to look at as they are good to eat. Be sure to roll the pasta dough very thin. A *sagra*, or food festival, dedicated to this pasta is held in the Piacenza province in the town of Vigolzone every summer.

SERVES 4

PASTA
4   cups unbleached all-purpose flour or oo flour
5   large eggs

FILLING
4   ounces spinach
11 ounces (1¼ cups) ricotta
2   cups grated Parmigiano Reggiano
2   large eggs, lightly beaten
Salt to taste
Freshly grated nutmeg to taste

FINISHING
Unsalted butter to taste
Sage leaves
Salt to taste
Grated Parmigiano Reggiano to taste

For the pasta, on a work surface knead the flour with the eggs until you have a smooth and compact dough. Cover and set aside to rest for 30 minutes.

For the filling, blanch the spinach, squeeze dry, and mince. In a bowl, combine the ricotta, the spinach, the grated Parmigiano, and the eggs. Stir to combine well, then season with salt and nutmeg.

Roll out the dough very thin (1½ millimeters, or 1/20 inch) and cut into squares with 2-inch sides. Place a small amount of the filling slightly off center on each square. Place one square in the palm of your non-dominant hand (i.e., your left hand if you are right-handed). With your right hand, pinch over alternating sides of the dough (right-left-right-left) to form a braid down the center and a little tail at the end. Pinch to seal, but don't fold over the tail.

Melt butter for the sauce in a large skillet with some sage leaves. Bring a large pot of salted water to a boil and cook the pasta just until it rises to the surface. Remove with a skimmer and place in the skillet. Toss briefly, sprinkling with a generous amount of grated Parmigiano.

RAVIOLI DI RICCIOLA CON SUGO DI LUPINI 🪔
Amberjack Ravioli with Tiny Lupini Clams
Ristorante Sirio, Formia (Latina), Lazio

Amberjack is similar to sea bass and the two types of fish can substitute for each other. Both have firm, somewhat dense flesh. Lupini are tiny, tender clams with gray shells. Soak them in cold salted water for several hours to clean them.

SERVES 4

- 3 cloves garlic, minced
- 2 tablespoons extra-virgin olive oil, plus more for sautéing
- 14 ounces skinless amberjack fillet, chopped
- Salt to taste
- ¼ cup dry white wine
- 1½ cups minced parsley (about 1 bunch)
- 12 ounces borage
- ½ cup grated Parmigiano Reggiano
- 3½ cups unbleached all-purpose flour
- 2 large eggs
- 8 egg yolks
- 2½ pounds lupini clams
- ¼ cup tomato puree

For the filling, in a skillet sauté 1 clove minced garlic in olive oil. Add the amberjack fillet and season with salt. Cook, stirring, for a few minutes, then add the wine and let it evaporate. Add all but about 1 tablespoon of the minced parsley and all of the borage. Cook until the greens have shrunk down and the mixture is well combined. Mince by hand (a food processor will make the mixture too fine). Stir in the grated Parmigiano and mix to combine.

For the dough, combine the flour, eggs, egg yolks, 2 tablespoons olive oil, and a pinch of salt and knead into a dough. It should not be overly soft. Roll into a thin sheet with a rolling pin and cut into small squares. Place a bit of the filling in the center of each square and neatly gather up the corners and sides of one square to meet at the top so that the piece of pasta looks like a drawstring purse. Pinch to seal and repeat with the remaining squares.

For the sauce, place the clams in a pot with a few spoonfuls of water and cook over high heat until they have opened. (Discard any unopened clams.) Shell the clams and strain any cooking liquid. In skillet large enough to hold the pasta, sauté the remaining 2 cloves minced garlic in olive oil. When they turn golden, add the remaining 1 tablespoon parsley and the clams. Cook for 1 minute over medium heat, then add the strained cooking liquid from the clams and the tomato puree. Season with salt and simmer. Meanwhile, bring a large pot of salted water to a boil for the pasta and cook al dente. Remove gently with a slotted spoon or skimmer and transfer to the skillet with the clams. Toss to combine and serve.

AGNOLOTTI AL SUGO DI ARROSTO
Agnolotti in Roasted Meat Sauce
Osteria Ai Binari, Mombarone di Asti (Asti), Piemonte

These agnolotti may appear similar to the *agnolotti dal plin* on page 196, but to those in the Piemonte region, they are completely different. While that pasta can be enjoyed unadorned, these demand a meaty sauce.

SERVES 8 TO 10

FILLING
- 1 rabbit, about 2 pounds
- 1 pound veal chuck
- 1 pound pork shoulder
- 1 carrot, chopped
- 1 medium yellow onion, chopped
- 1 rib celery, chopped
- Extra-virgin olive oil for drizzling
- Salt to taste
- About 1 cup dry white wine
- 1 pound spinach, blanched and squeezed dry
- Parmigiano Reggiano to taste
- 6 large eggs, lightly beaten
- Freshly ground black pepper to taste

PASTA
- 4½ cups stoneground semolina flour
- 5 large eggs, lightly beaten
- 1 pinch salt

SAUCE
- 1 veal marrow bone
- Meat scraps from mixed boiled meat or roasted veal and pork
- ¼ yellow onion, chopped
- ½ carrot, chopped
- ½ rib celery, chopped
- Leaves of 1 sprig rosemary
- 2 bay leaves
- Extra-virgin olive oil for drizzling
- Salt to taste

For the filling, place the rabbit, the chuck, and the pork shoulder in 3 separate baking pans. Divide the carrot, onion, and celery among the pans. Drizzle with extra-virgin olive oil and season with salt. Roast all 3 in the oven for 30 minutes, shaking the pans occasionally to keep the meat from sticking. After 30 minutes, add a little of the wine to each pan and roast for an additional 30 minutes.

While the meat is roasting, make the pasta dough. Shape the flour into a well on the work surface and place the eggs and a pinch of salt in the center of the well. (Don't overdo the salt; the filling is heavily seasoned.) Gradually draw in flour from the side of the well, then knead the dough, adding as much lukewarm water as necessary to make a compact and elastic dough. Set aside to rest for 30 minutes.

For the filling, grind the spinach and roasted meats together. Combine with the Parmigiano and the eggs and season with salt and pepper.

Roll out the pasta with a rolling pin into a thin sheet. Position small pieces of the filling in a row on the sheet of pasta, spacing them a little less than ½ inch apart and leaving a border a little less than ½ inch wide at the edge. Fold the border over the filling to cover, press with your fingertips around the portions of filling to seal, and with a serrated wheel cutter cut the strip of pasta the long way to separate it from the unused dough, then cut in between each portion of filling to make small individual pieces of filled pasta. Repeat with the remaining filling and dough and let the filled pasta rest for at least 1 hour.

For the sauce, place the bone, meat scraps, onion, carrot, celery, rosemary, and bay leaves in a baking pan and toss with oil. Roast for 1 hour. Strain the pan juices and season with salt. To serve, bring a large pot of salted water to a boil, cook the pasta until it rises to the surface, then remove with a skimmer and transer to a serving bowl. Top with the sauce.

CAICC
Stuffed Pasta with Meat and Amaretto Filling
Vecchia Trattoria Ca' Bianca, Breno (Brescia), Lombardia

These large ravioli are a signature dish of Breno.

SERVES 4 TO 6

PASTA

3¾ cups unbleached all-purpose flour,
    plus 1 tablespoon
¼ cup buckwheat flour
4 large eggs
Salt to taste
2 tablespoons milk

FILLING AND SAUCE

5 ounces boiled lean veal
5 ounces roast pork
5 ounces cooked or cured salami
4 ounces mortadella
11 ounces chard, steamed
1 clove garlic
Leaves of 1 sprig parsley
1½ cups walnuts
6 amaretto cookies
20 golden raisins, soaked in warm water
    for 30 minutes and squeezed dry
    (optional)
Freshly grated nutmeg to taste
3 large eggs
2 to 3 tablespoons breadcrumbs
Unsalted butter to taste
3 to 4 sage leaves
Salt to taste
½ cup grated Parmigiano Reggiano
Freshly ground black pepper to taste

For the pasta, combine the 3¾ cups all-purpose flour and the buckwheat flour, shape into a well on the work surface, and place a pinch of salt and 3 eggs in the center of the well. Begin to draw in flour from the sides of the well and then knead until all the flour has been incorporated. Add as much water as needed to make a soft dough, then shape into a ball and set aside to rest.

For the filling, grind the boiled and roasted meats, the salami, the mortadella, the chard, the garlic, the parsley, the walnuts, the amaretto cookies, and the golden raisins, if using, and a pinch of nutmeg in a meat grinder, passing the mixture through the grinder twice. Combine with the eggs and mix well. Add breadcrumbs to make a firm mixture that clumps when you pinch off a piece; you may not need all the breadcrumbs.

Roll the pasta dough into a thin—but not extremely thin—sheet and cut out disks 4¾ to 5½ inches in diameter. In a bowl, break the remaining egg and use a fork to beat with the remaining 1 tablespoon flour and the milk. Brush the tops of the disks with this mixture. Place a small amount of filling on half of the disks of dough. Overturn the other disks and place them, brushed sides down, on top of the filling. Press around the edges to seal.

To serve, place the butter and sage leaves in a skillet and cook until golden brown. Meanwhile, bring a large pot of salted water to a boil and cook the pasta al dente. Drain the pasta and top with the browned butter. Sprinkle with the grated Parmigiano and a little pepper and serve.

PANSOTTI CON SALSA DI NOCI

Pansotti in Walnut Sauce

Osteria Panzallegra, Sarzana (La Spezia), Liguria

*P*ansotti are right-angled triangles of stuffed pasta often filled with a meatless mix of ricotta and greens. Traditionally, they are served in a rich walnut sauce.

SERVES 4

PASTA

2¾ cups unbleached all-purpose flour
4 large eggs
1 pinch salt

FILLING

2 cups grated young sheep's cheese
11 ounces (1¼ cups) ricotta
1½ cups grated Parmigiano Reggiano
2 egg yolks
Salt and freshly ground black pepper to taste

SAUCE

3¾ cups walnuts
2 tablespoons pine nuts (optional)
1 clove garlic, minced
3 tablespoons unsalted butter
½ cup whole milk
Salt to taste

For the dough, on a work surface, shape the flour into a well. Place the eggs, a pinch of salt, and a little water in the center of the well. Begin drawing in flour from the sides of the well and knead, adding as much water as required to make a soft elastic dough. Roll into a thin sheet, then cut into triangles with 4-inch sides.

For the filling, combine the three types of cheese in a bowl. Whisk in the egg yolks and season with salt and pepper. Place a clump of the filling about the size of walnut in the center of each triangle and fold in half to form a triangle. Press around the edges with your fingertips to seal firmly.

For the sauce, grind the walnuts with the pine nuts, if using. In a skillet, brown the garlic in

the butter. Add the nuts and cook, stirring frequently. When the nuts are nicely toasted, add the milk and cook until reduced to a creamy sauce. Taste and adjust salt. Bring a large pot of salted water to a boil and cook the pasta until it rises to the surface, which will take just a few minutes. Remove with a skimmer, toss briefly with the prepared sauce, and serve.

TORTELLONI DI CAPRA

Goat Cheese Robiola Tortelloni

Trattoria Madonna della Neve, Cessole (Cuneo), Piemonte

*R*occaverano robiola is a goat's milk cheese, and while the DOP version of this cheese may contain up to 85 percent cow's milk, under the Slow Food Presidium rules it is made with goat's milk only. If you have never had this kind of real robiola, it may surprise you: it is floral and herbaceous and has its own terroir, with distinct differences from farm to farm. It is delicious both young and aged.

SERVES 6

4 cups unbleached all-purpose flour
5 large eggs
1 egg yolk
14 ounces spinach
1 tablespoon unsalted butter
6 ounces young goat cheese
⅔ cup grated Parmigiano Reggiano
Salt to taste
Chopped toasted hazelnuts to taste
Grated Roccaverano robiola cheese to taste

For the pasta, combine the flour, 4 eggs, yolk, and ¼ cup water and knead to a soft dough. Roll into a thin sheet and set aside to rest while you make the filling.

For the filling, blanch the spinach, drain, sauté in the butter, then mince. Combine the goat cheese, grated Parmigiano, the 1 remaining egg, and the spinach. Taste and adjust salt.

With a serrated wheel cutter, cut the sheet of dough into squares. Set a small amount of the filling on each and fold into a triangle, pressing the edges firmly to seal. Bring a large pot of salted water to a boil and cook the pasta until it rises to the surface, then remove with a skimmer and transfer to individual serving dishes. Sprinkle on the chopped hazelnuts and grated Roccaverano robiola and serve immediately.

TORTELLI DI PRUGNE ▦
Plum Tortelli
Osteria Al Caret, San Siro di San Benedetto Po (Mantova), Lombardia

Tortelli are a classic of Mantova's cuisine; here the expected squash filling is replaced with prunes for a twist. Crumbled amaretto cookies—crisp almond cookies that have been made in the city of Saronno in Lombardia for centuries—are often used in the way that breadcrumbs might be used to stiffen a filling and add body, texture, and flavor. These tortelli can be served in sage butter or tomato sauce.

SERVES 6
3½ pounds Italian plums, pitted
20 amaretto cookies, crumbled
1 cup grated Parmigiano Reggiano
Breadcrumbs for making firm filling
1 pinch freshly grated nutmeg
Salt to taste
6⅔ cups all-purpose flour
8 large eggs
1 tablespoon extra-virgin olive oil
7 tablespoons unsalted butter
3 to 4 sage leaves

For the filling, place the plums in a pot and cook over medium heat, stirring frequently, until they have broken down into a puree. If they are soft but still chunky, puree in a blender. Combine the cooked plums with the crumbled amaretto cookies, the grated Parmigiano, and enough breadcrumbs to make a firm mixture. Season with nutmeg and salt, stir to combine well, and set aside to rest in a cool place.

Meanwhile, for the dough combine the flour, eggs, and olive oil and knead into a very soft dough. Set aside to rest for 4 to 5 hours. Then roll the dough, using a rolling pin or crank pasta machine, into a thin sheet and cut into squares with 4-inch sides. Place a heaping teaspoon of the filling in each square and fold in half. Press the edges to seal.

Melt the butter with the sage leaves. Bring a large pot of salted water to a boil and cook the pasta until it rises to the surface. Remove with a skimmer, drizzle with melted sage butter, and serve.

CARAMELLE DI TALEGGIO CON CULATELLO E TOMA 🐖
Taleggio-Stuffed Caramelle Pasta with Culatello and Toma Cheese
Trattoria Campanini, Busseto (Parma), Emilia-Romagna

Zibello culatello is a highly prized kind of cured pork haunch. It is a DOP product and also has a Slow Food Presidium whose members are long-standing butchers who follow very strict rules: they work only by hand and in winter using raw materials from Emilia-Romagna and Lombardia that are cured using natural processes. With their twisted ends, these pieces of pasta are meant to look like pieces of hard candy wrapped in cellophane.

SERVES 4

2¾ cups unbleached all-purpose flour or
    00 flour
3 large eggs
3 egg yolks
9 ounces mild taleggio
Freshly grated nutmeg to taste
¼ cup extra-virgin olive oil
½ cup heavy cream
¼ cup diced toma made from the milk of
    Italian brown cows
¼ cup diced Zibello culatello (see note on
    page 203)
Salt to taste

Combine the flour, eggs, and yolks to make a soft dough. Cover and set aside to rest for an hour or so.

Place the taleggio in the top of a double boiler and soften. Sprinkle with nutmeg. Roll the dough into a thin sheet about 1 millimeter (3/100 inch) thick and use a smooth wheel cutter to cut rectangles 2½ to 2¾ inches on their long sides and 1½ inches on their short sides. Place a small amount of the taleggio mixture in the center of each. Roll a rectangle into a cylinder and twist the ends, pinching to seal. Repeat with the remaining rectangles of pasta and filling.

In a skillet combine the olive oil, cream, toma, and culatello. Season with salt and simmer until slightly thickened. Meanwhile, bring a large pot of salted water to a boil and cook the pasta until tender, about 5 minutes, then remove with a skimmer and transfer to the skillet with the cream mixture. Toss gently over medium heat to combine and serve.

TORTELLI MAREMMANI
Tortelli Stuffed with Greens in Veal Sauce
Trattoria da Tronca, Massa Marittima (Grosseto), Toscana

These tortelli can also be served with melted sage butter.

SERVES 4

SAUCE
1 medium red onion, thinly sliced
Extra-virgin olive oil for sautéing
1½ pounds veal, coarsely ground
½ cup red wine
1 tablespoon tomato paste
Salt to taste

PASTA
4 cups unbleached all-purpose flour
6 large eggs
Salt to taste

FILLING
1½ pounds chard
1 pound (1¾ cups) sheep's milk ricotta
1 cup grated Parmigiano Reggiano
Salt to taste
Freshly grated nutmeg to taste

For the sauce, in a pot sauté the onion in oil. Add the veal and brown over high heat, then add the wine and cook until evaporated. Dilute the tomato paste in warm water and add. Season with salt and cook over medium heat for 2 hours.

For the pasta, combine the flour, eggs, salt, and a little water and knead for at least 15 minutes. Roll into a thin sheet with a rolling pin or crank pasta machine. Cut into strips about 4 inches wide.

For the filling, blanch the chard and mince in a meat grinder, then combine with the ricotta, Parmigiano, salt, and nutmeg. Shape the filling into small balls of equal size and place them off center on one of the strips of pasta, about 2 inches apart. Fold the empty border of the strip of pasta over and press to seal, then cut into individual pieces with a wheel cutter. Repeat with the remaining pasta strips and filling.

Bring a large pot of salted water to a boil. When the pasta rises to the surface of the cooking water, remove with a skimmer. Top with the veal sauce and serve.

CALZÙ DI CARNI, SALUMI E PATATE

Egg Pasta with Meat and Potato Stuffing

Ristorante Cavallino, Cané di Vione (Brescia), Lombardia

This pasta is made with all sorts of different fillings, such as grated cheese, cotechino sausage, or a combination of salami, cabbage, and potatoes.

SERVES 8

FILLING
- 1¾ pounds ground meat, such as pork, chicken breast, and beef
- Extra-virgin olive oil for sautéing
- Salt and freshly ground black pepper to taste
- 1 salamella pork sausage, casing removed and crumbled
- ¾ cup diced mortadella
- 8 potatoes
- 1 large egg, lightly beaten
- ½ cup grated Parmigiano Reggiano
- Freshly grated nutmeg to taste
- Grated zest of ½ lemon
- 1 medium yellow onion, sliced

PASTA
- 8 cups unbleached all-purpose flour
- 4 large eggs
- Extra-virgin olive oil for dough

FINISHING
- 3 tablespoons unsalted butter
- 3 to 4 sage leaves
- 1 to 2 cloves garlic, minced (optional)
- Salt to taste
- Grated Parmigiano Reggiano to taste

For the filling, brown the meat in a skillet in oil, then season with salt and pepper, cover, and cook over low heat, stirring occasionally so that the meat braises in its own juices. When the meat is cooked through, stir in the salamella and the mortadella and continue cooking until the sausage meat is cooked through. Set aside to cool. Cook the potatoes, then peel and crush them. Chop the meat and potatoes together, then combine with the egg, Parmigiano, nutmeg, and lemon zest. Sauté the onion in oil, then strain out and discard the onion and stir the onion-flavored oil into the filling mixture.

For the pasta, knead together the flour, eggs, a little oil, and some lukewarm water into a soft dough. Set aside to rest for 30 minutes. Roll the dough into a thin sheet and cut out disks of the dough. Place a ball of the filling about the size of a walnut in the center of each disk. Fold over a disk into a half-moon (don't trap air inside the pasta) and seal the edges with the tines of a fork. Repeat with the remaining disks and filling.

Melt the butter in a skillet with the sage leaves and the garlic, if using. Cook until the butter browns slightly. Meanwhile, bring a large pot of salted water to a boil and cook the pasta until tender, 5 to 6 minutes. Gently remove with a skimmer, then toss with the sage and butter, sprinkle with grated Parmigiano, and serve.

CANNELLONI DI SCRIPPELLE

Rolled Crepes with Meat Filling

Minuccia De Berardinis, Roseto degli Abruzzi (Teramo), Abruzzo

In a bowl, whisk 1 egg per person and then sprinkle in 1 tablespoon flour per person until no lumps remain. Whisk in water in a thin stream until you have a thin batter. Grease a nonstick pan with a piece of lardo or prosciutto fat, place over medium heat, and when the pan is very hot, add about ¼ cup of the batter, tilting the pan to cover the whole surface. Cook for 1 minute, then carefully use a skimmer to transfer to wax paper. Continue with the remaining batter. For the filling, cook equal amounts veal, pork, and chicken in a skillet in a little extra-virgin olive oil. Mince the cooked meat and combine with a few spoonfuls of ragù, some grated Parmigiano Reggiano, and a pinch of grated nutmeg. Beat in a little softened butter and enough egg yolk to keep the mixture stiff but pliable (not runny). Taste and adjust salt. Fill each crepe with a spoonful of the meat mixture (reserve a little for topping) and a few cubes of diced mozzarella and roll up the crepes tightly. Butter a skillet and place the rolled crepes in it. They should be pressed together fairly tightly. Pour in beef broth to come about ¾ of the way up the crepes or just to cover and top them with the reserved meat sauce. Cook over medium heat until the broth has reduced. Sprinkle with a little more Parmigiano Reggiano and serve.

SPOJA LORDA CON SALSICCIA E RADICCHIO 🌳
Pasta Smeared with a Little Cheese Served with Sausage and Radicchio
Trattoria Croce Daniele, Brisighella (Ravenna), Emilia-Romagna

S poja lorda literally means "dirty sheet of dough," because the sheet of pasta dough is just lightly smeared with the filling rather than being truly stuffed full of it, as with ravioli. Originally, this dish was invented as a way to use up a scant amount of leftover filling and trimmings, and the recipe, such as it was, consisted of wiping out the bowl that had contained the filling with leftover rolled pasta trimmings and then cooking them. Stracchino is a soft, spreadable cheese usually sold in small bricks or tubs—you will need a 250-gram package. Variations on this dish from the area in and around Forlì and Cesena sometimes incorporate a little meat in the filling, and this type of pasta is served in a rustic and hearty sauce or boiled in tasty beef broth.

SERVES 4
- 2¾ cups unbleached all-purpose flour or 0 flour
- 5 large eggs
- 9 ounces stracchino cheese
- 1 cup grated Parmigiano Reggiano
- Salt to taste
- Freshly grated nutmeg to taste
- 4 tablespoons unsalted butter
- 2 ounces sausage, casing removed and crumbled
- 1 cup loosely packed ribbons of Chioggia radicchio

For the pasta, form the flour into a well. Place 4 eggs in the center, beat with a fork, and begin drawing in flour from the side of the well. When you have a crumbly mass, knead into a firm, elastic dough. Cover with a kitchen towel and set aside to rest for 15 minutes.

For the filling, in a bowl combine the stracchino with the remaining egg, grated Parmigiano, salt, and nutmeg. Combine well and set aside.

With a rolling pin, roll out the pasta dough to a thin sheet (a little less than 1/10 inch), cut in half into two pieces of equal size and shape, and smear the filling on one half. Place the other piece of dough on top of the smeared dough. Press down to seal and make sure you don't create any air pockets in between the two pieces of dough. Use a serrated wheel cutter to cut into squares with ½- to ¾-inch sides. Spread out in a single layer and allow to dry briefly.

For the sauce, in a large skillet melt the butter over low heat. Add the crumbled sausage and brown for a few minutes, then add the radicchio. Season with salt and cook until the radicchio is wilted, 1 to 2 additional minutes. Bring a large pot of salted water to a boil and cook the pasta until it rises to the surface. Remove with a skimmer and transfer to the skillet with the butter mixture. Toss to combine and serve.

TORTELLI DI FONDUTA 🧀
Tortelli with Fontina Filling
Osteria Lalibera, Alba (Cuneo), Piemonte

Be sure to break up the fontina with your hands. It requires a little more effort than using a grater or food processor, but the end result is worth it. If you want to speed up the process, you can try cooking the fonduta in a heavy-bottomed pot over low heat for 20 minutes, but you will need to keep a close eye on it to prevent scorching. If you can get your hands on a white Alba truffle, skip the sage in the butter sauce and shave thin petals of truffle over the pasta just before serving.

SERVES 10

PASTA
4   cups unbleached all-purpose flour or 00 flour
10   large eggs
1   tablespoon extra-virgin olive oil
Salt to taste

FILLING
1¾ pounds fontina
1   cup whole milk
3   large eggs
6   egg yolks
2   tablespoons unbleached all-purpose flour
6   tablespoons unsalted butter
Salt and freshly ground black pepper to taste

FINISHING
Unsalted butter to taste
3 to 4 sage leaves
Salt to taste

For the pasta, knead the flour, eggs, olive oil, and a pinch of salt into a compact but elastic dough. If it feels too firm, knead in a little water. Then set aside to rest for at least 30 minutes.

Meanwhile, make the filling. Break apart the fontina by hand and place in the top of a double boiler with 1 cup water, the milk, the eggs and egg yolks, the flour, the butter, and salt and pepper to taste. Place on top of boiling water and cook over low heat, whisking briskly and constantly with a wooden spoon, for 45 minutes. Set aside to cool.

While the filling is cooling, roll the dough into a thin sheet and use a cookie cutter or glass to cut out disks or cut into squares with 2-inch sides using a wheel cutter. Place a portion of the filling in the center of each piece of pasta and fold into half-moons (circles) or triangles (squares). Take care not to trap any air inside the folded pasta, and press firmly around the edges to seal.

Melt butter with sage leaves for topping the pasta. Bring a large pot of salted water to a boil and cook just a few pieces of pasta at a time to keep them from getting stuck to each other. Remove with a skimmer and transfer to a serving bowl, then top with the sage butter and serve.

CRESPELLE ALLA VALDOSTANA 🧀
Crepes with Fontina and Prosciutto
Cotto Trattoria degli Amici, Saint-Vincent (Aosta), Valle d'Aosta

Though the world at large considers crepes a French invention, Italians from many different areas believe their crespelle predate their French cousins. Some say they were invented in Paleochristian Rome, others that Florentines first made thin pancakes as a riff on their medieval ritortelli. These crespelle, however, are a more modern invention: in the 1960s, a great effort was made to advertise locally made fontina cheese (not well known outside the area at the time), and restaurants in Valle d'Aosta began making these crepes with fontina in both the filling and the sauce. The dish became wildly popular with locals and visitors alike and is still a favorite today—a manufactured "traditional dish," but a delicious one nonetheless.

SERVES 4

BATTER
1   cup unbleached all-purpose flour or 00 flour
1   cup whole milk
2   large eggs, lightly beaten
1   pinch salt
3   tablespoons unsalted butter, softened

SAUCE
4   ounces fontina cheese, cut into cubes
1   cup whole milk
1   tablespoon unsalted butter
2   egg yolks

FILLING AND FINISHING
8   slices prosciutto cotto
8   slices semi-hard fontina cheese
Freshly ground black pepper to taste
Freshly grated nutmeg to taste
1   tablespoon unsalted butter

For the batter, in a bowl combine the flour and milk and whisk smooth. Whisk in eggs, salt, and about half of the butter. Set aside to rest for at least 1 hour. Butter a crepe pan or skillet with the remaining butter and cook the batter into 8 thin crepes, tilting the pan as you add the batter to cover the surface evenly, and flipping the crepes to cook both sides. Drain briefly on paper towels. Preheat the oven to 350°F.

For the sauce, place the fontina cubes in a bowl that can be used on top of a double boiler and pour the milk over them. Add 1 tablespoon butter to the bowl, place on top of a double boiler, and cook, whisking, until the cheese is completely melted. In a separate bowl, beat the egg yolks. Add the yolks to the cheese mixture. Whisk until completely incorporated, about 3 minutes.

Place 1 slice of prosciutto and 1 slice of fontina on each crepe, season with pepper and nutmeg, fold the crepes in half, and arrange them in a single layer or slightly overlapping in a baking pan. Drizzle on the prepared sauce, dot with the remaining 1 tablespoon butter, and bake in the preheated oven until browned, 10 to 15 minutes.

CJARSONS DI PATATE
Pasta Stuffed with Potato
Trattoria Stella d'Oro, Villa di Verzegnis (Udine),
Friuli-Venezia Giulia

Cjarsons are half-moons and almost always have a sweet component in their filling, whether chocolate, candied fruit, or preserves. If you can't get o flour and oo flour, just use 2 cups of all-purpose flour. The numbers refer to the coarseness of the grind.

SERVES 4

PASTA
1   cup unbleached all-purpose flour or
    o flour
1   cup unbleached all-purpose flour or
    oo flour
1   pinch salt

FILLING
3 to 4 potatoes
1   tablespoon unsalted butter
1   bunch aromatic herbs, such as parsley,
    mint, melissa, marjoram, and tarragon,
    minced
1   tablespoon breadcrumbs
1   tablespoon golden raisins, soaked in
    warm water and squeezed dry
1   tablespoon cherry preserves
1   tablespoon ground cinnamon
Salt to taste

FINISHING
Clarified butter to taste
2   sage leaves
Salt to taste
Grated aged latteria cheese to taste
Grated smoked ricotta to taste

For the pasta, combine the flours, a pinch of salt, and enough warm water to make a soft dough. Cover with a kitchen towel and set aside to rest while you prepare the filling.

For the filling, boil the potatoes until tender, then peel, crush, and pass through a sieve. Melt the butter in a skillet and sauté the herbs for 5 minutes. Add the herbs to the potatoes, then stir in breadcrumbs, raisins, cherry preserves, and cinnamon. Mix until well combined. Season with salt.

On a work surface, roll the pasta dough into a thin sheet, then use an overturned drinking glass to cut out disks 2¾ to 3½ inches in diameter. Place a portion of the filling on each disk and fold the disks in half, pressing to seal along the border.

Place clarified butter in a large skillet with the sage and cook over low heat. Bring a large pot of salted water to a boil and cook the pasta until it rises to the surface, 5 to 6 minutes. Drain thoroughly and add to the skillet with the clarified butter. Sprinkle on a little latteria cheese and toss to combine. Arrange the pasta on plates in a fan shape, sprinkle with smoked ricotta, and serve hot.

CAPPELLACCI AL RAGÙ
Squash Cappellacci in Meat Sauce
Stefania Ricci, Ferrara, Emilia-Romagna

Mantova and Ferrara have both laid claim to pasta stuffed with a squash filling since the mid-1400s. Those in Ferrara are slightly larger and made with a slightly thicker dough and called *cappellacci*, while those in Mantova are known as *tortelli*. Subtle regional differences abound. In and around Modena, the pasta is served with a sausage ragù. In Bologna, a little mortadella makes its way into the filling. In the areas around the Lombardia border, crumbled amaretto cookies are added. In Reggio Emilia and Parma, the pasta takes the form of rectangular ravioli. Since 1994, Slow Food has organized an annual national competition for the makers of this delicious pasta.

For the sauce, brown minced beef, crumbled sausage (casing removed), and diced pancetta in olive oil with minced onion, carrots, and celery. When the meat has lost its raw red color, add white wine and cook until evaporated, then add tomato puree. Season with salt and pepper and cook over very low heat. For the filling, roast halved seeded butternut squash until tender, then force through a sieve. In a bowl, beat the squash with enough egg and grated Parmigiano Reggiano to make a rather dry mixture. Add breadcrumbs if necessary to achieve the right consistency. Season with salt and freshly grated nutmeg. If the squash is not particularly sweet, add a pinch of sugar. Make a pasta dough with whole eggs and all-purpose or 00 flour and roll out a little thicker than usual. Cut into squares with 2⅓-inch sides or larger. Place a spoonful of the filling on each square and fold in half diagonally, pressing to seal the edges. Cook the pasta in boiling salted water with a drop of olive oil to keep the pasta from opening or sticking together. As soon as the pieces of pasta rise to the surface, remove with a skimmer. Arrange in a serving bowl with the meat sauce in alternating layers. Sprinkle with a generous amount of grated Parmigiano Reggiano. Leftover cappellacci are delicious the next day: reheat in a skillet with a little butter over high heat so that they brown in spots.

PALACINKE ALLA MANDRIERA 🌿
Crepes with Basil Filling
Trattoria Suban, Trieste, Friuli-Venezia Giulia

Palatschinke are crepes served all over the former territories of the Austro-Hungarian empire. They may be sweet (filled with fruit, honey, or chocolate) or savory (filled with cured meat, cheese, mushrooms, greens).

SERVES 4

1   cup unbleached all-purpose flour or 00 flour
1   cup whole milk
1   large egg
2   egg yolks
Salt to taste
Leaves of 1 bunch basil
2   cloves garlic
Extra-virgin olive oil for drizzling
Unsalted butter for buttering pan and browning crepes
¼   cup rich stock or pan juices from roasted meat
¼   cup heavy cream
Grated aged cheese (such as Parmigiano Reggiano) to taste
Freshly ground black pepper to taste

For the crepe batter, sift the flour into a bowl and then gradually whisk in the milk, the egg, and the yolks. Season with salt and whisk to be sure there are no lumps. Set aside to rest for at least 30 minutes. Meanwhile, puree the basil leaves, garlic, and a pinch of salt while drizzling in enough oil to make a creamy sauce.

Preheat the oven to medium heat (about 350°F, but if you have the oven on for another use, you can be flexible). Butter a nonstick pan, then heat the pan over medium heat. Add enough batter to coat the pan thinly, turning it to cover the entire surface, then cook over medium heat until browned and set. Flip and cook the other side. Repeat with the remaining batter, buttering the pan as needed.

Spread basil sauce on each crepe, then fold them in half. In a large ovenproof skillet, brown the crepes in a little butter. Remove from the heat. Whisk together the stock and cream and add the mixture to the skillet. Sprinkle on the grated cheese and season with pepper, then bake until browned on top, 8 to 10 minutes.

❦{ B A K E D   P A S T A }❧

LASAGNA BOLOGNESE
Lasagna Bolognese
Trattoria Serghei, Bologna, Emília-Romagna

If you have only eaten overstuffed types of lasagna, you will be pleasantly surprised by a classic lasagna Bolognese, which judiciously balances spinach noodles with a meaty sauce and béchamel. It can be assembled in advance and baked before serving. A traditional meat ragù cooks very slowly over low heat. The incorporation of milk keeps the meat soft and sweet.

SERVES 6

- 2¾ cups unbleached all-purpose flour
- 3 large eggs
- 7 ounces spinach, blanched, squeezed dry, and minced
- 2 ribs celery, minced
- 1 carrot, minced
- ½ medium yellow onion, minced
- Extra-virgin olive oil for sautéing
- ¼ cup diced pancetta
- 5 ounces finely ground pork
- 1 chicken liver and giblets, chopped
- 1 pound finely ground beef
- ½ cup whole milk
- 2 cups chopped tomatoes
- Salt and freshly ground black pepper to taste
- 1 tablespoon unsalted butter
- 2 cups béchamel (page 47 or 214)
- 2 cups grated Parmigiano Reggiano

For the pasta, on a work surface knead the flour with the eggs and minced spinach until you have a firm and elastic dough. Cover with a kitchen towel and set aside to rest.

Meanwhile, for the meat sauce, sauté the minced celery, carrot, and onion in a little oil until soft, then add the pancetta and cook over low heat for 3 additional minutes. Add the ground pork and cook, stirring frequently, for 5 minutes. Then add the chicken liver and giblets. Cook for a few minutes, then add the ground beef and cook for 30 minutes, stirring frequently. The meat should not brown. Add the milk and cook until liquid has evaporated, then add the tomatoes and about ½ cup lukewarm water. Season with salt and pepper and cook, covered, over the lowest possible heat for 1½ hours.

Meanwhile, roll the pasta dough into a thin sheet less than 1/10 inch thick and cut into large rectangular noodles. Bring a large pot of salted water to a boil and cook the pasta al dente, then transfer to an ice bath to stop the cooking. Spread the noodles in a single layer on a kitchen towel to dry thoroughly.

Preheat the oven to 350°F. Butter a large baking pan with 1 tablespoon butter and spread a little of the sauce on the bottom. Cover with a layer of noodles, then some of the béchamel, then a sprinkling of grated Parmigiano, and continue to build layers in that order until you have used up all of the ingredients, ending with a layer of the sauce and a sprinkling of grated cheese on top. Bake in the preheated oven until browned and bubbling, about 1 hour. Let the lasagna rest for a few minutes before cutting.

LASAGNA NAPOLETANA 🌿
Neapolitan Lasagna
Trattoria 'O Romano, Sarno (Salerno), Campania

Neapolitans incorporate small meatballs into their lasagna, which makes it look especially pretty when sliced. Don't over-cook the noodles, as they'll continue to grow softer in the oven.

SERVES 6
1   rib celery, minced
1   carrot, minced
1   medium yellow onion, minced
Extra-virgin olive oil for sautéing and pan-frying
1   pound ground veal
4½ cups tomato puree
Salt and freshly ground black pepper to taste
3   large eggs
1½ cups grated Parmigiano Reggiano
11 ounces curly lasagna noodles
9   ounces (1 cup) ricotta
2   cups diced fior di latte mozzarella
4   ounces salami, cut into strips

In a pot, sauté the celery, carrot, and onion in olive oil. Add about half of the ground veal and cook until it has lost its rare red color, then add the tomato puree. Season with salt and pepper and cook, stirring occasionally, over very low heat for 2 hours.

Combine the remaining ground veal with 1 egg and season with salt and pepper. Stir in about ¼ cup Parmigiano and shape into small meatballs (the size of a walnut). Pan-fry the meatballs in olive oil until browned on all sides. Hard-boil the 2 remaining eggs and dice them.

Preheat the oven to 350°F. Bring a large pot of salted water to a boil and cook the noodles very al dente—about half of their regular cooking time. Drain and cool, but make sure they don't stick together.

Smear some of the meat sauce on the bottom of a baking pan and toss the rest with the noodles. Make at least 3 layers of the ingredients in the pan (you may be able to make more, depending on the size of the pan) in this order from the bottom upward: noodles with sauce, ricotta, mozzarella, meatballs, salami, hard-boiled egg. End with a layer of the noodles, then sprinkle on the remaining grated Parmigiano and bake until browned and bubbling, about 35 minutes.

LASAGNA DI RADICCHIO E CARCIOFI 🌳
Radicchio and Artichoke Lasagna
Antica Osteria Al Tiglio, Moruzzo (Udine), Friuli-Venezia Giulia

Radicchio is bitter when raw but turns sweet when cooked. If you are not a fan of robiola cheese, you can use milder quartirolo in its place.

SERVES 4
2¾ cups plus 1 tablespoon unbleached all-purpose flour
3   large eggs, lightly beaten
Salt to taste
3   medium heads Treviso radicchio, cored and separated into leaves
Extra-virgin olive oil for braising
3   artichokes, trimmed and sliced
7   ounces aged robiola, thinly sliced
3   tablespoons unsalted butter, melted
½   cup grated Parmigiano Reggiano
Freshly ground black pepper to taste

On a work surface, shape 2¾ cups flour into a well and place the eggs, a little salt, and a small amount of water in the middle of the well. Begin to draw in flour from the sides of the well, then knead into a firm dough, adding as much water as needed. Roll into a sheet about ⅒ inch thick.

In a skillet, braise the radicchio with a pinch of salt in oil over high heat until wilted. Remove with a slotted spoon or skimmer and drain on paper towels. Bring a pot of salted water to a boil and stir in the remaining 1 tablespoon flour. Cook the artichokes until tender, then drain on paper towels. Cut the sheet of pasta dough into squares the size of the small baking pan you plan to use. Bring a large pot of salted water to a boil and cook the pasta for just a few seconds, then transfer to an ice water bath. Spread on a clean kitchen towel to dry.

Preheat the oven to 400°F. Butter the small baking pan. Cover the bottom with a square of pasta, then top with a few leaves of radicchio (spread open) and slices of robiola. Make another layer of pasta and top with artichokes and robiola. Continue making alternating layers until you have used up all of these ingredients, ending with a layer of pasta. Drizzle on the melted butter, sprinkle on the grated Parmigiano, season with salt and pepper, and bake until browned, about 15 minutes.

PASTA CHINA
Baked Pasta with Provolone and Beef
Da Pepè La Vecchia Osteria, Catanzaro, Calabria

Pasta china is local dialect for "filled pasta." Traditionally, this is made with "half zite," i.e., long tubes of dried semolina pasta about ⅓ inch in diameter that are snapped in half. But you can use any medium-short tubular pasta that is not too wide, such as penne. Soppressata is a spicy salami.

SERVES 6

- 5 large eggs
- 7 ounces soppressata
- 7 ounces provolone or mozzarella
- About 2 cups tomato puree
- Salt to taste
- 9 ounces ground beef
- Leaves of 1 sprig parsley, minced
- 1 clove garlic, minced
- Extra-virgin olive oil for pan-frying
- 1 pound zite, snapped in half, or other medium-short tubular pasta
- Grated aged sheep's cheese for sprinkling on top

Hard-boil 4 of the eggs. Slice or dice the hard-boiled eggs, the soppressata, and the provolone. (In other words, slice all or dice all.) Place the tomato puree in a saucepan and reduce to a sauce, seasoning with salt if necessary. For the meatballs, combine the ground beef, parsley, garlic, and a pinch of salt. Lightly beat the remaining egg and add to the mixture. Shape the mixture into small meatballs and pan-fry in olive oil, then drain on paper towels.

Preheat the oven to 350°F. Bring a large pot of salted water to a boil and cook the pasta al dente. Drain and toss with about half of the tomato sauce. Spread the remaining sauce on the bottom of a baking pan. In the pan make a layer of the pasta, then meatballs, then hard-boiled egg, provolone, and soppressata. Continue to make layers in this order until you have used up the ingredients. End with a layer of pasta on top, then sprinkle on the grated aged sheep's cheese. Bake in the preheated oven until browned and bubbling. Let the pasta set for a few minutes before serving.

LASAGNA ALL'ORTICA 🌿
Nettle Lasagna
Trattoria Le Panzanelle, Radda in Chianti (Siena), Toscana

ettle leaves are covered in little prickly hairs and must be handled with care when raw—wear gloves. Once cooked, they're harmless (and tasty).

SERVES 4

FILLING AND FINISHING
Blossoms and leaves of 50 sprigs nettle
8   *tablespoons (1 stick) unsalted butter,*
    plus more for sautéing
1   *cup unbleached all-purpose flour or*
    00 flour
2   *quarts whole milk*
Salt and freshly ground black pepper to taste
Freshly grated nutmeg to taste

Extra-virgin olive oil for sautéing
2   *cloves garlic*
2   *tablespoons crumbled mild Gorgonzola*
1½ *cups grated Parmigiano Reggiano*

PASTA
1   *cup unbleached all-purpose flour or*
    0 flour
1   *cup semolina flour*
1   *pinch salt*
3   *large eggs*

Bring a large pot of water to a boil and cook the nettles for about 2 hours. Meanwhile, for the pasta, combine the flours and salt and form into a well on the work surface. Place the eggs in the center of the well and knead into a soft, elastic dough. Set aside to rest for a while, then roll into a thin sheet and cut into rectangles.

In a saucepan, melt the 8 tablespoons butter and whisk in the flour, then whisk in the milk. Season with salt, pepper, and nutmeg and reduce to a creamy béchamel sauce, whisking constantly. Puree the cooked nettles with a little of their cooking water to make a smooth but not runny mixture. Melt a combination of butter and oil in a skillet and add the garlic and the nettle mixture and cook over medium heat, stirring, until the garlic begins to color. Remove and discard the garlic and stir in the Gorgonzola.

Preheat the oven to 350°F. Bring a large pot of salted water to a boil and cook the pasta very al dente, 3 to 4 minutes. Drain. Smear a little of the béchamel on the bottom of a baking pan with high sides. Cover with a layer of one sixth of the noodles, then béchamel and about one fifth of the nettle mixture. Use a rubber spatula to combine the two, then sprinkle with some of the Parmigiano. Continue to make layers in this order, ending with a layer of noodles so that you have five layers of nettles and béchamel and six of noodles. Top the noodles with the last of the béchamel and sprinkle the remaining Parmigiano on the top. Bake in the preheated oven until browned and bubbling.

PASTICCIO DI CARCIOFI 🌳
Baked Pasta with Artichokes
Ristorante Taverna della Torre, Cisternino
Brindisi), Puglia

A *pasticcio* is literally a "mess"—usually a tangle of pasta and other ingredients baked in the oven. This one, made with charmingly irregular little rags of pasta, is inverted and unmolded, much like a timbale.

SERVES 6

3⅓ cups unbleached all-purpose flour or
    00 flour
⅔ cup semolina flour
Salt to taste
6 artichokes, trimmed and sliced
½ cup minced shallot
Extra-virgin olive oil for sautéing
½ cup white wine
¼ cup vegetable broth
7 ounces young caciotta, cut into small dice
Leaves of 1 sprig parsley, minced
Freshly ground black pepper to taste

Preheat the oven to 350°F.

For the pasta, combine the flours with a pinch of salt and knead with enough water to make a firm, elastic dough. Roll into a thin sheet and cut into irregular shapes. Cook the pasta in boiling salted water just until it rises to the surface. (Keep in mind that it will go into the oven afterward.) Drain and set aside.

In a small pot, sauté the artichokes and shallot in a little oil. Add the wine and cook until evaporated, then add the broth and cook for 2 to 3 minutes. Remove from the heat and stir in the caciotta and parsley. Season with salt and pepper and cook, covered, 2 to 3 additional minutes.

Fill a baking pan with alternating layers of the pasta and the artichoke mixture. Bake in the preheated oven until browned. Allow to rest for a few minutes, then place a platter upside down over the pan. Wearing oven mitts, flip both pan and platter. Lift off the pan and serve.

LASAGNE DI VERDURE 🥕
Vegetable Lasagna
Osteria Il Lupo, Sarzana (La Spezia), Liguria

W e think of lasagna as a baked pasta dish, but the name really refers to the large noodles. This version is not baked in the oven—layers are constructed directly on the serving plate.

SERVES 6

4 cups unbleached all-purpose flour
5 large eggs
1 medium yellow onion, chopped
1 carrot, chopped
1 rib celery, chopped
Extra-virgin olive oil for sautéing
14 ounces tomatoes, chopped
Ground chili pepper to taste
1 bay leaf
Salt to taste
1 bunch chard
5 to 6 leaves borage
2 cups grated Parmigiano Reggiano
11 ounces (1¼ cups) sheep's milk ricotta
Freshly grated nutmeg to taste

Shape the flour into a well on the work surface. Lightly beat 3 eggs and add to the well along with a little lukewarm water. Begin drawing in flour from the sides of the well, then knead into a soft, smooth dough, adding water as needed. Roll into a thin sheet and cut into 4¾-inch squares.

In a pot, sauté the onion, carrot, and celery in a little oil. Add the tomatoes, chili, and bay leaf, season with salt, and cook over low heat for 45 minutes. Meanwhile, bring a pot of salted water to a boil and blanch the chard and borage. Drain and mince, then combine with 1½ cups of the Parmigiano, the 2 remaining eggs, the ricotta, and a little nutmeg and set aside. Remove the bay leaf from the sauce and discard.

Bring a large pot of salted water to a boil and cook the pasta al dente. To serve, make alternating layers on each serving plate of noodles, tomato sauce, ricotta mixture, and a sprinkling of Parmigiano, ending with Parmigiano.

GATTÒ SALSICCE E FRIARIELLI

Sausage and Pepper Potato Cake

La Compagnia del Ragù, Giugliano in Campania (Napoli), Campania

Sometimes this dish is called a Santa Chiara, as nuns who were members of the Order of Saint Clare (*Santa Chiara* in Italian) are thought to have invented it.

SERVES 6

- 4½ pounds (10 to 14) white potatoes
- ½ cup whole milk
- 1 tablespoon unsalted butter, plus more for buttering pan
- ½ cup grated Grana Padano cheese
- Salt and freshly ground black pepper to taste
- 1 large bunch young and tender broccoli rabe
- 1 tablespoon extra-virgin olive oil, plus more for sautéing and oiling fingers
- 1 clove garlic, crushed
- 1 chili pepper, minced
- 9 ounces fennel sausage, casing removed and crumbled
- Breadcrumbs for coating pan and sprinkling on top
- 9 ounces smoked provolone, cut into thin matchsticks

Cook the potatoes in boiling water until tender enough to pierce with a fork. Drain, peel, and crush with a potato ricer while still warm. Mix the crushed potatoes with the milk, butter, grated cheese, salt, and pepper. Blanch the broccoli rabe in boiling water for 5 minutes, then drain, squeeze dry, chop, and sauté in a skillet in olive oil with the crushed garlic and chili pepper for about 5 minutes.

In a skillet, combine the 1 tablespoon olive oil and about ¼ cup water over medium heat. Add the sausage and cook, stirring, for a few minutes until the meat is lightly cooked.

Preheat the oven to 350°F.

Butter a baking pan. Sprinkle with breadcrumbs to coat, then turn over and tap out any excess. Place the sautéed broccoli rabe in the pan, then top with the sausage. Spread the provolone in a single layer on top. Cover with the potato mixture. Dip your fingers in olive oil and spread even and smooth. Sprinkle with additional breadcrumbs and bake in the preheated oven until browned, about 30 minutes. Serve warm.

TIMBALLO DI ANELLINI

Baked Pasta Timbale with Veal, Pork, and Vegetables

Fîlippa Gatì, Palermo, Sicîlia

To serve 4 people, slice an eggplant and salt the slices, then let them drain for a couple of hours. Sauté ½ minced onion, ⅔ cup diced prosciutto cotto, 2 cups shelled peas, minced parsley, and 1 whole garlic clove in extra-virgin olive oil. Add 1 cup water and cook over medium heat until evaporated. In a separate pot, sauté another ½ minced onion with ½ pound each ground veal and ground pork. Add 1 tablespoon tomato paste diluted in a little water, season with salt, and cook over low heat for at least 1 hour, adding small amounts of water, if necessary, to keep from sticking. Fry the eggplant and drain on paper towels. Cook about 14 ounces (4 cups) *anellini* (small ring-shaped) pasta very al dente. Drain and toss with the meat sauce. Butter a baking pan and coat with breadcrumbs. Arrange the fried eggplant to cover the bottom of the pan. Top with a layer of half the pasta. Add the prosciutto and peas mixture in an even layer. Top with the remaining pasta. Sprinkle 1 cup grated aged sheep's cheese on top, and bake at 350°F for 20 minutes. Allow to cool somewhat before serving warm.

VINCISGRASSI AL SUGO DI CARNI E RIGAGLIE
Rich Lasagna with Meat and Giblets
Osteria dei Fiori, Macerata, Marche

incisgrassi is a very rich baked pasta from the province of Macerata believed to have been created for an Austrian officer named Windisch Grätz, who fought against Napoleon's army in the area. It should have at least seven layers, so choose your baking pan accordingly.

SERVES 6

PASTA
8   cups unbleached all-purpose flour or 0 flour
8   large eggs
2   tablespoons vino cotto

BÉCHAMEL
1   quart whole milk
⅓   cup extra-virgin olive oil
1   pinch salt
½   cup unbleached all-purpose flour or 0 flour

SAUCE
1½ pounds mixed meat on the bone, such as pork, veal, rabbit, and chicken
Extra-virgin olive oil for sautéing
Salt and freshly ground black pepper to taste
1   cup dry white wine
½   cup tomato paste
5   ounces chicken giblets
1   medium yellow onion
3 to 4 whole cloves
1   carrot, minced
2   ribs celery, minced
2   cups canned peeled tomatoes, chopped
Unsalted butter for buttering pan
Grated Parmigiano Reggiano to taste

For the pasta, on a work surface knead together the flour, eggs, and vino cotto into a smooth and elastic dough, cover, and set aside to rest.

Make the béchamel. Gently heat the milk in a saucepan over low heat, then add the oil and a pinch of salt. Sprinkle in the flour while whisking constantly and cook, still whisking, until the mixture has the consistency of sour cream. Remove from the heat and set aside.

Bone the meat and chop, reserving the bones. Place the bones in a large pot, coat with olive oil, and brown them, then add salt, pepper, and ½ cup of the wine. Cook until the wine has evaporated and add tomato paste and water just to cover. Cook over low heat at length to make a strong stock. Strain and reserve.

Meanwhile, in a small skillet, sauté the chicken giblets in a little oil and when they are browned, mince them. In another pot, brown the meat over high heat until it gives up its juices. Stud the onion with the cloves. Season

the meat with salt and pepper and add the carrot, celery, and onion. Brown for a few minutes, then add the remaining ½ cup wine. When the wine has evaporated, add the giblets, chopped tomatoes, and the prepared stock. Cook over the lowest possible heat for at least 1½ hours, adding small amounts of water if the sauce seems to be getting overly dense.

Roll the pasta dough into a thin sheet and cut into large rectangles. Bring a pot of salted water to a boil and cook the pasta briefly, then run under cold water and spread in a single layer on a kitchen towel to dry.

Preheat the oven to 350°F. Thickly butter a large baking pan, then line the bottom with a layer of pasta. Top with some of the meat sauce, then some béchamel, and a sprinkling of Parmigiano and continue to make layers until you have used up all of the ingredients, ending with Parmigiano. Bake until crisp and browned on top and soft in the center, about 40 minutes.

{DUMPLINGS}

GNOCCHI ALLA ROMANA ⬤
Roman Semolina Dumplings
Osteria del Velodromo Vecchio, Roma, Lazio

These gnocchi are a Roman classic and are often served on holidays. They are also great for entertaining, because they can be prepared in advance and browned at the last minute. The egg yolks will make this an even richer dish.

SERVES 4
- 1 quart whole milk
- 2½ cups semolina flour
- Salt to taste
- Freshly grated nutmeg to taste
- About 1 cup grated Parmigiano Reggiano
- 2 egg yolks (optional)
- 10 tablespoons (1 stick plus 2 tablespoons) unsalted butter

Place the milk in a pot and bring to a boil, then slowly drizzle in the semolina flour, stirring constantly with a wooden spoon to avoid lumps. Season with salt and nutmeg and cook over low heat, stirring constantly, for 30 minutes. Remove the semolina from the heat and whisk in 1 tablespoon grated Parmigiano and the egg yolks, if using. Brush a marble surface with water, then pour the mixture onto the surface, smoothing the top and making it an even thickness a little less than ½ inch. Allow to cool.

With a cookie cutter or glass, cut out as many circles as you can from the cooled semolina, with as few scraps as possible. Thickly butter a baking pan and melt the remaining butter. In the prepared pan, arrange the disks in rows, overlapping slightly, like shingles on a roof. (You can hide any scraps on the bottom so they don't go to waste.) Sprinkle each row with some of the grated cheese and drizzle on the melted butter as you go. Bake or broil until a golden crust forms on top, about 10 minutes, then allow to rest briefly before serving.

GNOCCHI DI COLLA ⬤
Bread Dumplings
Renata Nonis, Rovetta (Bergamo), Lombardia

Renata Nonis learned this recipe from the Fantoni family of Bergamasco, who have been sculpting and carving wood and marble for centuries. Soak stale bread in milk to soften. Meanwhile, boil diced peeled white potatoes in salted water until tender. Remove potatoes with a slotted spoon or skimmer and reserve cooking water and keep at a boil. Crumble the bread into a bowl and mix with flour and egg. The mixture should be fairly dry and stiff. Gradually add water until the mixture is medium density and holds together when you squeeze some in your palm. Use a teaspoon (not the measuring spoon, but a spoon for tea) to form small balls of the mixture and then hold the spoon in the boiling water where you cooked the potatoes until the dough detaches. Repeat with the remaining dough, working very quickly. Cook the dumplings for about 15 minutes. Drain the dumplings and place them with the cooked diced potatoes in a serving dish. Drizzle with melted butter and top with sage leaves and grated cheese. You can also add strips of pancetta crisped on a griddle.

LANDEIRES ⊞⊞⊞⊞
Egg Dumplings in Melted Butter
Secondina Turin, Oulx (Torino), Piemonte

These soft dumplings are the very definition of comfort food, and they are made with ingredients you likely have on hand. Beat 1 large egg per person in a bowl, adding enough all-purpose flour and milk to make a soft but not runny dough. Season with salt and pepper and beat to combine thoroughly. Bring a generous amount of water to a boil and season with salt. Use a tablespoon to make dumplings about the size of an egg or a walnut and drop them into the boiling water. As soon as they rise to the surface, remove with a slotted spoon or skimmer and set aside. Toss the dumplings in melted butter and sprinkle with a generous amount of grated toma cheese, a semi-soft cow's milk cheese.

GNOCCHETTI BIANCHI AL BURRO VERSATO
Small Bread Dumplings with Potatoes and Melted Butter
Osteria Crotasc, Mese (Sondrio), Lombardia

Latteria (literally dairy) is a mild cow's milk cheese aged for at least two months and up to one year. There is a Slow Food Presidium dedicated to the *latteria turnaria*, the traditional cooperative dairy where this type of cheese is made by a rotating series of farmers. While there used to be many such small local dairies in the North, they are now disappearing.

SERVES 4

- 5 to 6 cups white bread cubes
- ½ cup whole milk, warm
- 2½ cups unbleached all-purpose flour or 00 flour
- 2 teaspoons salt, plus more for salting water
- 4 ounces new potatoes, peeled and cut into ½-inch dice
- 7 tablespoons Alpine butter
- 4 sage leaves, minced
- 2 cloves garlic, minced
- 2 ounces young latteria, cut into small dice
- ½ cup grated Parmigiano Reggiano

Place the bread in a large bowl and pour the warm milk over it. Let sit until softened, then mix in the flour, 2 teaspoons salt, and about ½ cup water. Knead until you have a soft and elastic dough, adding more water in small amounts if it feels too dry and more flour in small amounts if it feels too wet. Set aside to rest for 30 minutes.

Place the dough on a cutting board or work surface and use a spoon to shape the dough into small, irregularly shaped dumplings. Bring a large pot of salted water to a boil and add the dumplings and potatoes. Cook until both are tender, about 20 minutes. Preheat the oven to a medium temperature (or if the oven is on for another use, just keep it at that temperature; you can even use the broiler if you keep a close eye on the pan).

Meanwhile, in a skillet, melt the butter with the sage and garlic until the butter is foamy. When the dumplings and potatoes are cooked, drain them and place them in a baking pan. Sprinkle on the latteria and the Parmigiano, drizzle on the butter, and bake until the cheese is melted, about 3 minutes. Stir to combine dumplings and cheese and serve immediately.

PASTA SFRITTA
Bread Dumplings with Pork Belly
Federico Valicenti, Terranova di Pollino (Potenza), Basilicata

Soak stale bread in milk until very soft, then crumble into a bowl. Add a pinch of salt and enough beaten eggs to make a soft dough. Knead by hand. Sauté cubes of pork belly in a skillet in a small amount of oil. Bring a large pot of salted water to a boil and drop the bread mixture in by the spoonful. The dumplings should cook in about 5 minutes. Remove them with a skimmer to a bowl and combine with the cooked pork belly. Sprinkle with a generous amount of grated aged ricotta.

PISAREI E FAS

Tiny Bread Dumplings with Beans and Sausage

Antica Trattoria Cattivelli, Monticelli d'Ongina (Piacenza), Emilia-Romagna

A signature first course of the Piacenza area, this dish has roots in Renaissance-era recipes for bread dumplings. While recipes vary widely, the size of the dumplings does not: they should be very small—the same size as the beans—in order best to absorb the loose, brothy sauce.

SERVES 4

- 3 cups dry breadcrumbs
- ¾ cup unbleached all-purpose flour
- 2½ cups dried borlotti beans, soaked overnight
- 1 medium yellow onion, quartered
- 3 cloves garlic
- 1 sprig rosemary
- Unsalted butter for sautéing
- 2 sausages, casing removed and crumbled
- ¼ cup tomato paste
- Extra-virgin olive oil for drizzling
- Salt to taste
- ½ cup grated Parmigiano Reggiano

In a bowl combine the breadcrumbs and flour. Add boiling water while stirring with a wooden spoon until the mixture forms a dough. Knead briefly until soft and elastic. Pinch off a piece of the dough and on a work surface roll to a rope the diameter of a pencil. Cut into pieces no bigger than a bean. Press down on one piece with your thumb and twist your thumb against the work surface to shape the dumpling—they should look like small, elongated orecchiette. Repeat with the remaining dough.

Set the dumplings aside to rest. Fill a large pot with 1½ quarts water and bring to a boil. Drain the beans, add to the pot, and cook until tender. In a large pot, sauté the onion, garlic, and rosemary in butter over low heat until browned. Remove the onion, garlic, and rosemary, and add the sausage meat and cook over low heat until cooked through.

Remove the cooked beans with a slotted spoon or skimmer, reserving their cooking water, and transfer to the pot with the sausage. Add enough of the cooking water from the beans to make the mixture a little loose. Stir in the tomato paste, drizzle in a little oil, and cook over low heat until well combined and thickened to the consistency of a stew, 30 to 35 minutes. Season with salt.

Bring a large pot of salted water to a boil and cook the dumplings until tender, 5 to 6 minutes. Transfer to a serving bowl and top with the beans. Sprinkle with grated Parmigiano and serve.

KNÖDEL DI RAPE ROSSE 🌰
Beet Dumplings
Patscheiderhof, Signato-Signat di Renon-Ritten
(Bolzano-Bozen), Trentino-Alto Adige

The people of Trentino–Alto Adige are crazy for bread dumplings of all kinds. They are served in soups, with sauces, and as side dishes. There are even sweet dumplings for dessert. You can also serve these with a chive sauce or some reduced milk or cream.

SERVES 4
- 10 ounces (about 2) beets, peeled
- Salt to taste
- ¼ yellow onion, minced
- 1 clove garlic, minced
- ½ teaspoon freshly ground cumin seed
- 1 sage leaf, minced
- 2 tablespoons unsalted butter, plus more for serving
- 2 large eggs, lightly beaten
- 2 ounces (¼ cup) low-fat ricotta
- 1½ cups crumbled white bread
- Grated Parmigiano Reggiano for serving

Cook the beets in boiling salted water until tender, then grind with a food mill or in a food processor fitted with the metal blade. In a skillet, sauté the onion, garlic, cumin, and sage leaf in 2 tablespoons butter. Transfer to a bowl and allow to cool, then mix with the eggs, ricotta, and bread. Stir in the beets and set aside to rest for 10 minutes.

Melt butter for serving dumplings. Bring a large pot of salted water to a boil. Form the beet mixture into dumplings about 2¾ inches in diameter and cook until tender, about 10 minutes. Remove with a skimmer, toss with melted butter, and serve warm with Parmigiano.

FREGOLOZ ALLE ERBE
Dumplings with Wild Greens
Borgo Poscolle, Cavazzo Carnico (Udine),
Friuli-Venezia Giulia

Fregoloz are bumpy irregular dumplings, and these are packed with the flavor of foraged herbs and greens. If you like, you can reserve a few whole blanched leaves for garnish.

SERVES 4
- Salt to taste
- 1 pinch baking soda
- 12 ounces foraged greens, such as nettles, dandelion, bladder campion, and amaranth
- 8 tablespoons unsalted butter
- 1 shallot, minced
- ¼ cup to 1 cup whole milk
- 2 cups unbleached all-purpose flour or 00 flour
- 1 large egg
- Freshly ground black pepper to taste
- Freshly grated nutmeg to taste
- 1 cup grated smoked ricotta

Fill a pot with water, add salt and a pinch of baking soda, and bring to a boil. (If you add baking soda to boiling water, it may bubble up and spill out of the pot.) Blanch the greens, then drain and dunk in a cold-water bath to stop them from cooking further and maintain their color. Chop and sauté in a skillet in 1 tablespoon butter with the shallot. Then puree the mixture in a blender, adding enough milk to create a creamy mixture. Transfer to a bowl and stir in the flour and egg and season with salt, pepper, and nutmeg. Knead into a dense and well-combined dough that falls heavily off a spoon. If it seems too thick, add a little more milk.

Bring a large pot of salted water to a boil, lower the heat so that it simmers, and drop in irregular spoonfuls of the dough. As they rise to the surface, remove with a slotted spoon or skimmer and place in a cold-water bath to stop them from cooking further.

In a skillet, melt the remaining 7 tablespoons butter and gently toss the dumplings in the melted butter. Top with the grated cheese and serve.

RAVIOLES
Cheese and Potato Dumplings
Locanda Codirosso, Stroppo (Cuneo), Piemonte

Despite the name, these are not ravioli but potato dumplings from the Valle Varaita. They were traditionally served to celebrate an engagement or betrothal, as well as the baptisms of male children, back in the days when girls' baptisms engendered less excitement and were acknowledged with a simpler snack of bread and cheese. These dumplings are also closely connected to the Baio di Sampeyre, a traditional festival held every five years in the area to commemorate the expulsion of invading Moors in the late tenth century. Toma di montagna is a DOP Alpine cheese aged for a few months. Toma cheeses are basically divided into two groups: those from the mountains, like this type, and those from the plains.

SERVES 6

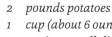

- 2 pounds potatoes
- 1 cup (about 6 ounces) toma di montagna, cut into small dice
- 1 egg yolk
- 2½ cups unbleached all-purpose flour or oo flour
- Salt to taste
- 6 tablespoons unsalted butter
- 2 tablespoons heavy cream or whipping cream

Boil the potatoes until tender, peel, and while still warm crush with a potato ricer. Stir the cheese into the warm potatoes—it should melt. Transfer the mixture to a work surface, knead in the egg yolk and flour, and continue kneading until you have a smooth dough. Pull off a piece of the dough and roll into a long rope ¾ inch in diameter. Cut into small dumplings. Repeat with the remaining dough. One by one, rub the dumplings between the palms of your hands to shape them—each should have a round "belly" in the center and elongated ends that are thinner.

Bring a large pot of salted water to a boil. At the same time, melt the butter in a pot large enough to hold the dumplings. Cook the dumplings in the boiling water until they rise to the surface, then remove them with a slotted spoon or skimmer and transfer to the pot with the melted butter. Drizzle on the cream, toss gently to combine, and serve.

PALLOTTE DI PANE
Fried Bread Dumplings in Tomato Sauce
Anna Maria Carnevale, Capracotta (Isernia), Molise

Make a tomato sauce: cook minced onion in a skillet with a clove of garlic. Add some tomato puree and a pinch of salt and cook over low heat, uncovered, for about 20 minutes. Soften stale crumbled bread (crusts removed) in milk and squeeze dry, then combine with grated aged sheep's cheese, a pinch of salt, minced parsley, and enough beaten egg to make a soft mixture. (Add the eggs one at a time, but if the mixture is too soft, whisk in a little flour.) Form the mixture into small balls, dust them lightly with flour, and brown them in a generous amount of hot oil. (Opt for a less aromatic olive oil, if possible.) Drain briefly on paper towels, then add to the skillet with the tomato sauce and cook for about 10 minutes, tossing frequently, to combine. Sprinkle with additional grated sheep's cheese just before serving.

RABATÓN 🌳
Baked Dumplings with Greens and Ricotta
Locanda dell'Olmo, Bosco Marengo (Alessandria), Piemonte

Bosco Marengo was the birthplace of sixteenth-century Pope Pius V, a great gourmand. Rabatón are tossed with flour, which gives them their particular slightly slippery texture after cooking. Use vegetables you have on hand for making the broth here—a carrot, a rib of celery, and an onion are a good start.

SERVES 6

2 pounds wild greens, such as nettles, dogtooth, and hops, or chard or spinach
Vegetables for broth
1 clove garlic
3 tablespoons fresh marjoram
½ cup tightly packed flat-leaf parsley leaves
3 large eggs
1 egg yolk

1½ cups grated Parmigiano Reggiano
14 ounces (1⅔ cups) ricotta
Salt and freshly ground black pepper to taste
Freshly grated nutmeg to taste
Unbleached all-purpose flour for coating dumplings
1 tablespoon unsalted butter, plus more for buttering pan
2 tablespoons whole milk
3 to 4 sage leaves

Bring a large pot of unsalted water to a boil and cook the greens until tender. Remove with a slotted spoon or skimmer to drain. Add the vegetables for broth to the water and simmer to make a broth. Meanwhile, squeeze the cooked greens dry, then mince them with the garlic, marjoram, and parsley. In a large bowl, lightly beat the eggs and egg yolk. Add ¾ cup of the grated Parmigiano, the ricotta, and the minced greens mixture and combine. The mixture should be firm and form a clump when you pinch off a piece. If it is too loose, add some more of the Parmigiano (or a handful of bread-crumbs). Season with salt, pepper, and nutmeg.

Shape the dough into oval dumplings about 2½ to 2¾ inches long and 1 inch in diameter. Toss in a generous amount of flour until thickly coated.

Preheat the oven to 350°F. Butter a baking pan and set aside. Remove and discard the vegetables from the broth and bring the broth to a boil, then add the dumplings. Cook until tender, just a few minutes, then remove with a skimmer or slotted spoon and transfer to the prepared pan. Sprinkle on the remaining grated Parmigiano, drizzle on the milk, dot with the butter, and scatter on the sage leaves. Bake in the preheated oven until lightly browned, about 10 minutes. Serve hot.

STRUKI LESSI 🌿
Potato Dumplings Stuffed with Raisins, Pine Nuts, Grappa, and Cinnamon
Trattoria Sale e Pepe, Stregna (Udine), Friuli-Venezia Giulia

Traditionally, these stuffed dumplings were made by the girls and young women in the family, and the people of Friuli used to claim they could identify who had made which dumplings by studying the fingerprints left on the dough as they were formed. The inclusion of sugar in a savory dish is a hallmark of the area's offerings.

SERVES 10 TO 12
2 pounds potatoes

2½ to 3 cups unbleached all-purpose flour or 00 flour

1 large egg

Salt to taste

Freshly grated nutmeg to taste

¼ cup pine nuts

1 tablespoon unsalted butter, plus melted butter for serving

2¾ to 3¾ cups walnuts, ground

¼ cup golden raisins, soaked in warm water and squeezed dry

1 tablespoon grappa

1 pinch ground cinnamon, plus more for serving

2 to 3 tablespoons sugar, plus more for serving

For the dough, cook the potatoes in boiling water until tender, peel, and crush with a potato ricer, then combine with the flour, the egg, salt, and a little nutmeg. Knead until you have a soft dough as for gnocchi. Set aside to rest in a cool place.

For the filling, toast the pine nuts in 1 tablespoon butter. Combine the pine nuts, walnuts, raisins, and grappa and toss to combine thoroughly. Stir in cinnamon and sugar.

Pinch off a piece of the dough and shape into a large-diameter rope. Cut into pieces the size of a large dumpling. Roll out one piece of dough to a disk, place some of the filling in the center, and fold in half to make a half-moon. Pinch the border together to seal, then set the dumpling with the pinched border facing upward and use an index finger to press down on the top in the center to indent it. The ends will curve upward a little. Repeat with remaining dough and filling.

Bring a large pot of salted water to a boil and cook the dumplings until they rise to the surface. Remove with a slotted spoon or skimmer and transfer to a serving dish. Drizzle with melted butter, sprinkle with cinnamon and sugar, and serve either warm or cold.

GNOCCHI CON TALEGGIO E BIRRA 🧀
Gnocchi with Taleggio and Beer
Luciano Piana, Gravellona Lomellina (Pavia), Lombardia

Combine boiled, peeled, mashed, and cooled potatoes with flour, egg, and a pinch of nutmeg to make gnocchi dough and make small gnocchi, pressing them against the tines of a fork to create the typical lines on them. In a pot, reduce double malt beer by about one third. Remove from the heat and add cubes of taleggio cheese (the cheese aged in the grottoes of Valsassina is particularly excellent) and whisk until melted. Cook the gnocchi in boiling salted water just until they rise to the surface, then remove with a skimmer and toss them with the taleggio and beer sauce. Spread in a baking pan, sprinkle with grated Grana Padano, and bake until evenly browned on top, 5 to 6 minutes.

GNOCCHI DI PATATE E PRUGNE ❗
Potato and Prune Gnocchi
Osteria di Borgomarturi, Poggibonsi (Siena), Toscana

hianti spice mix combines black pepper, nutmeg, mace, cinnamon, and cloves in varying proportions and is used to flavor soprassata pork salami. The same spice mix—heavy on the cinnamon—is used in several desserts from the Siena area.

SERVES 4

- 1½ cups unbleached all-purpose flour, plus more for flouring work surface
- 14 ounces yellow potatoes
- 5 to 6 pitted prunes (dried plums), minced
- Salt to taste

- 1 day-old roll, crusts removed
- 3 tablespoons extra-virgin olive oil
- 1 cup diced soprassata
- ½ teaspoon Chianti spice mix, plus a pinch for serving

Arrange the 1½ cups flour in a well on a work surface. Place the potatoes in a pot with cold water to cover and bring to a boil, then cook until just tender. Drain the potatoes, peel, and crush them while still warm with a potato ricer, letting them fall right onto the flour on the work surface. Add the prunes and a pinch of salt and knead into a soft, elastic dough. Flour the work surface and roll a piece of the dough into a rope the thickness of your thumb, then cut into thumb-length pieces. Spread the dumplings out on a tray in a single layer and refrigerate.

Crumble the roll coarsely and toast in a nonstick pan in 2 tablespoons of the olive oil, then remove with a slotted spoon or skimmer and drain on paper towels. In a large skillet, sauté the soprassata in the remaining tablespoon oil very briefly. Do not brown.

Bring a large pot of salted water to a boil and cook the dumplings. Stir about ¼ cup of the cooking water into the soprassata mixture. Remove the skillet from the heat and stir in the ½ teaspoon spice mix. When the gnocchi rise to the surface of their cooking water, transfer to a serving bowl and top with the soprassata mixture. Sprinkle on the toasted breadcrumbs, add a pinch more of the spice mix, and serve.

GNOCCHI DI SUSINE
Plum Dumplings
Antica Osteria da Giusi, Malborghetto-Valbruna
(Udine), Friuli-Venezia Giulia

These dumplings clearly evince the area's Austrian heritage. They can also be made with apricots. The inclusion of sugar is typical of the region.

SERVES 4

2   pounds potatoes
1¾ cups unbleached all-purpose flour
2   large eggs, lightly beaten
Salt to taste
30 small plums, pitted
16 tablespoons (2 sticks) unsalted butter
¼   cup sugar
Ground cinnamon to taste

Boil the potatoes until easily pierced with a fork. Peel, crush with a potato ricer, and set aside to cool. On a work surface combine the potato puree, the flour, the eggs, and a pinch of salt and knead until soft and dry. Roll a piece of the dough into a rope about 3 inches in diameter and cut into slices ½ to ⅔ inch thick. You should have about 30 pieces of dough.

Place a pitted plum in the center of a piece of dough. Gently stretch the dough so that it encases the plum and is an even thickness of a little less than ½ inch all around. Eliminate any excess dough. Repeat with the remaining plums and dough. Scraps can be rerolled and used to cover additional plums.

Melt the butter in a pot and leave over medium heat until lightly browned, then add the sugar and keep warm. Bring a large pot of salted water to a boil and cook the dumplings for a few minutes. Remove with a skimmer or slotted spoon to individual serving plates, drizzle with the butter sauce, and sprinkle with ground cinnamon.

GNOCCHETTI DI ZUCCA CON CREMA DI AMARETTI
Squash Gnocchi with Amaretto Sauce
Ristorante Collina, Almenno San Bartolomeo
(Bergamo), Lombardia

Delica squash is round and dark green on the outside with orange flesh on the dry side. It is similar to kabocha squash.

SERVES 6

½   cup whole milk
3   amaretto cookies, crumbled
Salt to taste
2   tablespoons rhubarb liqueur
4   tablespoons unsalted butter
1½ pounds delica winter squash, seeded, peeled, and thinly sliced
11 ounces white potatoes
5   large eggs, lightly beaten
2¼ cups all-purpose flour or 00 flour
⅓   cup grated Grana Padano cheese

For the sauce, place the milk and the cookies in a saucepan and bring to a boil. Add 1 pinch salt, then remove from the heat. Grind in a food processor fitted with the metal blade, then force through a sieve to make a perfectly smooth mixture. Over medium-low heat, reduce the rhubarb liqueur to a syrupy consistency.

For the dumplings, melt 1 tablespoon butter in a large skillet and sauté the squash until soft, turning occasionally and adding as much water as necessary to keep it from sticking to the bottom of the skillet. Remove the squash from the heat when it begins to break down. Meanwhile, bring a large pot of unsalted water to a boil and cook the potatoes until tender, then peel and dice. Process the potatoes and the squash with a food mill, letting the puree fall into a bowl. Add the eggs, a pinch of salt, and the flour and mix until the mixture has the consistency of thick sour cream. Transfer to a pastry bag fitted with a smooth tip a little less than ½ inch in diameter. Bring a large pot of salted water to a boil and pipe dumplings about ¾ inch long, letting them fall directly into the boiling water. As the dumplings rise to the surface of the cooking water, gently remove with a slotted spoon or skimmer and distribute among individual serving plates. Top with the prepared sauce. Melt the remaining 3 tablespoons butter and drizzle over the dumplings. Sprinkle on the grated Grana Padano and add a few drops of the reduced liqueur to each plate, then serve.

GNOCCHI AL SUGO DI CAVEDANO
Potato Gnocchi with Chub
Osteria al Pescatore, Castelletto di Brenzone (Verona), Veneto

When potato gnocchi are paired with a delicate fish sauce, the flavor of the tubers shines. You can make this with any kind of white fish fillet.

SERVES 6
2 pounds potatoes
Salt to taste
2 large eggs, lightly beaten
3 tablespoons unsalted butter, softened
2½ cups unbleached all-purpose flour
3 tablespoons extra-virgin olive oil
About 1½ pounds skinless chub fillet, minced
½ cup white wine
1 carrot, minced
1 rib celery, minced
½ medium yellow onion, minced
Freshly ground black pepper to taste
Leaves of 1 bunch aromatic herbs, such as
	parsley, sage, and rosemary, minced
3 tablespoons tomato puree

Cook the potatoes in boiling water until easily pierced with a fork, about 20 minutes. Peel the potatoes and crush them into a large bowl. Add 1 pinch salt, the eggs, the butter, and the flour. Knead by hand until dry and elastic. Spread out on a plate and set aside to cool.

Meanwhile, in a large skillet heat 3 tablespoons olive oil and add the fish. Sauté briefly, then add the wine. When the wine has evaporated, add the carrot, celery, and onion and cook, stirring frequently, until the vegetables soften and begin to color. Season with salt and pepper, add the herbs and the tomato puree, and cook, covered, over low heat for 30 minutes.

Pull off a small portion of the potato mixture, roll into a rope with your palms, and cut into small dumplings with a knife. Bring a large pot of salted water to a boil and cook the dumplings until they rise to the surface. With a slotted spoon or skimmer, remove them and transfer them to the skillet with the fish. Toss briefly over medium heat and serve.

GHINEFLE
Rye Bread and Potato Dumplings
Alberto Bergoin, Sauze d'Oulx (Torino), Piemonte

To serve 4, boil, peel, and mash 2 pounds potatoes. When they are cool, combine with 2 minced onions browned in a small amount of butter, 6 to 8 slices stale dark rye bread softened in milk and crumbled, 1 cup grated toma cheese, 2 whole eggs and 2 egg yolks (lightly beaten), and enough flour to make a soft dough. Season with salt, pepper, and grated nutmeg and knead to combine.

Bring a large pot of water to a boil, salt lightly, then shape the dough into dumplings about the size of an egg using a spoon. Drop a few at a time into the water and remove with a skimmer as they float to the surface. Combine with a generous amount of melted butter and sprinkle on 1 additional cup grated toma cheese before serving. You can vary this recipe by adding cabbage or spinach to the dumplings. Augusta Allemand of Bardonecchia places the dumplings in a baking pan, dots them with butter and shavings of toma, and bakes them at 350 to 400°F for a few minutes to brown them.

GNOCCHI DI NOCCIOLE ALLE GALITORE 🌰
Hazelnut Dumplings in Chanterelle Sauce
Ristorante La Coccinella, Serravalle Langhe (Cuneo), Piemonte

When mushrooms aren't available, the restaurant serves these nutty dumplings in a creamy sauce made with young castelmagno cheese. Mombarcaro in the Valle Belbo is known for producing potatoes that are on the small side with a pronounced mineral flavor due to the sandy soil. There is a special consortium in the area devoted to these local treasures.

SERVES 6

- 2 pounds Mombarcaro potatoes or other starchy potatoes
- 1 egg yolk
- 1 cup ground hazelnuts
- 1½ cups unbleached all-purpose flour or 00 flour, plus more for work surface
- 2 tablespoons grated Parmigiano Reggiano
- Salt and freshly ground black pepper to taste
- 1 shallot, minced
- Extra-virgin olive oil for sautéing
- 7 ounces chanterelle mushrooms, stemmed and caps cut into julienne
- 2 tomatoes, peeled, seeded, drained, and diced
- Leaves of 1 sprig parsley, minced

Boil the potatoes until tender, about 45 minutes. Peel and crush with a potato ricer. Place the puree on a work surface and knead in the egg yolk, the hazelnuts, the 1½ cups flour, and the grated Parmigiano. Season the dough with salt and pepper. Lightly flour the work surface. Pinch off a piece of dough and roll under your palms on the work surface into a rope about ¾ inch in diameter. Cut into dumplings. Press each dumpling against the tines of a fork to curve and imprint it with lines and set aside on a lightly floured tray. Repeat with the emaining dough.

In a large skillet, sauté the shallot in a little oil until golden. Add the mushrooms and cook over high heat for 2 minutes. Add the tomatoes and cook for a few more minutes, then season with salt and pepper, sprinkle on the parsley, and remove from the heat.

Bring a large pot of salted water to a boil and cook the dumplings until they rise to the surface. Remove with a slotted spoon or skimmer and transfer to the skillet with the mushrooms. Toss over medium heat to combine and serve.

GNOCCHETTI AL PESCE 🌶

Small Potato Gnocchi with Seafood

Ristorante Kursaal, Grottammare (Ascoli Piceno), Marche

Purge clams of sand by soaking them in cold salt water for a couple of hours. Look for the smallest clams, calamari, and scampi, as they will remain tender. Scampi should still have their heads attached. Whether or not you shell them is up to you. If you are unsure about how much flour to add to your potatoes for the gnocchi, pinch off a little piece and boil it in salted water. If it disintegrates, you still need more flour. Go slowly and add in small amounts, though—the gnocchi should still taste of potato.

SERVES 4

2 pounds potatoes
Salt to taste
1 large egg, lightly beaten
About 1½ cups unbleached all-purpose flour
½ medium yellow onion, minced
Extra-virgin olive oil for sautéing

7   ounces baby calamari
10 ounces tiny lupini clams
1   small piece chili pepper, minced
4   ounces small scampi
½   cup white wine
Leaves of 1 sprig parsley, minced

Cook the potatoes in boiling salted water until tender. Peel and crush with a potato ricer and once they have cooled combine with a pinch of salt, the egg, and enough flour to make a firm dough, probably a little more than 1 cup. Knead until well combined, then set aside to rest. Pull off a piece of the dough and roll it under your palms on a lightly floured work surface into a rope. Cut into small pieces (about ½ inch) and shape the pieces by pressing them against the tines of a fork to curve them and to imprint them with lines. Arrange in a single layer on a floured tray or baking sheet and set aside.

In a large skillet sauté the onion in oil. Add the calamari and the clams, a pinch of salt, and the chili pepper and cook, stirring, until golden, 3 to 4 minutes. Add the scampi and cook for an additional 2 minutes, then add the wine and cook until evaporated. Crush the heads of the scampi with a wooden spatula to extract their flavor. Add about ¼ cup water to the skillet and cook until well combined and the scampi and calamari are cooked and clams have opened, about 2 additional minutes. Remove and discard any unopened clams.

Bring a large pot of salted water to a boil and cook the gnocchi until they rise to the surface. Remove with a slotted spoon or skimmer and transfer to the skillet. Toss over medium heat to combine, sprinkle with parsley, and serve.

GNOCCHI AL SUGO DI SPUNTATURE

Potato Gnocchi with Pork Ribs

Osteria Flavio al Velavevodetto, Roma, Lazio

This is more of a one-dish meal than a first course, and a hearty meal at that. You may have sauce left over, and you may even want to keep some of the gnocchi for another day. (You can also decrease the amount of tomatoes in the recipe.) Spread them on a tray and freeze them, then transfer to plastic freezer bags. You can cook frozen gnocchi without thawing them—simply drop them into boiling salted water.

SERVES 8

4½ pounds pork ribs
2   tablespoons extra-virgin olive oil
½   cup dry white wine
6   (16-ounce) cans (about 12 cups) canned, peeled tomatoes, chopped
4   pork sausages, halved
4½ pounds (10 to 14) potatoes
5   cups unbleached all-purpose flour or 00 flour
2   large eggs, lightly beaten
Grated zest of ½ lemon
1   cup grated Parmigiano Reggiano
Freshly grated nutmeg to taste
Salt to taste
Grated pecorino Romano for serving

In a large pot, brown the pork ribs in the olive oil on all sides. Add the wine and cook until evaporated. Add the canned peeled tomatoes, lower the heat, and cook, covered, for 45 minutes. Add the sausages and continue cooking for an additional 40 minutes.

Meanwhile, to make the gnocchi, cook the potatoes in boiling water until easily pierced with a fork, then drain, peel, and crush with a potato ricer while still warm. Allow the potatoes to cool, then form in to a well on a work surface. Add the flour, the eggs, the lemon zest, the Parmigiano, nutmeg, and a pinch of salt. Knead until well combined, then set aside to rest for 30 minutes. Pinch off a piece of dough and roll it under your palms on the work surface into a rope about ¾ inch in diameter, then cut into gnocchi your preferred length.

Bring a large pot of salted water to a boil and cook the gnocchi until they rise to the surface. Remove with a slotted spoon or skimmer and transfer to a serving bowl. Top with a generous amount of the sauce and accompany with the grated Pecorino Romano, the ribs, and the sausages.

GNOCCHI DI MELE

Apple Dumplings

Chiara Veronesi, Egna-Neumarkt (Bolzano-Bozen), Trentino-Alto Adige

There are eleven different varieties of apple in the Adige, Venosta, and Isarco Valleys that may bear the IGP (Protected Geographic Origin) marking, and apples appear in recipes for both savory and sweet dishes in the area. For these dumplings, boil potatoes in lightly salted water and steam peeled, cored, and seeded apples until soft. (Aim for about twice as many potatoes as apples by weight.) Peel the potatoes and mash the potatoes and apples together. Sprinkle in salt, flour, and eggs. If the mixture is too soft, add a little more flour; if it is too stiff, add a little more egg. When the mixture is a soft dough, shape it into ropes and cut them into pieces about ¾ inch long. Cook the dumplings in salted boiling water and serve with a sauce of grated Parmigiano beaten into heavy or whipping cream.

GNUDI DI ORTICHE CON FIORI DI ZUCCA ❦
Nettle Gnudi with Zucchini Blossoms and Pine Nuts

Ristorante Albergo Aiuole, Arcidosso (Grosseto), Toscana

Gnudi are like ravioli without the pasta wrapper on the outside. Instead, the finished dumplings are coated in flour. Always wear gloves when working with nettles—they have prickles that sting painfully when fresh. Once cooked they are harmless. Zucchini blossoms are very delicate: shake them out over the sink to remove any dirt or insects and pinch off their pistils and stems. Rinse very lightly and dry on paper towels.

SERVES 6

- 10 ounces nettles
- 1 pound (1¾ cups) ricotta
- 4 large eggs, lightly beaten
- 1 cup grated Parmigiano Reggiano
- Salt and freshly ground black pepper to taste
- Freshly grated nutmeg to taste
- ½ cup unbleached all-purpose flour
- 1 medium yellow onion, thinly sliced
- Extra-virgin olive oil for sautéing
- 12 zucchini blossoms
- ½ cup whole milk
- 1 teaspoon pine nuts

For the dumplings, blanch the nettles, drain, and mince. In a bowl combine the nettles, ricotta, eggs, and Parmigiano. Season with salt, pepper, and nutmeg and mix well to combine. Spread the flour on a work surface. Pinch off small pieces of the nettle mixture, shape into balls or ovals, and toss in the flour until coated. Leave the dumplings spread out on the work surface to dry slightly while you prepare the sauce.

In a saucepan, sauté the onion in olive oil until golden. Add the zucchini blossoms and sauté for a few minutes, then add the milk and pine nuts. When the sauce has thickened, remove from the heat and puree to a smooth sauce.

Bring a large pot of salted water to a boil. Shake any excess flour off of the dumplings and add them to the water. Cook until they rise to the surface, then remove with a slotted spoon or skimmer, transfer to a serving bowl, and toss with the prepared sauce.

GNOCCHI DI PATATE CON LUGANEGA E RADICCHIO
Potato Gnocchi with Luganega Sausage and Radicchio
Osteria dai Mazzeri, Follina (Treviso), Veneto

The amount of flour needed to make gnocchi will depend on the potatoes you use and the amount of water they absorb while cooking. Begin with about 1 cup flour, then add more in small amounts until the dough reaches the right consistency. If you are uncertain, incorporate the egg, but it's not really necessary. Luganega is a pork sausage that is one long coil and is sold by weight rather than by link.

SERVES 4

- 2 pounds (about 6) potatoes
- Salt to taste
- About 1⅓ cups unbleached all-purpose flour
- 1 large egg (optional)
- 1 shallot, minced
- Extra-virgin olive oil for sautéing
- 5 ounces luganega or other pork sausage (see note), casing removed and crumbled
- ½ cup white or red wine
- 7 ounces (1 small head) late-season radicchio, cut into ribbons
- ½ cup grated smoked ricotta

For the gnocchi, cook the potatoes in boiling water until easily pierced with a fork, then drain, peel, and crush with a potato ricer while still warm. Transfer the potatoes to a work surface and allow to cool, then knead with a pinch of salt and enough flour to make a soft dough, probably a little more than 1 cup, but start with 1 cup and add flour in small amounts. If the dough feels very loose and crumbly, you can knead in the egg. Pinch off a piece of dough and roll it under your palms on the work surface into a rope about the same diameter as your thumb, then cut into pieces about ¾ inch long. Spread out the gnocchi in a single layer, not touching, and let them dry slightly while you make the sauce.

In a pot, sauté the shallot in a little oil. When it turns golden, add the sausage and cook until browned, then add the wine and cook until evaporated. Add the radicchio and season with salt. Cook over the lowest possible heat, covered, for 10 minutes.

Bring a large pot of salted water to a boil and cook the gnocchi until they rise to the surface. Remove with a slotted spoon or skimmer and transfer to the pot with the sausage and radicchio. Toss over medium heat until well combined. Sprinkle with grated smoked ricotta and serve.

GNOCCHI DI CASTAGNE
Chestnut Gnocchi
Ristorante La Speranza, Farigliano (Cuneo), Piemonte

Fulvia Calvi of Edolo makes gnocchi with equal parts chestnut flour, buckwheat flour, and wheat flour, and sometimes she replaces the chestnut flour with dried chestnuts that are soaked in cold water, then boiled in water aromatized with bay leaves until tender and crushed.

SERVES 6

- 6 medium potatoes
- 1½ cups unbleached all-purpose flour
- 1 cup chestnut flour
- 1 tablespoons unsalted butter
- 2 sage leaves
- 1¼ cups cream
- ½ cup grated Parmigiano Reggiano
- 6 boiled chestnuts, crumbled
- Salt to taste
- Freshly ground white pepper to taste

Boil the potatoes until tender enough to pierce with a fork. Peel, mash with a potato ricer, and while still warm knead with both types of flour to make a well-combined dough. Pull off a piece of dough the size of an egg, roll into a rope, then cut into gnocchi.

In a skillet, melt the butter with the sage. Add the cream, the Parmigiano, and the chestnuts and cook, stirring constantly, over medium heat for 1 minute.

Bring a large pot of salted water to a boil and cook the gnocchi. As soon as they rise to the surface, remove with a skimmer or slotted spoon and transfer to the skillet. Toss to combine, season with pepper, and serve.

GNOCCHI LONGHI CON SPUNTATURE 🐷
Long Flour Dumplings with Pork Ribs
Trattoria Bacco, Pisoniano (Roma), Lazio

The dumplings here are not the usual squat shape but instead are rolled into thin strings like spaghetti. They have a pleasantly chewy texture.

SERVES 6

- 8 cups unbleached all-purpose flour or 00 flour
- Salt to taste
- 6 pork ribs
- 3 tablespoons extra-virgin olive oil
- 4 bay leaves
- 1 clove garlic, minced
- 1 carrot, minced
- 1 rib celery, minced
- 1 small yellow onion, minced
- ½ cup dry white wine
- 10 ounces ripe tomatoes, chopped
- 1 chili pepper, minced
- 1¼ cups canned peeled tomatoes, pureed
- 1 cup grated Pecorino Romano

Combine the flour with 2 cups salted ice water and knead to make an elastic dough. With a rolling pin, roll out about ⅕ inch thick. Cut into wide strips. Roll one strip with your palms, beginning at the center and moving outward, to form thick spaghetti similar in diameter to bucatini and about 12 inches long. Repeat with the remaining strips of dough.

In a large pot, brown the ribs in 3 tablespoons olive oil over high heat. Add the bay leaves, garlic, carrot, celery, and onion. Cook, stirring frequently, until the vegetables start to brown. Add the wine and cook until evaporated, then add the chopped tomatoes and the chili pepper. Season with salt and cook until combined, 5 to 6 minutes. Add the pureed canned tomatoes to the pot and bring to a simmer, then turn the heat to the lowest possible setting and cook for 45 minutes. Remove and set aside the ribs and remove and discard the bay leaves.

Bring a large pot of water to a boil and cook the gnocchi, then remove with a skimmer or slotted spoon. Toss in the pot with the sauce over medium heat. Distribute among individual serving dishes, including one rib per serving. Serve with grated Pecorino Romano on the side.

CANEDERLI CON MORTANDELA SU FONDUTA DI CASOLET ❙
Large Dumplings with Mortandela in Cheese Sauce
Ristorante Nerina, Malgolo di Romeno (Trento), Trentino-Alto Adige

Mortandela is a cured pork product from the Val di Non (not to be confused with mortadella). Rather than being packed into a casing, ground pork and spices are formed into patties and are dried on wooden boards and then smoked. They look a little like large mushroom caps, but when cut reveal marbled dark-red interiors. Casolét from the Val di Sole (and the neighboring Pejo and Rabbi Valleys) is protected by a Slow Food

Presidium. It is a soft raw-milk cheese. Replace with another mild, soft cow's milk cheese of your choosing if it is unavailable.

SERVES 4

1 pound day-old bread, cut into cubes
2 cups whole milk
2 large eggs, lightly beaten
1 tablespoon diced mortandela
2 tablespoons grated Trentingrana cheese
1 tablespoon snipped fresh chives
1 tablespoon unbleached all-purpose flour
Salt to taste
Beef broth for boiling dumplings
7 ounces casolét cheese (see note), cut into small dice
1 cup whipping cream

Place the bread in a heatproof bowl. Heat the milk to a boil, then pour it over the bread. Toss and set aside to soften for at least 30 minutes. Crumble the bread into another bowl (it should have absorbed most of the milk, but if not, leave behind any milk that has not been absorbed) and mix in the eggs, the mortandela, the Trentingrana, the chives, the flour, and salt to taste. Mix by hand until well combined, and then form the mixture into large dumplings, about the size of an egg. Place the broth in a large pot and bring to a boil, then cook the dumplings in the broth until firm, about 10 minutes.

While the dumplings are cooking, place the casolét in a heatproof bowl. Scald the cream and pour it over the cheese. Whisk to melt. Season with a pinch of salt, if needed. When the dumplings are cooked, remove with a slotted spoon or skimmer and transfer to a serving bowl. Top with the cheese sauce and serve.

STRANGULAPRIEVETE VERDI
Spinach Dumplings
Federico Valicenti, Terranova di Pollino (Potenza), Basilicata

Brown an onion and cooked spinach in a skillet together, then mince or grind with a food processor and combine with breadcrumbs. Beat in egg, grated Parmigiano Reggiano, and a handful of flour. If the dough seems too loose, add more breadcrumbs. If it seems dry, stir in more egg. Season with salt and pepper. Roll the dough into thin ropes and cut into pieces about ¾ inch long. Cook in boiling salted water and remove with a skimmer as soon as they rise to the surface. Serve with butter melted with sage leaves; a thick, spicy tomato sauce; a ragù with pancetta, sausage, and mushrooms; or even a vegetarian sauce made with asparagus.

GNOCCHI DI RISO
Rice Dumplings
Giuseppina Steffanoni, Milano, Lombardia

Cook rice, stirring frequently, in a generous amount of broth until al dente. Season with salt, then drain the rice, reserving the broth. Combine the rice with beaten eggs and breadcrumbs to make a firm dough. Form the dough into small dumplings and cook them in the reserved broth (brought back to a boil). When they are cooked (about 5 minutes), remove with a skimmer and toss with butter and grated cheese.

ᎧᏰ{RICE & OTHER GRAINS}Ꭶᏼ

RISI E BISI 🌱
Rice and Peas
Locanda da Condo, Farra di Soligo (Treviso), Veneto

Risi e bisi is *the* dish of the Veneto region and is de rigueur on April 25 for the feast of Venezia's patron, Saint Mark. It is sometimes mislabeled a risotto, but really it is soupier than risotto, yet not quite brothy enough to be called a soup. In Italian this is described as *all'onda*, or "wavy." The finished dish should be loose enough to ripple if you tilt the skillet a little. The peas used at the Locanda da Condo are the sweet and tender Borso del Grappa variety from the nearby town of that name. The earliest versions of this recipe, which date back to the time of the doges, call for a teaspoon of anise seed in the broth.

SERVES 4

- 5 sprigs parsley
- 1 medium yellow onion
- 1 carrot
- 1 rib celery
- 2 to 3 celery leaves
- Salt to taste
- 1¼ to 1½ pounds organic peas in their pods
- 2 ounces pancetta, roughly chopped
- 18 tablespoons (2 sticks plus 2 tablespoons) unsalted butter
- 1 medium spring onion
- 1½ cups carnaroli rice
- ½ cup dry white wine
- Freshly ground black pepper to taste
- 1 cup grated Grana Padano cheese

Mince the leaves of 1 sprig parsley and set aside. In a stockpot, combine the yellow onion, carrot, celery, celery leaves, remaining 4 parsley sprigs, and a little salt. Add cold water to cover and simmer to make a vegetable broth. Strain, transfer to a pot, and keep at a low simmer.

Shell the peas. Boil the pods in a small amount of salted water until very soft, then puree through a food mill to make a dense mixture. Set aside and reserve. In a small skillet, sauté the pancetta in 3 tablespoons butter, then puree through a food mill to make an almost completely smooth mixture and set aside.

In a large skillet, melt 7 tablespoons butter and sauté the spring onion until softened. Add the rice and cook, stirring, until it begins to sizzle, then add the wine and cook until evaporated. Add the peas and the pureed pancetta, then add the pea pod puree, about ½ cup at a time, stirring to absorb between additions. When all the pea pod puree has been added, begin adding the vegetable broth in small amounts, stirring constantly and waiting until the last addition has been absorbed somewhat before adding the next. After about 20 minutes, sprinkle in the minced parsley, then continue adding broth until the rice is cooked al dente and the rice is very moist. Season with salt and pepper. Cut up the remaining 8 tablespoons butter and sprinkle into the skillet. Sprinkle on the grated Grana Padano as well. Stir until the butter and cheese have melted and serve.

RISO IN CAGNONE ❗
Rice with Butter and Young Cheese
Ristorante Baracca, Biella, Piemonte

No one is really sure what the name *riso in cagnone* means, and different dishes bear that name in different places: in Lombardia, it indicates rice cooked in water and flavored with garlic and sage; in Veneto, it refers to rice topped with sage butter; and in Liguria, it indicates al dente rice with meat sauce and sausage. Ristorante Baracca highly recommends the use of macagn cheese, which has its own Slow Food Presidium and is made in the Alps in the summer from raw cow's milk immediately after milking.

SERVES 4
- 1 quart beef broth
- 2¼ cups Sant'Andrea or carnaroli rice
- 7 tablespoons unsalted Alpine butter, cut into pieces
- 14 ounces young toma cheese, preferably tuma macagn, cut into small dice
- Freshly ground black pepper to taste

Place the broth in a pot and bring to a boil. Add the rice and cook, stirring frequently, until al dente. Stir in the butter and cheese until melted. The mixture should be a little oily. Sprinkle with a generous amount of pepper and serve.

RISO ALLA PITOCCA
Rice with Chicken and Chicken Livers
Dispensa Pani e Vini, Torbiato di Adro (Brescia), Lombardia

Traditionally, the broth for this dish would be made with the rest of the chicken: the neck, head, stomach, and bones, simmered with onion, celery, and carrot. If you are not starting with a whole chicken, you can use beef broth instead—just make sure it's high quality. A similar dish is made in the Veneto, but it usually includes veal along with the chicken.

SERVES 4
- 2 tablespoons unsalted butter
- 1 medium yellow onion, very thinly sliced
- ½ free-range chicken (wing and thigh), boned and chopped
- 2 quarts broth
- 1½ cups carnaroli rice
- 2 ounces chicken livers, chopped
- Salt to taste
- ¼ cup grated Parmigiano Reggiano
- 2 tablespoons minced parsley

In a pot, melt 1 tablespoon of the butter and sauté the onion until very soft. Add the chicken wing and thigh, add just enough broth to cover, and cook, covered, for 20 minutes. Stir in the rice and remaining broth and cook for 15 additional minutes. Add the chicken livers, season with salt, and cook for just a couple of additional minutes. Stir in the remaining tablespoon butter and the Parmigiano until melted, then sprinkle with the parsley and serve.

RISO CON FILETTI DI PERSICO

Rice with Perch Fillets

Ristorante Mella, San Giovanni di Bellagio (Como), Lombardia

Small fillets can be left whole, but if they are large you may want to cut them into strips. This is a first course, but one on the substantial side, so it makes an excellent dinner on its own.

SERVES 4

- 2 large eggs
- ½ cup whole milk
- Salt to taste
- 1½ pounds perch, gutted and filleted
- ½ cup breadcrumbs
- ⅔ cup Italian short-grain rice
- 6 tablespoons unsalted butter
- Leaves of 1 sprig sage
- ¼ cup grated Parmigiano Reggiano

In a bowl, beat the eggs with the milk and a pinch of salt. Dredge the fillets first in the milk and egg mixture and then in breadcrumbs. Set aside. Bring a large pot of salted water to a boil and cook the rice as you would pasta, stirring frequently, until al dente, about 15 minutes.

In a skillet, melt the butter with the sage leaves and fry the dredged fillets until golden on both sides, working in batches if necessary to keep from crowding the pan. Set aside.

Drain the cooked rice, arrange in a serving dish, and sprinkle with the grated Parmigiano. Arrange the fish fillets on top of the rice, strain the butter in the pan and drizzle on top, and serve.

RISOTTO COI FENOCI

Fennel Risotto

Dora Vittorini, Venezia, Veneto

To serve 4 people, in a large skillet, melt 3 tablespoons butter and sauté a thinly sliced onion. Add 5 to 6 bulbs fennel cut into strips. Season with salt, add a little water, and cook until soft, about 10 minutes. Stir in 1½ cups vialone nano or arborio rice and cook risotto-style, adding about 1 quart hot vegetable broth in small amounts, until cooked al dente. Sprinkle on ½ cup grated Parmigiano, stir to combine, and serve. If you like, you can include 1 minced rib celery and some diced pancetta with the onion at the start and sprinkle about ½ cup dry Marsala on the risotto just before serving.

RISOTTO CON CAVOLO NERO

Tuscan Kale Risotto

Letizia Castagnoli, Cecina (Livorno), Toscana

This should be made with the leaves and tender sprouts of Tuscan kale. The latter are available just before the old plant is removed to make way for a new one. They are added at the end because they don't need much cooking and indeed may be eaten raw. In a large skillet, sauté minced garlic and onion in olive oil and lard. Season with salt and pepper. Add leaves of Tuscan kale cut into ribbons, tomato puree, and a small spoonful of tomato paste. Stir to combine and cook over high heat for a few minutes. Add arborio rice and cook, stirring, until the rice is translucent, then cook risotto-style by adding hot broth in small amounts and stirring constantly. When the rice is almost cooked, add kale sprouts, stir to combine, and serve.

RISO IN TORTIERA
Baked Rice with Meat and Tomato Sauce
Rosaria Salvatore, Tropea (Vîbo Valentia), Calabria

To serve 4 to 6 people, sauté a minced onion in a skillet in a little oil until browned, then add 14 ounces veal (in one piece) and a sausage (casing removed). Cook until browned, add ½ cup red wine, 1 pound peeled and seeded tomatoes, and 1 tablespoon tomato paste diluted in ¼ cup water. Season with salt. Turn down the heat to the barest simmer and cook, covered, for 1½ hours, stirring occasionally and adding a little warm water if it begins to stick. Remove the veal and mince it. Return about half of the minced veal to the sauce and transfer the rest to a bowl. Mix with 1 egg, a handful of grated aged sheep's cheese, and enough breadcrumbs to form a dough. Knead by hand, then shape into small balls and cook them in a generous amount of oil until browned on all sides. Drain on paper towels. Combine 4 cups of cooked rice (2 cups raw) with the meat sauce and spread about half of the rice mixture in the bottom of an oiled baking pan coated with breadcrumbs. Cover with diced mozzarella (about 7 ounces), the browned meatballs, 3 hard-boiled eggs cut into wedges, some of the reserved sauce, and about ⅓ cup grated aged sheep's cheese. Top with the remaining rice and smooth the surface. Cover with the remaining meat sauce, a drizzle of olive oil, and another ⅓ cup grated aged sheep's cheese. Bake at 350°F for about 20 minutes, then let rest briefly before serving.

RISOTTO CON FAVE E ORTICHE ❦
Risotto with Fava Beans and Nettles
Agriturismo La Vecchia Posta, Avolasca (Alessandria), Piemonte

To peel fava beans, blanch in salted water for 30 seconds, then transfer to an ice bath. The skins should slip off easily.

SERVES 4

Leaves of 1 bunch nettle
1½ cups carnaroli rice
Extra-virgin olive oil for sautéing
½   cup dry white wine
1   quart vegetable broth, warm
2   pounds young fava beans, shelled and peeled
3   tablespoons unsalted butter
¼   cup grated Parmigiano Reggiano
Salt to taste

Blanch the nettle leaves, squeeze dry, and puree. In a large skillet, toast the rice in a little oil. When the rice is coated, add the wine and cook until evaporated. Begin adding the broth in small amounts, stirring constantly and waiting for the broth to be absorbed before the next addition. Cook for about 10 minutes, then add the fava beans and cook until the rice is tender, about 10 additional minutes. Stir in the nettles, butter, and cheese, taste and adjust salt, and let rest, covered, off the heat for a few minutes.

RISOTTO CON I CARLETTI 🥕
Risotto with Maidenstears
Pironetomosca, Treville di Castelfranco Veneto (Treviso), Veneto

Silene vulgaris, known in English as maidenstears, is considered a weed in some places, but in Italy these greens are enjoyed as a vegetable—especially the younger shoots and leaves.

SERVES 6

1   medium yellow onion
1   carrot
1   rib celery
1   leek, halved
Salt to taste
9   ounces maidenstears shoots and leaves
1   spring onion, minced

Extra-virgin olive oil for sautéing and
     drizzling
2⅔ cups carnaroli rice
½   cup dry white wine
3   tablespoons unsalted butter
½   cup grated Grana Padano cheese
Freshly ground black pepper to taste

For the broth, in a large pot combine 12 cups cold water, the yellow onion, the carrot, the celery, and ½ leek. Add a pinch of salt, bring to a boil, and cook for about 1 hour to extract all the flavor from the vegetables. Strain, place in a small pot, and keep warm. Meanwhile, bring a large pot of water to a boil and blanch the maidenstears for 1 minute, then drain and mince.

Mince the remaining leek and set aside. In a skillet, sauté the spring onion in oil, then add the maidenstears and cook for 5 minutes. In a separate large skillet, sauté the minced leek in oil until golden, then add the rice and cook, stirring, until coated and transparent. Add the wine and cook, stirring constantly with a wooden spoon, until the liquid has evaporated. Begin adding the broth in small amounts, stirring constantly and waiting for the broth to be absorbed before the next addition. Cook for about 20 minutes, then add the maidenstears and cook until the rice is tender, about 20 additional minutes, continuing to stir in broth so that the skillet never dries out completely. Stir in the butter and cheese, taste and adjust salt, drizzle with oil, season with pepper, stir to combine, and serve.

RISOTTO CON ASPARAGINE
Risotto with Wild Asparagus
Antica Trattoria del Teatro, Lugo (Ravenna), Emilia-Romagna

Wild asparagus are thin and flavorful, while their cultivated cousins are more mild. This risotto can also be made with less desirable end-of-season asparagus, as you can simply cook the stalks as long as required for them to be tender. The Antica Trattoria del Teatro favors asparagus foraged in pine forests. Cervia salt is from salt flats on the Adriatic in the region.

SERVES 4

1   bunch wild asparagus
Extra-virgin olive oil for sautéing
1   cup dry white wine
About 1½ quarts beef or vegetable broth
4   Romagna shallots, thinly sliced
2   cups vialone nano rice
3   tablespoons unsalted butter
Cervia salt to taste
Grated Parmigiano Reggiano

Break off the woody ends of the asparagus and chop the stalks. You should have 10 to 11 ounces of asparagus. Sauté in a little oil, then add about ½ cup wine and cook, covered, until very tender. If the pan looks dry before the asparagus is tender, add a little broth.

Heat the broth in a small pot and keep warm. In a large skillet, sauté the shallots in a little oil, then add the rice and butter and cook, stirring constantly, until the rice looks transparent. Add the remaining ½ cup wine and cook, stirring constantly until evaporated. Begin adding the broth in small amounts, stirring constantly and waiting until the last addition has been absorbed before adding the next. Stir constantly with a wooden spoon. When the rice is cooked al dente and has released its starch, taste and adjust salt and stir in the cooked asparagus. Remove from the heat and sprinkle on the Parmigiano, stir to combine, cover, and allow to rest for 2 minutes before serving.

RISOTTO CON LE BEVARASSE
Risotto with Venus Clams
Luigino Bissaco, Chioggia (Venezia), Veneto

Venus clams are small saltwater clams. Cook carefully cleaned clams in a skillet with a little water, covered, over high heat until they open, a couple of minutes. Remove from the shells and strain any grit out of the cooking liquid. In a skillet, sauté minced Chioggia onion until golden. Add rice and cook for a few minutes, stirring, then add the clams. Cook risotto-style with the strained cooking liquid. If you run out of liquid before the rice is cooked, use hot water. Season with salt, drizzle with extra-virgin olive oil, sprinkle on minced parsley, and serve.

RIS E VERZ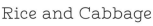
Rice and Cabbage
Pino Bagagli, Milano, Lombardia

Sauté peeled, seeded, diced tomatoes in butter with a clove or two of garlic. Remove and discard the garlic. Bring a pot of beef broth to a boil and add the tomatoes, some lardo (cured fatback) and parsley minced together, and cabbage leaves cut into ribbons. When the broth returns to a boil, add a generous amount of vialone nano rice and cook, stirring occasionally, until the rice is cooked through. Sprinkle with grated Grana Padano just before serving. You may also omit the tomatoes and start by sautéing diced pancetta with some onion in butter in a pot. Then add cabbage, moisten with some white wine, season with salt and pepper, and lastly add hot broth and rice and simmer until rice is cooked through.

RISOTTO CON PORCINI ❗
Risotto with Porcini Mushrooms
Federico Valicenti, Terranova di Pollino (Potenza), Basilicata

Sauté minced shallot in a large skillet in olive oil and butter until golden. Add carnaroli or vialone nano rice and cook, stirring, for a few minutes. Add red wine and cook, stirring, until evaporated, then add rehydrated dried porcini mushrooms that have been squeezed dry and chopped. Use the strained soaking water from the mushrooms to cook the risotto. If the soaking water runs out before the rice is cooked, proceed with hot vegetable broth. When the rice is cooked, taste, adjust salt, and mount with a little butter and a sprinkling of minced parsley. Remove the skillet from the heat, cover, and set aside to rest for 5 minutes before serving.

At the Hostaria La Trisa in the Bergamo province, winter savory is used in the porcini mushroom risotto, and strachitunt cheese is stirred into the dish with the butter and Parmigiano. *Strachitunt* is a herbaceous cheese from the northern Val Taleggio made by combining the results of morning and evening milkings of Bruna Alpina cows and aged for at least two months.

RRISOTTO AI BRUSCANDOLI 🌿
Risotto with Hop Shoots
Locanda Solagna, Vas (Belluno), Veneto

Grumolo delle Abbadesse rice, protected under a Slow Food Presidium, is a variety of vialone nano rice cultivated in the area of Veneto between Vicenza and Padova—a popular locale for Venetian nobles to build luxurious villas and play the role of gentleman farmer. The rice is highly absorbent and assertively flavored. Hop shoots pop up in early spring and look and taste a little like asparagus.

SERVES 4
Salt to taste
7   ounces hop shoots (see note)
About 1 quart vegetable broth
3   tablespoons extra-virgin olive oil
1   shallot, minced
1   heaping cup Grumolo delle Abbadesse (see note) or other vialone nano rice
½   cup Prosecco
Freshly ground black pepper to taste
3   tablespoons unsalted butter
½   cup grated Grana Padano cheese

Bring a pot of salted water to a boil and boil the hop shoots for 3 minutes. Drain, chop, and reserve. Place the broth in a small pot and keep warm. In a large skillet, heat the olive oil and cook the shallot until it begins to color. Add the hops and cook for a few minutes, then add the rice and cook, stirring, until the rice is translucent. Add the wine and cook until evaporated. Season with salt and pepper, then begin adding the broth in small amounts, stirring constantly and waiting for the broth to be absorbed before the next addition. Cook until rice is just tender. Stir in the butter and cheese, then allow to melt off the heat and serve.

RISOTTO CON MUSCIARULI
Sibari Rice Risotto with Prugnolo Mushrooms
Ristorante Luna Rossa, Terranova di Pollino (Potenza), Basilicata

Prugnolo mushrooms go by a few dozen different names in Italy, where they are widely appreciated for their firm flesh and delicate floury aroma. These creamy white mushrooms with sturdy stems grow in sunny grassy fields. Cutting them differently (some are sliced and some are halved) and varying the cooking time adds pleasant texture to this dish. That said, you can make a delicious risotto using almost any type of wild mushroom. Rice is usually associated with northern Italy, but for a couple of decades now some high-quality short-grain carnaroli rice has been grown on the Sibari plain in Calabria. Senise peppers are sweet and slightly smoky.

SERVES 6

- 1 rib celery
- 1 carrot
- 1 medium yellow onion
- Salt to taste
- 6 ounces prugnolo mushrooms (see note)
- 6 tablespoons unsalted (preferably buffalo milk) butter
- 3 tablespoons extra-virgin olive oil
- 1 tablespoon bone marrow (optional)
- 2½ cups Sibari or other carnaroli brown rice
- 1 teaspoon ground Senise pepper
- ½ cup grated smoked scamorza

For the broth, place the celery, carrot, and onion in a large pot with a generous amount of cold water. Season with salt and bring to a boil, then remove from the heat and cover. Let the liquid sit for 30 minutes, then bring to a boil again. Repeat this cycle 5 times in all, then strain the broth—it should be light and clear, and you should have at least 1½ quarts. Place the broth in a small pot and keep warm.

Thinly slice about two thirds of the mushrooms and halve the rest. In a large skillet, melt 3 tablespoons of the butter with the oil. Add the bone marrow, if using, and the halved mushrooms and sauté briefly until softened. Add the rice and cook, stirring constantly. Begin adding the broth and the sliced mushrooms in small amounts, stirring constantly and waiting until the last addition of broth has been absorbed before adding the next. Stir constantly with a wooden spoon and cook until the rice is just tender. Stir in the ground pepper and taste and adjust salt. Off the heat, stir in the remaining 3 tablespoons butter until melted. Sprinkle with grated cheese and serve.

RISOTTO AL BAROLO
Barolo Wine Risotto
Locanda dell'Arco, Cissone (Cuneo), Piemonte

This dish highlights Piemonte's most famous wine—rich red Barolo. Be sure to purchase a high-quality bottle, as it is the star of the show.

SERVES 4

½ cup minced shallot
1 clove garlic, minced
Extra-virgin olive oil for sautéing
4 ounces bone marrow, chopped
2 cups vialone nano rice
2 cups Barolo wine (see note)
1 quart beef broth
1 medium tomato, peeled, seeded, and chopped, or ½ cup canned peeled tomatoes, chopped
Salt and freshly ground black pepper to taste
2 to 3 sage leaves, minced
Leaves of 2 sprigs rosemary, minced
3 tablespoons unsalted butter
Grated Parmigiano Reggiano to taste

In a large skillet, sauté the shallot and garlic in a little olive oil, then add the bone marrow and cook for 1 minutes, stirring. Add the rice and cook, stirring constantly, over high heat until the rice is coated and translucent. Add the wine and cook over high heat until the alcohol has evaporated. Remove from the heat and allow to rest for 30 minutes.

After 30 minutes, place the broth in a small pot and keep warm. Place the skillet over medium-low heat. Add the tomato, season with salt and pepper, then begin adding the broth in small amounts, stirring constantly and waiting until the last addition has been absorbed before adding the next. With each addition, this will take a little longer. Stir constantly with a wooden spoon and cook until the rice is just tender with a tiny bit of crunch still in the center. Stir in the minced sage and rosemary and cook for 1 minute, then remove from the heat and stir in the butter and grated Parmigiano until melted.

RISOTTO ALLA MARINARA 🌿
Seafood Risotto
Locanda di Mare, Amantea (Cosenza), Calabria

Superfino rice does not refer to a variety or quality but to the small size of the grains. Always clean shellfish thoroughly to remove any grit or sand.

SERVES 4

- 1 tablespoon extra-virgin olive oil, plus more for cooking shellfish
- 20 clams
- 10 mussels
- Salt to taste
- 1 small yellow onion, thinly sliced
- 1 tablespoon unsalted butter
- 10 shrimp, shelled
- 3 baby squid, cut into strips
- 2¼ cups superfino rice (see note)
- ¼ cup heavy cream or whipping cream
- ¼ cup grated aged sheep's cheese
- Leaves of 1 large sprig parsley, minced
- Freshly ground black pepper to taste

Drizzle a little oil in a pot and place over medium heat. Add the clams and mussels and cook, covered, until they have opened. (Discard any clams or mussels that stubbornly refuse to open.) Strain any cooking liquid and reserve. Shell the clams and mussels. (You can reserve a few shells to garnish the finished dish if you like.)

Combine the strained cooking liquid with enough water to make 1 quart, season with salt, and place in a small pot. Keep warm. In a large skillet, sauté the onion in the 1 tablspoon oil and butter. Add the mussels, clams, shrimp, and squid and cook, stirring, for 2 minutes. Add the rice and cook, stirring, until it begins to stick to the bottom of the skillet. Begin adding the cooking liquid mixture in small amounts, stirring constantly and waiting until the last addition of liquid has been absorbed before adding the next. Stir constantly with a wooden spoon and cook until the rice is tender on the outside but still crunchy in the center, 12 to 13 minutes. Stir in the cream and grated cheese and continue cooking, adding broth in small amounts and stirring constantly, until the rice is tender. Stir in the parsley and a generous amount of black pepper, stir for 1 more minute, then set aside to rest for 10 minutes before serving.

RISOTTO ALLA CERTOSINA
Risotto with Shrimp and Tomatoes
Mariangela Fasoli, Pavia, Lombardia

Sauté a crushed garlic clove in extra-virgin olive oil, then remove and discard and add minced onion, celery, and carrot to the skillet. Add shelled freshwater shrimp and cook. Add minced fresh oregano and rosemary, then add rice and a small amount of Cognac. Cook, stirring, until it has evaporated. Add milk and pureed tomatoes, then finish cooking risotto-style by adding small amounts of hot vegetable broth. Season with salt and stir in a generous amount of grated Parmigiano Reggiano. Sprinkle with minced parsley and season with black pepper. For a heartier dish, use butter and beef broth. You can also use saltwater shrimp or even fillets of perch. Cistercian monks reportedly make this dish with a broth made by boiling freshwater shrimp and frogs and then incorporating the shelled shrimp and frog's legs into the finished dish.

RISOTTO GIALLO CON OSSOBUCO
Saffron Risotto with Ossobuco
Trattoria Ponte Rosso, Milano, Lombardia

Ossobuco is a dish but also a cut of meat—a cross-cut veal shank. Be sure to purchase foreleg shanks, as they provide the more tender meat.

SERVES 6

MEAT

6   cuts pieces cross-cut veal shank
1   tablespoon unbleached all-purpose
    flour, plus more for dredging
1   medium yellow onion, minced
Extra-virgin olive oil for sautéing
Leaves of 1 sprig rosemary
3 to 4 sage leaves
3 to 4 bay leaves
Salt and freshly ground black pepper to taste
½   cup dry white wine
2   cups beef broth

1   tablespoon unsalted butter, softened
Grated zest of ½ lemon
1   tablespoon minced parsley

RICE

About 1 quart beef broth
7   tablespoons unsalted butter
1   medium yellow onion, minced
2¾ cups carnaroli rice
½   cup dry white wine
1   pinch ground saffron
1   pinch saffron threads
Salt to taste
½   cup grated Parmigiano Reggiano

For the meat portion of the dish, trim the shank cuts of any excess fat and cut a shallow line around the perimeter of each one. Dredge them in flour very lightly. In a large skillet, sauté the minced onion in a small amount of olive oil until golden, add the rosemary, sage, and bay leaves. Brown the veal on both sides and season with salt and pepper. Add the wine and cook until evaporated. Add the beef broth, cover, and cook over low heat until the meat is quite tender and there is some very nicely reduced liquid cloaking it. (You can also do this in the oven.) Remove the meat and set aside. Work the butter with the remaining 1 tablespoon flour until it forms a paste, then mount the sauce remaining in the skillet by whisking in the butter and flour. Strain the sauce through a sieve (discard sage, rosemary, and bay leaves). Combine the lemon zest and parsley, then stir the mixture into the strained sauce and set aside.

While the meat is cooking, prepare the rice. Place the broth in a small pot and keep warm. In a large skillet, melt 3 tablespoons unsalted butter and sauté the onion until just golden. Add the rice and toast, stirring, just until translucent. Add the white wine and cook until evaporated. Add the ground saffron and begin adding the broth in small amounts, stirring constantly with a wooden sppoon and waiting until the last addition of liquid has been absorbed before adding the next. Cook until the rice is tender, 15 to 18 minutes total, then stir in the saffron threads until dissolved. Season with salt. Remove from the heat and briskly stir in the remaining 4 tablespoons butter and the grated Parmigiano until melted.

Divide the rice among individual shallow bowls, keeping it to one side if possible. Add the meat on the other side. Make an indentation in each portion of rice and fill with the prepared sauce.

RISOTTO CON LE NOCCIOLE
Risotto with Hazelnuts
Rosanna Dotta, Novello (Cuneo), Piemonte

Sauté minced shallot in extra-virgin olive oil, then add diced pancetta and rice. Stir for a few minutes, then add a small amount of dry white wine and let it evaporate. Season with salt and pepper and finish cooking risotto-style, adding small amounts of hot vegetable broth. When the rice is cooked al dente, remove from the heat and stir in butter and toasted, peeled, chopped hazelnuts. Cover and set aside to rest for a few minutes, then serve, garnished with whole hazelnuts.

RISOTTO PICANTE
Spicy Risotto
Rosaria Salvatore, Tropea (Vibo Valentia), Calabria

Risotto traditionally hails from the North of Italy, but here it has been made southern with the addition of hot pepper. To serve 4, brown 1 clove garlic in a generous amount of extra-virgin olive oil, then remove the garlic and add 2 green chili peppers and 2 red chili peppers, cut into strips. Immediately add 2⅔ cups fino or superfino rice for risotto. Cook, stirring, for a few minutes, then add a small amount of dry white wine. When the wine has evaporated, cook risotto-style by adding hot vegetable broth in small amounts. When the rice is almost cooked, add 6 to 8 crushed cherry tomatoes. Remove from the heat, taste and adjust salt, then sprinkle on ½ cup grated Parmigiano Reggiano and ¼ cup pine nuts. Tear 5 to 6 basil leaves over the risotto and serve.

COTECHINO NEL RISOTTO
Cotechino Risotto
Nuova Osteria Tripoli, San Giorgio di Mantova (Mantova), Lombardia

Cotechino is a wide-diameter pork sausage that is cooked long and slow.

SERVES 4

- 10 ounces cotechino
- 2 quarts beef broth
- 3 tablespoons unsalted butter
- 1 tablespoon extra-virgin olive oil
- ½ medium yellow onion, thinly sliced
- ¼ head Savoy cabbage, cut into ribbons
- Salt and freshly ground black pepper to taste
- 1¾ cups vialone nano rice
- ½ cup white wine
- 1 cup grated Grana Padano cheese

Soak the cotechino in cold water for at least 1 hour, then pierce with a toothpick all over and simmer over low heat until cooked, at least 2 hours. Remove from the casing and mince or crumble.

Place the broth in a small pot and keep warm. In another larger pot melt 1 tablespoon butter with the oil and sauté the onion for 2 minutes. Add the cabbage, about ¼ cup water, and salt and pepper. Cook over high heat for 5 minutes, then add the rice and cook until translucent. Add the wine and cook until evaporated. Add broth to cover and cook over low heat, stirring constantly. Begin adding the broth in small amounts, stirring constantly with a wooden spoon and waiting until the last addition of liquid has been absorbed before adding the next. After 10 minutes of cooking, stir in the cooked sausage. When the rice is tender but still has just a little bite, remove from the heat and stir in the grated cheese and remaining 2 tablespoons butter until melted.

RISOTTO AL PICON
Veal Risotto
Nuova Osteria Tripoli, San Giorgio di Mantova
(Mantova), Lombardia

This was originally invented as a way to use up leftover roasted meat. A similar risotto is made with pork.

SERVES 4

- 14 ounces veal bones
- Salt to taste
- 1½ yellow onions
- 2 to 3 whole cloves
- 1 leek, chopped
- 1 carrot, chopped
- 1 rib celery, chopped
- 1 bay leaf
- 2 tablespoons extra-virgin olive oil
- 7 ounces veal, cut into small dice
- 1 clove garlic, minced
- 3 to 4 sage leaves
- ¾ cup white wine
- 3 tablespoons unsalted butter
- 1¾ cups vialone nano or carnaroli rice
- 1 pinch saffron
- Freshly ground black pepper to taste
- 1 cup grated Grana Padano cheese

The day before you plan to make the risotto, make the veal stock. Rinse the bones and place them in a pot with 3 cups cold water. Season with salt and bring to a boil. Stud 1 onion with the cloves and add the studded onion, leek, carrot, celery, and bay leaf to the pot. Cook over low heat for 3 hours, skimming any foam that rises to the surface. Strain and set aside to cool. Degrease the stock once it has cooled.

The next day, warm the stock slightly. In a skillet, heat 1 tablespoon oil and sauté the veal with the garlic and sage leaves. Add about half of the wine and cook until evaporated. Add a few tablespoons of the prepared veal stock and cook until the veal is cooked through.

Thinly slice the remaining ½ onion. In a pot, melt 1 tablespoon butter with the remaining 1 tablespoon olive oil. Sauté the onion over high heat until golden, then add the rice and cook until translucent. Add the remaining wine and cook until evaporated. Add enough of the prepared veal stock to cover the rice and simmer gently to absorb for 10 minutes. Dissolve the saffron in about ¼ cup of the stock and add to the rice along with a generous amount of pepper. Continue cooking, adding stock as needed, until the rice is tender. Remove from the heat and stir in the grated cheese and remaining 2 tablespoons butter until melted.

Divide among individual serving plates and make an indentation in the center of each portion. Place the veal in these indentations. Top with a drizzle of veal stock and serve.

RISOTTO CON SALTARELLI
Freshwater Shrimp Risotto with Lemon
Bianca Remelli, Goito (Mantova), Lombardia

Fry small freshwater shrimp (shells on) in a neutral extra-virgin olive oil until red and crispy. Drain on paper towels and keep warm. In a large skillet, sauté thinly sliced onion until golden. Remove and discard the onion and strain the oil, then return it to the skillet. Add rice and cook for a few minutes, then finish cooking risotto-style with hot fish or vegetable broth. When the rice is cooked al dente, stir in a generous chunk of butter and sprinkle with grated Grana Padano cheese. Top with the reserved fried shrimp. Spritz with lemon juice and serve. There are also versions of this recipe that call for boiling local water chestnuts, sautéing them in butter with onion and partially crushing them with a fork, then adding them to the finished risotto. Still other versions include pancetta or tomatoes.

RISOTO DE GÔ
Goby Fish Risotto
Ofelia Facco Trevisan, Cavallino Treporti
(Venezia), Veneto

Gô is a species of goby fish that lives in the Venezia lagoons. It is very flavorful, but the flesh is delicate and breaks down easily, so it almost always appears in the form of soup or broth. There are many different varieties of the fish, including one that Venetian fishermen caught with their hands at one time. Boil gutted and scaled goby fish (or any other delicate white fish) with onion, celery, garlic, salt, and green peppercorns for about 1½ hours. Remove and discard the vegetables and peppercorns and force the fish and liquid through a sieve lined with cheesecloth. In a skillet, sauté rice with minced garlic and ginger in extra-virgin olive oil. Cook, stirring constantly, adding the goby broth in small amounts. When the rice is almost cooked, add a spoonful of brandy and cook until al dente. Sprinkle with minced parsley before serving.

Annalisa Scarpa in Chioggia makes a similar risotto but omits the ginger and uses dry white wine in place of the brandy.

RISOTTO ALLA MILANESE
Milanese Risotto with Saffron and Bone Marrow
Enrica Tagliabue, Desio (Mîlano), Lombardia

To make traditional Milanese risotto, first cook butter and bone marrow (ideally from the knee of a cow) in a skillet. Add onion and cook until just golden. (Some cooks remove the onion to avoid any bitterness; others leave it in.) Add rice and cook for a few minutes until coated in fat, then finish cooking risotto-style by stirring in small amounts of beef or chicken broth. Meanwhile, heat a few pistils of saffron over a flame in a spoon, then dilute them slightly in a small amount of hot broth. Add that broth toward the end of cooking. When the rice is cooked, stir in a few more pistils of saffron for additional color and flavor. Stir in additional butter along with grated Granone Lodigiano, Grana Padano, or Parmigiano Reggiano. (There is much debate about which is proper.) As the butter and cheese melt from the heat of the risotto, the rice should form characteristic waves.

RISOTTO AL SALTO
Milanese Risotto Cake
Simonetta Riva, Giussano (Mîlano), Lombardia

This is the best way to use any leftover Milanese risotto. Crush the risotto with a wooden spoon so that it forms a disk of even thickness. In a nonstick skillet melt a generous amount of butter and when it begins to foam, slide in the disk of rice. Cook until brown and crusty underneath, then flip and cook until browned on the other side as well. Sprinkle with a generous amount of grated Parmigiano Reggiano and cut into wedges. A similar dish is baked in the oven and topped with sautéed mushrooms, stewed snails, or stewed frogs.

RISOTTO CON MIDOLLO E CARDO GOBBO
Risotto with Bone Marrow and Gobbo Cardoons
Pino Osella, Carmagnola (Torino), Piemonte

Vermouth, which appears in this traditional recipe, was invented in Torino in the eighteenth century. In a skillet, sauté pieces of bone marrow (boiled for a few minutes in broth) in extra-virgin olive oil with a few pieces of boiled and minced cardoons. When they begin to turn golden, add rice and cook, stirring, over high heat for a few minutes until the rice is translucent. Add a dose of vermouth and cook until evaporated, then cook risotto-style, adding small amounts of hot beef broth. After about 10 minutes, add a little more bone marrow and more boiled cardoons cut into large dice. Continue cooking by adding broth until rice is al dente, about an additional 10 minutes. Stir in a generous amount of butter and grated Parmigiano Reggiano.

RISOTTO CON ANIMELLE ⫷
Risotto with Sweetbreads
Agriturismo Il Giardino degli Ulivi, Castelraimondo (Macerata), Marche

This dish provides an excellent way to use up "discards" from butchering. Soak the sweetbreads in several changes of cold water for at least 12 hours to remove any impurities.

SERVES 4

3   sprigs rosemary
3   sprigs thyme
2   cloves garlic
1   cup dry white wine
Salt to taste
7   ounces veal sweetbreads, soaked and membrane removed
1   quart veal broth
1   medium yellow onion, minced
¼   cup extra-virgin olive oil
2   cups carnaroli rice
5   tablespoons unsalted butter
2   sage leaves
Leaves of 1 sprig marjoram
Grated young pecorino or Parmigiano Reggiano to taste
Freshly ground white pepper

In a pot combine 2 sprigs rosemary, 2 sprigs thyme, 2 cloves garlic, about ½ cup white wine, salt, and 1 quart water. Bring to a boil, simmer for 10 minutes, then blanch the sweetbreads in this liquid. Remove the sweetbreads and

strain the cooking liquid, then return the liquid to the pot and combine with 1 quart veal broth. Keep warm.

In a skillet, sauté the onion in 3 tablespoons oil. Add the rice and cook until translucent. Add the remaining ½ cup wine and cook until evaporated. Begin adding the broth in small amounts, stirring constantly with a wooden spoon and waiting until the last addition of liquid has been absorbed before adding the next.

While the rice is cooking, slice the sweetbreads. Mince the leaves of the remaining sprigs rosemary and thyme. In a small skillet, melt 3 tablespoons unsalted butter over high heat. Add the sliced sweetbreads and the minced thyme and rosemary. Brown the sweetbreads on both sides.

Mince the sage leaves and marjoram and combine with the grated cheese. When the rice is tender, stir in the remaining 2 tablespoons butter, remaining 1 tablespoon oil, grated cheese mixture, and white pepper until butter and cheese have melted. Serve sweetbreads on top of rice.

SARTÙ
Baked Rice with Mushrooms, Peas, and Meat
Antonio Rizzo, Napoli, Campania

Sartù is a rich dish that was invented to feed the aristocracy of Napoli. These days, some home cooks make a simpler version by lining the top and sides of the pan with cooked rice tossed with butter and grated Parmigiano, then filling the center with mozzarella, fried zucchini, and more grated Parmigiano. For the traditional version, in an earthenware pot, sauté minced onion in a little extra-virgin olive oil. Add chopped rehydrated dried porcini mushrooms, peas, and a little tomato paste diluted in warm water. Season with salt and pepper and cook until the peas are soft, about 10 minutes. Add a whole cervellatina (long, thin, and spicy) sausage and cook for

249

30 minutes. While the sausage is cooking, combine ground beef, egg, a handful of grated Parmigiano, and salt and pepper and form into small meatballs, then dredge them in bread-crumbs and pan-fry them in olive oil until browned on all sides. Separately, cook cleaned chicken livers with a little lard and some broth until tender. Cook a generous amount of rice with about half of the peas and sauce (reserve sausage) and enough broth to keep it moist but not soupy.

When the rice is cooked, remove it from the heat and stir in a little lard and an egg (stir briskly to keep it from curdling) and set aside to cool completely. Oil a deep but not very wide baking pan and fill it with about three fourths of the cooked rice mixture, spreading it so that it covers the bottom and the sides evenly. In the center, make a layer of the meatballs, top with a spoonful of the peas and sauce, then a layer of the chicken liver mixture, diced mozzarella, slices of the cervellina sausage, a sprinkling of Parmigiano, and shreds of thinly sliced pro-sciutto and slices of hard-boiled egg. Continue to build layers in this order, ending with the reserved rice on top. Press down firmly to seal, sprinkle with breadcrumbs, and dot with lard. Bake at 325°F until the top is golden, 30 to 35 minutes. Allow the sartù to rest for about 10 minutes, then invert onto a serving platter and carefully lift off the pan.

BOMBA DI RISO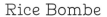
Rice Bombe
Mercedes Spiaggi, Piacenza, Emilia-Romagna

The aristocrats of Piacenza were fond of this dish, which has existed for centuries and can be seen on a menu prepared for members of the House of Farnese circa 1550. Traditionally, the copper mold used to make a *bomba di riso* was part of the eldest daughter's dowry—it was a symbol of the family's wealth. Piacenza poet Valente Faustini (1858–1922) even wrote a poem dedicated to the dish

that reads, in part, "You're beautiful on the outside, and you're good on the inside with your sausage and squab." This recipe was passed down to Mercedes Spiaggi from her great-grandmother, who worked as a cook for the Farnese family.

In a sauté pan with high sides, sauté minced shallot in butter until golden, then add whole squab (plucked and cleaned). Season with salt, pepper, and nutmeg. Cook for about 15 minutes, then add minced rehydrated dried mushrooms, chicken giblets, bay leaf, and some minced parsley. Cook over low heat until tender, keeping the pan moist by adding small amounts of broth and a splash of the local Gutturnio red wine. When the squab are cooked, bone them and cut the meat into small pieces, then add back to the pan with the mushroom mixture. Crumble in some sau-sage meat (casing removed) and cook briefly to combine. Prepare a pan for the bombe by buttering it thickly and then coating with breadcrumbs. Combine a generous amount of boiled and cooled balilla rice (enough to fill the pan when combined with the squab mixture) with a generous amount of melted and cooled butter and grated Grana Piacentino cheese. Combine with enough beaten egg to make a mixture stiff enough to stand on its own but still amalgamated. Pour half of the rice mix-ture into the pan, forming an indentation in the center. Place the squab mixture and sauce in the indentation. Top with the remaining rice and smooth the top. Sprinkle with bread-crumbs and dot with butter. Bake in a hot oven until golden. Let the baked bombe rest for about 10 minutes, then invert onto a serving platter and lift off the pan.

ORZOTTO ALLE VERDURE 🌿
Risotto-Style Barley with Vegetables

Ristorante Taverna Kus, San Zeno di Montagna (Verona), Veneto

Barley makes a nice change from rice in this light summer dish.

SERVES 6

Salt to taste
1¼ cups pearled barley
½ cup dried borlotti beans, soaked overnight
About 3 cups vegetable broth
1 medium yellow onion, minced
Extra-virgin olive oil for sautéing
3 zucchini, diced
⅔ cup shelled peas
3 plum tomatoes, peeled, seeded, and diced
¼ cup minced chives
3 basil leaves
1 tablespoon unsalted butter
¼ cup grated Parmigiano Reggiano

Bring a large pot of salted water to a boil and cook the barley al dente, about 20 minutes, then drain and set aside. Drain the beans and cook in lightly salted water in another pot until tender, about 40 minutes. Drain the beans.

Place the broth in a small pot and keep warm. Sauté about half the minced onion in a skillet in oil. Add the zucchini and a couple tablespoons of the broth and braise until soft, about 10 minutes. In a separate skillet, sauté the remaining minced onion and add the peas. Add 2 tablespoons broth and braise until tender.

Place the barley in a pot with broth to cover and simmer for 5 minutes. Add the zucchini, peas, and beans and cook, stirring and adding more broth in small amounts, until tender and well combined, about 10 minutes. Remove from the heat and stir in the tomatoes and chives, tear in the basil leaves, then stir in the butter and cheese until melted.

TIELLA DI ORZO, PATATE E COZZE 🖤
Barley, Potato, and Mussel Casserole

Trattoria Antichi Sapori, Montegrosso di Andria, Puglia

Hulled barley has had only the very tough outer husk removed and takes longer to cook than pearled barley. An overnight soak helps speed the process along. Puglia is known for this kind of hearty vegetable casserole—the varieties are almost limitless.

SERVES 4

1½ cups hulled barley, soaked overnight in water to cover
2 pounds mussels
Extra-virgin olive oil for oiling pan and drizzling
2 medium yellow onions, sliced
2 zucchini, sliced into rounds
1 pound (about 3) potatoes, peeled and sliced
Salt and freshly ground black pepper to taste
1 pound tomatoes, sliced
¼ cup grated aged pecorino cheese
3 to 4 basil leaves

Boil the barley in its soaking water for 30 minutes, then drain. Shell the mussels, reserving and straining any liquid and discarding the beards.

Preheat the oven to 350°F. Generously oil a baking pan and arrange about half the onions in a single layer. Cover with a layer of half the zucchini, then a layer of all the potato slices. Season with salt and pepper. Make a layer of the mussels on top of the potatoes, then cover with the barley. Drizzle on the liquid from the mussels and layer the tomato slices on top. End with another layer of the remaining zucchini and another of the remaining onion.

Sprinkle on the cheese and tear on the basil leaves. Season with a generous amount of pepper, a pinch of salt, and a drizzle of olive oil. Bake for 45 minutes. Serve hot or cold.

FARROTTO CON PORCINI
Risotto-Style Farro with Porcini Mushrooms
Osteria Giocondo, Rivisondoli (L'Aquîla), Abruzzo

arro's nutty flavor and firm texture stand up beautifully to meaty porcini mushrooms. You can really adapt the risotto cooking method to almost any grain there is. The cooking time of farro can vary widely by brand and depending on the age of the farro and how pearled it is.

SERVES 4

- About 1 quart beef broth
- 4 tablespoons unsalted butter
- 1 medium yellow onion, thinly sliced
- ¾ cup pearled farro
- ½ cup dry white wine
- 2 cloves garlic
- 1 small piece chili pepper
- Extra-virgin olive oil for sautéing
- 1 pound porcini mushrooms, sliced or diced
- Salt to taste

Place the broth in a small pot and keep warm. In a large skillet, melt 2 tablespoons butter and sauté the onion until golden. Add the farro and cook, stirring, for a couple of minutes until it is coated in the butter. Add the wine and cook until evaporated, then begin adding the broth in small amounts, stirring constantly with a wooden spoon and waiting until the last addition of liquid has been absorbed before adding the next.

Meanwhile, in a separate skillet, cook the garlic and chili pepper in olive oil until browned. Remove and discard the garlic and chili pepper and add the porcini mushrooms and a pinch of salt. When the mushrooms are soft and browned, stir them into the farro, which should be about halfway cooked. Continue cooking by adding broth in small amounts until the farro is tender, about 20 additional minutes. When it is cooked, remove from the heat and stir in the remaining 2 tablespoons butter until melted.

FARROTTO ALLA ZUCCA
Risotto-Style Farro with Squash
Bianca Remelli, Goito (Mantova), Lombardia

immer cubes of winter squash in vegetable broth (made with carrot, onion, celery, leek, garlic, rock salt, and a bouquet garni of bay leaf, parsley, thyme, and peppercorns) until soft, then puree both the squash and the cooking liquid. Taste and adjust salt. In a large skillet, sauté thinly sliced onion in a little extra-virgin olive oil until golden. Add farro. Add white wine and cook, stirring, until the liquid has evaporated. Continue to cook by adding small amounts of hot vegetable broth, stirring constantly and waiting for the broth to be absorbed between additions, for about 10 minutes. Stir in the squash puree and continue to cook, adding broth in small amounts and stirring constantly, until farro is tender. Taste and adjust salt.

RISOTTO ALLA BONARDA CON LUMACHE
Risotto with Bonarda Wine and Snails
Trattoria San Giovanni, Piacenza, Emilia-Romagna

Bonarda is a fruity red wine. Chop about half the snails roughly and the other half more finely for textural interest.

SERVES 4 OR 5

- 7 tablespoons unsalted butter
- 2 shallots, minced
- ¼ cup plus 2 tablespoons sugar
- 2 cups sweet Bonarda wine (see note)
- 1 medium yellow onion, minced
- 2 cloves garlic, minced
- 1 carrot, minced
- 2 ribs celery, minced
- 14 ounces snails, shelled and chopped
- 1 tablespoon tomato paste
- Salt and freshly ground black pepper to taste
- About 1½ quarts vegetable broth
- Extra-virgin olive oil for sautéing
- 2 cups carnaroli or vialone nano rice
- 1 cup grated Grana Padano
- ¼ cup minced herbs, such as thyme, chives, marjoram, rosemary, and dill

In a pot, melt 2 tablespoons of the butter and sauté 1 shallot until soft. Add ¼ cup plus 1 tablespoon sugar. Stir until the sugar melts, but before it caramelizes add 1½ cups of the Bonarda and cook over low heat until thick and syrupy. Remove from the heat and strain through a sieve, then reserve.

In an earthenware pot, melt 3 tablespoons butter and sauté the onion and garlic until golden. Add the carrot and celery and cook until softened, then add the snails. Cook until browned, then add the tomato paste and remaining 1 tablespoon sugar. Add the remaining ½ cup wine and cook until evaporated. Season with salt and pepper and cook until very tender, about 2 hours, adding small amounts of broth to keep the pot moist. Remove from the heat and keep warm.

When the snails are cooked, place the remaining broth in a small pot and keep warm.

In a large skillet, sauté the remaining shallot in olive oil. Add the rice and cook, stirring, until translucent. Begin adding the broth in small amounts, stirring constantly with a wooden spoon and waiting until the last addition of liquid has been absorbed before adding the next. Cook until the rice is tender on the outside but still crunchy in the center. Begin adding the Bonarda reduction in small amounts, alternating with the broth. The rice should turn a rich red color. Season with salt. When the rice is tender, remove from the heat and stir in the remaining 2 tablespoons butter and grated cheese until melted. Allow to rest for a few minutes. To serve, form the rice in a well on a serving platter and place the snails in the center of the well. Sprinkle with the minced herbs, drizzle on any pan juices from the snails, and season with black pepper.

POLENTA MARITATA ❗
Polenta with Spicy Beans
Giada Bruni, Viterbo, Lazio

Polenta is traditionally cooked in a copper pot called a *paiolo* that has gently convex sides and a single arched handle over the top (dating back to the days when the pot was hung over an open flame in a fireplace rather than set on a stove). Copper cookware is prized for its ability to conduct heat quickly and evenly. If you are lucky enough to own a large copper pot, use it to make polenta the traditional way, but if not, a sturdy cast-iron or even stainless steel pot will do. Just be sure to use a pot with a heavy bottom so the polenta doesn't scorch.

In a large, preferably copper, pot, bring salted water to a boil, then drizzle in polenta, being sure to mix until no lumps remain. Turn the heat down to low until the mixture barely bubbles and cook, stirring, until the polenta no longer tastes raw, about 40 minutes. In a skillet sauté strips of pancetta in a small amount of extra-virgin olive oil until the fat on the pancetta is translucent. Add cooked borlotti beans and crumbled dried chili pepper, season with salt, and cook for 10 minutes. Stir the bean mixture into the polenta and cook, stirring, for a few minutes, then sprinkle with a generous amount of freshly ground pepper and a handful of grated aged sheep's cheese and serve.

POLENTA CON LA SALVIA 🍃
Polenta with Sage
Antonella Riva, Lecco, Lombardia

In a skillet, sauté diced onion in a few tablespoons of olive oil, then add rehydrated dried mushrooms that you have squeezed dry, the minced leaves of 1 bunch sage and 1 bunch flat-leaf parsley, and 2 minced anchovy fillets. Bring salted water to a boil in a copper polenta pot, slowly drizzle in polenta, and cook, stirring very frequently, until the polenta begins to pull away from the sides of the pot, about 45 minutes. Stir in the sage mixture and finish cooking. Spread the cooked polenta on a board and level to an even thickness of about ¾ inch. When the polenta has cooled, cut it into slices and dredge the slices of polenta in flour. Heat a couple of inches of olive oil in a skillet with a few sage leaves. When it begins to sizzle, pan-fry the polenta slices until golden, turning to brown both sides. Drain briefly on paper towels and serve.

ZUF 🎃
Polenta with Winter Squash Puree
Dorina Treppo, Tarcento (Udine), Friuli-Venezia Giulia

In a copper polenta pot, cook diced winter squash in a small amount of butter with a little water until falling apart. Mash with a fork or wooden spoon, then add milk and bring to a boil. Drizzle in polenta and cook, stirring constantly, until the polenta is cooked and the mixture is creamy, 30 to 45 minutes. If the mixture is getting too stiff before it has finished cooking, add water or milk in small amounts.

POLENTA CON CAURIGLI 🌿
Polenta with Broccoli
Matteo Iannacone, Venafro (Isernia), Molise

Bring salted water to boil in a large copper polenta pot for making polenta and briefly cook chopped broccoli in the water on its own, then slowly drizzle polenta into the water, mixing to be sure no lumps form, and cook, stirring, until the polenta is creamy and the broccoli has broken down and mixed into the polenta and turned it green, about 45 minutes. Sauté thinly sliced garlic cloves (remove any green shoots) in extra-virgin olive oil with crumbled chili pepper and stir the mixture into the polenta. This dish is also excellent the day after it is made and can be reheated briefly in the oven.

POLENTA INCATENATA 🌿
Polenta with Beans and Kale
Carlotta Olivieri, Sarzana (La Spezia), Liguria

Back when meat was a luxury reserved for holidays like Christmas and maybe a wedding banquet, this was a typical dish in the lower Val Magra, where it served as both a first and second course. In a large pot, combine thin ribbons of Tuscan kale, diced peeled potatoes, diced carrots, and chopped onion and garlic with borlotti beans that are cooked but still firm. Add water to cover by a couple of inches and simmer for 30 minutes. Sprinkle in polenta, stirring constantly to keep lumps from forming, and cook until the polenta no longer tastes raw, about 45 minutes. The polenta should be soft—if it is getting too thick and isn't cooked yet, stir in some boiling water. Serve with grated cheese and a drizzle of extra-virgin olive oil.

FARINATA CON LE LEGHE 🌿
Polenta with Tuscan Kale
Osteria Il Cibreo, Firenze, Toscana

This dish was traditionally cooked in the evening, and then the next morning firm polenta was sliced and reheated. Tuscan kale is available in early winter, after the first frost. Discard any tough, fibrous stems.

SERVES 6
Salt to taste
3   bunches Tuscan kale, cut into ribbons
4¾ cups polenta
2   cloves garlic, minced
½   cup extra-virgin olive oil, plus more for drizzling
2   cups grated Parmigiano Reggiano, plus more for serving

In a large pot, bring 5 quarts water to a boil. Salt the water and add the kale and then drizzle in the polenta very slowly, whisking constantly. Continue to whisk, always in the same direction, until all the polenta has been added, then whisk for a minute or two more. Cook over low, very even heat (on a griddle or a flame tamer), stirring occasionally with a wooden spoon. Do not scrape the bottom of the pot. After 40 minutes, stir in the garlic. Taste (very carefully—it will be extremely hot) and adjust salt.

When the polenta is cooked (it will be a little looser than normal polenta, but it should no longer taste raw), stir in the ½ cup olive oil and 2 cups grated Parmigiano, whisking so that everything is thoroughly combined. Serve very hot with a drizzle of olive oil on top and additional grated cheese on the side.

POLENTA INCACIATA
Polenta with Beef and Dried Porcini
Ristorante Il Pozzo, Pieve Fosciana (Lucca), Toscana

ttofile means "eight rows" and refers to an ancient variety of corn that may be red, white, or yellow.

SERVES 6

2 *cups dried porcini mushrooms*
½ *medium yellow onion, minced*
1 *carrot, minced*
1 *rib celery, minced*
Extra-virgin olive oil for sautéing and
    drizzling
14 *ounces ground beef*
½ *cup dry white wine*
Salt to taste
Whole black peppercorns to taste
About ½ cup vegetable broth
3½ *cups red Ottofile polenta (see note)*
1 *cup grated aged sheep's cheese*

Soak the dried porcini in warm water. In a pot, sauté the onion, carrot, and celery in a little oil. Add the ground beef and the wine and cook over low heat, stirring occasionally, until evaporated. Add a pinch of salt, a few peppercorns, and ¼ cup vegetable broth and cook for 30 minutes. Remove the dried porcini from their soaking water, chop, and add to the pot. Strain a few tablespoons of their soaking water and add that as well. Cook over low heat, adding more vegetable broth if the pot looks dry, for 1½ hours. Remove and discard peppercorns.

Bring a large pot of salted water to a boil and very gradually whisk in the polenta in a thin stream. Cook the polenta over the lowest possible heat, whisking constantly, until it is thick and bubbling like lava, about 50 minutes. Remove from the heat, cover with a damp kitchen towel, and set aside to rest for a few minutes.

Place about ½ cup of the meat sauce in the bottom of a terra-cotta serving dish. Top with a layer of the polenta, a handful of grated sheep's cheese, and a drizzle of oil. Continue to make layers in this order until you have used up the polenta and sauce. Cover and set aside to rest for 10 minutes, then serve.

CACIUF
Polenta with Beans, Meat, and Tomatoes
Trattoria Entrà, Massa Finalese di Finale Emîlia (Modena), Emîlia-Romagna

In Ferrara, this type of polenta is cooled, cut into diamonds or rectangles an inch or two thick, and then fried golden brown in olive oil.

SERVES 6

2 *cups dried Lamon beans, soaked for*
    12 hours
1 *medium yellow onion, minced*
2 *tablespoons extra-virgin olive oil*
1 *tablespoon lardo (cured fatback)*
7 *ounces ground beef*
7 *ounces seasoned ground pork*
7 *ounces sausage, casing removed and*
    crumbled
¼ *cup tomato puree*
Salt and freshly ground black pepper to taste
6 *cups medium-grind polenta*

Drain the beans and place in a pot with a generous amount of water to cover. Bring to a boil, then simmer over medium heat until tender. Meanwhile, for the meat sauce, in a pot sauté the onion in the oil and lardo. Add the ground beef, ground pork, and sausage and cook over low heat for 1½ hours. Add the tomato puree and cook for an additional 1½ hours. Season with salt and pepper.

Place 4 quarts water in a copper polenta pot and bring to a boil. Salt lightly, then drizzle in the polenta very slowly while stirring constantly. The mixture should be very thin. Stir in the beans, then the meat sauce. Season with salt and cook over low heat for 45 minutes. Serve warm, but not piping hot, in individual bowls.

POLENTA GRASSA 🧀
Rich Polenta with Milk and Cheese
Letizia Palesi, Champorcher (Aosta), Valle d'Aosta

Polenta mixed with various types of cheese is commonly served in the Alps. Combine equal amounts water and milk in a pot. Season with salt and drizzle in coarsely ground polenta between your fingers very slowly, stirring constantly. Stir in clarified butter and cook the polenta, stirring constantly, until it is thick and no longer tastes raw. Stir in cubes of toma cheese until melted, then remove from the heat. Sprinkle with grated aged cheese if you like.

VIANDON 🍴
Polenta with Rye Bread Croutons and Cheese
Franca Gallo, Aosta, Valle d'Aosta

In a copper polenta pot, bring equal amounts water and milk to a boil. Salt and sprinkle in polenta, mixing with a whisk so that no lumps form. Cook the polenta, stirring constantly, for at least 1 hour. About 10 minutes before the polenta is fully cooked, stir in cubes of stale rye bread toasted in a generous amount of melted butter, diced fontina cheese, and a few tablespoons of butter. Finish cooking and serve piping hot.

POLENTA MITONÀ 🍴
Baked Polenta with Gorgonzola and Toma Cheese
Adriano Ravera, Boves (Cuneo), Piemonte

Bring a pot of water to a boil and add salt and some oil. Sprinkle in polenta and cook, stirring slowly, for about 1 hour. Pour polenta onto a wooden board and cut into slices. Butter an earthenware baking dish that is on the small side in diameter but has high sides. Arrange a layer of polenta slices in the dish, then sprinkle with grated aged local cheese, a few diced pieces of toma (soft or semi-soft cow's milk) cheese, and some Gorgonzola. Continue making layers of polenta and cheese. Top the last layer of polenta with Gorgonzola and dot with butter. Pour milk into the pan so that it comes up the sides and just covers the polenta. Sprinkle with a little salt and bake at 325°F for 1 hour.

PIZZA DI GRANONE 🥬
Baked Polenta with Sausage and Broccoli Rabe
Antonio Rizzo, Napoli, Campania

Blanch broccoli rabe briefly, then drain and chop. In a skillet, brown a thinly sliced spring onion in a drizzle of extra-virgin olive oil, then add the broccoli rabe. After a few minutes, add some crumbled pork sausage. Stir to combine, adjust seasoning, and cook until the sausage is browned. In a large copper polenta pot, bring salted water to a boil, then slowly drizzle in polenta and mix with a whisk to keep lumps from forming. Cook, stirring constantly, for 45 minutes. When the polenta is almost ready, stir in the sausage mixture and finish cooking. Pour the polenta into an oiled baking pan, sprinkle on a generous handful of grated aged sheep's cheese, and bake at 350°F until a golden crust forms on top. Allow to rest for a couple of minutes before serving.

CRESC' TAJAT AI CARCIOFI 🌰
Polenta Pasta with Artichokes
Ristorante La Baita, Costa di Arcevia (Ancona), Marche

This dish obviously was developed to use up leftover polenta, but it is so delicious that you will want to make polenta just for this purpose. Remember to drop the artichokes into cold water spiked with lemon juice as you trim and slice them to keep them from browning.

SERVES 4
Salt to taste
2⅓ cups polenta
1   large egg, lightly beaten
2½ cups unbleached all-purpose flour
½   cup grated aged sheep's cheese
Freshly ground black pepper to taste
½   medium yellow onion, minced
1   chili pepper

Extra-virgin olive oil for sautéing and drizzling
1   thick slice speck, about 4 ounces, diced
½   cup Verdicchio dei Castelli di Jesi white wine
3   artichokes, trimmed and cut into julienne
4   ripe tomatoes, peeled, seeded, and diced
Leaves of 1 sprig parsley, minced

For the pasta, bring a large pot of salted water to a boil and drizzle in the polenta, stirring to avoid creating lumps. Cook over low heat, stirring constantly, until thickened, about 40 minutes. Remove the polenta from the heat and allow to cool, then transfer to a bowl. Beat in the egg, the flour, and the grated cheese. Knead until well combined. Season with salt and pepper. Spread the mixture about 1/10 inch thick and use a smooth wheel cutter to cut into medium-sized lozenges or diamonds.

For the sauce, in a large pot, sauté the onion and the chili pepper in oil. Add the speck and then add the wine and cook until evaporated. Add the artichokes and cook until tender, 5 to 6 minutes. Add the tomatoes and cook until well combined and soft. Season with salt.

Bring a large pot of salted water to a boil and cook the polenta pasta al dente, 2 to 3 minutes. Remove with a slotted spoon or skimmer and add to the pot with the artichokes. Cook, stirring, to combine, then drizzle with a little olive oil, sprinkle on parsley, and serve.

CALZAGATT
Polenta with Beans, Pancetta, and Rosemary
Gina Piccinini and Renato Graziosi, Vignola (Modena), Emîlia-Romagna

Sauté minced pancetta in a pot with crushed garlic and a few sprigs of rosemary tied with kitchen twine. When the pancetta has begun to render its fat, add a small amount of extra-virgin olive oil, then add cooked borlotti beans and tomato paste. Season with salt, add water to cover, and cook until reduced slightly, about 20 minutes. In a copper polenta pot, prepare polenta in a mixture of milk and water (1 part milk to every 3 parts water), stirring constantly. After about 40 minutes, when the polenta is nice and thick and almost cooked, stir in the beans and sauce, then cook over low heat for an additional 15 minutes. Serve warm (not piping hot) or cool, or fry bits of calzagatt as described in the note for caciuf (page 256).

PULEINTA E GRASEI
Polenta with Pork Cracklings
Massimo Volpari, Cortemaggîore (Piacenza), Emîlia-Romagna

Bring a pot of salted water to a boil, drizzle in polenta, and cook, stirring to keep lumps from forming, until the polenta is cooked. In a skillet, melt a little lard and sauté thinly sliced onion over low heat, without letting it brown. Add pork cracklings and continue cooking over low heat for 15 minutes. When the polenta begins to pull away from the sides of the pot, stir the onion mixture into it and continue cooking for an additional 10 minutes. Remove from the heat, pour onto a wooden board or platter, and serve.

POLENTA CON SALSICCIA E PEPERONI CRUSCHI
Polenta with Sausage and Dried Peppers
Federico Valicenti, Terranova di Pollino (Potenza), Basîlicata

This dish uses IGP (Protected Geographic Origin) *peperoni cruschi* from Senise, sun-dried sweet peppers that can either be crumbled or ground. Sauté cubes of pancetta in a little olive oil. Add sausages sliced into disks and ground dried peppers. Sauté for a few minutes, then add some tomato puree. Cook for about 20 minutes, taste, and adjust salt. Meanwhile, bring salted water to boil in a large pot. Slowly sprinkle in polenta and cook, stirring constantly with a wooden spoon to avoid letting lumps form, until the polenta pulls away from the sides of the pot. Melt lard in a small skillet and stir in a little bit of ground dried Senise peppers. Cook briefly, then taste and adjust salt and add the lard mixture to the polenta, stirring until well combined. Pour the hot polenta onto a clean cloth and squeeze tightly so that it is very firm. Unwrap, slice, and arrange the slices on plates. Serve with the sausage and its sauce on top.

PAPPA SCIANSCA
Wheat-Flour Porridge with Cinnamon, Sugar, and Wine
Giovanna Barzan, San Donˆ di Piave (Venezia), Veneto

Combine all-purpose flour with enough white wine to make a paste, then stir in enough milk to make it rather soupy. Stir in a small amount of sugar, a pinch of salt, and a pinch of ground cinnamon. Cook over low heat, stirring constantly, until thickened into a porridge, about 20 minutes. Cinnamon was used widely in the Venetian Republic, as it was involved in the spice trade.

259

PUCCIA 🌿
Polenta, Cabbage, and Beans
Benedetta Rizzolo, San Giorgio Scarampi
(Asti), Piemonte

Cook borlotti beans that have been soaked in cold water overnight in water with a piece of celery, sage, rosemary, and parsley wrapped in cheesecloth. Sauté ribbons of Savoy cabbage in extra-virgin olive oil with a little lardo (cured fatback), then add that to the pot with the beans. Add water to cover by a couple of inches, bring to a boil, then drizzle in polenta, whisking to keep any lumps from forming. Season with salt, remove the cheesecloth, and cook, stirring constantly with a wooden spoon, until the polenta is cooked, about 45 minutes. Serve hot with melted butter and grated Grana Padano, serve cold, or cut into slices and pan-fry in extra-virgin olive oil. You can also stir a little stewed pork into the polenta while it is cooking.

POLENTA E OSEI 🍃
Polenta with Game Birds
Franca Mangili, Bergamo, Lombardia

In the most strictly traditional version of this recipe, the small birds used here (usually a type of lark) are not gutted and their heads and feet are left intact so that the meat takes on a slightly bitter flavor. Even if you do choose to gut your birds (or they are sold to you already gutted), do try to keep the heads attached. As you thread them onto the skewers, tuck their heads under their wings. Loanghina is a kind of dried sausage from the Bergamo area made from pork leg, shoulder, and neck that is finely minced and larded with pork fat from the belly and neck and flavored with red wine and spices. Thread skewers with alternating small game birds, slices of pancetta, and sage leaves. You will need about five small birds per person, and five should fit on one skewer. Cook polenta in salted water in a copper polenta pot, stirring frequently, until the polenta pulls away from the sides of the pot, about 45 minutes. Cook the skewers with the birds and the pancetta and coils of loanghina sausage fixed with a toothpick in a generous amount of butter for 15 to 20 minutes, adding small amounts of additional butter, water, or broth if the pan begins to dry out. Serve the skewers and sausage over the polenta and drizzle on the pan juices.

PASTICCIO DI POLENTA 🪶
Twice-Cooked Polenta with Walnuts and Cheese
Bottiglieria da Pino, Milano, Lombardia

This is one of the many ways to use leftover cooked polenta. Chop the polenta (it will be firm) and force it through a potato ricer, letting it fall into a nonstick skillet. Add diced Gorgonzola, Taleggio, and mozzarella or Asiago in more or less equal amounts. Pour in enough milk to come up the sides of the polenta but not quite cover it. Cook for 10 minutes, stirring constantly and adding more milk in small amounts until the polenta is at a consistency that you like—it can be served more or less firm. Divide among individual serving bowls, top with walnuts, and sprinkle with grated Grana Padano.

POLENTA E BACCALÀ 🐟
Biancoperla White Corn Polenta with Baccalà
Osteria da Paeto, Pianiga (Venezia), Veneto

Biancoperla corn has large white kernels that resemble glass beads. Unfortunately, hybrid varieties took over in the 1950s, but today through a Slow Food Presidium, Biancoperla is making a comeback. Confusingly, what the people in this area call baccalà is actually stockfish, or fish that has been dried rather than salted for long-term storage. Traditionally in the Veneto, polenta is stirred with a flat-headed wooden spatula designed to reach into all corners of the pot. You can use a wooden spoon in its stead.

14 ounces to 1 pound stockfish (dried cod), skinned, boned, and soaked in several changes of water for 3 days
Rock salt to taste
2 to 3 cloves garlic, minced

1¼ cups extra-virgin olive oil
Fine salt to taste
Freshly ground black pepper to taste
2⅓ cups white Biancoperla polenta (see note)

If the stockfish is in one large piece, chop it. Place the stockfish in a pot with cold water to cover and salt with rock salt. Bring to a boil, then remove from the heat and let the fish rest in the pot for 20 minutes.

Remove the fish from the pot and place it in a bowl with the garlic. Beat with a wooden spoon, slowly drizzling in the oil as you do until the garlic and the fish have broken down into a smooth puree. Season with fine salt and a grinding of black pepper.

For the polenta, bring 1 quart water to a boil in a large pot. Season with a heaping spoonful of rock salt, then add the polenta in a very thin stream, whisking constantly as you do. When the water and polenta are a smooth mixture with no lumps, cook, stirring with a wooden polenta spatula (see note) and folding from the bottom of the pot to the top, until the polenta begins to pull away from the sides of the pot and no longer tastes raw, about 50 minutes. If the polenta gets very thick but doesn't seem to be cooked yet, add boiling water in small amounts.

Pour the cooked polenta onto a board and serve hot with the whipped fish mixture.

POLENTA CON SPUNTATURE DI MAIALE 🍅
Polenta with Pork Ribs
Agriturismo Il Ruspante, Castro dei Volsci (Frosinone), Lazio

The kind of goat cheese used here should be white and rather soft and crumbly. As with many polenta dishes, this is a one-course meal on its own with no need for a separate entrée. You'll want about 2 ribs per person.

SERVES 4

- 1 tablespoon unsalted butter
- Salt to taste
- 3 cups polenta
- 1½ pounds sausage, casing removed and crumbled
- Extra-virgin olive oil for sautéing
- 6 cups tomato puree
- 1 clove garlic
- 1 pound pork ribs
- Shavings of young goat cheese to taste

Grease the bottom of a large, heavy pot with the butter, add 1½ quarts water, and bring to a boil. As soon as the water begins to boil, add a pinch of salt and add the polenta, letting it drizzle in a very thin stream between your fingers and whisking constantly to avoid lumps. Simmer until cooked, about 45 minutes.

Meanwhile, in a skillet brown the sausage in a little olive oil. Add 4 cups tomato puree, season with salt, and cook until reduced, about 30 minutes. In a separate large pot, brown the garlic in a little oil. Brown the ribs, then add about ½ cup water and the remaining 2 cups tomato puree. Season with salt and cook until any liquid has evaporated, about 30 minutes.

To serve, pour the cooked polenta onto a wooden board. Spread the tomato sauce with the sausage on top and pass the ribs and cheese shavings on the side.

'NGRITOLI 🐖
Wheat-Flour Porridge with Sausage
Adele Ciceri, Rieti, Lazio

To make enough to serve 4, brown chunks of sausage in a small amount of olive oil. Keep warm. Bring 1½ quarts water to a boil in a large pot, season with salt, and add 4 cups unbleached all-purpose flour, letting it drizzle in slowly between your fingers. Cook over low heat, stirring constantly and in the same direction with a wooden spoon, until the mixture forms a slightly lumpy porridge, about 30 minutes. Pour onto a board, top with the cooked sausage, and sprinkle with a generous amount of grated aged sheep's cheese. 'Ngritoli (the name means "lumps") can also be topped with sliced mushrooms sautéed with minced garlic and parsley.

POLENTA DI FARRO CON MOSTO COTTO 🍇
Farro Polenta with Cooked Grape Must
Nuccia Barîle, Termoli (Campobasso), Molise

Crush Aglianico (black) grapes and collect the juice in a pot. Bring to a boil, then lower the heat and cook over low heat until the juice has been reduced to one third, 4 to 5 hours. Add cinnamon sticks, whole cloves, and a handful of sugar (if you like) and cook for an additional 10 minutes. Remove and discard cinnamon sticks and cloves. Bring a pot of water to a boil and sprinkle in farro flour. Season with salt and cook, stirring, until the mixture is stiff and no longer tastes raw. Stir in cubes of young sheep's cheese and cook until the cheese has melted. Serve with a generous amount of the grape must drizzled on top of each serving.

POLENTA DI FAVE CON CICORIELLE
Fava Polenta with Chicory
Nunzia Rutigliano, Bitetto (Bari), Puglia

Soak dried fava beans overnight in room temperature water. The next day, cook them in salted water, stirring frequently, until they break down into a puree. Stir in blanched, chopped wild chicory and a very generous amount of extra-virgin olive oil and serve.

POLENTA DI FORMENTON CON BOTIRO DI MALGA
Buckwheat Polenta with Butter and Cheese
Nereo Pederzolli, Stravino di Cavedine (Trento), Trentino-Alto Adige

Bring a large pot of water to a boil, season with salt, and stir in a spoonful of oil, then slowly add buckwheat flour while stirring constantly to keep lumps from forming. When the flour is smooth, cover the pot with a lid and cook for less than 1 minute. Then remove the lid and turn the heat to low and cook, stirring almost constantly, with a traditional polenta spatula (see note on page 261), until the polenta begins to pull away from the sides of the pot. Pour the cooked mixture onto a wooden board and top with Primiero Mountain butter (a Slow Food Presidium) and grated young or semi-aged malga cheese.

POLENTA SARACENA CON PORRI E FUNGHI
Buckwheat Polenta with Leeks and Mushrooms
Ristorante Il Borgo, Ormea (Cuneo), Piemonte

Buckwheat cooks into an earthy polenta that matches well with equally earthy mushrooms. This is pure comfort food.

SERVES 6
- 2 tablespoons extra-virgin olive oil
- 1 leek, minced
- ¼ cup dried porcini, soaked to rehydrate, squeezed dry, and minced
- 1 quart whole milk
- ⅔ cup heavy cream or whipping cream
- Salt to taste
- 2 pounds potatoes, peeled and halved
- 2½ cups whole-wheat flour
- ¾ cup buckwheat flour

In a saucepan, heat 2 tablespoons olive oil and brown the leek. Add 2 tablespoons water, the mushrooms, and the milk. Cook over low heat, stirring occasionally, for 1 hour, then add the cream, season with salt, and simmer for 10 additional minutes to reduce slightly.

Meanwhile, place the potatoes in a large pot with water to cover, bring to a boil, and cook until tender, about 30 minutes. Combine the two flours and drizzle the mixture into the pot with the potatoes and the boiling water in a thin stream. Cook over low heat for 30 minutes without stirring so that the mixture steams. Then beat with a wooden spoon so that the potatoes break down and the mixture is smooth. Serve with the leek sauce on top.

POLKA RIVOLTA

Baked Corn and Wheat Polenta with Onions

Trattoria Da Bussè, Pontremoli (Massa-Carrara), Toscana

A similar recipe appears in the recipe book of an anonymous Neapolitan from the fifteenth century that since 1948 has been housed in the Pierpont Morgan Library in New York.

SERVES 4

- 2 cups cornmeal
- 2½ cups unbleached all-purpose flour
- 2 teaspoons salt
- 2 large white onions, sliced
- 3 tablespoons extra-virgin olive oil

Preheat the oven to 350°F. Combine the corn-meal, flour, and salt and whisk in enough water to make a fairly loose mixture. Stir in the onions and 1 tablespoon oil. Oil a baking pan with 1 tablespoon oil and transfer the mixture to the pan. Drizzle the remaining tablespoon oil on the surface and bake in the preheated oven until firm, 40 to 50 minutes.

POLENTA TARAGNA CON LUGANEGHE

Buckwheat Polenta with Pork Sausage

Mariateresa Bettini, Teglio (Sondrio), Lombardia

Bring a large pot of salted water to a boil. Drizzle in coarsely ground buck-wheat polenta, stirring constantly to keep lumps from forming. When the mixture begins to thicken, turn the heat as low as possible and let it simmer very gently for 15 minutes, stirring with a wooden spatula so that the polenta doesn't stick to the bottom of the pot. Add a generous amount of butter cubes and continue cooking for 1 hour. When the polenta is cooked, stir in cubes of young Casera or Bitto cheese until melted. Pour the polenta onto a board and serve with boiled or griddle-cooked luganega pork sausages.

PAPAROTTA

Semolina Polenta with Dried Peppers

Trattoria La Pergola, Gesualdo (Avellino), Campania

This simple dish highlights the sweetness of sun-dried peppers, which intensify as their liquid evaporates.

SERVES 4

- 1 medium yellow onion, thinly sliced
- ¼ cup extra-virgin olive oil
- 4 sun-dried red peppers, seeded and sliced into rounds
- 1 cup finely milled semolina flour
- Salt to taste

In a pot, sauté the onion in the olive oil over low heat. When the onion browns, remove it and add the peppers to the hot oil. Sauté briefly, then remove the peppers as well. Add 2 cups water to the pot and crumble in the peppers. Bring to a boil, then add the semolina in a very thin stream, whisking to keep lumps from forming. Cook over medium heat for 15 minutes, adding additional hot water if the pot begins to look dry. Season with salt, divide among individual serving dishes, and allow to rest for a few minutes before serving.

POLENTA DI PATATE CON PECLIN
Potato Polenta with Smoked Herring
Nereo Pederzolli, Stravino di Cavedine (Trento), Trentino-Alto Adige

Salted smoked Atlantic herring used to be hung from the kitchen ceiling over the large table where the extended family would gather, and diners would then simply brush their slices of polenta against the fish. The strong flavor rubbed off on the polenta, and the fish lasted a long time, yet gave those eating somewhat meager meals of plain polenta the feeling that they were enjoying something a little heartier. Clean and fillet smoked herring and arrange the fillets in a large glass container with alternating layers of bay leaf, garlic cloves, and juniper berries. Pour over a neutral oil (not olive oil) to cover and refrigerate for at least 1 week. To make potato polenta, boil potatoes, peel them, and crush them thoroughly with a potato masher or food mill. Melt a large amount of butter in a copper polenta pot and stir in some corn polenta, stirring constantly to keep lumps from forming. Add water and milk and the crushed potatoes. Season with salt and cook over low heat, stirring constantly, until the polenta mixture begins to scorch on the bottom of the pot and pull away from the sides, about 30 minutes. Drain the herring fillets and heat them in the oven on low heat and serve with polenta. The herring fillets can also be served with slices of grilled polenta, thinly sliced rings of raw onion, and a drizzle of aromatic oil.

SMACAFAM
Baked Buckwheat Polenta with Sausage
Albergo Passo Brocon, Castello Tesino (Trento), Trentino-Alto Adige

Smacafam means "hunger beater," and this filling dish (and other similar porridgelike dishes) has satisfied appetites for centuries. Luganega is a pork sausage from the Trento area. It is sometimes labeled "lucanica."

SERVES 6

- 4 cups buckwheat flour
- 1 quart beef broth (not skimmed), warm
- Salt to taste
- 2 ounces lardo (cured fatback), diced
- 1 fresh luganega or other pork sausage (see note), sliced
- 3 tablespoons grated cheese
- Lard for greasing pan
- Unsalted butter for dotting top of polenta
- Freshly ground black pepper to taste

Preheat the oven to 300°F.

In a wooden bowl, beat the buckwheat flour with the broth and a little salt until thoroughly combined and beginning to bubble as if it were boiling. This will take quite a while. In a saucepan, melt the lardo, then brown most of the sausage in it, reserving a little. Beat the browned sausage into the buckwheat mixture and again beat for a long time. Beat in the grated cheese.

Grease a copper baking pan with the lard and pour in the mixture. The pan should be large enough that the buckwheat mixture is no more than 1¼ inches deep. Top with the reserved sausage and dot with butter, then bake in the preheated oven for at least 1 hour. Season with black pepper and serve warm.

Polpette di Verza
Carciofi Ripieni al Sugo
Verdure Ripiene
Melanzane al Cioccolato
Agnello a Scottadito
Spigola al Forno
Frittedda

SECONDI PIATTI

Ciaudella
Cinghiale al Civet
Bistecca di Chianina
Bombas cun Bagna
Fricassea di Agnello
Porcetto Arrosto
Cipolle Rosse Ripiene
Tonno a Cipollata
Coniglio all'Ischitana
& Many More

VEGETARIAN & VEGETABLE DISHES

FRITTEDDA 🌳
Spring Vegetable Stew
Trattoria Da Salvatore, Petralia Soprana
(Palermo), Sicilia

*f*rittedda is a great dish to have in your repertoire. It can serve as a main course, but also as a side dish, a soup, or even a topping for pasta. Salvatore Ruvutuso, owner of Trattoria Da Salvatore, notes that this spring dish frequently features *rubbunedda*, which is the dialect term for the smallest and most tender fava pods. Since the lettuce is cooked, choose a type with some substance, such as Romaine.

SERVES 4

Juice of ½ lemon
4 *artichokes*
1 *clove garlic, minced*
1 *medium yellow onion, minced*
Extra-virgin olive oil for sautéing
½ *head lettuce (see note), cut into ribbons*
Leaves of 1 sprig wild fennel, chopped
4½ *pounds very fresh young fava beans, shelled*
2 *pounds fresh peas, shelled*
Salt and freshly ground black pepper to taste

Add the lemon juice to a bowl of cold water. Trim the artichokes, removing any hard outer leaves and sharp tips and removing and discarding the chokes. Cut into wedges and drop the wedges into the lemon water.

Sauté the garlic and onion in olive oil, then add the lettuce, fennel, artichokes (drained), fava beans, and peas. Cook over medium heat for 5 minutes, then continue cooking until tender, adding small amounts of water to keep the pan moist. Season with salt and pepper and allow to rest before serving.

PALLOTTE CAC' E OVE 🍳
Vegetarian "Meatballs"
Hostaria del Pavone, Vasto (Chieti), Abruzzo

*T*he pairing of eggs and cheese is widely used in the Abruzzo region. If possible, let the mixture rest overnight before pan-frying. You can serve these plain or with a simple tomato and basil sauce.

SERVES 6

14 *ounces stale bread*
1 *cup whole milk*
2 *cups grated Parmigiano Reggiano*
2 *cups grated aged sheep's cheese*
2 *cloves garlic, minced*
Leaves of 1 sprig parsley, minced
Freshly ground black pepper (optional)
4 to 6 large eggs
Extra-virgin olive oil for frying

Soak the bread in the milk, then squeeze dry and crumble it into a bowl. Add the cheese, the garlic, and the parsley and season with black pepper if using (no need for salt). Lightly beat 4 eggs, add, and mix. The mixture should clump together when you squeeze a bit in your hand. If it is too dry, add another egg, and then another, if necessary. Set the mixture aside to rest for a few hours or overnight.

Form the mixture into small ovals about the size of an egg. Flatten them slightly, then pan-fry in olive oil for about 10 minutes. Serve warm.

POLPETTE DI VERZA
Stuffed Cabbage
Osteria della Villetta, Palazzolo sull'Oglio
(Brescia), Lombardia

The stuffing for these cabbage packets includes a little salami, which adds punch to a dish that can sometimes be bland.

SERVES 4

1   small head Savoy cabbage
Salt to taste
Sliced white bread for stuffing
Whole milk for soaking
2   ounces soft salami
Leaves of 1 sprig parsley, minced
Freshly ground black pepper to taste
Extra-virgin olive oil for drizzling
     and frying
Unbleached all-purpose flour for dredging
¼   yellow onion, minced
1   clove garlic, minced
½   cup canned peeled tomatoes

Remove the outer leaves of the cabbage and cook in boiling salted water for 5 minutes, then drain well in a colander. Cut the remaining cabbage into ribbons, and then chop the ribbons. Set the chopped cabbage aside. Soak the bread in milk until crumbly, then squeeze dry and crumble into a bowl. Remove the casing from the salami and crumble that into the bowl as well. Stir in parsley, season with salt and pepper, and drizzle in a little extra-virgin olive oil to moisten. Form the mixture into round balls and press lightly to flatten them a little bit. Wrap each ball of filling in a cooked cabbage leaf. Dredge the stuffed leaves in flour and pan-fry in hot oil. As they cook, the leaves should firm up around the filling.

In a separate skillet, cook the onion, garlic, tomatoes, and reserved chopped cabbage until slightly thickened and serve on the side with the stuffed cabbage.

VERDURE RIPIENE ❦
Stuffed Vegetables
Trattoria Nuovo Piccolo Mondo, San Remo
(Imperia), Liguria

Liguria loves its vegetables, especially in summer, when all along the coast stuffed vegetables and all kinds of salads are on the menu. Everyone's stuffing is a little different. Though most are vegetarian, some incorporate mortadella, leftover boiled meat, flaked tuna, or veal.

SERVES 4

¼   cup extra-virgin olive oil plus more for
     oiling baking dish
2   pounds young vegetables such as
     zucchini, onions, bell peppers,
     and eggplant
4   ounces snow peas or green beans,
     trimmed and blanched
3   medium potatoes, boiled, peeled,
     and crushed
3   large eggs, lightly beaten
½   cup grated Parmigiano Reggiano
Leaves of 1 sprig marjoram, minced
Salt to taste
¼   cup breadcrumbs

Preheat the oven to 400°F. Lightly oil a baking dish and set aside. Blanch the young vegetables, except for peppers and eggplant, for 5 minutes, leaving them whole. If using bell peppers, cut in half the long way, remove and discard seeds, salt the interiors, and set aside to drain. If using eggplant, cut in half the long way, scoop out the pulp while leaving the shell whole, salt lightly on the cut sides, and set aside to drain.

Drain any blanched vegetables. Scoop out the flesh of any zucchini and reserve it. Scoop out the centers of the onions and reserve, keeping the large external layers for stuffing. The goal is to prepare the vegetables to be used as containers.

Mince the blanched snow peas with any reserved zucchini and onion pulp. In a bowl, combine the minced snow pea mixture, crushed potatoes, eggs, Parmigiano, marjoram,

3 tablespoons olive oil, and a pinch of salt. With a wooden spatula, mix the filling until well combined, then use it to fill the prepared vegetables. Place them in the prepared dish. They should be close together. Sprinkle on the breadcrumbs and drizzle on the remaining 1 tablespoon olive oil. Bake in the preheated oven for 30 minutes.

IMPASTICCIATA
Baked Endive with Cheese
Hostaria de Dadà, Spello (Perugia), Umbria

You can replace the mozzarella in this recipe with young (not aged) caciotta of about the same weight, or use half of one type of cheese and half of the other. At the restaurant these are sometimes served in Parmigiano Reggiano baskets.

SERVES 4
2   heads curly endive
1   (6-ounce) mozzarella, diced
½   cup grated Parmigiano Reggiano
Salt to taste
¼   cup plus 2 tablespoons extra-virgin
    olive oil
Freshly ground black pepper to taste

Preheat oven to 400°F. Mince the endive as finely as you can by hand (discard any hard cores). In a bowl, combine the endive and the mozzarella. Stir in ¼ cup plus 2 tablespoons of the Parmigiano. Season with salt. Stir in ¼ cup of the olive oil. Divide the mixture among 4 single-serving earthenware casserole dishes and bake in the preheated oven for 15 minutes.

Unmold the baked endive cakes and place on individual serving plates. Drizzle with the remaining 2 tablespoons olive oil and sprinkle on the remaining 2 tablespoons Parmigiano. Season with pepper and serve.

ZUCCHINE RIPIENE E POLPETTE
Stuffed Zucchini with Small Meatballs
Trattoria Serghei, Bologna, Emilia-Romagna

The secret to great meatballs is great meat. Meatballs can be cooked any number of ways—stewed or fried. This dish calls for some crusty bread for dipping in the sauce.

SERVES 6
1   pound rump steak
5   egg yolks
1   tablespoon extra-virgin olive oil
8   tablespoons (1 stick) unsalted butter
1½   cups grated Grana Padano cheese
⅓   cup breadcrumbs
Salt and freshly ground black pepper to taste
3½   pounds (9 to 10) medium zucchini
1   carrot, cut into small dice
1   rib celery, cut into small dice
1   cup whole milk
2   cups tomato puree

To make the meat mixture, grind the meat and combine thoroughly with the egg yolks, 1 tablespoon olive oil, 1 tablespoon butter, the Grana Padano, and the breadcrumbs. Season with salt and pepper. Use a paring knife or corer to remove the pulp from the zucchini while leaving them intact. Stuff with some of the meat mixture.

Melt the remaining 7 tablespoons butter in a large sauté pan with high sides. Sauté the carrot and celery until soft. Season with salt and pepper, then add the stuffed zucchini and cook for 10 minutes, turning occasionally. Add the milk, cover, and cook over low heat for 30 minutes. Add the tomato puree to the pan. Form the remaining meat mixture into small balls and add them to the pan. Cook, turning occasionally until the sauce has thickened and the meat is cooked, about 1 additional hour.

TEGAMINO DI ASPARAGI E UOVA ●
Asparagus and Eggs
Trattoria La Tana del Grillo, San Pietro in Casale (Bologna), Emilia-Romagna

Another local variation on this dish uses asparagus from Altedo (the site of an annual asparagus fair) cooked for 15 minutes in lightly salted water (in an asparagus pot with a tight-fitting lid), then patted dry and topped with fried eggs. In Cremona, cooked asparagus is topped with a sprinkling of grated Parmigiano Reggiano and then topped with fried or scrambled eggs cooked in butter.

SERVES 4
- 1 bunch (12 to 14 ounces) asparagus
- Extra-virgin olive oil for sautéing
- ½ medium yellow onion, minced
- Salt to taste
- 3 large eggs
- 1 cup grated Parmigiano Reggiano

Trim the asparagus and peel the stalks. Mince the asparagus and then sauté in an earthenware pot in oil with the onion for 15 minutes. Season with salt. Break the eggs directly on top of the asparagus, quickly add the grated cheese, and cook over low heat while beating. Serve in the earthenware pot.

CARCIOFI RIPIENI AL SUGO 🍈
Stuffed Artichokes in Tomato Sauce
Elisabetta Antelmi, Agropoli (Salerno), Campania

Trim the stalks and hard leaves and remove the chokes from young, firm artichokes, at least 1 per person, more if they are small, dropping them into acidulated water as you do to keep them from turning brown. In a bowl, combine grated Parmigiano

Reggiano, minced garlic, and minced parsley. Beat in enough eggs to make a firm filling. Drain the trimmed artichokes, gently open them up, fill them with the egg mixture, and fry stem side up in a generous amount of hot oil. In a pot large enough to contain the artichokes, sauté a clove of minced garlic in extra-virgin olive oil, then add chopped canned tomatoes (you can simply crush them with your hands) and their juices. Season with a pinch of salt, then arrange the artichokes in the sauce and cook for 30 minutes.

PARMIGIANA DI CARDI
Cardoon Parmigiana
Trattoria del Borgo, Perugia, Umbria

This cardoon casserole is a traditional rustic dish from the Umbria countryside. Clean about 1 pound cardoons per person, peeling off any fibrous strings and dropping them into acidulated water as you do. Boil the cardoons in salted water, then cool them and cut them into 1½- to 2-inch pieces. Dredge them in flour and then in beaten eggs and fry in hot oil, working in batches if necessary. Drain briefly on paper towels.

Preheat the oven to 350°F. In a buttered baking dish, arrange a layer of fried cardoons, cover with a layer of tomato sauce with ground pork or veal (or a combination of the two), and sprinkle on a generous amount of grated Parmigiano Reggiano. Dot with butter and make another layer of cardoons, sauce, and cheese. Continue until you have used up the cardoons, ending with a layer of cheese on top. Bake in the preheated oven for 20 minutes and serve piping hot.

A similar dish calls for alternating layers of breaded and fried cardoons, tomato sauce, browned ground veal, and chicken livers cooked in butter. Sprinkle on some grated cheese and bake as described above.

PARMIGIANA DI MELANZANE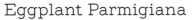
Eggplant Parmigiana
Osteria Nunzia, Benevento, Campania

In the Napoli area, the eggplant for parmigiana is dredged only in flour before frying, whereas in other parts of Campania (including at Osteria Nunzia in Benevento) the eggplant is dredged in flour and egg. This dish is so rich and satisfying that it serves as a one-dish meal, with no need for a pasta or soup course.

In Alberobello in the province of Bari in the Puglia region, Giuseppina Palmisano makes a Puglia-style parmigiana by wrapping slices of eggplant around a filling of beaten eggs, grated Parmigiano Reggiano, grated stale bread, minced garlic, and minced parsley. She arranges these rolls in a baking pan and tops them with tomato sauce and a generous sprinkling of grated Parmigiano, then bakes them. They may be served either cold or at room temperature. Rosaria Salvatore of Tropea in Calabria's Vibo Valentia province alternates her layers of eggplant with sliced hard-boiled eggs and fennel sausage; she also uses grated aged sheep's cheese in place of the Parmigiano Reggiano and young caciocavallo cheese in place of the mozzarella.

SERVES 6

3½ pounds (2 to 3 medium) eggplant
Salt to taste
1   medium yellow onion, minced
Extra-virgin olive oil for sautéing
    and frying
3½ pounds plum tomatoes, diced

Unbleached all-purpose flour for dredging
6   large eggs, lightly beaten
Leaves of 1 sprig basil
1½ pounds fior di latte mozzarella, cut into
    small dice
½   cup grated Parmigiano Reggiano

Cut the eggplant the long way into slices a little less than ¼ inch thick. Salt and place in a colander to drain.

In a small pot, sauté the onion in some olive oil until soft. Add the tomatoes and cook for 30 minutes, then process through a food mill to make a tomato sauce. Set aside.

Rinse and dry the eggplant. Line a baking sheet with paper towels. In a pot with high sides, bring a generous amount of oil to frying temperature. Dredge the eggplant slices first in flour, then in beaten egg (reserve any left-over beaten egg), then fry in the hot oil until golden. Work in batches if necessary to keep from crowding the pan. Remove with a slotted spatula or skimmer and drain briefly on the prepared pan.

Preheat the oven to 350°F.

Cover the bottom of a baking pan with some of the tomato sauce and sprinkle on a few of the basil leaves. Arrange some of the eggplant in a layer, overlapping slightly. Make a layer of mozzarella. Sprinkle with Parmigiano. Repeat layers in the same order until you have used up all of the eggplant and mozzarella. Mix together any remaining beaten egg and the remaining tomato sauce and pour it over the top. Sprinkle on the remaining Parmigiano and basil leaves. Bake in the preheated oven until the cheese has melted and the casserole is hot, about 30 minutes. Allow to cool either to room temperature or completely before serving.

MELANZANE AL CIOCCOLATO ❦
Chocolate Eggplant
Ristorante Da Gemma, Amalfi (Salerno), Campania

Chocolate eggplant might sound like some newfangled invention, but it is actually a traditional dish from the Amalfi Coast that is prepared for the Feast of the Assumption. Historians consider it likely that Spain, which controlled the Kingdom of Napoli for many years, brought both Arab eggplant and Aztec cocoa to the area. *Liquore concerto* is so named because it is a "concert" of fifteen different herbs all working together to make beautiful music.

SERVES 4

4 *purple eggplant*
Extra-virgin olive oil for frying
2 *large eggs*
Unbleached all-purpose flour for batter
8 *cups whole milk*
1 *vanilla bean, split lengthwise*
1 *cinnamon stick*
1½ *cups sugar*
11 *ounces dark chocolate*
2½ *cups unsweetened cocoa powder*
½ *cup herb liqueur, such as liquore concerto (see note)*
1 *tablespoon pine nuts, toasted*
1 *tablespoon minced candied orange peel*

Cut the eggplant the long way into slices about ½ inch thick. Line a baking sheet with paper towels and bring a generous amount of oil to the correct temperature for frying. Fry the eggplant slices, working in batches if necessary, then remove with a skimmer (reserve frying oil) and drain briefly on the prepared pan. In a bowl beat the 2 eggs. Add enough flour to make a thin batter. Dredge the fried eggplant slices in the batter and fry them a second time.

In a saucepan, combine the milk, vanilla bean, and cinnamon stick. Scald the milk and remove the cinnamon stick and vanilla bean. Whisk in the sugar. Place the saucepan with the milk over a pot of boiling water to create a double boiler and whisk in the chocolate and cocoa powder. When the chocolate has melted completely and the sugar has dissolved completely, stir in the liqueur.

Arrange the eggplant on a serving platter, pour the warm chocolate sauce over it, and garnish with pine nuts and candied orange peel.

MELANZANE DELLA MADONNA 🍆
Madonna Eggplant
Ristorante Parco Pingitore, Serrastretta (Catanzaro), Calabria

The best eggplant to use for this dish are the long, dark purple varieties. This is prepared in Serrastretta for the Feast of Our Lady of Sorrows, the Madonna Addolorata in Italian, on September 15, hence the name. In Siderno Superiore in the province of Reggio Calabria, the Fragomeni family's osteria Zio Salvatore stuffs eggplant with a similar filling softened with a little of the vegetable cooking water, but then fries the eggplant and skips baking it in tomato sauce. The Locandiera in Bernalda in the province of Matera in Basilicata includes ground veal in the stuffing.

SERVES 6

4½ *pounds (3 to 5) long eggplant*
Salt to taste
7 *ounces (about 1½ to 2 cups cubed) stale bread*
1 *pound ripe tomatoes*
6 *large eggs, lightly beaten*
Leaves of 1 sprig parsley, minced
Leaves of 1 sprig basil
2½ *cups grated aged sheep's cheese*
Breadcrumbs to firm up filling
Extra-virgin olive oil for frying

Cut the eggplant in half or in quarters the long way, depending on their size. Boil in lightly salted water for 20 minutes. Soak the stale bread in water to cover until soft. Pass the tomatoes through a food mill and set aside.

Drain the eggplant, squeeze dry, and use a spoon to scoop out the flesh. Place the eggplant shells on a clean dish towel to dry. In a bowl, crush the eggplant flesh with a fork. Squeeze dry the stale bread and crumble it into the bowl with the eggplant pulp. Add the eggs and parsley. Mince about half of the basil and add. Add about 2¼ cups of the sheep's cheese. Add enough breadcrumbs to make a mixture that is firm but not too dry. Sprinkle the insides of the eggplant shells with the remaining grated cheese and then stuff with the mixture.

Preheat the oven to 325°F to 350°F. Fill a pot with high sides with a generous amount of oil for frying and bring to high temperature. Line a baking sheet with paper towels and set aside. Fry the stuffed eggplant in the oil until golden, working in batches if necessary. Drain briefly on the prepared pan, then spread half of the tomato puree in the bottom of a baking dish. Arrange the eggplant on top of the puree and drizzle on the remaining puree. Scatter on the remaining basil leaves, tearing them into smaller pieces if they are large. Bake in the preheated oven for 15 minutes.

SERVES 6

- 6 *Romanesco artichokes*
- 1 *large egg, lightly beaten*
- 11 *ounces ground pork, preferably the Cinta Senese or Pesante Pisano breed*
- 1 *cup grated aged sheep's cheese*
- *Leaves of 1 sprig parsley, minced*
- 6 *cloves garlic*
- *Salt and freshly ground black pepper to taste*
- ½ *cup extra-virgin olive oil*
- 7 *ounces thinly sliced pancetta*

Trim the artichokes of hard outer leaves and cut off the stems and any hard tips of the remaining leaves and the choke, if any. Gently open the artichokes, then turn them upside down on the work surface and press down (again, gently) to open them up as much as possible.

For the stuffing, combine the egg and pork, the grated cheese, and the parsley. Mince 3 cloves garlic and add to the mixture. Season with salt and pepper. Stuff the artichokes with the pork mixture. Place the oil in a pot with high sides and add the artichokes and the three remaining cloves garlic. Arrange the slices of pancetta on top, cover the pot, and cook over medium heat for 1 hour. Serve hot and drizzle any juices from the bottom of the pan over the artichokes.

MAMME RIPIENE
Artichokes Stuffed with Ground Meat and Pancetta
La Taverna dell'Ozio, Corazzano di San Miniato (Pisa), Toscana

This recipe calls for Romanesco artichokes, which are large and round. When you cover the pot, it's a good idea to wrap the lid in a damp dish towel. This keeps all the steam the artichokes release inside and allows the artichokes to cook more evenly.

MELANZANE ABBOTTONATE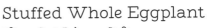
Stuffed Whole Eggplant
Filippa Gatì, Palermo, Sicilia

Select 1 small round eggplant per person and make slices in them the long way, without peeling them. Salt generously and let the eggplants sit for a couple of hours so that their bitter liquid drains. Meanwhile, thinly slice a yellow onion and cook in a pot in some extra-virgin olive oil. Add a little tomato sauce—about 2 tablespoons per eggplant—and cook for a few minutes more, then stir in minced parsley and basil leaves. Rinse the eggplant under running water, pat dry, and stuff slices of garlic and mint into the cuts. Place in a lightly oiled pan that can hold the eggplant in a single layer and cook over low heat for 20 minutes. Pour the prepared tomato sauce over the eggplant (thin with a little water if it's not a pourable consistency), season with salt, cover, and cook over low heat for an additional 30 minutes. Serve hot.

MELANZANE ROSSE DI ROTONDA RIPIENE

Stuffed Rotonda Red Eggplant

Ristorante da Peppe, Rotonda (Potenza), Basîlicata

Red eggplant have grown in and around Rotonda since the late nineteenth century and are believed to come from Africa. They are small, round, and really more orange than red. Some have green streaks. The flesh of this eggplant does not discolor when cut, and it has an intense and fruity scent and a slightly spicy flavor with a bitter finish. It can be preserved in oil or vinegar and is often stewed. The leaves are edible. Rotonda red eggplant are part of the Slow Food Ark of Taste (as are white poverello beans).

SERVES 10

¾ cup fresh white poverello beans or dried white poverello beans (or similar white beans, such as cannellini), soaked overnight
2 cups sliced fresh porcini mushrooms
Extra-virgin olive oil for sautéing
1 clove garlic
20 medium Rotonda red eggplant
Salt to taste
2½ cups fresh breadcrumbs
¾ cup grated Parmigiano Reggiano
1 large egg, lightly beaten
Leaves of 1 sprig parsley, minced
Freshly ground black pepper to taste

If using dried beans, drain them. Cook the beans in boiling water until soft, about 1 hour. Drain and set aside.

Sauté the porcini in a skillet in some olive oil with the garlic until soft. Discard the garlic.

Cut off the cap of each eggplant and set aside. Use a paring knife to hollow out the eggplant, reserving the pulp. Cook the eggplant shells in salted boiling water for 10 minutes and remove with a slotted spoon or skimmer to drain. Boil the eggplant pulp for 5 minutes and drain. When the pulp is cool enough to handle, squeeze dry.

Preheat the oven to 350°F. In a bowl, crush the eggplant pulp and combine with the porcini, beans, breadcrumbs, Parmigiano, and the egg. Stir to combine. Stir in the parsley and season with pepper, then stuff the eggplant shells with the mixture. Arrange in a baking pan and place the reserved caps on top. Bake in the preheated oven for 7 minutes.

INVOLTINI DI MELANZANE ALLA MENTA

Eggplant Rolls with Mint

Ristorante Peppe Zullo, Orsara di Puglia (Foggîa), Puglia

This is just one of a rich trove of eggplant recipes from southern Italy. Do not even dream of purchasing pre-shredded mozzarella: use your fingers to crumble fresh mozzarella into crumbs. You'll need about 4 ounces. Also, buy the prosciutto in one thick slice rather than the usual thin ones.

SERVES 4

1 eggplant
4 ounces prosciutto crudo, cut into julienne
¾ cup shredded mozzarella
Leaves of 1 sprig mint, minced
Salt to taste
Extra-virgin olive oil for drizzling and oiling pan
½ cup dry white wine

Preheat the oven to 400°F. Very thinly slice the eggplant, using a slicer or mandolin if you have one.

For the filling, combine the prosciutto, mozzarella, and mint. Season with salt and moisten with a drizzle of olive oil. Arrange some of the filling on an eggplant slice, then roll it up and secure it with a toothpick. Repeat with the remaining filling and eggplant slices. Lightly oil a baking pan and arrange the eggplant rolls in it. Pour the wine into the pan and bake in the preheated oven for 10 minutes.

Preheat the oven to 350°F. Drain the vegetables and puree all but the hollowed-out onion shells through a food mill. In a bowl, combine the resulting puree, the mortadella, the parsley, about half of the grated Parmigiano, the eggs, the marjoram, salt, pepper, and nutmeg. Stir to combine.

Stuff the onion shells with the mixture and place them in a baking pan. Sprinkle the remaining Parmigiano on top, then bake in the preheated oven for 30 minutes.

CIPOLLE RIPIENE ALLA LIGURE 🌿
Ligurian Stuffed Onions
Trattoria Armonia, Bajardo (Imperia), Liguria

All kinds of vegetables are stuffed in Liguria: in addition to onions, try stuffing bell peppers, zucchini, zucchini blossoms, or eggplants.

SERVES 4

- 8 white onions
- 2 pounds starchy potatoes, peeled and diced
- 12 ounces green beans, trimmed and chopped
- 2 cups diced zucchini
- ¾ cup diced mortadella
- Leaves of 1 sprig parsley, minced
- 1½ cups grated Parmigiano Reggiano
- 3 large eggs, lightly beaten
- Leaves of 1 sprig marjoram, minced
- Salt and freshly ground black pepper to taste
- Freshly grated nutmeg to taste

Peel the onions, boil them in salted water until cooked al dente, then remove with a slotted spoon. Halve the onions and set aside to cool. When the onions are cool enough to handle, scoop out the centers and boil them with the potatoes, beans, and zucchini until very tender.

SECRA E SURIATA 🌶
Spicy Bean and Chard Cake
Luisa Sanfile, Monterosso Calabro (Vîbo Valentia), Calabria

To make enough to serve 4, the night before you plan to serve the beans, soak 1¼ cups of any type of beans in cold water. In the morning, drain them and boil them in a pot with a generous amount of water, a pinch of salt, 1 chili pepper, and 1 yellow onion. Separate the green leaves from the stems of 2 pounds (2 to 3 bunches) chard. Cut the stems into ¾-inch pieces and tear the leaves by hand. Blanch the stems in salted water for 5 minutes, then add the greens and cook until tender. Drain and squeeze dry. Tear a generous hunk of stale bread into bite-size pieces and toast them in a skillet with a generous amount of olive oil and 1 whole clove garlic. Add the chard and sauté for 5 minutes, then add the beans and cook over medium heat for an additional 15 minutes. Sprinkle on a generous amount of grated aged sheep's cheese and adjust salt to taste. Use a wooden spoon to press the mixture into a cake and cook until browned underneath, then use a lid to flip the cake and brown the other side. Allow to cool before serving.

PASTICCIO DI PATATE E PORCINI ◖

Potato and Porcini Casserole

Trattoria Castello, Castello di Serle (Brescia), Lombardia

The number of layers in this tasty casserole will depend on the size of the pan you use, but you'll want a minimum of two layers of potatoes with a layer of mushrooms in between. The potatoes should be cooked in advance, but don't overdo it—they'll continue cooking in the oven.

SERVES 6

5   medium white potatoes
Extra-virgin olive oil for oiling pan and
    drizzling
2 to 3 cloves garlic, minced
1   bunch chives, snipped
Leaves of 1 sprig parsley, minced
Leaves of 1 sprig oregano, minced, or 1 pinch
    dried oregano
Salt and freshly ground black pepper to taste
1½ pounds porcini mushrooms, sliced about
    ¼ inch thick

Boil the potatoes until just tender and drain. As soon as they are cool enough to handle, peel them and cut into slices about ¼ inch thick.

Preheat the oven to 350°F. Lightly oil a baking pan and arrange a layer of potato slices in it. Sprinkle on some of the garlic, chives, parsley, and oregano and drizzle with extra-virgin olive oil. Season with salt and pepper. Top with a layer of sliced mushrooms. Again, sprinkle on garlic, chives, parsley, and oregano and drizzle with oil, then season with salt and pepper. Continue layering the potatoes and mushrooms, ending with a layer of potatoes on top. Drizzle with oil and season with salt and pepper. Cover the pan with aluminum foil and bake in the preheated oven until the mushrooms are cooked and potatoes are completely tender, about 20 minutes.

PATATE E UOVA IN SALSA VERDE ❦

Potatoes and Eggs in Green Sauce

Pier Antonio Cucchietti, Stroppo (Cuneo), Piemonte

To make this simple entrée vegetarian, use vegetable broth. To serve 4 people, sauté a thinly sliced yellow onion in equal parts oil and butter (about 2 tablespoons each). Add roughly chopped chard leaves (at least half of a standard bunch) and a minced garlic clove and sauté for a few minutes to wilt the greens. Add about ½ cup broth, cover, and cook over medium-low heat until the greens have shrunk down considerably. This should take only a few minutes. Add 4 hard-boiled eggs cut in half the long way and 8 small boiled and peeled potatoes to the skillet. Season with salt and add more broth if the pan looks dry. Cook for a few more minutes, then sprinkle with a generous amount of flat-leaf parsley minced using a mezzaluna (which will be more flavorful than if it were minced with a knife) and stir very carefully so as not to break the eggs and potatoes. Season with pepper, simmer for a few more minutes, then serve hot.

CIPOLLE ROSSE RIPIENE

Stuffed Red Onions

Rosaria Salvatore, Tropea (Vibo Valentia), Calabria

To serve 4 people, cut a couple of eggplant into small dice, toss with salt, and let drain for a couple of hours. Sauté a very thinly sliced spring onion in olive oil, then add about 2 cups chopped, seeded ripe plum tomatoes and the eggplant and sauté for 5 minutes. Season with salt, pepper, and minced fresh oregano. Trim 8 Tropea red onions per person and boil them in salted water for 5 minutes. Hollow them out and stuff them with the eggplant mixture. Arrange in an oiled baking pan and bake at 400°F for 45 minutes.

PORRI GRATINATI E UOVA AL TEGAMINO ●
Baked Leeks and Eggs
Osteria Burligo, Burligo di Palazzago
(Bergamo), Lombardia

Use the white portion of the leeks in this recipe, but don't discard the green parts—they add a subtle flavor to soups and can be minced and used in savory pies of all kinds. Always rinse leeks very thoroughly—they tend to contain a lot of grit. This dish is usually served with polenta.

SERVES 4
10 small leeks, white only
2 to 3 tablespoons heavy cream or whipping cream
1 cup grated Grana Padano cheese
1 tablespoon unsalted butter
8 large eggs
Salt to taste

Preheat the oven to 350°F. Boil the leeks in lightly salted water until tender. Drain and cut each leek into 2 pieces. Arrange the leeks in 4 individual baking dishes (2 to 3 leeks per portion). Pour the cream over them, then sprinkle on the grated cheese. Bake in the preheated oven until nicely browned on top, about 10 minutes.

While the leeks are baking, melt the butter in a nonstick skillet and fry the eggs, leaving the yolks very soft. Season the eggs with salt and place 2 fried eggs in each individual baking dish on top of the leeks. Serve very hot.

PREVE ❗
Cabbage Stuffed with Rice
Trattoria La Baita, Gazzo di Borghetto d'Arroscia (Imperia), Liguria

Serve these stuffed cabbage packets in tomato sauce and garnish with toasted pine nuts.

SERVES 4 TO 6
1 large head white cabbage
Salt to taste
2 cups whole milk
1 cup short-grain rice for soup
½ cup extra-virgin olive oil, plus more for oiling pan
4 large eggs
2 cups grated Parmigiano Reggiano
Vegetable broth for simmering

Core the cabbage but leave whole. Bring a pot of salted water to a boil and boil the cabbage until tender, about 5 minutes. Rinse with cold water and allow to dry thoroughly. Remove and reserve about 10 of the largest cabbage leaves. Mince the rest.

Combine the milk, rice, and ½ cup oil in a saucepan and bring to a boil. Season with salt, turn down to a simmer, and cook until the rice is tender and has absorbed all of the liquid. Remove from the heat and add the minced cabbage.

Preheat the oven to 400°F. In a bowl, beat the eggs with the Parmigiano, then add the rice and cabbage mixture. Lightly oil an ovenproof skillet. Stuff the whole leaves with the rice mixture and arrange them in the skillet in a single layer. Add enough vegetable broth to come halfway up the sides of the cabbage packets. Place over medium heat until the broth comes to a simmer, then transfer to the preheated oven and bake until all of the broth has been absorbed and the pan is dry. Serve hot.

❧{ FISH & SEAFOOD DISHES }❧

ACCIUGHE RIPIENE 🐚
Stuffed Fresh Anchovies
Trattoria Barisone, Genova, Liguria

Anchovies have a long history as part of Liguria's cuisine. Traveling fishmongers used to boast about their goods, freshly plucked from the nearby waters by shouting, *Gente che belle ancioe! Ancioe che pan polastri! Vendo l'argento do ma!* ("People, look at these beautiful anchovies! So plump they look like chickens! I'm selling the silver of the sea!") The anchovies in this recipe are boned, but their tails are left intact and they should remain in one piece.

SERVES 4
- Interior (crumb) of 2 rolls
- 1 cup milk
- 1¾ pounds large fresh anchovies
- 1 head lettuce
- Leaves of 1 sprig parsley
- Leaves of 1 sprig marjoram
- 2 cloves garlic, minced
- 3 large eggs
- Grated Parmigiano Reggiano to taste
- Salt to taste
- Extra-virgin olive oil for frying
- ¼ cup dry breadcrumbs

Soak the crumb of the rolls in the milk until soft. Clean, gut, and bone the anchovies, leaving them attached at the tail. Rinse in cold water, then arrange them open on a slanted cutting board to drain.

Meanwhile, mince the lettuce and herbs together. In a bowl, combine the lettuce mixture with the garlic. Remove the crumb of the rolls from the milk and squeeze, then crumble into the bowl. Stir in 2 of the eggs and a little grated Parmigiano. Season with salt and mix to combine. The mixture should form a clump when you grasp some in your fist.

Beat the remaining egg in a shallow bowl. Fill a pot with high sides with several inches of oil for frying. Line a baking sheet with paper towels and set aside. Spread about 1 tablespoon of the filling on each anchovy. Without closing up the anchovies, very gently dredge them in the beaten egg. Sprinkle them with the breadcrumbs. Fry the anchovies on both sides until golden, working in batches if necessary to avoid crowding the pot. Remove with a skimmer to the prepared pan to drain briefly, then transfer to a warm platter and serve immediately.

SARDELLA ⬅
Preserved Whitebait
Trattoria Max, Cirò Marina (Crotone), Calabria

Traditionally, this was made with very young sardine whitebait. These days, we don't recommend eating young sardines, but the technique can work with other very small whitebait (though technically that would make *sardella* a misnomer). This mixture, also known as the caviar of the South, is excellent served with a tomato and red onion salad, or it can be used as a topping for pasta. Sardella isn't a paste exactly—you should be able to see the individual fish in it. You must use tiny whitebait no more than 3 hours after it is fished.

Place the whitebait in a colander, salt, and let drain for about 10 minutes. Rub wild fennel fronds between your fingers to break them up. Make alternating layers of the whitebait, red chili peppers broken into big pieces, and crushed wild fennel in a bowl. Cover with a linen cloth and set aside for 2 days at room temperature. Toss the whitebait with red pepper and fennel using two forks. Fill an earthenware container called a *terzaluro* or a wooden container to the top and seal hermetically (a terzaluro will have its own special lid, known as a *timpagno*). Place a river rock on top to keep firmly closed. Store in a cool, dark place (the traditional method used by sailors) or refrigerate. Drizzle with a little extra-virgin olive oil before serving.

ALICI FARCITE DI SCAMORZA ❧
Fresh Anchovies Stuffed with Scamorza Cheese
Trattoria 'A Paranza, Atrani (Salerno), Campania

Stuffed fried anchovies are also eaten along the coastline in Calabria. At the Locanda di Mare in Amantea (province of Cosenza) about 20 fresh anchovies are stuffed with a mixture of stale bread that has been soaked, squeezed dry, and crumbled, 1 tablespoon dry breadcrumbs, 1 tablespoon grated hard cheese, minced flat-leaf parsley, freshly ground black pepper, 2 eggs, and 5 or 6 finely chopped walnuts. The anchovies are then fried for a couple of minutes (they are not coated in flour or breadcrumbs before frying). The anchovies in Sardegna are larger, and they are often filled with a piece of young local cheese and a rinsed salted anchovy fillet before they are dredged in flour, then beaten eggs, then breadcrumbs and, finally, fried until golden.

SERVES 4
- 1½ cups unbleached all-purpose flour or 00 flour
- 14 ounces fresh anchovies, scaled and filleted
- 7 ounces smoked Scamorza cheese
- 1 tablespoon chopped wild fennel fronds
- 2 large eggs
- Salt to taste
- 1 cup dry breadcrumbs
- Extra-virgin olive oil for frying

Arrange the flour in a shallow bowl. Dredge the anchovy fillets in the flour.

Cut the Scamorza into strips—you will need half as many strips as you have fillets. Arrange half of the fillets on a work surface and place 1 strip of Scamorza on each. Sprinkle the wild fennel over them. Top with the remaining fillets. Beat the eggs in a shallow bowl with a bit of salt. Arrange the breadcrumbs in another shallow bowl. Fill a pot with high sides with several inches of oil for frying and bring to the correct temperature. Dredge the stuffed pairs of fillets first in the eggs, then in the breadcrumbs, and fry in the oil until golden, working in batches if necessary to keep from crowding the pan. Serve hot.

TORTIERA DI SARDE ❧
Baked Sardine Cake
Carmen Fontana, Bari, Puglia

Preheat the oven to 350°F. Lightly oil a cake pan, sprinkle the inside lightly with salt, and set aside. In a bowl combine equal parts breadcrumbs and grated aged sheep's cheese with minced parsley, minced fresh mint, and minced fresh or dried oregano. Season with salt and pepper. Sprinkle on a thin layer of the breadcrumb mixture. Arrange sardine fillets (2½ pounds of sardines will serve about 6 people) in a single layer on top. Make alternating layers of the breadcrumb mixture and sardines, ending with the breadcrumb mixture. Drizzle on a generous amount of olive oil. Beat eggs (2 to 4, depending on the size of pan) with a little salt and pepper and spread the beaten eggs evenly over the surface. Bake in the preheated oven until cooked through, about 40 minutes (but cooking time will depend on the number of layers). Allow to cool to room temperature before serving.

BACCALÀ ALLA ROMANA
Roman-Style Baccalà with Pine Nuts
Osteria del Velodromo Vecchio, Roma, Lazio

Baccalà is very stiff and dry when purchased. Soak the salt cod in several changes of cold water over several days until it is pliable. Check carefully to be sure all bones have been removed and peel off any skin before proceeding.

SERVES 4

2 pounds baccalà, soaked in several changes of cold water
½ cup unbleached all-purpose flour
Extra-virgin olive oil for frying and sautéing
1 clove garlic, minced
2 medium yellow onions, thinly sliced
2 tablespoons black raisins
3 tablespoons pine nuts
½ anchovy fillet, rinsed, drained, and minced
½ cup dry white wine
About 8 cups fish fumet
Salt and freshly ground black pepper to taste
Leaves of 1 sprig parsley, minced

Cut the baccalà into fillets, dry thoroughly, dredge in the flour, and fry in a generous amount of hot oil, working in batches if necessary to keep from crowding the pan. When the pieces are browned and crisp on both sides, arrange them on a tray lined with paper towels to drain.

In a skillet large enough to hold the baccalà in a single layer, sauté the garlic in oil. When the garlic begins to brown, add the onions, then the raisins, pine nuts, and anchovy. When the onion begins to brown, add the wine and cook, stirring frequently, until it has evaporated. Add about 3 cups fish fumet and cook, covered, over medium heat until the liquid has almost completely reduced. Add another 3 cups fish fumet. As soon as the liquid begins to boil, transfer the fried baccalà to the pan. Cook, covered, until the liquid has reduced and created a silky sauce, turning the fish occasionally and adding more fumet as needed to keep the pan from drying out. Season with salt and pepper and sprinkle on minced parsley, then transfer to a warm serving platter.

SARAGHINE RIPIENE
Stuffed Sprats
Osteria La Canonica, Casteldimezzo di Pesaro (Pesaro and Urbino), Marche

Saraghine are sprats—plump, oily small fish found in the Adriatic (and elsewhere) that are related to the sardine and have the same silvery skin. Serve with a lightly dressed green salad.

SERVES 4

Extra-virgin olive oil for oiling pan
About 1 cup stale bread
3 salted anchovy fillets, rinsed, drained, and minced
1 cup grated Parmigiano Reggiano
Grated zest of 1 lemon
1 to 2 cloves garlic, minced
Leaves of 1 sprig parsley, minced
1 large egg, lightly beaten
Salt and freshly ground black pepper to taste
20 sprats, scaled, gutted, and boned but left whole

Preheat the oven to 350°F. Lightly oil a baking pan and set aside. Soak the bread in cold water until softened, then squeeze dry and crumble into a bowl. Add the minced anchovies, the grated Parmigiano, and the zest. Stir to combine, then stir in the garlic, parsley, and egg. Season with salt and pepper.

Stuff the sprats with this mixture and place in the prepared pan. Bake in the preheated oven just until opaque, 5 to 8 minutes, depending on the size of the fish. Do not overbake.

MERLUZZO AL VERDE 🍆
Baccalà with Vegetables
Trattoria del Belbo da Bardòn, San Marzano Oliveto
(Asti), Piemonte

In the Langhe area of Piemonte, this dish is made with spinach, but in Monferrato cooks are more likely to rely on chard.

SERVES 6

- 2 pounds baccalà, soaked under running water for 2 days in several changes of water
- Unbleached all-purpose flour or 00 flour for dredging
- Extra-virgin olive oil for frying and sautéing
- 1 cup spinach or chard leaves
- ½ rib white celery, diced
- 1 leek, diced
- 1 bell pepper, diced
- Beef or vegetable broth for moistening
- ¼ cup minced parsley
- 2 cloves garlic, minced
- 4 sage leaves, minced
- 3 tablespoons capers, rinsed and drained
- 4 ripe plum tomatoes, peeled, seeded, drained, and chopped
- Salt to taste

Divide each piece of baccalà into 3 pieces. Pat dry, dredge lightly in flour, and fry in a generous amount of hot olive oil until golden. Transfer to a serving platter and keep warm.

For the sauce, chop the spinach or chard and sauté with the celery, leek, and bell pepper in a few tablespoons of olive oil in a large skillet or saucepan for 15 minutes. When the vegetables are soft and very dry, add a small amount of broth, then mix in the parsley, garlic, sage, and capers. Stir to combine.

Cook the chopped tomatoes separately for 5 minutes, then add to the sauce. Finally, add the cooked baccalà to the skillet, taste and adjust salt, and cook for a few minutes over medium heat to combine the flavors.

BACCALÀ ALLA VICENTINA 🌿
Vicenza-Style Baccalà with Milk
Ostaria da Mariano, Mestre (Venezia), Veneto

The Ostaria da Mariano in Mestre, outside Venezia, serves this Venetian-style baccalà: Cut baccalà that has been soaked in several changes of water into chunks, season with salt and pepper, then place in an ovenproof saucepan in a single layer with milk to cover and a pinch of ground cinnamon, as well as thinly sliced onion. Bring the mixture to a boil, then cover and simmer until the milk has been absorbed completely. Sprinkle the baccalà with grated Parmigiano Reggiano, then turn and sprinkle with minced garlic and parsley. Place minced rinsed salted anchovy fillets on top, drizzle with extra-virgin olive oil, and bake at 275°F for 15 to 20 minutes, and then at 250°F for about 3½ hours. Serve hot with polenta.

Elvira Menegon in Orgiano in the province of Vicenza makes this local baccalà dish: To make enough to serve 4, soak about 1½ pounds baccalà, then slice it and open it up like a book. Sauté 5 thinly sliced yellow onions in extra-virgin olive oil along with 2 crushed garlic cloves, which should be discarded once they brown. Add minced parsley and 2 minced anchovy fillets. Spread a little less than half of this mixture on both sides of the baccalà, then sprinkle on a little all-purpose flour, ½ cup grated Parmigiano Reggiano, salt, and pepper. Close the fish back up and truss with kitchen twine, leaving about 1 inch between the loops of twine. Cut the trussed fish into even slices, dredge them in flour, and arrange them in an earthenware pot. Mix the remaining onion mixture with 2 cups milk and a drizzle of extra-virgin olive oil and cover the fish with the mixture. Cook over the lowest possible heat, moving the fish occasionally to be sure it doesn't stick, until the liquid has been absorbed and the fish is very tender, 4 to 5 hours. Taste and adjust salt once it is cooked. The flavor improves if it is made a day in advance and reheated. Serve hot with polenta.

MERLUZZO CON POLENTA 🌱
Salt Cod with Polenta
Trattoria della Luna, San Giorgio Canavese
(Torino), Piemonte

Baccalà and polenta are a classic combination throughout northern Italy. Be sure to add the polenta to the pot in a very thin stream—letting it fall from your fist as if you were playing with sand at the beach—to keep any lumps from forming. The polenta takes a long time to cook, so be sure to start far enough in advance. In Piemonte, polenta is traditionally cooked in a copper pot and then poured onto a wooden board.

SERVES 4
1   tablespoon rock salt
2   cups medium-grind polenta
⅔   cup coarse-grind polenta
Leaves of 2 bunches parsley
½   clove garlic
1   rib celery
½   small yellow onion
1   carrot
1   teaspoon capers in vinegar, rinsed and drained
4   salted anchovy fillets, rinsed and drained
1   tablespoon unsalted butter
½   cup dry white wine
Salt and freshly ground black pepper to taste
1½ pounds baccalà, soaked (under running water if possible) for 2 days in several changes of water
Unbleached all-purpose flour or oo flour for dredging
Extra-virgin olive oil for frying

Place 6 cups water in a copper pot, add 1 tablespoon rock salt, and place over high heat. Before the water comes to a full boil, add both types of polenta in a very thin stream, stirring constantly and energetically with a wooden spoon or spatula to keep any lumps from forming. When the polenta has all been added and

begins to boil, turn the heat to medium-low and cook, stirring constantly, until the polenta no longer has a raw flavor and is very thick, about 1 hour and 15 minutes.

For the baccalà, mince the parsley, garlic, celery, onion, carrot, capers, and anchovies together. Sauté the mixture in the butter in a skillet large enough to hold the baccalà in a single layer. Add the wine and cook until it has evaporated, then add enough hot water to fill the pan an inch or two (there should be enough liquid to cover or almost cover the baccalà once it is added, but without overflowing the pan). Season with salt and pepper.

Meanwhile, drain the baccalà and cut into 4-inch pieces. Dredge the pieces in all-purpose flour and fry in a generous amount of olive oil. Drain briefly on paper towels or butcher's paper, then transfer to the skillet with the parsley mixture and keep warm. When the polenta is ready, serve it steaming hot with the baccalà and the sauce.

TIELLA DI BACCALÀ CON PATATE 🌿
Baccalà and Potato Casserole
Ristorante Medioevo, Monte Sant'Angelo, Puglia

A tiella is a casserole from Puglia and also the name of the kind of baking dish used to cook it. Home ovens were relatively rare in Italy until modern times, so home cooks would prepare their casseroles at home, then carry them to a communal wood oven, or simply bake them on a grill, covered with a lid in an attempt to distribute the heat as evenly as possible. This recipe first cooks the tiella on the stovetop, then finishes it in the oven, so be sure to use a pan that can go from burner to oven.

SERVES 6

1¾ pounds baccalà in one piece (no tail), soaked for 2 days in several changes of water

Unbleached all-purpose flour for dredging

¼ cup plus 3 tablespoons extra-virgin olive oil

3 cloves garlic, minced

¾ cup flat-leaf parsley leaves, minced

Freshly ground black pepper to taste

2 pounds (about 6 medium) potatoes, peeled and sliced into rounds about ½ inch thick

1 cup grated aged sheep's cheese

5 medium yellow onions, sliced

1 pint cherry tomatoes, halved

2 to 3 tablespoons fresh breadcrumbs

Cut the baccalà into 6 strips of equal size. Dredge lightly in flour and brown in 2 tablespoons olive oil until lightly golden.

In a bowl, combine the garlic, about two thirds of the parsley, 3 tablespoons oil, and pepper. In another bowl, toss the potato slices with a little of the parsley mixture to coat. Cover the bottom of a (preferably rectangular) ovenproof pan with a layer of potatoes. Sprinkle on some grated cheese. Make a layer of onions and then a layer of baccalà. Drizzle on a little of the parsley mixture. Make another layer of potatoes and continue to make layers in this order until you have used up the ingredients, ending with the onions. Arrange the cherry tomato halves on top of the last layer of onions. Drizzle on 1 tablespoon olive oil. Pour ½ cup water gently down the side of the pan and cook over low heat, uncovered, until the potatoes are tender, about 30 minutes. If the pan appears to be getting excessively dry during cooking, add small amounts of water as it is cooking.

Preheat the oven to 475°F. Combine the breadcrumbs, the remaining parsley, and the remaining 1 tablespoon olive oil and scatter on top. Bake in the preheated oven until the crumb topping is crisp and golden, 10 to 20 minutes.

BRANDACUJUN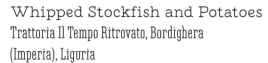

Whipped Stockfish and Potatoes
Trattoria Il Tempo Ritrovato, Bordighera (Imperia), Liguria

*B*randacujun is the Ligurian version of whipped stockfish, or brandade. It is also made in slightly different form in Piemonte, at the Osteria del Diavolo in Asti and elsewhere. In Piemonte, the fish is cooked for just 30 minutes, and the ratio of fish to potatoes is higher. The final mixture, which includes thyme and marjoram as well as parsley, is whipped until the potatoes have fallen apart completely, but the pieces of fish retain their texture. The dish is then shaped into oval balls and served at room temperature.

SERVES 10

2 pounds dried cod (stockfish), pounded and soaked in several changes of cold water until pliable

4½ pounds potatoes, peeled

1 clove garlic, minced

Extra-virgin olive oil for sautéing and drizzling

Salt and freshly ground black pepper to taste

¾ cup heavy cream or whipping cream

Juice of ½ lemon

Leaves of 1 sprig parsley, minced

Place the cod and the potatoes in a pot with water to cover and boil for 1 hour. Carefully remove any bones from the fish and remove and discard the skin, then mince the potatoes and cod together.

In a large skillet, sauté the garlic in a small amount of oil, then add the dried cod mixture. Stirring constantly over medium heat, season with salt and pepper and stir in the cream, lemon juice, and parsley. Drizzle in a little additional oil and cook until the ingredients are thoroughly combined, 3 to 4 minutes.

STOCCAFISSO ACCOMODATO 🍀
Stockfish with Tomatoes, Potatoes, and Olives
Trattoria Da Iolanda, Campomorone (Genova), Liguria

This stockfish dish has long been a classic choice for Fridays in Liguria, a seafaring region where both the local fish and preserved fish products such as salt cod and stockfish are the focus of many different imaginative preparations. Sometimes this recipe includes raisins along with the pine nuts, and if you prefer you can replace the dried tomatoes with fresh tomatoes.

SERVES 6
- 1¾ pounds dried cod (stockfish), soaked in several changes of water until pliable
- 1 clove garlic, minced
- 1 spring onion, minced
- Leaves of 1 sprig parsley, minced
- ⅓ cup pine nuts
- ½ cup extra-virgin olive oil
- ½ cup dry white wine
- 1 tablespoon diced sun-dried tomatoes
- 1 tablespoon tomato paste
- 1 pound potatoes, peeled and chopped
- 20 Taggiasca black olives, pitted
- Salt to taste

Boil the stockfish until soft, then bone and skin it and chop. In a saucepan, sauté the garlic, onion, parsley, and pine nuts in the oil. When the onions are lightly golden, add the wine, sun-dried tomatoes, and tomato paste. When the wine has evaporated, add the chunks of stockfish, the potatoes, and the olives (left whole). Season with salt and add warm water to cover. Cook over medium heat until the potatoes are soft, about 30 minutes, adding small amounts of water to the pan if necessary to keep it from getting too dry.

STOCCO ALLA MULINARA 🌿
Stockfish with Green Olives and Capers
Trattoria La Mamma, Cittanova (Reggio Calabria), Calabria

Stockfish (dried cod) benefits from being pounded before it is soaked. It grows pliable more quickly as it absorbs the water more readily.

SERVES 4
- 1¾ pounds dried cod (stockfish), pounded and soaked in several changes of cold water
- Salt to taste
- Unbleached all-purpose flour for dredging
- Extra-virgin olive oil for frying and drizzling
- 1 medium Tropea red onion, thinly sliced into rounds
- Leaves of 1 sprig parsley, minced
- ½ cup pitted green olives
- ¼ cup capers, rinsed and drained

Cut the fish into 1–inch pieces. Season with salt, dredge lightly in flour, and fry in a generous amount of hot oil until golden on both sides. Set aside to cool. When the cooked fish is cool, place it in a pot and add water to come halfway up the height of the fish. Add the onion, about half of the parsley, the olives, and the capers. Season with salt, then simmer over very low heat until fish is very soft, 35 to 40 minutes. Sprinkle on the remaining parsley and drizzle with a little extra-virgin olive oil before serving.

STOCCAFISSO CON PRUGNE SECCHE E UVETTA
Stockfish with Prunes and Raisins
Ilda Cardinali, Passignano sul Trasimeno (Perugia), Umbria

To make enough to serve 4, pound and then soak 1 pound dried cod (stockfish) for 3 to 4 days in several changes of water. Drain, skin, and carefully inspect for bones. In a pot, sauté a thinly sliced onion in extra-virgin olive oil. Chop the soaked cod and add it to the pot. Sauté for a few minutes. Add 1 tablespoon tomato paste, about 1½ cups prunes, and about 1¼ cups sultana raisins (soaked in warm water to rehydrate if necessary, then drained and squeezed dry before they are added to the pot). Add a couple of tablespoons of honey and cook over medium heat until very soft, at least 45 minutes. Season to taste with salt and pepper and serve hot.

STOCCO A SFINCIONE
Stockfish with Wild Fennel Seed and a Breadcrumb Crust
Marco Lombardo, Milazzo (Messina), Sicilia

To make enough to serve 6, soak about 2 pounds of stockfish (dried cod) in several changes of water until pliable. (This may take several days.) Preheat the oven to 350°F. Lightly oil a baking pan and arrange the soaked and drained stockfish (cut into fillets if it is one large piece) and about 3 peeled and cubed potatoes. Thinly slice an onion and spread the slices on top, then sprinkle on minced garlic, minced flat-leaf parsley, and wild fennel seeds. Season with salt, pepper, and dried oregano, and drizzle on a generous amount of extra-virgin olive oil. Finally, sprinkle on a couple of handfuls of breadcrumbs to form a crust. Bake in the preheated oven until breadcrumbs are crispy and potatoes and fish are tender, 40 to 50 minutes.

STOCCO CON LE AMAREII
Stockfish with Broccoli Rabe
Trattoria La Scaletta, San Giorgio Morgeto (Reggio Calabria), Calabria

Both stockfish and baccalà have a little more resistance than fresh cod once cooked, and they hold up to longer cooking better than fresh fish. Here, that chewy texture pairs beautifully with the slightly bitter taste of broccoli rabe.

SERVES 4
- 1½ pounds dried cod (stockfish), pounded and soaked in several changes of cold water
- 1¼ pounds broccoli rabe
- Salt to taste
- 1 clove garlic
- Extra-virgin olive oil for sautéing
- Freshly ground black pepper to taste

Drain the stockfish, remove and discard skin and any bones, and chop. Trim the broccoli rabe, removing and discarding any thick stalks and damaged leaves, and chop roughly. Bring a large pot of lightly salted water to a boil and blanch the broccoli rabe until tender. Drain and set aside.

In a saucepan, sauté the garlic in a generous amount of oil. When the garlic turns golden, add the chunks of stockfish. Season with salt and pepper, then add the broccoli rabe and cook, stirring frequently, over medium heat for 15 minutes.

CODA DI STOCCAFISSO RIPIENA ⚑
Stuffed Dried Cod Tail
Trattoria degli Amici, Isolabona (Imperia), Liguria

For this recipe, you'll need a dried cod tail in one piece with the skin on. The slices of the finished dish are quite lovely. Pigato is an aromatic white wine from Liguria.

SERVES 4

1	large dried cod (stockfish) tail, pounded and soaked in several changes of cold water
1	roll
½	cup whole milk
2	cloves garlic
	Leaves of 2 sprigs parsley
2	lettuce leaves
2	large eggs, lightly beaten
	Minced fresh marjoram leaves to taste
	Salt and freshly ground black pepper to taste
1	medium yellow onion
3	tablespoons extra-virgin olive oil
1	bay leaf
1	cup Pigato white wine (see note)
¼	cup Taggiasca black olives, pitted

Drain the soaked cod tail. Scale it (but do not skin) and remove and discard any bones, then hollow it out by carving away and reserving some of the flesh.

Soak the roll in the milk until soft, then squeeze dry and crumble. Mince together 1 clove garlic, the leaves of 1 sprig parsley, the lettuce leaves, the crumbled bread, and the reserved cod flesh. Add the eggs, marjoram, salt, and pepper. Stuff the cod tail with this mixture and truss it closed with kitchen twine.

Mince together the remaining clove garlic, the onion, and the remaining parsley. Heat 3 tablespoons olive oil in a skillet large enough to hold the tail and cook the onion mixture and the bay leaf until the onion softens. Add the wine and arrange the stuffed cod tail in the pot. Season with salt and pepper and cook over low heat, adding warm water to the pot in small amounts as it gets dry and shaking the skillet occasionally, until the cod is tender and the stuffing is cooked through, about 1 hour. Add the olives just before the fish has finished cooking. Remove the twine and cut the cod tail into slices. Serve with the juices from the pan.

BRANZINO AL SALE
Branzino Cooked in Salt
Carlotta Olivieri, Sarzana (La Spezia), Liguria

A whole fish cooked in salt is a good choice for serving a crowd, and when you break the salt crust at the table it always makes an impression. Don't worry about the abundance of salt here: it forms a crust that helps the fish remain moist as it cooks, but it doesn't leave the cooked fish overly salty. A whole fish that weighs about 2½ pounds (or two smaller fish that weigh 1¼ pounds each) will serve 4 people. Scale, gut, and clean a branzino. Fill the cavity with a generous amount of rosemary sprigs and black peppercorns. Drizzle the outside of the fish with a little extra-virgin olive oil. Make a layer of 2 pounds (1 kilogram) rock salt in the bottom of a baking dish with high sides. Arrange the fish on top and cover it with another 2 pounds (1 kilogram) rock salt, pressing gently with your hands to be sure the fish is covered. Bake at 350°F until the fish is cooked through, about 20 minutes.

SPIGOLA AL FORNO 🐟
Baked Sea Bass
Letizia Castagnoli, Cecina (Livorno), Toscana

A whole sea bass that weighs about 2½ pounds will serve 4. Scale, gut, and clean and stuff the cavity with sprigs of rosemary and tarragon and a bay leaf or two. Place ¼ cup extra-virgin olive oil in a baking pan and place the fish in the pan. Pour another ¼ cup olive oil over the fish, then season with salt and pepper. Sprinkle with minced parsley. Bake in a 350°F oven, splashing with a little white wine every once in a while to keep it from drying out (about ¼ cup total). After 15 minutes, turn the fish carefully and season the other side with salt and pepper. Bake until the flesh is opaque, about 30 minutes total. Serve the fish on a platter with any juices from the pan on the side.

DENTICE ARROSTO 🧅
Roasted Snapper
Gina Semeria, Imperia, Liguria

To make enough to serve 6, scale, gut, and rinse a snapper that weighs about 4 pounds. If you would like the fish to cook a little more quickly, make some slashes in the sides. Rehydrate ¼ cup dried porcini mushrooms in warm water, then squeeze them dry and mince them together with 2 cloves garlic and a generous handful of parsley. Season the fish with salt and place it in a lightly oiled pan. Combine some of the mushroom mixture with salt, pepper, and 1 tablespoon oil and insert in the cavity of the fish. Brush the fish with another 2 tablespoons oil and sprinkle on the remaining mushroom mixture. Season again with salt, cover (use aluminum foil if the pan doesn't have a lid), and bake at 400°F for 10 minutes. Turn the oven down to 350°F and bake for an additional 20 minutes. Uncover the pan and baste the fish with the juices in the pan. If the fish looks excessively dry, add a few tablespoons of water. Cook the fish uncovered until the flesh is opaque, about 10 minutes.

DENTICE CON PATATE E CAPPERI 🐝
Snapper with Potatoes and Capers
Ristorante Lido Azzurro da Serafino, Marina di Ragusa, Sicilia

Dentice, a kind of Mediterranean snapper, is also delicious when cut into slices, especially if you get one large fish. Another interesting recipe calls for dredging strips of snapper in flour, frying them, and smearing them in mint sauce, then serving them cold.

SERVES 4
14 ounces scorpionfish or other fish scraps for broth (including heads and bones)
1 rib celery, chopped
1 medium yellow onion, chopped
1 small carrot, chopped
1¼ cups dry white wine
⅓ cup extra-virgin olive oil
2 to 3 cloves garlic, minced
¼ cup plus 1 tablespoon Salina capers, rinsed and drained
1 whole snapper, about 3½ pounds, scaled, gutted, and cleaned
2 medium potatoes, peeled and thinly sliced
Salt and freshly ground black pepper to taste
Leaves of 1 sprig parsley, minced

Place the fish scraps in a pot with the celery, onion, and carrot and 8 cups water. Add ¼ cup of the white wine and simmer over low heat for 1 hour. Strain the broth and discard solids. Keep the broth warm.

Place the oil in a large pot and sauté the garlic and capers until golden. Place the fish on top, add the remaining 1 cup white wine, then the potatoes and cook over medium heat. Once the wine has evaporated, add the warm fish broth in small amounts to keep the pot moist. Cook until the potatoes are tender and the fish flesh is opaque. Season with salt and pepper and sprinkle on minced parsley.

ORATA AL FORNO CON PATATE 🌿
Baked Dorade
Giovanni Petrucci, Follonica (Grosseto), Toscana

In southern Italy, dorade is handled as follows: make an emulsion of minced garlic and parsley in extra-virgin olive oil. Thinly slice potatoes and grate some aged sheep's cheese. Arrange about half of each of those ingredients in the bottom of a baking dish, top with a whole dorade, and cover with the remaining potatoes, garlic mixture, and cheese. Drizzle with a little more olive oil and bake in a hot oven (about 400°F) until the flesh is opaque and the potatoes are tender, shaking the pan occasionally to keep the fish and potatoes from sticking to the bottom.

SERVES 4

1   pound potatoes, peeled and cut into medium rounds

Extra-virgin olive oil for oiling pan and sautéing

2   cloves garlic, minced

Leaves of 1 sprig rosemary

Salt to taste

1   whole dorade (about 2¼ pounds), scaled, gutted, and cleaned

Unbleached all-purpose flour for dredging

1   cup dry white wine

Preheat the oven to 350°F. Place the potatoes in a lightly oiled baking pan. Add the garlic, rosemary, and a little salt and bake in the preheated oven until almost baked through, about 10 minutes.

Lightly dredge the fish in flour and brown on both sides in a skillet in a little olive oil. Transfer the fish to the pan on top of the potatoes, pour the wine over, and bake until the fish flesh is opaque, about 20 additional minutes.

PEZZOGNA ALL'ACQUAPAZZA 🥕
Sea Bream in "Crazy Water"
Trattoria 'A Paranza, Atrani (Salerno), Campania

No one is certain of the derivation of the expression *acquapazza*, or "crazy water," for fish cooked in this manner. Some speculate that it refers to sailors drinking seawater and losing their minds, while others feel it's just a nod to how insanely good this dish tastes. This is particularly delicious made with the small tomatoes known as *piénnolo* that grow along the Amalfi Coast. Because the preparation is relatively simple, all the ingredients must be as fresh as possible—their flavor will make or break the dish.

SERVES 4

1   whole sea bream (about 4¾ pounds), scaled, gutted, and cleaned

1   pint cherry tomatoes

1   rib celery, minced

2   carrots, minced

2   cloves garlic, minced

Leaves of 1 sprig parsley, minced

Salt to taste

Extra-virgin olive oil for drizzling

Place the fish in a pan with just enough water to cover. Add the tomatoes, celery, carrots, garlic, parsley, and salt to taste. Drizzle with a generous amount of oil and cook at a brisk simmer over medium heat until the fish flesh is opaque, about 20 minutes. Serve the fish with the pan juices and vegetables poured over it.

PALAMITA CON PISELLI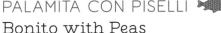
Bonito with Peas
Ristorante Il Gusto Etrusco, San Vincenzo
(Livorno), Toscana

Bonito is related to tuna and mackerel. It has rosy pink flesh and can be cooked or preserved in oil. Bonito fished using sustainable methods around the Archipelago Toscano are part of a Slow Food Presidium.

SERVES 4

1   whole bonito (about 3½ pounds)
¼   cup extra-virgin olive oil
2   spring onions, thinly sliced
1   pound ripe plum tomatoes, diced
1   chili pepper, minced
Leaves of 1 sprig parsley, minced
2   cloves garlic, minced
Salt to taste
2   pounds young peas in their pods, shelled

Fillet the fish and cut into at least 6 pieces. Fill a large bowl with water and add 10 ice cubes. Soak the fish in the ice water until it turns white, about 45 minutes.

In a saucepan, heat the olive oil and sauté the onions until golden. Drain the fish, pat dry, and add to the pan. Cook, turning once, for 8 minutes. Add the tomatoes, cook briefly, and then add the chili pepper, parsley, and garlic. Season with salt, cook for 10 minutes, then add the peas and cook over low heat until the peas are cooked but still firm and the liquid has reduced to a creamy sauce. Add warm water in small amounts if the pan begins to look dry before the dish is fully cooked.

FILETTI DI NASELLO FRITTI
Fried Hake Fillets
Secondina Lanteri, Ceriana (Imperia), Liguria

For 4 hake fillets, make a marinade of ¾ cup extra-virgin olive oil, thinly sliced garlic, a generous amount of minced parsley, and the juice of 2 lemons. Marinate the fillets in this mixture for about 1 hour, turning them occasionally. Drain the fish from the marinade and remove any pieces of garlic or parsley that are stuck to the fillets. Strain the marinade and beat 1 tablespoon of it with a large egg. Dredge the fillets lightly in flour, then in the egg mixture, and pan-fry in several inches of very hot olive oil until browned, 3 minutes per side, working in batches if necessary to avoid crowding the pan. Season with salt and serve.

RICCIOLA AL FORNO CON POMODORI RIPIENI ●
Baked Amberjack with Stuffed Tomatoes
Marco Lombardo, Milazzo (Messina), Sicilia

Halve 1 large beefsteak tomato per person and scoop out the seeds. Place thinly sliced pitted black olives, rinsed capers, minced garlic, and minced parsley in the middle of the hollowed tomatoes. Sprinkle with minced fresh oregano and freshly ground pepper and drizzle with extra-virgin olive oil. Arrange 7 ounces amberjack fillet per person in a lightly oiled baking dish. Season lightly with salt and place the tomato halves cut sides down on the fish. Crush the tomatoes gently, season them lightly with salt, and drizzle on a little oil. Bake at 400°F for 10 minutes, then add about ½ cup dry white wine to the dish and return to the oven until the fish is opaque, about 10 additional minutes, basting occasionally with the juices.

Amberjack may also be baked with sliced artichokes that are first sautéed in butter over low heat, then tossed with lemon juice and a few tablespoons of heavy cream. Make alternating layers of these artichokes and amberjack fillets in a baking dish and bake, basting frequently with the liquid that collects in the pan.

TRANCE DI RICCIOLA ALLA BRACE
Grilled Amberjack Fillets with Calamint and Lemon
Ristorante Margherita, Massa Lubrense (Napoli), Campania

Because amberjack flesh is thick and rather firm, it holds up well to grilling, but this recipe can also be made using an oven: place the fillets in a lightly oiled pan, sprinkle with minced garlic and parsley, and add a small amount of water. Season with salt, bake until opaque, and drizzle on the lemon juice after the fish is cooked. Calamint, *mentuccia* or *nepitella* in Italian, is similar to mint but with a more muted (less toothpaste-like) flavor and hints of basil.

SERVES 4

4 amberjack fillets, about 10 ounces each
½ cup extra-virgin olive oil, plus more
   for brushing fillets
3 to 4 cloves garlic, minced
Leaves of 1 sprig calamint (see note), minced
Juice of 1 large lemon
Salt to taste

Prepare a charcoal or gas grill. Brush the fillets lightly with oil and grill, turning every 3 minutes, until they are just cooked through. While the fish is cooking, whisk together the garlic, calamint, lemon juice, and ½ cup olive oil. Season the grilled fish with salt, transfer to a serving platter, pour the mixture over the fillets, and serve immediately.

LUSERNA INCOVERCIÀ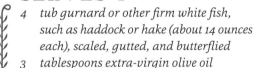
Preserved Grilled Fish
Osteria Da Penzo, Chioggia (Venezia), Veneto

This cooking method was originally conceived as a way to preserve leftover grilled fish and was used not only for tub gurnard (a firm white fish), but also for gray mullet, weever, bass, and other types of fish. These days, restaurants like Osteria Da Penzo start with fresh fish—not leftovers—and use a little less vinegar, as the fish isn't really being preserved long-term with the vinegar, just flavored with it. Serve the fish with crispy polenta (cooked, cooled, sliced, and crisped in a pan or on the grill).

SERVES 4

4 tub gurnard or other firm white fish,
   such as haddock or hake (about 14 ounces
   each), scaled, gutted, and butterflied
3 tablespoons extra-virgin olive oil
2 cloves garlic, minced
1 cup dry white wine
1 cup white wine vinegar
Salt to taste

Grill the fish, turning, until barely opaque, 6 to 7 minutes. Combine the oil, garlic, wine, and vinegar in a (cold) saucepan or skillet large enough to hold the fish in a single layer. Add the fish, season with salt, cover, and cook over medium heat until the liquid has reduced, about 10 minutes. Serve hot. The fish may be refrigerated and then reheated before serving.

SCALOPPE DI MUGGINE 🦪
Breaded Mullet Fillets with Potato Cake
Antica Trattoria del Teatro, Oristano, Sardegna

Mullet is a firm-fleshed fish that does not have an overly strong flavor. Ask your fishmonger to clean the fish for you and to cut it into four fillets.

SERVES 4

- 7   ounces (about 2 medium) potatoes
- 2   large eggs, beaten
- 1   cup heavy cream
- Salt and freshly ground black pepper to taste
- Freshly grated nutmeg to taste
- 1   whole mullet (about 2¼ pounds), skinned and filleted
- 1   cup whole-wheat breadcrumbs
- 3   tablespoons extra-virgin olive oil, plus more for drizzling
- 1   clove garlic
- 1   cup loosely packed basil leaves
- ¼   cup black olives, pitted

Preheat the oven to 400°F. Bake the potatoes in parchment until tender.

Peel the potatoes and crush them (through a potato ricer or with a fork) in a bowl. Add the eggs, cream, salt, pepper, and nutmeg. Stir to combine and transfer the mixture to a baking ring on a parchment-lined baking sheet. Bake until firm, about 30 minutes.

Meanwhile, dredge the fish fillets in the breadcrumbs. Heat 3 tablespoons oil in a nonstick skillet with the garlic. When the garlic turns brown, remove and discard, then brown the breaded fillets on both sides in the oil. Salt lightly and drain briefly on paper towels, then transfer to the oven and bake for 5 minutes to finish cooking.

To serve, wilt the basil leaves, then use them to line a platter. Unmold the potato cake onto the basil leaves. Arrange the fillets on the platter. Drizzle with additional olive oil and garnish with olives.

TRIGLIE ALLA LIVORNESE 🦪
Livorno-Style Red Mullet
Ristorante La Gattabuia, Rosignano Marittima (Livorno), Toscana

This is clearly the descendant of an ancient Sephardic Jewish dish, which is logical enough, given that Livorno has a long history as a safe haven for Jews. Indeed, in 1593 the grand duke introduced a law welcoming "people of all ethnicities and religions" to the city.

SERVES 4

- 2   cloves garlic, crushed
- ½   cup extra-virgin olive oil
- 1   pound plum tomatoes or 1¼ cups drained canned peeled tomatoes, roughly chopped
- Salt and freshly ground black pepper to taste
- 12 whole small red mullet (3 to 4 ounces each), scaled and gutted
- Leaves of 1 sprig parsley, minced

In a skillet large enough to hold the fish in a single layer, sauté the garlic in the oil. When the garlic browns, remove and discard and add the tomatoes. Add water to cover and season with salt and pepper. Cook over medium heat, stirring occasionally, until reduced, about 20 minutes. Add the mullet to the skillet and cook, uncovered, until just opaque, about 10 minutes. Do not turn the fish while it is cooking. If you must, you can shake the pan a little to keep the fish from sticking. Sprinkle with parsley and serve.

NASELLO CON CARCIOFI 🌳
Hake with Artichokes
Felicita Marengo, Savona, Liguria

A whole hake weighing about 2 pounds should feed 2 or 3 people. Place 1 crushed clove garlic in the cavity of a scaled and gutted hake. Season inside and out with fresh rosemary, salt, and pepper, and drizzle generously with extra-virgin olive oil. In an ovenproof skillet with a tight-fitting lid, sauté ½ thinly sliced yellow onion and 1 minced clove garlic in some extra-virgin olive oil just until wilted, then add the fish and brown on both sides. Add about ½ cup dry white wine to the pan and wait for it to evaporate, then cover and bake in a 425°F oven for 15 minutes. Add 1 to 2 sliced lemons and blanched artichoke quarters to the pan. Season with salt and pepper and add about ½ cup vegetable broth to keep the fish from sticking. Return to the oven and bake for an additional 30 minutes.

FILETTI DI PESCE GALLO AL MARSALA 🐟
John Dory Fillets in Marsala
Caterina Rizzo, Castelvetrano (Trapani), Sicilia

Ask your trusted fishmonger to fillet a whole fish for you, butterflying it and leaving the fillets attached, but do request the head and bones, as you can use them to prepare a fish stock. One fish weighing about 2 pounds should feed 2 or 3 people. Dredge the fillets lightly in flour and brown on both sides in extra-virgin olive oil. Add about ¼ cup dry Marsala and 1 cup fish stock to the pan. Season with salt and pepper and cook over low heat until the liquid has reduced by half.

SGOMBRI AL FINOCCHIO SELVATICO
Mackerel with Wild Fennel
Ristoro della Cooperativa Coomarpesca, Fano (Pesaro and Urbino), Marche

Oily fish such as mackerel benefit from a healthy dose of acidity, which in this recipe comes from the lemon juice. Mackerel is also delicious marinated after cooking in vinegar and then topped with minced garlic and fresh mint leaves.

SERVES 4
1 whole mackerel (2½ to 3 pounds), scaled and gutted
Salt to taste
10 cipollini onions
4 carrots
1 rib celery
1 sprig wild fennel
Leaves of 1 sprig parsley
1 clove garlic
1 strip orange zest
3 tablespoons extra-virgin olive oil
Freshly ground black pepper to taste
1 tablespoon tomato paste, dissolved in warm water or broth
Juice of ½ lemon

Boil the mackerel in lightly salted water until the flesh is opaque. Bone the fish and cut into fillets.

Mince the cipollini, carrots, celery, wild fennel, parsley, garlic, and orange zest and sauté in the olive oil until very fragrant, about 10 minutes. Season with salt and pepper and add the tomato paste. When the mixture has thickened, add the lemon juice. Arrange the fish fillets on a platter and pour the sauce over them. Serve warm or refrigerate and serve cold.

TROTA IN CARTOCCIO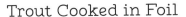
Trout Cooked in Foil
Trattoria Campagna, Arona (Novara), Lombardia

Like cooking in parchment, cooking in foil packets keeps food moist and tender. It is an especially effective method for fish.

SERVES 4

4   whole trout (about 7 ounces each), scaled and gutted
Salt and freshly ground black pepper to taste
4   sprigs wild fennel
1   shallot, minced
1   tablespoon dry vermouth
½   cup fish stock
Extra-virgin olive oil for drizzling
1   lemon, sliced

Preheat the oven to 450°F. Season the fish with salt and pepper and place a sprig of fennel in the cavity of each one. Prepare four pieces of aluminum foil 12 inches long. Arrange one fish on each piece of foil. Scatter on the shallot and sprinkle on the vermouth, fish stock, and a generous drizzle of olive oil. Fold up the foil packets envelope-style, crimping the top to seal. Place them on a baking sheet and cook in the preheated oven for 10 minutes. Carefully open one packet (steam will escape) and check that the flesh is opaque. Garnish the fish with lemon slices and serve.

TEMOLO ALLE NOCCIOLE
Grayling Fish with Hazelnuts
Renato Dominici, Carmagnola (Torino), Piemonte

Grayling is a delicate fish (similar to trout in texture, but less fishy in flavor) that deserves to be better known. It cannot be farmed and lives in streams and rivers with high oxygen levels. To serve 6 people, clean and fillet 3 fish (about 1 pound each) to make 6 fillets. Mince 2 anchovy fillets and mix with 7 tablespoons softened butter. Spread the anchovy butter thickly on both sides of the fillets. Place the fillets in a baking dish thickly buttered with another 3 tablespoons butter. Toast, peel, and finely chop ¼ cup hazelnuts and sprinkle them on the fillets. Season with salt and pepper and top each fillet with 1 large sage leaf and some calamint leaves, if desired. Bake at 270°F until opaque, 20 to 30 minutes. Sprinkle the juice of 1 lemon over the cooked fish, then transfer to a serving platter. Spoon any cooking liquid out of the baking pan and drizzle it over the fish.

TROTE AL VINO
Trout Cooked in Wine
Brasserie Les Pertzes, Cogne (Aosta), Valle d'Aosta

Blanc de Morgex et de la Salle is an ice-wine, meaning that the grapes used to make it grow at the highest possible altitude. Juniper berries also grow at high elevations and in snowy climates. Serve this dish with steamed potatoes sautéed in butter with chopped wild thyme, and pour the same wine used in the dish to accompany it. It is recommended that you use the previous year's vintage if possible.

SERVES 4

2   whole brown trout (about 1½ pounds each), scaled, gutted, and filleted
½   cup unbleached all-purpose flour
1   tablespoon unsalted butter
2   tablespoons extra-virgin olive oil
Salt and freshly ground black pepper to taste
Freshly ground dried juniper berries to taste
½   cup Blanc de Morgex et de La Salle wine

Preheat the oven to 350°F. Dredge the trout fillets in the flour and then brown them on both sides in an ovenproof skillet in the butter and oil. Season with salt and pepper and a pinch of ground dried juniper berries (a little goes a long way). Add the wine and transfer to the oven. Cook until opaque, about 10 minutes.

SOGLIOLE AL SUGO 🍅
Sole in Pepper and Tomato Sauce

Ugo Rossano, Gerace (Reggio Calabria), Calabria

In a large skillet, sauté 1 thinly sliced yellow onion and 2 whole cloves garlic in extra-virgin olive oil. Remove and discard the garlic once it browns. Add 2 minced bell peppers and 4 plum tomatoes that have been peeled, seeded, and crushed with a fork. Cook over medium heat for 10 minutes. Add 1 to 2 sole fillets (skin removed or left on—it's up to you) per person. Cover the skillet and cook until the fish is opaque, shaking the pan occasionally to keep it from sticking. Adjust salt to taste, transfer the fish and sauce to a serving platter, and serve hot.

SOGLIOLE AL VINO 🍇
Sole Cooked in Wine

Luca Prati, Cervia (Ravenna), Emilia-Romagna

Dredge sole fillets in unbleached all-purpose flour and shake off the excess. Brown the fillets in equal amounts butter and extra-virgin olive oil in a skillet. Add a little dry white wine and a little fish stock and cook over medium heat. When the fish is just opaque, drizzle on lemon juice and season with salt and pepper. Remove from the heat and transfer the fish to a serving platter. Pour pan juices over the fish and garnish with minced flat-leaf parsley.

TINCA DEL TRASIMENO FARCITA 🐟
Stuffed Tench

Ristorante L'Acquario, Castiglione del Lago (Perugia), Umbria

The stuffing for this tench dish is made with an ingredient that is relatively easy to find on the shores of Lake Trasimeno: carp roe. This caviarlike substance can be sprinkled on pasta or sautéed in oil and used to garnish bread soup. Tench is a member of the carp family; substitute with another type of carp if you can't find tench in your area.

SERVES 6

- 2   whole tench (about 1½ pounds each), scaled, gutted, and boned, but left whole
- Salt and freshly ground black pepper to taste
- ½   clove garlic, minced
- Leaves of 1 sprig parsley, minced
- 1½ cups breadcrumbs
- ¼   cup grated Parmigiano Reggiano
- ¼   cup carp roe
- 1   egg white
- 1   tablespoon wine vinegar
- 2   tablespoons extra-virgin olive oil, plus more for oiling pan

Season the fish cavities with salt and pepper and set aside to rest for at least 30 minutes. Preheat the oven to 350°F. Meanwhile, prepare the stuffing by combining garlic, parsley, breadcrumbs, Parmigiano, carp roe, the egg white, vinegar, 2 tablespoons oil, and salt and pepper to taste. Stuff the fish with the mixture and truss with kitchen twine. Season the outside of the fish with salt and pepper, place in a lightly oiled baking pan, and bake in the preheated oven until flesh is opaque, about 1 hour. To serve, remove twine and cut into slices about ¾ inch thick.

TINCHE FRITTE 🍃
Fried Tench
Cantina dei Cacciatori, Monteu Roero (Cuneo), Piemonte

Lightly salt the cavities of scaled, gutted small tench (2 or 3 per person) and place a sage leaf in the cavity of each. Dredge the fish in flour, then bring several inches of extra-virgin olive oil to high temperature for frying and cook the fish in the oil, turning once, 6 minutes per side. Salt and drain briefly on paper towels, then transfer to a serving platter and scatter lemon quarters, halved cherry tomatoes, and thin ribbons of lettuce over the top before serving.

FILETTI DI SPATOLA AL PANE SAPORITO 🌿
Breaded Scabbard Fish Fillets
Ristorante al Duomo, Taormina (Messina), Sicîlia

Because scabbard fish has no scales, it is easy to clean. It is also excellent simply cut into 2½-inch batons, dredged in a little flour, and fried, then served with lemon slices or tomato sauce.

SERVES 4
- 2 cups dry breadcrumbs
- Leaves of 1 bunch flat-leaf parsley, minced
- ½ cup grated mild sheep's cheese
- Extra-virgin olive oil for moistening and oiling pan
- Freshly ground black pepper to taste
- 14 ounces scabbard fish fillets
- 2 to 4 Pachino tomatoes or other small, flavorful tomatoes, sliced
- Salt to taste

Preheat the oven to 350°F. Combine the breadcrumbs, parsley, and grated cheese with a little oil to moisten and season with pepper. Lightly oil a baking pan large enough to hold the fillets in a single layer and place the fish in it. Sprinkle the breadcrumb mixture on top. Arrange the tomato slices on top of the fillets in a single layer. Season with salt and bake in the preheated oven until the fish is just cooked, about 3 minutes.

PESCE LAMA IN CROSTA DI PATATE 🌿
Scabbard Fish in a Potato Crust
Osteria Magiargè, Bordighera (Imperia), Liguria

This dish pairs beautifully with ratatouille, which complements both its flavor and its appearance.

SERVES 4
- ½ cup whole milk
- 2 tablespoons fresh thyme leaves
- 2 tablespoons fresh rosemary leaves
- 2 medium potatoes
- 2 teaspoons poppy seeds
- 14 ounces scabbard fish fillets
- Salt to taste
- Extra-virgin olive oil for oiling pan

Preheat the oven to 350°F. Simmer the milk with the thyme and rosemary to infuse it with their flavor, then strain the milk. Meanwhile, boil the potatoes until tender, peel, and mash them with the milk. Add the poppy seeds and mash until smooth. Transfer the mashed potatoes to a pastry bag fitted with a ridged tip.

Season the fish with salt and place in a single layer in a lightly oiled baking pan. Pipe the mashed potatoes over the fish in a regular pattern. Bake until just cooked through, 10 to 15 minutes.

SCALOPPA DI SPATULA 🍅
Thin Scabbard Fish Fillets with Tomatoes, Onion, and Oregano
Trattoria Max, Cirò Marina (Crotone), Calabria

Scabbard fish is a long, silvery fish that looks like the metal blade of a sword or a silver belt. It does not have scales. A classic caponata is a good choice for a side dish. Cirò bianco is a Calabrese white wine made from Greco Bianco grapes, which Greek settlers brought to the region thousands of years ago.

SERVES 4
- 1 medium Tropea red onion, thinly sliced
- 2 tablespoons extra-virgin olive oil
- 1½ pounds scabbard fish fillets
- Unbleached all-purpose flour for dredging
- ½ cup Cirò bianco white wine
- 1 tablespoon tomato paste
- 2 tomatoes, sliced
- Salt to taste
- Leaves of 1 sprig oregano, minced
- Leaves of 1 sprig thyme, minced
- Freshly ground black pepper to taste

In a skillet large enough to hold the fish in a single layer, sauté the onion in the olive oil. Dredge the fish fillets in flour, add them to the skillet, and brown them on both sides, then remove from the pan. Add the wine to the skillet and allow it to evaporate. Stir in the tomato paste and fresh tomatoes. Stir, cook briefly to combine, then season with salt and sprinkle on the oregano and thyme and a generous amount of pepper. Pour the contents of the skillet over the fish and serve hot.

FILETTI DI TROTA ALLE NOCCIOLE 🍴
Hazelnut-Crusted Trout Fillets with Golden Zucchini
Ristorante La Fioraia, Castello d'Annone (Asti), Piemonte

Look for small brown trout, or river trout (preferably wild and not farmed), for this dish. The color of the pink-fleshed trout now available does not mark them as a particular species, but is a result of diet: they are fed ground shrimp and other shellfish. If you are purchasing whole fish and filleting them yourself, look for 4 small trout, about 10 ounces each.

SERVES 4
- ⅔ cup hazelnuts, toasted and skinned
- ⅔ cup semolina flour
- 1 large egg
- Salt to taste
- 8 small brown trout fillets
- 1 tablespoon clarified butter
- Extra-virgin olive oil for frying
- 4 small zucchini, cut into julienne
- ¼ cup unbleached all-purpose flour

Use a meat pounder to crush the hazelnuts and combine them with the semolina flour in a shallow bowl. In a separate shallow bowl, beat the egg with a pinch of salt. Dredge the fillets first in the egg, then in the hazelnut mixture. Fry the dredged fillets in the butter until browned, about 6 minutes total. (Work in batches if necessary to avoid crowding the pan.) In a pan with high sides, bring several inches of oil to high temperature. Dredge the zucchini in the flour and brown in the oil, about 3 minutes. Season with salt.

To plate the dish, mound a portion of the zucchini in the center of each individual serving plate and arrange 2 fillets on either side.

CARPA REGINA IN PORCHETTA

Carp Cooked Porchetta Style

Ristorante L'Acquario, Castiglione del Lago (Perugia), Umbria

Porchetta is one of the most famous dishes from Umbria: a larded suckling pig stuffed with garlic, rosemary, and fennel and then roasted. Carp—a freshwater fish frequently eaten in landlocked Umbria—is given the same treatment with delicious results.

SERVES 4

1   cup diced lardo (cured fatback) or pancetta
2   sprigs wild fennel
Leaves of 1 sprig rosemary
1   clove garlic
Salt and freshly ground black pepper to taste
1   large whole carp (about 4½ pounds), scaled and gutted
2   tablespoons plus 1 teaspoon white wine vinegar
Extra-virgin olive oil for oiling pan
Dry white wine for cooking

Finely mince together the lardo, 1 sprig wild fennel, rosemary leaves, and garlic. Season with salt and pepper.

Make multiple cuts the long way (head to tail) in the cavity and outside of the fish. Season the cuts with salt and pepper, then fill the cuts with small amounts of about ¾ of the lardo mixture. Reserve the remaining lardo mixture. Chop the remaining sprig fennel and combine with the 2 tablespoons vinegar, then sprinkle that mixture into the cuts in the fish as well. Rub the remaining lardo mixture all over the inside and outside of the fish.

Let the fish rest for 12 hours, then preheat the oven to 350°F to 400°F. Place the fish in a lightly oiled pan and bake, basting it with small amounts of white wine and the pan juices occasionally, until the fish is cooked through, about 1 hour. Drizzle on the remaining 1 teaspoon vinegar just before serving.

COREGONE AL FINOCCHIETTO

Whitefish with Wild Fennel

Osteria La Piazzetta del Sole, Farnese (Viterbo), Lazio

This recipe will work with almost any type of whole fish, including oily varieties such as mackerel.

SERVES 4

4   whole whitefish (about 10 ounces each), scaled and gutted
Salt and freshly ground black pepper to taste
Wild fennel flowers to taste
3   cloves garlic (1 unpeeled)
Extra-virgin olive oil for drizzling

Preheat the oven to 350°F. Season the fish inside and out with salt and pepper, then sprinkle with fennel flowers. Chop 2 cloves garlic and sprinkle those on, too. Line a baking pan large enough to hold the fish in a single layer with parchment. Drizzle a little oil in the pan and add the third garlic clove, which should still have its skin. Place the fish in the pan and bake in the preheated oven until the flesh is opaque, about 20 minutes. Serve immediately.

LAVARELLO AL FORNO

Baked Whitefish

Ilda Cardinali, Passignano sul Trasimeno (Perugia), Umbria

Scale and gut 1 small whitefish (about 1 pound) per person. Lightly oil a baking pan and sprinkle the bottom with some rock salt. Place the fish in the pan and sprinkle with lemon juice and white wine. Mince together garlic, parsley, wild fennel, and rosemary and mix with some breadcrumbs. Sprinkle the mixture over the fish, season with pepper, drizzle with extra-virgin olive oil, and bake in a 400°F oven until opaque, about 30 minutes.

ROMBO AL FORNO CON PATATE
Baked Turbot with Potatoes
Paola Cutinelli, Pozzuoli (Napoli), Campania

Preheat the oven to 400°F. Scale and gut a large turbot (at least 3½ pounds) and make 2 cuts on each side. Insert halved garlic cloves and some rosemary leaves into the slits. Peel several potatoes and cut them into thick slices. Toss them with a couple of tablespoons of extra-virgin olive oil, salt, and pepper, then place them in a baking dish large enough to hold the whole fish and bake until they are cooked, but still have a little resistance in the middle, about 10 minutes. Set the fish on top of the potatoes with the light-skinned side upward. Pour in about ½ cup wine, season with salt and pepper, and cook until the fish flesh is opaque and potatoes are completely tender, about 15 minutes. Serve very hot.

LAVARELLO ALLE MANDORLE
Whitefish with Almonds
Crotto del Sergente, Como, Lombardia

Whitefish is commonly found in the lakes at the foot of the Alps and in the volcanic lakes of Lazio. It has—as the name indicates—very white flesh. It also has very few bones, making it a pleasure to clean. Roasted potatoes make a great accompaniment.

SERVES 6
Unbleached all-purpose flour for dredging
1   large egg
Salt to taste
2   tablespoons unsalted butter
4 to 6 sage leaves
6   whitefish, scaled, gutted, and butterflied
⅓   cup sliced almonds

Preheat the oven to 400°F. Place flour in a shallow bowl. Lightly beat the egg with a pinch of salt in another shallow bowl. Line a baking sheet with paper towels and set aside. In a non-stick pan, melt the butter with the sage leaves. Dredge the fish first in flour and then in the egg and brown in the butter on both sides. Work in batches if necessary to keep from crowding the pan. Drain briefly on the prepared pan, then transfer to a baking pan. Sprinkle on the almonds and bake in the preheated oven until the flesh is opaque, about 2 minutes.

LUCCIO ALLA GONZAGA
Simmered Pike
Ristorante Il Porticciolo, Lazise (Verona), Veneto

In Acquanegra sul Chiese in the province of Mantova, the osteria Al Ponte covers its simmered pike in a sauce made by blending 1 tablespoon mustard, ½ cup extra-virgin olive oil, 3 tablespoons unsalted butter, 3 tablespoons wine vinegar, 1 tablespoon balsamic vinegar, 2 tablespoons grated Parmigiano Reggiano, and a pinch of salt. The fish marinates in that sauce for at least 4 hours, and then is sliced and served with toasted polenta.

SERVES 4
2   lemons
½   cup white wine vinegar
1   bay leaf
1   rib celery
1   carrot
1   medium yellow onion, halved
1   whole pike (about 2¼ pounds), scaled and gutted
Salt and freshly ground black pepper to taste
¼   cup grated Parmigiano Reggiano
Ground cinnamon to taste
½   cup extra-virgin olive oil

Halve one of the lemons. Grate the zest of and juice 1½ lemons. Make a court-bouillon with 8 cups water, the vinegar, the remaining ½ lemon, and the bay leaf, celery, carrot, and onion. Simmer the fish in the court-bouillon until the flesh is opaque, then let it cool in the broth. When it has cooled, peel and bone it.

Arrange the cooked pike on a serving platter. Season with salt and pepper. Sprinkle on the Parmigiano, cinnamon, and grated lemon zest. Whisk together the lemon juice and olive oil and drizzle the mixture over the fish. Allow to rest for at least 12 hours before serving.

STORIONE AL FORNO
Baked Sturgeon with Pancetta and Sage
Antica Trattoria Cattivelli, Monticelli d'Ongina (Piacenza), Emilia-Romagna

Covering the pan keeps the fillets an attractive white color.

SERVES 4
1   tablespoon unsalted butter
4   slices pancetta
4   sturgeon fillets (about 7 ounces each), skinned
Salt to taste
4   basil leaves
4   sage leaves
¼   cup dry white wine (optional)

Preheat the oven to 350°F. Lightly grease a baking pan with the butter and arrange the slices of pancetta in the pan. Place one sturgeon fillet on each slice of pancetta. Season with salt and top each fillet with 1 basil leaf and 1 sage leaf. Sprinkle on a little water and the wine, if using. Cover the pan and bake in the preheated oven until the fish is translucent, about 15 minutes.

LUCIOPERCA CON VERDURE
Pike-Perch with Vegetables
Ristorante Castel Toblino, Calavino (Trento), Trentino-Alto Adige

Pike-perch is a freshwater fish with flavorful flesh. It has very few bones, but it does require rather lengthy cooking.

SERVES 4
1   whole pike-perch (about 1½ pounds), halved but still on the bone
Extra-virgin olive oil for drizzling and sautéing
Salt and freshly ground black pepper to taste
1   bunch chives, minced
1   sprig dill, minced
2   potatoes, peeled and diced
1   yellow bell pepper, diced
1   red bell pepper, diced
2   carrots, diced
2   zucchini, diced
1   clove garlic (unpeeled)

Steam the fish until opaque, 7 to 8 minutes, and skin and bone it while it is still warm. (This is easier to do after it is cooked.) Place the fish halves in a bowl and drizzle them with olive oil, season with salt and pepper, and sprinkle on most of the chives and dill, reserving some for garnish.

Blanch the vegetables separately to keep them from discoloring. In a skillet, sauté the vegetables in some olive oil with the unpeeled garlic. To serve, place the vegetables in the center of each plate, arrange the fish on top, drizzle with a little more olive oil, and garnish with the reserved chives and dill.

SAMPIETRO IN UMIDO CON PATATE

Stewed Saint Peter's Fish with Potatoes

Ristorante Delfina & Giovanni, Lido di Tortoreto (Teramo), Abruzzo

Saint Peter's fish, sometimes called John Dory, is a flat fish that forms a classic duo with potatoes. Possible alternatives include sole and turbot. For this recipe, do not turn the fish. If you are afraid it is sticking, gently shake the pot to move it. At Antichi Sapori they sprinkle the fish with white wine and then roast it.

SERVES 4

Extra-virgin olive oil for oiling pot and
    drizzling
1   whole Saint Peter's fish
    (about 2½ pounds), scaled and
    gutted but head left on
1⅓ pounds potatoes, peeled and cut into
    medium-thick rounds
10 cherry tomatoes
1   clove garlic, minced
Salt to taste
Leaves of 1 sprig parsley, minced

Lightly oil a pot large enough to hold the fish with extra-virgin olive oil and place the fish inside of it. Arrange the potatoes on top of it. Scatter on the tomatoes and garlic. Season with salt and sprinkle on the parsley. Drizzle on additional oil, then add enough water to cover the fish. Cover the pot with a lid and cook over high heat until the water has almost completely reduced, about 20 minutes.

INVOLTINI DI STORIONE

Sturgeon Rolls

Osteria Grand Hotel, Milano, Lombardia

Rather than purchasing a whole fish, you can use fillets for this recipe. Either ask your fishmonger to slice them or do it yourself at home. These rolls also make an interesting appetizer.

SERVES 4

Juice of 2 lemons
Extra-virgin olive oil for marinade,
    drizzling, and sautéing
1   whole sturgeon (about 1¾ pounds),
    scaled, gutted, boned, skinned, and cut
    into thin slices
12 cherry tomatoes
Salt to taste
Leaves of 1 sprig oregano, or calamint,
    minced
1   large eggplant
1   shallot, minced
2   peeled and seeded (jarred) plum
    tomatoes, passed through a food mill,
    or ½ cup tomato puree

Combine the lemon juice with a generous amount of extra-virgin olive oil and marinate the fish slices in this mixture for 12 hours.

Meanwhile, preheat the oven to 400°F. Place the cherry tomatoes in a baking pan, salt, and bake in the preheated oven for 50 minutes. Remove the tomatoes from the oven and drizzle with a little olive oil and the oregano. Set aside at room temperature for a couple of hours. Cut the eggplant into slices about ¼ inch thick, salt them, and drain them for about 1 hour. Briefly bake until just tender.

When you are ready to cook the fish, turn down the oven temperature to 300°F. On each slice of fish place a slice of eggplant, 2 to 3 cherry tomatoes, and a pinch of salt. Roll up and close with a toothpick. As you make the rolls, place them in a baking dish. When you have used all of the fish, eggplant, and tomatoes, cover the baking dish and bake in the preheated oven for

10 minutes, then remove the cover and bake until golden, an additional 10 to 15 minutes.

Meanwhile, in a small skillet sauté the shallot in olive oil. Add the tomato puree, season with salt, and cook for a few minutes until reduced slightly. When the fish is cooked, remove it from the oven, pour the tomato sauce over, and serve hot.

TONNO A CIPOLLATA
Tuna in Onion Sauce
Ristorante Al Duomo, Taormina (Messina), Sicília

Tuna in a sweet and sour sauce with plenty of onions is a Sicilian classic. The onions here should be cooked slowly until golden—they shouldn't be overly browned.

SERVES 4
4   Tropea red onions, peeled and cut into julienne
Extra-virgin olive oil for sautéing
2   tablespoons sugar
¼   cup wine vinegar
½   cup red wine
8   mint leaves, chopped
Salt and freshly ground black pepper to taste
4   slices of tuna (about 4 ounces each)

Cook the onions in a little olive oil in a skillet over low heat until golden. Add the sugar, vinegar, wine, and mint leaves. Cover and braise over low heat for 30 minutes. Season with salt and pepper and allow to cool.

Heat a skillet and sear the tuna, 30 seconds per side. Add the onion mixture to the pan and cook until the tuna is cooked to your preference, then serve.

TOMBARELLO FRITTO
Fried Frigate Tuna
Giovanni Addamo, Corleone (Palermo), Sicília

Frigate tuna must be meticulously fresh for this recipe, as it is a fairly oily fish. Simply dredge pieces of frigate tuna (about 7 ounces per person) in unbleached all-purpose flour, then pan-fry in a generous amount of extra-virgin olive oil until golden. Drain briefly on paper towels, then transfer to a serving platter. Season with salt, scatter minced parsley over the fish, and garnish with lemon wedges. Serve piping hot.

FRITTO DI PESCI D'ACQUA DOLCE
Fried Freshwater Fish
Antica Trattoria Cattivelli, Monticelli d'Ongina (Piacenza), Emília-Romagna

This is delicious when made with almost any type of fish, including pike, pike-perch, tench, catfish, or carp. Baby eels will work as well.

SERVES 4
2   pounds freshwater fish (see note)
Unbleached all-purpose flour or 00 flour for dredging
4½ cups extra-virgin olive oil
Salt to taste

Clean the fish, fillet where appropriate, and dry thoroughly. Dredge lightly in flour.

Line a platter with paper towels and set aside. In a large skillet with high sides, heat the oil over high heat and add the fish. Lower the heat to medium. Freshwater fish need a longer cooking time than saltwater fish, so give them time to cook without burning or sticking to the pan, about 10 minutes. Remove with a skimmer or slotted spoon and transfer to the platter. Season with salt and serve immediately.

TONNA ALLA MENTA 🌿
Tuna with Garlic and Mint
Trattoria Don Ciccio, Bagheria (Palermo), Sicilia

Brothers Francesco and Salvatore Castronovo specialize in cooking tuna. This recipe combines two traditional recipes: *tunnina a raù* (tuna in a tomato sauce from Palermo) and *tuccu di tunnina* (a Trapani dish that calls for baking tuna with garlic, mint, and oregano).

SERVES 5
2½ *pounds fresh tuna*
4   *cloves garlic*
Leaves of 1 sprig mint
¾   *cup caciocavallo cheese shavings*
½   *cup unbleached all-purpose flour*
Extra-virgin olive oil for pan-frying
   and sautéing
1   *medium yellow onion, diced*
2   *tablespoons tomato paste*
2   *cups shelled peas*
1   *chili pepper, minced*
Salt to taste

Cut the tuna into 5 equal pieces and cut a slit into each. Halve 3 of the garlic cloves. Stuff each piece of tuna with 1 garlic half, 1 to 2 mint leaves (reserve a few), and cheese shavings. Dredge the tuna in the flour and pan-fry until browned.

Mince the remaining 1½ cloves garlic and set aside. For the sauce, in a skillet sauté the onion in oil until golden, then add the tomato paste, peas, minced garlic, and chili pepper. Season with salt and tear in the reserved mint leaves, then stir in about ½ cup water, add the tuna to the skillet, and simmer over low heat until the tuna is cooked through and sauce has reduced, 15 to 20 minutes.

TONNO CON PEPERONATA
Tuna with Peppers
Salvo Miligi, Pachino (Siracusa), Sicilia

In a skillet, heat a couple of tablespoons of extra-virgin olive oil and brown 1 to 2 crushed garlic cloves. Add bell peppers seeded and sliced into rings, peeled cubes of potatoes, and seeded and peeled tomatoes. Season with salt, cover, and cook for 30 minutes. Sprinkle on a few tablespoons red wine vinegar. Meanwhile, in a separate skillet, sauté a chunk of tuna belly preserved in oil in a couple of tablespoons of extra-virgin olive oil. Dredge slices of fresh tuna (about 7 ounces per person) in flour and add to the pan. Cook until golden, then add the bell pepper mixture to the pan with the tuna. Mix gently to combine. Taste and adjust seasoning. Serve hot.

TONNO BRIAO
Tuna in Red Wine
Ristorante Il Garibaldi Innamorato, Piombino (Livorno), Toscana

When purchasing tuna for this or any other recipe, we recommend that you follow the guidelines of our campaign for sustainability and avoid buying tuna species that are at risk. There is no lack of alternatives. Bonito caught off of Toscana is part of the Slow Food Presidium and is absolutely delicious.

SERVES 4
1   *pound fresh tuna*
Salt and freshly ground black pepper to taste
2   *tablespoons unbleached all-purpose*
   flour
1   *cup extra-virgin olive oil*
1   *medium red onion, minced*
Leaves of 1 sprig parsley, minced
1   *clove garlic, crushed*
1½ *cups young red wine*

Cut the tuna into slices. Season lightly with salt and pepper and dredge in the flour. Heat the oil in a skillet large enough to hold the tuna in a single layer. Add the onion, parsley, and garlic and sauté until fragrant, about 30 seconds. Add the tuna and cook until browned on both sides, turning once. Add the wine and cook, uncovered, until it has evaporated.

FRITTO DI PARANZA
Mixed Fried Fish
Trattoria La Darsena, Viareggio (Lucca), Toscana

This dish is eaten up and down the Italian coastline, but the species of fish used varies according to location. Ask your fishmonger for the best, freshest fish available, but look for young, small fish in general. At Sirio di Formia in Lazio, a fried fish platter typically uses mullet, flounder, small sole, baby calamari, and young cod. Cleaned appropriately, they are dredged in flour and then moistened with a sprinkling of water—this keeps them from absorbing too much of the fat when they are fried. In Campania at A Ridosso di Bacoli, fried fish is made with young cod, mullet, spotted flounder, calamari, and shrimp; goby are thrown into the mix in the summer. At Delfina & Giovanni on the Abruzzo coastline, the dish usually includes young cod, mullet, anchovies, flounder, young monkfish, scampi, baby calamari, and small shrimp.

SERVES 4
2½ pounds mixed fresh fish, such as sole, goby, gurnard, rockfish, conger eel, red bandfish (which look like pink eels), anchovies, and mullet
2 cups unbleached all-purpose flour or 00 flour
1½ cups semolina flour
4 cups extra-virgin olive oil
Salt to taste
1 lemon, cut into wedges

Scale and gut the fish and fillet, where appropriate. (This is by far the most time-consuming part of preparing the dish.) Dry thoroughly. Combine the two flours and dredge the fish in the flours, taking care to coat lightly.

Line a platter with paper towels and set aside. Place the oil in a pot with high sides and bring to 300°F. Cook the fish in the oil, working in batches if necessary to avoid crowding, until browned and very crisp. Remove with a slotted spoon or skimmer to the prepared platter. Salt lightly, garnish with lemon wedges, and serve hot.

CROCCHETTE DI PERSICO E PATATE
Perch and Potato Croquettes
Ristorante Sauro, Tuoro sul Trasimeno (Perugia), Umbria

You may not want to use all of the smoked fish, depending on how strongly flavored it is. Smoked trout can be used if smoked tench is hard to track down. You also may not need all of the potatoes—the potatoes and perch fillets should be served in about equal amounts.

SERVES 4
14 ounces perch fillets
1 pound potatoes
2 ounces smoked tench (see note), minced
Leaves of 1 sprig thyme, minced
Leaves of 1 sprig sage, minced
Salt and freshly ground black pepper to taste
Breadcrumbs for dredging
Extra-virgin olive oil for frying

Steam the fillets and mince them. Scrub the potatoes and place them (unpeeled) in a pot with cold water to cover. Bring to a boil and cook until soft, then peel and crush with a potato ricer.

Place the minced fish in a bowl and add an equal amount of potatoes. Add smoked tench to taste, as well as thyme and sage. Season with salt and pepper and mix to make a well-combined mixture.

Pinch off a piece of the mixture and roll it between your palms into a ball the size of a walnut. Repeat with remaining mixture. Dredge the croquettes in breadcrumbs, then fry in hot oil until golden, just a few minutes. Drain briefly on paper towels, season with salt, and serve.

LUPO ALLA MARINARA 🍅
Wolffish with Tomatoes
Ristorante Casina dei Mille, Melito di Porto Salvo (Reggio Calabria), Calabria

Wolffish is in the cod family and lives in sandy and muddy waters. It is very tasty, but does not keep well. The tomato sauce resulting from this recipe can also be served over pasta.

SERVES 4
1 wolffish (about 2½ pounds)
2 cloves garlic, thinly sliced
Extra-virgin olive oil for sautéing
2 plum tomatoes, peeled, seeded, and chopped, juices reserved
Salt and freshly ground black pepper to taste
Leaves of 1 sprig parsley, minced

Scale, gut, clean, and fillet the fish. Extract any flesh from the head and reserve separately. (It will be in small pieces; if not, chop.)

In a skillet, sauté the garlic in oil until browned. Add the pieces from the head. Cook for a few minutes, then add the tomatoes and their juices. Season with salt and pepper and add the fillets. Add about ½ cup water and cook over low heat until fillets are opaque, 10 to 15 minutes. Sprinkle with minced parsley and serve.

POLPETTINE DI LAVARELLO CON POMODORO E BASILICO 🌿
Whitefish "Meatballs" with Tomato and Basil
Ristorante La Terrazza, Nago-Torbole (Trento), Trentino-Alto Adige

Coregonus lavaretus is a whitefish in the salmonid family that lives in deep-water lakes. In Italy, it is found mostly in the Benaco area. These can be served with a salad or with some polenta. Drizzle the finished dish with extra-virgin olive oil from the northern basin of Lake Garda, the northernmost olive-growing area.

SERVES 4
1 whitefish (about 14 ounces)
¼ cup unbleached all-purpose flour or 00 flour
Extra-virgin olive oil for sautéing
Salt and freshly ground black pepper to taste
1 small leek, thinly sliced
½ cup dry white wine
3 pear tomatoes, diced
Leaves of 1 sprig basil, thinly sliced

Clean and fillet the fish. Mince the flesh. Shape the minced flesh into small balls and dredge in the flour. In a skillet, heat a small amount of extra-virgin olive oil. Cook the balls of fish until golden on all sides. Season with salt and pepper and sprinkle on the leek. Add the wine and cook until it has evaporated, then add the tomatoes. Sprinkle on the basil, stir to combine, and serve hot.

FRITTO DI PIGNOI
Fried Goby
Gigi Boscolo, Chioggia (Venezia), Veneto

Cut and scale small goby, and remove the heads. Rinse and dry thoroughly. Dredge lightly in semolina flour, which will result in extra-crispy fish with a soft center. Fry in very hot extra-virgin olive oil until golden, about 5 minutes, and drain briefly on paper towels. Season with salt. Sprinkle with lemon juice, and serve with hot polenta or grilled slices of cooled polenta.

POLPETTE DI CAVEDANO
Chub "Meatballs"
Ristorante Fior di Roccia, Lon di Vezzano (Trento), Trentino–Alto Adige

At the Taverna del Capitan in Porto di Brenzone, similar meatballs are made with chub, milk, garlic, parsley, grated cheese, breadcrumbs, and eggs. They are moistened with a few drops of white wine after they are cooked and then served piping hot.

SERVES 4

10 ounces chub fillets
1 egg white
Leaves of 1 sprig marjoram
½ cup minced shallots
1 small piece of white bread (about 2 by 2 inches)
¾ cup heavy cream
Salt and freshly ground black pepper to taste
Fish broth for cooking
6 cups mesclun
Wine vinegar for dressing
Extra-virgin olive oil for dressing
Ground ginger to taste
¼ cup hop shoots

In a food processor fitted with the metal blade, grind the fish and then add the egg white. Add a couple of ice cubes to keep cold while you mix to incorporate. Add the marjoram and shallots. Moisten the bread with a little cream and add to the food processor. Whip the remaining cream to soft peaks and fold into the mixture. Season with salt and pepper and mix until well combined.

Form the mixture into small meatballs and simmer in the fish broth. While the meatballs are cooking, make a vinaigrette for the mesclun, flavor the vinaigrette with ginger, season with salt, and toss to combine. To serve, line each plate with some of the dressed mesclun, place the fish meatballs on top, and scatter on the hops.

POLPETTE DI RICCIOLA
Amberjack "Meatballs"
Alfonso La Rosa, Catania, Sicilia

To serve 4 people, mince about 14 ounces amberjack flesh. In a bowl, beat 1 large egg, then mix with the minced fish and a minced garlic clove. Add minced capers (about 1 tablespoon), a pinch of oregano, a few tablespoons of breadcrumbs, and a little water. Season with salt and pepper. Adjust breadcrumbs and/or water to make a mixture that forms a ball when you squeeze it in your hand. Shape into small balls and fry them in hot oil until golden brown on all sides. Drain briefly on paper towels and serve hot.

MEDAGLIONI DI PESCATRICE AL VINO 🌿

Monkfish Medallions in Wine

Trattoria La Taverna, Cortellazzo di Jesolo (Venezia), Veneto

After the wine—Malvasia Istriana, a dry white wine—has evaporated, you can vary this dish by adding capers and or chopped cherry tomatoes, as well as basil. Serve with 1 pound (about 6 medium) carrots, sliced into rounds and boiled until tender.

SERVES 4

1 monkfish (about 3⅓ pounds)
Unbleached all-purpose flour for dredging
1 tablespoon unsalted butter
1 tablespoon extra-virgin olive oil
Salt and freshly ground black pepper to taste
1 cup Malvasia Istriana wine (see note)

Remove and discard the head and skin from the monkfish. Wash, dry thoroughly, and cut the tail into medallions. Dredge the medallions in flour.

In a skillet, heat the butter and oil. Brown the monkfish medallions on both sides, season with salt and pepper, then add the wine and let it evaporate. Serve hot.

CODA DI ROSPO CON VERDURE E MANDORLE 🥕

Monkfish with Vegetables and Almonds

Osteria del Borgo Antico, Gioia del Colle (Bari), Puglia

This dish is a perfect illustration of Italy's waste-not-want-not cooking philosophy: not a single part of the monkfish goes to waste. Monkfish is difficult to clean, so you would be wise to ask your fishmonger to do it for you, but do request that the scraps and head be set aside for this recipe.

SERVES 4

4 monkfish (about 9 ounces each)
3 medium carrots
3 ribs celery
1 to 2 bulbs fennel
1 to 2 zucchini
1 to 2 yellow onions
Extra-virgin olive oil for sautéing, browning, and drizzling
1 sprig wild fennel, chopped
Salt and freshly ground black pepper to taste
Leaves of 1 sprig sage, chopped
Leaves of 1 sprig thyme, minced
⅓ cup almonds, finely chopped

Clean the monkfish, reserving scraps and heads to make broth.

Cut 2 carrots, 2 ribs celery, fennel bulbs, and zucchini into lozenges. Bring a pot of water to a boil and add first the carrots, celery, and fennel. Cook for 5 minutes, then add the zucchini. Continue cooking until all are tender. Remove the vegetables with a slotted spoon or skimmer, drain well, and set aside. Reserve broth.

To make the sauce, chop 1 carrot, 1 rib celery, and the onions. Sauté briefly in a small amount of oil, then add the wild fennel and reserved fish scraps and heads. Add enough of the reserved vegetable cooking water to cover by several inches and cook for 1 hour. The liquid should be greatly reduced.

Preheat the oven to 350°F. Slice the monkfish into fillets, season with salt and pepper, and brown in a little oil in an ovenproof nonstick pan. Scatter on the sage and transfer to the oven. Bake until the fish is cooked through.

In a skillet, sauté the cooked vegetables in a little oil with the thyme. Season with salt and pepper. Arrange on a platter and place the monkfish on top. Sprinkle on the almonds. Strain the reduced sauce and drizzle it over the fish, along with a little extra-virgin olive oil.

PESCE RAGNO IN UMIDO 🐚
Stewed Monkfish
Libero Federici, Castiglione della Pescaia (Grosseto), Toscana

Preheat the oven to 350°F. Place a whole gutted monkfish (about 2½ pounds to start) with gills and fins removed in a baking pan. Season with salt and pepper. Sprinkle on minced garlic, minced parsley, and fennel seeds. Add about 1 pound plum tomatoes that have been seeded and crushed. Drizzle on a generous amount (about ½ cup) extra-virgin olive oil and 1 cup white wine. Bake in the preheated oven until cooked through, about 20 minutes. Skin the fish, fillet it, and serve the fillets with the tomatoes and pan juices on top.

RANA PESCATRICE ALLA CACCIATORA 🌿
Hunter's Style Monkfish
Ristorante Circolo della Vela, Pescara, Abruzzo

In northern Italy, something cooked *alla cacciatora*, or hunter's style, is generally stewed with tomatoes and onion and often lardo or pancetta. In central Italy, the same phrase indicates a dish scented with garlic, rosemary, and sometimes vinegar. In both cases, this treatment is usually lavished on meat, but here it is used with fish—and the results are fantastic.

SERVES 4
½ cup extra-virgin olive oil
1 monkfish (about 2½ pounds), cleaned, filleted, and sliced
Salt to taste
1 clove garlic, minced
Leaves of 1 sprig parsley, minced
Leaves of 1 sprig rosemary
10 Pachino cherry tomatoes, diced
Black olives in brine, pitted, to taste
1 cup dry white wine

Place the olive oil in a skillet off the heat. Add the monkfish to the skillet and season with salt. Scatter on the garlic, parsley, rosemary, tomatoes, and olives. Place over medium heat, and as soon as the monkfish begins to brown, add the white wine. Cook for 10 additional minutes. Serve hot.

RANA PESCATRICE ALLA BRACE CON IL SUO FEGATO 🌿
Grilled Monkfish and Monkfish Liver
Trattoria da Maria, Fano (Pesaro and Urbino), Marche

For this dish you will need whole monkfish with their heads and skin, and preferably with their livers, as monkfish liver is a delicacy. No need to remove the livers—they will grill along with the monkfish.

SERVES 2
2 monkfish (about 2 pounds each)
Extra-virgin olive oil for coating fish
Leaves of 1 sprig parsley, finely minced
Salt to taste

Preheat a grill (preferably charcoal) to low heat. Skin the monkfish. Remove their eyes, mouths, and gills. Soak in cold water for about 10 minutes. Dry thoroughly with a thick cotton dish towel. Coat with a generous amount of olive oil. Scatter the minced parsley over the fish. Cook on the prepared grill until the flesh is very soft. Salt and serve.

CACCIUCCO ALLA LIVORNESE 🌶
Livorno-Style Fish and Shellfish Stew
Trattoria In Caciaia, Antignano di Livorno, Toscana

acciucco is Toscana's answer to the brodetto found along the Adriatic coast (see recipe at right). The name *cacciucco* is a Turkish word meaning "little bits and pieces." This is a typical recipe from the Livorno area; the fish stew in Viareggio is less spicy and often features additional types of fish, including mullet and monkfish.

SERVES 12

- 3½ pounds saltwater fish, such as gurnard, dogfish, weever, scorpionfish
- 2 carrots
- 2 ribs celery
- 2 medium yellow onions
- 1 pound cuttlefish
- 1 pound octopus
- ¼ cup plus 2 tablespoons extra-virgin olive oil
- 4 cloves garlic
- Crushed chili pepper to taste
- Salt to taste
- 1 cup white wine
- 2 tablespoons tomato paste
- 1 pound mantis shrimp and other types of shrimp
- 12 mussels
- 24 clams
- 12 slices Tuscan (unsalted) bread

Scale and gut the saltwater fish. Cut off the heads and remove the bones. Roughly chop 1 carrot and 1 rib celery and quarter 1 onion. Combine the heads, bones, chopped carrot, chopped celery, and quartered onion in a pot with a generous amount of water to cover. Bring to a boil, skim, and simmer until you have a flavorful broth. Strain the broth and set aside, but keep warm. Cut any large fillets of fish into strips.

While the broth is cooking, clean the cuttlefish and octopus and cut into strips. In a pot heat ¼ cup olive oil and brown 2 cloves garlic. Add the cuttlefish, cook for a few minutes, then add the octopus. Season with chili pepper and salt and add ½ cup of the wine. Dissolve 1 tablespoon tomato paste in a small amount of warm water and add that as well. Cook for 10 minutes.

In a large pot, heat the remaining 2 tablespoons oil. Add 1 clove garlic and brown. Add the saltwater fish and the shrimp. Season with salt. When they begin to brown, add the remaining ½ cup wine. When the wine has evaporated, dissolve the remaining 1 tablespoon tomato paste in the reserved warm broth and add a pinch of chili pepper, then add the broth to the pot. Cook over medium heat.

In a separate pot, very briefly cook the mussels and clams just until most of the shells open.

Toast the bread, rub it with the remaining garlic clove, and sprinkle it with chili pepper if desired. Place the toast on a platter. Arrange the cuttlefish and octopus on top, then the fish and shellfish with their cooking liquid. Arrange the clams and mussels on top and serve.

BRODETTO SAMBENEDETTESE
San Benedetto-Style Fish and Shellfish Stew
Associazione Mare Bunazz, San Benedetto del Tronto (Ascoli Piceno), Marche

Every town on the Adriatic coast has its own version of fish stew, or *brodetto*. San Benedetto del Tronto in the Marche region boasts a brodetto that is yellow-green in color and on the acidic side due to the inclusion of not-fully-ripe tomatoes, green peppers, and vinegar. The latter is probably a throwback to the days when fishing boats could only be stocked with food and drink that would not risk going bad, so the men on board drank a mixture of water and vinegar, known as *masa*, in place of wine.

SERVES 4

- 1 medium yellow onion, thinly sliced
- ½ cup extra-virgin olive oil
- 1 pound firm tomatoes, chopped
- 1 pound green bell peppers, chopped
- 1 chili pepper, chopped
- Salt to taste
- ¼ cup white wine vinegar
- 2 to 4 cuttlefish, cleaned
- 1 monkfish, scaled and gutted
- 2 dogfish fillets
- 1 turbot, scaled and gutted
- 1 tub gurnard, scaled and gutted
- 1 scorpionfish, scaled and gutted
- 1 sole, scaled and gutted
- 2 to 3 mullet, scaled and gutted
- 2 skate wings
- 2 to 4 crabs
- 2 to 4 mantis shrimp

In a large pot, sauté the onion in the olive oil. Add the tomatoes, bell peppers, and chili pepper. Season lightly with salt and cook over medium-low heat for 15 minutes, stirring occasionally. Add the vinegar and cook for an additional 10 minutes.

Add the cuttlefish and let them cook for a few minutes, then add the other fish in layers, from the heartiest and largest to the smallest and most delicate: monkfish, dogfish, turbot, tub gurnard, scorpionfish, sole, mullet, skate wings, crabs, mantis shrimp. Shake the pot occasionally to avoid sticking, but don't stir, as you want to leave the fish whole. If necessary, add a little water to keep from sticking. Once all the fish are in, cook for about 20 minutes.

BRODETTO ALLA TERMOLESE
Termoli-Style Fish Stew
Ristorante San Carlo, Termoli (Campobasso), Molise

It is preferable to cook this in a terra-cotta pot. You can serve it right in the pot, accompanied by slices of bread that you have browned in some olive oil and then sprinkled with vinegar.

SERVES 4

- 4 to 6 mussels
- 4 to 6 clams
- 1 clove garlic
- 1 small yellow onion, thinly sliced
- Extra-virgin olive oil for sautéing
- 2 plum tomatoes, diced
- Salt to taste
- 2 pounds mixed fish, such as skate, monkfish, sole, baby cod, baby cuttlefish, and scampi, scaled, gutted, and cleaned as appropriate
- Leaves of 1 sprig parsley, minced

Place the mussels and clams in a pot, cover (do not add water), and place over medium heat until the shells have opened. Discard any unopened shells and strain any liquid remaining in the pan to remove any grit. Set aside.

In a pot, sauté the garlic and onion in olive oil. Add the tomatoes, season lightly with salt, and add about ¼ cup water and ¼ cup of the shellfish cooking liquid. Bring to a boil, turn down to a brisk simmer, and gradually add the fish to the pot, beginning with the thicker fish that will take longer to cook and ending with those that will cook quickly.

When all the fish is cooked, remove from the heat, garnish with parsley, and serve.

BURIDDA DI MOSCARDINI ALLE ERBE
Musk Octopus with Herbs and Garlic
Ristorante Pippo, Spotorno (Savona), Liguria

*B*uridda is usually a mixed seafood stew, but this elegant variation uses only musk octopus, a variety of octopus from the Mediterranean. Baby octopus can be used as a substitute. Ligurian herbs typically include thyme, sage, rosemary, tarragon, chives, marjoram, and basil. Pigato is a white wine.

SERVES 4

3½ pounds musk octopus (see note), cleaned
2 cloves garlic
A generous amount mixed aromatic Ligurian herbs (see note)
Extra-virgin olive oil for sautéing
1 cup Pigato wine
¼ cup pine nuts
1 tablespoon capers, rinsed and drained
¼ cup Taggiasca olives, pitted
1 small piece chili pepper (optional)
Salt and freshly ground black pepper to taste
2 tomatoes, cut into small dice
3 to 4 basil leaves

Steam the octopus for 10 minutes. Pat dry. Meanwhile, mince together the garlic and the herbs. Marinate the cooked octopus in this mixture for at least 1 hour. Remove the octopus from the herb mixture. Strain the herb mixture and reserve any liquid. Sauté the octopus in a skillet in a small amount of olive oil. Add the wine and when it has evaporated add the liquid from the herbs, the pine nuts, the capers, the olives, and the chili pepper, if using. Season with salt and pepper. Cook until the octopus are very tender. Add the tomatoes and stir to combine. Tear the basil leaves into the dish and serve hot.

MOSCARDINI ALLA DIAVOLA
Spicy Musk Octopus
Osteria Vino e Farinata, Savona, Liguria

*T*his dish is delicious with a generous amount of chili pepper, but of course you can adjust to suit your own tastes. Musk octopus can be replaced with baby octopus.

SERVES 4

1 medium yellow onion
1 carrot
1 clove garlic
Leaves of 1 sprig parsley
Extra-virgin olive oil for sautéing
2 pounds musk octopus, cleaned
1 cup dry white wine (Pigato or Vermentino)
4 canned seeded and peeled tomatoes
Salt to taste
Ground chili pepper to taste

Mince together the onion, carrot, garlic, and parsley and sauté in a skillet in hot oil. Add the octopus and cook over high heat until the octopus has given off all its liquid. Add the wine, and when it has evaporated crush the tomatoes with a fork and add those as well. Season with salt and chili pepper, then cover and cook over medium heat until tender.

POLPO IN GALERA ❗
"Imprisoned" Octopus
Trattoria dell'Abbondanza, Pistoia, Toscana

The name of this dish refers to the cooking method: the octopus must remain "imprisoned" in a covered pot for a long period of time. You can either use small octopus here and leave them whole, or purchase a large octopus and cut it into strips.

SERVES 4

2 cloves garlic
Leaves of 1 sprig parsley, minced
Extra-virgin olive oil for sautéing
1 to 1½ pounds octopus, cleaned
Salt and freshly ground black pepper to taste
1 cup dry white wine
1 cup red wine vinegar
5 medium potatoes, peeled and diced
Juice of 1 lemon

Mince together the garlic and about half of the parsley and sauté in a pot in hot oil. When the garlic begins to brown, add the octopus and salt and pepper. Add the wine and once it has evaporated, cover and cook over low heat for 30 minutes.

After 30 minutes, add the vinegar and potatoes. Cover and cook over low heat for an additional 30 minutes. The potatoes should be tender—if not, cook until they are.

Sprinkle on the lemon juice and the remaining parsley. Stir and cook over low heat for 2 to 3 additional minutes to combine the flavors.

CALAMARI RIPIENI 🌿
Squid with Shellfish Stuffing
Vecchia Cantina, Napoli, Campania

Stuffed calamari are eaten in many areas along the Italian coastline. Sometimes the tentacles are chopped and sautéed in olive oil, then combined with lemon juice, breadcrumbs, egg, parsley, grated caciocavallo cheese, pine nuts, and raisins for the stuffing. The stuffed calamari can also be cooked in tomato sauce flavored with garlic, parsley, and basil, or with black olives and minced garlic. In Sardegna, calamari are stuffed with garlic, parsley, anchovies, breadcrumbs, eggs, and minced cooked tentacles and grilled or baked. In Puglia, too, stuffed calamari are traditionally grilled or baked, and in Liguria they are baked and the stuffing often incorporates a little minced mortadella.

SERVES 4

2 cloves garlic
Leaves of 1 sprig parsley
6 to 8 mussels or clams, shelled
8 shrimp, shelled
¼ cup breadcrumbs
2 lemons
½ cup dry white wine
Extra-virgin olive oil for moistening and sautéing
Salt and freshly ground black pepper to taste
4 large calamari, 6 to 8 inches long, cleaned

Mince together the garlic, parsley, mussels, and shrimp. (You can steam the mussels briefly to open the shells if you like.) Combine with the breadcrumbs, juice of ½ lemon, 2 tablespoons white wine, and a little oil to moisten. Season with salt and pepper. Mix to combine thoroughly, then stuff the calamari bodies with this mixture. Don't overstuff them—the filling shouldn't be leaking out. Seal the calamari by closing the tentacles over the openings and fixing them in place with toothpicks.

Brown the stuffed calamari in olive oil in a skillet for a few minutes, adding a little water if necessary to keep them from sticking. When the outside of the calamari is a dark pink color, add the remaining wine to the skillet and cook until it has evaporated. Slice the remaining 1½ lemons and garnish the calamari with the lemon slices.

TOTANI E PATATE 🖤
Squid and Potatoes
Trattoria Il Sestante, Villa Rosa di Martinsicuro (Teramo), Abruzzo

The flavor of the squid really comes through in this simple preparation. Cooking time will depend on how small you cut the potatoes.

SERVES 4
14 ounces baby squid, cleaned
Extra-virgin olive oil for sautéing
¼ cup dry white wine
7 ounces (2 small) potatoes, peeled and diced
¼ cup mixed aromatic herbs, minced
Leaves of 1 sprig rosemary, minced
1 bay leaf
Salt to taste

If the squid are very small, cut them in half, but if they are on the larger side, chop them into pieces.

In a skillet, heat a little olive oil for sautéing and add the squid. When they begin to brown, add the wine and cook until it has evaporated. Add about ¼ cup water to the skillet and cook over medium heat for 10 minutes, then add the potatoes, herbs, and the bay leaf and cook until the potatoes are tender. Season with salt and serve.

TOTANI RIPIENI
Stuffed Squid with Tomatoes
Osteria Al Moro, Campo nell'Elba (Livorno), Toscana

This is a traditional recipe from the island of Elba, where stuffed squid are as popular as they are in Liguria. Use a high-quality olive oil from Toscana.

SERVES 6
3 to 4 slices Tuscan (unsalted) bread, crusts removed
½ cup whole milk
8 calamari, about 10 ounces each, cleaned
Extra-virgin olive oil for sautéing
3 cloves garlic
Salt to taste
About 1 cup loosely packed chard, blanched, squeezed dry, and minced
Grated Parmigiano Reggiano to taste
1 large egg, lightly beaten
Leaves of 1 sprig parsley
Freshly ground black pepper to taste
Freshly grated nutmeg to taste
Ground chili pepper to taste
1 cup red wine
1½ cups chopped tomatoes
Fish broth for moistening pan, if needed

Soak the bread in the milk. Cut the tentacles off of the calamari. Chop about half the tentacles and set aside. In a skillet, heat a small amount of oil. Add 1 clove garlic and salt, then 2 of the calamari bodies and the remaining half of the tentacles.

Mince the cooked calamari and transfer to a bowl. Remove the bread from the milk, squeeze dry, and crumble into the bowl. Add the chard, Parmigiano, and the egg. Mince the remaining garlic and the parsley and add about 1 tablespoon to the bowl with the cooked calamari mixture, reserving the rest. Season the mixture with salt, pepper, and nutmeg. Mix to combine, then reserve about 1 tablespoon of the stuffing mixture. Stuff the remaining calamari bodies with the remaining mixture. Do not overfill. Close with toothpicks.

In a wide, shallow skillet, sauté the remaining garlic and parsley with some chili pepper in olive oil. Add the stuffed calamari. When they are browned on all sides, add the wine. When the wine has evaporated, add the reserved chopped tentacles and the remainder of the stuffing, and the chopped tomatoes. If the pan seems dry, moisten with a small amount of fish broth.

Season with salt and cook over low heat until cooked through, 20 to 25 minutes, piercing the calamari occasionally with a fork so they don't break.

SEPPIE CON PISELLI

Cuttlefish with Peas

Enoteca Corsi, Roma, Lazio

When cooked for a long time over low heat, cuttlefish are tender, moist, and creamy.

SERVES 4

9 ounces cuttlefish, cleaned
½ medium yellow onion, thinly sliced
Extra-virgin olive oil for sautéing
1 small piece chili pepper
2 cloves garlic, halved
½ cup dry white wine
1 cup quartered Pachino cherry tomatoes
1⅓ cups peas
Salt to taste
Broth (optional)

Cut the cuttlefish into strips 1 to 1½ inches long and ½ inch wide. In a skillet, sauté the onion in olive oil with the chili pepper and garlic. As soon as the garlic browns, remove and discard it and add the cuttlefish to the pan. Cook, stirring occasionally, for 5 minutes, then add the wine. When the wine has evaporated, add the tomatoes and the peas. Season with salt, cover, and cook over low heat for 40 minutes. Check occasionally to make sure the pan isn't getting to dry, and if it is, moisten with hot broth or hot water.

SEPPIE AL NERO

Cuttlefish in Their Ink

Trattoria Ballarin, Mirano (Venezia), Veneto

If you have pan juices left over after serving this delicious dish, use them to flavor a risotto—they shouldn't go to waste! The traditional accompaniment to this dish is white polenta.

SERVES 4

2 pounds medium cuttlefish, cleaned and ink reserved
¼ cup extra-virgin olive oil
1 clove garlic
½ cup dry white wine
Salt and freshly ground black pepper to taste
Juice of ½ lemon
Leaves of 1 sprig parsley, minced

Cut the cuttlefish into strips. Heat the oil in a skillet and add the garlic. When the garlic has browned, remove it and add the cuttlefish. Cook, stirring, over medium heat for 3 minutes. Add the wine and when it has evaporated, cover and cook over low heat.

While the cuttlefish are cooking, thin the cuttlefish ink with a little warm water, then strain through cheesecloth and add to the skillet with the cuttlefish. Cook until cuttlefish are tender, about 30 minutes. When the cuttlefish are cooked, season with salt and pepper.

Combine the lemon juice and parsley and add to the dish off the heat.

CAPPON MAGRO ♣
Classic Ligurian Seafood Salad
Ristorante Da Casetta, Borgio Verezzi (Savona), Liguria

no doubt cappon magro was created as a way for intrepid sailors to recycle leftovers, as it consists of cooked vegetables and leftover fish stew. Traditionally it is presented in a big pyramid, though, which gives it a rather opulent look. It is one of the signature dishes of the Liguria region. This version calls for tuna mosciame, which is cured, dried tuna. Another unusual ingredient is sailors' rusks—a kind of dry cracker that could be kept on board almost indefinitely. You can steam or boil beets for this dish if you like, but it's convenient to purchase vacuum-packed cooked beets.

SERVES 15
1 hake (about 7 pounds)
Vegetable broth for boiling hake
4½ pounds clams
4½ pounds shrimp
7 pounds mussels
2 pounds zucchini
1 pound green beans
2 pounds potatoes
2 pounds black salsify
2 pounds (about 12) carrots
6 young artichokes
1 pound celery
3 cups extra-virgin olive oil
1 pound cooked beets
2 rolls
1¼ cups wine vinegar
8 anchovy fillets, rinsed and drained
1 clove garlic
2 cups loosely packed parsley leaves
¾ cup pine nuts
6 hard-boiled large eggs
1½ cups capers, rinsed and drained
½ cup pitted olives
14 ounces sailors' rusks
10 ounces tuna mosciame (see note), thinly sliced

Boil the hake in vegetable broth. Cook the clams, shrimp, and mussels separately until just done. Boil the zucchini, green beans, potatoes, black salsify, carrots, artichokes, and celery whole in separate pots, as they will all have different cooking times. Cut the zucchini, green beans, salsify, carrots, and celery into small dice and toss to combine. Cut out the fuzzy choke of the artichokes and pull off and discard leaves. Dice the hearts and bottoms and add to the other diced vegetables. Toss with 1 cup olive oil. Peel the potatoes and slice. Peel the beets and slice. (Leave separate.)

For the sauce, soak the rolls in ¾ cup vinegar until soft. Mince together the anchovy fillets, garlic, parsley, pine nuts, hard-boiled eggs, capers, olives, and rolls. Stir in 1 cup olive oil and set aside.

Fillet the cooked hake and dice. Peel the shrimp and shell the clams and mussels and combine. Toss with the remaining 1 cup olive oil.

Combine the remaining ½ cup vinegar with ½ cup water and dip the rusks in the liquid to soften. To construct the dish, on a large patter with a ¾-inch border arrange a base of moistened rusks. Brush on some of the sauce, then arrange the potato slices in a layer and brush on some sauce. Place the mosciame in a layer on top and brush with a thin layer of sauce. Place the beets in a layer and top with sauce. Make a layer of about half of the hake, shrimp, mussels, and clams and top with sauce. Make a layer of about half of the diced vegetables and top with sauce. Make a layer of the remaining fish and shellfish and top with the sauce. Make a layer of the remaining diced vegetables. Brush the remaining sauce on the top and sides and serve.

SEPPIE IN UMIDO
Stewed Cuttlefish
Buffet da Siora Rosa, Trieste, Friuli–Venezia Giulia

Stewed cuttlefish can be served with polenta, but they are also delicious with pasta or rice.

SERVES 4

1 clove garlic, minced
Leaves of 1 sprig parsley, minced
Extra-virgin olive oil for sautéing
3½ pounds cuttlefish, cleaned and cut into strips
½ cup dry white wine
2 to 3 tablespoons tomato puree (optional)
Salt to taste
Ground chili pepper to taste

In a skillet, sauté the garlic and parsley in oil. Add the cuttlefish and cook for a few minutes to flavor. Add the wine and the tomato puree, if using. Cook over high heat for 3 minutes, then cover and cook over low heat for 1 hour. Check occasionally to make sure the cuttlefish liquid is not evaporating too quickly and adjust the heat if it is, but don't add water to the pan as it will cause the cuttlefish to get tough. Remove from the heat, season with salt, and sprinkle with a pinch of ground chili pepper before serving.

CAPPESANTE AL FORNO
Baked Scallops
Enoteca Al Calice, Venezia, Veneto

Another scallop dish from the Veneto region calls for simply tossing the scallops with olive oil and minced parsley and broiling or baking them for a few minutes, just until they begin to brown. Scallops are also delicious when lightly dredged in flour or sprinkled with a small amount of grated cheese, and they can topped with thinly sliced truffle or chopped mushrooms.

SERVES 4

8 scallops in their shells
⅔ cup breadcrumbs
¼ cup thyme leaves, minced
Extra-virgin olive oil for moistening breadcrumbs
Salt and freshly ground black pepper to taste

Preheat a convection oven to 325°F.
   Open the scallop shells, detach the scallops, and wash and dry them. Reserve the shells. Combine the breadcrumbs and thyme with enough oil to make a moist mixture. Season with salt and pepper. Toss the scallops with the breadcrumb mixture and return them to their shells. Arrange on a baking sheet and bake in the preheated oven until the scallops are just golden, 10 to 12 minutes. Serve immediately.

SEPPIE RIPIENE AL VERDE
Stuffed Cuttlefish
Osteria dell'Acquasanta, Mele (Genova), Liguria

Cuttlefish are similar to squid but larger, and they tend to be thicker as well.

SERVES 4

1 roll, crust removed
2 cloves garlic
4 ounces prosciutto cotto
Leaves of 1 sprig marjoram
3 egg yolks
½ cup grated Parmigiano Reggiano
2 pounds cuttlefish, cleaned and ink reserved
1 medium yellow onion, chopped
Extra-virgin olive oil for sautéing
Leaves of 1 sprig parsley, minced
½ cup dry white wine
Salt and freshly ground black pepper to taste
Fish broth, if needed

Soak the roll in water to soften. Mince 1 clove garlic, the prosciutto, and the marjoram leaves together. Squeeze the soaked roll dry and crumble into the bowl. Add the prosciutto mixture, egg yolks, and grated cheese. Mix to combine.

Set aside 1 cuttlefish and stuff the others with the prosciutto mixture. Close with toothpicks and arrange them with their tentacles in place. Sauté the onion and the remaining clove garlic in oil in a large skillet. Cut the reserved cuttlefish into strips and add to the skillet with the parsley. Cook for 10 minutes, then add the wine. Cook briefly to let some of the wine evaporate, then arrange the stuffed cuttlefish in the skillet in a single layer. Season with salt and pepper, cover with a heavy lid, and cook until the cuttlefish are tender and opaque, checking frequently to make sure the pan isn't getting too dry; if it is, moisten with broth.

GRANZOPORO AL ROSMARINO

Crabs with Rosemary
Trattoria La Taverna, Cortellazzo di Jesolo (Venezia), Veneto

In Venezia and the surrounding area, crab is usually served in its shell. In some areas, the crabmeat is eaten raw topped with warm garlic butter and minced parsley.

SERVES 4

4 crabs
Extra-virgin olive oil for sautéing
2 cloves garlic, minced
Leaves of 1 sprig rosemary, minced
½ cup dry white wine
2 tablespoons unsalted butter
Leaves of 1 sprig parsley, minced
Salt and freshly ground black pepper to taste

Steam the crabs for 15 minutes. Let them cool, then extract the meat (take care not to crack the shells if you'd like to serve the meat on them) and chop. In a skillet, heat some oil and sauté the crabmeat with the garlic and rosemary. Cook for 5 minutes, stirring frequently, then

add the wine, butter, and parsley. Season with salt and pepper and cook until the crabmeat is tender and wine has almost completely evaporated but not quite.

MAZZANCOLLE CON PATATE

Tiger Shrimp with Potatoes
Osteria Teatro Strabacco, Ancona, Marche

Tiger shrimp, sometimes called striped shrimp, are large, meaty shrimp fished in the Mediterranean. Be sure to purchase the type of pancetta that comes in a slab for this dish, and not the rolled type.

SERVES 4

1 pound (3 medium) potatoes
Salt to taste
2 tablespoons unsalted butter, softened
½ cup grated Parmigiano Reggiano
Freshly ground white pepper to taste
3 tablespoons extra-virgin olive oil
1 medium yellow onion, thinly sliced
8 medium tiger shrimp, peeled
8 slices pancetta (see note)
Leaves of 1 sprig parsley

Boil the potatoes in a generous amount of salted water until tender. Let them cool in the cooking water, then drain, peel, and crush. Heat the crushed potatoes in the top of a double boiler. Stir in the butter and whisk energetically. Whisk in the Parmigiano and season with salt and pepper.

In a skillet, heat 2 tablespoons extra-virgin olive oil and brown the onion. Wrap each shrimp in a slice of pancetta and add to the pan. Cook for 10 minutes.

Arrange the mashed potatoes on a serving platter. Arrange the cooked shrimp on top. Sprinkle with the parsley, drizzle on the remaining 1 tablespoon oil, and serve.

MUSCOLI RIPIENI 🍅
Stuffed Mussels
Antica Hostaria Secondini, Sarbia di La Spezia, Liguria

Stuffed mussels are eaten all over Italy. In the Marche region, mussels are often stuffed with tomatoes, prosciutto, and parsley. In Toscana, a little mortadella is often included in the mix. Serve toasted bread rubbed with a garlic clove alongside this version from Liguria.

SERVES 4

- 4 pounds mussels
- 1 piece of bread (2 by 2 inches), crusts removed
- ¼ cup whole milk
- ¾ cup minced mortadella
- ½ cup grated Parmigiano Reggiano
- 2 large eggs, lightly beaten
- Leaves of 1 sprig thyme, minced
- 2 cloves garlic, minced
- Leaves of 1 sprig parsley, minced
- ⅓ cup tuna in olive oil, drained
- Salt and freshly ground black pepper to taste
- Extra-virgin olive oil for sautéing
- 1 carrot, minced
- 1 medium yellow onion, minced
- 1 sun-dried tomato, minced
- 1 cup dry white wine
- 2 cups chunky tomato puree

Pick out the 24 best-looking mussels and scrub them until they are very shiny and smooth. Use a paring knife to open the shells, keeping the shells intact and the mussels attached.

Place the remaining mussels in a pot and steam them until the shells open. Shell the mussels, discard the shells, and mince the meat. Strain and reserve the cooking liquid. Discard any mussels that refuse to open.

Soak the bread in the milk. In a bowl, combine the minced mortadella and about half of the minced mussels. Add the grated Parmigiano and the eggs. Remove the bread from the milk, squeeze dry, and crumble into the bowl. Add a pinch of minced thyme, 1 tablespoon minced garlic, and about half of the parsley. Flake in the tuna. Season with salt and pepper. Mix until you have a compact, smooth mixture. Stuff the opened mussels with this mixture and seal tightly.

In a pot, sauté in extra-virgin olive oil the remaining garlic and parsley, the carrot, the onion, and the sun-dried tomato. Add the remaining minced mussel meat, then add the wine and cook, stirring occasionally, until it has evaporated. Add the tomato puree and cook for 5 minutes, then add the stuffed mussels and cook for 25 minutes. If the pan begins to dry out, add the reserved strained cooking liquid in small amounts. Let the mussels cool slightly and serve warm.

POLPETTI ALLA LUCIANA 🐙
Baby Octopus in the Style of the Santa Lucia Neighborhood
Concetta De Carlo, Napoli, Campania

The Santa Lucia neighborhood of Napoli was once home to fishermen and their families, who lived on simple seafood dishes like this one. Place cleaned baby octopus in a large pot with water just to cover and cook over medium heat until tender, 25 to 45 minutes, depending on their size. Drain and cut into small pieces, then dress with a mixture of minced garlic, a generous amount of extra-virgin olive oil, lemon juice, a generous amount of minced parsley, salt, and pepper. Let sit at room temperature for at least 10 minutes before serving.

COZZE ALLA CATALANA 🌿
Mussels with Cherry Tomatoes
Ristorante Da Gesuino, Olbia, Sardegna

The best way to clean the outside of mussel shells is to rub them briskly against each other. This dish needs to rest for a couple of hours, but will be even more strongly flavored if you refrigerate it overnight.

SERVES 4
2 *pounds mussels*
¼ *cup cherry tomatoes, halved*
½ *medium yellow onion, thinly sliced*
1 *bunch basil, chopped*
¼ *cup extra-virgin olive oil*
1 *tablespoon wine vinegar*
Juice of ½ lemon
Salt to taste

Place the mussels in a pot, cover, and place over medium heat. Cook until the shells have opened, about 5 minutes. Shell the mussels and transfer to a bowl. Discard any unopened mussels. Add the tomatoes, onion, and basil.

In a separate bowl, whisk together the olive oil, vinegar, lemon juice, and a pinch of salt. Pour this dressing over the mussels and toss until well combined. Refrigerate for at least 2 hours and up to 24 hours before serving.

CHIOCCIOLE ALLA PAESANA 🍅
Snails Stewed in Tomato Sauce
Ristorante La Panzanella, Empoli (Firenze), Toscana

Land snails are often harvested in fields and gardens after it rains, though, of course, you can also purchase farmed snails. To clean snails, place them in a box and sprinkle with salt to encourage them to purge their liquid and innards. Then wash them in several changes of cold water. Serve these with small forks or picks so that diners can extract the meat.

SERVES 4
Extra-virgin olive oil for sautéing
1 *medium yellow onion, minced*
1 *carrot, minced*
1 *rib celery, minced*
Wild thyme leaves to taste, minced
1 *pinch ground chili pepper*
100 snails, cleaned
1 *cup dry white wine*
1 *pound ripe tomatoes, chopped, or 2 cups canned peeled tomatoes and their juices*
Salt and freshly ground black pepper to taste
About ½ cup hot broth (optional)

Heat a generous amount of olive oil in a skillet and sauté the onion, carrot, celery, wild thyme, and chili pepper. As soon as the onion begins to brown, add the snails. Add the wine and tomatoes. Season with salt and pepper and cook over low heat for 2 hours, adding hot broth or water in small amounts to keep the pot moist. Allow to cool slightly before serving.

LUMACHE ALL'ISCHITANA 🌿
Ischia-Style Snails
Ristorante Il Focolare, Flaiano di Barano d'Ischia
(Napoli), Campania

Land snails can still be collected in many parts of the island of Ischia, where they remain a popular ingredient. *Freselle* are rusks that are usually round with a hole in the center. They soak up the juices of the dish with delicious results.

SERVES 4
- 2 tablespoons extra-virgin olive oil
- 3 cloves garlic, minced
- 1 carrot, minced
- 1 small yellow onion, minced
- 1 rib celery, minced
- 48 snails, cleaned
- ½ cup dry white wine
- 2 bay leaves
- 1 tablespoon calamint
- Leaves of 1 sprig parsley
- Leaves of 1 sprig sage
- 1 strip lemon or orange zest
- 1 cup canned peeled tomatoes
- Salt to taste
- Ground chili pepper to taste
- Vegetable broth, as needed (optional)
- 4 to 5 freselle rusks

In a large skillet heat the olive oil and sauté the minced garlic, carrot, onion, and celery. Add the snails and cook for 2 minutes, then add the wine, bay leaves, calamint, parsley, sage, and zest. Add the tomatoes. Season with salt and chili pepper and cook, stirring occasionally, for 30 minutes. If the pan begins to dry out, add vegetable broth or water in small amounts. Arrange the freselle in a single layer on a serving platter and pour the snails and sauce over them.

LUMACHE IN UMIDO 🍃
Snails Stewed in White Wine and Herbs
Antica Bettola da Marisa, Rive d'Arcano (Udine),
Friuli-Venezia Giulia

Snails should be foraged in the spring, as soon as they wake up from their winter hibernation. To clean them, place them in a large non-metallic container with a couple handfuls of cornmeal for 3 to 4 days. Then boil them for 20 minutes. Drain, dry, and pick out of the shells using a knitting needle. Cut off and discard the black ends and the stomachs. Wash the remaining snail meat with a paste of cornmeal and vinegar and then rinse several times in a mixture of water and vinegar until they are completely free of any trace of slime. Of course, there's no shame in buying farmed snails. Serve these with soft polenta cooked with a little milk.

SERVES 4
- 48 snails, cleaned and prepped (see note)
- 1 medium yellow onion, minced
- 1 carrot, minced
- 1 clove garlic, peeled
- ¼ cup loosely packed parsley, minced
- Leaves of 1 sprig rosemary, minced
- 2 sage leaves, minced
- 1 cup Tocai or other dry white wine
- 2 cups beef broth
- Salt to taste

Cut each snail into 2 or 3 pieces. In a pot, combine the snails with the onion, carrot, garlic (left whole), parsley, rosemary, sage, wine, and broth. Cook until the liquid has reduced greatly, about 30 minutes. Take care not to overcook the snails, as they will go quickly from tender to tough. Remove and discard the garlic, season with salt, and serve.

POLLO ALLA CACCIATORA
Hunter's Style Chicken
Ristorante del Belbo da Bardòn, San Marzano Oliveto
(Asti), Piemonte

This classic dish is popular all over northern Italy. It can be served hot or at room temperature.

SERVES 4

4   medium yellow onions, minced
Leaves of 1 sprig rosemary, minced
Extra-virgin olive oil for sautéing
1   free-range chicken, cut up
1   cup dry white wine
1½ cups beef broth
2   ribs celery, diced
1   red bell pepper, seeded and diced
1   yellow bell pepper, seeded and diced
3 to 4 carrots, diced
Salt and freshly ground black pepper to taste
4 to 5 plum tomatoes, peeled, seeded,
     and diced
1   tablespoon sugar
Leaves of 1 sprig basil

In a large pot, sauté the onions and rosemary in olive oil until the onions begin to brown. Add the chicken pieces and brown on all sides. Add the wine and when it has evaporated add the broth and mix to combine. Simmer for 40 minutes, then add the celery, peppers, and carrots and season with salt and pepper.

Toss the tomatoes with the sugar. Chop the basil leaves and toss with the tomatoes. When the chicken is almost cooked through, an additional 30 to 35 minutes after adding the carrots, peppers, and celery, gently stir in the tomato mixture. Cook for about 10 additional minutes.

POLLO ALLA DIAVOLA
Devil's-Style Chicken
Salvatore Grieco, Firenze, Toscana

The name probably refers to both the high heat of the grill and the spicy pepper. Spatchcock a young chicken (a butcher will do this for you), season with salt and brush with extra-virgin olive oil, and grill until the outside is crisp and the meat is thoroughly cooked. When it is almost fully cooked, sprinkle on freshly ground black pepper, ground chili pepper, and breadcrumbs, which will help create a crust and will keep the spices from burning. Brush the chicken all over with a sprig of rosemary dipped in extra-virgin olive oil. Grill for a few more minutes and serve piping hot.

POLLO CON PEPERONI
Chicken with Peppers
Enoteca Corsi, Roma, Lazio

This is an ideal dish for summer, when peppers are at their peak.

SERVES 4

½   cup unbleached all-purpose flour
Salt and freshly ground black pepper to taste
1   chicken, cut into 8 pieces
¼   cup plus 2 tablespoons extra-virgin
     olive oil
1   clove garlic, halved
1   bay leaf
1   medium yellow onion, cut into julienne
2   yellow bell peppers, seeded and diced
2   red bell peppers, seeded and diced
12 Pachino cherry tomatoes, halved
1   cup dry white wine
½   cup beef broth
Leaves of 1 sprig parsley, minced

Season the flour with salt and pepper and dredge the chicken in it. In a skillet, heat 3 tablespoons olive oil and brown the chicken for 15 minutes.

In a separate large skillet, heat the remaining 3 tablespoons olive oil and add the garlic and bay leaf and cook until golden. Add the onion and stir to combine. Add the peppers. Cook for 5 minutes, stirring occasionally, then add the tomatoes and cook for an additional 5 minutes. Add the wine and cook for an additional 5 minutes. Adjust salt to taste.

Add the chicken to the skillet with the peppers and combine gently with the peppers. Add the broth and cook, stirring occasionally and turning the chicken, until the chicken is opaque and liquid has reduced, about 10 minutes. Remove and discard the bay leaf, garnish with parsley, and serve.

SPIEDO VALSABBINO
Grilled Poultry and Sage Skewers
Trattoria Castello, Castello di Serle (Brescia), Lombardia

These skewers are cooked in the traditional manner of the Val Sabbia. This is great for serving a crowd. Pair with soft polenta.

SERVES 10
- 1 chicken
- 1 rabbit
- 4 boneless spare ribs
- 10 thrushes or other game birds, plucked and cleaned
- 4 large potatoes
- Leaves of 1 bunch sage
- 20 slices pork loin or pork shoulder, or a combination of the two
- Salt to taste
- 13 sticks plus 2 tablespoons unsalted butter

Bone the chicken and skin and bone the rabbit, reserving any trimmings. Cut the chicken, rabbit, and spare ribs into pieces roughly the same size as the thrushes. Peel the potatoes and cut them into about 15 very thick slices. Place 1 sage leaf and any reserved trimmings (minced if necessary) in the center of each slice of pork loin or shoulder, season with salt, and roll up.

Thread the skewers in this order: potato slice, sage leaf, rib, sage leaf, chicken, sage leaf, rabbit, sage leaf, thrush, sage leaf, loin or shoulder roll. Prepare a grill with a generous amount of charcoal. Grill the skewers over low heat for 30 minutes, then, with a dripping pan in place, melt the butter with a few sage leaves and pour the butter over the skewers. Cook for an additional 4 to 5 hours, collecting the drippings in the dripping pan and basting occasionally. Season with salt four times during the cooking process, but not at the same time you are basting the meat with the drippings. Remove the meat from the skewers and serve hot with pan drippings.

ROLATA DI POLLO
Rolled and Sliced Chicken
Trattoria della Posta, Monforte d'Alba (Cuneo), Piemonte

This is a take on a traditional Piemontese recipe that uses veal rather than chicken. A good butcher will be able to bone a whole chicken for you while keeping it in one piece. This is lovely looking when sliced.

SERVES 6
- 6 ounces ground veal
- 6 ounces pork sausage, casing removed
- ¼ cup minced prosciutto cotto
- 1 carrot, minced
- Salt and freshly ground black pepper to taste
- 1 chicken, about 2½ pounds, cleaned and boned but kept in 1 piece
- 4 hard-boiled eggs
- ¼ cup extra-virgin olive oil

Preheat the oven to 325°F.

Combine the ground veal, sausage meat, prosciutto cotto, and minced carrot and mix by hand. Season with salt and pepper. Arrange the chicken flat, skin-side down, on a work surface and spread the veal mixture over it. Arrange the hard-boiled eggs in a line slightly off center and then roll up the chicken and truss with kitchen twine. Brush the exterior with the oil, place in a pan, and bake in the preheated oven for 30 minutes or until cooked through. Remove the twine and slice. Serve hot.

GALLINA RIPIENA DI VERZE E AMARETTI
Hen with Cabbage and Amaretto Cookie Stuffing
Hostaria San Carlo, Colombare di Moscazzano (Cremona), Lombardia

Like many dishes from the Cremona area, this is a legacy of the kind of Renaissance food that was served at court. During that era, dishes often combined savory and sweet flavors. Dark amaretti are a specialty of the Cremona region—they are crumbly rather than soft and owe their dark color to cocoa powder.

SERVES 6

1 small Savoy cabbage
½ medium yellow onion, sliced
3 tablespoons unsalted butter
1 cup crumbled dark amaretto cookies
½ cup grated Grana Padano
1 large egg, lightly beaten
Salt and freshly ground black pepper to taste
Freshly grated nutmeg to taste
1 free-range hen with yellow skin

Preheat the oven to 350°F.

Cut the cabbage into strips, discarding the hard core. Blanch the cabbage in boiling water, then drain. In a skillet sauté the onion in the butter, then add the drained cabbage and cook until it is very dry. Remove from the heat and add the crumbled cookies, grated cheese, and the egg. Season with salt, pepper, and nutmeg. Mix to combine thoroughly.

Stuff the chicken with the cabbage mixture, then sew closed with kitchen twine. Place in a baking pan and bake in the preheated oven until the juices run clear and flesh is opaque, about 1½ hours.

TACCHINO AL LIMONE
Turkey with Lemon
Trattoria Serghei, Bologna, Emília-Romagna

Columbus brought turkey to Europe from the Americas, and in the period following the Renaissance in Italy, it became a very popular kind of poultry and quickly replaced the peacock, which tended to be rather tough and leathery. Serve this simple yet satisfying dish warm with its pan juices. Cooked greens make a nice accompaniment, as does a high-quality sweet mustard.

SERVES 6

2 turkey hindquarters, boned
Juice of 2 lemons
Salt and freshly ground black pepper to taste
2 tablespoons extra-virgin olive oil
Leaves of 1 sprig rosemary

Preheat the oven to 350°F.

Rinse the turkey with the lemon juice. Roll up the turkey and truss with kitchen twine. Season with salt and pepper. Brush the turkey with the oil and place in a baking pan. Sprinkle the rosemary on all sides of the turkey. Bake in the preheated oven for 2 hours.

ANATRA IN PORCHETTA
Porchetta-Style Duck
Osteria dell'Acquolina, Terranuova Bracciolini
(Arezzo), Toscana

This is a recipe for duck that uses the classic flavors of porchetta. In Venice, stuffed duck appears on the menu for the Feast of the Most Holy Redeemer in July. A lot of delicious juices will collect in the pan as the duck cooks—be sure to drizzle them over the duck when serving.

SERVES 4 TO 6
8   *cloves garlic, unpeeled*
1   *Muscovy duck, gutted and cleaned*
4   *bay leaves*
1   *pinch wild fennel seed*
1   *thick slice pancetta*
Salt and freshly ground black pepper to taste
About 1 cup dry white wine

Preheat the oven to 350°F.

Place 4 cloves unpeeled garlic inside the duck, along with the bay leaves, fennel seeds, and pancetta. Season inside and out with salt and pepper. Place the duck in a baking pan and place the remaining 4 cloves garlic in the pan. Bake in the preheated oven for 1½ hours, splashing with a bit of wine occasionally and frequently turning the duck. To serve, carve the duck and drizzle the strained pan juices over it.

OCA CON LE CASTAGNE
Goose with Chestnuts
L'Usteria, Treviglio (Bergamo), Lombardia

At L'Usteria, the local sausage used in this dish is made of pork rib meat, broth, and cheese. This is a rich and complex dish that makes a wonderful centerpiece for a celebratory meal.

SERVES 6 TO 8
1   *goose (6½ to 9 pounds)*
3   *tablespoons unsalted butter*
12   *slices pancetta*
Salt and freshly ground black pepper to taste
2   *cups white wine*
Leaves of 1 sprig sage, minced
Leaves of 1 sprig rosemary, minced
Leaves of 1 sprig thyme, minced
20   *cipollini onions*
20   *shallots*
½   *cup beef broth*
1   *tablespoon wine vinegar*
1   *pound chestnuts, roasted, shelled, and peeled*
3 to 4 *carrots, cut into julienne*
1   *local sausage, diced*

Preheat oven to 350°F. Truss the goose with kitchen twine and brown in 2 tablespoons butter in a large ovenproof skillet with high sides. Transfer to the preheated oven and bake for 30 minutes.

Remove the goose from the oven, scrape any drippings and juices out of the skillet, and reserve. Line the pan with half of the pancetta slices and place the goose on top of them. Season with salt and pepper. Add about ½ cup wine to the pan and return to the oven.

Meanwhile, degrease the reserved drippings and juices and in a saucepan combine with the remaining 1½ cups wine. Add the sage, rosemary, and thyme and bring to a boil. Add the cipollini onions and the shallots. Stir in the remaining 1 tablespoon butter, the broth, and the vinegar. Simmer until the liquid has reduced somewhat and glazed the onions. Remove the onions with a slotted spoon or skimmer, reserving the liquid.

Add the glazed onions, the chestnuts, the carrots, and the sausage to the pan around the goose. Cover the top of the goose with the remaining slices of pancetta and cook until the goose is opaque and juices run clear, 10 to 15 additional minutes. Reheat the reserved liquid and drizzle over carved slices of goose just before serving.

OCA RIPIENA
Stuffed Goose
Ristorante Prato Gaio, Montecalvo Versiggia (Pavia), Lombardia

The two most common forms of stuffed goose in Italy are packed with minced veal, lardo, aromatics, and rice, or boiled or roasted chestnuts, sausage, and goose liver. This is a third, more unusual version.

SERVES 6

- 2 lemons, halved
- 1 large goose
- 3 cups breadcrumbs
- ¼ cup beef broth, plus more if needed
- 1 cup minced mortadella
- Leaves of 1 sprig parsley, minced
- 1 (4-ounce) fresh pork sausage, casing removed and crumbled
- 1½ cups grated Parmigiano Reggiano
- 3 large eggs, lightly beaten
- Salt and freshly ground black pepper to taste
- Extra-virgin olive oil for oiling pan
- 3 slices lardo (cured fatback)
- Leaves of 1 sprig sage
- Leaves of 1 sprig rosemary
- 1 cup red wine

Preheat the oven to 400°F. Rub the cut sides of the lemons all over the goose inside and out, squeezing the juice over it.

In a pan, heat the breadcrumbs with the broth. Set aside to cool. In a bowl combine the mortadella, parsley, sausage, Parmigiano, and eggs. Season with salt and pepper. Remove the breadcrumbs from the broth with a skimmer and add to the bowl. Mix to combine.

Stuff the goose with the breadcrumb mixture, truss with kitchen twine, and transfer to a lightly oiled baking pan. Arrange the lardo on top of the goose and scatter on the sage and rosemary. Season with salt and pepper. Roast in the preheated oven for 1 hour, then add the wine to the pan. Continue roasting until the outside is golden and the juices run clear, about 3 hours total, depending on the size of the goose.

QUAGLIA FARCITA
Stuffed Quail
Trattoria Molin Vecio, Caldogno (Vicenza), Veneto

Torcolato is a sweet wine from the Veneto similar to Sauternes. Malga butter is made with raw milk from cows that graze in Alpine pastures. You can ask your butcher to spatchcock the quail for you.

SERVES 4

- Extra-virgin olive oil for oiling pan
- Leaves of 1 sprig thyme
- 4 ounces ground veal
- 4 ounces ground pork
- Salt to taste
- Ground cinnamon to taste
- Freshly grated nutmeg to taste
- 4 small black truffles (or 1 large truffle, quartered), preferably from the Berici Hills
- 4 large spinach leaves, blanched and drained
- 4 thin slices lardo (cured fatback)
- 4 quail, boned and spatchcocked but left whole (see note)
- ¼ cup Torcolato wine
- 1 tablespoon unsalted butter, preferably Malga butter (see note)

Preheat the oven to 400°F. Lightly oil a baking dish, sprinkle on the thyme leaves, and set aside.

Combine the veal and pork. Season with salt, cinnamon, and nutmeg and form this mixture into four balls, each about the size of a plum. Place a truffle in the center of each ball and wrap each ball in a blanched spinach leaf and then in a slice of lardo. Stuff one of these balls into the center of each quail and then close the birds, returning them to their original shape as best as possible, and place seam side down in the prepared dish.

Bake in the preheated oven for 15 minutes, adding the wine to the pan about halfway through the cooking time.

Slice the quail or cut them in half. Make a sauce by mounting the strained pan juices with the butter in a saucepan over low heat, then drizzle the sauce over the quail and serve.

QUAGLIA RIPIENA DI VERZA E SPECK CON MOSTO
Quail Stuffed with Cabbage and Speck with Wine Must Sauce
Ristorante Mezzosoldo, Mortaso di Spiazzo (Trento), Trentino-Alto Adige

You can use either wild quail or farm-raised quail for this dish. Wild quail are usually larger and fattier, and their meat is more flavorful. Serve over salad greens dressed in vinaigrette with a scoop of apple compote on the side. Speck is smoked cured pork.

SERVES 4

Leaves of ½ head Savoy cabbage
3   tablespoons extra-virgin olive oil
4   quail, boned
12 slices speck (see note)
2   tablespoons unsalted butter, softened
2   tablespoons unbleached all-purpose flour
⅔   cup red wine must
1⅔ cups heavy cream

Preheat the oven to 350°F. Blanch the cabbage leaves, drain, squeeze dry, and sauté in a skillet with 1 tablespoon olive oil. Set aside.

Arrange the quail flat on a work surface. Place 3 slices speck on each quail and divide the cabbage among them. Roll up the quail. (Tie with twine or close with toothpicks if necessary.) Brown the quail in an ovenproof skillet in 2 tablespoons olive oil, then transfer the skillet to the oven and bake until cooked through.

Blend together the butter and flour. In another skillet, reduce the wine must by two thirds. Add the butter and flour and stir until melted. Whisk in the cream and cook until thickened.

Slice the quail and drizzle the sauce over the top.

PETTO DI PICCIONE IN RETE DI MAIALE
Squab Breast in Caul Fat
Agriturismo Il Giardino degli Ulivi, Castelraimondo (Macerata), Marche

Caul fat is a lacy webbing that surrounds the stomach of a pig. As it cooks, it turns transparent.

SERVES 4

2   squab
Salt and freshly ground white pepper to taste
4   potatoes
7   tablespoons unsalted butter
¼   cup extra-virgin olive oil
3 to 4 sage leaves
1   clove garlic
1   medium yellow onion, minced
1   rib celery, minced
1   carrot, minced
Minced aromatic herbs to taste
4   pieces pork caul fat (see note)

Preheat the oven to 350°F. Mince the squab hearts and chop the livers. Detach the legs from the breasts and bone both the breasts and legs. Cut the breasts in half. Mince any trimmings, season with salt and white pepper, and stuff the squab legs with this mixture. Wrap the narrow ends of the legs in aluminum foil and set aside. Peel the potatoes and slice very thinly—less than ¹⁄₁₀ inch thick. (A mandoline is handy for this.)

In a skillet melt 2 tablespoons of the butter and 2 tablespoons of the oil. Add the sage leaves and the garlic and brown. Remove the garlic and sage. Season the squab breasts with salt and white pepper and brown on both sides over high heat so that the interior remains rare.

In a skillet, heat the remaining 2 tablespoons olive oil and sauté the onion, celery, and carrot. Add the hearts and sauté until browned. Add the livers and cook over high heat for 3 minutes.

Melt the remaining 5 tablespoons butter in a skillet 5 to 6 inches in diameter. Add one eighth of the potato slices in a single layer, overlapping slightly, and cook until golden on both sides, turning them as if they were a frittata. Repeat with the remaining potatoes so that you have 8 golden disks of potatoes.

Place 4 of the potato disks on parchment-lined baking sheets. Slice the squab breasts without going all the way through and fan out one of the sliced breast halves on top of each of the potato disks. Divide the sauce with the hearts and livers on top of each breast. Place a second disk on top and press the edges together to seal. Sprinkle on the aromatic herbs and wrap each packet in caul fat. Bake the stuffed legs and the potato packets in the preheated oven until the caul fat has melted and turned golden brown and the legs are cooked through. Serve hot.

CONIGLIO ALL'ISCHITANA
Ischia-Style Rabbit
Ristorante Il Focolare, Flaiano di Barano d'Ischia (Napoli), Campania

A Slow Food Presidium has revived the practice of raising rabbits in caves on the island of Ischia, which had nearly disappeared. The rabbits live in holes dug 10 to 13 feet into the ground connected by a complex series of long tunnels. This dish is cooked in a clay pot for maximum moisture. Diners can pop the garlic cloves from their skins and eat them—they are soft and sweet.

SERVES 4
Extra-virgin olive oil for sautéing
1 whole head garlic (unpeeled)
1 rabbit, cut into 10 pieces
1 cup dry white wine
Leaves of 1 sprig parsley
Leaves of 1 sprig basil
Leaves of 1 sprig thyme
Leaves of 1 sprig rosemary
10 tomatoes, seeded and chopped
1 piece chili pepper
¼ cup vegetable broth (optional)
Salt to taste

Heat a small amount of oil in a large skillet over high heat. Add the head of garlic (left whole) and the rabbit and cook, turning occasionally, until browned on all sides, about 20 minutes. Remove the rabbit and the garlic and transfer to a terra-cotta pot. Place the pot over medium heat and add the wine. Chop the herbs together. When the wine has evaporated, add the herbs, tomatoes, and chili pepper and cook over medium heat, turning the rabbit pieces occasionally, until the rabbit begins to stick to the pot. Add the broth or ¼ cup water to moisten the pot and simmer until the rabbit meat is very tender and falling off the bone. If the pot appears to be getting dry before the rabbit is fully cooked, add more vegetable broth or water in small amounts. Season with salt at the end of cooking. To serve, place the terra-cotta pot in the middle of the table on a wooden board.

CONIGLIO IN CASSERUOLA
Rabbit and Potatoes Cooked in a Terra-Cotta Pot
Trattoria Luigina, Genova, Liguria

This is another classic way with rabbit from Liguria. The initial step is intended to remove the slight gaminess that some rabbit has, especially wild rabbit.

SERVES 6
1 rabbit (about 4 pounds), cut into pieces
7 tablespoons unsalted butter
¼ cup extra-virgin olive oil
3 medium white onions, sliced
1 tablespoon pine nuts
2 to 3 bay leaves
Salt and freshly ground black pepper to taste
¼ cup dry white wine
2 pounds potatoes, peeled and diced

Rinse the rabbit in running water and without draining or drying it place it in a terra-cotta pot. Place over medium heat for 10 minutes until all of the water has evaporated.

In another terra-cotta pot, melt the butter with 2 tablespoons of the oil and sauté the onions. Add the pine nuts and bay leaves and sauté briefly, then add the rabbit. Season with salt and pepper and cook, turning occasionally, for 30 minutes. Add the wine and simmer for an additional 30 minutes, stirring frequently.

Meanwhile, in a skillet, pan-fry the potatoes in the remaining 2 tablespoons oil until tender enough to pierce with a fork. When the rabbit is tender, stir the potatoes into the pot and cook for a few additional minutes. Remove and discard the bay leaves before serving.

CONIGLIO ALL'ACETO BALSAMICO 🌿
Rabbit in Balsamic Vinegar
Osteria di Rubbiara, Nonantola (Modena), Emília-Romagna

Rabbit is eaten all over Emilia-Romagna, especially in the area around Modena. The Osteria di Rubbiara has been in the Pedroni family since 1861 and makes its own balsamic vinegar. Serve this with boiled potatoes to soak up the juices.

SERVES 4
- 12 cups (4 bottles) dry white wine
- ½ cup strong wine vinegar
- 1 rabbit, about 4½ pounds, cut up
- 1 medium yellow onion, minced
- 1 rib celery, minced
- Extra-virgin olive oil for sautéing
- 1 (16-ounce) can whole peeled tomatoes in their juices, pureed and strained
- 1 clove garlic, minced
- 1 teaspoon fine sea salt
- 1 tablespoon minced rosemary
- About 6 cups broth, preferably a combination of beef and chicken
- 7 tablespoons unsalted butter
- ¼ cup traditional balsamic vinegar of Modena

In a large stainless steel pot, combine 8 cups white wine and the wine vinegar. Marinate the rabbit in this mixture for at least 8 hours.

When you are ready to cook the rabbit, sauté the onion and celery in olive oil in a small saucepan. As soon as the onion begins to brown, add the tomatoes and simmer over very low heat until thickened.

Combine the garlic, salt, and rosemary. (This mixture is known as *aglione,* and the amount and proportions can be varied to taste.) Remove the rabbit from the marinade, reserving liquid, and drain thoroughly. Coat the rabbit with most of the garlic mixture, reserving a pinch for later. Place the broth in a small pot and bring to a boil, then turn down to a simmer and keep warm.

In another large pot, melt the butter. Brown the rabbit in the butter. Add the remaining 4 cups wine (the same wine you used in the marinade), which should cover the rabbit about halfway (use a little less if necessary), cover the pot, and cook over medium heat until the wine has evaporated. Stir in the tomato mixture. Add enough hot broth to cover the rabbit. Bring to a boil, then turn down to a simmer, cover, and cook over low heat. Check occasionally and if the pan seems to be drying out too quickly, add a little more broth. (The broth must always be hot when it is added to the pot.) When the rabbit is cooked through, add the balsamic vinegar and stir gently, then remove the pot from the heat and transfer the rabbit and strained juices to a serving platter. Serve hot.

CONIGLIO CON OLIVE E PINOLI 🌿
Rabbit with Olives and Pine Nuts
Circolo dar Magasin, Lerici (La Spezia), Liguria

The cuisine of the Liguria region can be sharply divided into two categories: sea and land. In the latter category, rabbit plays a starring role. Use a generous hand with the herbs in this dish for the most authenticity—the people of Liguria indulge heavily in the herbs that flourish in the area. You can pit the olives or leave the pits in, but be sure to inform your guests if you choose the latter method.

SERVES 6

1   clove garlic, minced
½   medium yellow onion, minced
Minced marjoram to taste
Minced thyme to taste
Minced rosemary to taste
Minced sage to taste
Minced chili pepper to taste
Extra-virgin olive oil for sautéing
⅓   cup Taggiasca olives
¼   cup pine nuts
1   rabbit, about 2½ pounds, cut into small pieces
2   cups dry white wine
Salt and freshly ground black pepper to taste

In a large saucepan, sauté the minced garlic, onion, marjoram, thyme, rosemary, sage, and chili pepper in olive oil. Add the olives and pine nuts and stir to combine, then add the rabbit. Cook, turning occasionally, until browned on all sides. Add the wine and cook over medium heat for 5 minutes, then cover and cook over low heat until the rabbit is tender and the liquid has reduced to coat the meat in a thick sauce. Season with salt and pepper.

CONIGLIO IN PORCHETTA 🍃
Porchetta-Style Rabbit
Agriturismo A Casa da Angelo, Grottammare (Ascoli Piceno), Marche

All over central Italy, rabbit, goose, and duck are cooked "porchetta style." This is a popular dish in the interior of the Marche region. The rabbit is cooked bone-in, but you can ask the butcher to cut through the backbone at regular intervals to make it easier to slice once cooked.

SERVES 6

1   rabbit (about 4 pounds), spatchcocked (see note)
¼   cup white wine vinegar
1   bunch wild fennel
2   fresh bay leaves
2   sage leaves
Leaves of 1 sprig rosemary
Salt and freshly ground black pepper to taste
3   cloves garlic, crushed
½   cup extra-virgin olive oil
½   cup dry white wine
Juice of 1 lemon

Start a fire in a wood-burning oven or preheat a standard oven to 350°F. Rinse the rabbit thoroughly. Sprinkle it with the vinegar and set aside for 10 minutes.

Mince the green parts of the fennel with the bay and sage leaves and the rosemary. Rinse the rabbit, pat it dry, and set it in a baking pan. Season with salt and pepper. Scatter the crushed garlic cloves inside and fill with the minced herb mixture.

Close the rabbit tightly with toothpicks. Drizzle the oil and white wine over the rabbit. Roast in the preheated oven for 45 minutes. Turn the rabbit over and drizzle on the lemon juice. Return to the oven and roast until tender and cooked through, about an additional 45 minutes. Remove toothpicks and slice to serve.

BISTECCA DI CHIANINA
Grilled Chianina Steak
Locanda Borgo Antico, Greve in Chianti
(Firenze), Toscana

A grilled Chianina steak—the pride of Toscana—is actually quite simple to prepare. The biggest challenge is finding the top-quality meat required. The steak should be at least 1½ inches thick and on the bone—a steak weighing about 3 pounds will feed 2 people. It should be loin from Chianina breed cattle that has aged for at least 1 week. It must be grilled with no air currents, as those will cause the flames to jump up and lick the meat, and burnt meat will taste bitter, not sweet as a proper Chianina steak does. At least 1 hour before you plan to serve the steak, build a wood-burning fire in a grill using oak. Remove the steak from the refrigerator at least 30 minutes before you plan to cook it. When the fire is very hot, place the steak on the grill. Let it sit until it no longer sticks to the rack, about 3 minutes, then turn the steak (use tongs, never a fork). When you turn the steak, move it to a different spot over the flames, as the spot where it was before will have absorbed some of the moisture from the meat, so it won't be quite as hot. Liberally season the cooked side of the steak with salt and pepper. The salt will turn the meat a lighter color, but it will absorb only what it needs. Cook again for about 3 minutes, just until the steak doesn't stick and the salt is no longer visible on the surface of the steak. Turn it again and season the other side with salt and pepper. The steak should be ready, meaning quite rare in the center with a salty crust on the surface. Always use a warm platter and warm plates for the cooked steak. Serve with a green salad, or cannellini or zolfini beans, or radicchio dressed with extra-virgin olive oil from Chianti.

FILETTO DI MANZO CON SALSA AL TEROLDEGO 🌿
Beef Fillet with Teroldego Wine Sauce
Ristorante Alpino, Brez (Trento), Trentino-Alto Adige

Teroldego red wine is made only in the Campo Rotaliano area. It marries with roasted, stewed, and braised meats. The sauce in this recipe can be prepared in advance and refrigerated after it is strained.

SERVES 4
- 2 cups Teroldego red wine
- ½ medium yellow onion
- 1 clove garlic
- 1 rib celery
- 1 carrot
- 10 juniper berries
- 1 cinnamon stick
- 10 whole black peppercorns
- 4 whole cloves
- Salt to taste
- 1¾ pounds beef fillet
- Extra-virgin olive oil for browning
- 1 tablespoon unsalted butter, softened
- 1 tablespoon unbleached all-purpose flour

In a pot combine the wine, onion, garlic, celery, carrot, juniper berries, cinnamon stick, peppercorns, cloves, and a pinch of salt. Bring to a boil, then simmer over low heat until the liquid is reduced by two thirds, about 45 minutes. Strain and set aside.

Cut the fillet into 4 equal pieces and flatten them slightly with the palm of your hand. In a large skillet, brown the meat on both sides in extra-virgin olive oil, turning once, for 5 minutes total. Remove the beef from the skillet, drain off any excess fat, then return the beef to the skillet and add the wine reduction. It should almost cover the beef. Cook over high heat until the sauce is reduced and silky, 4 to 5 minutes. While it is cooking, blend the butter and flour.

Remove the beef from the skillet and mount the sauce with the butter and flour mixture. Slice the beef and arrange on individual serving plates, then top with the sauce and serve hot.

TAFELSPITZ
Boiled Beef with Horseradish
Ristorante Gummer, Bolzano-Bozen, Trentino-Alto Adige

*T*afelspitz is the name given to boiled beef in the German-speaking part of Alto Adige. Piquant horseradish adds zing to this tasty dish. Grate it at the last minute, and don't lean over the bowl—it's powerful stuff.

SERVES 6
Salt to taste
2   *pounds top blade steak*
2   *carrots, chopped*
1   *rib celery, chopped*
2   *pounds potatoes*
1   *medium yellow onion, chopped*
3   *tablespoons unsalted butter*
Grated fresh horseradish for serving

Bring a large pot of salted water to a boil. Add the meat, carrots, and celery and cook until very tender, about 2 hours.

Meanwhile, bring another pot of water to a boil and boil the potatoes until easily pierced with a fork. Drain, let cool slightly, peel, and slice. In a skillet, brown the onions in the butter. Add the potatoes and cook, turning occasionally, until golden.

Cut the meat into slices and serve with the potatoes. Pass grated horseradish on the side.

BISTECCA PANATA ALLA PALERMITANA
Breaded Palermo-Style Steak
Trattoria Il Maestro del Brodo, Palermo, Sicilia

*L*egend has it that cooking meat in breadcrumbs in this way developed in 1492, when the residents of Sicilia wanted to grill meat and offer it to the Jews who were being expelled from the then-Spanish island under the Inquisition. They didn't have quite enough meat to go around, though, so they dipped it in breadcrumbs to make it a heartier meal.

SERVES 4
½   *cup breadcrumbs*
¼   *cup grated caciocavallo cheese*
4   *slices veal breast or loin, about*
      7 ounces each
Extra-virgin olive oil for brushing meat
Salt and freshly ground black pepper to taste
Leaves of 1 sprig oregano, minced
Leaves of 1 sprig parsley, minced

Heat a cast-iron griddle or charcoal grill. Combine the breadcrumbs and the cheese in a shallow bowl. Brush the meat with oil and dredge it in this mixture, then cook on the griddle or grill. While it is cooking, season with salt, pepper, oregano, and parsley. When the breadcrumbs have browned, the meat should be cooked through. Serve hot.

PEPOSO 🐚
Traditional Beef Stew
Trattoria Da Burde, Firenze, Toscana

Though this dish is prepared all over Toscana, citizens of Impruneta, a city that borders Firenze, claim it as their own. Impruneta is known for its earthenware pots and it is believed that this was traditionally prepared in a kiln after pottery had been fired as the kiln was cooling. Serve this with plenty of the local unsalted bread and Chianti wine. The tomato paste is not traditional, but it does give the finished dish a pleasant color. You can also prepare this on the stovetop over medium-low heat. In that case, it will probably need only 3 hours rather than 4.

SERVES 6
2½ pounds stew beef, cut into large chunks
1 teaspoon black peppercorns
1 pinch salt
2 tablespoons Tuscan extra-virgin olive oil
4 cloves garlic
1 tablespoon tomato paste (optional)
1 bottle (about 3 cups) Chianti wine

Preheat the oven to 250°F. Place the meat in an earthenware pot with a tight-fitting lid. Wrap the peppercorns in a cheesecloth sachet. Stir the salt into the oil in the pot. Add the garlic, peppercorn sachet, oil, and tomato paste, if using. Add the wine, which should just barely cover the meat, then cover and roast in the preheated oven. Check occasionally to be sure the pot hasn't dried out. If the liquid evaporates, add small amounts of water as necessary.

Roast until the meat is tender enough that it falls apart when you pierce it with a fork, about 4 hours. Remove from the oven and place on the stovetop over medium heat. Cook until the cooking liquid has reduced to a thick sauce. Remove and discard the sachet before serving.

SPEZZATINO DI MANZO CON FAGIOLI BRONTOLINI 🍃
Beef Stew with Beans
Hosteria Il Carroccio, Siena, Toscana

Make this when fresh cannellini are in season, from May to October, and you won't need to soak the beans. Otherwise, soak dried beans overnight. Chianina is Toscana's famed ancient breed of cattle.

SERVES 4
1½ cups fresh shelled cannellini beans or dried cannellini beans soaked overnight in cold water and drained
1 clove garlic
3 to 4 sage leaves
1 pound Chianina or other veal
Extra-virgin olive oil for sautéing
2 medium yellow onions, minced
½ cup red wine (optional)
Salt and freshly ground black pepper to taste
1 tablespoon tomato paste
1 cup beef broth

Place the beans in a pot with cold water to cover, add the garlic and the sage leaves, and bring to a boil, then simmer until the beans are soft, 30 minutes to 1 hour. Drain and keep warm.

Meanwhile, chop the veal into cubes. In a large pot, heat olive oil and brown the onions. Add the wine, if using, and season with salt and pepper. Cook over medium heat until reduced. Add the meat and cook, stirring occasionally with a wooden spoon, over low heat for 30 minutes. Add the tomato paste and broth and simmer until the meat is very tender. Serve with the beans.

FRICANDÒ VALDOSTANO ●
Valle d'Aosta Beef Stew with Potatoes, Peas, and Green Beans
Trattoria Perret, Bonne di Valgrisenche (Aosta), Valle d'Aosta

In an earlier era, this stew was made with salted beef that was then rinsed to remove excess salt. A good choice for the white wine here is to look for a bottle from Morgex et de La Salle, a heroic vineyard that is growing grapes in the shadow of glaciers. Seek out beef that is not too lean and that still has a few pieces of bone and cartilage in it. The amount of broth needed will vary depending on several different factors. If at the end of the cooking time your cooking liquid is too thin, remove the meat and vegetables with a slotted spoon and thicken the sauce by adding 1 tablespoon all-purpose flour diluted in 1 tablespoon water and whisking continuously for a few minutes. You can use all peas or all green beans for this dish, or substitute any other vegetable in season.

SERVES 4

- 1¾ pounds stew beef, chopped into chunks
- ¾ cup unbleached all-purpose flour
- 2 tablespoons unsalted butter
- 1 medium yellow onion, thinly sliced
- 2 slices lardo (cured fatback), diced
- Leaves of 1 sprig sage
- Leaves of 1 sprig rosemary
- 1 cup dry white wine
- Salt and freshly ground black pepper to taste
- About 4 cups beef broth
- 4 potatoes, peeled and diced
- 1 cup shelled peas
- 8 ounces green beans, trimmed

Dredge the meat in the flour.

Melt the butter in a Dutch oven and brown the onion in it. Add the lardo, the meat, the sage, and the rosemary. Add the wine and simmer until evaporated. Season with salt and pepper. Add beef broth to cover and bring to a simmer. Continue cooking over medium heat, adding small amounts of broth to keep the meat covered, until the meat is tender, about 1½ hours. Add the potatoes, peas, and green beans and cook until tender. Continue to add broth if necessary to keep the pot from drying out. Serve hot.

GENOVESE
Stewed Beef
Francesca Pappaianni, Catanzaro, Calabria

Strangely, this specialty is not from Genova at all but from Napoli. There are a range of possible reasons for the misnomer. In any case, this dish dates back at least to the 1800s, and, more importantly, it makes good use of some of the tougher cuts of meat. If you like, you can serve the meat as a second course and for a first course cook linguine or other pasta al dente, then toss it briefly in a skillet with the creamy onion mixture. Serve grated aged sheep's cheese on the side.

SERVES 6

- 4½ pounds (12 to 14 medium) white onions, thinly sliced
- 2 pounds beef shoulder or other stew meat, cut into chunks
- 6 ounces ground veal
- Salt to taste
- 1 to 2 cups dry white wine
- 4 cherry tomatoes
- Leaves of 1 sprig basil
- Extra-virgin olive oil for drizzling

Combine the onions, beef shoulder, and ground veal in a pot off the heat. Add water to cover and a pinch of salt. Cook over low heat for 1 hour, then add wine to cover, cherry tomatoes, and basil. Cook until the onions have completely dissolved into a puree. Remove from the heat and drizzle with a generous amount of olive oil. Slice the meat and serve.

BOLLITO MISTO ALLA PIEMONTESE 🍲
Mixed Boiled Meat Piemonte Style
Ristorante Moderno, Carrù (Cuneo), Piemonte

wo Thursdays before Christmas, Carrù stages a festival, the Fiera del Bue Grasso, that involves large platters of mixed boiled meats. The seven classic ingredients are beef ribs, calf's head, shank, tongue, rump, capon, and cotechino sausage. Capon is only available at Christmastime, however, so in this recipe it's been replaced by a hen. Be sure to follow the instructions for cooking the meats in separate pots. The fat from the calf's head and the spices from the cotechino will cover up the flavors of the other ingredients if you mix them. There are several different sauces that can be served with the dish: a spicy tomato sauce; a green sauce made with chopped hard-boiled eggs, parsley, garlic, anchovies, capers, breadcrumbs, oil, and vinegar; or *cognà* (page 416).

SERVES 8
1   large yellow onion
2   ribs celery
3   cloves garlic
1   sprig rosemary
5   stalks parsley
Rock salt to taste
Whole black peppercorns to taste
1   pound ribs

1   pound rump
1   pound beef tongue
1   pound shank
½   whole hen
1   pound calf's head
1   cotechino sausage (about 10 ounces)
Sauces for serving (see note)
Fine sea salt for serving

You will need 3 pots. Fill a large pot with 10 quarts water. Add the onion, celery, garlic, rosemary, parsley, rock salt, and peppercorns and bring to a boil. Remove 3 quarts from the first pot and place it in the second pot.

Place the ribs, rump, tongue, shank, and hen in the boiling liquid in the first pot and cook for 10 minutes, then turn the heat to low and simmer, covered, for 2½ hours total. After the first 1 hour and 15 minutes, check the hen. If it is cooked, remove and set aside in a warm spot.

In the second pot with the 3 quarts liquid, place the calf's head. Boil for 10 minutes, then turn down and simmer for 3 hours.

Pierce the cotechino with a fork and place it in the third pot with unsalted cold water. Bring to a boil, then simmer briskly for 1 hour.

When all the meat is very tender and falling off the bone, drain and transfer to a large platter. Slice the meats at the table and pass sauce on the side, though true connoisseurs will likely prefer their boiled meats dipped in a little fine sea salt and nothing more.

FRITTO MISTO ALLA PIEMONTESE 🍴
Piemonte-Style Fritto Misto
Agriturismo da Elvira, Montegrosso d'Asti (Asti), Piemonte

There are three hard and fast rules for fritto misto: 1. Use a cast-iron pan. 2. Use extra-virgin olive oil that is frequently replaced. 3. Serve freshly fried foods piping hot. This is a Piemontese version, but there are other versions from Ascoli-Piceno, Bologna, Liguria, Milano, Roma, and Toscana. Griva is a pork (including organ meats) sausage made with grated cheese, nutmeg, and juniper berries.

SERVES 4

2 cups whole milk
1 cup sugar
Grated zest of 1 lemon
1 cup fine ground semolina flour
½ calf's brain
7 ounces veal marrowbones
1 sweetbread
4 large eggs
Breadcrumbs for dredging
¼ cup unbleached all-purpose flour
4 amaretto cookies
4 veal cutlets
4 chicken cutlets
8 goat ribs (in season)
2 mushrooms (in season), sliced
6 ounces ground veal
½ cup grated Parmigiano Reggiano
Freshly ground black pepper to taste
Extra-virgin olive oil for deep-frying
Salt to taste
4 slices liver
8 small sausages
8 griva sausages (see note)
2 lemons, quartered

Combine the milk, sugar, and lemon zest in a pot and bring to a boil. Slowly add the semolina, letting it drizzle between your fingers. Whisk to break up any lumps. Cook, whisking constantly, for 5 minutes, then spread evenly on a plate or baking sheet and allow to cool and set for 1 day.

Blanch the calf's brain, marrowbones, and sweetbread for 3 minutes, then drain. Cut the cold semolina into small squares. Slice the sweetbread.

Beat 1 egg in a shallow bowl. Place some breadcrumbs in a second shallow bowl. Place 2 tablespoons of the flour in a third bowl. Dredge the semolina squares and amaretto cookies in flour, then in egg, then in breadcrumbs. Beat another 2 eggs in a clean bowl and dredge the cutlets, brain, marrowbones, and sweetbread in the egg and then in breadcrumbs. Do the same with the goat ribs and mushroom slices, if using.

Combine the remaining egg with the ground veal, Parmigiano, and a generous dose of pepper. Form the mixture into small meatballs and dredge them in breadcrumbs.

Bring a large pot of extra-virgin olive oil to high temperature and fry all of the breaded items separately. Start with the sweet items, then move on to the savory items. Change the oil between each item so that it remains clean. Salt the items as they are fried.

Dredge the liver in the remaining flour and brown the liver and the sausages separately in a skillet.

Transfer to a large platter. Serve hot with lemon quarters.

CREMA FRITTA
Fried Milk Dumplings
Trattoria Il Tubino, San Pietro in Casale (Bologna), Emilia-Romagna

Though it is lightly sweetened, crema fritta is served as a side dish with meat. It also makes a nice snack with a drink. Frequently a mixed plate of fried foods, such as the fritto misto at left, will include a few cubes (especially in Bologna).

SERVES 6

5	large eggs
½	cup sugar
1	cup plus 2 tablespoons unbleached all-purpose flour or 00 flour
14	cups whole milk, scalded
2	tablespoons unsalted butter, cut into pieces
¼	cup breadcrumbs
	Extra-virgin olive oil for frying

Beat 4 eggs with the sugar in a saucepan. Gradually add ¼ cup plus 2 tablespoons of the flour, whisking to combine between additions. Gradually add the scalded milk (it should not be overly hot), whisking constantly. Bring to a boil while whisking constantly and whisk for 2 minutes, then remove from the heat and whisk in the butter.

Spread this mixture about ¾ inch thick on a clean platter and set aside to cool. Once it has cooled, cut it into cubes. Place the remaining ¾ cup flour in a shallow bowl, beat the remaining egg in a second bowl, and place the breadcrumbs in a third bowl. Bring a large pot of several inches of oil to high heat for frying. Line a baking sheet with paper towels. Pat the cubes dry and dredge them first in the flour, then in the beaten egg, and lastly in the breadcrumbs. Fry until golden and transfer to the prepared pan to drain briefly before serving.

MANZO ALL'OLIO
Stewed Beef with Anchovies
Osteria della Villetta, Palazzolo sull'Oglio (Brescia), Lombardia

The anchovies really make this dish. In Italy, this is made with a cut known as *cappello da prete*, or "priest's hat"; beef brisket is probably the closest cut in the United States. This is best made with the excellent beef raised in Rovato, near Palazzolo sull'Oglio, and with the delicate olive oil produced in the region. Serve with polenta.

SERVES 6 TO 8

3½	pounds beef brisket in one piece
1	cup extra-virgin olive oil, plus more for drizzling
2	cloves garlic
3	large salted anchovies, rinsed, drained, and filleted
	About 4 cups beef broth
3	tablespoons breadcrumbs
1	tablespoon grated Parmigiano Reggiano
	Salt to taste
¼	cup minced parsley

Place the meat, the 1 cup oil, the garlic, and the anchovies in a Dutch oven. Brown over low heat for 30 minutes, then gradually add the broth. The broth should not cover the meat. Cook over low heat for another 2 hours and 30 minutes. Add the breadcrumbs and grated cheese and remove from the heat.

Remove the meat and puree the contents of the pot. (An immersion blender works well.) Season to taste. Cut the meat into ½-inch slices and arrange on a platter. Pour the sauce over it. Garnish with parsley and a drizzle of additional olive oil.

STRACOTTO DI MANZO
Long-Cooked Beef Stew
Trattoria San Bernardo, Verzuolo (Cuneo), Piemonte

Alberto Mellano, chef at Trattoria San Bernardo, says there are two key ingredients for this dish: patience for the long cooking time and the quality of the meat, which should be of the local Fassone type, a genetic variant of Piemontese cattle that has been making a comeback in Italy lately, thanks in no small part to the Slow Food Presidium and veterinarian Sergio Capaldo, who is involved in defending traditional animal-raising practices. This is delicious with mashed potatoes or a cauliflower gratin.

SERVES 8

¼ cup plus 2 tablespoons extra-virgin olive oil

2 tablespoons unsalted butter

2 to 3 carrots, chopped

3 to 4 ribs celery, chopped

3 to 4 large yellow onions, chopped

1 clove garlic

2 bay leaves

2 to 3 whole cloves

5½ pounds Fassone brisket in one piece (see note)

½ bottle (about 1½ cups) Barbera or Nebbiolo wine

Salt and freshly ground black pepper to taste

Freshly grated nutmeg to taste

4 cups vegetable broth

Heat the olive oil and butter in a Dutch oven or other large pot. Add the carrots, celery, onions, garlic, bay leaves, and cloves and brown, stirring occasionally, over medium heat for about 10 minutes. Brown the meat on all sides, then cook uncovered, adding small amounts of wine to keep it from sticking, until it has lost its raw red color, 20 to 30 minutes. Season with salt, pepper, and nutmeg and add the remaining wine, about 1 cup. Add the vegetable broth to cover the meat, turn the heat to low, and cook at a gentle simmer, covered, for 2 hours.

Strain the sauce and discard solids. Let the meat cool, then cut into slices ½ to ¾ inch thick. Just before serving, reheat the meat and sauce.

MANZO LESSO CON PATATE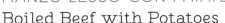
Boiled Beef with Potatoes
Trattoria dal Maestro del Brodo, Palermo, Sicilia

This is a tasty way to enjoy beef that was boiled to make broth. Added bonus: serve the resulting broth on its own, or with pasta as a first course.

SERVES 4

3½ pounds veal ribs and veal marrowbones

3 medium yellow onions

4 ribs celery

¼ cup plus 1 tablespoon tomato puree

Rock salt to taste

Extra-virgin olive oil for sautéing

2 carrots, minced

1 pinch saffron threads

3½ pounds (about 10) potatoes, peeled and diced

¼ cup minced parsley

Salt and freshly ground black pepper to taste

Place the meat and bones in a large pot and add cold water to cover. Bring to a boil and skim any foam and fat that rise to the surface. Add 2 onions, celery, tomato puree, and a generous amount of rock salt and cook until the meat has given up its flavor and is very tender, about 1 hour 30 minutes.

Mince the remaining onion. In a separate pot heat a generous amount of olive oil and sauté the minced onion and carrots. Add the saffron and stir until dissolved, then add the potatoes. Stir to combine, then add water to cover and cook at a low simmer until the potatoes are tender. Stir in the parsley and season to taste with salt and pepper.

Serve the potatoes with the meat. Strain and reserve the broth for another use.

GULASCH ALLA GORIZIANA 🍅
Gorizia-Style Goulash
Gostîlna Korsic, San Floriano del Collio (Gorizia), Friuli-Venezia Giulia

Hungarian goulash is prepared throughout northwestern Italy, which was once part of the Habsburg Empire. Many variations exist, including some with pork, lamb, venison, and other game. This is best made a day in advance and then reheated. Serve with bread dumplings, potato gnocchi, or slices of polenta.

SERVES 5
- 2 pounds (about 6) yellow onions, thinly sliced
- Extra-virgin olive oil for sautéing
- 2 pounds beef, cut into chunks
- Salt to taste
- Ground paprika to taste
- 1 tablespoon unbleached all-purpose flour
- 1 cup tomato puree, warm
- About 2 cups beef broth, warm

Brown the onions in olive oil over low heat. Add the beef and season with salt. Brown the beef, then add the paprika and the flour, tossing everything together until the meat is coated on all sides. Add the tomato puree and enough broth to cover the meat. Cook over low heat, semi-covered (keep the lid on but ajar), until the meat is very tender, about 2 hours.

STINCO DI MANZO AL FORNO
Roasted Beef Shank
Nereo Pederzolli, Cavedine di Stravino (Trento), Trentino-Alto Adige

Place 1 shank per person in an ovenproof pot with cubes of butter, extra-virgin olive oil, chopped carrots, onions, and celery, sage, and rosemary. Brown the meat over high heat, then add 1 cup dry white wine and cook for at least 1 hour 30 minutes, turning the shanks frequently and adjusting the level of the liquid with additional wine or warm water. Season with salt and pepper and sprinkle on a couple of tablespoons of grappa. Transfer to a preheated oven (about 350°F) and roast for at least 1 hour, preferably more. Serve the shanks whole, or cut them in half the long way. Sauerkraut and roasted potatoes are the ideal accompaniments.

GULASCH SUDTIROLESE 🌿
Alto Adige-Style Goulash
Dorfnerhof, Montagna-Montan (Bolzano-Bozen), Trentino-Alto Adige

The Bolzano area has its own type of goulash. Both that and this contain the Italian addition of tomato, which does not appear in the Hungarian original. Signaterhof in Renon-Ritten serves an equally tasty lamb goulash that contains no spices, but incorporates cabbage, potatoes, and carrots.

SERVES 4
- 2 bay leaves
- 1 sprig basil
- 1 sprig marjoram
- 1¾ pounds beef shoulder
- 1 medium yellow onion, minced
- Extra-virgin olive oil for sautéing
- 1 tablespoon double-concentrate tomato paste
- 1 tablespoon unbleached all-purpose flour
- 1 cup red wine
- 3 cloves garlic
- Cumin seeds to taste
- Sweet paprika to taste
- Salt and freshly ground black pepper to taste

Tie the bay leaves, basil, and marjoram into a bouquet garni and set aside. Chop the meat into about 20 cubes. Brown the onion in olive oil. Add the meat and brown over high heat. Stir in

337

the tomato paste and flour and then the wine. Cook, stirring occasionally, until evaporated. Add the prepared bouquet garni, the garlic, the cumin, and the paprika. Season with salt and pepper. Add 2 cups water, turn the heat to low, and simmer until the meat is extremely tender, at least 1 hour. Remove and discard bouquet garni before serving.

BRASATO AL BAROLO
Beef Braised in Barolo Wine
Trattoria Dai Saletta, Torino, Piemonte

This is a classic pairing of Piemonte's revered wine and its equally revered beef. You can use the breast or rump, or even the shoulder, but anyone from the Piemonte region would insist that it can only be made with the local breed of cattle.

SERVES 10

3½ pounds Piemontese beef (see note)
½ cup extra-virgin olive oil
Leaves of 1 sprig rosemary
2   bay leaves
3   cloves garlic
4   carrots, diced
4   medium yellow onions, diced
1   rib celery, diced
5   whole cloves
Salt and freshly ground black pepper to taste
6   cups Barolo wine

Tie the meat with kitchen twine and brown in the oil in a Dutch oven. Add the rosemary, bay leaves, garlic, carrots, onions, and celery, then the cloves. Season with salt and pepper.

When the vegetables have browned, add the wine to cover the meat, cover the pot, and cook over low heat, turning the meat occasionally, until the meat is very tender and the wine has reduced. Let the meat cool slightly, then remove the twine and slice. Strain the sauce and pour it over the meat and serve.

BOMBAS CUN BAGNA
Large Meatballs
Sa Piola della Vecchia Trattoria, Cagliari, Sardegna

These oversized meatballs are made using the red beef of Sardegna from Modica breed cattle, created by breeding local Podolico cows with Modica bulls from Sicilia. These cows today are protected as part of a Slow Food Presidium and are raised year-round in the fields of Montiferru in the province of Oristano.

SERVES 6

12 ounces red beef (see note)
12 ounces pork
12 ounces chicken
6   large eggs, lightly beaten
2   cups grated semi-aged Pecorino Sardo
2   tablespoons extra-virgin olive oil, plus
    more for pan-frying meatballs
1 to 2 cups breadcrumbs
2 to 3 carrots, minced
1   medium yellow onion, minced
1   rib celery, minced
1   clove garlic
7 to 8 ripe tomatoes, peeled, seeded,
    and chopped
Salt to taste
Leaves of 1 sprig basil
Beef broth, if needed

Trim the meat and chop the beef, pork, and chicken very finely together. Place in a large bowl. Add the eggs, grated cheese, 1 tablespoon oil, and enough breadcrumbs to make a mixture that clumps together when you grab some in your fist. There should be no need to salt the mixture.

For the sauce, in a skillet, heat 1 tablespoon oil and add the carrots, onion, celery, and garlic. When the vegetables start to brown, add the tomatoes, season with salt, and cook for 5 minutes. Remove from the heat and puree along with the basil leaves.

Line a baking sheet with paper towels. Form the meat mixture into large meatballs and pan-fry in hot oil for a few minutes, turning to form a golden brown crust on all sides and retain the juices. Drain on the prepared pan.

Transfer the sauce to a skillet and add the meatballs. Cook uncovered over low heat until the meatballs are cooked through, about 20 minutes. If the pan seems to be drying out, add broth in small amounts.

NOSECC ☙
Meatballs Wrapped in Cabbage
Trattoria La Conca Verde, Trescore Balneario (Bergamo), Lombardia

These tasty meatballs are used as a stuffing for cabbage leaves. If you have any cabbage left over, braise it and serve it as a side dish. These go beautifully with polenta.

SERVES 8

1   large yellow onion, thinly sliced
Extra-virgin olive oil for sautéing
5   ounces luganega sausage, casing removed and crumbled
7   ounces veal, chopped
7   ounces beef, chopped
5   ounces pork loin, chopped
Leaves of 1 sprig rosemary
3 to 4 sage leaves
½   cup dry white wine
2   heads Savoy cabbage
Salt to taste
2   large eggs, lightly beaten
⅓   cup breadcrumbs
⅓   cup grated Parmigiano Reggiano
Freshly grated nutmeg to taste
1   slice pancetta, diced
½   cup beef broth

Sauté the onion in oil, then add the sausage, veal, beef, and pork, rosemary, and sage. Add the wine and cook until most of the liquid has evaporated, about 10 minutes. Allow to cool.

Meanwhile, blanch the larger cabbage leaves for 2 minutes in salted water, then drain. If the central ribs are hard, cut them out and discard, leaving the leaves whole. Mince any small leaves in the center and set aside.

Preheat the oven to 300°F.

Mince the cooled meat mixture and combine with the eggs, breadcrumbs, grated Parmigiano, and reserved minced cabbage. Season with salt and nutmeg. Knead with your hands to combine thoroughly.

Arrange the blanched cabbage leaves flat on a work surface and place a small ball of the meat mixture in each one. Roll up the cabbage leaves envelope style. Place a small amount of oil in an ovenproof skillet large enough to hold the cabbage bundles in a single layer and sauté the pancetta for 1 minute. Arrange the cabbage bundles in the skillet and pour in the broth. When the broth is beginning to bubble, transfer the skillet to the preheated oven and bake until most of the liquid has been absorbed, about 20 minutes.

SALTIMBOCCA ALLA ROMANA
Veal Saltimbocca
Clarissa Monnati, Roma, Lazio

Pound veal cutlets very thin. Place them on a work surface and top each with a sage leaf. Top that with a slice of prosciutto and secure with toothpicks. Melt some butter in a skillet and as soon as it begins to sizzle, add the veal cutlets and cook for a couple of minutes per side. Add a little white wine and when it has evaporated season to taste with salt and remove from the heat. Transfer the veal to a serving platter, then return the pan with the cooking liquid to the heat, add a little water to the pan, and reduce to a sauce. Pour over the veal and serve immediately.

POLPETTE IN UMIDO
Stewed Meatballs
Antica Trattoria della Gigina, Bologna, Emilia-Romagna

These meatballs are stewed, but they would be equally delicious pan-fried. The ideal accompaniment is wild radicchio or freshly picked dandelion greens dressed with olive oil, vinegar, and plenty of garlic. You could buy ground meat for these meatballs, but you'll get better results if you buy the best meat possible and chop it yourself by hand.

SERVES 6

1 medium yellow onion, minced
1 rib celery, minced
1 carrot, minced
3 tablespoons extra-virgin olive oil
2 tablespoons tomato puree
1 cup heavy cream
1 tablespoon unsalted butter
Salt and freshly ground black pepper to taste
10 ounces sirloin
5 ounces pork loin
7 ounces mortadella
2 ounces sausage, casing removed
1 large egg, lightly beaten
1½ cups grated Parmigiano Reggiano
Freshly grated nutmeg to taste
Breadcrumbs for dredging

Sauté the onion, celery, and carrot in the olive oil. When they begin to brown, add the tomato puree, cream, and butter. Stir to combine, season lightly, and cook at a very low simmer.

Meanwhile, chop together the sirloin, pork loin, and mortadella. Crumble in the sausage. Mix with the egg, Parmigiano, salt, pepper, and nutmeg. Combine well and form into balls about 6 inches in circumference. Dredge the meatballs in breadcrumbs and add to the pan with the cream and stew, turning occasionally, until the meatballs are cooked through.

SOÇA
Stewed and Baked Salted Beef
Ristorante Lou Tchappé, Lillaz di Cogne (Aosta), Valle d'Aosta

You can use broth in place of the water if you prefer. Another variation calls for adding a fistful of rice to the pot.

SERVES 4

1½ pounds beef
Rock salt for salting beef
Aromatic herbs for salting beef
1 bay leaf
2 sage leaves
½ clove garlic
1 leek, thinly sliced
Leaves of 1 small head Savoy cabbage
2½ pounds (about 6) potatoes, peeled and sliced
1 cup cubed fontina cheese
1 tablespoon butter, melted

Salt the beef for 4 to 5 days with the rock salt and aromatic herbs. Rinse thoroughly to remove excess salt, then cut into cubes.

In a large pot, combine 8 cups water with the bay leaf, sage, garlic, and leek. Bring to a boil and add the chopped meat and the leaves of the cabbage (discard core) and simmer for 50 minutes. Add the potatoes and cook until the potatoes are tender, about 50 additional minutes.

Preheat the oven to 350°F. Transfer the contents of the pot to a baking pan, sprinkle on the fontina and drizzle on the butter, and bake until the cheese has melted and top is brown, about 10 minutes.

QUAJËTTE 🌿
Beef Rolls with Herbs
Vineria Turné, Canelli (Asti), Piemonte

The name of this dish is local Piemontese dialect for quail, as the little rolls of meat resemble the small birds. This is a dish with ancient origins. The writer Primo Levi described a similar dish made with turkey (and, obviously, without lardo) that he and other Piemontese Jews ate on Passover.

SERVES 10

- 7 ounces salted lardo (cured fatback)
- ½ cup plus 1 tablespoon finely minced parsley
- 2 cloves garlic, finely minced
- 10 slices Piemontese beef from the shoulder
- Extra-virgin olive oil for sautéing
- Unsalted butter for sautéing
- 1 medium yellow onion, thinly sliced
- Leaves of 1 sprig rosemary
- 2 pounds ripe tomatoes, peeled, seeded, squeezed, and diced
- Salt and freshly ground black pepper to taste
- 1 teaspoon sugar, if needed
- Grated zest of ½ lemon

Mince the lardo until it is creamy. Mix in ¼ cup of the parsley and garlic and stir to combine. Spread a scant tablespoon of this mixture on each slice of meat. Roll up the meat jelly-roll style and close with toothpicks.

In a skillet, heat equal amounts olive oil and butter and sauté the onion until golden. Add the rolls of beef and rosemary and brown the meat, then add the tomatoes. Season with salt and pepper. If the tomatoes are very acidic, add the sugar. Add ¼ cup parsley and cook, uncovered, over low heat until the meat is tender and soft. Taste and adjust salt, then sprinkle on the remaining 1 tablespoon parsley and the lemon zest. Transfer to a platter and drizzle with the pan juices, then serve.

BRACIOLE AL SUGO CON POLPETTE 🍅
Veal Rolls and Dumplings
Osteria del Tempo Perso, Ostuni (Brindisi), Puglia

In the South, *braciole* (which are bone-in chops in other areas of Italy) are slices of meat rolled up around a filling, known elsewhere as *involtini*. At Osteria del Tempo Perso, the filling is a spicy Mediterranean mix of tomatoes and herbs. They're served with what are essentially meatless meatballs.

SERVES 4

- Leaves of 2 sprigs parsley
- 1 piece chili pepper
- 4 cloves garlic
- 8 slices veal, 3 to 4 ounces each, pounded thin
- 1½ cups grated aged pecorino cheese
- Salt to taste
- 1 medium yellow onion, chopped
- 3 bay leaves
- ½ cup plus 2 tablespoons extra-virgin olive oil
- ½ cup red wine
- 2 pounds tomatoes, pureed through a food mill
- 3 slices stale bread
- 3 to 4 fresh mint leaves
- 4 large eggs, lightly beaten
- Freshly ground black pepper to taste

For the rolls, mince together about half the parsley, the chili pepper, and 2 cloves garlic. Place the slices of veal on a work surface and divide the minced herb mixture evenly among them. Sprinkle on ½ cup grated cheese (divided evenly), and season with a pinch of salt. Roll up jelly-roll style and close with toothpicks.

In a skillet large enough to hold the rolls in a single layer, sauté 1 whole clove garlic, the onion, and the bay leaves in 2 tablespoons olive oil. Add the veal rolls and cook for 10 minutes, turning to brown on all sides. Add the wine and let the alcohol evaporate, then add the tomato puree and cook over very low heat until the veal is tender and tomatoes have reduced, about 1 hour.

Meanwhile, to make the dumplings, soak the bread in water to soften, then squeeze dry and crumble into a large bowl. Mince the remaining clove garlic, remaining parsley, and the mint and add to the bread. Stir in the remaining 1 cup grated cheese and the eggs, season with salt and pepper, and mix to combine thoroughly. Form the mixture into balls. Heat the remaining ½ cup olive oil in a large skillet and brown the dumplings on all sides, working in batches if necessary. As they cook, remove them from the skillet, drain briefly, then add to the skillet with the veal rolls.

STINCO DI SANTO 🐄
Roasted Veal Shank for the Holidays
Claudia Nicolino, Riva Presso Chieri (Torino), Piemonte

This is a dish fit for a family celebration. Buy a large veal shank and ask your butcher to make slits down into the bone so that the marrow will emerge while cooking. In an oval baking pan, heat olive oil and butter until the butter has melted. Briefly cook sage and rosemary leaves. Add the shank and turn it with a wooden spoon to brown on all sides. Add white wine and cook until evaporated. In a separate skillet, brown a couple of roughly chopped onions, then add vegetable broth to cover and simmer until very soft. Add the onions to the pan with the shank and season with salt. Transfer the pan to a preheated 350°F oven and roast at length until meat is falling off the bone, about 2½ hours. (You can also simmer it on the stovetop, which will take 3 to 4 hours.) To serve, remove the shank to a platter. Process the contents of the pan through a food mill to make a sauce and serve on the side.

TOMAXELLE 🏮
Sautéed Veal Rolls
Osteria Vegia Arbà, Genova, Liguria

This is one of the few classic dishes of Liguria that showcases meat rather than fish. It makes creative use of leftovers. Austrian officials who were taken prisoner during the siege of Genova in 1800 are said to have been served this dish.

SERVES 4
1 roll
Beef broth for soaking roll and for moistening pan
4 ounces veal breast
4 ounces lean veal
1 clove garlic
Leaves of 1 sprig parsley
Leaves of 1 sprig marjoram
1 cup dried mushrooms, soaked in warm water and drained
1 tablespoon pine nuts
2 large eggs, lightly beaten
About ½ cup grated Parmigiano Reggiano
Salt to taste
8 thin slices veal (about 2 ounces each)
1 tablespoon unsalted butter
Freshly ground black pepper to taste
½ cup dry white wine
1 cup meat jus
Tomato puree for sauce (optional)

Soak the roll in broth until soft, then squeeze dry. Blanch the veal breast and the lean veal in boiling water, drain, and mince with the garlic, parsley, marjoram, mushrooms, pine nuts, and roll. Transfer the minced mixture to a bowl and add the eggs, Parmigiano Reggiano, and salt. The mixture should hold together; if not, add a little more grated cheese until it does. Pound the veal slices as thin and wide as possible. Arrange them on a work surface and divide the mixture evenly among them. Roll up jelly-roll style and tie closed with kitchen twine.

In a skillet large enough to hold the rolls in a single layer, melt the butter and brown the rolls on all sides. Season with pepper and add the wine, then allow almost all of the wine to evaporate over high heat. Add the meat jus and the tomato puree, if using, and cook over medium heat until the veal is tender and the sauce has thickened, 15 to 20 minutes. If the pan looks dry, add broth in small amounts. To serve, cut off and discard the twine and place the veal rolls on a platter. Force the sauce through a sieve and pour it over the rolls.

OSSOBUCO ALLA MILANESE CON GREMOLADA
Ossobuco with Gremolata
Enrica Tagliabue, Desio (Milano), Lombardia

ssobuco is traditionally served with risotto alla Milanese. Buy 1 *ossobuco* (a thick cross-cut of veal shank with bone and marrow intact) per person. Season the meat with salt and pepper, dredge in flour, and brown on both sides in a generous amount of olive oil. Cook minced onion, celery, carrot, and a little pancetta in butter in a heavy pot or Dutch oven. Add the browned meat to the pot along with bay leaves and sage leaves. Place over medium heat and add dry white wine to cover, then let it evaporate. Add a generous amount of diced peeled and seeded tomatoes. Cover and cook for a few minutes, then add some tomato sauce made with ground veal and a little beef broth to cover or almost cover the meat. Braise until the meat is very tender, adding broth or water in small amounts if the pot looks dry.

Meanwhile, prepare a gremolata by mincing parsley, garlic, and grated lemon zest together. When the ossobuco is cooked, remove from the pot. Puree the remaining contents of the pot through a food mill and degrease. Thin with a little broth or water if the result is very thick or scanty. Stir that puree into the minced mixture for the gremolata. Return the meat to the pot with the gremolata on top of the meat. Cook over low heat for an additional 10 minutes.

CODA ALLA VACCINARA
Braised Oxtail
Trattoria Zarazà, Frascati (Roma), Lazio

xtail is one of the many items in what in Roma is termed the *quinto quarto*, or "fifth quarter," a category composed of the organ meats and other cheap cuts that were once given to cowhands and butchers' apprentices.

SERVES 4
- 4 carrots
- 8 ribs celery
- 2 medium yellow onions
- 1 chili pepper
- Extra-virgin olive oil for sautéing
- 12 pieces oxtail
- ½ cup Castelli Romani white wine
- Salt to taste
- 1 (14-ounce) can peeled tomatoes

Mince 2 carrots, 2 ribs celery, and 1 medium yellow onion and sauté with the chili pepper in a pot in oil. Add the oxtail and brown lightly. Add the wine, let it evaporate, and add water to cover. Bring the water to a boil and when it boils add 2 whole ribs celery and the remaining 2 carrots, and chop the remaining onion and add that as well. Season with salt. Cook for about 1 hour, then add the peeled tomatoes and continue cooking over low heat until the meat is very tender.

Meanwhile, bring a pot of salted water to a boil. Peel any thick strings from the remaining 4 ribs celery, cut them into 4-inch pieces, and cook them in the water until tender, then drain. When the oxtail is cooked, add the celery to the pot.

PANTASCA AI FUNGHI PORCINI

Rolled Veal with Porcini Mushrooms

Il Gastronomo dal 1908, Montemarano (Avellino), Campania

Porcini mushrooms abound in this part of Campania. Aglianico del Vulture is a red wine more closely associated with Basilicata, but this restaurant is located just a few miles from the border between Campania and Basilicata.

SERVES 6

- 4 slices stale bread, crumbled
- ¼ cup dry white wine
- ¼ cup grated aged sheep's milk cheese
- Leaves of 1 sprig parsley, minced
- 2 large eggs, lightly beaten
- Salt and freshly ground black pepper to taste
- 2 tablespoons extra-virgin olive oil
- 2 porcini mushrooms, diced
- 2 cloves garlic, minced
- 1 pound veal belly in a single slice
- 2 cups Aglianico del Vulture wine (see note)

Preheat the oven to 350°F. Make a paste of the stale bread, white wine, grated cheese, parsley, and eggs. Season with salt and pepper. Heat the oil in a skillet and when it is hot brown the diced mushrooms with the garlic. Add to the bread mixture.

Arrange the veal belly on a work surface and spread the bread mixture on top. Roll up the veal and tie with kitchen twine. Place in a baking pan, pour the Aglianico wine over it, and roast in the preheated oven for 50 minutes. To serve, remove the twine, cut into slices, and pour the cooking juices over the slices as a sauce.

SCARAMELLA AL FORNO

Roasted Veal Belly with Herbs

Piccolo Sanremo dal Baròn, Canelli (Asti), Piemonte

Veal belly is a very versatile cut that contains both fatty and lean parts. The secret to a great roasted veal belly is to cook it long and slow and never let it dry out.

SERVES 6

- 4½ pounds veal belly
- 3 tablespoons extra-virgin olive oil
- 5 cloves garlic
- Leaves of 1 sprig rosemary
- 3 bay leaves
- 1 tablespoon dried aromatic herbs such as thyme, marjoram, oregano, and tarragon
- 2 cups dry white wine
- 2 cups beef broth, warm, plus more for moistening pan (optional)
- Salt and freshly ground black pepper to taste

Preheat the oven to 400°F. In a heavy pot or Dutch oven, brown the veal belly on one side in the olive oil with the garlic cloves (left whole), the rosemary, and the bay leaves, then add the dried herbs. Turn the meat to brown the other side, then add the wine. Cook over high heat until the wine has evaporated, about 10 minutes, then add the broth and bring to a boil. Season with salt and pepper. Transfer to the preheated oven and roast until the meat is very tender, about 2½ hours, turning the meat occasionally and adding water or broth in small amounts to keep the pan moist.

PUNTA DI VITELLO RIPIENA AL FORNO 🌿
Baked Stuffed Veal Breast
Trattoria Nonna Bianca, Trecasali (Parma), Emília-Romagna

Veal breast is eaten in Parma and Piacenza, though it also has a following in Bologna. It can be cooked either by boiling or roasting, as it is here. As long as you're turning on the oven, roast potatoes to serve alongside this dish.

SERVES 8

1   medium yellow onion, minced
1   carrot, minced
2   tablespoons unsalted butter
About 8 cups beef broth
3   cups breadcrumbs
3   cups grated Parmigiano Reggiano
3   large eggs, lightly beaten
Salt and freshly ground black pepper to taste
3½ pounds veal breast
Extra-virgin olive oil for browning and
      drizzling
15   slices pancetta
Leaves of 1 sprig rosemary, minced
1   clove garlic, minced
1   cup dry white wine

Preheat the oven to 350°F. Brown the onion and carrot in 1 tablespoon butter. Add 2 cups broth and simmer until reduced, about 30 minutes. In a bowl, combine the reduced broth with the breadcrumbs while still warm. When the mixture has cooled, add the grated cheese and eggs. Season with salt and pepper and combine thoroughly.

Cut a "pocket" in the meat and fill it with this stuffing. In a large pot, brown the meat on all sides in olive oil. Transfer the meat to a roasting pan and cover with the slices of pancetta. Drizzle on a little additional oil. Melt the remaining 1 tablespoon butter and drizzle that on as well. Sprinkle on rosemary and garlic. Pour the wine into the pan and roast until the wine has evaporated, then add the broth, about 1 cup at a time, replenishing it each time the pan starts to look dry. (You may not need all the broth.) Roast until tender, about 2 hours total. To serve, strain the cooking juices to create a sauce.

MILANESE 🍴
Breaded Veal Cutlets
Caterina Bossi, Milano, Lombardia

Ask your butcher to cut 1 bone-in veal cutlet a little more than ½ inch thick per person from a suckling veal loin and to make cuts around the edge so that it won't curl up when cooked. Dredge the veal cutlets in egg beaten with freshly ground black pepper, then in breadcrumbs. Pan-fry in clarified butter until golden, 6 to 7 minutes per side, working in batches if necessary to avoid crowding the pan. Season with salt, drizzle on a little of the cooking butter, and serve.

FEGATO ALLA VENEZIANA 🌱
Venetian Liver with Onions
Ostaria Da Mariano, Venezia Mestre, Veneto

Slightly bitter calf's liver and sweet onions are a classic combination and for good reason. Don't even attempt this dish unless you can obtain very high quality calf's liver. Grilled slices of polenta or mashed potatoes are wonderful with this dish.

SERVES 4

1 pound calf's liver
¼ cup extra-virgin olive oil
1 pound (about 3) yellow onions, sliced
About ½ cup broth
Salt to taste
Lemon juice or vinegar to taste (optional)
Freshly ground black pepper to taste
¼ cup minced flat-leaf parsley

Clean the liver, removing the membrane, rinse, and cut into very thin slices, less than ¹⁄₁₀ inch. Heat the oil in a skillet and add the onions. Cook, covered, over low heat until golden, about 30 minutes, adding broth to the pan in small amounts to keep the onions from sticking. (You may not need all the broth.) Raise the heat to high and add the liver and cook, turning occasionally, until cooked through, 4 to 5 minutes. Season with salt and sprinkle with the lemon juice or vinegar, if using.

Transfer the liver and the onions to a warm platter and season with pepper. Sprinkle on the parsley. Serve hot.

TRIPPA ALLA FIORENTINA 🥕
Florentine Tripe
Trattoria Il Cibreo, Firenze, Toscana

This dish calls for blanket tripe, which is smooth and thick and comes from the first stomach of the cow (as opposed to honeycomb tripe, from the second stomach). Naturally, it should be of the highest quality. Tripe should be rinsed in several changes of cold water and boiled and drained before using. Your butcher may already have taken care of this, so be sure to ask.

SERVES 6

2 medium yellow onions, minced
1 carrot, minced
1 rib celery, minced
½ cup extra-virgin olive oil
1 cup canned peeled tomatoes and their juices, crushed with a fork
Salt to taste
1½ pounds blanket tripe, cleaned and cut into strips
Beef broth (optional)
1 whole clove
3 tablespoons unsalted butter
½ cup grated Parmigiano Reggiano
Freshly ground black pepper to taste

Sauté the onions, carrot, and celery in the olive oil in a large aluminum or copper pot. When the vegetables begin to turn golden, add the tomatoes. Season lightly with salt and cook for a few minutes to combine the flavors. Add the tripe and cook for a few more minutes, then add water or broth, if using, to cover and the clove. Cook over low heat, checking that the pot doesn't dry out too much and adding liquid in small amounts if it does, until the tripe is tender, about 1 hour 15 minutes. Remove the clove and stir in the butter, grated cheese, and pepper. Serve hot.

CODA DI VITELLO IN SALSA VERDE 🌿
Veal Oxtail in Salsa Verde
Ristorante Bistek, Trescore Cremasco (Cremona), Lombardia

The most traditional version of this dish is made with cartilage, which is boiled, pressed, and then thinly sliced. Oxtail is a tasty (and easier to find) substitute.

SERVES 6

- 1 carrot, chopped
- 1 rib celery, chopped
- 1 medium yellow onion, chopped
- 2 bay leaves
- Rock salt to taste
- 3 pieces veal oxtail
- ¼ cup plus 1 tablespoon white wine vinegar, plus more for dressing
- ¼ cup plus 1 tablespoon extra-virgin olive oil, plus more for dressing
- 1 salted anchovy fillet, rinsed
- 1 clove garlic
- Salt to taste
- Leaves of 1 bunch flat-leaf parsley
- 1 large egg, hard-boiled
- Freshly ground black pepper to taste
- 3 cups cooked large white runner beans
- 1 spring onion

Combine the chopped carrot, chopped celery, chopped onion, bay leaves, and rock salt with a generous amount of water in a stockpot and simmer to make a vegetable broth. Place the oxtail in the broth and simmer until the meat is tender and falling off the bone, about 3 hours.

Meanwhile, in a blender puree ¼ cup plus 1 tablespoon vinegar and ¼ cup plus 1 tablespoon oil, the anchovy fillet, and the garlic. Season to taste with salt. Blend until smooth. Add the parsley leaves a little at a time, blending smooth between additions. If the mixture seems too thick (you will thicken it with the egg), add equal amounts oil and vinegar to thin. When all the parsley has been added, add the hard-boiled egg and puree to thicken. Set aside.

Strip the meat from the bones and cut the meat into thin strips. Make a dressing of oil and vinegar and season with salt and pepper. In a bowl combine the meat and the beans and toss with the dressing.

Spread the sauce on a serving platter. Arrange the meat and bean mixture on top. Slice the spring onion and scatter it on top.

AGNELLO CON PATATE ARRAGANATE

Lamb with Oregano Potatoes

Ristorante Al Becco della Civetta, Castelmezzano (Potenza), Basilicata

In the South, oregano is used frequently, and it is often paired with potatoes. Castelmezzano is a small town in the Dolomiti Lucane mountains. Pecorino Lucano is the local sheep's cheese

SERVES 4

2   pounds (about 6) potatoes, peeled and quartered
2   cloves garlic, minced
Leaves of 1 sprig parsley, minced
Leaves of 1 sprig oregano, minced
½   cup grated Pecorino Lucano (see note)
2   pounds lamb
Salt and freshly ground black pepper to taste

Preheat the oven to 400°F. Combine the potatoes, garlic, parsley, oregano, and cheese. Season the lamb lightly with salt and pepper and add it to the mixture. Toss to combine.

Make a layer of half the potatoes in a baking pan. Top with a layer of the lamb. Arrange the remaining potatoes in a layer on top. Bake in the preheated oven until the lamb is tender and potatoes are cooked through, about 1 hour 30 minutes.

ABBACCHIO ALLA ROMANA

Roman Braised Suckling Lamb

Ristorante La Briciola di Adriana, Grottaferrata (Roma), Lazio

Suckling lamb is a classic of Rome and the entire region of Lazio. It is also frequently roasted.

SERVES 4

¼   cup extra-virgin olive oil
1   leg of lamb (3½ to 4½ pounds), boned and cut into chunks
2   medium yellow onions, minced
2   cloves garlic, minced
Leaves of 3 to 4 sprigs rosemary, minced
1   chili pepper, crumbled
Salt to taste
½   cup white wine vinegar
2   tablespoons balsamic vinegar
½   cup dry white wine

Heat the oil in a pot. Add the lamb and brown over medium heat. Add the onions, garlic, rosemary, and chili pepper. Season with salt and cook for a few minutes, stirring occasionally, then add both types of vinegar and the wine. Cook over low heat until the liquid has thickened and the lamb is cooked to your liking.

COTOLETTE IMBOTTITE

Veal Cutlets with Béchamel

Letizia Palesi, Champorcher (Aosta), Valle d'Aosta

Pound veal cutlets thin. Brown in butter, season with salt, and set aside. Make a béchamel by melting more butter and whisking in flour and scalded milk. Whisk until thickened, then remove from the heat and season with salt. Whisk together a small amount of grated Parmigiano Reggiano and an egg yolk, then whisk that mixture into the béchamel. Whisk until cool, then spread the béchamel on both sides of the cutlets. Dredge the coated cutlets in beaten egg, then breadcrumbs, and fry in a combination of oil and lard until browned. Serve with lemon wedges.

AGNELLO CAC' E OVE ●
Lamb with Cheese and Eggs
Osteria Antiche Mura, L'Aquila, Abruzzo

Variations on this Abruzzo Easter specialty include adding garlic to the pan and moistening the lamb with a little white wine during cooking. Goat may also be used in place of the lamb.

SERVES 4
3½ pounds lamb leg and shoulder, boned and chopped
Extra-virgin olive oil for sautéing
Leaves of 1 sprig rosemary
Salt and freshly ground black pepper to taste
3 large eggs
½ cup grated aged sheep's milk cheese
Juice of 1 lemon

Brown the meat in olive oil in a skillet with the rosemary. Season with salt and pepper and continue cooking.

In a bowl, beat the eggs. Beat in the grated cheese and lemon juice. When the lamb is cooked to the desired degree, pour the egg mixture into the skillet, tossing vigorously with the meat until the egg is firm. Serve hot.

COSCIOTTO DI AGNELLO NELLA CRETA ◀◀◀
Leg of Lamb Cooked in Clay
Trattoria La Collinetta, Martone (Reggio Calabria), Calabria

This dish probably dates back to the days when Calabria was a Greek colony. Cooking in clay really seals in the flavors. You will need about 7 pounds of clay and 2 sheets of parchment. Ask your butcher to bone the lamb and leave it as intact as possible. Most home ovens don't go up to 650°F. Set your oven as high as it will go and adjust the cooking time accordingly.

SERVES 6
1 clove garlic
Leaves of 1 sprig rosemary
2 sage leaves
Rock salt
1 leg of lamb (about 3½ pounds), boned
4 ounces pork rind
1 tablespoon unsalted butter
1 pinch oregano

Preheat the oven to 650°F (or as high as your oven will go). Very finely mince together the garlic, rosemary, and sage. Season with salt. Spread this mixture on the lamb and insert the pork rind into the lamb. Place the lamb on parchment paper and dot it with the butter. Sprinkle on the oregano, then wrap the lamb in the parchment and fold the ends of the paper over to seal.

Using water to moisten the clay, shape the clay around the lamb packet, pressing firmly so that there are no air pockets. When the lamb is completely sealed in the clay, bake in the preheated oven for at least 2 hours.

Let the lamb rest for 15 to 20 minutes, then transfer the clay-wrapped lamb to a platter. To serve, break the clay at the table.

AGNELLO A SCOTTADITO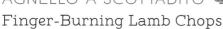
Finger-Burning Lamb Chops
Ristorante Sportellino, Spoleto (Perugia), Umbria

In Spoleto and throughout much of central Italy, the migration of sheep and cows has left its mark. Grilled lamb chops are one of the most obvious legacies of that tradition. The quick sauce of aromatic herbs and prosciutto fat counters the bitter taste lamb can sometimes impart. Reserve the lean prosciutto for another preparation, or slice and eat it on its own.

SERVES 4
⅔ cup diced prosciutto fat
2 to 3 cloves garlic
Leaves of 1 sprig rosemary
4 to 5 marjoram leaves
2 pounds lamb chops
Salt to taste

Mince together the prosciutto fat, garlic, rosemary, and marjoram. Spread this mixture on both sides of the lamb chops. Prepare a grill and grill the lamb chops until rare, about 10 minutes. Season with salt and serve piping hot.

SPEZZATINO DI AGNELLO CON I CARCIOFI
Braised Lamb and Artichokes
Anna Sulis, Cagliari, Sardegna

Chop lamb shoulder and boneless ribs (about 2 pounds to serve 6) into small pieces. Clean artichokes (about 2 per person) and slice the artichokes 1 to 1½ inches thick. Drop into acidulated water to keep them from discoloring. In a pot or Dutch oven, sauté a whole clove of garlic with minced parsley in extra-virgin olive oil until browned. Add the lamb and brown over high heat to form a golden crust. Lower the heat and begin to add Vernaccia wine in small amounts, allowing it to evaporate between additions. (You will need about 4 cups wine total.) After about 30 minutes, season with salt and add the sliced artichokes. Continue to cook, adding wine, until the artichokes are tender but not falling apart, about 30 additional minutes. Taste and adjust salt and serve hot.

AGNELLO SOTTO LA COPPA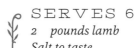
Lamb Cooked Under a Coppa
Ristorante Da Adriano, Carovîlli (Isernia), Molise

In earlier times, every house in the region of Molise had a *coppa*, a dome that was used to create an "oven" in the fireplace, as the actual oven was usually only turned on once a week to bake bread. This metal dome retained the heat from the stones in the hearth; embers were placed all around and on top for even heat. It was used to cook potatoes, onions, sausage, focaccia, cornmeal pizza, and—as in this recipe—simple roasted meats. The aroma that then filled the house was irresistible.

SERVES 6
2 pounds lamb
Salt to taste

Build a fire in the fireplace. Chop the meat and season with salt. Arrange the meat on a sheet of straw paper. Arrange the paper on the floor of the fireplace. Cover with a coppa. Shovel embers and ashes all around and on top of the dome. Cook until the meat is cooked to the desired degree, at least 1 hour and likely a little longer. Remove the dome and serve hot.

CASTRADINA CON RADICCHIO DI TREVISO 🍃
Leg of Lamb with Radicchio
Ristorante La Ragnatela, Mirano (Venezia), Veneto

A lamb stew called *castradina* is traditionally prepared for the feast day of the Madonna della Salute on November 21, widely celebrated in the Venezia area. This is a less soupy version served with delicious radicchio. At that time of year, intensely flavored salt-cured lamb is available specifically for use in this dish, but fresh lamb is used here. Preserved lamb can also be minced and used in traditional rice dishes, most of which mute the intense flavor of the meat with spices.

SERVES 8

- 1 leg of lamb (about 4½ pounds)
- 1 rib celery, chopped
- 1 yellow onion, chopped
- 2 carrots, chopped
- 6 bay leaves
- 15 juniper berries
- ⅔ cup red wine vinegar
- 1¼ cups extra-virgin olive oil, plus more for sauce
- 4 heads Treviso radicchio, quartered
- 2 heads cabbage, shredded
- 2 sardines preserved in salt, rinsed and boned
- 1 tablespoon capers, rinsed and drained
- ½ tablespoons grated horseradish
- 1 clove garlic
- Salt to taste
- 1 pinch chili pepper

Place the lamb in a pot with water to cover by several inches. Bring to a boil, then simmer for 1 hour 30 minutes. Remove from the heat and allow to cool for 10 to 12 hours. Rinse out the pot, place the lamb back in the pot with fresh water, and add the celery, onion, carrots, 2 bay leaves, and 5 juniper berries. Cook over medium heat until the meat is very tender and falling apart, 5 to 6 hours.

In a pot combine the vinegar, 1¼ cups oil, the remaining 4 bay leaves, and remaining 10 juniper berries. Place over medium heat and when the mixture is sizzling, add the radicchio. Cook over medium heat until soft, 10 to 12 minutes. Remove and discard the bay leaves and juniper berries and transfer the radicchio and the oil and vinegar mixture to a glass container. Allow to cool for at least 6 hours. (The radicchio will be served at room temperature.)

For the sauce, blanch the cabbage and set aside to cool. In a blender, puree the cabbage, the sardines, the capers, the horseradish, and the garlic. Season with salt and chili pepper and whisk in enough oil to make a loose sauce.

To serve, slice the meat and serve the radicchio and sauce on the side.

FRICASSEA DI AGNELLO 🌿
Lamb Shepherd's Pie
Ristorante L'Antica Locanda, Noci (Bari), Puglia

This dish has roots in the sheepherding culture of the Puglia region. Tassel hyacinth bulbs are foraged in Puglia and Basilicata and must be carefully cleaned before using. Replace with a few spring onions if you can't locate them where you live—the flavor won't be exactly the same, but they are hard to find.

SERVES 4
- 1 cup breadcrumbs
- 1 ball of fresh mozzarella, drained and diced
- 1 cup grated aged sheep's milk cheese
- Leaves of 1 sprig parsley, minced
- 2 large eggs, lightly beaten
- 2 pounds boned leg of lamb, diced
- Extra-virgin olive oil for sautéing and drizzling
- ½ cup dry white wine
- 4 cloves garlic, minced
- Salt and freshly ground black pepper to taste
- 2 yellow onions, chopped
- 2 medium artichokes, trimmed and quartered
- 7 ounces hyacinth bulbs (see note), boiled, drained, and chopped

Combine the breadcrumbs, mozzarella, ½ cup grated cheese, parsley, and the eggs. Stir in enough water to make a soft mixture.

Sauté the lamb in a skillet in oil. As soon as the meat browns, add the wine and then stir in the minced garlic. Season with salt and pepper. Cook for 30 minutes over low heat.

In another skillet, sauté the onions in oil until golden. Add the artichokes and sauté for 5 minutes, then add the hyacinth bulbs. Season with salt and pepper and cook for an additional 20 minutes, stirring occasionally and adding water in small amounts if the skillet looks dry.

Preheat the oven to 350°F. Add the onion mixture to the lamb mixture and toss to combine, then transfer to a baking pan. Spread the breadcrumb mixture on top, smoothing with an offset spatula. Sprinkle on the remaining ½ cup grated cheese. Drizzle on a little oil and bake in the preheated oven for 40 minutes. Serve hot.

PECORA ALLA PIGNATA 🍃
Mutton Cooked in a Clay Pot
Ristorante Luna Rossa, Terranova di Pollino (Potenza), Basilicata

This dish is traditionally cooked in a *pignata*, an earthenware or clay jug with a rounded belly and a small opening at the top that keeps food especially moist.

SERVES 6 TO 8
- 4 bay leaves
- ½ cup white wine vinegar
- 2 pounds mutton, chopped
- 2 medium yellow onions, sliced
- 2 to 3 tomatoes, diced
- 1 pound (about 3 medium) potatoes, peeled and diced
- Extra-virgin olive oil for stewing
- Salt and freshly ground black pepper to taste
- 1 cup grated aged sheep's cheese

In a large bowl, combine the bay leaves and vinegar. Add the mutton and cold water to cover and let rest, refrigerated, for at least 2 hours.

Place the onions, tomatoes, and potatoes in a pignata or other earthenware pot. Add a generous amount of olive oil and season with salt and pepper. Add enough cold water to cover the vegetables and bring to a boil. When the water boils, drain the mutton and add it to the pignata. Season with a little more salt, add enough water to fill the pot, and cook over medium-low heat until the meat is tender and the liquid has reduced, 4 to 5 hours. Sprinkle on the grated cheese, cook for 5 additional minutes, and serve.

ARISTA AL FORNO
Roast Pork
Osteria Mangiando Mangiando, Greve in Chianti
(Firenze), Toscana

rista, which derives from the Greek word
for "excellent," is a traditional dish of
pork loin with garlic and rosemary (or
sometimes fennel seeds) roasted on a spit,
though these days it is often roasted in an
oven. It dates back to at least the fourteenth
century. If at all possible, use Cinta Senese
breed pork. The classic accompaniment is
simple cannellini beans.

SERVES 4
4   cloves garlic
Leaves of 1 sprig rosemary
Leaves of 1 sprig sage
3 to 4 juniper berries
1   pound pork loin with the belly attached
Salt and freshly ground black pepper to taste
Extra-virgin olive oil for brushing pan
1   cup red wine

Preheat the oven to 300°F. Mince together the
garlic, rosemary, sage, and juniper berries.
Open up the pork loin on a work surface and
season with salt and pepper, then spread on
the garlic mixture. Roll the loin with the belly
on the bottom and tie the roast in a cylinder
with kitchen twine. Brush a roasting pan with
oil, place the pork in the pan, and bake in the
preheated oven for 1 hour.

Raise the oven temperature to 350°F, add the
wine to the pan, and roast until the outside of
the pork is golden and crisp, about 20 minutes.
To serve, remove the twine, cut into thick slices,
and drizzle any pan juices on top.

COSTINE DI MAIALE CON VERZE E CHIODINI
Pork Ribs with Cabbage and Chiodini Mushrooms
Trattoria Tre Rose, Valli di Castelleone
(Cremona), Lombardia

hiodini mushrooms (their Latin name is
Armillariella mellea) are small and flavorful. This dish is redolent with fall flavors.

SERVES 6
1   carrot, minced
1   medium yellow onion, minced
1   rib celery, minced
1   clove garlic
Extra-virgin olive oil for sautéing
3½ pounds pork ribs
Salt and freshly ground black pepper to taste
2   pounds chiodini mushrooms or other
    wild mushrooms
½   cup broth
2 to 3 heads Savoy cabbage, cored and cut
    into ribbons
Leaves of 1 sprig parsley, minced

In a large pot, sauté the carrot, onion, celery, and
garlic in olive oil. Add the ribs, season with salt
and pepper, then add the mushrooms and the
broth. Bring to a boil, then simmer for 30 minutes. Add the cabbage and cook for an additional
30 minutes. Sprinkle on the parsley and serve.

PORCHETTA
Porchetta
Orazio Falchi, Foligno (Perugia), Umbria

orchetta is eaten throughout central Italy.
Start with a one-year-old pig, gutted and
cleaned. It will weigh about 330 pounds.
Slit it along the belly and arrange on a work
surface. Arrange the ears, organ meats, and
shanks in large roasting pans. Scatter the

cloves from 3 to 4 heads garlic (chopped if large), 1 bunch wild fennel, chopped, and 1 cup salt on all pieces of meat. Lastly, sprinkle on about ¼ cup freshly ground black pepper. Chop the liver and place it inside the body of the pig. Close up the pig (it is useful to insert a long pole down the middle for the purposes of moving the pig) and truss it with hemp string about ⅒ inch thick. Roast the pig and the organs and shanks in a very hot oven (about 450°F) until tender, at least 4 hours. Arrange the pans with the organs and shanks so that they catch any drippings. Let the porchetta cool before slicing, and serve cold.

PECORA IN CAPPOTTO
Stewed Mutton with Dried Tomatoes
Gianni Mereu, Bari Sardo (Ogliastra), Sardegna

To make enough to serve 4, cut 2 pounds lean, meaty cuts of mutton into chunks on the bone using a large knife. (Or ask your butcher to do it for you.) Place the meat in a large pot—traditionally a copper pot hung in a fireplace. Add 8 cups water, a generous amount of chopped wild fennel, and 5 sun-dried tomatoes and cook, covered, over low heat for 1 hour 30 minutes, occasionally skimming grease and foam from the surface and discarding. The cooking time will depend on the cut of meat you have used and the age of the animal. Cook until it is tender enough to be pulled apart with a fork. When it is, peel and chop 3 potatoes and 2 large yellow onions and add to the pot. Chop 2 to 3 ribs celery and add those as well. Season with salt and cook until the potatoes are tender, about 30 additional minutes. Add water in small amounts if the pot appears to be getting dry. The resulting dish should be moist, but not a soup. Allow to rest for 10 to 15 minutes off the heat, then drizzle with extra-virgin olive oil. Serve with slices of toasted bread.

PORCETTO ARROSTO
Roast Suckling Pig
Agriturismo Muzzu, Padru (Sassari), Sardegna

Roast suckling pig and boiled mutton have sustained shepherds in Sardegna for centuries. The pork for this dish should be butchered at 20 to 25 days of age and should weigh somewhere between 17½ and 20 pounds. It will serve 20 people. Cut the pig (naturally it should be gutted, the skin charred to remove bristles, scalded, scraped, rinsed, and dried) into quarters (or, if you prefer to roast it on a spit, cut it in half the long way and insert the spit). Build a fire in a wood-burning oven and roast the meat, turning to cook both sides—leaving the skin side down longer—until tender and cooked through, about 2 hours. Remove from the oven, slice, salt lightly, and eat. If you prefer to eat it cold, wrap the slices in myrtle to cool and unwrap just before serving.

LOMBELLO DI MAIALE INCAMICIATO
Pork Loin in Caul Fat
Orazio Falchi, Foligno (Perugia), Umbria

Caul fat is the omentum, a thin stomach membrane from a pig or sheep that may be used to wrap food while cooking. This keeps the enclosed items from being exposed too directly to heat, and the fat melts as it cooks. Season a boneless pork loin with salt and pepper. Arrange a few bay leaves on top, then wrap the loin and leaves in caul fat. Insert a spit or skewer the long way. Cook over a hot fire for about 1 hour, turning frequently. Serve in slices.

STINCO DI MAIALE AL FORNO 🐖
Roasted Pork Shank
Trattoria Alla Terrazza, Interneppo di Bordano (Udine), Friuli-Venezia Giulia

This dish may also be made with a smoked pork shank. Indeed, that's a more common version in the mountains and in the more Germanic areas of Friuli and Alto Adige. Be sure to use an olive oil that is not terribly fruity for this dish.

SERVES 4
- 2 pork shanks, halved the long way
- ¼ cup extra-virgin olive oil
- 3 tablespoons unsalted butter
- 4 bay leaves
- ½ cup dry white wine
- Salt and freshly ground black pepper to taste

Preheat the oven to 400°F. Off the heat, place the shanks in an ovenproof pot where they will fit together tightly. Add the oil, butter, and bay leaves. Place over high heat and brown on all sides. When the shanks are browned, add the wine and cook until it has evaporated. Season with salt and pepper, turn cut sides up, and add a little warm water to the pot. Roast in the preheated oven for 1 hour, then turn the shanks cut sides down. If the pan appears to be getting dry, lower the oven temperature. Cook until cooked through and golden brown, about 30 additional minutes.

MAIALINO ALLE MELE
Pork Loin with Apples
Trattoria Maso Cantanghel, Civezzano (Trento), Trentino-Alto Adige

Firm rennet apples are very popular in Italy, especially in the Trentino area, where they are a major crop. The salty-sweet contrast accented by a final sprinkling of sugar (don't go overboard) makes this dish special. Serve with polenta.

SERVES 4
- 3 tablespoon unsalted butter
- 1 medium yellow onion, minced
- 1 boneless pork loin, about 2 pounds
- Salt to taste
- ½ cup dry white wine
- 1 rennet apple (see note), peeled, cored, and chopped
- 20 medium spring onions
- 2 bulbs celery root, peeled and cut into julienne
- Leaves of 1 sprig parsley, minced
- Sugar to taste

Preheat the oven to 425°F. Melt 2 tablespoons of the butter in an ovenproof pot. Add about half of the minced yellow onion and sauté briefly, then add the loin to the skillet, fat side down, and cook until browned on that side. Turn the loin, season with salt, and add the wine. Add the remaining yellow onion and the apple. Set aside 1 spring onion and add the rest to the pot. Cover and roast in the preheated oven until cooked through, about 1 hour 30 minutes.

Mince the reserved spring onion. Sauté the celery root and the minced spring onion in the remaining 1 tablespoon butter for 20 minutes, stirring frequently. Add ½ cup water and the parsley to the pan and cook, covered, for an additional 20 minutes.

Remove the pork loin from the pan and slice. Sprinkle a small amount of sugar into the pan, whisk to combine with the pan juices and apples, and pour over the sliced pork. Serve with the sautéed celery root.

COSTOLETTE DI MAIALE CON LA MENTA 🌿
Pork Ribs with Mint
Nicola Magnifico, Mattinata (Foggia), Puglia

Season pork ribs (about 1 per person) with salt and black pepper. In a pot large enough to hold the ribs in one layer, heat some extra-virgin olive oil. Arrange the ribs in a single layer and cook for 15 minutes, turning occasionally. With tongs, remove the ribs to a platter and keep warm. Sauté minced onion and a few whole cloves of garlic in the pork fat. Cover the pan with a lid, tilt the pan, and spoon out any excess fat without removing the onion and garlic. To the pot add lemon juice, fresh mint leaves, a few seeded slices of tomato, and a few slices of peeled orange. Add 1 to 2 cups veal stock and cook until the liquid is reduced by one third. Season with salt and pepper. Whisk in 1 to 2 tablespoons butter to thicken the sauce. Arrange the ribs on plates. Cover with additional seeded tomato and orange slices, drizzle on the sauce, and garnish with more mint leaves.

TORTIERA DI SALSICCIA, PATATE E LAMPASCIONI ●
Sausage, Potato, and Hyacinth Bulb Casserole
Grazia Galante, San Marco in Lamis (Foggia), Puglia

Place peeled and sliced potatoes in a baking pan with boiled and cleaned hyacinth bulbs (or wild or cultivated onions) and chopped fresh pork sausage. Add seeded tomatoes cut into strips, minced parsley and garlic, grated aged sheep's cheese, a drizzle of extra-virgin olive oil, and salt. Pour water in the side of the pan until it comes about halfway up the height of the ingredients. Roast until the potatoes are tender and most of the water has evaporated. Add water in small amounts if the pan looks too dry. Serve warm with slices of rustic bread.

CIAUDELLA 🌿
Fresh Fava Beans and Sausage
Ristorante La Vecchia Quercia, Cerreto Sannita (Benevento), Campania

This dish is made with sausage preserved in lard. Dried sausage is packed in a glass or ceramic jar filled with lard for long-term preservation. The dried sausage grows softer over time, but its flavor and color remain the same. If you obtain very young fava beans, they will not yet have developed a skin (inside the pods) that needs to be removed and they will cook quickly. You should have about 2 pounds of fava beans, maybe a little more, once they are shelled.

SERVES 6
8 to 9 pounds young fresh fava beans
1   medium yellow onion, thinly sliced
Extra-virgin olive oil for sautéing
12   ounces dried sausage preserved in lard
*   (see note), diced*
Salt and freshly ground black pepper to taste

Shell the beans, discarding the pods. If the beans have developed tough outer skins, remove and discard the skin around each bean. In a large skillet, sauté the onion in olive oil. Add the sausage and cook for a few minutes, then add the fava beans. Cook until the beans are tender, 20 to 30 minutes, adding a little water if the pan begins to look dry. Season with salt and pepper and serve hot.

VERZA RIPIENA DI SALSICCIA
Stuffed Cabbage with Sausage
Ristorante Altran, Cortona Alta di Ruda (Udine), Friuli-Venezia Giulia

If you prefer, you can replace one quarter to one third of the pork sausage with ground pork loin. Rather than individual packets of stuffed cabbage, this recipe makes a large dome-shaped terrine that resembles a head of cabbage.

SERVES 4
- 1 medium head Savoy cabbage
- Salt to taste
- 2 carrots, cut into small dice
- 2 ribs celery, cut into small dice
- Extra-virgin olive oil for sautéing and drizzling
- 7 ounces pork sausage, casing removed
- 2 egg whites, lightly beaten
- 2 to 4 wild fennel seeds, ground
- 1 tablespoon tomato paste
- ¾ cup grated Parmigiano Reggiano
- Freshly ground black pepper to taste
- 1 (2-ounce) piece pork caul fat
- 1 tablespoon unsalted butter
- ¼ cup beef broth

Detach the leaves from the cabbage. Discard the core and cut out any thick ribs with a paring knife, leaving the leaves intact. Blanch in salted water until soft. Drain and cool, then arrange between flat-weave dish towels and roll over them with a rolling pin to flatten and dry them. Briefly sauté the carrots and celery in oil until just tender.

Preheat the oven to 350°F. Combine the sausage, egg whites, carrot and celery mixture, the fennel seeds, the tomato paste, and the Parmigiano. Season with salt and pepper (if the sausage is very heavily seasoned it may not need much or any additional seasoning). Line a dome mold with blanched cabbage leaves. Spread on a layer of the sausage mixture. Arrange another layer of leaves and continue alternating layers, following the shape of the mold and ending with a small piece of filling on top. Cover the top with a layer of cabbage leaves. Carefully unmold the stuffed cabbage and wrap with the caul fat. It should resemble a small head of cabbage.

Melt the butter in an ovenproof pot and brown the stuffed cabbage, then transfer to the preheated oven and bake for 15 minutes. Skim off any excess fat from the pot and add the beef broth. Return to the oven until sausage is cooked through and caul fat has melted.

Arrange the stuffed cabbage on a warm platter. Drizzle with pan juices and extra-virgin olive oil. Cut wedges at the table to reveal the interior layers.

PEPERONATA CON LA SALSICCIA 🍅
Sautéed Peppers with Sausage
Pier Antonio Cucchietti, Stroppo (Cuneo), Piemonte

In olive oil, sauté thinly sliced onion and minced garlic. Add strips of red and yellow bell peppers. Cook over medium heat until softened. Add seeded tomatoes, either breaking them up with your hands as you add them or pureeing them with a food mill in advance. Cook uncovered over high heat. Drain dried sausage preserved in oil and add to the pan. Season with salt, cook for 5 additional minutes, and serve.

SALSICCE E LENTICCHIE 🌶
Sausage and Lentils
Ilda Cardinali, Passignano sul Trasimeno (Perugia), Umbria

Place Castelluccio lentils (which are smaller and more tender than standard brown lentils) in a pot of cold water with 1 clove garlic and 1 rib celery. Bring to a boil, then simmer for about 20 minutes. Meanwhile, in a skillet, sauté minced celery and garlic in oil. Add pork sausages and cook until browned, 5 to 6 minutes. Add tomato puree and a pinch of chili pepper and cook, stirring frequently, until the sausages are cooked through. When the lentils are cooked al dente, drain them and transfer them to the skillet with the sausages. Add enough water to come about halfway up the side of the pan and simmer for an additional 10 minutes, adding more water if the skillet looks dry. Adjust salt and serve.

LUGANEGHE E FASO 🐚
Luganega Sausage and Beans
Enoteca del Soave, Monteforte d'Alpone (Verona), Veneto

Luganega is a mild pork sausage eaten throughout northeastern Italy. It is sometimes sold in one long coil and sometimes sold in links. This dish is traditionally served over polenta.

SERVES 4
2½ cups dried cannellini beans
1   clove garlic, minced
½   medium yellow onion, minced
2   tablespoons extra-virgin olive oil
1   tablespoon unsalted butter
Vegetable broth for simmering
1   cup tomato puree
1½ pounds luganega pork sausage, cut into 4- to 5-inch lengths if long
Salt to taste
Ground chili pepper to taste

Soak the beans in cold water to cover by several inches for 12 hours. Drain and rinse in running water. In a pot, sauté the garlic and onion in 1 tablespoon of the oil and the butter until softened. Add the drained beans and enough vegetable broth to cover by several inches. Bring to a boil and simmer for 20 minutes. Add the tomato puree and continue cooking.

Meanwhile, line a baking sheet with paper towels. In a separate skillet, brown the luganega briefly in the remaining 1 tablespoon oil, working in batches if necessary, then transfer to the prepared baking sheet to drain briefly. When you think the beans are 5 to 10 minutes from being fully cooked, add the sausage to the pot with the beans. When the beans are soft, season with salt and chili pepper. Serve hot.

COTECHINO CREMONESE ALLA VANIGLIA

Cotechino Sausage with Vanilla

Caffè La Crepa, Isola Dovarese (Cremona), Lombardia

To make your own cotechino, a fresh pork sausage, grind together pork rind, meat from the neck and head, and pork fat, preferably from the base of the skull. Season with salt, spices (nutmeg, allspice, cinnamon, black pepper, and cloves are all traditional choices), and the seeds of a vanilla bean. Moisten with red wine and stuff into wide-diameter natural casing. Age in a cool place for at least 15 days.

To cook cotechino, soak in cold water for at least 1 hour, then wrap tightly in aluminum foil or parchment paper. Poke holes all over with toothpicks, leaving them inserted into the sausage. Place the sausage in a pot, fill with water to cover, and simmer very gently for at least 3 hours. The cooking time can be even longer, but be sure the casing of the sausage doesn't split, or water will infiltrate. Serve hot with lentils (a New Year's classic) or beans, mashed potatoes, spinach sautéed in butter, braised cabbage, mostarda, and polenta.

CINGHIALE AL CIVET

Stewed Boar

Ristorante Il Sentiero dei Franchi, Sant'Antonino di Susa (Torino), Piemonte

Boar, the wild cousin of the pig, has an intense gamy flavor that responds well to long cooking and pairs with assertive flavors. Boar is available from specialty butchers. Serve this over polenta.

SERVES 6

- 6 cups Barbera d'Alba wine
- ½ cup red wine vinegar
- 1 cup or more aromatic herbs
- 6 whole cloves
- ½ cinnamon stick
- 2 pounds boar meat, chopped
- ½ cup extra-virgin olive oil
- 1 medium yellow onion, chopped
- 1 carrot, chopped
- 1 rib celery, chopped
- 2 tablespoons brandy
- ½ cup broth
- Salt to taste

In a nonreactive bowl combine 2 cups of the Barbera d'Alba, the vinegar, about half of the aromatic herbs, the cloves, and the cinnamon stick. Add the boar, toss to combine, and marinate for 12 hours.

When you are ready to cook the boar, drain it and discard the marinade and herbs and spices. Pat the meat dry. Place the oil in a large pot and brown the meat over high heat, along with the onion, carrot, and celery. When the meat is browned on all sides, add the remaining aromatic herbs and the brandy. Gradually add the remaining 4 cups wine in small amounts, about ¼ cup at a time, stirring and waiting a few minutes between additions, until it has all been incorporated. Add the broth, season with salt, and cook over low heat for 2 hours 30 minutes. Remove the chunks of meat to a platter. Puree the pan juices through a food mill and pour the resulting sauce over the meat. Serve hot.

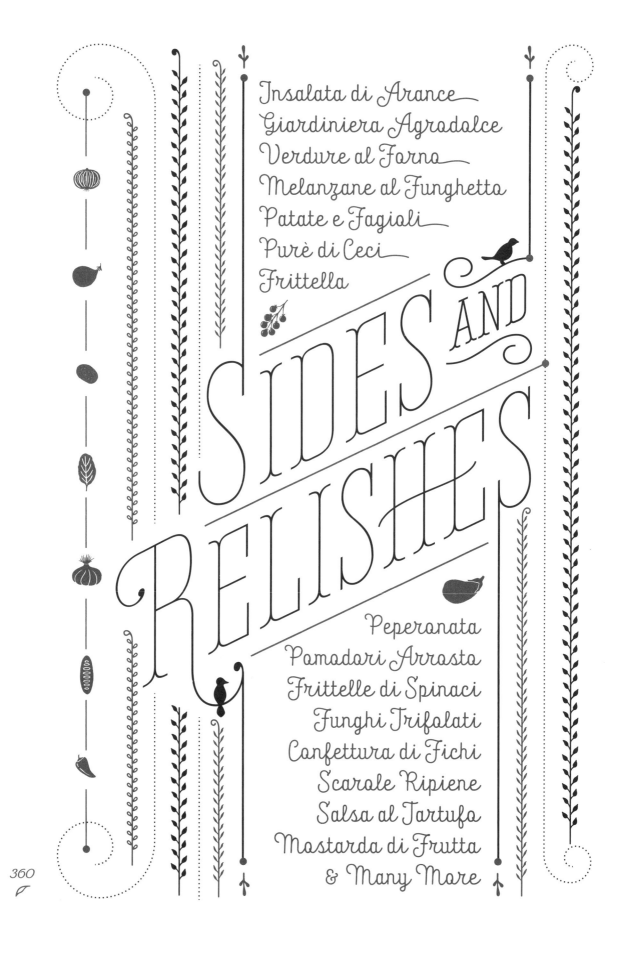

Insalata di Arance
Giardiniera Agrodolce
Verdure al Forno
Melanzane al Funghetto
Patate e Fagioli
Purè di Ceci
Frittella

SIDES AND RELISHES

Peperonata
Pomodori Arrosto
Frittelle di Spinaci
Funghi Trifolati
Confettura di Fichi
Scarole Ripiene
Salsa al Tartufo
Mostarda di Frutta
& Many More

❧{ S A L A D S }❧

INSALATA DI ARANCE
Orange and Oregano Salad
Osteria U Locale, Buccheri (Siracusa), Sicilia

Brothers Sebastiano and Giuseppe Formica serve this salad in their Sicilian osteria. The oranges may be one of the several varieties of blood oranges available in the area or the more common light-colored variety. Vary this recipe by using minced parsley leaves in place of the oregano, adding thinly sliced spring onions, incorporating thinly sliced fennel and sun-dried tomatoes, or including herring or anchovies and olives.

SERVES 4
4 oranges
Extra-virgin olive oil for dressing
1 pinch minced fresh oregano leaves
Salt and freshly ground black pepper to taste

Peel the oranges and slice them thinly, then cut them into cubes, removing and discarding any seeds.

Place the orange cubes in a salad bowl and dress with a generous pour of olive oil. Add the oregano and season with salt and pepper.

Stir to combine and allow to rest for 15 minutes at room temperature before serving.

INSALATA DI CETRIOLI
Cucumber Salad
Christine Richter, Merano-Meran (Bolzano-Bozen), Trentino-Alto Adige

This summer salad can be enhanced with any number of acidic ingredients, such as sour cream or yogurt. Fresh mint and minced garlic are tasty as well. You can also add tomatoes to the salad along with the cucumbers. Peel, seed, and thinly slice cucumbers, about 1 per person. Arrange in a single layer on a rack or a cutting board set at an angle, sprinkle with salt, and wait for excess water to drain from the cucumbers, about 1 hour. Rinse the cucumber slices, blot dry, and make a dressing with extra-virgin olive oil and wine vinegar. Just before serving, sprinkle with a pinch of paprika and some freshly ground white pepper.

TARASSACO, MELE ED ERBA CIPOLLINA
Dandelion and Apple Salad
Osteria Bohemia, Sozzigalli di Soliera (Modena), Emilia-Romagna

Dandelion leaves get increasingly bitter as they grow, so this salad is best made in early spring, when tender young greens are still available. Even then, dandelion has a refreshing bite that is tempered here by the sweetness of the apples.

SERVES 4
1 small bunch dandelion leaves
1 bunch chives
3 apples
Juice of ½ lemon
Extra-virgin olive oil for dressing
Salt to taste
16 borage flowers

Rinse the dandelion and chives and dry them. (It's best to use a salad spinner.) Reserve a few whole dandelion leaves for garnish, then cut the dandelion leaves into ribbons and slice the chives.

Peel, quarter, and core the apples and cut into thin slices, about 1/10 inch thick. Arrange the apple slices in a salad bowl and drizzle the lemon juice over them to stop discoloration. Add the dandelion and the chives.

Dress with oil and salt and toss gently. Divide the salad among individual salad plates and garnish with the reserved leaves and borage flowers.

RAVANELLI IN CAZZIMPERIO ♣
Radishes, Fennel, Carrots, and Celery Dipped in Oil
Carla Magliozzi, Gaeta (Latina), Lazio

Cazzimperio is basically the southern Italian equivalent of *pinzimonio* (raw vegetables dipped in olive oil), though the earliest recipes actually call for a cheese, egg, and broth sauce more complex than the simple dipping sauce provided here. No matter what you call it, the tasty pairing of vegetables and extra-virgin olive oil is always a treat and an excellent inclusion in a dinner with friends featuring heavier meat or cheese dishes. In addition to the vegetables indicated below, you can use bell peppers, Belgian endive, or artichokes in this dish.

Scrub about 4 radishes per person, but leave them whole. Peel 1 carrot per person and cut into quarters lengthwise. Peel the fibrous strings off of 1 rib celery per person and cut into sticks about 4 inches long. Trim the greens off of fennel bulbs (about ½ bulb per person), remove the outermost layers, and divide the hearts into quarters. Season a generous amount of extra-virgin olive oil with salt and pepper. You can also whisk in a little white wine vinegar, but it's not necessary. To serve, divide the oil into small individual dipping dishes and place the vegetables on a communal platter. Invite diners to help themselves to vegetables and dip them in the oil.

INSALATA DI PRIMAVERA ♣
Salad of Spring Greens
Rosina Idrame, San Damiano d'Asti (Asti), Piemonte

This dish was traditionally served on Easter Monday and was made with a combination of garden lettuce and foraged greens. Sometimes *gianchetti*, salt-preserved anchovy whitebait, were included in the mix. In the morning, children were sent into the fields, where they considered it great fun to gather the greens that would be served for lunch. To serve 6 people, tear up 4 small heads of lettuce and, in a bowl, toss with about 4 cups mesclun, such as mâche, dandelion, rampion, sorrel, watercress, arugula, mallow, and chervil. (Obviously, all greens should be washed in several changes of water.) Place in a salad bowl. Whisk together red wine vinegar and extra-virgin olive oil to make a vinaigrette. Add a pinch of salt and pour the dressing over the salad. Toss to coat the leaves, then snip 1 bunch of chives over the salad and toss again.

INSALATA DI CAVOLFIORE
Cauliflower Salad
Mario Carpentieri, Napoli, Campania

Be sure to toss the cauliflower with the dressing while it is still warm, as its heat softens the flavors and brings them together. Cauliflower is a little bland, which works perfectly here—it's a great canvas for the sharp flavor of capers, anchovies, and olives.

SERVES 4
- 1 head cauliflower
- Salt to taste
- Extra-virgin olive oil for dressing
- Wine vinegar for dressing
- 12 black olives, pitted
- 1 tablespoon capers, rinsed and drained
- 2 salted anchovies, rinsed, drained, boned, and minced
- 1 bell pepper preserved in vinegar, drained and cut into thin strips

Divide the cauliflower into florets and rinse well. Bring a large pot of salted water to a boil and cook the cauliflower until tender and easily pierced with a knife. Drain briefly in a colander.

Toss the warm cauliflower with a dressing of oil and vinegar, the olives, the capers, the anchovies, and the pepper. Toss gently to combine and serve.

RAVANELLI IN MISTICANZA ❧
Radishes and Mesclun Greens
Irma Stirpe, Grottaferrata (Rome), Lazio

Mesclun—*misticanza* in Italian—was originally composed of greens collected close to home. Depending on the area and the season, a typical combination would incorporate up to ten different types of greens and herbs, such as lettuce, chervil, arugula, mâche, dandelion, saltwort, chicory, endive, arugula, burnet, monk's beard chicory, lambsquarters, and mallow. These days, it can be hard to find someone expert enough in foraging to recognize which greens are edible and which are not; on the other hand, many stores sell mesclun mixes (though these are not foraged—they're a mix of cultivated greens such as chicory, endive, escarole, and arugula). This salad can also be varied with additions of chopped anchovy fillets that have been boned and rinsed, thin shavings of caciotta cheese, or thinly sliced raw fennel. You can also use lemon juice in place of the vinegar. Simply rinse about 1 scant cup mesclun per person. Scrub radishes (2 to 3 per person) and slice very thinly. Toss the mesclun and radishes in a salad bowl. Make a vinaigrette of extra-virgin olive oil, wine vinegar, and a pinch of salt, whisk briskly, pour over the salad, and toss to coat the leaves well.

INSALATA DI BUCCE DI PISELLI 🐚
Pea Pod Salad
Antonella Iadevaia, Cuneo, Piemonte

Naturally, you will want to know the origin of the peas for this salad: they should not have been treated with any pesticides or grown near any sources of pollution. Remove the strings from pea pods (1 pound will serve about 6 people). Bring a large pot of salted water to a boil, add the pea pods, and boil until tender, 3 to 4 minutes after the water returns to a boil.

Drain and cool the pea pods. Pat them dry, then make a dressing with extra-virgin olive oil, wine vinegar, and a pinch of salt. Crush a garlic clove and toss it into the dressing. Whisk the mixture vigorously, then pour it over the pea pods and toss to combine. Remove and discard the garlic clove before serving.

INSALATA EOLIANA 🌿
Eolian Islands Salad with Cherry Tomatoes, Potatoes, Cucumber, Onion, Capers, and Basil
Assunta Giuffrè, Santa Marina Salina (Messina), Sicilia

Capers from the Eolian Islands of Salina are part of a Slow Food Presidium.

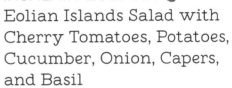

SERVES 4
- 1 medium yellow onion
- Salt to taste
- 4 potatoes
- 10 cherry tomatoes
- 1 cucumber
- 2 tablespoons salted capers, soaked, rinsed, and drained
- Extra-virgin olive oil for dressing
- Minced fresh oregano to taste
- 3 to 4 leaves basil

Thinly slice the onion. Soak in salted cold water for about 10 minutes to leach out any bitterness.

Boil the potatoes (unpeeled) until easily pierced with a fork, then drain, peel, and cut into ¾-inch cubes. Cut each of the tomatoes into quarters. Peel, seed, and slice the cucumber.

In a salad bowl, combine the potato cubes, tomatoes, cucumber, and capers. Dress with a generous amount of oil and season with salt and a pinch of oregano. Tear the basil leaves into the salad, toss once to combine, and serve.

INSALATA DI CAVOLO CAPPUCCINO 🍴
Green Cabbage Salad with Speck and Croutons
Ristorante Martinelli, Ronzo-Chienis (Trento), Trentino-Alto Adige

If at all possible, use olive oil from the Trentino area around the northern end of Lake Garda in this dish. Speck is cured pork haunch that is boned, then salt cured and, finally, cold smoked.

SERVES 4

1   pound (1 large or 2 medium heads) green cabbage
Extra-virgin olive oil for dressing and for croutons
Salt and freshly ground black pepper to taste
4   ounces speck in one slab (see note)
Stale bread for croutons

Remove the outer leaves from the cabbage and cut into quarters. Remove the hard cores and cut the leaves into thin ribbons. Arrange the cabbage in a salad bowl and dress with oil, salt, and pepper.

Cut the speck into small cubes and cut the bread into cubes the same size. In a pan over medium heat, toss both the speck and the bread cubes in a small amount of olive oil until the bread is toasted.

Sprinkle the bread and speck over the salad, toss to combine, and serve.

TARTUFI NERI 🥮
Mushroom and Black Truffle Salad
Piero Saturnia, Perugia, Umbria

Though mushrooms and black truffles are no wallflowers, it's the extra-virgin olive oil that is really the star of this salad.

SERVES 4

7   ounces mushrooms
Juice of 1 lemon
4   ounces black truffle
4   ounces Emmental (Swiss) cheese
4   ounces prosciutto cotto in one slice
1   rib white celery
Extra-virgin olive oil for dressing
Salt and freshly ground black pepper to taste

Clean the mushrooms thoroughly and slice them with a truffle slicer into very thin slices. Place them in a bowl with the lemon juice, toss gently to combine, and set aside for 15 minutes. Meanwhile, peel the truffle with a sharp paring knife.

Cut the cheese and the prosciutto cotto into julienne. Slice the celery thinly and add the cheese, prosciutto cotto, and celery to the bowl with the mushrooms. Toss gently to combine. Dress with oil and season with salt and pepper. Toss gently again and transfer to a serving platter. Slice the truffle over the top and serve.

INSALATA DI CAVOLO VERZA 🌰
Savoy Cabbage Salad with Hot Dressing
Anna Maria Marcarino, Ceva (Cuneo), Piemonte

Heads of Savoy cabbage are generally small. Figure about 1 head for every 2 people. Discard the outer leaves, quarter the cabbage, and discard the cores. Cut into thin ribbons and place in a heatproof bowl. In a small pan, heat a couple of cloves of garlic in extra-virgin olive oil. Add rinsed, boned, and minced salted anchovy fillets and cook until the anchovies dissolve. Add wine vinegar, then remove from the heat. Whisk the hot mixture and pour it over the cabbage. Toss to combine and set aside for a few minutes to wilt slightly. Taste and adjust salt, then serve.

VEGETABLE SIDE DISHES & PRESERVED VEGETABLES

FRITTELLA 🌳
Lightly Cooked Spring Vegetables
Trattoria Primavera, Palermo, Sicîlia

This side dish can be served room temperature or cold and may also be served as an appetizer. It's best prepared in advance so that the flavors have time to develop. The fava beans used here should be young enough that you simply need to remove them from the pods—in other words, they should not have had time to develop the tough outer skin around each individual bean.

SERVES 4
Juice of 1 lemon
7 ounces very young tender fava beans
7 ounces fresh shell peas
7 ounces artichokes
2 yellow onions, thinly sliced
Extra-virgin olive oil for sautéing
½ cup white wine vinegar
¼ cup sugar
Salt to taste

Prepare a large bowl of cold water and add the lemon juice. Shell the fava beans and peas. Trim the artichokes, discarding the outer leaves, spiny tips of any leaves, and the chokes, and cut them into wedges. Drop them into the water with lemon juice to keep them from discoloring.

In a pan, sauté the onions in olive oil until golden. Add first the fava beans, then the artichokes (drained), and, lastly, the peas. Cook over medium heat, stirring occasionally with a wooden spoon. When the vegetables are tender (they should cook fairly quickly) add the vinegar, sugar, and salt. Stir to combine and allow to rest off the heat for at least 10 minutes before serving.

ARRABBIATA 🌶
Spicy Mixed Vegetables
Marco Lombardo, Mîlazzo (Messina), Sicîlia

This delicious side dish pairs equally well with meat or fish.

SERVES 4
1½ pounds fava beans
4 potatoes, peeled
3 fresh tomatoes
10 ounces (2 to 3 medium) carrots
4 zucchini
10 ounces (1 small head) cauliflower
1 medium yellow onion, minced
1 clove garlic, minced
Extra-virgin olive oil for sautéing
½ red chili pepper
1 cup canned diced tomatoes
Salt to taste

Shell and peel the fava beans. Cut the potatoes and tomatoes into dice. Slice the carrots and zucchini into rounds. Separate the cauliflower into florets.

In a large pan with a tight-fitting lid, sauté the onion and garlic in olive oil. Chop the chili pepper and add to the pan, then add the fava beans, potatoes, tomatoes, carrots, zucchini, and cauliflower to the pan. Add the diced tomatoes, season with salt, cover the pan, and cook over low heat, adding water in small amounts if necessary to keep the vegetables from sticking. Cook until the vegetables are very soft, about 30 minutes.

CIAKI-CIUKA
Sautéed Zucchini and Other Vegetables
Trattoria La Vela, Pantelleria (Trapani), Sicîlia

The name *ciaki-ciuka* is a Sicilian interpretation of a Berber word meaning "mixture." While ciaki-ciuka is, indeed, a mixture and its ingredients may vary, it always includes zucchini. The zucchini that grow on Pantelleria are justly renowned.

SERVES 4
4 zucchini
1 eggplant
2 potatoes, peeled
2 tomatoes
1 medium yellow onion
Extra-virgin olive oil for sautéing
Salt to taste

Cut the zucchini, eggplant, potatoes, tomatoes, and onion into julienne about 2½ inches long and ¾ inch wide.

In a large pan, heat a generous amount of olive oil and add the vegetables. Cook, stirring frequently with a wooden spoon to keep them from sticking, until they begin to turn golden. Add about ¼ cup water and season with salt. Braise over medium heat until soft, about 20 minutes, and serve hot.

CIAMBOTTELLA
Stewed Vegetables
Trattoria La Pergola, Gesualdo (Avellino), Campania

This dish is known by several different names. One alternative name is *cianfotta*, as it was invented by Vincenzo Cianfotti, a cook from Abruzzo who worked for the king of Napoli. This stew is most flavorful at room temperature.

SERVES 4
10 ounces (1 small) eggplant, diced
9 ounces (about 2 medium) zucchini, diced
7 ounces (about 2) red bell peppers, diced
Extra-virgin olive oil for sautéing
1 medium yellow onion, thinly sliced
1 pint cherry tomatoes
2 pounds potatoes, peeled and diced
Salt to taste
Leaves of 1 sprig basil

Sauté the eggplant, the zucchini, and the peppers separately in oil until soft. Drain separately on paper towels.

Over medium heat in a large pot, sauté the onion in a generous amount of olive oil until golden. Remove the onions with a slotted spoon and add the tomatoes to the pot. Add ½ cup water and cook over high heat for 5 minutes. Add the potatoes and water to cover and cook until the potatoes are falling apart, about 30 minutes.

Add the other vegetables to the potato mixture and season with salt. Tear in the basil leaves. Mix gently to combine and remove from the heat. Allow the dish to rest until it reaches room temperature, then transfer to a platter and serve.

VERDURE AL FORNO 🍆
Roasted Vegetables
Fattoria La Piastra, Cutigliano (Pistoia), Toscana

This is a summer dish, but you can make a winter version with seasonal vegetables such as leeks, fennel, and winter squash. You can add potatoes, too, but only if you're planning on serving the vegetables as soon as they are cooked—they don't hold up well. Roasted vegetables are a wonderful accompaniment to meat, especially roasted pork.

SERVES 6
2   zucchini, cut into ¾-inch dice
1   eggplant, cut into ¾-inch dice
1   yellow bell pepper, cut into ¾-inch dice
1   red bell pepper, cut into ¾-inch dice
2   white onions, cut into ½-inch dice
3   carrots, cut into ½-inch dice
2   tablespoons extra-virgin olive oil
Salt to taste
Crushed or ground chili pepper (optional)

Preheat the oven to 350°F. In a baking pan, combine all of the vegetables and the oil. Season with salt and chili pepper, if using, and toss to combine. Cover with aluminum foil and cook in the preheated oven until tender, about 30 minutes.

VERDURE AMMOLLICATE 🫐
Greens and Potatoes with Breadcrumbs
Trattoria La Collinetta, Martone (Reggio Calabria), Calabria

You can use spinach, borage, and other greens in place of the beet greens and chicory if you like.

SERVES 4
6   ounces (about ½ bunch) beet greens or chard
6   ounces (about ½ bunch) chicory leaves
Salt to taste
3   potatoes
1   clove garlic
3   tablespoons olive oil
1   dried chili pepper, ground (optional)
½   cup small cubes of bread
⅓   cup grated aged sheep's milk cheese

Clean the greens, tear them, and steam them briefly to soften. Bring a pot of salted water to a boil and cook the potatoes until they are easily pierced with a paring knife. Peel and chop roughly.

In a large pan, sauté the garlic in the olive oil. Add the chili pepper if using. Add the greens and potatoes, season with salt, and sauté over medium heat, stirring frequently, until combined, about 5 minutes. Add the bread cubes and continue to cook, stirring frequently, until the bread has soaked up any remaining cooking liquid and crumbles. Sprinkle on the cheese, stir to melt, and remove from the heat. Allow to rest for a few minutes before serving.

ASPARAGI SELVATICI IN TEGAME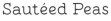
Sautéed Wild Asparagus
Bruna Guarneri, Solarino (Siracusa), Sicîlia

Wild asparagus are similar to cultivated asparagus, but they have thinner stems and a more decisive flavor. They are available in spring and are often sold on the street in Italy by foragers. In Sicilia wild asparagus are more common than the culti-vated type, and they are often cooked simply as in this recipe. They can also be used to top pasta. This recipe uses only the tips of the asparagus, but don't throw away the stems— boil them in lightly salted water and use them elsewhere.

SERVES 4
9 ounces wild asparagus
Extra-virgin olive oil for sautéing
¼ onion, minced
Salt to taste
½ cup dry white wine

Snap off the stems of the asparagus and reserve for another use. Heat olive oil in a pan and add the onion and the asparagus tips. Season with salt. Cook, stirring occasionally, until the aspar-agus and onion begin to turn golden. Add the wine to deglaze the pan and cook until the liq-uid has evaporated, 2 to 3 additional minutes.

PISELLI IN TEGAME
Sautéed Peas
Antonella Iadevaia, Cuneo, Piemonte

Shell fresh peas, reserving the pods for making the pea pod salad on page 363. In a medium skillet with a tight-fitting lid, sauté a thinly sliced onion in olive oil until soft. Add the peas and cook over high heat, stirring frequently with a wooden spoon, for 5 minutes. Add enough hot vegetable broth to cover the peas, season with salt and pepper, cover the skillet, and cook the peas until soft, about 20 minutes. Check occasionally and if the pan appears to be drying out, add more broth. Taste, adjust salt, and serve.

CARCIOFI ARROSTITI
Roasted Artichokes
Ristorante Fenesta Verde, Giugliano in Campania (Napoli), Campania

These artichokes are redolent of a little char from the fire.

SERVES 4
4 medium artichokes
2 cloves garlic
Leaves of 1 bunch parsley
Salt and freshly ground black pepper to taste
Extra-virgin olive oil for drizzling

Trim the tops of the artichokes and use a spoon to scoop out the chokes, leaving the artichokes intact. Cut off stems and reserve for another use. Rinse and pat dry. Roughly chop the garlic and parsley together and stuff the artichokes with the mixture. Season with salt and pepper.

Build a fire in a fireplace with a grate or in a charcoal grill. Drizzle the artichokes with olive oil and cook in the prepared fire (a grill basket is useful for turning) until tender, about 20 minutes.

Remove the artichokes from the fire and set aside to cool. When the artichokes are cool enough to handle, remove and discard any tough outer leaves. Arrange on a serving platter, drizzle with additional extra-virgin olive oil, and serve.

BAGGIANATA
Braised Sugar Snap Peas
Nando Cellini, Viggiù (Varese), Lombardia

This delicious dish can be made with other vegetables in place of the sugar snap peas. Bell peppers, eggplant, and zucchini are all good choices.

SERVES 4

2 pounds sugar snap peas
1 clove garlic
Leaves of 3 sprigs parsley
3 to 4 basil leaves
¼ cup (about 2 ounces) diced lardo (cured fatback)
1 pound plum tomatoes, chopped
½ cup red wine
Salt and freshly ground black pepper to taste
8 slices country-style bread, toasted

Remove and discard any fibrous strings from the sugar snap peas.

Mince together the garlic, parsley, and basil. Heat the lardo in a saucepan with a tight-fitting lid over high heat until it begins to render some of its fat. Add the garlic mixture and cook until the garlic begins to give off its aroma, about 2 minutes. Add the tomatoes and sugar snap peas and cook, stirring occasionally, for 2 to 3 minutes to combine. Add the wine and cook, stirring occasionally, until the alcohol has evaporated. Season with salt and pepper, turn the heat down to a brisk simmer, cover the pan, and cook for 30 minutes. Serve very hot with the slices of toasted bread on the side.

PISELLI ALLA FIORENTINA
Florentine-Style Peas with Pancetta
Trattoria Da Sergio, Firenze, Toscana

Chef Sergio Gozzi recommends that you not go overboard with the seasoning and that you not cook this traditional dish at too high a heat in order to preserve the natural sweetness of the fresh peas. For the 3½ cups of shelled peas called for here, you'll want to start with about 3½ pounds of peas in their pods. These are an excellent foil for strongly flavored stews.

SERVES 6

3 tablespoons extra-virgin olive oil
½ cup (about 4 ounces) diced pancetta
3½ cups shelled peas (see note)
1 clove garlic, thinly sliced
Leaves of 1 sprig parsley, minced
Salt and freshly ground black pepper to taste
Beef broth (optional)

Heat the oil in a large pan with a tight-fitting lid over medium heat and add the pancetta. Add the peas, the garlic, and the parsley. Add water just to cover the peas, turn down to a simmer, cover the pan, and simmer until the peas are soft, about 30 minutes.

Season with salt and pepper and add enough water or broth, if using, to make the peas very moist. Allow to cool slightly and serve warm, but not piping hot.

CARCIOFINI SOTT'OLIO 🌿
Baby Artichokes Preserved in Oil
Silvana Borgna, Pamparato (Cuneo), Piemonte

Yes, the amounts given here are quite large, but this is a rather time-intensive recipe, so you might as well prepare a large amount, and you may even want to double the recipe. The same technique can be used to preserve eggplant.

MAKES ABOUT 4 (8-OUNCE) JARS OF BABY ARTICHOKES

Juice of 1 lemon
50 medium semi-ripe artichokes
1 cup dry white wine

1 cup white wine vinegar
¼ teaspoon rock salt
Extra-virgin olive oil for jars

Combine the lemon juice with cold water in a bowl or basin large enough to hold the artichokes. Trim the top of an artichoke and remove the outer leaves until you have reached the very tender leaves near the heart. Scoop out and discard the choke. Rinse the trimmed artichoke and immediately drop it into the prepared bowl to keep it from discoloring. Repeat with the remaining artichokes.

Combine the wine and vinegar and the rock salt in a large pot and bring to a boil. Line a few baking sheets with clean dishtowels. Add about half of the artichokes to the pot. Allow the liquid to return to a boil and cook the artichokes for 8 minutes after it does. Remove the artichokes with a skimmer and transfer to the prepared pans, leaving the pot on the heat. Arrange the artichokes facing upward. Cook the remaining artichokes the same way. Let the artichokes drain on the pans, facing upward, for about 20 hours. Turn the artichokes over

so that they are facing downward and let them drain for another 4 to 5 hours.

Place a small amount of oil in the bottom of a sterilized 8-ounce canning jar. Arrange a layer of artichokes in the jar, add olive oil until it covers the layer of artichokes, and then arrange a second layer of artichokes. Continue until the jar is full, adding oil in between each layer. You should be able to fit 13 or 14 artichokes in the jar. They should be tightly packed and oil should fill any space between them. Add enough oil to cover the top layer. Repeat with the remaining jars and artichokes. Cover the jars and let them rest for 12 hours, then top off with additional olive oil so that all the artichokes are fully covered. (Any air bubbles in the oil should have risen to the top, but if you do see air bubbles, continue letting the jars rest and adding oil until the level of oil remains stable.) Close the jars, hermetically seal them, and let rest in a cool, dark place for at least 2 months before opening.

CARCIOFI IN TEGAME
Slow-Cooked Artichokes
Trattoria Il Cibreo, Firenze, Toscana

These artichokes cooked slowly over a low flame become pleasantly tender without turning to mush.

SERVES 6

- 8 artichokes
- ½ lemon
- 2 cloves garlic
- Leaves of 1 sprig parsley
- ¼ cup diced pancetta
- Extra-virgin olive oil for drizzling
- ½ cup vegetable broth, plus more if needed
- Salt to taste

Remove and discard the hard outer leaves of the artichokes. Trim the stems to about 1 inch in length. Trim the tops and use a spoon to scoop out the chokes. Rub all over with the cut side of the lemon, then quarter the artichokes and place the quarters in a stainless steel pan that holds them snugly in a single layer. Roughly chop the garlic and parsley and add those and the pancetta to the pan. Drizzle with oil and gently pour in the vegetable broth.

Season with salt and place over the lowest possible flame. Cook for 15 minutes, checking occasionally and adding broth in small amounts if the artichokes begin to stick to the pan.

CARCIOFI IN PASTELLA
Fried Battered Artichokes
Ristorante Barabau, Marina di Cecina (Livorno), Toscana

This type of artichoke preparation—used for lots of different kinds of vegetables—dates back to at least the sixteenth century.

SERVES 6

- ⅓ cup unbleached all-purpose flour
- ½ cup white wine
- ¼ cup extra-virgin olive oil
- Salt and freshly ground black pepper to taste
- 12 artichokes
- Oil for frying

Whisk together the flour, wine, olive oil, and salt and pepper to create a batter. Refrigerate for 2 to 3 hours.

When you are ready to fry the artichokes, trim away the tops and any hard outer leaves. Cut them into eighths and discard the chokes. Prepare a large pot of oil for frying. Dredge the artichoke wedges in the batter, then fry until golden. Remove with a skimmer, salt, and serve.

CARDI ACIDI
Cardoons with Lemon
Luisa Gargiulo, Marino (Roma), Lazio

This pleasantly tart traditional Roman Jewish dish can be eaten cold or at room temperature.

SERVES 4

- 4 lemons
- 2 pounds cardoons
- About ¾ cup extra-virgin olive oil
- Salt to taste

Prepare a bowl of acidulated water with the juice of 1 lemon. Trim the cardoons: discard any outer fibrous ribs and any leaves and peel off any strings. Chop into 1-inch lengths and drop the pieces into the prepared lemon water. Let sit, preferably overnight. Drain the cardoon pieces and transfer to a pot and add ¾ cup olive oil and ¾ cup water. If the liquid doesn't cover the vegetables, continue to add equal amounts of oil and water until they are fully submerged. Place the pot over low heat and cook until all the water has evaporated and only oil remains in the bottom of the pot, about 2 hours. Season with salt and add the juice of the remaining 3 lemons. Cook over low heat for an additional 10 minutes, then remove from the heat and allow the cardoons to cool to room temperature and absorb the lemon juice.

CARDI AL FORNO
Baked Cardoons
Gino Zampolini, Magione (Perugia), Umbria

When baked, cardoons have a tender texture and a more subtle taste akin to that of artichokes.

SERVES 4
2 lemons
2 medium cardoons
Salt to taste
½ cup heavy cream or whipping cream
¾ cup grated Parmigiano Reggiano
Freshly ground black pepper to taste

Prepare a bowl of acidulated water with the juice of 1 lemon. Trim the cardoons: discard any outer fibrous ribs and any leaves and peel off any strings. Chop into 4-inch lengths and drop the pieces into the prepared lemon water. Allow to rest in the water for 15 minutes. Preheat the oven to 350°F.

Fill a pot with water. Add the juice of the remaining lemon and salt to taste and bring to a boil. Drain the cardoons, add them to the pot, and cook until tender but still crisp. Drain and allow to cool.

Spread half of the cream in the bottom of a baking dish and sprinkle on about half of the grated cheese. Scatter the cardoons on top in a single layer. Pour the remaining cream over the cardoons, distributing it as evenly as possible. Season with salt and pepper and sprinkle on the remaining grated cheese. Bake in the preheated oven until the top is golden, about 20 minutes.

CARDO IN BIANCO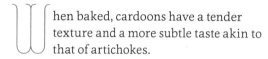
Slow-Cooked Cardoons
Luisa Tibaldi, Alba (Cuneo), Piemonte

A long, slow cooking time is the secret to creamy, soft, and delicious cardoons.

SERVES 4
1 tablespoon lemon juice
1¾ pounds very tender gobbo or straight cardoons
¼ cup extra-virgin olive oil
10 cloves garlic
3 salted anchovies from Sicilia or Liguria, rinsed, boned, and chopped
About 1½ cups whole milk
¼ cup plus 1 tablespoon heavy cream or whipping cream
Freshly ground black pepper and salt to taste

Prepare a bowl of acidulated water with the lemon juice. Trim the cardoons: discard any outer fibrous ribs and any leaves and peel off any strings. Drop into the prepared lemon water and allow to rest for about 10 minutes. Drain the cardoons, dry them thoroughly, and chop them into ¾-inch pieces.

Heat the oil in a pan over low heat with the garlic. Add the anchovies and cook, stirring with a wooden spoon, until dissolved. Add the cardoons and cook, stirring occasionally, for about 3 minutes. Add enough milk to moisten the pan without fully submerging the cardoons and cover the pan. Cook over very low heat until the cardoons are tender and the garlic is creamy, about 1 hour 15 minutes, stirring occasionally and checking to be sure the cardoons are moist but not soupy. If the pan looks dry, add milk in small amounts. When the cardoons are cooked, add the cream. Cook for a few additional minutes. Season with pepper and salt, then serve immediately while still very hot.

CARDI FRITTI 🍴
Fried Cardoons
Caterino Rizzo, Castelvetrano (Trapani), Sicilia

Wild cardoons grow in central and western Sicilia and are one of the area's great vegetable assets. Fried cardoons are often served with grilled meat such as lamb, goat, and pork sausage. A variation on this recipe calls for beating eggs with plenty of pepper and dredging the cardoons first in flour, then egg, then breadcrumbs for an extra-crunchy texture. Whether you're foraging for wild cardoons or buying them, for this recipe be on the lookout for the smallest ribs, which will be tender and crisp.

SERVES 4
- 1¾ pounds small wild cardoons
- Juice of 1 lemon
- Salt to taste
- Extra-virgin olive oil for frying
- ⅓ cup unbleached all-purpose flour

Trim the cardoons and sprinkle them with lemon juice. Cook in a generous amount of salted boiling water until al dente.

Drain the cardoons and dry them thoroughly. Prepare a large pot of olive oil for frying. Line a baking sheet with paper towels and set aside. Dredge the cardoons in the flour, fry them until golden, then drain briefly on the prepared baking sheet, salt to taste, and serve.

GOBBI TRIPPATI 🍅
Gobbo Cardoons with Tomato Sauce
Ristorante La Ribotta, Castagneto Carducci (Livorno), Toscana

In other parts of Toscana, this recipe incorporates onion and a pinch of ground cinnamon.

SERVES 4
- Lemon juice or white wine vinegar for acidulated water
- 1 bunch gobbo cardoons
- ½ cup unbleached all-purpose flour
- Extra-virgin olive oil for browning and drizzling
- 4 cloves garlic
- Salt and freshly ground black pepper to taste
- ¾ cup tomato puree
- ¾ cup grated aged sheep's cheese or Parmigiano Reggiano

Prepare a bowl of acidulated water with the lemon juice or vinegar. Trim the cardoons: discard any outer fibrous ribs and any leaves and peel off any strings. Chop the cardoons, then drop into the prepared acidulated water. Bring a large pot of water to a boil, drain the cardoons, and boil until tender, then drain, pat dry, and dredge in the flour. Place a generous amount of oil (just shy of the amount you would use to deep-fry the cardoon pieces) in a pot and place over medium heat. Add the cardoons and the garlic and brown. Season with salt and pepper to taste. When the cardoons are browned, drizzle in a small additional amount of oil and stir in the tomato puree. Cook briefly, but keep a close eye on the pot to guard against sticking.

Just before serving, sprinkle on the grated cheese. If you are a strict traditionalist, you will want to use the local sheep's cheese from this part of the Maremma area, but Parmigiano is a reliable substitute.

CAROTE AL MARSALA 🥕
Carrots in Marsala
Mattea Magistri, Messina, Sicilia

This simple side dish brightens any meal. Use about 1 pound carrots for every four people you are serving. Peel the carrots by scraping them with a knife, then rinse them, pat dry with a dishtowel, and cut into rounds or julienne. Melt a few tablespoons of butter in a skillet. Add the carrots and a pinch of salt and cook over medium-high heat, stirring occasionally, until browned, about 10 minutes. Add a couple of tablespoons of dry Marsala, cook until it has evaporated, then cover the skillet, turn the heat to low, and cook until the carrots are tender enough to pierce easily with a fork. Remove from the heat and serve.

CAROTE BRASATE 🌿
Carrots Braised in Wine
Trattoria Castello, Castello di Serle (Brescia), Lombardia

This makes an excellent side dish for pork cheeks, which can even be browned right in the pan with the carrots.

SERVES 4
- 1 pound (about 6 medium) carrots
- 1 rib celery
- 1 medium yellow onion
- Extra-virgin olive oil for sautéing
- 1 clove garlic
- 1 bay leaf
- ½ cup red wine
- Beef broth for braising
- Salt and freshly ground black pepper to taste
- 1 tablespoon tomato paste

Trim and wash the carrots. If they are very young, you don't need to peel them, but if they are more mature, scrape them with a knife and wash them under running water. If they are large, cut them to manageable size, but if they are small, leave whole. Rinse and dry the celery rib and slice it thinly. Peel the onion, slice it thinly, and sauté it in olive oil with the garlic and bay leaf. Add the carrots and the celery. Sauté briefly, then add the wine and enough broth just to cover the vegetables. Turn the heat down to a simmer. When the carrots are cooked, season with salt and pepper and stir in the tomato paste.

CAROTE IN AGRODOLCE 🥕
Sweet and Sour Carrots
Elvira Menegon, Orgiano (Vicenza), Veneto

If you cannot obtain goose or chicken fat, it can be replaced with extra olive oil.

SERVES 6
- ¼ cup plus 1 tablespoon black raisins
- ½ cup red or white wine
- 2 pounds young carrots
- Extra-virgin olive oil for sautéing
- 2 to 3 tablespoons diced goose or chicken fat (see note)
- Salt to taste
- 3 tablespoons pine nuts
- 2 to 3 tablespoons vinegar

Soak the raisins in the wine. Slice the carrots into rounds. In a pot large enough to hold the carrots in two or more layers, heat enough oil to cover the carrots once they are in the pot over medium heat. Arrange the carrots in layers in the oil with the cubes of fat scattered between the layers and each layer seasoned lightly with salt. Cover the pot and turn the heat down very low. Cook until the carrots are tender enough to be pierced with a fork. Drain the raisins, squeeze dry, and add to the pot along with the pine nuts. Stir to combine and cook uncovered for a few additional minutes until the ingredients are well combined.

If there is a layer of fat in the pot, pour it off and discard it. Add the vinegar and cook over medium heat until the carrots are browned. Serve immediately.

ZUCCHINE ALLA POVERELLA 🌳
Sautéed Zucchini
Osteria delle Travi, Bari, Puglia

The Italian name of this dish translates literally as "zucchini in a poor person's style," but you will not feel deprived when eating it! Another variation of this dish calls for frying the zucchini until golden, then draining them and sprinkling them with salt, vinegar, and some minced parsley.

SERVES 4
8   very young and fresh zucchini
2   tablespoons extra-virgin olive oil
1   clove garlic
Salt to and freshly ground black pepper
    to taste

Slice the zucchini into rounds. Heat the oil in a large pot and brown the garlic clove in it. Add the zucchini, season with salt and pepper, and cook, stirring occasionally, until evenly golden, about 15 minutes. If at any time the zucchini appears to be sticking to the pot, add a small amount of water.

ZUCCHINE TRIFOLATE 🌿
Zucchini with Parsley and Garlic
Nanni Ricci, Firenze, Toscana

These zucchini are not only a great side dish, but also can be used as a topping for pasta.

SERVES 4
12   young zucchini
2   tablespoons extra-virgin olive oil
1   clove garlic, crushed
Leaves of 1 sprig parsley or calamint,
     chopped
Salt to taste

Slice the zucchini into thin rounds. Heat the olive oil in a skillet over medium heat and brown the garlic clove in it. Add the zucchini and turn the heat to high. Cook, stirring constantly, until the zucchini is beginning to color. Add the parsley, season with salt, cover the skillet, and cook over medium heat until soft and browned.

ZUCCHINE AL POMODORO 🍅
Zucchini Stewed with Tomatoes
Trattoria Pisturri, Magomadas (Nuoro), Sardegna

Zucchini and tomatoes are the stars of the summer table and always make a good team. Make sure to use a high-quality extra-virgin olive oil for this dish, as its flavor really shines through.

SERVES 4
1   clove garlic
1   small onion, minced
Extra-virgin olive oil for sautéing
8   very young and tender zucchini, diced
4   plum tomatoes, peeled, seeded, and diced
Salt to taste

In a pot, cook the garlic and onion in a generous amount of olive oil until they begin to turn golden. Add the zucchini and tomatoes. Moisten the pot with a little water and season with salt. Cook over medium heat until the zucchini is very soft, adding more water if the pot begins to look dry.

ZUCCHINE E FIORI DI ZUCCA IN SALSA DI POMODORO 🌿
Zucchini and Squash Blossoms in Tomato Sauce
Ristorante delle Rose, Mongrando (Biella), Piemonte

There are really three different parts to this recipe: stuffed blossoms, stuffed small zucchini, and a tomato sauce. You can prepare the blossoms and the zucchini in advance and bake them just before serving.

SERVES 4
8   zucchini blossoms
4   large eggs
½   cup ricotta
¾   cup grated Parmigiano Reggiano
Salt and freshly ground black pepper
1   pinch thyme
Unsalted butter for dotting
8   small zucchini

6   ounces veal roast
6   ounces prosciutto cotto
5 to 6 hard amaretti cookies
2   cloves garlic
Extra-virgin olive oil for sautéing
1   pound tomatoes, peeled, seeded, and chopped
3 to 4 basil leaves

Preheat the oven to 325°F. Gently rinse the zucchini blossoms and set them open sides down on a clean dish towel to drain.

In a small bowl, beat 2 of the eggs. Add the ricotta, about one quarter of the grated Parmigiano, salt, pepper, and thyme. Use a pastry bag to fill the blossoms with the ricotta mixture. Place them on a baking pan, sprinkle with another one quarter of the Parmigiano, dot them with butter, and bake them in the preheated oven for 10 minutes. Leave the oven at 325°F.

Meanwhile, blanch the zucchini in lightly salted water, then cut them in half lengthwise and scoop out the flesh. (Reserve for another use.) Mince together the veal and the prosciutto cotto, then lightly beat the remaining 2 eggs and combine them with the meat. Crush the amaretti and stir them in. Stir in about one quarter of the Parmigiano Reggiano, and season with salt and pepper. Stuff the zucchini with this mixture and place in a baking pan. Dot with butter, sprinkle on the remaining grated Parmigiano, and bake in the preheated oven for 10 minutes.

To make a tomato sauce, sauté the garlic cloves in extra-virgin olive oil. Add the tomatoes and the basil leaves and cook until reduced. Serve the warm tomato sauce with the zucchini blossoms and stuffed zucchini.

ZUCCHINE MARINATE
Marinated Zucchini
Martina Dotta, Carignano (Torino), Piemonte

Marinated zucchini will keep in the refrigerator for about 10 days; for longer storage, hermetically seal them in glass jars. If you prefer a more subtle garlic flavor, you can leave the garlic cloves whole or eliminate them completely.

SERVES 4 TO 6
- 2 pounds zucchini, cut into julienne
- 1 medium yellow onion, thinly sliced
- 3 cloves garlic, minced
- Leaves of 1 sprig basil
- ¼ cup dry white wine
- ¼ cup white wine vinegar
- ½ cup extra-virgin olive oil
- 2 teaspoons salt
- 3 to 4 whole cloves

Combine the zucchini, onion, and garlic in a pot. Add the basil leaves, wine, vinegar, oil, salt, and cloves. Stir, bring to a boil, cook for 5 minutes, then remove from the heat. Allow to cool in the pot, remove cloves, and serve.

CIAUDEDDA
Stewed Eggplant and Peppers
Ristorante La Tana, Maratea (Potenza), Basilicata

Feel free to replace some of the olive oil in this vegetable stew with lardo (preserved fatback). You can also incorporate legumes, such as fava beans. This makes a great antipasto when served on slices of toasted bread and drizzled with additional extra-virgin olive oil.

SERVES 4
- ¼ cup plus 1 tablespoon extra-virgin olive oil
- 1 clove garlic
- 2 bell peppers, chopped
- 2 eggplant, chopped
- 7 ounces cherry tomatoes, halved
- 3 potatoes, peeled and cut into thick rounds
- 2 zucchini, cut into thick rounds
- Salt to taste
- ¼ teaspoon oregano
- Leaves of 1 sprig basil
- Vegetable broth for moistening (optional)

Place the oil and garlic in a skillet with high sides. Add the peppers and eggplant and fry, stirring frequently, until browned, about 10 minutes. Add the tomatoes, potatoes, and zucchini, a generous pinch of salt, the oregano, and the basil leaves (do not tear). Cook over low heat, stirring occasionally very gently so as not to break up the potatoes and zucchini, until the vegetables are tender. If the pan looks dry, add water (or hot vegetable broth) in small amounts to moisten.

MELANZANE AL FUNGHETTO
Eggplant Sautéed in the Style of Mushrooms
Anna Cappellotto, Venezia, Veneto

For this simple side dish, eggplant is cooked until it collapses. Cut 4 long eggplant into quarters and then into long strips. Sauté 3 to 4 minced garlic cloves in a generous amount of extra-virgin olive oil just until fragrant, then add the eggplant and season with salt. Add a little water, cover, and cook over low heat until the eggplant is very soft. Uncover and continue cooking, stirring occasionally, until the eggplant has collapsed into a dark puree with oil on the surface.

ZUCCHINE PROFUMATE ALLA NEPITELLA
Preserved Zucchini with Calamint
Antonella Biagioni, Sesto Fiorentino (Firenze), Toscana

Calamint is commonly used in Toscana and throughout central and southern Italy and adds a refreshing touch to a wide array of foods. In addition to zucchini, it goes well with artichokes, mushrooms, snails, and frittate. Of course, you can swap in a different herb if you'd like to experiment with other flavors—zucchini are a blank canvas for almost anything.

SERVES 4 TO 6
1   small yellow onion, thinly sliced
2 to 3 cloves garlic, green shoots removed
2   pounds zucchini, diced
¼   cup dry white wine
¼   cup white wine vinegar
½   cup to 1 cup extra-virgin olive oil
2   teaspoons salt
1   sprig calamint

Place the onion, garlic, and zucchini in a pan with the wine and vinegar. (You can dilute them with a little water if you prefer a less strong flavor.) Add oil (the exact amount depends on your taste), the salt, and the calamint sprig. Stir, bring to a boil, and cook at a brisk simmer for just a few minutes, until just tender, then remove from the heat.

Transfer the zucchini to sterile jars while still hot and hermetically seal.

RATATOIA AGRODOLCE
Sweet and Sour Ratatouille
Trattoria Tre Merli, Morano sul Po (Alessandria), Piemonte

This ratatouille improves if it has a day to sit before being served.

SERVES 4
1   cup extra-virgin olive oil
2   yellow onions, diced
3   carrots, diced
1   rib celery, diced
9   ounces zucchini, diced
2   yellow bell peppers, diced
1   red bell pepper, diced
1   cup wine vinegar
¼   cup sugar
Salt to taste
10   cloves
¾   cup tomato sauce

In a large skillet, heat the oil, then add the onions and cook until soft. Add the carrots and celery and cook for 10 minutes, then add the zucchini and peppers and cook for 15 minutes. Add the vinegar, sugar, salt, cloves, and tomato sauce. Cook for an additional 10 minutes, then remove from the heat and allow to cool.

INVOLTINI DI MELANZANE SOTT'OLIO
Stuffed Eggplant Rolls Preserved in Oil
Ristorante Liviù, Dipignano (Cosenza), Calabria

For a simpler alternative to this dish, sprinkle a few drops of vinegar on some grilled eggplant slices, then scatter minced chili pepper, garlic, and parsley on top. You can also flake some drained tuna canned in olive oil into the filling along with the anchovies if you like.

SERVES 4

- 2 long eggplant
- ¼ cup breadcrumbs
- 1 heaping tablespoon salted capers, rinsed, drained, and chopped
- 1 teaspoon minced oregano leaves
- Leaves of 1 sprig calamint, minced
- Leaves of 1 sprig wild fennel, minced
- 2 salted anchovies, rinsed, boned, and chopped
- White wine vinegar for moistening
- Extra-virgin olive oil for moistening and filling container
- Salt to taste

Cut the eggplant the long way into ¼-inch-thick slices. Grill, turning, until soft and set aside.

In a bowl combine the breadcrumbs, capers, oregano, calamint, and fennel. Stir in the anchovies. Moisten with a little vinegar and a generous amount of extra-virgin olive oil. Season the mixture with salt and arrange on the eggplant slices. Roll up the slices and arrange them packed snugly together in a container. Add enough olive oil to fill the container and close it. The eggplant will keep in the refrigerator for 1 week. For longer storage, hermetically seal in sterilized jars.

CONFETTURA DI POMODORI VERDI 🍅
Green Tomato Preserves
Teotiste Griva, Cavoretto (Torino), Piemonte

Use those last few tomatoes that will never fully ripen in these excellent preserves. They are a terrific addition to a cheese plate. To make four 8-ounce jars of preserves, wash, dry, and seed about 4½ pounds green tomatoes, then chop them and place in a pot with 5 cups sugar, a vanilla bean, and the grated zest of 1 lemon. Cook over low heat for 1 hour. Remove the vanilla bean and puree the tomato mixture through a food mill. Return the puree to the pot and continue cooking over low heat until the mixture has reached the consistency you desire. Transfer to sterile jars and hermetically seal.

GIARDINIERA AGRODOLCE 🍶
Sweet and Sour Giardiniera
Osteria della Villetta, Palazzolo sull'Oglio (Brescia), Lombardia

Giardiniera is a mix of vegetables usually preserved in jars. You can buy giardiniera, but it's never as good as the homemade version. If you like a more acidic flavor, decrease the amount of water and increase the amount of vinegar.

MAKES 3 QUARTS

- 1½ cups white wine vinegar
- 1½ cups white wine
- Salt and freshly ground black pepper
- 2 bay leaves
- 2 cloves garlic
- 14 ounces celery, cut into ¾-inch dice
- 14 ounces green beans, cut into ¾-inch lengths
- 14 ounces carrots cut into ¾-inch dice
- 14 ounces zucchini, cut into ¾-inch dice
- 14 ounces cauliflower, cut into ¾-inch florets
- 4 cups extra-virgin olive oil, or more as needed

In a large pot combine 8 cups water, the vinegar, wine, salt, pepper, bay leaves, and garlic. Bring to a boil and add the celery, green beans, and carrots. When the liquid returns to a boil, add the zucchini, and when it returns to a boil again, add the cauliflower. Cook until the vegetables are soft but have not lost their shape. Drain and cool in a *bastardella* (a deep metal bowl with handles). Dress the cooled vegetables with olive oil, taste and adjust salt, and refrigerate. This giardiniera will keep in the refrigerator for a couple of days; hermetically seal in sterilized jars for longer storage.

GIARDINIERA DI PEPERONI, MELANZANE E CIPOLLE
Pepper, Eggplant, and Onion Giardiniera
Luisa Sanfile, Monterosso Calabro (Vibo Valentia), Calabria

Giardiniera is typically prepared in the summer, when its ingredients are in season, and then preserved in jars. Its fresh flavors are much appreciated in winter and the taste actually improves as it sits in a cool, dark place. It's a Christmas classic.

Seed round green bell peppers and cut into thin strips. Toss with salt, place in a sieve, set a plate and a weight on top, and set aside for 24 hours to drain. Cut eggplants into thin strips and do the same in a separate sieve. Slice onions and do the same in a third sieve. When the vegetables have given up their liquid, squeeze them dry and set them in separate bowls. Add white wine vinegar to cover in each bowl, place a plate and a weight on top, and set aside for 24 hours again.

Drain the vegetables again, squeezing them dry, and mix to combine. Place the vegetable mixture in a sterile jar or jars, adding thin slices of garlic and chopped chili pepper. (Don't mince the chilies too small—they should be visible.) Pour in enough extra-virgin olive oil to cover completely, seal hermetically, and allow to age for at least 2 weeks before opening.

GIARDINIERA ROSSA
Red Giardiniera
Livia Cotto, San Marzanotto di Asti (Asti), Piemonte

Giardiniera can be served cold as an antipasto and is often accompanied by wedges of hard-boiled egg, canned tuna, olives, and capers. The mixture can also be jarred in hermetically sealed sterile jars. The Ristorante del Casot di Castell'Alfero (Asti) makes giardiniera with tomatoes, bell peppers, zucchini, cauliflower, green beans, carrots, onion, and celery cooked in a mixture of one part white wine vinegar to two parts extra-virgin olive oil, along with rock salt and sugar. The mixture is seasoned with a pinch of nutmeg and tossed with pitted green olives before it is hermetically sealed in sterile jars. Use the smallest, sweetest onions you can find. In Piemonte, onions from the town of Ivrea, which are one inch or less in diameter, are used to make a particularly tasty giardiniera.

MAKES 3 QUARTS
- 4½ pounds ripe tomatoes, preferably San Marzano, chopped
- 9 ounces carrots, diced
- 9 ounces spring onions
- 1 rib celery, diced
- 9 ounces green beans, trimmed and cut into thirds
- 1 head cauliflower, divided into florets
- 1 pound red and yellow bell peppers, seeded and diced
- 1 cup vinegar
- Salt to taste
- 2 tablespoons sugar
- ½ cup extra-virgin olive oil

Place the tomatoes in a pot and cook over low heat for 45 minutes to 1 hour, stirring occasionally, until they have collapsed. Use a food mill or sieve to strain out the seeds and peels. Return the tomato puree to the pot and place over medium heat.

Add the carrots and cook for 5 minutes, stirring occasionally. Add the whole onions and cook for 5 minutes, stirring occasionally. Continue to add, in this order, the celery, green beans, cauliflower florets, and peppers, stirring to incorporate and cooking for 5 minutes between additions. Lastly, add the vinegar and salt and cook at a low simmer until the vegetables are soft, 40 to 50 minutes. Keep a close watch and don't let the vegetables turn mushy. When the vegetables are cooked, add the sugar and oil and adjust salt to taste.

POMODORI ARROSTO 🍅
Roasted Tomatoes with Wild Fennel
Paola Braccioni, Urbania (Pesaro and Urbino), Marche

This same technique can be used with bell peppers, zucchini, onions, or eggplant. The tomatoes can also be grilled, crushed, and then slicked with extra-virgin olive oil and served on slices of fresh bread.

SERVES 4
3   cloves garlic
Leaves of 1 sprig wild fennel
2   cups breadcrumbs
3   tablespoons extra-virgin olive oil, plus more for pan
Salt to taste
8   tomatoes

Preheat the oven to 350°F. Mince the garlic and fennel together. Combine with the breadcrumbs and oil and season with salt. Halve the tomatoes horizontally. Lightly oil a baking pan and place the tomatoes in it cut sides down. Roast in the preheated oven for 30 minutes.

Remove the pan from the oven, flip the tomatoes over, and sprinkle the breadcrumb mixture all over them. Return to the oven and bake until all of the liquid they have given off during cooking has evaporated, about 20 additional minutes. Serve hot or cold.

POMODORI GRATINATI 🌿
Tomatoes with Breadcrumbs
Maîla Carpentieri, Udine, Friuli-Venezia Giulia

Tomatoes are more than just a salad ingredient. Cooking tomatoes brings out their flavor and lends them an interesting texture.

SERVES 4
4   San Marzano tomatoes
Salt to taste
Leaves of 1 sprig parsley, minced
1   clove garlic, minced
About ¼ cup breadcrumbs
Extra-virgin olive oil for moistening and oiling skillet
1   tablespoon unsalted butter

Halve the tomatoes horizontally, seed them, and salt them. Combine the parsley, garlic, and breadcrumbs. Moisten with oil and season with salt. Stir until well combined.

Lightly oil a skillet and arrange the tomatoes cut sides up. Dot them with the butter and sprinkle on the parsley mixture. Cover the skillet and cook over medium heat for 5 minutes. Turn the tomatoes over and cook for another 5 minutes. Serve hot or cold.

PESTO PANTESCO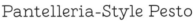
Pantelleria-Style Pesto
Ristorante La Nicchia, Pantelleria (Trapani), Sicilia

Pantelleria-style pesto is excellent on spaghetti, and it can also be served with fried or roasted fish or spread on toasted bread (it's perfect with firm Castelvetrano black bread, which has a Slow Food Presidium).

SERVES 6
4 to 5 cloves garlic
30 large basil leaves
1   mint leaf
1   pound plum tomatoes, peeled and diced
Salt to taste
Freshly ground chili pepper to taste
1   teaspoon minced fresh oregano
½   cup extra-virgin olive oil

With a mortar and pestle, grind the garlic with the basil and mint. Stir this mixture together with the tomatoes and season with salt, chili pepper, and oregano. Stir in the oil.

PEPERONATA
Sautéed Peppers
Trattoria dell'Alba, Vho di Piadena (Cremona), Lombardia

This can be perked up with minced parsley or basil, or with a tablespoon of vinegar and a pinch of sugar. It can also be served as a light entrée, and it may be either warm or cold. As a side dish, it marries beautifully with sausages and other meat dishes. The peppers can also be preserved, but if you plan to do this, remove them from the heat when they are still crisp in the center (and, of course, follow the appropriate steps for preserving in sterile jars). The Trattoria Cortevecchia in Polesella (province of Rovigo) serves a similar vegetable medley: to prepare it, cook bell peppers, carrots, and onions in oil over low heat for 5 minutes, then add diced potatoes and zucchini, and after an additional 5 minutes add diced, seeded ripe tomatoes. Cover and cook over low heat for 1 hour, stirring occasionally.

SERVES 6

- 7 tablespoons unsalted butter
- ¼ cup extra-virgin olive oil
- 2 small onions, thinly sliced
- 1 clove garlic
- 2 carrots, thinly sliced
- 6 to 7 canned peeled tomatoes, crushed
- 1 large red bell pepper, seeded and diced
- 1 large yellow bell pepper, seeded and diced
- 1 large green bell pepper, seeded and diced
- Salt and freshly ground black pepper to taste

Melt the butter with the oil in a large skillet over medium heat. Add the onions and cook until they begin to color. Add the garlic, carrots, and tomatoes. Cook, stirring occasionally, until the carrots are cooked halfway through, then add the peppers, season with salt and pepper, and cook over very low heat until all the vegetables are soft and combined.

PEPERONATA CON ACCIUGHE
Sautéed Peppers with Anchovies
Rosetta Castello, Cocconato (Asti), Piemonte

This and other pepper dishes from the Piemonte region were once made with the peppers from Motta di Costigliole d'Asti in the Tanaro valley area. Sadly, today those once renowned peppers have all but vanished. (Even worse, much of the formerly fertile farmland in this area is now the 231 highway that runs from Cuneo to Asti, and many farmers grow flowers rather than produce, with the result that shiny, beautiful, and utterly tasteless hydroponic peppers imported from Holland can be found in many home and restaurant kitchens.) There are still some local peppers available, though—look for the varieties grown in Carmagnola, Cuneo, and Bra. This dish can be served hot or warm (better in summer) as a side dish to accompany boiled meats, or even on its own.

SERVES 4

- ¼ cup extra-virgin olive oil
- 2 cloves garlic, halved
- 1 large firm yellow bell pepper, seeded and cut into medium dice
- 1 large firm green bell pepper, seeded and cut into medium dice
- 1 large firm red bell pepper, seeded and cut into medium dice
- 4 salted anchovies, rinsed, boned, and chopped, or 1 tablespoon anchovy paste whisked with a small amount of extra-virgin olive oil
- Salt to taste

Heat the oil in a skillet and sauté the garlic cloves until browned. Add the diced peppers and cook over medium heat, stirring with a wooden spoon, briefly, then turn the heat up to high. When the peppers begin to color (obviously, do not allow them to burn), turn the heat to low and cook for 5 minutes. Add the anchovies and crush with a fork to dissolve them. Cook, stirring occasionally, for an additional 25 minutes.

Remove and discard the garlic. Taste and adjust salt (you may not need any salt unless the peppers are very sweet), stir to combine, and remove from the heat.

PEPERONI MOLLICATI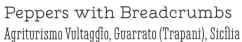
Peppers with Breadcrumbs
Agriturismo Vultaggio, Guarrato (Trapani), Sicilia

This dish should be prepared in advance and allowed to rest at room temperature for a few hours before serving. Nubia red garlic is particularly flavorful and intense. If you like your peppers to have an assertive personality and you are using standard garlic, feel free to add an extra clove.

SERVES 4
Extra-virgin olive oil for pan-frying
1⅓ pounds green bell peppers, trimmed and diced
Salt and freshly ground black pepper to taste
4 cloves garlic, preferably Nubia red garlic, minced (see note)
Leaves of 1 sprig parsley, minced
1⅓ cups breadcrumbs

In a generous amount of extra-virgin olive oil, pan-fry the peppers over medium heat, uncovered, until not quite cooked through, about 10 minutes. Season with salt and pepper and stir in the garlic and parsley. Cook for an additional 5 minutes and stir in the breadcrumbs. Cook for 2 additional minutes, adding a little additional oil to the pan if it begins to look dry. Remove from the heat and allow to rest at room temperature for a few hours before serving.

PEPERONATA CON OLIVE VERDI 🌿
Sautéed Peppers with Green Olives
Casa-Museo Da Nunzio Bruno, Floridia (Siracusa), Sicilia

You can add a little vinegar about halfway through cooking—when you add the olives—for a slightly different flavor. Potatoes are also a nice addition and can temper the strong flavor of this dish a little. For a heartier dish, add a scant pound of cubes of a relatively fatty cut of pork after the onion has turned golden, and cook it through before adding the peppers and other ingredients.

SERVES 4
1 medium yellow onion, chopped
Extra-virgin olive oil for sautéing
1 pound ripe bell peppers, roasted, peeled, and cut into strips
2 cloves garlic, minced
2 plum tomatoes, peeled, seeded, and chopped
½ cup green olives, pitted
Salt and freshly ground black pepper or hot pepper to taste

Sauté the onion in olive oil and when it is golden, add the peppers, garlic, and tomatoes. Cook over low heat, stirring occasionally with a wooden spoon, until the tomatoes and peppers have softened but not collapsed. Add the olives, season to taste with salt and pepper, and continue to cook over low heat, stirring occasionally, until mixture is soft and thoroughly combined.

PEPERONI CON POMODORI
Peppers and Tomatoes
Mimmo Folino, Vibo Valentia, Calabria

This side dish can also be used to make a really tasty frittata, or use it as a sauce for pasta. To make enough to serve 4, seed 1 pound bell peppers and cut them into julienne. Peel about 10 ounces plum tomatoes, squeeze them to remove the seeds and liquid, and cut into dice. Sauté the peppers in a generous amount of extra-virgin olive oil for a minute or two, then add the tomatoes and cook, stirring frequently, until the peppers are tender but still crisp in the center. Tear in some basil leaves and remove from the heat.

PEPERONI SOTT'OLIO
Bell Peppers with Anchovies Preserved in Oil
Claudia Nicolino, Riva presso Chieri (Torino), Piemonte

Prepare several jars of this Piemonte classic in jars and you'll always have a tasty antipasto at hand. Chop 2 pounds yellow bell peppers: quarter them if they are small, or cut them into more pieces if they are larger. Blanch for 10 minutes in equal parts water and vinegar seasoned with salt. Drain the peppers and dry them on a clean dish towel, turning once to blot both sides. Rinse and bone half as many salted anchovies as you have pieces of pepper and cut each one into 2 fillets. Place a fillet on a piece of pepper, fold the pepper, and use a toothpick to hold it closed. Repeat with the remaining peppers and anchovy fillets. Arrange the peppers in sterile jars and add enough olive oil to submerge them completely. Seal hermetically for longer storage.

FAGIOLINI AGRODOLCI
Green Beans in Sweet and Sour Sauce
Flavio Righetti, Milano, Lombardia

Trim about 1½ pounds green beans and blanch them in salted water until al dente. While the beans are cooking, in a small pot beat 2 large eggs with ¼ cup sugar, 2 tablespoons vinegar, and 2 tablespoons water. Cook in a hot water bath, whisking constantly to stop any lumps from forming, over medium heat. When the beans are cooked, drain them and spread them on a serving platter. Pour the sauce over the beans and serve immediately. You can also add some spring onions sautéed until golden and minced parsley to this dish.

DIAVOLICCHI RIPIENI SOTT'OLIO
Stuffed Chili Peppers Preserved in Oil
Ristorante Già Sotto l'Arco, Carovigno (Brindisi), Puglia

Like bell peppers, chili peppers can be eaten whole, as long as you can take the heat! Diavolicchio peppers are long, thin red chili peppers.

MAKES 2 PINTS

- 1 pound diavolicchio chili peppers, trimmed, halved, and seeded
- White wine vinegar for soaking
- 1 (500-gram) can Italian tuna, drained and flaked
- 3 ounces salted anchovies, rinsed, boned, and minced
- ¼ cup plus 2 tablespoons small capers, rinsed and drained
- 1 chunk stale bread, crumbled (optional)
- Extra-virgin olive oil for moistening stuffing and filling jars

Place the peppers in a bowl and add vinegar to cover. Allow to sit for 24 hours, then drain. Combine the remaining ingredients to make a stuffing. Stuff the peppers with that mixture and transfer to sterile jars and add enough oil to submerge them completely. Hermetically seal the jars.

FAGIOLINI AL POMODORO 🍅
Green Beans with Tomatoes
Trattoria Matteuzzi, San Casciano in Val di Pesa (Firenze), Toscana

For this recipe, look for green beans that are about 4 inches long. You can also use yellow wax beans if they are available. This should be made in an earthenware pot. Just don't boil the green beans first—they'll be limp and flavorless.

SERVES 4
1   rib celery
1   carrot
1   small yellow onion
2   cloves garlic
Leaves of 1 sprig parsley
4 to 5 basil leaves
1¾ pounds green beans, trimmed
1   pound fresh tomatoes, chopped,
    or 1 (1-pound) can peeled tomatoes
Extra-virgin olive oil for sautéing
Salt and freshly ground black pepper to taste

Mince together the celery, carrot, onion, garlic, parsley, and basil and place in an earthenware pot with the green beans and the tomatoes. Add a generous amount of oil, season with salt and pepper, cover the pot, and cook over low heat until the green beans are tender, 50 to 60 minutes.

FINOCCHI GRATINATI
Baked Fennel
Salvatore Grieco, Firenze, Toscana

Fennel seeds are very popular in Toscana, where they appear in pork dishes and the salami known as *finocchiona*. But the bulbs are eaten as well, especially the Dolce di Firenze fennel variety, and can be served raw in salads or baked until tender and sweet as they are here. For a richer version of this dish, spread béchamel over the fennel before adding the cheese.

SERVES 6
3   tablespoons unsalted butter, plus more
    for baking pan
Juice of 1 lemon
¼   teaspoon unbleached all-purpose flour
1   tablespoon wine vinegar
3⅓ pounds fennel bulbs
¾   cup grated Parmigiano Reggiano
Salt to taste

Butter a baking pan and set aside.
    Fill a pot of water and add the lemon juice. Dissolve the flour in the vinegar and add that mixture to the water as well (this will keep the fennel from discoloring as it cooks). Bring to a boil. Meanwhile, cut an X in the bottom of each fennel bulb. When the water boils, add the fennel and cook until they are just tender but not too soft. Drain, cut into slices, and arrange in the prepared baking dish. Preheat the broiler.
    Sprinkle on the grated cheese. Dot with the butter, season with salt, and broil until the top is browned and the cheese has melted, about 5 minutes.

FAGIOLINI CON POMODORO E CACIORICOTTA
Green Beans with Cherry Tomatoes and Cheese
Trattoria La Piazza, Poggiardo (Lecce), Puglia

Cacioricotta is aged ricotta that is firm enough to be shaved or grated. For this recipe, seek out cheese with a bit of bite.

SERVES 4
1   pound green beans
Salt to taste
1   clove garlic
1   medium yellow onion, diced
Extra-virgin olive oil for sautéing
7   ounces cherry tomatoes, diced
2   ounces cacioricotta cheese

Trim the beans and cook in boiling salted water until al dente. In a pot, sauté the garlic and onion in olive oil. When the garlic has browned, remove it and discard it and add the tomatoes and green beans and cook for 10 minutes. Adjust salt to taste and shave the cheese over the dish just before serving.

BARBABIETOLE IN AGRODOLCE
Sweet and Sour Beets
Alda Baglioni, Cavedine di Stravino (Trento), Trentino–Alto Adige

Beets may be baked, steamed, or boiled. They pair naturally with pork and other roasted meats and their sweet taste calls for an acidic complement. The vacuum-packed cooked beets available in many supermarkets are handy and can be used here—simply skip boiling the beets. Double the sugar if you like your beets sweet.

SERVES 4
4   medium beets
Salt to taste
½   cup white wine vinegar
1   tablespoon sugar
Whole black peppercorns to taste
1   bay leaf
1   clove garlic, unpeeled
Extra-virgin olive oil for drizzling
Freshly ground black pepper to taste

Boil the beets in lightly salted water until tender. Drain, peel, and set aside to cool. (Be careful where you leave them, as they can stain.) Meanwhile, gently heat the vinegar and stir in the sugar until dissolved. Add a few black peppercorns, the bay leaf, and the garlic.

Slice the beets and transfer to a bowl or platter, then pour the vinegar mixture over them. Allow to sit and absorb the flavors, then remove and discard the peppercorns, bay leaf, and garlic. Season the beets with a drizzle of olive oil, season with salt and ground black pepper, and serve.

FINOCCHIO SPACCATO
Crushed Fennel Salad
Trattoria Font'Artana, Picciano (Pescara), Abruzzo

This is the perfect simple side dish for a stuffed rabbit or duck, but you will need young, tender fennel bulbs to make it. Simply trim the fennel, then crush it firmly against the work surface to break it apart. Crushing it releases more flavor, but if you prefer you can cut it into slices. Dress the fennel with a dressing made by whisking red or white wine vinegar with extra-virgin olive oil and salt. Add a generous grinding of black pepper and serve. In Sansepolcro (Arezzo), Beatrice Ligi makes a salad of fennel and cooked beans. In Palermo, Filippa Gatì makes a salad of fennel, olives, vinegar, garlic, oregano, chili pepper, and minced parsley.

FINOCCHI CON CAPPERI E ACCIUGHE
Fennel with Capers and Anchovies
Rosaria Puccia, Modica (Ragusa), Sicilia

The mild flavor of fennel is enhanced by the salty tang of anchovies and capers. When cooked, fennel no longer tastes like anise.

SERVES 4

- 1 pound fennel
- Salt to taste
- 2 salted anchovies, rinsed, boned, and chopped
- 3 tablespoons extra-virgin olive oil
- ¼ cup breadcrumbs
- Freshly ground black pepper to taste
- 1½ teaspoons capers, rinsed and drained
- Freshly ground chili pepper to taste
- Aged sheep's cheese shavings for serving

Thinly slice the fennel and blanch in lightly salted water. Drain and transfer to a bowl. Sauté the anchovies in the oil until dissolved, then add the breadcrumbs and season with black pepper. Pour the anchovy mixture over the fennel and toss to combine, then add the capers and a little chili pepper and toss again. Top with a generous amount of cheese and serve.

CAVOLO RAPA SOFFOCATO
Smothered Kohlrabi
Klaus Mayr, Renon-Ritten (Bolzano-Bozen), Trentino-Alto Adige

Kohlrabi is a kind of turnip eaten in northern Italy.

SERVES 4

- 6 tablespoons unsalted butter
- 1 tablespoon sugar
- 4 kohlrabi, diced
- 1 tablespoon unbleached all-purpose flour
- Salt and freshly ground black pepper to taste
- ½ cup heavy cream or whipping cream

Melt the butter in a pot and add the sugar. Cook, stirring, over medium heat until it begins to caramelize. Add the kohlrabi. Sprinkle on the flour and season with salt and pepper. Cook, stirring constantly to avoid sticking, until browned. Add ½ cup cold water, cover the pot, and cook over low heat for 1 hour. Check every once in a while to make sure the pan isn't dry and add a small amount of additional water if the vegetables are beginning to stick.

After 1 hour, uncover the pot and stir in the cream. Cook, stirring frequently, for a few minutes to thicken, then serve.

CAVOLFIORE IN UMIDO
Stewed Cauliflower
Nanni Ricci, Firenze, Toscana

This cauliflower dish is brilliant for soaking up the juices of any meat dishes. Discard the tough base of the cauliflower, or reserve for another use, but keep any tender leaves and add them to the pot along with the florets. They are delicious!

SERVES 6

- ¼ cup extra-virgin olive oil
- 2 cloves garlic
- Leaves of 1 sprig fresh rosemary
- 1 piece chili pepper to taste
- 3 ripe tomatoes, peeled, seeded, and diced, or 1 small jar peeled tomatoes
- 12 olives in brine, drained and pitted
- 1 large, firm head cauliflower, divided into medium florets
- Salt and freshly ground black pepper to taste

Place the olive oil in a pot with the garlic, rosemary, and chili pepper and place over medium heat. When the garlic begins to color, add the tomatoes and the olives. Stir to combine, then cook until thickened slightly. Add the cauliflower florets and any leaves and stir to combine.

Season with salt and pepper and add enough lukewarm water just to cover the cauliflower. Cover and simmer until the cauliflower is soft, but not falling apart, 15 to 30 minutes.

CUCUZZA ALL'AURUDUCI
Sweet and Sour Squash
Filippa Gatì, Palermo, Sicilia

This sweet and sour squash, which probably has Arab roots, is a Sicilian classic. At one time, hawkers sold this dish from the stalls in the Vucciria market. It was meant to be squash cooked in a manner that made it resemble meat, giving rise to an old proverb: *Cònzala comu voi, sempri cocuzza jè*, or, "Cook it however you like; it's still squash." This dish is great with sausages, roasted veal rolls, or breaded Palermo-style roast and can also be served as an antipasto.

SERVES 4 TO 6
Extra-virgin olive oil for pan-frying and dressing
1   *firm cucuzza squash, about 2 pounds, peeled, seeded, and cut into slices*
Salt and freshly ground black pepper to taste
1   *cup white wine vinegar*
¼   *cup sugar*
2 to 3 *cloves garlic, crushed*
¼   *cup small mint leaves*

Heat a generous amount of olive oil in a pan with high sides and fry the squash slices, turning to cook both sides, until browned. Season with salt and pepper, remove with a slotted spoon, and drain.

In a small pot, combine a small amount of extra-virgin olive oil with the vinegar and sugar

and cook, stirring constantly with a wooden spoon, over low heat until the sugar has dissolved completely.

Arrange the squash slices on a platter. Pour the warm dressing over them. Scatter on the garlic cloves and the mint leaves.

CIME DI RAPA AFFOGATE AL VINO
Broccoli Rabe Smothered in Wine
Ristorante Al Fornello da Ricci, Ceglie Messapica (Brindisi), Puglia

Broccoli rabe—known by a multitude of names and available in a multitude of varieties in Italy, along with its close cousins turnip greens and mustard greens—is one of the vegetables most frequently eaten in Puglia.

SERVES 4
¼   *cup extra-virgin olive oil*
¼   *cup diced lean pancetta*
1   *clove garlic*
4½ *pounds broccoli rabe, roughly chopped*
1   *cup dry white wine*
Freshly ground black pepper to taste
Ground chili pepper to taste
10 *cherry tomatoes*
Salt to taste

Heat the olive oil in a skillet with high sides or a pot. Sauté the pancetta and garlic clove until the garlic clove browns, then remove and discard the garlic. Add the broccoli rabe and ½ cup of the wine, then cover and cook over low heat for 15 minutes.

Uncover, add the remaining ½ cup wine and the black and chili pepper and the tomatoes. Taste and season with salt, then cover again and cook over low heat until very tender, at least 15 additional minutes.

BROCCOLETTI AFFOGATI
Smothered Broccoli
Domenica Lo Dico, Petralia Soprana (Palermo), Sicilia

This dish can also be made with cauli-flower.

SERVES 4

1   medium yellow onion, sliced
Extra-virgin olive oil for sautéing
2   pounds broccoli, chopped
Salt and freshly ground black pepper to taste
½   cup dry white wine
2 to 3 salted anchovy fillets, rinsed, boned, and chopped
12   black olives, pitted
2   ounces aged sheep's cheese, shaved with a vegetable peeler
8   slices country-style bread

In a large pot, sauté the onion in olive oil until browned. Add the broccoli. Season with salt and pepper and add 1 cup water. Cook over medium heat, covered, adding water occasionally so that the broccoli is just barely covered. You want it to be simmered, not boiled. After 30 minutes, add the wine and cook until evaporated. Add the anchovies, olives, and cheese and cook for 15 additional minutes, then remove from the heat.

Toast or grill the bread just before serving. Serve the broccoli hot.

POLPETTE DI CAVOLFIORE
Cauliflower Dumplings
Ristorante Vicolo Duomo, Caltanissetta, Sicilia

These are basically vegetarian meatballs with crushed cauliflower standing in for the ground meat with mouthwatering results. They can be served as a side dish or as an appetizer. You can also prepare these as fritters by making a looser mixture (more egg, less breadcrumbs, or both) and dropping tablespoons of the mixture into hot oil, then scooping the fritters out with a skimmer.

SERVES 4

1   head cauliflower (1⅓ to 1½ pounds)
Salt to taste
2   cloves garlic
Leaves of 1 sprig mint
Leaves of 1 sprig parsley
¼   cup breadcrumbs
2   large eggs, lightly beaten
1   tablespoon grated aged sheep's cheese
1   tablespoon grated Parmigiano Reggiano
Olive oil for frying

Trim the cauliflower and boil it in lightly salted water until soft. Mince together the garlic, mint, and parsley. Drain the cauliflower and transfer it to a large bowl. Crush the cauliflower with a fork, then stir in the breadcrumbs, beaten eggs, both types of cheese, and the minced herbs and garlic.

Form the mixture into balls about 2 inches in diameter. Line a baking sheet with paper towels and set aside. Prepare a large pot of olive oil for frying. Fry the dumplings until golden on all sides, then remove with a slotted spatula to the prepared baking sheet and drain briefly before serving.

SCAROLE AFFOGATE
Smothered Escarole
Ristorante Europeo, Napoli, Campania

Escarole is widely used in Italy. It can be eaten raw in salads, but it is most often cooked. Escarole with capers, raisins, anchovies, olives, and pine nuts is a classic combination from the Campania region.

SERVES 4

2 pounds escarole, roughly chopped
Salt to taste
2 cloves garlic
¼ cup extra-virgin olive oil
1 ounce salted anchovies, rinsed, boned, and chopped
¼ cup pitted olives
¼ cup capers, rinsed and drained
¼ cup black raisins, soaked in water to rehydrate, then drained
⅓ cup pine nuts

Blanch the escarole in lightly salted water. Drain of excess water but do not squeeze.

In a pot, sauté the garlic in the olive oil. When the garlic turns golden, remove and discard and add the escarole to the pot and cook over medium heat for a few minutes. Add the anchovies, olives, capers, raisins, and pine nuts. Stir to combine. Taste and adjust salt. Cover and cook over low heat until the escarole is very soft and liquid has evaporated.

CAVOLINI DI BRUXELLES ALLA PARMIGIANA
Brussels Sprouts Parmigiana
Alberto Colombo, Vigevano (Pavia), Lombardia

Preheat the oven to 350°F. Butter a baking pan and set aside. Bring a pot of lightly salted water to a boil, turn down to a gentle simmer, and cook Brussels sprouts for about 15 minutes. (Be sure to cook at a low temperature so as not to break apart the Brussels sprouts.) Drain and arrange in the buttered pan. Drizzle on a generous amount of melted butter and sprinkle on a generous amount of grated Parmigiano. Season with freshly ground white pepper and/or freshly grated nutmeg, if desired. Bake until golden, about 15 minutes.

Alternatively, cook the Brussels sprouts in salted water and then sauté them in a skillet with a little oil and add some meat jus or a small amount of broth and let them absorb it over medium heat for a few minutes, stirring frequently.

SCAROLE RIPIENE
Stuffed Escarole
Ristorante Sirio, Formia (Latina), Lazio

Stuffed escarole comes in many forms and may be served as side dish, appetizer, or even a main course. If you don't have time to stuff the leaves, you can simply tear the escarole leaves and then scatter the filling on top and cook them on the stovetop. Nunzia Grimaldi of Giffoni Sei Casali in the province of Salerno stuffs her escarole with a caper filling and cooks it on the stovetop over low heat in garlic-infused olive oil for 15 minutes or so.

SERVES 4

3 tablespoons dried currants
4 heads escarole
15 Gaeta olives, pitted
¼ cup pine nuts
2 salted anchovies, rinsed, boned, and minced
Extra-virgin olive oil for drizzling
Salt to taste

Preheat the oven to 325°F. Place the currants in a small bowl and add warm water to cover. Let sit for about 10 minutes. Wash the escarole, discarding any torn or discolored leaves, but leaving the heads whole.

Drain and squeeze dry the currants. In a small bowl, combine the currants, olives, pine nuts, and anchovies. Mix to combine thoroughly.

Gently open the heads of escarole and stuff them with the currant mixture. Tie closed with kitchen twine. Drizzle oil on all sides of the escarole and salt them, then arrange in a baking pan in a single layer. Bake in the preheated oven for 45 minutes. Cut off and remove the twine and serve hot.

SPINACI CON PANE RAFFERMO E PANCETTA
Spinach with Bread and Pancetta
Ristorante L'Elfo, Capracotta (Isernia), Molise

This dish originates with the shepherds of the tiny Molise region. They used wild spinach, but today's cultivated spinach works just as well, as would chard. Shepherds also used cured sheep's belly, *pancetta di pecora*, but since that isn't widely available, feel free to substitute pork-belly pancetta.

SERVES 4
Salt to taste
1   pound spinach
2   cups stale bread cubes
1   tablespoon extra-virgin olive oil
1   clove garlic
⅓   cup diced sheep or pork pancetta
Grated aged sheep's cheese to taste (optional)

Bring a small amount (an inch or two) of salted water to a boil in a pot and add the spinach. Cook for 5 minutes, then add the bread and cook until softened. Drain the mixture and crush with a fork or in a mortar and pestle.

In a small skillet, heat the olive oil and cook the garlic until golden. Remove and discard the garlic and cook the pancetta until crisp. Sprinkle the pancetta over the spinach and stir to combine. Taste and adjust salt. Transfer to a serving bowl and top with grated cheese, if using.

COSTE DI BIETOLE ALLA VENEZIANA
Chard Stems with Garlic and Parsley
Ofelia Facco, Cavallino Treporti (Venezia), Veneto

Chard stems can also be chopped, dredged in beaten egg and then flour, and fried.

SERVES 6
3½ pounds (4 to 5 bunches) chard
½   cup extra-virgin olive oil
1   clove garlic, minced
Leaves of 1 sprig parsley, minced
Salt to taste
2   tablespoons white wine vinegar

Tear the greens off the chard stems and reserve for another use. Wash and chop the stems. Transfer the stems to a pot, add water to cover, and bring to a boil. Cook at a simmer for 15 minutes, then remove some of the water, leaving a little liquid in the pot, and add the oil, garlic, and parsley and season with salt. Cover and cook until all the liquid has evaporated, then add the vinegar and cook until that has evaporated as well.

FRITTELLE DI SPINACI
Spinach Fritters
Palmira Giovannini, Bologna, Emilia-Romagna

Spinach fritters are a nice light supper when paired with some slices of good prosciutto.

SERVES 4
1   pound spinach
4   large eggs
¾   cup all-purpose flour or 00 flour
2   cups grated Parmigiano Reggiano
1   tablespoon extra-virgin olive oil, plus more for frying
Salt and freshly ground black pepper to taste

Steam the spinach, drain, squeeze dry, and chop. In a medium bowl, beat the eggs. Beat in the flour, grated Parmigiano, spinach, 1 tablespoon extra-virgin olive oil, salt, and pepper.

Line a baking sheet with paper towels and set aside. In a skillet with high sides, heat a generous amount of olive oil. Drop the batter by spoonfuls into the oil and cook, turning gently, until both sides are browned. Drain on the prepared pan briefly before serving.

COSTE AL BRUSCH ❗
Chard Stems with Eggs
Rosina Idrame, San Damiano d'Asti (Asti), Piemonte

This recipe uses only the meaty white stems of the chard. Reserve the tender greens for another use—they are terrific in a frittata or soup, or simply braised.

SERVES 6
3½ pounds (4 to 5 bunches) chard
Salt to taste
3 large eggs, separated
2 tablespoons unbleached all-purpose flour
½ cup red wine vinegar
Extra-virgin olive oil for sautéing

Tear the greens off the chard stems and reserve for another use. Wash and chop the stems and boil them in lightly salted water until tender.

While the chard stems are cooking, separate the eggs and beat the whites to stiff peaks. Beat the yolks separately and then beat them into the whites. Sift in the flour and beat again, then add the vinegar and ½ cup water and beat to combine into a rather liquid batter.

Drain the cooked chard stems and place in an aluminum pot with a small amount of oil and cook, stirring frequently with a wooden spoon, over medium heat for 5 minutes. Turn the heat as low as it will go and pour in the egg mixture. Cook, stirring constantly, until the eggs firm up. Taste and adjust salt. Serve very hot.

SECRA CU PANA
Chard Cake with Bread and Cheese
Luisa Sanfile, Monterosso Calabro (Vîbo Valentia), Calabria

Depending on many factors, you may need a little more than ⅓ cup sheep's cheese to make this cake bind together, so have extra on hand, but don't grate it until you need it.

SERVES 4
2 pounds chard
Salt to taste
Extra-virgin olive oil for sautéing
1 clove garlic
2 cups stale bread cubes
About ⅓ cup grated aged sheep's cheese
1 chili pepper, minced (optional)

Separate the green leaves from the white stems of the chard. Chop the stems into pieces about ¾ inch by ½ inch (this will probably mean cutting the stems in half or in thirds lengthwise before chopping them). Tear the green leaves into rough pieces. Bring a pot of lightly salted water to a boil. Add the stems and cook for 5 minutes, then add the leaves and cook until tender. Drain and squeeze dry.

In a skillet, heat a generous amount of olive oil with the garlic and toast the bread cubes until crisp. Remove and discard the garlic. Add the cooked chard and cook, stirring frequently, for 5 minutes. Stir in ⅓ cup of the grated cheese. The mixture should bind together. If it does not, add cheese in small amounts until it does. Taste and adjust salt and add the chili pepper if using. Use a wooden spoon to press the mixture together firmly into a cake. Cook until the underside is nicely browned, then use a lid to turn the cake as you would a frittata and cook until the other side is browned as well. Allow to cool before serving.

POLPETTE DI VURRANIA ▦
Borage Fritters
Sabina Zuccaro, Siracusa, Sicilia

Borage is an herb that grows in warm dry places. The largest borage leaves are excellent battered and fried, stuffed with prosciutto and mozzarella or anchovy fillets, and the most tender leaves are a lovely addition to a salad mix.

SERVES 4
Salt to taste
2 pounds borage
4 large eggs, lightly beaten
Leaves of 1 sprig parsley, minced
1 clove garlic, minced
1 cup grated aged Sicilian sheep's cheese
About 1 cup breadcrumbs
Freshly ground black pepper to taste
Extra-virgin olive oil for pan-frying

Bring a pot of lightly salted water to a boil and cook the borage for 15 minutes. Drain, squeeze gently, and chop.

In a bowl, combine the cooked borage, the eggs, the parsley, the garlic, the cheese, and the 1 cup breadcrumbs and season with salt and pepper. Mix until you have a soft mixture that holds together when squeezed. If the mixture is too liquid, add breadcrumbs a little at a time to stiffen.

Line a baking sheet with paper towels and set aside. In a skillet with high sides, heat a generous amount of olive oil. Drop the batter by spoonfuls into the oil and cook, turning gently, until both sides are browned. Regulate the temperature to avoid burning. Drain on the prepared pan briefly before serving.

CAVOLFIORE GRATINATO ▨
Baked Cauliflower with Cheese and Breadcrumbs
Luigi Grassi, Cecina (Livorno), Toscana

In Monopoli, in the province of Bari, Paolo Giangrande first sautés cauliflower in an ovenproof pan with a few chopped cloves of garlic, a bay leaf, 3 or 4 chopped tomatoes, a piece of hot chili pepper, and some parsley leaves. Next he adds water to cover and cooks over high heat for 15 minutes, before sprinkling on grated aged sheep's cheese and baking the dish in a preheated 400°F oven.

SERVES 4
1 head cauliflower, broken into medium florets
Salt to taste
6 tablespoons unsalted butter, plus more for buttering pan
⅓ cup unbleached all-purpose flour
2 cups whole milk, warm
Freshly grated nutmeg to taste
Freshly ground white pepper to taste
1½ cups grated aged sheep's cheese
1 cup breadcrumbs
Leaves of 1 sprig parsley, minced

Cook the cauliflower in lightly salted boiling water until tender, about 10 minutes. Preheat the oven to 350°F. Butter a baking pan and set aside.

Melt 3 tablespoons of the butter in a small pot and whisk in the flour until smooth. Add the warm milk, season with salt, nutmeg, and pepper, and bring to a boil, whisking constantly. Cook until thickened to the consistency of sour cream, about 2 minutes, then remove from the heat and whisk in about half of the sheep's cheese.

Drain the cauliflower and arrange it in the prepared pan. Pour the béchamel over it and sprinkle on the remaining sheep's cheese. Dot with the remaining 3 tablespoons butter and sprinkle on the breadcrumbs. Bake until the top is browned, 10 to 20 minutes. Sprinkle with minced parsley just before serving.

CIME DI RAPA INFUOCATE 🌶
Spicy Broccoli Rabe
Luisa Greco, Scorrano (Lecce), Puglia

This recipe combines two ingredients essential to the cooking of Puglia: broccoli rabe and hot pepper.

SERVES 4

2   cloves garlic, crushed
1   red chili pepper, minced
3 to 4 tablespoons extra-virgin olive oil
1¾ pounds broccoli rabe, roughly chopped
Salt to taste
½   cup vegetable broth
Ground chili pepper to taste

In a skillet with high sides or a pot, sauté the garlic and the minced chili pepper in the oil. When the garlic begins to brown, remove and discard it and add the broccoli rabe. Season with salt and stir to combine. Add the vegetable broth, cover, and cook until the broccoli rabe is wilted, about 10 minutes. Uncover and cook, stirring occasionally with a wooden spoon, until the greens are very tender. Season with a pinch of ground chili pepper before serving.

CIME DI RAPA SOFFRITTE 🧅
Braised Broccoli Rabe
Paolo Giangrande, Monopoli (Bari), Puglia

This is a simple way to obtain very tender broccoli rabe, as the greens can sometimes be rather chewy. Serve with roasted pork or sausages.

SERVES 4

2   cloves garlic, crushed
3 to 4 tablespoons extra-virgin olive oil
1¾ pounds broccoli rabe, roughly chopped
Salt to taste

In a large pot, sauté the garlic in olive oil. When the garlic browns, remove and discard it and allow the oil to cool. Add the broccoli rabe, 3 tablespoons water, and salt. Cover the pot and cook over medium heat until the broccoli rabe is wilted, then uncover and continue to cook, stirring frequently, until very tender.

AMAREDDI AL POMODORO 🍅
Wild Broccoli Rabe with Tomato Sauce
Ristorante Il Giardino di Bacco, San Giovanni La Punta (Catania), Sicilia

Wild broccoli rabe is closely related to the cultivated type, but it has a more bitter flavor. This recipe calls for cooking the greens first to remove some of that bitterness. You can use broccoli rabe, mustard greens, or any other of the heartier greens in the *Brassica* genus in this recipe.

SERVES 4

2   pounds wild broccoli rabe
2   cloves garlic, sliced
½   cup extra-virgin olive oil
½   cup tomato sauce
Salt to taste
⅔   cup diced young sheep's cheese with pepper (pecorino pepato)

Rinse the broccoli rabe but do not dry thoroughly. With the water still clinging to the leaves, place the broccoli rabe in a pot, cover, and cook until soft. Drain, squeeze dry, and chop.

In a skillet with high sides, sauté the garlic in the oil, then add the greens and cook for a few minutes. Add the tomato sauce and season with salt. When the sauce begins to bubble, add the cheese and stir to combine and distribute the cheese thoroughly. Cook until the cheese melts and serve immediately.

RAPE ACCOMMODATE ♣
Turnips Cooked in Milk
Agriturismo Cascina di Maggio, Moncucco Torinese
(Asti), Piemonte

The milk in this recipe helps to soften the bitterness of the turnips with very mild results that make a wonderful foil for sausage, particularly cotechino sausage. Not that we encourage subterfuge, but some parents have reported managing to get their children to eat turnips by passing them off as "Hungarian potatoes."

SERVES 6
5 to 6 turnips
Extra-virgin olive oil for sautéing
½ cup whole milk
Salt and freshly ground black pepper to taste
*1 tablespoon unsalted butter, cut into a
    few pieces*

Peel and quarter the turnips, then cut into medium-thick slices. Heat oil in a skillet, then add the turnips and cook, turning once or twice until they begin to caramelize, about 5 minutes. Add the milk, season with salt and pepper, and cook over low heat until the turnips are soft. Scatter on the butter and cook, stirring occasionally, until the butter has melted and the turnips are shiny and glazed, about 3 minutes.

RAPE ALLE ACCIUGHE 🐟
Turnips with Anchovies
Milvia Tardito, Cengio (Savona), Liguria

The humble turnip comes to life when paired with anchovies.

SERVES 4
Salt to taste
1 pound turnips, peeled and sliced
Leaves of 3 sprigs parsley
½ medium yellow onion, thinly sliced
2 cloves garlic
3 tablespoons extra-virgin olive oil
4 salted anchovies, rinsed and boned

Bring a pot of salted water to a boil and boil the turnips for 10 minutes, then drain. Mince the leaves of 2 of the sprigs of parsley.

Over medium heat, sauté the onion and garlic in the oil in a skillet. Add the anchovies, crushing them a little with a fork, and 2 tablespoons water. Cook for 1 minute, then add the turnips. Cook, stirring, until the turnips have begun to brown. Stir in the minced parsley. Transfer to a serving platter, garnish with the remaining whole parsley leaves, and serve.

NUSET
Savoy Cabbage Cake
Guglielmo Zani, Cremona, Lombardia

This type of cabbage cake is usually served with a selection of cheeses, with polenta, or with boiled meats. The osteria Il Postiglione di Montodine in the province of Cremona serves a cabbage flan made by sautéing cabbage in butter with garlic, then mixing it with a fairly stiff béchamel, eggs, and a generous amount of grated Parmigiano Reggiano and baking it in a water bath at 300°F for 1 hour.

SERVES 6
2 pounds Savoy cabbage
Salt to taste
1 large egg
2½ cups grated Parmigiano Reggiano
1 clove garlic, minced
Freshly ground black pepper to taste
1 tablespoon unsalted butter

Core the cabbage and cut into ribbons. Boil in lightly salted water for 15 minutes, then drain and squeeze dry.

In a bowl, beat the egg and the grated cheese. Beat in the garlic, black pepper to taste, and the cabbage. Cover and set aside to rest for 3 to 4 hours.

Melt the butter in a skillet and add the egg mixture. Cook as you would a frittata (see pages 24 to 25) until golden on both sides.

CAVOLI STRASCINATI
Cabbage with Croutons
Gino Zampolini, Magione (Perugia), Umbria

Ruffled Savoy cabbage (named for the Savoy region of the Alps) is more tender than standard red and green cabbage. Look for tight heads that sport green leaves without soft or brown spots. This dish is a good choice with sausage or pork cutlets.

SERVES 4
1 head Savoy cabbage
2 to 3 potatoes
Salt to taste
2 cloves garlic
½ cup extra-virgin olive oil
2 to 3 slices bread, cut into cubes

Remove and discard the outer leaves of the cabbage. Scrub the potatoes but do not peel them. Bring two pots of lightly salted water to a boil and cook the cabbage and the potatoes separately until soft. Drain the cabbage and squeeze dry, pulling off small pieces and forming them into balls. Peel the potatoes and cut into dice. In a skillet, sauté the garlic in the olive oil. When the garlic browns, remove and discard it and add the bread cubes. As soon as the bread begins to color, add the cabbage and potatoes and cook, stirring gently to avoid breaking apart the vegetables, until combined. Taste and adjust salt and serve hot.

CIPOLLE ROSSE CARAMELLATE
Caramelized Red Onions
Ristorante La Baritlera, Chianocco (Torino), Piemonte

These onions are often served with meat, but they can be a refreshing part of a vegetarian meal as well.

SERVES 4
4 red onions, sliced
2 tablespoons extra-virgin olive oil
Salt to taste
¼ cup turbinado sugar
Red wine for simmering

Place the onions in a skillet with high sides and add the olive oil and a pinch of salt. Cook over high heat until the onions have wilted, then add the sugar. Continue to cook, stirring, until the sugar has melted, then add wine to cover, turn the flame down to low, cover, and cook until the onions are falling apart, at least 1 hour.

STUFATO DI CAVOLO ROSSO
Stewed Red Cabbage
Ristorante Altran, Cortona Alta di Ruda (Udine), Friuli-Venezia Giulia

Red cabbage is a natural with smoked and roasted pork shoulder. Start with a boned pork shoulder and for about every 5½ pounds meat make a brine of ¾ pound salt, 4¼ cups water, 2 teaspoons sugar, bay leaves, and whole cloves. Brine the meat for 2 days in this mixture, then smoke it over cherry or oak wood chips and aromatic herbs such as thyme, rosemary, and sage. Finally, brown it in butter on the stovetop, then roast for 15 minutes. Slice and serve with this stewed red cabbage for a perfect meal.

SERVES 4

- 2 cups red wine
- ¼ cup red wine vinegar
- 1 apple
- 1 orange
- 1 large head red cabbage, enough for 1 pound once trimmed
- ½ medium yellow onion, thinly sliced
- Unsalted butter for sautéing
- Beef broth for braising
- Salt to taste

In a bowl, combine the wine and vinegar. Peel and core the apple and grate it into the bowl. Grate the orange zest into the bowl, then juice the orange and add the juice as well. Core the cabbage, cut into ribbons, and marinate in the wine mixture overnight.

The next day, drain the cabbage. Sauté the onion in butter until golden. Add the drained cabbage and just enough broth to film the bottom of the pan. Cook at a simmer until very soft, adding small amounts of broth at a time, just enough to keep the pan from drying out. Season with salt.

CIPOLLE IN UMIDO
Stewed Onions

Bruno Burchini and Gina Martini, Chiusi della Verna (Arezzo), Toscana

This onion side dish is great with polenta. Peel 4 large yellow onions and slice as thinly as possible. Peel and seed 2 to 3 plum tomatoes. Sauté the onion and about ½ cup diced pancetta (preferably lean rigatino pancetta) in extra-virgin olive oil. Add the tomatoes, season with salt, and cook, stirring frequently, until soft.

UMIDO DI CIPOLLINE AL CERFOGLIO ✿
Stewed Cipollini Onions with Chervil

Osteria Bohemia, Sozzigalli di Soliera (Modena), Emilia-Romagna

Chervil (*Anthriscus cerefolium*) should be used right after you cut it and should be incorporated after cooking, as it loses much of its flavor when exposed to heat.

SERVES 4

- Rock salt for cooking water
- 1 pound cipollini onions, peeled and trimmed
- ¼ cup extra-virgin olive oil
- 3 tablespoons unsalted butter
- ½ cup beef broth
- 2 bay leaves
- ¼ cup white wine
- Authentic balsamic vinegar from Modena for drizzling
- Leaves of 1 bunch chervil, minced

Bring a large pot of salted water to a boil and cook the onions for 15 minutes. Drain, blot to remove excess water, and sauté in the oil and butter. When the onions begin to color, add the broth and bay leaves. Cook for a few minutes to combine, then add the wine and cook over low heat until the onions are soft enough that you can easily insert a toothpick all the way into the center. Remove and discard the bay leaves.

Drain the onions and transfer to a serving platter. Drizzle with vinegar and scatter on the chervil and serve hot.

SMARITATA DI LAMPASCIONI E CIPOLLA
Hyacinth Bulbs and Onions with Wild Thyme and Lardo
Osteria Antichi Sapori, Montegrosso di Andria (Bari), Puglia

Lampascioni are tassel hyacinth bulbs. They are foraged frequently in Puglia. They are a bit of a bother to clean, but their flavor is unique. If you can't find any where you live and want to try this recipe, you can double the onions and will still get good results. Please note that lardo is not lard, but a kind of cured fatback. These bulbs and onions are cooked long and slow over the lowest possible heat—it is best to use a flame-tamer to do so.

SERVES 4

7   ounces hyacinth bulbs, peeled
Salt and freshly ground black pepper to taste
3 to 4 leaves wild thyme, minced
½   cup grated aged sheep's cheese
Extra-virgin olive oil for drizzling
10   ounces (4 to 5) small white onions, peeled and halved
2   ounces lardo slices

Soak the hyacinth bulbs overnight to leach out the bitterness. Drain them (still whole and uncooked) and place them in a terra-cotta pot where they fit in a single layer. Season lightly with salt and pepper, scatter on about half of the thyme and about half of the cheese, and drizzle with olive oil. Arrange the white onion halves on top in a single layer. Season again with salt and pepper, scatter on the remaining thyme and cheese, and drizzle with oil. Arrange the slices of lardo in a single layer on top.

Pour in ½ cup water (pour it down the side of the pot to avoid disturbing the onions), cover, and cook over the lowest possible heat for 3 hours.

CIPOLLINE GLASSATE
Glazed Cipollini
Salvatore Grieco, Firenze, Toscana

Glazed onions are always a visually attractive and tasty accompaniment to roasted meats. To make enough to serve 6 people, peel 1¾ pounds cipollini onions, preferably the Borettana variety (an especially mild heirloom variety with a flattened shape), and blanch in very hot water. Drain and set aside. In a skillet, melt 3 tablespoons butter. Add ½ cup sugar and stir until a caramel forms. Stir in ½ cup white wine vinegar and cook over high heat until the mixture thickens, about 3 minutes. Add the onions and 5 bay leaves and cook over medium heat, turning occasionally, until the onions are coated in the glaze.

Another technique for glazing onions is simply to place them in a skillet with high sides where they fit in a single layer and add broth to cover. Dot the surface with butter, then cook over low heat until the liquid has been reduced by a third. Turn the onions and cook until the liquid has reduced down to a thick 2 or 3 tablespoons. For sweet and sour glazed onions, do the same but add 1 tablespoon vinegar to the pan along with the broth.

SCALOGNI GLASSATI
Glazed Shallots
Riccardo Baiocchi, Carpi (Modena), Emília-Romagna

These shallots use honey rather than sugar for the glaze, which suggests the recipe is based on ancient traditions. In a large skillet, combine 2 tablespoons unsalted butter, 1 tablespoon extra-virgin olive oil, and 1 tablespoon honey. Add 20 peeled shallots. Cook over low heat, adding a tablespoon or two of chicken broth occasionally to keep the onions from sticking to the pan. Cook until the onions are soft and glazed, but keep a close eye on the heat to keep the mixture from burning, as the honey can caramelize quickly.

ZOLLE SOTT'OLIO
Garlic Scapes Preserved in Oil
Taverna de li Caldora, Pacentro (L'Aquíla), Abruzzo

Zolle are the scapes (stems) of garlic, in this case the area's Sulmona red garlic. Garlic scapes pop out of the soil and if left unpicked grow flowers. Scapes are harvested on early May mornings, because they are easier to pluck when the dew is still keeping the soil moist. They can be eaten in salads and frittatas, or preserved as they are here— 10 ounces scapes will serve as a side dish for 4 people. Chop the scapes and boil them for 5 minutes in a solution of water, salt, and white wine vinegar. Drain and dry on a clean dish towel, then transfer to sterile jars and add extra-virgin olive oil to cover. Hermetically seal and wait at least 5 months before eating. These are an interesting addition to a platter of cheese and salumi.

FUNGHI TRIFOLATI
Mushrooms with Garlic and Parsley
Ristorante Il Vecchio Mulino, Saline di Volterra (Pisa), Toscana

This cooking technique is most often used with mushrooms, but it is also a good way to handle other vegetables and some organ meats. This recipe may seem to call for a lot of mushrooms, but they shrink drastically when cooked.

SERVES 4
⅓ cup extra-virgin olive oil
1 sprig calamint
2 cloves garlic
1 piece chili pepper
Salt to taste
1 pound 6 ounces mixed mushrooms, small ones left whole and larger ones sliced (about 8 cups)
Leaves of 1 sprig parsley, minced

Place the oil, calamint sprig, garlic, chili pepper, and salt in a large pot or skillet with high sides. Add the mushrooms and cook until the mushrooms are very soft and have given up all their liquid, and then the liquid has evaporated, about 20 minutes.

Remove from the heat, discard the garlic and calamint sprig, and sprinkle on parsley.

COMPOSTA DI CIPOLLE
Tropea Onion Jam
Francesca Maggio, Pino Torinese (Torino), Piemonte

This onion jam can be eaten immediately or preserved in sterile glass jars according to proper canning techniques. It is a wonderful addition to a cheese plate. Thinly slice 2 pounds Tropea onions, which are an elongated, red, extra-sweet variety. Place the onion slices in a pot with ½ cup Malvasia wine, 3 tablespoons apple cider vinegar, 1 cinnamon stick, 1 pinch ground cinnamon, 1¾ cups sugar, 3 tablespoons golden raisins (soaked in water to rehydrate if dry), and 1 tablespoon pine nuts (optional). Cook over low heat, stirring occasionally, for 2 hours. The onions should be so soft that they are falling apart. Allow to cool to room temperature before serving or preserving in jars.

FUNGHI FRITTI ALL'OLIO DI LENTISCHIO
Mushrooms Fried in Mastic
Ristorante Letizia, Nuxis (Carbonia-Iglesias), Sardegna

Mastic (*Pistacia lentiscus*) is an evergreen shrub that grows in the Mediterranean. Its oil is intensely aromatic and lends a unique flavor to dishes from Sardegna; the oil is also used in Greek cooking, so Greek specialty stores may carry it. About 2 pounds of mixed mushrooms will serve 6 people. Use any combination you like, including varieties such as porcini and white mushrooms. Trim the stems and wipe the mushrooms clean, keeping them as dry as possible. Spread coarsely ground semolina flour on a work surface and gently toss the mushrooms in it. Fill a pot with high sides with several inches of a mixture of 1 part mastic oil for every 5 parts extra-virgin olive oil and bring to the correct temperature for frying. Meanwhile, line a baking sheet with paper towels and set aside. Fry the mushrooms until golden, turning them to cook them on all sides, and working in batches if necessary to avoid crowding the pot. As they are cooked, remove them with a skimmer to the prepared pan to drain briefly and season with salt. For serving, line a platter with butcher paper and scatter the mushrooms on it. As with all fried foods, serve hot.

FUNGHI IN UMIDO
Stewed Mushrooms
Osteria Bagnoli, Castagneto Carducci (Livorno), Toscana

This recipe is best with a mix of different varieties of mushrooms. You can also add boiled beans and sage leaves for a heartier dish: add about 1 cup cooked beans and 4 sage leaves.

SERVES 4
- 2 cloves garlic, minced
- Leaves of 1 sprig parsley, minced
- Extra-virgin olive oil for sautéing
- 1 pound 6 ounces mushrooms, roughly chopped if large (about 8 cups)
- ¾ cup tomato puree
- Leaves of 1 sprig marjoram
- Salt and freshly ground black pepper to taste

In a large skillet, sauté the garlic and parsley in oil very briefly. Add the mushrooms, tomato puree, and marjoram and cook until the mushrooms have given off their liquid and the liquid has evaporated, about 30 minutes. Season with salt and pepper.

FUNGHI CHIODINI SOTT'OLIO 🌶
Chiodino Mushrooms Preserved in Oil
Ristorante In Contrada Serio, Crema (Cremona), Lombardia

Mushrooms are preserved in oil through-out Calabria, Liguria, and Puglia. You can include various flavoring agents in the vinegar solution used to cook them, or put the flavorings directly in the oil in the jars. In addition to the cloves and hot pepper used here, bay leaves, white peppercorns, and cinnamon sticks are popular choices. Look for small chiodino mushrooms (also known as honey mushrooms, beech mushrooms, and shimeji) without any soft spots and wipe them gently with a damp cloth to clean. Use a high-quality extra-virgin olive oil here—the flavor will be noticeable. As always, exercise caution if you are foraging for your own mushrooms. Chiodino mushrooms resemble several toxic varieties. Also, they cannot be consumed raw. You can use this technique with any other small mushrooms.

MAKES ABOUT 8 CUPS PRESERVED MUSHROOMS
Extra-virgin olive oil for boiling and preserving
1 *pinch ground chili pepper*
2 *cups vinegar*
¾ *teaspoon salt*
1 *whole clove*
2 *pounds chiodino mushrooms, trimmed*

Place a small amount of oil and the chili pepper in a pot. Add the vinegar and 2 cups water, the salt, and the clove. Bring to a boil and add the mushrooms. When the liquid returns to a boil, cook the mushrooms for 1 additional minute; do not allow them to get soft. Drain the mush-rooms and allow them to cool in a sterilized jar. When the mushrooms are cool, add enough extra-virgin olive oil to cover them completely. Hermetically seal for longer storage.

SALSA AL TARTUFO 🌿
Truffle Sauce
Cesaria Gioia, Terni, Umbria

Unlike its cousin the white truffle, black truffle, or *Tuber melanosporum*, is at its best when heated (though not to a piping hot temperature). This sauce can be refrigerated and brought back to room tem-perature before serving. It is tasty with roasted veal, whether the veal is served hot or cold.

Sauté 1 clove garlic in 3 tablespoons butter in a small pot. When the garlic colors, remove and discard it and let the butter cool. Mince a black truffle (about ⅓ ounce) and add it to the pot. Incorporate the juice of ½ lemon and salt and freshly ground black pepper to taste. Return the pot to the heat and bring it to a boil, then remove from the heat immediately.

CIANFOTTA DI PATATE E CARCIOFI 🌱
Stewed Potatoes and Artichokes
Ristorante Europeo, Napoli, Campania

Cianfotta is a summer vegetable dish from Napoli. Every recipe for cianfotta is unique (see also the recipe on page 366). Feel free to adjust them to suit your tastes.

SERVES 4
4 *potatoes*
Juice of 1 lemon
4 *artichokes*
Extra-virgin olive oil for sautéing
1 *medium yellow onion, diced*
Salt to taste
Oregano to taste
¼ *cup pitted black olives*
¼ *cup capers, rinsed and drained*
Leaves of 1 sprig parsley, minced
Calamint leaves (optional)

Parboil the potatoes, drain, peel, and cut into dice. Prepare a bowl of cold water and lemon juice and trim and quarter the artichokes (or cut smaller if they are very large), dropping them immediately into the bowl of water so they don't discolor.

Heat olive oil for sautéing in a pot. Add the onion and potatoes. Drain the artichokes and add those as well. Season with salt and oregano. Add the olives, capers, and parsley and stir to combine. Cover and cook over low heat until vegetables are very soft.

Uncover and allow any liquid in the pan to evaporate. Tear in calamint leaves if using.

If you are using ripe tomatoes, pass them through a food mill to remove the seeds and peels and puree them. If you are using canned tomatoes, crush them with a fork and set aside.

Heat the oil in a large pot with the garlic and rosemary. Just before the garlic begins to brown, add the potatoes and cook, stirring frequently, for 3 minutes. Add the tomatoes and season with salt and pepper. Add enough warm (not hot) water just to cover the vegetables.

Cover the pot and cook over low heat, stirring occasionally, until the potatoes are very soft. If the dish appears excessively thick during cooking, thin it with small amounts of beef broth.

PATATE ALLA CONTADINA
Country-Style Potatoes with Tomatoes, Garlic, and Rosemary
Trattoria Mario, Firenze, Toscana

Originally, this simple dish was made by home cooks in farmhouses, who simply placed all of the ingredients in a pot in the morning, then left the pot in a corner of the hearth, where the potatoes would cook gently and be ready by mealtime. There is no overcooking this dish, which should remain on the flame until just before serving. It's perfectly acceptable for some or all of the potatoes to fall apart.

SERVES 6
1   pound ripe tomatoes, or 1 (28-ounce) can peeled tomatoes
¼   cup extra-virgin olive oil
2   cloves garlic
Leaves of 1 sprig rosemary, minced
2   pounds (about 6 medium) potatoes, peeled and chopped
Salt and freshly ground black pepper to taste
About ¼ cup beef broth, if needed

PATATE E FAGIOLI
Potatoes and Beans
Trattoria Roma, Castelletto Stura (Cuneo), Piemonte

This side dish pairs well with hearty meat dishes, but in a pinch you can also add broth and turn it into a soup. This recipe is easily made in larger quantities, but be sure to keep the ratio of potatoes to beans balanced. The cooking time is lengthy, but once everything is in the pot there's no real work involved.

SERVES 4
1   medium yellow onion
1   leek
1   carrot
1   rib celery
Leaves of 1 sprig rosemary
Extra-virgin olive oil for sautéing and drizzling
2   medium potatoes, peeled and diced
1½ cups kidney beans, soaked in cold water overnight
Salt to taste
Freshly ground black pepper or chili pepper to taste

Mince together the onion, leek, carrot, celery, and rosemary and sauté in olive oil in a pot.

Add the potatoes. Drain the beans of their soaking water, rinse, then add those to the pot as well. Cook, stirring, over medium heat for a few minutes to combine flavors, then add enough water to cover. Bring to a boil, still stirring, then lower the heat to a simmer and cook, stirring occasionally with a wooden spoon, until the beans and potatoes are extremely soft and most of the liquid has evaporated, 4 to 5 hours. Season with salt after cooking. Ladle into bowls and drizzle with olive oil and season with black pepper or chili pepper before serving.

PATATE AL FORNO
Roasted Potatoes
Osteria di Rubbiara, Rubbiara di Nonantola (Modena), Emília-Romagna

This recipe calls for Bologna variety potatoes, the only potato variety in Italy with DOP status. Peel the potatoes (figure 2 to 3 small potatoes per person) and cut them into slices or wedges. Arrange them in a baking pan, sprinkle with salt, and pour in about 1 inch water. Bake in a preheated 350°F oven until very soft, about 2½ hours. Drizzle with a few drops of authentic balsamic vinegar from Modena and serve immediately.

In Potenza, Mimma Tancredi fills a pan with alternating layers of potatoes and sliced onions and tomatoes. She drizzles each layer with extra-virgin olive oil and sprinkles grated aged sheep's cheese, breadcrumbs, and oregano over the top before baking. She also peels and thinly slices boiled potatoes and lets them cool, then sautés hot pepper in some olive oil and pours the mixture over the potatoes to delicious effect. Celestino Mariani in Castellafiume (province of L'Aquila) cooks potatoes in the fireplace with a cast-iron pot overturned on top to protect them from direct contact with the flames. He then seasons the roasted potatoes with salt, extra-virgin olive oil, and red wine vinegar.

PATATE E POMODORI
Potatoes and Tomatoes
Luigia Bevione, Monteu da Po (Torino), Piemonte

This side dish can be paired with almost any main course, but it's so delicious that it may end up being the star of the meal.

SERVES 4
8 potatoes
Unbleached all-purpose flour for dredging
¼ cup extra-virgin olive oil
2 cloves garlic
1 sprig rosemary
2 sage leaves
Salt and freshly ground black pepper to taste
2 cups vegetable broth
6 tomatoes
Leaves of 1 sprig parsley, minced

Peel the potatoes, pat them dry, and cut them into rather thick slices. Dredge the potatoes in flour.

In a pot, heat the extra-virgin olive oil. Add the garlic and fry until golden, then remove and discard the garlic and add the rosemary and sage leaves. Let the herbs flavor the oil for a few minutes, then add the potatoes and brown. Season with salt and pepper. Add the vegetable broth (beware of sputtering), cover, and cook over medium heat for 15 minutes.

While the potatoes are cooking, peel and seed the tomatoes, then chop them. Add them to the pot with the potatoes and cook until the tomatoes have collapsed, 5 to 6 minutes. Sprinkle on the parsley and serve.

PURÈ DI PATATE
Mashed Potatoes
Claudia Nicolino, Riva presso Chieri (Torino), Piemonte

Place (scrubbed but unpeeled) potatoes in a pot with cold water to cover and bring to a boil. Simmer until soft enough to pierce easily with a fork. Drain the potatoes (reserving the cooking water if you don't plan to use milk), and as soon as they are cool enough to handle, peel them and mash them with a potato ricer. Place the potatoes in a *polsonetto*, a round-bottomed pan, and place it directly on the stovetop or in the top of a double boiler if you prefer frothier mashed potatoes. Add a bit of softened butter and mix it in with enough milk to make a smooth puree. (Use some of the potato cooking water in place of the milk if you prefer.) Season with salt. The potatoes are already cooked, so there is no need to leave them on the heat for very long. If desired, season with freshly ground pepper or freshly grated nutmeg as well.

Vittorio Fusari, owner and chef at the Dispensa Pane e Vini in Torbiato di Adro (province of Brescia), makes his mashed potatoes by cutting peeled potatoes into dice and placing the cubes in a pot with milk, cream, butter, and ground cinnamon. When the potatoes are cooked, he forces the mixture through a sieve to create a dense puree.

PATATE IN PADELLA
Sautéed Potatoes
Franca Gallo, Aosta, Valle d'Aosta

Potatoes came to Italy from France via the Valle d'Aosta region in the late 1700s. This combination of potatoes and leeks—another favorite in the region—was traditionally served to workers in the fields on the day wheat was threshed. To make a side dish to serve 4 people, wash 4 potatoes and place in a pot of cold salted water. Bring to a boil and cook until tender, but still with some resistance in the middle. Peel and slice. Mince 1 yellow onion and the white of 1 leek and sauté in a pan in 1 tablespoon butter. Add the potatoes and brown well on all sides. Season with salt and serve.

PATATE MARITATE
Potatoes with Garlic, Parsley, and Cheese
Ristorante Plistia, Pescasseroli (L'Aquila), Abruzzo

No one seems to know how these came to be named "married potatoes," but we'd hazard a guess that it's because the flavors exist in such perfect harmony.

SERVES 4
- Extra-virgin olive oil for oiling pan and drizzling
- 2 pounds (about 4 medium) potatoes
- 1½ cups crumbled stale crustless bread
- Leaves of 1 sprig parsley, minced
- 2 cloves garlic, minced
- Salt and freshly ground black pepper to taste
- 2 forms aged Scamorza cheese cut into cubes (about 3 cups)
- 1 cup grated aged sheep's cheese

Preheat the oven to 400°F. Oil a baking pan and set aside. Peel the potatoes and cut them into rounds a little less than ¼ inch thick. In a large bowl, combine the crumbled stale bread with the parsley and garlic. Season with salt and pepper and mix to combine.

Arrange one third of the potatoes in a single layer in the bottom of the prepared pan. Season with salt and sprinkle on about one third of the bread mixture, one third of the Scamorza cubes, and one third of the grated sheep's cheese. Make two additional layers in the same order. Drizzle on a generous amount of extra-virgin olive oil and bake in the preheated oven for 1 hour 15 minutes. Pour off any excess oil before serving.

PATATE SILANE 'MPACCHIATE AI FUNGHI

Potatoes with Basil and Porcini Mushrooms

Ristorante Parco Pingitore, Serrastretta (Catanzaro), Calabria

Sila potatoes are extra-starchy and firm. They grow in sandy soil at a high altitude. Look for potatoes with dense flesh and preferably cook in a cast-iron or blue steel pot.

SERVES 4

1 pound starchy potatoes, preferably Sila potatoes
Extra-virgin olive oil for frying
1 tablespoon lard (optional)
9 ounces porcini mushrooms, preferably from the Sila area, wiped clean and sliced (about 3 cups)
Salt to taste
Ground chili pepper
Leaves of 1 sprig basil

Peel the potatoes, dry them with a clean dishtowel, and cut them into rounds. Pour a generous amount of olive oil into a pot with high sides and bring to a high temperature. If using lard, add that to the oil and allow it to melt. Add the potatoes and cook until golden, 5 to 6 minutes, then add the porcini. Turn gently to cook on all sides. Season with salt and chili pepper. When the potatoes and mushrooms are cooked through, remove from the heat and tear in the basil leaves.

Transfer the contents of the pot to a container with a tight-fitting lid and seal tightly so that the potatoes continue to cook in the steam produced.

PATATE VOIANI E CUCUZZEDJA

Spicy Potatoes with Beans and Squash

Luisa Sanfile, Monterosso Calabro (Vibo Valentia), Calabria

This dish combines potatoes with classic ingredients from Calabria: the flat beans known as *voiani* and the long squash known as *cucuzzedja*.

SERVES 4 TO 6

Salt to taste
3 to 4 potatoes, peeled
2 pounds voiani flat beans or other flat beans, trimmed
2 pounds cucuzzedja or other squash, trimmed
2 cloves garlic
Extra-virgin olive oil for dressing
1 chili pepper, minced (optional)

Bring a large pot of salted water to a boil. Add the potatoes and cook until somewhat tender, then add the beans and cook until those are somewhat tender, and, finally, add the squash and cook until all three are tender. Drain the vegetables. Crush the potatoes and dice the squash while they are still warm, and in a bowl combine those with the beans (left whole). Combine the garlic and olive oil and season with salt, and chili pepper, if desired, and pour over the warm vegetables. Toss gently to combine. Serve at room temperature.

PATATE GRATINATE
Potatoes Baked with Fontina
Letizia Palesi, Champorcher (Aosta), Valle d'Aosta

This recipe pairs the humble potato and the most revered cheese from this area. Longer aged Fontina can be used here, since the starchy potatoes will counterbalance its sharpness. Boil medium unpeeled potatoes (1 per person is a good measure) until tender, then peel and thinly slice. Arrange the potato slices in a buttered baking pan, cover with slices of Fontina, season with salt and pepper and sprinkle with a little freshly grated nutmeg, then bake until the cheese melts.

RÖSTI
Potato Cake
Trattoria Altavilla, Bianzone (Sondrio), Lombardia

For this recipe, seek out small potatoes, each one about the size of an apricot. These are often more easily found in a farmers market than in a grocery store.

SERVES 4
20 small potatoes
Salt to taste
1 small onion, cut into julienne
2 tablespoons unsalted butter

Cook the potatoes in a generous amount of boiling salted water. Allow them to cool, then peel them and grate them on the medium holes of a grater.

In a skillet, cook the onion in the butter. Add the grated potatoes and sauté, stirring gently. Season with salt and cook for 10 minutes.

Use a wooden spoon to pack the potatoes together to form a cake. Cook until golden on the bottom, then gently flip in the pan and cook until the other side is golden as well. Serve very hot.

CUCULLI
Potato and Marjoram Fritters
Rosanna Orlandini, Genova, Liguria

Genova has a long tradition of fritters and croquettes, including these potato fritters, which are traditionally served with breaded lamb chops, but are also sometimes simply eaten on their own as a snack.

SERVES 4
2 pounds potatoes
7 tablespoons unsalted butter, cut into pieces
Leaves of 1 sprig marjoram, minced
¼ cup grated Parmigiano Reggiano
⅓ cup pine nuts, crushed
Salt to taste
3 large eggs, separated
Extra-virgin olive oil for frying
Breadcrumbs for dredging

Boil the potatoes until soft and then peel them while they are still warm. Crush them in a bowl with a fork or use a potato ricer, then add the butter and crush to combine. Add the marjoram, Parmigiano Reggiano, pine nuts, and a little salt. Add the egg yolks one at a time, stirring with a wooden spoon to combine between additions. The resulting dough should be soft and creamy. Beat the egg whites. Use a spoon to create small balls of the dough—each about the size of a large walnut.

In a pot with high sides, bring a generous amount of oil for frying to the correct temperature. Dredge the balls of dough first in the beaten egg whites, then in the breadcrumbs. Working in batches if necessary, fry them until puffed, golden, and soft. Season with salt and serve very hot.

KIFFEL
Potato Fritters
Antica Trattoria Valeria, Opicina (Trieste),
Friuli-Venezia Giulia

*K*iffel are an excellent side dish to serve with roasts, braised meat, and all kinds of stews. You can also make sweet kiffel: simply omit the cheese and sprinkle them with a generous amount of sugar after frying.

SERVES 6 TO 8
Salt to taste
2   *pounds potatoes*
1¾ *cups unbleached all-purpose flour*
5   *tablespoons unsalted butter, softened*
2   *large eggs, lightly beaten*
¼   *cup grated Grana Padano (optional)*
Extra-virgin olive oil for frying

Bring a large pot of salted water to a boil and cook the potatoes. When they are soft, drain, peel, and mash them with a potato ricer.

Let the potatoes cool on a work surface and then mix them with the flour, butter, eggs, salt, and cheese, if using. Knead to form a soft dough with the ingredients evenly distributed. Form the dough into cylinders and cut into 4-inch-long pieces. Curve each piece into a U shape.

Line a baking sheet with paper towels. In a pot with high sides, bring a generous amount of oil for frying to the correct temperature, about 275°F. Add the fritters, working in batches if necessary, and fry until puffed and golden, about 5 minutes. Remove with a skimmer and drain briefly on the prepared pan. Serve very hot.

TORTA DI PATATE
Potato Tart
Marianna Baldassini, Aulla (Massa-Carrara), Toscana

*I*n the Lunigiana region of Tuscany, vegetable cakes are a pillar of the area's cooking. This one is well suited to meat dishes.

SERVES 4
4   *potatoes*
2   *large eggs, lightly beaten*
1   *cup grated aged sheep's cheese*
Leaves of 1 sprig parsley, minced
2   *cloves garlic, minced*
Leaves of 1 sprig thyme, minced
Salt and freshly ground black pepper to taste
1½ *cups unbleached all-purpose flour*
Extra-virgin olive oil for oiling pan

Boil the potatoes until tender, peel them, and pass through a potato ricer. Mix with the eggs, cheese, parsley, garlic, and thyme. Season with salt and pepper. Mix the flour with a little salt and as much room temperature water as needed to create a soft dough. Knead briefly, then refrigerate for 20 minutes.

Preheat the oven to 350°F. Lightly oil a baking pan. Roll out the dough to fit the prepared pan and cover the dough with the potato mixture. Bake in the preheated oven for 40 minutes.

PATATE SAPORITE
Potatoes with Chives
Ristorante Martin Pescatore, Milano, Lombardia

*T*his simple side dish makes a good counterpart to a whole fish baked in a salt crust and other fish main courses.

SERVES 4
1   *pound (about 2 medium) potatoes*
Salt to taste
Extra-virgin olive oil for dressing
Freshly ground black pepper to taste
1   *bunch chives*

Boil the potatoes in salted water for 30 minutes. Drain and peel the potatoes . In a bowl, crush the potatoes with a fork. Drizzle on a generous amount of olive oil, season with salt and pepper, and stir. Rinse and dry the chives and chop them very fine. Sprinkle on the chives and serve immediately.

MAÜSC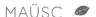
Buckwheat, Green Beans, Sage, and Potatoes
Oliana Maccarini, Berbenno di Valtellina (Sondrio), Lombardia

This dish hails from the Teglio area of the Lombardia region. *Tarozz* is another dish from the Sondrio area made with potatoes and green beans, as well as semi-soft cheese and sautéed onions. Bitto is a DOP cheese made from the milk of cows and goats that graze in Alpine areas, while casera is a cow's milk cheese. Both have a mild, slightly grassy flavor. This dish is baked in a cake pan, but it won't cut neatly into wedges and should be served with a spoon. A tasty salami will highlight its flavor.

SERVES 6

- 1 cup buckwheat flour
- Salt to taste
- 1 pound white potatoes, peeled and chopped
- 10 ounces green beans or yellow wax beans, trimmed
- 1 small onion, minced
- 3 to 4 sage leaves
- 13 tablespoons (1 stick plus 5 tablespoons) unsalted butter
- ⅔ cup cubed bitto cheese (see note)
- ⅔ cup cubed casera cheese (see note)
- 1 cup grated Grana Padano cheese

Make a dough with the buckwheat flour and water and roll out the dough to a sheet about ⅛ inch thick. Cut into large pieces. Bring a large pot of salted water to a boil and add the buckwheat dough pieces, the potatoes, and the green beans. When all three items are soft, drain and then puree them together through a food mill. Preheat the oven to 350°F.

In a pot, sauté the onion and sage in the butter. Remove the sage and set aside. Add the buckwheat mixture to the pot and sauté, stirring frequently, until well combined. Sprinkle in all three types of cheese and stir to combine. Transfer the mixture to a cake pan with sides at least 2 inches high and smooth the top level. Arrange the reserved sage leaves on top. Bake in the preheated oven for 15 minutes.

BIETE E FAVE
Chard and Fava Beans
Adriana Mastrodicasa, Francavilla al Mare
(Chieti), Abruzzo

To make 4 side-dish servings, boil 2 cups fresh shelled fava beans and 2 pounds chard or beet greens until soft, about 30 minutes, then drain. In a skillet, sauté 3 cloves garlic in a generous amount of extra-virgin olive oil. Add the drained beans and greens, a crumbled or minced chili pepper, and salt to taste. Cook, stirring, for 5 minutes, then serve. This springtime delight can also serve as a light main course. Cerasuolo d'Abruzzo is the perfect wine pairing.

FAGIOLANE AL VERDE
Val Borbera Fagiolane Beans with Parsley
Ristorante Stevano, Cantalupo Ligure
(Alessandria), Piemonte

Val Borbera fagiolane beans are the signature beans of the Borbera and Spinti valleys. They are picked by hand. The quality of both the extra-virgin olive oil and the vinegar used here is paramount.

SERVES 4
- 1¼ cups dried Val Borbera fagiolane beans, soaked 18 to 24 hours
- Salt to taste
- 1 clove garlic
- Leaves of 1 sprig parsley
- 2 to 3 tablespoons wine vinegar
- ¼ cup to ½ cup extra-virgin olive oil

Drain the beans of their soaking water and cook them in a generous amount of salted water until soft, then allow them to cool in their cooking water.

Mince the garlic and parsley very finely. Whisk together the vinegar and oil, season with salt, and whisk in the garlic and parsley. Drain the warm beans and pour the dressing over them. Mix to combine and serve warm.

FAGIOLI AL FIASCO
Beans Cooked in a Flask
Trattoria San Lorenzo da Ghigo, Suvereto
(Livorno), Toscana

Toscanelli beans are a small off-white variety similar to cannellini beans but slightly larger. They have a very creamy interior. To prepare this dish, you will need a round-bellied flask, similar to a traditional Chianti flask, without any straw around it. It should be made of thick, heat-resistant glass and have a wide mouth. Do not soak the beans.

SERVES 6
- 2½ cups dried Toscanelli beans
- 3 to 4 cloves garlic, peeled
- Leaves of 1 sprig sage
- 7 ounces Pachino cherry tomatoes, halved (optional)
- Salt to taste
- Extra-virgin olive oil for drizzling

Place the beans, garlic, sage leaves, and the tomatoes, if using, in the flask. Season with salt. Fill the flask with water and close the top with a ball of flax or a piece of white muslin folded over several times and tied with twine. The idea is to keep as much steam as possible in the flask without sealing it off completely.

Arrange the flask in a tilted position on the ashes around the edge of the hearth. After 1 hour, move the flask to the center of the embers and leave it there until the beans are so soft that they begin to fall apart, 2 hours or longer. Serve on individual plates with a little extra-virgin olive oil drizzled on top.

FAGIOLANE ALLA BARBERA ✿
Val Borbera Fagiolane Beans with Barbera Wine Sauce
Ristorante Stevano, Cantalupo Ligure (Alessandria), Piemonte

This side dish can be transformed into a tasty main-dish stew with the addition of tripe or goat. Val Borbera fagiolane, or beans from the Borbera Valley, are large white or off-white beans. The variety is part of the Slow Food Ark of Taste. They should be soaked anywhere from 18 to 24 hours. Of course, you can use this cooking technique with other types of beans as well.

SERVES 4
- 1¼ *cups dried Val Borbera fagiolane beans, soaked 18 to 24 hours*
- 1 *tablespoon unsalted butter*
- 1 *tablespoon extra-virgin olive oil*
- 1 *slice lardo (cured fatback), minced*
- 1 *medium yellow onion, minced*
- *Leaves of 1 sprig rosemary, minced*
- 2 *bay leaves, minced if fresh, left whole if dried*
- *Salt and freshly ground black pepper to taste*
- ½ *cup Barbera wine*

Drain the beans of their soaking water and cook them in a generous amount of water until soft, then allow them to cool in their cooking water.

Meanwhile, in a pot heat the butter and oil. Add the lardo, onion, rosemary, and bay leaves. Season with salt and pepper. Sauté this mixture until it begins to color, then add the wine and cook, stirring occasionally, until the wine has evaporated completely. Continue to cook, adding water in small amounts to keep the mixture moist, then waiting for it to evaporate before adding more, for 30 minutes. Drain the cooled beans and in a serving bowl combine them with the onion mixture. Stir to combine and serve.

FAGIOLI ALL'UCCELLETTO
Cannellini Cooked in the Style of Game Birds
Osteria Il Vignaccio, Santa Lucia di Camaiore (Lucca), Toscana

This is a standout when made with Bigliolo beans, which are sweet and tender and have a very delicate skin. Fresh beans are sold in their pods. This amount should yield about 2 cups shelled beans. You can replace the fresh beans with about 2 cups dried cannellini beans that you have soaked overnight then drained. They will take a bit longer to cook. This dish is best served with veal or pork.

SERVES 6
- 1¾ *pounds fresh cannellini beans, preferably the Bigliolo variety*
- *Salt to taste*
- 4 *cloves garlic*
- 8 *sage leaves*
- *Extra-virgin olive oil for sautéing*
- 14 *ounces plum tomatoes, chopped*
- 2 *basil leaves*
- *Freshly ground black pepper to taste*

Shell the beans and boil them in a generous amount of salted water with 2 garlic cloves and 4 sage leaves, until soft. Transfer to a colander or sieve to drain, but reserve cooking water.

Mince the remaining 2 garlic cloves and 4 sage laves and sauté briefly in oil. Add the beans, tomatoes, and basil leaves. Season with salt and pepper, add enough of the cooking water to cover, and cover the pan with a tight-fitting lid. Simmer until most of the liquid has evaporated and the beans are extremely soft, adding additional cooking water if needed.

PURÈ DI FAGIOLI DI LAMON CON RADICCHIO
Lamon Bean Puree with Radicchio

Trattoria Da Doro, Solagna (Vicenza), Veneto

Lamon beans have been grown in the area around the Lamon plateau in the Belluno area of the Veneto since the sixteenth century. For this recipe, use either the spagnolit or the calonega variety. The former are large and round; the latter are flatter and an off-white color with red streaks. This is served as a side dish in the restaurant, but it would also make a nice rustic appetizer.

SERVES 4

- 1½ cups dried Lamon beans, soaked overnight
- 7 ounces (2 small) potatoes, peeled
- 1 rib celery
- 1 medium yellow onion, peeled
- 1 clove garlic, peeled
- 1 head Treviso radicchio
- 1 bulb fennel, trimmed and quartered
- 2 salted anchovy fillets, rinsed
- Extra-virgin olive oil for dressing
- Wine vinegar for dressing
- Salt and freshly ground black pepper to taste
- 1 chive, snipped, or leaves of 1 sprig parsley, minced
- 8 slices grilled polenta
- 4 slices salami, or 8 slices speck or lardo

Drain the beans of their soaking water and place them in a pot with a generous amount of fresh water. Cook until the beans are soft and some are falling apart.

Meanwhile, in a separate pot, boil the potatoes, celery, onion, and garlic until the potatoes are tender enough to pierce with a fork. Set aside and reserve the cooking water.

Trim the radicchio and cut into ribbons. Make a sauce for the radicchio by boiling the fennel in water to cover until tender and pureeing it in a blender while still warm with the anchovies, a generous amount of extra-virgin olive oil, a few drops of vinegar, and salt and pepper to taste. Use this sauce to dress the radicchio.

When the beans are cooked, process them through a food mill with the potatoes, celery, onion, and garlic. Thin with a little of the vegetable cooking water (rather than the bean cooking water, which will make the resulting puree heavy) to make a creamy puree. Adjust salt and pepper.

For each serving, place about one quarter of the bean puree (which should still be warm) in the center of an individual plate and garnish with chives. Arrange one quarter of the dressed radicchio around it. Place 2 slices of polenta to one side. Place 1 slice of the salami on top of the puree, where it should soften from the heat and flavor the puree further. Serve hot.

FAGIOLI NEL TIANO
Beans Cooked in a Terra-Cotta Pot

Trattoria La Collinetta, Martone (Reggio Calabria), Calabria

A tiano is a traditional terra-cotta pot from southern Italy. Earthenware pots lend themselves to very long, slow cooking. You can use any type of medium-sized bean you like in this dish, and you can also serve the beans in a spicy tomato sauce with some diced pancetta in it or a porcini mushroom sauce.

SERVES 6

- 3⅓ pounds fresh shell beans in their pods, or 2½ cups dried beans
- 2 ribs celery, chopped
- 1 medium yellow onion, chopped
- Salt to taste
- Extra-virgin olive oil for drizzling

If you are using fresh beans, shell them. If you are using dried beans, soak them for 8 to 12 hours, then drain and rinse off their soaking water. Place the beans in a terra-cotta pot with the celery and onion and a pinch of salt. Add just enough water to moisten the beans. Place off to the side of the fire in a wood-burning oven or hearth and cook until very soft, about 1½ hours for fresh beans and 3 hours for dried beans, adding warm water in small amounts each time the beans appear dry. Drizzle with olive oil before serving.

FASOI IN POTACIN
Slow-Cooked Borlotti Beans
Trattoria Cortevecchia, Polesella (Rovigo), Veneto

These can also be made without tomato and simply flavored with bay leaf and rosemary. Another similar dish calls for sautéing a mirepoix of minced onion, celery, carrot, and parsley in olive oil, adding the beans and a little water, covering, and cooking over very low heat until the liquid has evaporated.

SERVES 4

1 medium yellow onion, minced
2 cloves garlic, minced
¼ cup diced guanciale
½ cup extra-virgin olive oil
3 cups fresh shelled borlotti beans (about 2 pounds in their pods)
1 tablespoon tomato paste
1 bay leaf or leaves of 1 sprig rosemary
Salt and freshly ground black pepper to taste

In a pot, sauté the minced onion and garlic and the guanciale in the oil until softened. Add the beans, tomato paste, and bay leaf. Season with salt and pepper and add enough water to cover by at least a couple of inches and bring to a boil.

Turn down to a simmer and cook until the beans are very tender, about 1 hour.

FASOI IN SALSA 🌿
Beans in Herb Sauce
Maria Rigodanza, Lonigo (Vicenza), Veneto

This dish is eaten widely in the Veneto region, both at home and in osterie. If you cannot locate fresh borlotti beans, use dried beans: soak them for at least 8 hours, drain and rinse, and extend the cooking time to about 3 hours.

SERVES 4

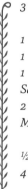

3 cups fresh shelled borlotti beans (about 2 pounds in pods)
1 carrot, roughly chopped
1 rib celery, roughly chopped
1 medium yellow onion, roughly chopped
Salt and freshly ground black pepper to taste
2 cloves garlic, minced
Minced herbs, such as parsley, basil, calamint, sage, and rosemary, to taste
½ cup extra-virgin olive oil
4 to 5 salted anchovy fillets, rinsed and chopped
½ cup wine vinegar
Ground cinnamon to taste

Boil the beans in a generous amount of water with the carrot, celery, onion, salt, and pepper until soft. When the beans are almost cooked, in a skillet, sauté the garlic and herbs in the extra-virgin olive oil. When the garlic begins to color, add the anchovies and cook until they have dissolved. Add the vinegar and cook at a brisk simmer for 10 minutes. Season with cinnamon and pepper. Drain the beans and pour the sauce over the beans. Both should be hot. Stir to combine, cover, and allow to rest at room temperature for 2 hours before serving.

PURÈ DI CICERCHIE DI CASTELVECCHIO

Castelvecchio Cicerchia Bean Puree

Trattoria La Conca alla Vecchia Posta,
L'Aquila, Abruzzo

Cicerchia beans are ivory-colored irregularly shaped legumes that resemble pebbles. They are also excellent served whole, simply drizzled with a little extra-virgin olive oil.

SERVES 4

¾ cup dried cicerchia beans
Salt to taste
Leaves of 1 sprig rosemary
1   bay leaf
1   clove garlic (unpeeled)
Freshly ground black pepper, ground chili
    pepper, thyme, marjoram, or oregano
    to taste (optional)
Extra-virgin olive oil for drizzling

Soak the beans in cold water overnight. Drain them of their soaking water and place them in a pot with fresh water. Season with salt. Add the rosemary, bay leaf, and the unpeeled garlic. If desired, season with black pepper, chili pepper, thyme, marjoram, or oregano. Cover the pot and cook over low heat until the beans are soft, about 2½ hours.

Pop the garlic from its skin or remove completely. Remove and discard the bay leaf. Puree the beans in a blender, adding small amounts of cooking water until they are smooth and have reached the desired consistency. They should be creamy, but not too runny. Drizzle with extra-virgin olive oil before serving.

LENTICCHIE DI ONANO STUFATE

Smothered Onano Lentils

Elvira Alfonsi, Onano (Viterbo), Lazio

Onano lentils, which are part of the Slow Food Ark of Taste, have a skin so thin it's almost nonexistent. They have a delicate flavor that recalls hay or chamomile. When stewed or smothered, they match wonderfully with game, especially partridge. To serve 4 people, rinse 1¾ cups Onano lentils and place them in a pot with cold water, along with 1 chopped rib celery, 1 chopped onion, 1 chopped carrot, 1 clove garlic, and salt to taste. You can also include rosemary or bay leaves. Place the pot over medium heat and cook for about 20 minutes, uncovered, after the water reaches a boil. If the lentils appear dry as they are cooking, add boiling water to the pot in small amounts.

PURÈ DI CECI

Chickpea Puree

Trattoria Martin Pescatore, Milano, Lombardia

At Trattoria Martin Pescatore, this puree is served as a side dish with shrimp, or sometimes on its own with slices of toasted bread rubbed with a garlic clove. It is also tasty topped with chicory leaves that have been boiled, chopped, and sautéed with garlic and oil.

SERVES 4

2½ cups dried chickpeas
1   pinch baking soda
1   bay leaf
1   spring onion
2 to 3 sage leaves
½   cup extra-virgin olive oil
Salt and freshly ground black pepper to taste

Soak the chickpeas for 12 hours in cold water to cover by several inches and the baking soda. Drain, rinse under running water, and boil with the bay leaf, onion, and sage until the beans are soft.

When the beans are cooked, remove and discard the bay leaf and puree the beans (an immersion blender is handy, though you may want to remove the beans with a slotted spoon and then add cooking water back in to the mixture to reach the correct consistency) while drizzling in the oil until you have a creamy puree. Season with salt and freshly ground black pepper.

FAVE 'NGRECCE 🦪
Fava Beans with Garlic and Mint
Osteria de le Cornacchie, Petritoli (Ascoli Piceno), Marche

This satisfying dish can be made with either fresh or dried fava beans. Dried beans should be soaked overnight. The best time to make this, however, is in the spring, when the fresh legumes have just been picked and the mint variety known in the Petritoli area as *svelto*—which has broad leaves and a very strong flavor—is available. If you can't track down that mint, spearmint makes a serviceable substitute.

SERVES 4
- 2   cups fresh shelled fava beans (from about 2½ pounds beans in their pods), or 2 cups dried fava beans, soaked overnight
- 1   clove garlic
- 3 to 4 leaves svelto mint or spearmint
- Ground chili pepper to taste
- Salt to taste
- Extra-virgin olive oil for dressing

Drain the beans if you used dried beans. Place them in a pot of unsalted boiling water and cook until soft, about 20 minutes for fresh beans and at least 1 hour for dried beans. When the beans are soft, drain them and transfer them to a bowl. Mince the garlic and mint leaves together and mix with a pinch of chili pepper and salt, then stir in enough extra-virgin olive oil to coat the beans nicely. Pour this dressing over the beans and toss to combine.

LENTICCHIE DI CASTELLUCCIO IN UMIDO 🌱
Stewed Castelluccio Lentils
Taverna Castelluccio, Norcia (Perugia), Umbria

Castelluccio, in the municipality of Norcia, in the heart of the Monti Sibillini National Park, is known for its flavorful lentils, which have a softer skin than standard lentils, making them extra tender. This recipe is simple because Castelluccio lentils need little enhancement.

SERVES 4
- 2   cups Castelluccio lentils
- 1   clove garlic
- 1   rib celery, chopped
- Salt to taste
- Extra-virgin olive oil for drizzling

In a small-diameter pot with high sides (preferably terra-cotta), combine 4 cups water, the lentils, the garlic, and the celery. Cook over low heat until the lentils are soft, adding boiling water in small amounts if needed to keep the lentils moist. Cooking time will depend on how hard the water is in your area, but it should take about 45 minutes from the time the lentils come to a boil. Season with salt and drizzle with oil, then serve.

{ MOSTARDA, RELISHES, COMPOTES & PRESERVES }

ALIVI CUNZATI ❧
Preserved Green Olives with Mint
Pippo Privitera, Misterbianco (Catania), Sicilia

Start with unripe (green) olives, preferably Nocellara Etnea, Ogliarola Messinese, or Tonda Iblea variety. Crush the olives and salt them with coarse salt, then arrange them in a terra-cotta or glass container with water, garlic, lemon wedges (preferably the Interdonato variety) and celery leaves. Change the water every day for 5 days. Next, to the container add a brine made with 1½ teaspoons coarse rock salt for every 4 cups water, along with lemon wedges, lightly crushed garlic cloves, bay leaves, mint leaves, and whole chili peppers. Finally, roll up a dry sprig of wild fennel and place it in the container so that it presses down on the ingredients and keeps them submerged in the brine. Hermetically seal the container and keep in a cool, dry place for at least 15 days before using.

Bring equal parts water and red wine vinegar to a boil and add the preserved olives. Cook for 5 minutes, then drain. Transfer the olives to a large bowl. Add minced garlic, mint leaves, a sprinkling of oregano, and toss to combine. Transfer to glass jars and add extra-virgin olive oil to cover.

MOSTARDA DI FRUTTA ◉
Fruit Mostarda
Osteria La Sosta, Cremona, Lombardia

Fruit mostarda—a kind of spiced fruit relish served with boiled meat—is a famous specialty of Cremona, and though you can purchase industrial varieties, they don't compare to the handmade mostarda served at the Osteria La Sosta, which is housed in a fifteenth-century building in Cremona.

Start with 4½ pounds mixed fruit. Apricots, cherries, pears, apples, and mandarin oranges are all good candidates. They should not be overly ripe. Pit and cut them into cubes the same size, then place all the fruit—except for cherries, if using—in a container with 5 cups sugar. Toss to combine and allow to macerate for 24 hours.

Drain the fruit, retaining the liquid, and place the fruit in a heatproof bowl and the liquid in a pot. Bring the liquid to a boil and simmer briskly for 30 minutes, then pour the hot liquid over the fruit. Cover with a linen dish towel and set aside to rest for an additional 24 hours. Repeat this process three times. On the last day, when the liquid comes to a boil add the cherries if using. Cook to the degree of caramelization that you prefer.

When you have poured the syrup over the fruit and the mixture has cooled, stir in 15 drops of mustard extract. You can experiment and add more if you like a spicier flavor, but the extract is strong, so proceed with caution.

Transfer the mixture to sterile jars and hermetically seal for storage in a cool, dry place.

MOSTARDA DI MELE 🍎
Apple Mostarda
Trattoria dell'Alba, Vho di Piadena (Cremona), Lombardia

In this area of Lombardia, tortelli filling combines amaretti, golden raisins, candied citron, mint candies, and wine must cookies with apple mostarda. To make it, peel 2 pounds firm apples (not overly ripe) and cut them into slices. Cut 1 unwaxed organic lemon into wedges and squeeze the juice from 2 additional lemons. In a bowl, combine the apple slices with 1½ cups sugar and the lemon juice and lemon wedges. Toss and let sit for 24 hours, stirring occasionally.

Drain the apples, retaining any liquid. Boil the liquid for 20 minutes, then pour the boiling liquid over the apples. Set aside for an additional 24 hours. Repeat three times. Finally, boil the apples and the syrup together in a nonstick pan to caramelize. Let the mixture cool, then stir in 10 drops mustard extract. Transfer to sterile jars and hermetically seal for longer storage.

La Sosta osteria in Cremona makes another version of apple mostarda that uses 4½ pounds not overly ripe Golden Delicious apples, 1 pound organic unwaxed lemons, 4 cups sugar, and 15 drops mustard extract. The apple-lemon version is particularly tasty with mild cheeses, such as ricotta, robiola, stracchino, young asiago, and pannerone.

fifth the original amount, 14 to 16 hours. Do not go too far away and check the progress every once in a while. Cooking time will depend on the sugar content of the grapes you have used—very sweet must will cook faster, but not much faster. To test doneness, pour a spoonful of the liquid onto a white ceramic plate and pass a finger through it. If the mark made by your finger remains visible—meaning the two portions of the liquid on either side do not run back together—the mostarda is ready. It should have a jammy consistency similar to honey.

Transfer the mostarda to sterile bottles or jars and store at room temperature (not in the refrigerator). If prepared correctly, it will last for years.

MOSTARDA D'UVA 🍇
Grape Mostarda
Ristorante Garibaldi, Cisterna d'Asti (Asti), Piemonte

This recipe has only one ingredient, but the process is a long one. At Ristorante Garibaldi, this is served as an accompaniment to cheese and, in an unusual move, over ice cream and custards. A classic grape mostarda from the area is made with Croatina grapes, but at the restaurant they have also used Barbera, Nebbiolo, and Moscato grapes, and even the strawberry grapes and Concord grapes that grow in their own arbors.

Start with 5 quarts freshly pressed grape must. It must be extremely fresh or the recipe won't work at all. Filter the must through a very fine sieve to eliminate any impurities. Place it in a stainless steel pot with a heavy bottom or in a large copper pot and bring to a boil over high heat. Then turn down the heat and very patiently, with a slotted ladle or skimmer, skim off and discard any dark foam (it will be almost brown) that forms on the surface. You will need to do this for at least 1 hour.

When all the foam has been eliminated, simmer, uncovered, until reduced to about one

COGNÀ 🍐
Raisin and Pear Relish
Ristorante Moderno, Carrù (Cuneo), Piemonte

Ristorante Moderno is famous for its classic Piemontese feasts of boiled meat, which this relish enhances, though it's equally good with polenta and soft cheeses. Anyone of a certain age who grew up in Piemonte will have fond memories of spreading a sweeter version of cognà on slices of bread for a snack. When the Dolcetto grape harvest ended in mid-September, an enormous pot of grape must was set to boil on the stove in every house. Vin cotto was made at the same time: this simply involved removing some of the must when it was halfway cooked, before the fruit was added. This was preserved in bottles and then on hot days was diluted with a little water and served to parched farmers as they worked in the fields. You can also use Barbera, Nebbiolo, or Moscato grapes here and add plums or winter squash. Martin Sec pears are part of the Ark of Taste. They are small pears grown in the Cuneo area. Tonda Gentile hazelnuts from the Langhe area are an IGP (Protected Geographical Origin) product and are known for their sweetness.

4½ pounds Dolcetto grapes (see note)
2 pounds Martin Sec pears
3 cups Tonda Gentile Langhe hazelnuts
2 cinnamon sticks
10 whole cloves

Press the grapes and strain the must so that it is free of any impurities, seeds, or skins. Peel, core, and slice the pears and place the pears and the must in a pot and cook over low heat until reduced to a thick syrup, at least 4 hours.

Meanwhile, toast the hazelnuts on the stovetop or in the oven and rub off the skins. Crush them into large pieces with a mortar and pestle and add them to the mixture when it is almost fully cooked. Add the cinnamon and cloves as well and let the mixture cook until reduced to a jamlike consistency.

Transfer the mixture to a terra-cotta container and cover with wax paper.

SABA 🐝
Saba (condiment)
Alberto Ferrari, Modena, Emília-Romagna

aba, sometimes written as "*sapa*," is an ancient condiment made from wine must. Saba is made in homes all over Romagna, but also in Sardegna, Puglia, Calabria, and the Marche. It is similar to vin cotto, but more concentrated. It is served with savory foods, but is also often served with pastries and cookies and can be used as a topping for ice cream. In winter, it is sometimes drizzled over fresh snow to make a kind of ad hoc granita.

Use extremely fresh, unfermented wine must. Place the must in a pot and add whole cloves and a piece or two of cinnamon stick if desired. Cook long and slow over low heat, skimming off any foam that forms on the top, until the mixture is very thick and sweet. (Saba is so sweet that it was for many years used as a sugar substitute.) Store in dark-colored glass jars.

CONFETTURA DI FICHI ❗
Fig Preserves
Ristorante Mediterraneo, Cirò (Crotone), Calabria

n a bowl, combine 3 cups sugar and the juice of 1 lemon for every 2 to 2¼ pounds peeled fresh figs. Set aside to macerate for 24 hours. Transfer the mixture to a pot and cook over medium heat, stirring occasionally and skimming any foam that forms on the top, until the mixture coats a wooden spoon or spatula. Transfer the hot preserves to sterile glass jars, seal them hermetically, turn them upside down, and let them cool. Store the jars in a cool dry place. These preserves are a wonderful counterbalance to aged cheeses.

CONFETTURA DI CASTAGNE ❗
Chestnut Preserves
Alda Baglioni, Cavedine di Stravino (Trento), Trentino-Alto Adige

arron chestnuts are large and meaty heart-shaped chestnuts without a skin between the two halves. If at all possible, procure Drena marron chestnuts for this recipe.

Boil about 4½ pounds marron chestnuts in lightly salted water. Carefully peel them and remove any skins, then grind them and pass them through a sieve to make a smooth, soft paste.

In a pot, combine 5 cups sugar with enough water to make a syrup. Simmer over low heat and stir with a wooden spoon until all of the sugar has dissolved. When large, viscous bubbles form on the surface, remove from the heat.

Wait a few minutes for the mixture to cool somewhat, then add the chestnut puree, 1 teaspoon vanilla extract, and a pinch of salt, and stir gently until thoroughly combined. Return the pot to the heat and cook, stirring slowly and constantly, for 1 hour.

Transfer the hot mixture to glass jars and hermetically seal. Cook them in a water bath for at least 10 minutes. Store in a dark, cool, place.

Panna Catta

Finocchini

Mostaccioli

Torta di Nocciole

Bauarese al Moscato

Spumone di Torrone

Margheritine di Stresa

Frittelle di Mele

Tiramisù

DOLCI

Fiordilatte

Dolcetti della Sposa

Tartufi di Cioccolata

Torta di Tagliatelle

Torrone alla Vaniglia

Fugassa Pasquale

Tortianata

di Mandorle

& Many More

CUSTARDS, MOUSSES, PUDDINGS, & OTHER SPOON DESSERTS

FIORDILATTE ▦
Milk Custard
Trattoria La Bolognese, Vignola (Modena), Emília-Romagna

For this simple custard, you can use store-bought caramel or make it yourself by combining ½ cup sugar with a little water and melting it on the stovetop. Just keep a close eye on it so that it doesn't burn. The finished custard is firm enough to be unmolded, but very soft.

SERVES 10
8   cups whole milk
1   cup sugar
Zest of 1 organic lemon
1   tablespoon vanilla sugar
2   large eggs
9   egg yolks
½   cup caramel

Combine the milk, sugar, lemon zest, and vanilla sugar in a small saucepan and bring to a very low simmer, keeping the heat low enough that it doesn't boil over or thicken quickly. Reduce by half, about 1 hour. Remove from the heat and allow to cool. Remove and discard the lemon zest and whisk in the whole eggs and egg yolks until combined.

Preheat the oven to 300°F.

Spread the caramel in the bottom of a mold. Pour in the milk mixture and cook in a water bath in the preheated oven until quite firm, refilling the water in the water bath as needed and turning down the heat if the water starts to boil. The cooking time will depend on the freshness of the eggs: it should take 1 hour 30 minutes at most. Serve lukewarm or cold.

PANNA COTTA ❗
Cooked Cream
Ristorante Belvedere, La Morra (Cuneo), Piemonte

Chef Marco Boschiazzo calls for Bourbon vanilla beans because he says they lend a more potent aroma to the finished dish, but you can use standard vanilla beans here too. This is delicious with fresh berries on the side.

SERVES 7
2   cups heavy cream or whipping cream
1   cup whole milk
1   Bourbon vanilla bean, halved
1   cup cane sugar
2   sheets gelatin, softened in water and
    drained
Caramel for lining molds

Combine the cream, milk, and vanilla bean in a stainless steel saucepan. Place over low heat until the cream mixtures reaches 175°F on a candy thermometer, then whisk in the sugar and the gelatin. Heat, whisking constantly, without allowing the liquid to come to a boil until thickened, about 10 minutes. Set aside to cool for 15 minutes, then remove the vanilla bean.

Fill the bottoms of 7 molds with caramel, turning them quickly as you add the caramel so that the bottoms are coated evenly. Divide the slightly cooled mixture among the molds and refrigerate overnight. Unmold once firm.

BAVARESE AL MOSCATO ✿
Moscato Pudding
Ristorante Locanda Fontanabuona, Mombercelli
(Asti), Piemonte

The restaurant serves diced peeled peaches, strawberries, or other summer fruit with this delicate pudding

SERVES 4 TO 6

4   *egg yolks*
⅔   *cup sugar*
½   *bottle Moscato d'Asti sparkling wine*
3   *sheets gelatin, softened in water and drained*
2   *cups heavy cream or whipping cream*

In a heatproof bowl, whisk the egg yolks and sugar until fluffy and light. Gradually pour in the Moscato while whisking constantly and cook in bain-marie for 5 minutes without bringing to a boil. Remove from the heat and add the gelatin. Set aside to cool. When the mixture has cooled, whip the cream to stiff peaks and fold it into the egg yolk mixture. Divide among individual serving dishes and refrigerate 6 to 8 hours before serving.

BIANCOMANGIARE DI MANDORLE DI NOTO 🥄
Noto Almond Blancmange
Caffé Sicîlia, Noto (Siracusa), Sicîlia

Long before almond milk became a trendy alternative to dairy, Sicilians made their own at home by crushing almonds in a marble mortar and pestle, wrapping the crushed almonds in a linen cloth and soaking them in water, and then pressing them. Some recipes for this preparation call for a little lemon peel. Traditionally, *biancomangiare* (a blancmange, or simple pudding) is made in terra-cotta molds with a variety of decorations on them—Caltagirone, famous for its

ceramics, makes many different varieties. At Dolceria Bonajuto in Modica, owner Franco Ruta makes a chocolate version by adding about 2 ounces chocolate that has been melted in a double boiler. In Cabras in the province of Oristano, Marina Bendico makes *papai biancu*, a similar blancmange that incorporates orange flower water and a strip or two of lemon zest that is removed before the pudding is chilled. Noto almonds have a stronger flavor than standard almonds. They are labor-intensive to produce, which makes them expensive, but they are still worth seeking out.

SERVES 4 TO 6

1   *heaping cup blanched Noto almonds*
¼   *cup sugar*
¼   *cup wheat starch*

Set aside 2 tablespoons of almonds. Grind the remaining almonds. Place 1½ cups warm water in a medium saucepan over medium heat until warm but not hot. Remove from the heat and whisk in the sugar, starch, and ground almonds. Strain and press as hard as you can on the almonds with the back of a wooden spoon to extract the liquid, then discard the solids. Bring to a simmer over medium heat, then pour into one large mold or individual molds and refrigerate until firm, 3 to 4 hours. To serve, unmold the blancmange. Chop the reserved almonds and sprinkle on top as garnish.

TIRAMISÙ ☕
Tiramisù
Ristorante Vecchia Cantina, Napoli, Campania

At the Vineria Derthona in Tortona in the province of Alessandria, this Italian classic is made with an equally classic zabaione made with egg yolks, sugar, and Marsala in place of the standard mascarpone (a creamy fresh cheese) and egg mixture.

SERVES 6 TO 8

½ cup sugar
3 large eggs, separated
1½ cups (about 12 ounces) mascarpone
12 espresso coffees (about 3 cups), warm
2 tablespoons rum
1 pound ladyfingers
Unsweetened cocoa powder for finishing

Combine the sugar and egg yolks in a large bowl and whisk to combine thoroughly. Fold in the mascarpone. In a separate bowl, whisk the egg whites to stiff peaks and fold those into the mascarpone mixture as well.

Place the coffee in a shallow bowl and stir in the rum. Dip the ladyfingers in the coffee mixture to moisten. In a serving bowl, arrange a layer of ladyfingers. Top that with a layer of the mascarpone mixture and smooth the top with a spatula. Continue alternating layers until you have used up both, finishing with a layer of the mascarpone mixture. Sprinkle the cocoa powder over the entire surface, cover, and refrigerate for at least 2 hours before serving.

MOUSSE DI ZABAIONE
Zabaione Mousse
Ristorante Garibaldi, Cisterna d'Asti (Asti), Piemonte

Zabaione is a simple and versatile custard. Here it is lightened with whipped cream for a more delicate effect.

SERVES 6

6 egg yolks
½ cup sugar
½ cup Marsala
½ cup Moscato d'Asti sparkling wine
2 cups heavy cream or whipping cream

Place the egg yolks in a saucepan with a heavy bottom. Whisk in the sugar and continue whisking until light and fluffy. Whisk in the Marsala and the Moscato. Place over low heat (use a double boiler if you are unsure of your-

self) and cook, whisking constantly, until thick and foamy. Transfer to a bowl and set aside to cool. When the mixture is cool, whip the cream to firm peaks and fold it into the zabaione. Divide among 6 individual serving bowls and refrigerate for at least 2 hours before serving.

BUDINO DI MARRONI CON CIOCCOLATO FUSO
Chestnut Pudding with Chocolate Sauce
Trattoria Alla Sorgente, Torrebelvicino (Vicenza), Veneto

At the Cucina della Sorgente, a rustic osteria at the mouth of the Val dei Mercanti, Claudia Brigo sometimes opts to steam the chestnuts in a steamer basket rather than boiling them. This keeps them from absorbing liquid and makes their flavor very intense.

SERVES 6 TO 8

1 pound chestnuts, peeled and skinned
1 bay leaf
1 pinch salt
3 tablespoons sugar
1 cup whole milk
7 ounces dark chocolate, chopped (about 1 ⅔ cups)

Combine the chestnuts and the bay leaf and salt in a pot with a generous amount of water to cover and boil for 15 minutes. Drain the chestnuts and discard the bay leaf. Toss the chestnuts with the sugar, and then force the chestnut mixture through a sieve with small holes. The mixture should be a soft puree. Scald the milk. Add the chocolate to the pot and cook, stirring constantly, until melted. Divide the chestnut pudding among individual serving plates, drizzle a little of the chocolate sauce on top, and serve.

ZUPPA INGLESE ⊞
Classic Zabaione Trifle
Trattoria dell'Alba, Vho di Piadena
(Cremona), Lombardia

In central Italy, slices of plain cake like the ciambellone on page 455 are often used in place of ladyfingers in this dessert. Be sure to use a fairly sweet liqueur to balance the alchermes, which is quite strong. A plum liqueur is a good choice.

SERVES 6
- ½ cup unbleached all-purpose flour
- ½ cup plus 2 tablespoons sugar
- ½ cup plus 2 tablespoons unsweetened cocoa powder
- 2 cups whole milk
- 6 egg yolks
- ¼ cup plus 2 tablespoons dry Marsala
- ¼ cup plus 1 tablespoon dry white wine
- Alchermes liqueur to taste
- Sweet fruit-flavored liqueur to taste (see note)
- 8 ounces (about 24) ladyfingers or sponge cake cut into rectangles

To make the chocolate cream, combine the flour, ¼ cup sugar, and the cocoa powder with enough milk to make a paste. Whisk until completely smooth, then whisk in the remaining milk. Place in a heavy-bottomed saucepan and bring to a boil over low heat, stirring constantly. Remove from the heat when bubbles begin to form and the mixture has thickened.

For the zabaione, whisk the egg yolks with the remaining ¼ cup plus 2 tablespoons sugar in the top of a double boiler. Whisk in the Marsala and the wine and cook on the top of the double boiler, whisking constantly, until thickened.

Combine alchermes with fruit-flavored liqueur and moisten the ladyfingers with this mixture. Arrange about half the ladyfingers in a bowl, top with about half of the chocolate cream and then the zabaione. Repeat, reserving a little of the chocolate cream to decorate the top. Refrigerate for at least 2 hours before serving.

BUDINO DI ALBICOCCHE ❧
Apricot Pudding
Ristorante Moderno, Carrù (Cuneo), Piemonte

This apricot pudding is tender with a layer of caramel on top. If you're unsure whether you can successfully unmold it, simply scoop it out of the pan with a spoon. It will still taste delicious. Fernet is a type of *amaro,* or bitter, often consumed as a digestif.

SERVES 8
- 2 pounds very ripe apricots, pitted
- ¾ cup plus 3 tablespoons sugar
- ½ cup rum
- ½ cup Moscato d'Asti sparkling wine
- 1 cinnamon stick
- 1 vanilla bean
- 8 large eggs
- 10 amaretto cookies
- 3 tablespoons Fernet (see note)

In a pot combine the apricots, ¼ cup plus 1 tablespoon sugar, ¼ cup rum, the Moscato, the cinnamon stick, and the vanilla bean. Cook over low heat for 30 minutes, then set aside to cool. When the mixture is cool, remove the cinnamon stick and vanilla and puree through a food mill. Beat the eggs and crush the amaretto cookies finely with a mortar and pestle. In a bowl combine the apricot puree, the eggs, the crushed cookies, the remaining ¼ cup rum, the Fernet, and ½ cup sugar.

Preheat the oven to 350°F. Place the remaining 2 tablespoons sugar in the pan you'll be using to cook the pudding. Place over the lowest possible heat and cook until it just begins to turn golden. Add 1 tablespoon water (watch for splashing) and turn the pan so that the bottom and sides are coated evenly with caramel. Set aside to cool. When the caramel has cooled, transfer the apricot mixture to the pan and smooth the top with a spatula. Cover the pan with foil, set it in a water bath, and cook in the preheated oven until firm, about 50 minutes. Remove from the oven and refrigerate for at least 2 hours before unmolding and serving.

BUDINO DI MANDORLE
Almond Pudding
Ristorante Enoteca Metrò, Catania, Sicîlia

You'll need to divide the almonds into three equal parts. Figure about 1 ounce each if you're using a scale. Avola almonds are an heirloom variety. They are smaller than standard almonds and flatter in shape. They have a higher oil content, which accounts for their pronounced taste. They are available in some gourmet stores and are also sold online. You can make this pudding with standard almonds, but it will be more mildly flavored. Puddings of this type are traditionally set in ceramic molds that have been carved with illustrations so that when they are unmolded they look like coins or engravings. Serve with warm melted chocolate on the side.

SERVES 4
- ⅔ cup raw Avola almonds (see note)
- ¾ cup sugar
- 2 cups whole milk
- 2 cups heavy cream or whipping cream
- 3 tablespoons almond liqueur
- 7 sheets gelatin, softened in water

Divide the almonds into three equal parts. Blanch and peel one third, toast the second third, and leave one third raw. Chop all of the almonds finely. In a pot, combine the almonds with the sugar, milk, cream, and liqueur. Bring to a boil over medium heat, stirring frequently and keeping a close eye on it so that it doesn't boil over. Drain the gelatin and add it to the pot. Stir to combine and remove from the heat. Divide the mixture among 4 small molds and refrigerate until firm, about 4 hours. Unmold and serve.

BONET
Chocolate Terrine
Osteria dell'Unione, Treiso (Cuneo), Piemonte

Bonet (the name is from Piemontese dialect for a kind of hat, which it resembles) has endless variations. At her osteria in Roddino, Gemma Boeri makes a version without amaretto cookies that incorporates coffee and an amaro. At the Osteria della Gallina Sversa di Calosso in the province of Asti a similar dessert uses both amaretto cookies and coffee, and Marsala is used in place of rum. Francesca Ronco at Dusino San Michele in the province of Asti makes her bonet with both ladyfingers and amaretto cookies. Keep the loaf pan warm while you make the caramel—it will be easier to coat the bottom and sides smoothly.

SERVES 8
- 4 large eggs
- ¼ cup plus 2 tablespoons sugar
- 2 tablespoons unsweetened cocoa powder
- 10 amaretto cookies, crumbled by hand
- 2 tablespoons rum
- 2 cups whole milk

Preheat the oven to 350°F.

Beat the eggs with ¼ cup sugar, the cocoa powder, the crumbled cookies, the rum, and the milk. Stir gently to combine. Make a caramel by cooking the remaining 2 tablespoons sugar over low heat until just golden, then stirring in a little water and rotating the pan over high heat until the caramel is dark and glassy looking. Pour the caramel over the bottom and sides of a warm loaf pan, tilting it to cover all surfaces evenly and working quickly to get it coated before the caramel hardens. Transfer the egg mixture to the pan, place the loaf pan in a water bath, and cook in the preheated oven for 30 minutes. Chill, unmold, and serve.

CAFFÈ IN FORCHETTA ☕
Coffee Pudding
Antica Fattoria del Grottaione, Castel del Piano
(Grosseto), Toscana

This is a kind of coffee pudding (the name literally means "coffee on a fork") that was for many years a home-cooking favorite. In the days before Italians commonly had ovens in their kitchens, this was made in a wood-burning stove.

SERVES 4
- 5 large eggs
- 2 egg yolks
- 1¾ cups sugar
- 4 cups whole milk
- 1¼ cups espresso, warm

Preheat the oven to 185°F. Beat the eggs and yolks with the sugar. Add the milk and espresso and stir to combine thoroughly. Divide among 4 molds or ramekins and cook in a water bath in the preheated oven until a crust forms on top, about 30 minutes.

MULUN CON SALSA DI CACHI
Cannellini Bean and Chestnut Mousse with Persimmon Sauce
Osteria del Crotto, Morbegno (Sondrio), Lombardia

This dessert is a sweet and modern take on a savory dish that farmers ate frequently because of its high protein content. A puree of beans and chestnuts was made in advance, cooled (it has a consistency similar to polenta once cooled), and brought into the fields in the days that followed. Start with about 4 pounds fresh beans in the shell and about 1 pound chestnuts in the shell to get 2 cups of each. If you have access to fresh beans, there's no need to soak them.

SERVES 10
- 2 cups fresh shelled cannellini beans or dried cannellini beans, soaked overnight in water to cover
- 2 cups peeled chestnuts, soaked overnight in water to cover
- ¼ teaspoon salt
- ¾ cup confectioners' sugar
- 7 ounces chopped white chocolate (about 1⅔ cups)
- 1½ cups heavy cream or whipping cream
- 1 vanilla bean, split lengthwise
- 3 sheets gelatin, softened in water
- 2 tablespoons granulated sugar
- 2 persimmons
- Juice of ½ lemon
- 1 teaspoon ground cinnamon

Drain the beans, if soaked, and the chestnuts and cook each separately in a generous amount of boiling water with about half of the salt in each pot. When the beans and chestnuts are soft, drain them and puree them, again separately, by forcing them through a sieve. Combine the two purees and ½ cup of the confectioners' sugar.

Place the chopped white chocolate in a heatproof bowl. In a saucepan combine ½ cup cream and the vanilla bean. Scald the liquid, then remove the gelatin from its soaking water and add it to the saucepan. Whisk to combine, then pour the warm liquid over the chocolate and whisk until melted. Stir the chocolate mixture into the chestnut and bean puree. Stir in 1 tablespoon of the granulated sugar and whisk energetically by hand or with an immersion blender for 1 minute.

Combine the remaining 1 cup cream with the remaining ¼ cup confectioners' sugar and whip to firm peaks. Fold the whipped cream into the bean and chestnut mixture. Divide the mixture among 10 individual serving bowls and chill in the refrigerator overnight.

When you are ready to serve the mousse, prepare the sauce: peel the persimmons and puree them with the lemon juice, cinnamon, and remaining 1 tablespoon granulated sugar. Serve on the side.

ZUPPA DI TOZZETTI ☕
Tozzetti Cookie Pudding
Trattoria 'L Richiastro, Viterbo, Lazio

*T*ozzetti are almond and hazelnut cookies from Lazio and Abruzzo that are similar to Toscana's *cantucci* (page 440)—the kind of nut cookies that have come to be known as "biscotti" in the United States. They are good keepers, and they are rather hard, which is why they're softened in espresso before being buried under a layer of soft custard.

SERVES 4
- 1   cup whole milk
- 2   tablespoons sugar
- ¼   cup unsweetened cocoa powder
- 1½ teaspoons potato starch
- 1   tablespoon unbleached all-purpose flour
- 8 to 12 tozzetti cookies (see note)
- 1   cup espresso
- ¼   cup sprinkles for decoration

Combine the milk with 1 cup water and bring to a boil. In a saucepan, combine the sugar, cocoa powder, potato starch, and flour. Gradually add the warm liquid in a thin stream, whisking constantly so as not to form any lumps. Place over low heat and cook, stirring constantly, until thickened. Set the mixture aside to cool.

Dip the cookies in the espresso and divide them among individual serving dishes. Top the cookies with the custard. Decorate with sprinkles and refrigerate until chilled.

CREMA DI PISTACCHI DI BRONTE ❗
Bronte Pistachio Custard
Ristorante Enoteca Metrò, Catania, Sicîlia

*B*ronte pistachios from Sicilia, which have a Slow Food Presidium, are used in many desserts and also in cured meats. They have a vibrant green color and are intensely flavorful. They grow at the foot of Etna in the eastern part of the island. You can order them online from several different sources, and it is worth seeking them out, especially when you are making a dish like this one, where the pistachios are the star of the show. To make chocolate curls for garnish, shave thin strips from a block of chocolate with a vegetable peeler.

SERVES 6
- 2   cups whole milk
- 2   cups heavy cream or whipping cream
- ¾   cup sugar
- 1   cup Bronte pistachios (see note)
- ¼   cup Avola almonds
- 2   tablespoons almond liqueur
- ¼   cup plus 2 tablespoons cornstarch or other starch
- *Dark chocolate curls for decoration*

In a saucepan, combine the milk, cream, sugar, pistachios, almonds, and almond liqueur. Bring to a boil over medium heat, stirring constantly with a wooden spoon.

Remove from the heat and allow to cool, then stir in the starch, taking care not to allow any lumps to form. Process the mixture in a food processor or with an immersion blender until perfectly smooth, then return to the saucepan and place over medium heat again. Cook, stirring constantly, until thickened and creamy. Transfer the mixture to 6 individual serving dishes or bowls and refrigerate for at least 4 hours. Decorate with chocolate just before serving.

CREMA CON LE VISCIOLE 🌿
Custard with Sour Cherries
Osteria del Cucco, Urbania (Pesaro and Urbino), Marche

Sour cherries—which in Italy include the visciole, amarena, and marasca varieties—are not eaten out of hand but are used to make all kinds of syrups and beverages (including maraschino liqueur) and also appear in many different desserts in Italy. For this simple dessert, make a custard by combining 2 cups whole milk, 4 egg yolks, 2 tablespoons sugar, and 2 tablespoons all-purpose flour in the top of a double boiler. Add a cinnamon stick and cook, whisking constantly, until thickened. Remove and discard the cinnamon stick and let the custard cool slightly. Brush sponge cake (it's fine if it's in odd-shaped pieces) with some of the syrup from a jar of visciole sour cherries (reserve whole cherries and remaining syrup) and line the bottom of a serving dish with the cake. Spread the custard on top and refrigerate 1 to 2 hours. Just before serving, scoop out the chilled cake and custard into individual dishes. Drizzle on additional syrup and garnish with whole cherries.

CREMA DI MASCARPONE CON BAICOLI ▦
Mascarpone Cream with Baicoli
Trattoria da Dino, Sîlea (Treviso), Veneto

Baicoli are very plain dry cookies that are not too sweet—almost a cross between a cookie and a piece of toast. They were created for sailors to take on long voyages. These days, they are generally eaten with a soft custard or cream for dipping. To make this, you will need the very freshest mascarpone, preferably purchased from a local cheese maker. To make enough to serve 8, separate 3 eggs. Beat the yolks with ¾ cup sugar, then beat in 1½ cups (about 12 ounces)

mascarpone—with an immersion blender, if you have one—until very light and fluffy. Separately whip the egg whites to firm peaks. Fold the egg whites into the yolk mixture until completely combined. Transfer to glasses or glass bowls, working gently to deflate the mixture as little as possible. Sprinkle on a couple of tablespoons of cocoa powder. Refrigerate or serve immediately with baicoli cookies (or other plain dry cookies) for dipping.

CUCCÌA DOLCE DI SANTA LUCIA 🍊
Sweet Ricotta and Wheat Berries for Saint Lucy
Pasticceria Artale, Siracusa, Sicîlia

This dessert is always made for the feast of Saint Lucy. Legend has it that during a terrible famine in Siracusa, ships miraculously appeared and unloaded wheat in the city's port. The people of Siracusa were so hungry that they ate it boiled rather than taking the time to grind it into flour. Saint Lucy is believed to have been behind that miracle.

SERVES 4
- 1 cup wheat berries
- ¾ cup sheep's milk ricotta
- ⅓ cup sugar
- ⅔ cup chopped candied orange peel
- ¼ cup dark chocolate chips
- 5 drops cinnamon extract
- ¼ teaspoon vanilla extract

Soak the wheat berries in water to cover for at least 2 days, changing the water every 12 hours. Boil the wheat berries in a generous amount of water until al dente. Drain and set aside to cool.

Meanwhile, force the ricotta through a sieve to make it very smooth and combine it with the sugar. Fold in the wheat berries, candied orange peel, chocolate, cinnamon extract, and vanilla. Serve in individual glass bowls.

TRIA DI SAN GIUSEPPE 🍇
Sweet Noodles in Wine Syrup for Saint Joseph
Ristorante Cîbus, Ceglie Messapica (Brindisi), Puglia

This unusual dessert consists of egg noodles tossed with a wine must reduction and is traditionally prepared to celebrate the Feast of Saint Joseph. This type of reduction, also known as *saba*, was once obtained by boiling grape juice (generally from green grapes) that had just begun to ferment in copper vats. The resulting liquid had a low alcohol content and well-developed sugars and was drizzled on polenta and aged cheese, as well as being featured in desserts. To serve 4 people, shape 1½ cups unbleached all-purpose flour into a well on a work surface and add 2 eggs to the center of the well. Gradually pull in flour from the sides of the well, then knead into a soft pasta dough. (Add a little water if the dough feels dry; add a little flour if the dough feels wet.) Roll the dough into a thin sheet and cut it into wide strips. In a large pot, combine about ¾ cup wine must and 1 teaspoon sugar and bring to a boil, then simmer until somewhat reduced. Meanwhile, cook the noodles in a large pot of salted water for just 2 minutes. Drain, add the noodles to the wine must mixture, and toss over medium heat until combined. Serve immediately.

CUSCUS DOLCE
Sweet Couscous with Chocolate, Pistachios, Almonds, and Candied Squash
Alessandro Sanfilippo, Agrigento, Sicîlia

Couscous is of Arab origin and is eaten up and down the southern coast of Sicilia in sweet and savory preparations. The nuns at the Monastero dello Spirito Santo in Agrigento make a particularly delicious version, but while they will prepare it for visitors who are wise enough to request the dessert in advance, they have never revealed their recipe. Candied squash is commonly used in Sicily alongside candied orange peel and candied citron. It is known as *zuccata*. You will need a couscousière to prepare this dish.

SERVES 6
- 3 cups semolina flour
- ⅓ cup confectioners' sugar
- ¾ cup raw almonds, toasted and finely chopped
- 1 cup pistachios, finely chopped
- 4 ounces chocolate, shaved (about 1 cup)
- ¼ cup chopped candied squash
- 1 tablespoon plus 1 teaspoon ground cinnamon

Gradually drizzle the semolina flour into a large terra-cotta container known as a *mafaradda* or another type of large mixing bowl. Moisten your hand and use it to stir the flour counterclockwise. Continue dipping your hand in water and stirring the flour in the same direction until the flour clumps together into pieces the size of the head of a pin. Spread the couscous on a canvas and let it dry for 3 hours.

Heat water in the bottom of a couscousière. When it begins to boil, place the couscous in the pot of the couscousière (which looks like a sieve), cover with a damp dish towel or parchment paper to keep the steam from escaping, and cook for 40 minutes.

Return the couscous to the terra-cotta container sprinkle with a little cold water, and let it rest for 15 minutes. Repeat the process of cooking it in the couscousière for an additional 20 minutes. Remove and allow to cool.

When the couscous has cooled, transfer it to a large bowl. Sprinkle on the confectioners' sugar, almonds, pistachios, chocolate, and candied squash and toss to combine. Sprinkle on the cinnamon and serve.

MAIASSA 🍎
Sweet Polenta Baked with Apples and Dried Figs
Trattoria Visconti, Ambivere (Bergamo), Lombardia

A traditional polenta pot is a large copper cauldron. Be sure to add the polenta very slowly to avoid creating any lumps. Use the most finely ground polenta you can find. Fox grapes (a large family of varieties that includes Concord grapes—the hallmark of fox grapes is that their skins slip off easily) are preferred here, but if they are out of season or unavailable to you, swap in ½ cup plus 2 tablespoons golden raisins, soaked to rehydrate then squeezed dry, in their place.

SERVES 4 TO 6
- 6 cups low-fat milk
- ¼ cup plus 1 tablespoon sugar
- 1 pinch salt
- 2 cups finely ground polenta
- 3 apples, peeled, cored, and thinly sliced
- 9 ounces (about 30) dried figs, diced
- 40 fox grapes (see note)
- 3 tablespoons unsalted butter

Preheat oven to 350°F. Place the milk, ¼ cup sugar, and salt in a polenta pot and place over medium heat. When just a few bubbles break on the surface, add the polenta in a very thin stream, whisking constantly. Cook for 30 minute, stirring constantly with a wooden spoon. Remove from the heat and stir in the apples, figs, and grapes.

Thickly butter a 12-inch-diameter baking pan with some of the butter. Pour in the polenta mixture and spread smooth. Sprinkle the remaining 1 tablespoon sugar on top. Cut the remaining butter into small pieces and dot the top with butter. Bake in the preheated oven for 50 minutes. Cool to room temperature before serving.

MONTEBIANCO 🍦
Chestnut Chocolate Puree with Whipped Cream
Livia Borgata, Montegrosso d'Asti (Asti), Piemonte

This rich dessert is named after Mont Blanc in the Alps. The chestnut puree is arranged roughly in a pyramid and then decorated to look like a mountain with whipped cream "snow." You can also decorate the finished dessert with pieces of candied chestnut, scattered dark chocolate shavings, or a sprinkling of sifted cocoa powder.

SERVES 6 TO 8
- 1 pinch salt
- 2 pounds chestnuts, scored
- About 4 cups whole milk
- ½ vanilla bean
- 1 cup sugar
- 1 tablespoon unsweetened cocoa powder
- 2 tablespoons rum
- 2 cups heavy cream or whipping cream

Bring a large pot of lightly salted water to a boil and boil the chestnuts for 20 minutes. Drain and peel off both the shells and the skin. Transfer the chestnuts to a pot with 4 cups milk, which should be enough to cover them. If not, add milk to cover. Add the vanilla bean, ¼ cup of the sugar, and the cocoa powder. Cover and simmer until the chestnuts are very soft, about 1 hour.

Drain the chestnuts, reserving the cooking liquid. Crush the chestnuts with a potato masher, and use a wooden spoon to mix the resulting puree with ½ cup of the sugar and the rum. If the mixture is very dense and dry, add a few tablespoons of the cooking liquid.

Force the puree through the large holes on a potato ricer to make thick "noodles," moving circularly over a tray as you do so that the puree forms a "mountain" that is taller in the center. Whip the cream with the remaining ¼ cup sugar to soft peaks and cover the mountain with the whipped cream.

LATTE E CAFFÈ CON PANE ABBRUSTOLITO 🍵
Coffee Trifle with Ricotta and Toasted Bread
Ristorante Borgo Spoltino, Mosciano Sant'Angelo (Teramo), Abruzzo

This deceptively simple dessert is inspired by a breakfast meal commonly eaten in farmhouses in the Abruzzo region: a cup of sheep's milk, barley coffee, and pieces of bread toasted over an open fire until crisp. Decorate the top with ground coffee for a pleasantly bitter touch.

SERVES 8
- 8 slices stale bread
- 2 cups whole milk
- ½ cup espresso, warm
- ½ cup extra-aged brandy
- 1¼ cups plus 2 tablespoons sugar
- 5 large eggs, separated
- 2¾ cups sheep's milk ricotta

Toast the bread on a grill or in a pan until fairly dark. Scald the milk, add the espresso, ¼ cup brandy, and ¼ cup plus 1 tablespoon sugar. Dip the bread in the milk mixture to soften, then arrange in a bowl or pan. Reserve the milk mixture. Beat the egg yolks with ¾ cup sugar until light and foamy. Beat the egg whites with the remaining ¼ cup plus 1 tablespoon sugar to stiff peaks.

Force the ricotta through a sieve to make it smooth and mix with the egg yolk mixture. Stir in some of the reserved milk mixture (enough to make a loose but not soupy mixture) and the remaining ¼ cup brandy. Fold in the whipped egg whites a little at a time. Transfer the egg mixture to the bowl on top of the bread. Refrigerate at least 4 hours before serving.

MACAFAME 🍎
Simple Bread Pudding with Apples and Figs
Pasticceria Dolci Pensieri, Schio (Vicenza), Veneto

The name of this cross between a bread pudding and a cake means "hunger killer," because a slice was considered substantial enough to keep diners full. It can be served hot, room temperature, or cold. You can vary the grind of the cornmeal to your liking—a coarser grind will result in a more rustic-style cake. Marano corn is a variety from northern Italy. In Belluno, Giulio Talamini makes *macafame* with stale bread soaked in milk, eggs, apple slices, melted butter, grated lemon zest, sugar, vanilla, baking powder, and enough flour to make a medium-thick batter. He then pours it into a buttered pan and bakes at moderate heat for 1½ hours.

SERVES 6 TO 8
- 14 tablespoons (1 stick plus 6 tablespoons) unsalted butter
- 4½ pounds (12 to 14 medium) apples, peeled, cored, and chopped
- 1¼ cups black raisins
- 2 cups whole milk
- ½ cup sugar
- 1 small piece cinnamon stick or star anise or bay leaf
- 2 cups crumbled stale bread
- 3 large eggs, beaten
- ⅔ cup honey
- 1⅓ cups dried figs, diced
- ¾ cup pine nuts
- 2¾ cups unbleached all-purpose flour
- 2⅓ cups cornmeal, preferably the Marano variety
- ¼ cup breadcrumbs

Preheat the oven to 400°F. Melt 10 tablespoons (1 stick plus 2 tablespoons) butter in a pot. Add the apples and raisins and cook over medium heat, stirring occasionally, until the apples are falling apart. In a medium saucepan, combine the milk with the sugar and cinnamon stick and heat just until the milk starts to boil. Remove and discard the cinnamon stick. In a bowl, combine the milk mixture and the apple mixture. Then, stirring constantly, add the bread, eggs, honey, figs, pine nuts, all-purpose flour, and cornmeal. Butter a terra-cotta baking dish with the remaining 4 tablespoons butter, coat the bottom and sides of the pan with the breadcrumbs, then transfer the batter to the pan. Cover and bake in the preheated oven for 15 minutes, then turn the oven temperature down to 350°F and bake until set, about 1½ hours.

ZUCCOTTO ●
Florentine Dome of Frozen Mousse
Eugenio Torrini, Fiesole (Firenze), Toscana

Make a cake layer by beating 3 whole eggs with ½ cup sugar, ¾ cup flour, and ¼ teaspoon vanilla extract. Pour into a cake pan and bake at 350°F for 30 minutes. Meanwhile, make a pastry cream with 1 egg yolk, ¼ cup sugar, 1 tablespoon flour, ¾ cup milk, and the grated zest of 1 lemon. When the cake layer is cool, cut it into slices about ½ inch wide. Brush some with maraschino or other sweet liqueur and use them to line a round mold or bowl. Whip 1½ cups cream with 1⅔ cups confectioners' sugar. Combine about two thirds of the whipped cream with half of the pastry cream and fold in ¼ cup chopped candied fruit and ¼ cup chopped toasted almonds. Combine the remaining whipped cream with the remaining pastry cream, 4 ounces melted dark chocolate, and ¼ cup unsweetened cocoa powder. Spread the mixture with the candied fruit on the cake lining the mold, then fill the center with the chocolate mixture. Place the remaining cake slices on the top and brush with a little more liqueur. Freeze for 4 hours. To serve, overturn a platter on top and flip both mold and platter, then lift off the mold. Decorate with confectioners' sugar and/or chocolate sauce.

STRACCHINO GELATO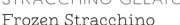
Frozen Stracchino
Trattoria San Giovanni, Piacenza, Emília-Romagna

Stracchino gelato, sometimes known as *lattemiele in cassetta*, is traditionally served on Christmas Eve. The components are frozen in special diamond-shaped molds of graduated sizes. These days, we use the freezer, but originally they were buried under the snow.

SERVES 8 TO 10
- 4 egg yolks
- ¼ cup sugar
- 2 tablespoons Marsala or sweet white wine
- 6 cups heavy cream or whipping cream
- 4 cups confectioners' sugar
- 2 cups blanched almonds, toasted and ground
- ¾ cup finely ground coffee
- Seeds of 1 vanilla bean, ground
- 7 ounces dark chocolate, grated (about 2 cups)

Make a zabaione by whisking the egg yolks, ¼ cup sugar, and Marsala in the top of a double boiler until thickened. Set aside to cool. Combine the heavy cream with the confectioners' sugar and whip to stiff peaks. Divide the whipped cream into 5 portions to fit 5 gradually sized molds. Fold the almonds into the largest portion, the coffee into the second largest, the vanilla bean seeds into the third largest, the prepared zabaione into the fourth, and the grated chocolate into the smallest. Transfer to the appropriate molds and freeze until firm.

To serve, unmold each section and stack them in a tower with the largest on the bottom and the smallest on top. Refrigerate until just before serving.

SEMIFREDDO AL TORRONCINO CON VINCOTTO 🌿
Nougat Semifreddo with Wine Syrup
Ristorante La Locandiera, Bernalda (Matera), Basilicata

A semifreddo is a frozen mousse that can be frozen in a loaf pan and then unmolded and sliced or simply scooped like ice cream.

SERVES 4

WINE SYRUP
- 4 cups Aglianico red wine
- 1 cup sugar
- 5 dried figs stuffed with almonds

CREAM
- 2 egg yolks
- ¼ cup sugar
- 1 cup whole milk

SEMIFREDDO
- 4 cups heavy cream or whipping cream
- 5 egg yolks
- 1¼ cups sugar
- 2 cups (about 1 pound) mascarpone
- 1 (300-gram) bar torrone (nougat candy), crushed

For the wine syrup, combine the wine and sugar in a saucepan and bring to a boil. Simmer for 1 hour. Add the figs and simmer for 1 additional hour. Let the syrup cool.

For the cream, in a heatproof bowl or the top of a double boiler beat the egg yolks with the sugar until foamy. Add the milk and place the bowl on top of a double boiler. Cook, whisking constantly, until thickened. Set aside to cool.

For the semifreddo, whip the cream to stiff peaks. Separately, beat the egg yolks and sugar. Beat the mascarpone into the egg yolk mixture, then fold in the whipped cream. Fold in the crushed torrone and freeze the semifreddo for at least 4 hours. Serve the semifreddo with the cream and syrup.

SPUMONE DI TORRONE 🎛
Nougat Spumone
Ristorante Bianca Lancia dal Baròn, Calamandrana (Asti), Piemonte

Spumone is a frozen mousse. This one is dotted with crushed pieces of torrone, the nougat candy eaten all over Italy at Christmastime. If you are interested in making your own, see the recipe on page 480 at the end of this chapter.

SERVES 6 TO 8

- 4 large eggs, separated
- 3 tablespoons plus 1½ teaspoons sugar
- 1 (300-gram) bar hard torrone (nougat candy), finely crushed
- 1⅔ cups heavy cream or whipping cream
- 1 pinch salt

In a bowl beat the egg yolks with the sugar until light and foamy, Stir in the crushed torrone. Separately, whip the cream to stiff peaks and whip the egg whites to stiff peaks with a pinch of salt. Gently fold both the whipped cream and the whipped egg whites into the egg yolk mixture. Pour the mixture into individual molds and freeze. Just before serving, rest the molds in a little hot water, then turn over and unmold onto individual serving plates.

BISCETTE 🍴

"Little Snakes" Butter Cookies

Virgílio Gandolfo, Alassio (Savona), Liguria

These biscuits hail from the tiny hamlet of Solva, part of the town of Alassio in Liguria, which legend says was invaded by snakes many years ago. Residents fled to higher ground, and a religious hermit chased away the snakes with prayer.

MAKES 3 TO 4 DOZEN COOKIES

- 18 tablespoons (2 sticks plus 2 tablespoons) unsalted butter, softened, plus more for buttering pans
- 2¾ cups unbleached all-purpose flour
- ¾ cup sugar
- 1 teaspoon salt
- 2 large eggs
- ½ cup confectioners' sugar

Beat the 18 tablespoons butter with the flour, sugar, and salt. Add the eggs one at a time, beating to combine between additions. The dough should be soft. Form the dough into a ball, place it in a bowl, cover with a dish towel, and refrigerate for 30 minutes.

Preheat the oven to 350°F. Pinch off pieces of dough, roll them into 3- to 4-inch lengths, and gently nudge them into S shapes. Transfer to buttered baking sheets and allow to rest for a few minutes, then bake in the preheated oven until golden on top, 10 to 20 minutes. Cool on the pans, then sprinkle with confectioners' sugar before serving.

TORCETTI 🍴

Yeasted Twist Cookies

Flavio Laurent, Gressoney-Saint-Jean (Aosta), Valle d'Aosta

These cookies have an unusual texture because the dough is yeast based. There is no sugar in the dough, so you can control the sweetness by deciding how much to sprinkle on top. Anywhere from ¼ cup to ½ cup should give good results.

MAKES ABOUT 10 DOZEN 1- TO 2-INCH COOKIES

- 1¾ teaspoons active dry yeast
- 4 cups unbleached all-purpose flour or 00 flour, plus more for flouring pans
- 1 pinch salt
- 14 tablespoons (1 stick plus 6 tablespoons) unsalted butter, softened, plus more for buttering pans
- Sugar for sprinkling on top

Dissolve the yeast in ½ cup warm water. Make a well out of the 4 cups flour on the work surface. Place the salt and yeast in the center and knead to a soft dough. Add a small amount of water if needed. Shape the dough into a ball, place in a bowl, cover, and set aside to rise for 2 hours.

Knead the dough again for about 10 minutes, kneading in the 14 tablespoons butter. Return to the bowl, cover, and set aside to rise for 1 hour.

Preheat the oven to 400°F. Butter and flour baking sheets and set aside. Knead the dough for a few minutes. Roll pieces of the dough on the work surface into long thin ropes. Sprinkle with a generous amount of sugar and cut into pieces about 4 inches long. Pick up one piece of dough and transfer it to one of the prepared pans, twisting it a little as you do and overlapping the ends so that it forms a rough teardrop shape with the two ends sticking out. Repeat with the remaining pieces of dough and bake in the preheated oven until golden, about 15 minutes. Cool before serving.

ESSE 🍵
S Cookies
Pasticceria Ardizzoni, Treviso, Veneto

These soft, plain cookies are perfect with tea or coffee. Sometimes they are dipped halfway in chocolate glaze.

MAKES 10 TO 12 DOZEN COOKIES

- 1¼ cups sugar
- 14 tablespoons (1 stick plus 6 tablespoons) unsalted butter, softened
- 1 large egg
- 2 egg yolks
- Scant ¼ cup grappa
- 1 pinch salt
- 1 teaspoon baking powder
- Grated zest of 1 lemon
- 4 cups unbleached all-purpose flour or 00 flour, plus more for work surface

Beat the sugar and butter, then beat in the whole egg and yolks. Beat in the grappa, salt, baking powder, and lemon zest, beating to incorporate between additions. Finally, beat in the 4 cups flour. When the dough is well combined, shape it into a ball, wrap in plastic, and refrigerate for 30 minutes.

Preheat oven to 350°F. Line a baking sheet with parchment and set aside. On a lightly floured work surface, shape the dough into a log with a diameter a little less than ½ inch. With a knife, cut the rope into 1½-inch pieces. Roll out each piece under the palms of your hands until 2¼ to 2¾ inches long. Transfer the pieces to the lined pan and shape them into an S shape. Bake in the preheated oven for 12 minutes.

QUAQUARE ▦
Piped Butter Cookies
Osteria La Torre, Cherasco (Cuneo), Piemonte

The name of these cookies is local dialect for "doodlebugs," as the ridged piping gives them a similar look, though presumably they're much tastier. These keep for a long time in a tightly sealed glass container.

MAKES ABOUT 8 DOZEN COOKIES

- 4¾ cups unbleached all-purpose flour
- 2 cups sugar or 3½ cups confectioners' sugar
- 1 pound (4 sticks) unsalted butter, cut into pieces
- 5 large eggs, lightly beaten
- 1 egg yolk
- Grated zest of 3 lemons

Preheat the oven to 350°F. Line baking sheets with parchment and set aside.

Make a well on a work surface with the flour (or place in the bowl of an electric mixer). In the center of the well place the sugar, butter, eggs, egg yolk, and lemon zest. Knead into a dough, working quickly so that the dough doesn't overheat. The dough should be soft but not sticky. Transfer the dough to a pastry tube or pastry bag fitted with a star-shaped tip. Pipe strips of the dough on the prepared baking sheets and then bring the ends of the strips close together to form them into teardrop shapes. (The ends should just barely touch but not overlap.) Bake in the preheated oven until golden, about 15 minutes.

433

MOSTACCIOLI

Honey Cookies

Trattoria Le Muraglie, Conflenti (Catanzaro), Calabria

Be sure to let these cookies "age" for a few days before eating them so that the flavors combine. Ammonium bicarbonate, sometimes labeled "baking ammonia," was used as a leavener in home baking before baking powder and baking soda replaced it. It is still used in some baked goods to impart a very crispy texture. It is available from baking specialty stores and also from some Greek gourmet shops. These cookies are very hard and are meant to be dunked in coffee or tea to soften.

MAKES 3 TO 4 DOZEN 2½-INCH COOKIES

Butter for buttering pans
4 cups unbleached all-purpose flour or 00 flour
1 tablespoon ammonium bicarbonate (see note)
1⅓ cups honey
2 egg yolks, lightly beaten

Preheat the oven to 350°F to 400°F. Thickly butter baking sheets and set aside. Combine the flour and ammonium bicarbonate and form the mixture into a well on the work surface. Heat the honey in the top of a double boiler and add it to the well. Knead into a dough until the ingredients are incorporated, working quickly as the dough gets sticky as it cools. Flour a rolling pin and work surface as needed and roll dough into a sheet a little more than ½ inch thick and cut into circles with a cookie cutter. Arrange the circles on the buttered baking sheet and bake in the preheated oven until dry, 10 to 20 minutes, watching carefully as the bottoms brown easily. Use a spatula to move the cookies to a rack and brush them with the egg yolks. Store in an airtight container.

MARGHERITINE DI STRESA

Crisp Butter Cookies from Stresa

Pasticceria Bistoletti, Arona (Novara), Piemonte

These cookies were invented in 1868 to mark the occasion of the wedding of Margherita and Umberto I of Savoy. They are sometimes cut in the shape of flowers, because margherita means "daisy" in Italian. No matter their shape, they are very crisp (due in part to the hard-boiled egg yolks used) and are actually better a few days after being baked. They will keep for up to two months.

MAKES ABOUT 8 DOZEN COOKIES

1 pound (4 sticks) unsalted butter, softened
2 cups confectioners' sugar, plus more for topping cookies
1¼ teaspoons vanilla extract
7 hard-boiled egg yolks
2½ cups unbleached all-purpose flour
2⅓ cups potato starch

In a large bowl, beat the butter with the 2 cups confectioners' sugar and the vanilla. Force the yolks through a sieve into a bowl and stir in to combine, then sift in the flour and potato starch. Stir until well combined and refrigerate overnight so that the dough is very firm.

Preheat the oven to 350°F to 375°F. Line baking sheets with parchment paper and set aside. Roll out the dough and with a small round cutter cut out circles and transfer them to the prepared baking sheets. Press with your thumb in the center of each cookie to make an imprint. Bake in the preheated oven until golden, about 20 minutes. Allow to cool completely, then sprinkle with confectioners' sugar.

UCCELLETTI RIPIENI ⬤
"Stuffed Bird" Cookies
Clarice Natelli, Castiglione Messer Marino
(Chieti), Abruzzo

These cookies, which resemble sleeping baby birds, are made in the shape of hearts or rings for weddings. Similar cookies called "birds" that are filled with fruit preserves and chocolate are made in Isola del Gran Sasso in the province of L'Aquila and in Teramano, where they are eaten for the Feast of Saint Anthony Abbott, the protector of animals. Ammonium bicarbonate is available from specialty baking stores and Greek gourmet shops.

MAKES ABOUT 5 DOZEN COOKIES

DOUGH
- 4 cups unbleached all-purpose flour or 00 flour
- 2½ teaspoons ammonium bicarbonate (see note)
- 2 large eggs
- 1 cup sugar
- 1 cup whole milk
- 1 cup olive oil

FILLING
- 1 pound walnuts in the shell
- 1 pound almonds in the shell
- 2 tablespoons grape preserves
- 1 tablespoon unsweetened cocoa powder
- Grated zest of 1 orange
- ½ cup vermouth

To make the dough, combine the flour, ammonium bicarbonate, eggs, sugar, milk, and olive oil. Knead at length until well combined and then set aside to rest for 1 hour. In the meantime, prepare the filling. Shell the walnuts and almonds, remove their skins, and chop them finely, then combine with the grape preserves, cocoa powder, orange zest, and vermouth.

Preheat the oven to 325°F. Roll out the dough—not overly thin—and cut into circles 2¾

inches in diameter. Top a circle of dough with a little of the filling and fold it in half, pressing the edges to seal. Bring the two corners together, as if shaping tortellini, overlapping slightly. They should touch but remain distinct. Repeat with remaining circles and filling and arrange the cookies on baking sheets. Bake in the preheated oven until golden, 10 to 20 minutes.

LINGUE DI GATTO 🥄
"Cat's Tongue" Butter Cookies
Maria Lorenzi, Frugarolo (Alessandria), Piemonte

These crisp butter cookies are named for their shape. They do spread a little while baking, so be sure to leave plenty of room around the cookies on all sides.

MAKES 8 TO 9 DOZEN COOKIES
- 14 tablespoons (1 stick plus 6 tablespoons) unsalted butter, softened
- 1⅔ cups confectioners' sugar
- 1½ cups unbleached all-purpose flour, sifted
- ¼ teaspoon vanilla extract
- 2 egg whites

Preheat the oven to 400°F. Line baking sheets with parchment paper and set aside.

In a bowl, beat the butter with the sugar with a whisk. Beat until foamy. Add the flour gradually and then the vanilla. In a separate bowl, beat the egg whites to stiff peaks and then fold into the butter mixture.

Transfer the batter to a pastry bag fitted with a narrow plain tip. Pipe 2- to 2½-inch-long strips of batter on the prepared baking sheets, leaving distance between them on all sides. Bake in the preheated oven just until the edges begin to darken, about 8 minutes. Cool on the pans for a few minutes, then remove the cookies to a rack to cool completely.

TEGOLE ❗
"Shingle" Cookies
Pasticceria Morandin, Saint-Vincent (Aosta),
Valle d'Aosta

These cookies were traditionally draped over a rolling pin to cool, which gave them a curved shape so that they looked like Italian terra-cotta roof shingles.

MAKES ABOUT
8 DOZEN COOKIES
- 1¼ pounds (about 4 cups) hazelnuts, toasted, skinned, and finely chopped
- ¾ cup walnuts, finely chopped
- 4 cups sugar
- 12 egg whites, whipped to soft peaks
- ¼ teaspoon vanilla extract
- 1¼ cups unbleached all-purpose flour

Preheat the oven to 350°F.

In a large bowl, fold the hazelnuts, walnuts, and sugar into egg whites. Fold in vanilla, then sift the flour over the mixture and fold to combine. Transfer to a pastry bag fitted with a plain tip and pipe circles 1 to 1½ inches in diameter on nonstick baking sheets. (Use a cookie cutter or round mold for assistance if you need to and leave a generous amount of space between the cookies, as they will spread.) Bake in the preheated oven until golden on top, 5 to 12 minutes.

BECCÙTE 🍇
Cornmeal, Raisin, and Nut Cookies
Marina Ferretti, Senigallia (Ancona), Marche

In Ancona and further inland in the Marche region, these cookies packed with dried fruit and nuts are served at Christmas, but in and around Fano they are served for Lent. To make the cookies, make a well on the work surface with 1¾ cups finely ground cornmeal.

In the center of the well, add a few tablespoons olive oil, ¼ cup plus 1 tablespoon black raisins (soaked in water to soften if necessary), and ⅓ cup pine nuts. Chop ⅓ cup blanched almonds, ½ cup walnuts, and ⅓ cup dried figs and add the mixture to the well. Add 1 tablespoon plus 1½ teaspoons sugar and a pinch each of salt and pepper. Knead together, and add as much boiling water as needed to make a soft dough. Shape the dough into small balls—about the size of a walnut or smaller—then place on baking sheets and flatten slightly. Bake in a preheated 300°F oven until golden and dry. Cool completely before serving.

BRIGIDINI ⬤
Thin Wafers
Pasticceria Carli, Lamporecchio (Pistoia), Toscana

Brigidini are made with a special tool— a flat-surfaced, round, cast-iron waffle iron that is held over the flame of a gas burner. They are very thin and crisp and often curl up after cooking.

MAKES ABOUT
60 WAFERS
- 5 large eggs
- ¾ cup sugar
- Anise extract to taste
- About 2½ cups unbleached all-purpose flour
- Oil for oiling iron

Beat the eggs with the sugar and some water. Beat in the extract, then begin beating in the flour a little at a time until you have a medium-thick dough. You may not need all of the flour. Divide the dough into balls, each about the size of a cherry. Heat both sides of the iron and oil one side. Place a ball of dough on the unoiled side of the iron. Close the iron firmly and hold it over the flame for 1 to 2 minutes, turning once. Open the iron, remove the wafer, and continue with the remaining dough.

ZALETI CON LE PRUGNE ❗
Cornmeal and Raisin Cookies with Prune Compote
Ristorante Il Desco, Verona, Veneto

These traditional cornmeal cookies can be a little dry, so they are paired here with a prune compote and some syrup. Sprinkle the cookies with a little confectioners' sugar just before serving if you like, then provide each guest with a small bowl containing a couple of prunes and a drizzle of syrup.

MAKES ABOUT 2 DOZEN COOKIES

- 20 to 24 pitted prunes
- 2¼ cups sugar
- 2 cups whole milk
- 1¾ cups finely ground cornmeal
- 7 tablespoons unsalted butter, softened, plus more for buttering pans
- 5 large eggs
- 1 pinch salt
- 1 cup golden raisins
- 1 cup pine nuts
- ¾ cup unbleached all-purpose flour or 00 flour
- 1 tablespoon plus 1 teaspoon baking powder

To make the compote and syrup, soak the prunes in 2 cups water until very soft, 6 to 7 hours. With a slotted spoon or skimmer, remove the prunes to a heatproof bowl. Add 1¼ cups sugar to the prune cooking water and cook over medium heat, whisking, until sugar has dissolved and the liquid has thickened slightly to form a syrup. Pour the hot syrup over the prunes and set aside to cool.

Place the milk in a pot, bring to a simmer, and add the cornmeal in a thin stream, stirring constantly. Cook over medium heat, stirring constantly, for 20 minutes. Set aside to cool.

Preheat the oven to 350°F. In a bowl beat the remaining 1 cup sugar with the butter. Add the eggs one at a time, beating to combine between additions, then beat in the salt, raisins, and pine nuts. Mix the flour with the baking powder and beat into the mixture. Beat in the cooked cornmeal.

Butter cookie sheets and drop heaping tablespoons of the batter onto the pans, leaving room between them. Press on the cookies with the back of a wet spoon. Bake in the preheated oven for 20 minutes. Cool before serving.

PASTE DI MELIGA ⬤
Cornmeal Cookies
Laboratorio Egidio Michelis, Mondovì (Cuneo), Piemonte

Piemonte is famous for many different cookies, but cornmeal *meliga* are among the region's best known and a Slow Food Presidium. These are ideal for dipping in two other Piemonte classics: a glass of good Barolo wine or a bowl of zabaione like the mousse version on page 421. For richer cookies, use 4 yolks and 2 whites in place of the 3 whole eggs.

MAKES 4 TO 5 DOZEN COOKIES

- 14 tablespoons (1 stick plus 6 tablespoons) unsalted butter, melted, then cooled to room temperature
- 1 cup sugar
- 3 large eggs
- 4¾ cups unbleached all-purpose flour or 00 flour
- 1¾ cups very fine stone-ground cornmeal, preferably the Ottofile variety
- 3 tablespoons baking powder
- Seeds of 1 vanilla bean, ground

Preheat the oven to 350°F. Beat the butter and sugar to combine. Add the eggs and beat until combined. Beat in the flour and cornmeal, then the baking powder and vanilla bean seeds. Transfer to a piping syringe with a wide mouth (or a pastry bag fitted with a wide tube) and pipe rectangular or round cookies onto a baking sheet. Bake in the preheated oven for 30 to 35 minutes.

FINOCCHINI
Anise Tea Cookies
Pasticceria Grossetti, Refrancore (Asti), Piemonte

These are sometimes called *maggiorini* after the pastry shop in Refrancore where they were created. Legend has it that they were the result of the baker accidentally spilling anise extract into cookie dough. These are crisp with a texture like toast, perfect for dipping into a cup of tea.

MAKES 4 TO 5 DOZEN COOKIES

- 2 tablespoons unsalted butter, plus more for buttering pans
- 7 large eggs
- 8 egg yolks
- 3 cups sugar
- 1 teaspoon honey
- 2 or 3 drops anise extract
- 4¾ cups unbleached all-purpose flour
- 1 tablespoon baking powder
- ½ cup potato starch

Preheat the oven to 425°F. Butter baking sheets and set aside. In a large bowl, combine the eggs and egg yolks and beat in the sugar. Beat until very foamy, then beat in the honey and anise extract. Gradually add the flour, baking powder, and starch. Beat until well combined into a soft dough. Roll out the dough into a rectangle or rectangles about ½ inch thick, transfer to the prepared pans, and bake until the top is golden, about 20 minutes.

Let the dough cool, then remove it from the pans and cut into slices about 2 by 4 inches. Place the cookies on baking sheets and bake in the preheated oven until lightly toasted, about 10 additional minutes.

BICCIOLANI
Spice Cookies
Pasticceria Follis, Vercelli, Piemonte

Eat these cookies within a week of baking them—they start to lose their fragrance and flavor after that.

MAKES ABOUT 6 DOZEN COOKIES

- 4 egg yolks
- 1 cup sugar
- 21 tablespoons (2 sticks plus 5 tablespoons) unsalted butter, softened, plus more for pans
- ½ cup acacia honey
- 2 to 3 vanilla bean seeds, ground
- 2¾ cups unbleached all-purpose flour or 00 flour, plus more for pans
- ⅔ cup potato starch
- 1 pinch ground cloves
- 1 pinch ground mace
- 1 pinch ground coriander
- 1 pinch freshly grated nutmeg
- 1 teaspoon ground cinnamon
- 1 pinch freshly ground white pepper
- 1 pinch salt

Beat the egg yolks, sugar, and 21 tablespoons butter until light and fluffy. Beat in the honey and vanilla bean seeds. In a small bowl, combine 2¾ cups flour, starch, spices, and salt, then beat into the mixture. Refrigerate for 24 hours.

Preheat the oven to 300°F. Butter and flour baking sheets. Knead the dough a few times, then roll it out to a little less than ¼ inch thick. With a knife or pastry wheel, cut it into rectangles 2¾ to 3 inches by 1 inch. Use a fork to make ridges on them the long way. Place on the prepared pans with about 1 inch between them on all sides. Bake in the preheated oven until crisp, about 20 minutes.

CHIFFEL
Crescents Filled with Jam or Pastry Cream
Ubaldo Balbi, Muggia (Trieste), Friuli-Venezia Giulia

Make a starter by dissolving 1 tablespoon active dry yeast in ¼ cup warm milk, then combining that mixture with about ¾ cup flour. Form into a ball, place in a bowl, slash an X in the top, cover with a dish towel, and set aside to rise for 1 hour. While the dough is rising, knead together another 1¾ cups flour, 3 whole eggs, 1 egg yolk, ⅓ cup sugar, 1 teaspoon salt, and the grated zest of ½ lemon. If the dough is dry and crumbly, loosen it with a little milk until it is soft. Knead in 10 tablespoons softened unsalted butter and the risen starter. Knead until very soft and elastic, then form into a ball, place in a bowl, cover, and set aside to rise for at least 2 hours. Finally, knead the dough briefly and then return it to the bowl, cover, and set aside to rise overnight. The next day, roll out the dough a little less than ¼ inch thick and cut into triangles with 4-inch sides. Place about 1 teaspoon of apricot or peach preserves (look for dense preserves, nothing watery or runny) or pastry cream in the center of each triangle. Roll each triangle from the long end and form into a crescent moon or letter C shape. Repeat with remaining triangles. Arrange on buttered and floured baking sheets and allow to rise for about 1 hour, then brush with beaten egg, sprinkle with a little sugar, and bake in a preheated 400°F oven until browned, about 20 minutes.

DOLCETTI DELLA SPOSA ●
Bride's Cookies
Ristorante Agorà, Civita (Cosenza), Calabria

Civita in Calabria has an Arbëreshë or Italo-Albanian community, where these white cookies are a must at weddings. Similar cookies are made for weddings in Puglia, but those are made with risen dough and are cut into rectangles. The best way to bake these is in a wood-burning oven, but lacking that, just turn your home oven as high as it will go.

MAKES 6 TO 8 DOZEN 1-INCH RINGS

- 1¼ cups unbleached all-purpose flour
- 4 large eggs
- 3 to 4 egg whites
- ½ cup confectioners' sugar, or more to taste
- A few drops lemon juice

Heat the oven as high as it will go, probably 500°F. Beat the flour and whole eggs to form a dough. Roll the dough into ropes about the thickness of a finger and cut the ropes into pieces about 2 inches long. Form the pieces into rings, overlapping the ends slightly and pinching them together. Transfer to baking sheets and bake in the preheated oven until golden, about 10 minutes. Set aside to cool.

Prepare a glaze by beating the egg whites to soft peaks. Add the confectioners' sugar and continue beating until they reach the firm-peak stage. Add the lemon juice and beat in. Glaze the cookies and let them dry completely.

CANTUCCI
Almond Cookies
Ristorante Grotta di Santa Caterina da Bagoga,
Siena, Toscana

*C*antucci are the crisp almond cookies commonly known outside of Italy as "biscotti." They are typically served with a glass of Vin Santo for dipping. There are numerous versions. In Pisa, Marianna Turchi makes cantucci that are soft and don't have almonds but are scented with Vin Santo, rosolio, Strega liqueur, star anise, and grated lemon zest. Giuliana Verni makes an extra-lemony version with the grated zest of four lemons and incorporates pine nuts as well as almonds.

MAKES 5 TO 6 DOZEN, DEPENDING ON THE SIZE

- 8 cups unbleached all-purpose flour or 00 flour
- 2 cups sugar
- 4 large eggs, lightly beaten
- 1 tablespoon Vin Santo
- 1 cup vegetable oil
- 2¾ cups raw almonds (with skins)

Preheat oven to 350°F. Line baking sheets with parchment and set aside.

In a large bowl, combine all the ingredients and knead until well combined. Divide the dough into equal parts and shape them into loaves about 2 inches high on the prepared baking sheets. Bake in the preheated oven until dry and golden, about 35 minutes. Remove from the oven and allow to cool slightly. When the loaves are cool enough to handle, slice them about ¾ inch thick. Cool completely before serving.

BIRBANTI
Pine Nut Meringue Cookies
Ilda Cardinali, Passignano sul Trasimeno
(Perugia), Umbria

*I*n a bowl combine 1¾ cups flour, 1¾ cups sugar, the grated zest of a lemon or orange, ¾ cup pine nuts, a pinch of salt, and a pinch of ground cinnamon. Beat 4 egg whites until they form stiff peaks and fold them into the flour mixture. Place walnut-sized portions of the dough on an oiled baking sheet. Bake in a 400°F oven until golden, about 10 minutes.

SUSUMELLE
Glazed Cinnamon Cookies
Agostino Tassone, Spadola (Vibo Valentia), Calabria

*D*issolve 2 tablespoons sourdough starter in about ¼ cup warm water and combine with about ¾ cup flour. Knead and set aside to rise until doubled, then combine with an additional 3¼ cups flour, 3 egg yolks, a pinch of ground cinnamon, and the grated zest of 1 lemon. Incorporate enough water to make a soft dough, knead at length, and set aside to rest for 15 minutes. Roll out the dough and cut into rectangles. Place on an oiled baking sheet and bake at 400°F until browned. Place the cookies on a rack, melt a few ounces of dark chocolate in a double boiler, and pour the chocolate over the cookies, or glaze with melted honey or a confectioners' sugar glaze.

RICCIARELLI ⬤
Sienese Almond Cookies
Pasticceria Bernardini, Fucecchio (Firenze), Toscana

These soft almonds cookies with a craggy cracked surface are the pride of Siena. They are good keepers and will last a long time if stored in a tin with a tight lid in a cool, dry place. You can sprinkle additional confectioners' sugar on the cooled cookies if you like. Along with standard sweet almonds, these cookies incorporate a small amount of bitter almonds; as their name implies, bitter almonds have a sharp flavor. Bitter almonds cannot be consumed raw and may be difficult to find—you can add a few drops of almond extract to the dough in their place if you can't track them down. Ammonium bicarbonate is available from baking specialty stores and Greek gourmet shops.

MAKES 7 TO 8 DOZEN COOKIES

- 7 cups raw sweet almonds
- Scant ¼ cup bitter almonds (see note)
- 5½ cups sugar
- Grated zest of 1 orange
- 1¼ teaspoons ammonium bicarbonate (see note)
- 3 to 4 egg whites
- 3 tablespoons honey
- Confectioners' sugar for work surface and pans
- Butter for pans

Blanch and finely chop both types of almonds. On a work surface, combine the almonds, sugar, orange zest, and ammonium bicarbonate and shape into a well. Add the egg whites to the center of the well one at a time, working in each egg white between additions, until you have a soft, smooth dough. (You may not need the fourth egg white.) Knead in the honey.

Sprinkle the work surface with confectioners' sugar. Divide the dough into equal parts and shape them into logs. Flatten the logs into rectangles and cut them at an angle to make the cookies. Butter baking sheets and sprinkle them with a generous amount of confectioners' sugar. Place the cookies on the prepared pans. Set aside to rest at room temperature, uncovered, until a dry crust forms on the surface, 12 to 24 hours.

When you are ready to bake the cookies, preheat the oven to 400°F. Bake the cookies for 5 minutes. Cool before serving.

BRUTTI MA BUONI ⬤
"Ugly but Good" Hazelnut Cookies
Ristorante Battaglino, Bra (Cuneo), Piemonte

The Piemonte region seems to offer an endless variety of tasty cookies. As the name of these humble cookies indicates, looks are not their strong suit, but they have plenty of flavor. Be sure to chop the nuts by hand so that they are slightly irregular. These keep for about one week.

MAKES ABOUT 6 DOZEN COOKIES

- 1 pound hazelnuts
- 3 egg whites
- 2¾ cups confectioners' sugar

Preheat the oven to 250°F to 275°F, preferably on the convection setting. Line baking sheets with parchment. Toast and skin the hazelnuts. Chop by hand (see note).

Beat the egg whites with the confectioners' sugar to stiff peaks. Gently fold in the hazelnuts. Place small balls of the mixture on the prepared baking sheets and bake in the preheated oven until dry to the touch and browned in spots, about 15 minutes, or a little longer if your oven doesn't have a convection setting. Let cool and harden on the pans (they will be soft when they come out of the oven).

CANESTRELLI ALLE NOCCIOLE
Hazelnut Butter Cookies
Osteria dell'Acquasanta, Mele (Genova), Liguria

O ther versions of these cookies include cornmeal and/or cocoa powder. The creator of this recipe highly recommends the use of DOP (Protected Designation of Origin) Piemonte hazelnuts, such as the Tonda Gentile variety, which have an intense flavor. For a different take, use walnuts in place of the hazelnuts. These cookies get their name from sea scallops, and they are traditionally cut with a specific daisy-shaped cookie cutter that gives them a scalloped edge and a hole in the center.

MAKES 5 TO 6 DOZEN 2½-INCH COOKIES

- ½ cup DOP Piemonte hazelnuts, toasted, skinned, and chopped (see note)
- 3¾ cups unbleached all-purpose flour
- ½ cup sugar
- 4 egg yolks
- ¼ teaspoon vanilla extract
- 14 tablespoons (1 stick plus 6 tablespoons) unsalted butter
- ⅔ cup confectioners' sugar

Mix together the hazelnuts, flour, and sugar and shape into a well on the work surface. Place the egg yolks and vanilla in the center of the well. Cut the butter into pieces and scatter the butter around the rim of the well. Knead into a soft dough, adding flour in small amounts if necessary. Refrigerate for 1 hour.

Preheat the oven to 350°F. Line baking sheets with parchment paper and set aside. Roll out the dough to ¼-inch thickness and cut out cookies with a daisy-shaped or round cookie cutter (see note). Transfer to the prepared pans and bake in the preheated oven until golden, about 10 minutes. Allow to cool, then sprinkle with the confectioners' sugar.

COPETA
Honey-Nut Wafer Cookies
Apicoltura Andrea Diale, Salmour (Cuneo), Piemonte

T hese cookies have a very unusual ingredient: *ostie*, or host wafers. These paper-thin wafers—the same as those eaten at Mass when taking communion—are for sale in some pharmacies in Italy, as they can be used by those who have trouble swallowing pills. You may be able to find edible wafer paper at a store that sells candy-making supplies. There are other versions of these cookies all over Italy, including in Toscana, Puglia, and Sicilia. Chop the nuts, but don't grind them—you don't want them to be too fine.

MAKES 60 COOKIES

- 3 cups acacia honey
- 2 pounds walnuts or skinned hazelnuts, chopped
- 120 round host wafers, 3½ inches in diameter (see note)

Place the honey in a pot and place over high heat until it is just about to boil, increases significantly in volume, and has lots of light foam on the surface, about 3 minutes. Continue cooking and as the water in the honey evaporates it should turn reddish amber—similar to a caramel. Stir in the nuts with a stainless steel spoon and turn down the heat.

As soon as the nuts and honey are combined, remove the pot from the heat and use a fork and spoon to take out a small portion of the mixture and place it on top of one host. Top with a second host and press lightly with a meat pounder until cool. You can make stacks of 8 or 10 cookies at a time and press down on them together. Just keep the pressure on until they are cool or the wafers will detach from the filling.

KINZICA 🍶
Pine Nut Meringues
Pasticceria Bernardini, Fucecchio (Firenze), Toscana

These meringue cookies take their name from a local heroine who is said to have saved the city of Pisa from invading Saracens in the year 1000.

MAKES ABOUT
4 DOZEN COOKIES

- 1¾ cups pine nuts
- 2 cups confectioners' sugar
- 4 egg whites
- 2 teaspoons honey

Finely chop 1½ cups of the pine nuts. In a bowl, combine with 1⅔ cups confectioners' sugar. In a separate bowl, beat the egg whites with the honey and the remaining ⅓ cup confectioners' sugar. Pour that mixture into a copper or stainless steel pot with a heavy bottom, fold in the chopped pine nuts, and cook, stirring constantly, over medium heat until the mixture pulls away cleanly from the sides of the pan. It will probably need to reach at least 140°F to do so.

Let the mixture cool and then transfer to a pastry bag. Pipe balls of the mixture and roll them in the remaining pine nuts so that they are coated on all sides. Place each ball in a small parchment pastry cup and allow to rest until dry on the surface, about 12 hours. Preheat the oven to 400°F, place the filled pastry cups on a baking sheet, and bake in the preheated oven until dry to the touch, 4 to 5 minutes. Allow to cool completely before serving.

BRAZZADELLE ⬤
Baked Rye Rings
Clelia Reghenzani, Teglio (Sondrio), Lombardia

Traditionally these not overly sweet rings are 12 inches in diameter. You may need to make smaller rings to fit in your home oven. Be sure to keep oven size in mind when shaping them. Also, remove them from the oven with care, as they break easily when hot. As they cool, they stiffen. These are often hung on a wooden rod.

MAKES 6 TO 8
LARGE RINGS

- 5¾ cups unbleached all-purpose flour
- ½ cup rye flour
- 2¼ teaspoons (1 envelope) active dry yeast, dissolved in 1 tablespoon water
- ½ teaspoon salt
- 1 cup plus 2 tablespoons sugar
- 10 tablespoons (1 stick plus 2 tablespoons) unsalted butter
- About ¾ cup whole milk, at room temperature
- 3 large eggs
- Cornmeal for surface

Make a starter by combining 1½ cups of the flour, the rye flour, and the yeast mixture in a bowl and adding enough water to make a fairly soft mixture. Cover and let rise in a warm place for 1 hour. Meanwhile, combine the remaining 4¼ cups flour, the salt, and 1 cup plus 1 tablespoon sugar. Place the butter in a saucepan with a teaspoon or so of milk and soften slightly (don't melt completely). Combine the flour mixture and the starter, then add the butter in small amounts, kneading to combine between additions. Add 2 eggs, kneading to combine between additions. Add as much milk as necessary to make a soft dough and knead until well combined.

Sprinkle some cornmeal on a large wooden peel and set aside. Tear off a piece of the dough about the size of your fist and form it into a ball. Pinch the ball of dough between your index finger and thumb to make a hole in the center, then rotate it until you have a round ring of dough about 12 inches in diameter, or a size that will fit in your oven. Set aside on the prepared board and repeat with remaining dough. Let the rings rise for 1 hour.

Preheat the oven with a baking stone to 350°F. Beat the remaining egg and brush the rings with it. Sprinkle on the remaining 1 tablespoon sugar. Transfer to the preheated oven and bake until browned, 25 to 30 minutes.

SPUMINI ALLE MANDORLE 🍴
Almond Meringues
Ristorante La Palomba, Mondavio (Urbino), Marche

Meringues are the perfect airy end to a meal and it also can be a nice touch to serve a couple of them alongside a more substantial dessert. The number of meringues you'll get from this recipe depends on what size you make them, but you will incorporate a lot of air into the egg whites as you whip them, so this will make quite a few.

MAKES 4 TO 6 DOZEN MERINGUES
- 7   egg whites
- 2½ cups sugar
- 3   cups blanched almonds, chopped

Preheat a convection oven to 175°F to 200°F. Line baking sheets with parchment paper and set aside. Whip the egg whites and sugar in an electric mixer for at least 30 minutes until very stiff. Fold in the almonds. Drop teaspoonfuls or pipe small amounts of the meringue mixture on the prepared baking sheets. Bake in the preheated oven until dry to the touch, about 1 hour 20 minutes.

CALCIONI ⊞
Sweet Cheese Turnovers
Ristorante Le Copertelle, Serra San Quirico (Ancona), Marche

Other versions of these little pies enclose a filling of pureed chickpeas, walnuts, pine nuts, orange zest, honey, and chocolate. These may be baked, as described below, or fried in olive oil.

MAKES ABOUT 20 TURNOVERS
- 16 large eggs
- 1½ cups sugar
- 2   pounds sheep's cheese aged at least three months, grated
- Grated zest of 7 lemons
- 8   cups unbleached all-purpose flour
- ¾   cup lard
- 1   egg yolk, beaten

Prepare the filling the night before by combining 8 eggs, ½ cup sugar, the grated cheese, and the zest of 5 lemons. Combine and refrigerate overnight.

Preheat the oven to 350°F. Line baking sheets with parchment paper and set aside. To make the pastry, combine the flour, the remaining 8 eggs, the remaining 1 cup sugar, the lard, and the remaining grated zest of 2 lemons. Roll out the dough (not overly thin) and cut into rounds about 3 inches in diameter. Place a piece of the filling about the size of a walnut on each round of dough. Fold them in half and seal the edges. Brush the pastries with the beaten egg yolk and slash a small cross (a little less than ½ inch long) in the top of each. Transfer to the prepared pans. Bake in the preheated oven until the pastries are golden and have opened where they were cut so that a little filling comes out, about 50 minutes.

KNÖDEL DI ALBICOCCA 🍑
Apricot Dumplings
Ristorante Kohlern, Bolzano-Bozen, Trentino–Alto Adige

These interesting dumplings can also be made with plums in place of the apricots. The trickiest part is pitting the fruit without cutting it in half completely. Use a sharp paring knife to make slits and extract the pits. If you do cut all the way around, just put the halves back together around the sugar cube and proceed. Once they are wrapped in the dough they should stay together.

SERVES 4
14 ounces (about 2) potatoes
2 egg yolks
4 tablespoons unsalted butter, softened
1 cup unbleached all-purpose flour
8 apricots
4 sugar cubes, halved
Salt to taste
¾ cup breadcrumbs
1 teaspoon ground cinnamon
¼ cup sugar
Melted butter for serving

Boil the potatoes, peel them, and puree them with a potato ricer. Combine with the egg yolks, butter, and flour until you have a smooth, well-combined dough. Roll out into a thick sheet and cut into 8 equal pieces.

Pit the apricots, leaving them intact. Slip a sugar cube half into each apricot where the pit was. Wrap each apricot in a piece of dough and form it into a ball that encloses the fruit, sealing the seams tightly. Bring a large pot of lightly salted water to a boil and boil the dumplings for 15 minutes.

Meanwhile, toast the breadcrumbs in a pan until golden. Remove from the heat and mix with the cinnamon and sugar. Drain the cooked dumplings, then roll them in the sugared breadcrumbs and drizzle on the melted butter.

BOCCONOTTI AL MOSTO DOLCE 🍎
Individual Apple, Pear, and Walnut Pies
Locanda La Corte, Acciano (L'Aquila), Abruzzo

At Al Ritrovo degli Amici in Martina Franca, in the province of Taranto, similar pies are filled with pastry cream.

MAKES 1 DOZEN SMALL PIES
2 large eggs
½ cup plus 2 tablespoons sugar
2 cups unbleached all-purpose flour
7 tablespoons unsalted butter, melted
Grated zest and juice of ½ lemon
1 tablespoon active dry yeast, dissolved in a little water
¼ teaspoon vanilla extract
2 medium or 3 small apples, peeled, cored, and diced
1 pear, peeled, cored, and diced
½ cup walnuts, chopped
1 pinch ground cinnamon
2 cups wine must reduction, warm

Beat the eggs with ½ cup sugar. Gradually add the flour, beating to combine between additions, and melted butter. Stir in the lemon zest, yeast, and vanilla. Knead, shape into a ball, place in a bowl, and refrigerate for at least 8 hours.

Preheat the oven to 350°F. For the filling, combine the apples, pears, walnuts, cinnamon, the remaining 2 tablespoons sugar, and lemon juice. Roll out the dough and cut into 24 pieces. Line 12 individual baking dishes or ramekins with dough, fill with the filling, and top with remaining pieces of dough. Place the baking dishes on baking sheets (to make it easier to take them in and out of the oven) and baking until browned, about 20 minutes. Let the pies cool completely and serve each with a few tablespoons of the wine must reduction.

CANDELAUS 🍪
Almond Pastries
Pasticceria Sorelle Piccioni, Quartu Sant'Elena
(Cagliari), Sardegna

These pastries can be made either filled (as here) or as flat circles or other shapes (hearts are common) that are not filled. The unfilled pastries are brushed with an icing made by melting sugar and orange flower water over medium heat, then decorated with edible gold leaf and other items so that they look like intricately embroidered pillows. The filled pastries, too, are iced and decorated. These are almost always made in large batches, in part because they are made for special occasions, and in part because the process is a long one (the cups must be allowed to dry for ten days before baking).

MAKES 4 TO 6 DOZEN 2-INCH CUPS

7½ cups sugar
Orange flower water to taste
¼ teaspoon vanilla extract
2 pounds blanched almonds, ground
Grated zest of 4 lemons
2 pounds blanched thinly sliced almonds
Confectioners' sugar for glaze and icing
Egg whites for icing

For the dough, place 2½ cups sugar in a saucepan over medium heat and melt. Stir in a little orange flower water and cook to a thick syrup. Add the vanilla and the ground almonds and cook, stirring continuously, until thoroughly combined. Remove from the heat, pour onto a work surface, and allow to cool. By hand, pinch off small balls of the mixture and shape them into small indented cups. Allow to dry for about 10 days. When the pastry cups are dry, preheat the oven to 300°F, transfer them to baking sheets, and bake them in the preheated oven for 15 minutes. Set aside to cool.

To make the filling, melt the remaining 5 cups sugar over medium heat. Add a generous amount of water, lemon zest, and the sliced almonds. Cook at a brisk simmer until the almonds have absorbed all the water and the mixture is dense and compact, about 45 minutes. Transfer the sliced almond mixture into the cups and set aside to cool for a few hours.

Make a thick glaze by combining confectioners' sugar with water until dissolved and glaze the tops of the pastries so that they are smooth and uniform. Make icing by cooking confectioners' sugar and egg whites over low heat for 30 minutes. Let the icing cool, then pipe it decoratively on top of the glazed surface using a pastry bag.

CASCHETTAS 🌿
Ribbon Pastries with Saba and Almond Filling
Marina Corda, Nuoro, Sardegna

These pretty pastries are open at the top to reveal their filling. Make a dough of 4 cups hard wheat flour, 2 tablespoons lard, a pinch of salt, and enough water to make a firm dough. Knead until well combined and set aside to rest. Cook 1½ cups white-grape saba (a syrup made with the wine must from the first pressing; see recipe on page 417) with 4¼ cups semolina flour over low heat for 15 minutes, stirring constantly and ensuring that no lumps remain. Let the saba mixture rest for 1 hour. It will get quite thick. Return to the heat and cook for an additional 10 minutes, stirring and gradually adding 3 cups ground almonds and the grated zest of 1 lemon or orange. Roll the dough into a very thin sheet and cut into strips with a pastry wheel. Spread some filling on a strip of dough and fold the long sides of the rectangle up to contain the filling, but don't seal them. Turn the piece so that it is standing on its fold, then shape as you prefer. (Caschettas can be in the form of half-moons, hearts, spirals, horseshoes, or any shape you like.) Repeat with the remaining dough and filling. Bake filled pastries in a preheated 325°F oven for 30 minutes.

SFOGLIATELLE RICE ⬛
Layered Sfogliatelle Pastries
Pasticceria O' Funzionista, Sorrento (Napoli), Campania

Sfogliatelle are clamshell-shaped flaky layered pastries (known as "lobster tails" in some parts of the United States). They are a signature of the Campania region in general and Napoli in particular. Some versions are filled with pastry cream or ricotta. Sfogliatelle are somewhat complex to make, but not really difficult. Just leave yourself plenty of time and don't skimp on chilling the dough—a buttery dough like this becomes unworkable if it sits at room temperature for too long.

MAKES ABOUT 16 LARGE PASTRIES

DOUGH
- 4½ cups 0 flour or unbleached all-purpose flour
- 1 cup 00 flour or unbleached all-purpose flour
- 1½ teaspoons salt
- 14 tablespoons (1 stick plus 6 tablespoons) unsalted butter, softened

FILLING
- 1 cup plus 2 tablespoons 0 flour
- ¼ cup semolina flour
- ⅔ cup sugar
- 1 pinch salt
- 2 cups whole milk
- 1 pinch ground cinnamon
- ¼ teaspoon vanilla extract
- Grated zest of 1 orange
- ½ cup diced candied orange peel
- 5 to 6 large eggs

For the dough, combine the two types of flour and the salt with 1½ cups water and knead until smooth and well combined. (Add more water in small amounts if the dough feels dry.) Cover and set aside to rest for at least 1 hour. Roll out the dough into a square or rectangle and spread the softened butter all over the surface. Very carefully roll up the sheet of dough fairly tightly into a roll about 4 inches in diameter without allowing air bubbles to form. Place the rolled dough on a tray or baking sheet and chill in the refrigerator for 12 hours.

To make the filling, in a large saucepan combine the two types of flour, sugar, and salt with the milk and 1 scant cup water. Cook over medium heat, stirring constantly, until thickened. Remove from the heat and allow to cool. When the filling is completely cool, stir in the cinnamon, vanilla, zest, and candied peel. Whisk in the eggs one at a time until you have a soft, smooth cream.

Preheat the oven to 400°F. Line baking sheets with parchment and set aside. Cut a disk a little less than ½ inch thick from the roll of dough, then by hand gently stretch it into a cone with the tip in the center. Try to maintain the butter "ribs" in the dough. Place a generous amount of filling in the center (the finished pastries should be pillowy, not flat) and fold in half to make a triangular pastry. Do not pinch the edges closed. Place a spoonful of the filling in the center and fold the disk in half to make a semi-circle. Place on the prepared pans and continue with remaining dough and filling. (If this is taking you a long time, cut a few disks at a time, then return the roll of dough to the refrigerator while you fill and seal them so that it stays firm.) Bake in the preheated oven until golden, 20 to 30 minutes. Cool on racks.

BABÀ AL RUM 🍴
Baba au Rum
Agriturismo Fattoria Terranova, Massa Lubrense
(Napoli), Campania

Individual baba molds or pans have high sides that encourage the pastries to rise into a sort of mushroom shape. These are a justly famous Neapolitan dessert—boozy, tender, and irresistible. Plating these with some fresh fruit and pastry cream is a nice touch. Fresh yeast is sold in cubes or cakes and is preferred for this recipe, but you can replace the yeast with 2 envelopes of active dry yeast if necessary.

SERVES 6
- 2 cakes fresh yeast (see note)
- 4 cups unbleached all-purpose flour, plus more for flouring pans
- 7 tablespoons unsalted butter, softened, plus more for buttering pans
- 5 large eggs, lightly beaten
- 1 pinch salt
- 1 cup whole milk
- 1¼ cups sugar
- ¼ cup plus 1 tablespoon rum

Make a sponge: crumble the yeast into a little warm water, then combine with ¾ cup flour in a large bowl. Stir to combine, cover with a dish towel, and set the starter aside for 45 minutes.

Form the remaining 3¼ cups flour into a well on a work surface. Place the starter in the center of the well with the butter, eggs, and salt. Pull in flour from the sides of the well until combined into a crumbly dough, then knead energetically for at least 15 minutes, adding the milk a little at a time to soften the dough as you do. Butter and flour 6 individual baba molds. Divide the dough into 6 equal pieces and place them in the molds. Cover with a dish towel and leave in a warm, dry place until the dough has risen to the rims of the molds.

Preheat the oven to 350°F and bake the cakes until golden and risen, about 35 minutes. Make a syrup by combining 2 cups water with the

sugar and rum and cook, stirring constantly, until the sugar is completely dissolved. Gently unmold the cakes and soak them in the hot syrup. Remove the cakes from the syrup, drain briefly, and serve.

CRESPELLE DI CASTAGNE 🍴
Chestnut Crepes
Osteria Lissidini, Stadolina di Vione (Brescia), Lombardia

The chestnut flour in these crepes gives them an earthy, nutty flavor. They are delicious served with almost any kind of ice cream. Don't be intimidated—crepes are actually very easy to cook.

MAKES 1 TO 2 DOZEN CREPES
- 2¼ cups chestnut flour
- 1 cup unbleached all-purpose flour
- 4 large eggs, lightly beaten
- Whole milk for thinning
- Olive oil for pan
- Ice cream for filling
- ⅓ cup confectioners' sugar

In a bowl combine the two types of flour with the eggs. Add enough milk to make a thin batter. Be sure there are no lumps.

Lightly oil a 6-inch nonstick pan and place over medium heat. When the pan is quite hot, add about ¼ cup of the batter and quickly tilt the pan in all directions so that it covers the pan completely in a thin layer. Cook until browned underneath, about 2 minutes, then flip and cook the other side for 1 minute. Set the crepe aside and continue until you have used up all of the batter. Allow the crepes to cool completely, then fill them with ice cream, fold them in packets, and sprinkle with confectioners' sugar.

DONUTS & OTHER FRIED PASTRIES

ANIME BEATE ▦
"Blessed Souls" Donuts
Rosaria Salvatore, Tropea (Vĭbo Valentia), Calabria

These small donuts are made for the Christmas holidays in Calabria. If you prefer, you can use a flavorful honey in place of the peach preserves.

MAKES 4 TO 6 DOZEN SMALL DONUTS

- 2 tablespoons olive oil, plus more for frying
- 1 pinch salt
- 4 cups unbleached all-purpose flour
- 6 large eggs
- Peach preserves for topping
- Confectioners' sugar for topping

Place 4 cups water in a pot. Add the 2 tablespoons olive oil and pinch of salt and place over medium heat. When the water starts to boil, add the flour very slowly, letting it fall in a thin stream between your fingers and stirring constantly with a wooden spoon. Continue stirring until the mixture pulls away cleanly from the sides of the pot. Remove from the heat and add the eggs one at a time, stirring constantly and waiting for each one to be incorporated before adding the next.

Line a baking sheet with paper towels and set aside. Place a generous amount of olive oil in a pot with high sides and bring to temperature for frying. Drop the dough in by the tablespoon and fry until golden. With a skimmer, remove to the prepared baking sheet to drain briefly, then transfer to the serving platter. Place a small spoonful of preserves on the center of each donut and sift confectioners' sugar over them all. Serve hot.

BUGIE 🌸
Fried Dough "Lies" for Carnival
Ristorante del Mercato da Maurizio, Cravanzana (Cuneo), Piemonte

These are one of the many fried dough treats made for Carnival in Italy. Some use milk in the dough; others incorporate raisins.

MAKES ABOUT 8 DOZEN PIECES

- 8 cups unbleached all-purpose flour or oo flour
- 1 teaspoon baking powder
- ½ cup sugar
- 1 pinch salt
- Grated zest of 1 lemon
- 4 large eggs, lightly beaten
- 7 tablespoons unsalted butter, melted
- 1 tablespoon dry Marsala
- 1 tablespoon dry white wine
- Olive oil for frying
- ⅓ cup confectioners' sugar

Combine the flour and baking powder and shape into a well on the work surface. Place the sugar, salt, lemon zest, and eggs in the center of the well. Work in the butter a little at a time, kneading between additions, then the Marsala and wine. Knead until smooth and compact.

Roll out some of the dough to a sheet less than ¹⁄₁₀ inch thick and use a fluted pastry wheel to cut it into triangles and diamonds 2 to 2½ inches in length.

Line baking sheets with paper towels and set aside. Place a generous amount of oil in a pot with high sides and bring to a high temperature for frying. Fry the pieces of dough in the hot oil a few at a time. When they puff up, turn them gently so that both sides cook. When golden, remove with a skimmer and transfer to the prepared pans. Drain and cool briefly, then sprinkle with confectioners' sugar.

CANNOLO DI RICOTTA
Cannoli
Osteria U Locale, Buccheri (Siracusa), Sicîlia

Cannoli (the plural form) are probably the most famous pastry from Sicilia and perhaps one of the most famous from all of Italy. The shells for cannoli are shaped around cylindrical molds. They can be either fried or baked, but either way they must be completely cool before you fill them, and they should be filled shortly before you plan to serve them so that they remain crisp.

MAKES ABOUT 4 DOZEN

SHELLS
2½ cups unbleached all-purpose flour or 00 flour
1¾ cups semolina flour
2 cups cornstarch
¼ teaspoon vanilla extract
1 pinch salt
2 tablespoons extra-virgin olive oil
3 large eggs
1 egg yolk
⅓ cup sugar
½ cup red wine
Peanut oil for oiling molds and frying (if frying) or oiling pans (if baking)

FILLING AND FINISHING
2 pounds sheep's milk ricotta, drained for 24 hours
1½ cups sugar
1 pinch ground cinnamon
Dark chocolate shavings for finishing
Confectioners' sugar for finishing

For the shells, place both types of flour, the cornstarch, vanilla, and salt on a work surface and shape into a well. Pour the oil in the center. Separate 1 egg. Reserve the white and add 2 whole eggs and 2 yolks to the center of the well, along with the sugar and wine. Knead, gradually pulling in the dry ingredients, until you have a firm, smooth dough. Roll the dough into a thin sheet and use a drinking glass to cut out rounds about 4 inches in diameter. Oil cannoli molds. Brush the two opposite sides of one of the rounds with a little of the reserved egg white and wrap the shell around the mold to shape. The two spots that you brushed with egg white should stick together so that the shell forms a tube. Repeat with remaining rounds of dough and molds. (Leave them on the molds.)

To fry, fill a pot with high sides (or an electric fryer if you have one) with a generous amount of peanut oil and bring to high temperature.

Line baking sheets with paper towels. Fry shells on the molds until golden. Work in batches if necessary to keep from crowding pan (or if you don't have enough molds). Remove from oil and gently slide the shell off of the mold and onto the prepared pans to drain. To bake, oil pans and preheat oven to 425°F. Place the shells (still wrapped around molds) on the prepared pans and bake until golden. Allow to cool slightly before gently sliding off of the molds. (Be careful, as the molds will be hot from the oven.)

For the filling, in a bowl combine the ricotta, sugar, and cinnamon. Stir with a fork at length until the mixture is creamy and dense. Remove the shells from the molds, cool completely, and then use a pastry bag to fill the shells with the ricotta mixture. Dip the ends in the chocolate shavings, sprinkle with confectioners' sugar, and serve.

CARFOGN 🍴
Fried Pastries with Chocolate, Poppy Seed, and Chestnut Filling
Pasticceria Colmean, Canale d'Agordo (Belluno), Veneto

These tasty little pastries come from the Biois Valley. They are served at weddings, Carnival, and other festive occasions. Poppy seeds—a main ingredient—were once grown in this area.

MAKES 20 DOZEN BITE-SIZED PASTRIES

DOUGH

4 *cups unbleached all-purpose flour*
1 *teaspoon vanilla extract*
3 *tablespoons sugar*
3 *tablespoons unsalted butter, softened*
1 *large egg*
1 *egg yolk*
½ *cup white wine*
1 *tablespoon grappa*
1 *tablespoon rum*
1 *pinch salt*
Grated zest of ½ lemon

FILLING AND FINISHING

1¾ *cups (about 8 ounces) poppy seeds, ground*
3 *dry plain cookies, such as tea biscuits, crumbled*
3 *tablespoons sugar*
Vanilla sugar to taste
2 *tablespoons chocolate spread*
2 *tablespoons chestnut preserves*
Grated zest of ½ lemon
1 *tablespoon grappa*
1 *tablespoon rum*
Milk as needed
Oil for frying

To make the dough, combine all of the ingredients. Knead until thoroughly combined, form into a ball, and set aside to rest.

Meanwhile, prepare the filling. Combine the poppy seeds, crumbled cookies, sugar, vanilla sugar, chocolate spread, chestnut preserves, lemon zest, grappa, and rum. Knead the mixture until well combined. If the mixture is too stiff to knead, stir in a small amount of milk until it is soft enough to handle.

Roll out the dough to a thin sheet. Drop small spoonfuls (¼ to ½ teaspoon) of the filling with about 1 inch between them (as if you were making ravioli) on half of the dough. Fold the other half of the dough over to cover and press down between the spoonfuls of filling to seal. Use a pastry wheel to cut 1-inch square pastries. Heat a generous amount of oil in a pot with high sides and fry briefly, working in batches if necessary, until golden.

CICERCHIATA 🥄
Fried Dough and Honey Cake with Almonds and Mistrà Liqueur
Gino Zampolini, Magione (Perugia), Umbria

Mistrà, sometimes called the poor man's sambuca, is a dry and strong-tasting liqueur. Make a dough of 3 eggs, 2 tablespoons mistrà, and 2½ cups flour, incorporating the grated zest of 1 lemon. The dough should be soft. Knead thoroughly, then form into ropes and cut those into small pieces the size of a chickpea. Fry the pieces in a generous amount of hot oil until golden, then drain on paper towels. In a large pot, heat ½ cup to 1 cup honey until it is liquid and begins to turn slightly darker. Remove from the heat and dip the pieces of fried dough into the honey, tossing gently to coat. Add about ¾ cup chopped blanched almonds and ¼ cup diced candied fruit. Transfer the mixture to an oiled ring pan, smooth the surface with an offset spatula, and allow to cool for at least 2 hours. Unmold onto a serving platter.

TESTA DI TURCO

"Turk's Head" Cream Puff

Ristorante Nangalarruni, Castelbuono
(Palermo), Sicilia

This pastry was traditionally shaped like a turban—hence the name. These days, the fried dough and pastry cream are simply layered.

SERVES 6

4   cups unbleached all-purpose flour
5   large eggs, lightly beaten
4   cups whole milk
1   cup sugar
1   cinnamon stick
Zest of 2 lemons
⅔   cup cornstarch or other starch
Extra-virgin olive oil for frying
Colored sprinkles for finishing
Ground cinnamon for finishing

Knead the flour and eggs into a soft dough, shape into a ball, and set aside to rest for 1 hour.

Meanwhile, place 3 cups of the milk in a saucepan with the sugar, the cinnamon stick, and the lemon zest (in strips) and place over medium heat. Combine the starch with the remaining 1 cup (cold) milk and whisk until dissolved. As soon as the milk mixture in the saucepan comes to a boil, stir in the starch and cold milk mixture and beat with a whisk until thickened. Remove and discard the lemon zest and cinnamon stick.

Roll out the dough into a fairly thin sheet. Cut into large diamonds and fry in a generous amount of hot oil. Drain on paper towels.

In a serving dish, make alternating layers of the fried pastry and the pastry cream. Finish with a layer of pastry cream on top, then decorate with sprinkles and a little ground cinnamon.

SEADAS

Fried Sheep's Cheese Pies with Honey

Ristorante La Margherita, Bosa (Oristano), Sardegna

Look for acidic fresh sheep's cheese for these tasty pies and grate it on the largest holes of a four-sided grater.

MAKES 12 TO 14 (3-INCH) PIES

1½   pounds fresh sheep's cheese, grated
Grated zest of 1 lemon or orange
1   cup unbleached all-purpose flour, plus more for work surface
1   cup semolina flour
2   large eggs
1   pinch salt
1   tablespoon sugar (optional)
¼   cup lard
Extra-virgin olive oil for frying
Honey for drizzling

Toss the cheese and zest together and set aside. Make the dough by combining the two types of flour, the eggs, the salt, and 1 tablespoon sugar, if using, and knead until very soft and smooth, adding warm water as needed. Add the lard a little at a time and knead until it is fully distributed. The dough should be soft. Roll out to a thin sheet and cut into 2 equal portions the same size and shape. Place one piece of dough on a lightly floured work surface. Place small amounts of the cheese mixture about ¾ inch apart. Place the second sheet of dough on top and press down between the cheese portions to seal the two sheets together. Cut the pies into circles using a serrated pastry wheel.

Transfer the pies to a floured dish towel and pierce holes in their surfaces with a needle, pressing gently to expel any air trapped inside. Place a generous amount of extra-virgin olive oil in a pot with high sides and bring to temperature for frying. Fry the pies until golden, then drain briefly on paper towels. Drizzle with honey and serve.

FRITTELLE DI MELE
Apple Fritters
Trattoria Eggerhoefe, Rasun Anterselva-Rasen
Antholz (Bolzano-Bozen), Trentino-Alto Adige

These fritters are often served as a mid-morning or mid-afternoon snack. Reinette apples are firm and hold their shape when cooked.

SERVES 8
- 2¾ cups unbleached all-purpose flour
- 8 large eggs
- 3 cups whole milk
- 1 pinch salt
- 4 Reinette or other firm apples
- ½ teaspoon ground cinnamon
- Sugar to taste
- Olive oil for frying
- Lingonberry preserves for serving

Whisk together the flour, eggs, milk, and a pinch of salt to make a batter. Peel and core the apples and cut them into slices a little less than ½ inch thick. Combine the cinnamon with enough sugar to cover the surface of a large plate or platter generously and spread out on the plate or platter. In a cast-iron pan, heat a generous amount of oil to medium-high heat for frying and drop the apples and batter in by the spoonful. Work in batches if necessary. As the fritters turn golden, remove them with a skimmer and toss them in the prepared cinnamon and sugar mixture. Serve warm with lingonberry preserves on the side.

FRITTELLETTI 'NCOTTI
Mistrà Fritters
Trattoria da Quintília Mercuri, Montefalcone
Appennino (Ascoli Piceno), Marche

Every recipe for *mistrà* is slightly different, but generally it includes an anise-flavored liqueur.

SERVES 6
- Zest of 1 lemon, in strips
- 1 cinnamon stick
- 2¾ cups unbleached all-purpose flour
- 1 pinch salt
- 6 large eggs, lightly beaten
- 2 tablespoons mistrà (anise liqueur)
- 2 tablespoons sugar, plus more for sprinkling
- Olive oil for frying

Place 8 cups water in a pot with the lemon zest and cinnamon stick and bring to a boil. Meanwhile, in a heatproof bowl, combine the flour and salt. Bring the water to a boil, then remove the zest and cinnamon stick and pour the hot water into the flour mixture while whisking. When no lumps remain, set aside to cool for about 45 minutes. With a wooden spoon, mix in the eggs, mistrà, and 2 tablespoons sugar.

Line baking sheets with paper towels and set aside. Fill a pot with a generous amount of oil and bring to high heat. Drop in the batter by the tablespoon, working in batches if necessary, and fry until golden. Remove with a skimmer to the paper towels to drain briefly, then sprinkle with sugar. Serve hot.

STRUFFOLI
Fried Dough and Honey Cake with Citrus
Elisabetta Antelmi, Agropoli (Salerno), Campania

Combine 4 cups flour and 1 tablespoon baking powder and make into a well on a work surface. Place 4 eggs, ¼ cup sugar, the grated zest of ½ lemon, a pinch of salt, and a generous amount of softened butter in the center and incorporate into a dough. Roll pieces of dough into ropes about as thick as your finger, then cut them at an angle into diamonds. Fry the diamonds, working in batches, in a generous amount of hot oil until puffed and golden and drain briefly on paper towels. Then, in a wide pan, heat ⅔ cup honey over medium heat. Add the grated zest of 2 oranges, chopped candied citron, and chopped candied orange peel (about ½ cup each). Add the pieces of fried dough and toss over heat for a few minutes until combined. Transfer to a serving platter. Oil your hands and use them to form into a ring or cone. Let the struffoli rest for a couple of hours to cool completely, then decorate with colored sprinkles or confectioners' sugar before serving.

ZEPPOLE
Potato Donuts
Locanda Pezzolla, Accettura (Matera), Basilicata

These can be made savory by omitting the honey and sugar, in which case they make a tasty appetizer. In the town of Accettura, these are often made to celebrate the feast of the local patron saint, Saint Julian.

MAKES ABOUT 1 DOZEN DONUTS

- 2 tablespoons active dry yeast
- 9 ounces (2 to 3) potatoes
- 3 cups semolina flour
- 1 pinch salt
- 4 cups extra-virgin olive oil
- 2 to 3 tablespoons honey
- ¼ cup sugar

Dissolve the yeast in about ½ cup warm (not hot) water. Boil the potatoes until easily pierced with a fork. Drain, peel, and mash smooth. Combine the potatoes with the semolina flour and dissolved yeast. Add the salt and knead vigorously. Shape into a ball, place in a ceramic container, cover with a dish towel, and set aside to rise for at least 30 minutes.

Shape pieces of the dough into rings, about 2 inches in diameter. Place the olive oil in a pot with high sides and bring to high temperature. Fry the donuts, working in batches if necessary, until golden brown. Drizzle with honey, sprinkle with sugar, and serve.

CRAFUN MÔRE
Donuts with Yogurt and Rum
Osteria Garsun, Marebbe-Enneberg (Bolzano-Bozen), Trentino-Alto Adige

As the name indicates, these are a riff on the Austrian-German *krapfen*, or donuts. There are also savory *crafun môre* that are filled with stewed game. The sweet version is served with either lingonberry preserves or stewed apples.

SERVES 8

- 1 tablespoon active dry yeast
- ½ cup plain yogurt, room temperature
- 1¾ cups unbleached all-purpose flour or 00 flour
- 1 large egg
- 3 egg yolks
- 1 tablespoon rum
- 2 tablespoons olive oil, plus more for frying
- 1 pinch salt

Mix the yeast into the yogurt, then combine with the flour, shape into a ball, cover, and set aside to rest for 15 minutes. Knead in the egg and yolks, the rum, 2 tablespoons olive oil, and salt. Knead for 15 minutes to make a very dense dough. Set aside to rest for 2 hours. Divide the dough into equal portions, shape them into balls, and cover loosely.

Place a generous amount of oil for frying in a pot with high sides and bring to high temperature. Use your hands to shape the balls of dough into rings and fry them until golden, working in batches if necessary.

❧{ CAKES & ROLLS }❧

....

CIAMBELLONE ●
Plain Ring Cake
Valeria Cappelli, Pienza (Siena), Toscana

There are numerous versions of *ciambellone*. Sometimes it is dotted with almonds to look like a snake and called a *serpentone*. For this version, in a large bowl combine 2¾ cups flour, 1¼ cups sugar, and 3 egg yolks (reserve whites). Beat in 6 tablespoons melted butter and 1 cup milk, then ¼ teaspoon vanilla extract and 2 tablespoons anise or orange liqueur, as well as the grated zest of 1 lemon. Mix until combined, then sift in 2 teaspoons baking powder. Whip 3 egg whites to stiff peaks and fold them in very gently. Pour the batter into a buttered ring pan and bake in a preheated 350°F for about 30 minutes. Allow to cool in the pan before unmolding.

BUCCELLATO TOSCANO ❙
Tuscan Ring Cake with Candied Citron
Franca Ridolfi, Lucca, Toscana

This firm cake will keep for up to two weeks. When it starts to get hard, simply cut it into slices and toast the slices in the oven. This was once the classic dessert in the region for celebrating a child's confirmation. Beat 3 tablespoons butter with 3 tablespoons lard until soft, then combine with 4 cups flour, 3 eggs, 1 cup sugar, grated zest of 1 lemon, about ¼ cup diced candied citron, ¾ cup milk, ½ cup Marsala, a pinch of salt, and 1 envelope (2¼ teaspoons) active dry yeast dissolved in a tablespoon or two of warm water. Knead until well combined and elastic. Place in a buttered and floured ring pan, cover with a dish towel, and set aside to rise for 1 hour. Brush the surface with egg white and bake in a preheated 475°F oven for 50 minutes.

TORTA MARGHERITA
Layer Cake
Panificio Valla, Ottone (Piacenza), Emîlia-Romagna

Light and airy *torta Margherita* (named for the queen) can also be eaten plain or filled with a different filling of your choosing. This looks especially lovely with some confectioners' sugar sifted over the top. Alchermes is a bright pink liqueur flavored with cinnamon, cloves, nutmeg, and vanilla.

SERVES 8 TO 10
- 14 tablespoons (1 stick plus 6 tablespoons) unsalted butter, softened, plus more for buttering pan
- 1 tablespoon unbleached all-purpose flour, plus more for flouring pan
- 1½ cups sugar
- 3 large eggs
- 1½ cups potato starch
- 2 teaspoons baking powder
- 2 egg yolks
- ½ cup plus 2 tablespoons fruit preserves
- Alchermes (see note) for brushing

Butter and flour a cake pan with 2-inch sides and set aside. Preheat oven to 300°F. Beat 7 tablespoons butter and 1 cup sugar until light and fluffy, then beat in the whole eggs one at a time, combining between additions. Add the potato starch and 1 tablespoon flour gradually. When the mixture is well combined, beat in the baking powder. Transfer to the prepared pan and bake in the preheated oven until a tester emerges clean, about 30 minutes. Cool in the pan, then unmold to a rack to cool completely.

Meanwhile, to make the filling beat together the egg yolks, the remaining ½ cup sugar, the remaining 7 tablespoons butter, and the fruit preserves. Slice the cooled cake in half horizontally and brush one side of each layer (the sides that will face the filling) with alchermes. Use an offset spatula to spread the prepared filling on the top of the bottom layer, then top with the second layer.

TORTA PARADISO 🍫
"Heaven" Cake
Trattoria dell'Alba, Vho di Piadena
(Cremona), Lombardia

Every city and town in Lombardia has laid claim to this cake at one time or another. It is eaten all over the region and is often served with wine for dipping. The most credible origin story is that the cake was invented in Pavia in 1878 by Enrico Vigoni, who, after admiring the pastries for sale in Milano, opened his own pastry shop near Pavia's university, the city's cultural center. The name supposedly derives from the enthusiastic exclamation of an aristocratic woman who declared it a little slice of heaven.

SERVES 6

- 14 tablespoons (1 stick plus 6 tablespoons) unsalted butter, plus more for buttering pan
- ⅓ cup unbleached all-purpose flour, plus more for flouring pan
- 1½ cups sugar
- 4 large eggs, separated
- Juice of ½ lemon
- 2 tablespoons liqueur
- 2 teaspoons baking powder
- 1⅔ cups potato starch
- 1 pinch salt

Preheat the oven to 350°F. Butter and flour a 10-inch pan with sides at least 2 inches high and set aside. Beat the butter with the sugar until light and fluffy. Beat in the egg yolks, lemon juice, liqueur, baking powder, starch, ⅓ cup flour, and salt. Whip the egg whites to stiff peaks and fold into the mixture.

Transfer to the prepared pan and bake in the preheated oven until a tester emerges clean, about 35 minutes.

TORTA SABBIOSA 🍴
"Sandy" Yellow Cake
Pasticceria Galletti, Garda (Verona), Veneto

This is a soft, airy, well-risen cake with a somewhat crumbly texture—hence the name. It is made throughout the Veneto, especially in and around Verona, and it is traditionally served with Recioto wine for dipping.

SERVES 10

- 18 tablespoons (2 sticks plus 2 tablespoons) unsalted butter, softened, plus more for buttering pan
- 1¼ cups sugar
- 5 large eggs
- 1 cup unbleached all-purpose flour
- ¾ cup potato starch
- 1¼ teaspoons vanilla-flavored baking powder
- 1 pinch salt
- Confectioners' sugar for finishing

Preheat the oven to 325°F. Butter a round cake pan and set aside. Beat the sugar with the butter. Gradually add the eggs, flour, starch, baking powder, and salt, beating to incorporate between additions. Transfer to the prepared pan and bake until a tester emerges clean, about 1 hour 10 minutes. Unmold and cool on a rack, then sprinkle with confectioners' sugar.

CASATIELLO ●
Ring Cake with Limoncello
Antonietta Gorga, Montecorvino Rovella
(Salerno), Campania

Beat 3 eggs with 1¼ cups sugar until light and creamy. Beat in 4 cups flour, a pinch of cream of tartar, 1¼ teaspoons baking soda, 2 sticks plus 2 tablespoons softened butter, 1 tablespoon limoncello (see recipe, below), and enough milk to make a batter. Pour into a buttered and floured ring pan and bake at 275°F to 300°F for 40 minutes.

If you want to make your own limoncello, place 7 freshly picked organic lemons in 1 quart 95-proof grain alcohol and allow to rest for 1 week. After 1 week, boil 1 quart water with 3½ cups sugar to form a syrup. Let the syrup cool, then transfer the lemons and alcohol to a stainless steel pot and add the syrup. Rinse out the container where the lemons were infused in the alcohol and add that water to the pot as well. Strain the liquid and transfer to bottles. After 1 week, strain it again, and after another week, strain it a third time. Continue straining weekly until the liqueur is perfectly clear.

TORTA TENERINA ☕
Tender Cake
Antica Trattoria Volano, Ferrara, Emília-Romagna

This is a signature dessert of Ferrara. As its name suggests, it is so feathery and light that it almost melts in your mouth.

SERVES 12 TO 14
- 10 ounces dark chocolate
- 18 tablespoons (2 sticks plus 2 tablespoons) unsalted butter
- 9 large eggs, separated
- 2 cups confectioners' sugar
- ¼ cup unbleached all-purpose flour or 00 flour
- 3 tablespoons potato starch

Preheat the oven to 300°F. Line a cake pan with parchment and set aside. Melt the chocolate and butter together in a double boiler. With a blender or mixer, beat the egg yolks with the sugar, flour, and potato starch. Beat in the melted butter and chocolate. Whip the egg whites to stiff peaks and fold into the mixture. Transfer to the prepared pan and bake until a tester emerges clean, about 40 minutes.

BERLINGOZZO ▦
Plain Cylindrical Cake with Anise Essence
Pasticceria Carli, Lamporecchio (Pistoia), Toscana

Berlingozzo was originally a Carnival dessert, but these days it's eaten year-round in the Pistoia area. When served for dessert, it is often dipped in vin santo; it may also appear on the breakfast table with milky coffee for dipping. At the Pasticceria Carli, the cake is made with a lower-protein 0 flour, which may be difficult to find outside of Italy. (The 0 or 00 in Italian flour refers to how finely the flour is milled.) Use pastry flour or cake flour for especially tender results.

SERVES 10
- 6 egg yolks
- 6 large eggs
- 5 cups sugar
- Anise extract to taste
- 7¼ cups low-protein 0 flour

Preheat the oven to 375°F. Beat the egg yolks and eggs together. Beat in the sugar and anise extract, then gradually add the flour in small amounts, beating to incorporate between additions. Form the dough into a log about 15¾ inches long. Place on a parchment-lined baking sheet and form into a ring, pressing the ends together. Bake in the preheated oven until a tester emerges clean, 20 to 25 minutes.

BENSONE ⬤
Cake with Anise Liqueur
Ines Mîlioli, Formigine (Modena), Emîlia-Romagna

Beat 2 eggs with ¾ cup sugar until light and foamy. Beat in 7 tablespoons melted butter, then beat in 2¾ cups flour, 2 tablespoons *sassolino* (an anise-flavored liqueur from Sassuolo in the Modena area), and 2 tablespoons milk. Lastly, beat in 2 teaspoons baking powder (vanilla-flavored if you can find it). Transfer this batter to a buttered ring pan. Brush the top with a little more milk and sprinkle with sugar (pearl sugar looks nice). Bake in a preheated 350°F oven for 40 minutes until a tester comes out clean.

Ivan Severi in Modena adds the grated zest of ½ lemon and a few drops of vanilla extract to his batter, and he bakes it in a wide pan so that the batter is a little less than ¼ inch high when it is added to the pan. He scatters sliced almonds all over the surface along with the sugar. In Bologna, a very similar ring cake is topped with pearl sugar and chocolate shavings.

BOLLO 🍴
Traditional Jewish Round Plain Cake with Anise Seed
Elena Servi, Pitigliano (Grosseto), Toscana

A *bollo* is a yeast-risen ring cake about 10 to 12 inches in diameters with a dark, shiny crust and an intense anise flavor. It was brought to Italy by Sephardic Jews fleeing the Spanish Inquisition in the fifteenth century. (The town of Pitigliano in Toscana has a long and fascinating Jewish heritage.) Combine 1¾ cups flour and ¾ cup sugar and shape into a well on a work surface. In the center place 2 lightly beaten eggs, about ½ cup water, a tablespoon or so of softened butter, a tablespoon or more of lightly crushed anise seeds, ¼ cup white wine, and 2 teaspoons active dry yeast dissolved in a little warm water. Knead into a dough, shape into a ball, cover, and let rise in a warm place for an entire day. When the dough is nicely risen, arrange it in a ring pan, brush the surface with an egg wash, and bake in a preheated 400°F oven until cooked through, 20 to 30 minutes.

TORTA DE FREGOLOTI 🍴
"Lumpy" Cake
Osteria Il Libertino, Trento, Trentino-Alto Adige

This is a typical cake from the Trento area. At the restaurant it is served with a vanilla-honey sauce. *Fregoloti* is local dialect for "lumps," as the batter is not particularly smooth.

SERVES 6
- 1¼ cups blanched almonds
- 1 large egg
- ¾ cup plus 2 tablespoons sugar
- 2 cups unbleached all-purpose flour
- 10 tablespoons (1 stick plus 2 tablespoons) unsalted butter
- 1 pinch salt

Preheat the oven to 350°F. Chop 1 cup of the almonds, reserving ¼ cup whole almonds for decoration. Beat the egg with the sugar, then beat in the flour, butter, salt, and chopped almonds until combined. The batter should be dense and a little crumbly. Transfer to a cake pan, sprinkle the whole almonds on top, and bake in the preheated oven until golden, about 35 minutes.

TORCIGLIONE 🍂
Almond "Snake" Cake
Ilda Cardinali, Passignano sul Trasimeno
(Perugia), Umbria

Torciglione is shaped into a loose spiral and decorated to look like a snake. Chop 3 cups blanched almonds and ⅓ cup blanched bitter almonds (may substitute sweet almonds plus a few drops of almond extract) and combine them with 1¾ cups sugar, a pinch of salt, the grated zest of 1 lemon, 2 tablespoons Zibibbo wine, and 3 egg whites whipped to firm peaks. Knead until the dough holds together, then shape it into a snake with a pointed tail and a narrow head. Brush the surface with a beaten egg yolk and then decorate, using pine nuts for scales, coffee beans for eyes, and 1 whole blanched almond as the tongue. Transfer to a buttered and floured baking sheet and bake in a preheated 325°F oven until cooked through, about 40 minutes.

TORTA DELLE ROSE 🥖
Yeast-Risen "Rose" Cake
Marina Conterno Ivaldi, Villafranca di Verona
(Verona), Veneto

Combine 2½ cups flour with 1 tablespoon sugar, the grated zest of 1 lemon, 3 egg yolks, 3 tablespoons olive oil, 2½ teaspoons active dry yeast dissolved in a little warm milk, and a pinch of salt into a dough. Separately, combine 7 tablespoons softened unsalted butter with ½ cup sugar. Use a rolling pin to roll out the dough. Spread the butter and sugar mixture on top of it. Roll up jelly-roll style without squeezing too tightly and then slice into 1-inch spirals. Arrange the spirals cut sides up in a buttered and floured 11-inch cake pan so that they fill the pan. Brush with beaten egg white and sprinkle with about ¼ cup pearl sugar. Let the cake rise in a warm, draft-free area for 1½ hours, then cover with foil and bake in a preheated 400°F oven for 15 minutes. Remove the foil, reduce the oven temperature to 350°F, and bake for 15 minutes more. Remove from the pan as soon as you take it out of the oven.

BISCIOLA 🍂
Yeast-Risen Dried Fig, Raisin, and Walnut Cake
Pasticceria Cattaneo, Sondrio, Lombardia

This dense yeast-risen cake packed with nuts and dried fruit is similar to the Christmas classic panettone.

SERVES 6 TO 8
- 1½ cups unbleached all-purpose flour or 00 flour
- 2 teaspoons active dry yeast
- 6 tablespoons unsalted butter, melted and cooled
- ¼ cup sugar, plus more for syrup
- 2 egg yolks
- 1½ cups chopped walnuts
- ½ cup black raisins, soaked to rehydrate and drained
- 1¾ cups chopped dried figs
- 1 large egg, lightly beaten

Preheat the oven to 100°F to 125°F. Combine ½ cup of the flour, the yeast, and enough warm water to make a soft batter. Set the starter aside to rise until bubbly, about 10 minutes. Knead together the starter, the remaining 1 cup flour, the butter, the ¼ cup sugar, and the 2 egg yolks. Set in the preheated oven to rise for about 5 minutes. Knead in the nuts, raisins, and figs and knead until well distributed. Shape the dough into a rectangular loaf, place on a parchment-lined baking sheet, and set in the oven to rise for about 20 minutes. Remove from the oven and increase the oven temperature to 375°F. Brush the cake with the beaten egg and bake at 375°F for 70 minutes. Make a simple syrup using equal parts sugar and water. Brush on the cake as soon as you remove it from the oven.

PINZA
Fennel Seed and Fruit Cornmeal Cake
Ofelia Facco Trevisan, Cavallino Treporti (Venezia), Veneto

There are endless versions of *pinza* in the Veneto. A now all-but-forgotten savory pinza uses beef broth in place of milk and was wrapped in cabbage leaves and then roasted in the embers of a fireplace overnight on January 5 to be eaten for the Epiphany on January 6. Another pinza made with spinach, hard-boiled eggs, ricotta, and nutmeg is traditionally served on Good Friday.

For this pinza, combine 2 cups milk and 2 cups water in a pot and bring to a boil. Slowly sprinkle in 1½ cups finely ground cornmeal, ¾ cup flour, 1 heaping tablespoon yeast, and ¾ cup sugar. Cook, stirring constantly, until thickened, then remove from the heat and allow to cool. Stir in 7 tablespoons melted butter, 1 egg, ¼ cup raisins soaked in a couple of tablespoons of grappa or anise liqueur, 2 thinly sliced cored and peeled apples, ¼ cup chopped dried figs, ¼ cup lightly crushed pine nuts, zest of 1 orange in strips and the grated zest of 1 lemon, a few drops of vanilla extract, a generous spoonful of fennel seeds, and a pinch of salt. When the mixture is well combined, transfer to a buttered pan, brush with beaten egg, sprinkle with a spoonful or two of sugar, and bake in a preheated 400°F oven for 45 minutes.

TORTA DI MELE
Apple Cake
Letizia Palesi, Champorcher (Aosta), Valle d'Aosta

Beat 7 tablespoons unsalted butter or 5 tablespoons olive oil with ¾ cup sugar. Beat in 2 eggs, 1 cup flour, 2 teaspoons baking powder, 2 or 3 peeled, cored, and chopped apples, and the grated zest of 1 lemon. Transfer to a buttered and floured pan. Peel, core, and thinly slice another 2 or 3 apples and arrange the slices on top—they should cover the entire surface. Warm 2 tablespoons apricot preserves with a little water, and then brush on the apples as a glaze. Bake in a preheated 400°F oven for 45 minutes. If you like the combination of chocolate and apples, you can also include chopped chocolate in the batter and/or sprinkle grated chocolate over the apples on the surface.

TORTA DI NOCCIOLE
Hazelnut Cake
Rosanna Dotta, Novello (Cuneo), Piemonte

The Tonda Gentile is no ordinary hazelnut—its meat is rich and dense with a crisp texture. It is prized in Piemonte, where hazelnuts in general are an object of almost cultlike celebration. If you are lucky enough to obtain some Tonda Gentile hazelnuts, use them to bake this cake, which shines a spotlight on their special flavor. Toast 2 cups hazelnuts, rub off the skins, and then grind to a paste. Beat 2 egg yolks (reserve the whites) with ¾ cup sugar. Beat in 6 tablespoons melted butter, a pinch of salt, ¼ teaspoon vanilla extract, 1 teaspoon cocoa powder, the hazelnut paste, and 1 tablespoon olive oil. Gradually add ¾ cup flour, beating to incorporate between additions. Stir in enough milk to make a medium-density batter. Dissolve 1¼ teaspoons baking powder in a little more milk and stir that in as well. Beat the 2 reserved egg whites to stiff peaks and fold into the batter. Transfer to a buttered pan. Sprinkle 1 tablespoon flour on top and bake at moderate heat, about 350°F, until a tester emerges clean, about 45 minutes.

TORTA DI FARRO CON FRUTTA 🌰

Farro Cake with Fresh Fruit

Ristorante La Rocca, San Leo (Rimini), Emîlia-Romagna

Farro flour and raw cane sugar lend an earthy flavor to this cake, and the fresh fruit balances the density more effectively than fruit baked on top of the cake would. Always use fruit that is in season, or opt for a layer of high-quality fruit preserves, drained canned fruit, or stewed dried fruit.

SERVES 6 TO 8

- 1¼ cups raw (turbinado) sugar
- 14 tablespoons (1 stick plus 6 tablespoons) unsalted butter, softened
- 1¾ cups unbleached all-purpose flour or 00 flour
- 1¾ cups farro flour
- 2 large eggs, lightly beaten
- 1 tablespoon plus 1 teaspoon baking powder
- Whole milk for kneading
- 1½ to 1¾ pounds apricots, peaches, or other fruit

Preheat the oven to 350°F. Beat together the sugar and butter until light and fluffy. Combine the flours and form them into a well on the work surface. Place the butter and sugar mixture, the eggs, and the baking powder in the center and knead into a dough. Add as much milk as needed to make a soft but dense dough. Shape the dough into a disk and bake in the preheated oven until golden. Peel, pit, and slice the fruit and spread it over the cooled cake.

TORTA DI PISTACCHI 🍴

Pistachio Cake

Marco Lombardo, Mîlazzo (Messina), Sicîlia

With a whisk beat 4 egg yolks with 1 cup sugar until foamy and light. Beat the 4 egg whites to stiff peaks. With a wooden spoon, beat 1 cup extra-virgin olive oil into the yolk mixture. Then, one at a time and beating to combine between additions, beat in 1 cup milk, the egg whites, a pinch of salt, ¾ cup finely chopped pistachios, 2¾ cups flour, and 1 tablespoon plus 1 teaspoon baking powder. Beat for 15 minutes, then transfer to a buttered and floured pan, smooth the surface, and bake in a preheated 350°F oven until a tester emerges clean, about 40 minutes. Unmold immediately and cool on a rack, then spread ¼ cup plus 1 tablespoon apricot preserves on top and sprinkle with 2 tablespoons confectioners' sugar. (Don't skip this step, as the glaze keeps the cake soft.)

BOCCONE DI DAMA ▦

Flourless Almond Cake

Trattoria La Tacchinella, Canzano (Teramo), Abruzzo

This simple treat is ready in the time it takes to preheat the oven.

SERVES 8

- Butter for pan (optional)
- Flour for pan (optional)
- 7 large eggs, separated
- 1½ cups sugar
- 2 cups almonds, chopped

Preheat the oven to 350°F. Butter and flour a cake pan or line with parchment paper and set aside. Beat the egg yolks with the sugar. In a separate bowl, beat the egg whites until they form firm peaks. Fold the two together and then fold in the almonds. Bake in the preheated oven until a tester comes out dry, 30 to 45 minutes.

CASTAGNACCIO ⫷

Tuscan Home-Style Cake with Chestnut Flour, Raisins, and Nuts

Trattoria L'Altana, Barga (Lucca), Toscana

This rustic cake was originally cooked (often fried) and sold by traveling salespeople who would set up their stalls outside of schools.

SERVES 4 TO 6

½   *cup olive oil, plus more for oiling pan*
4   *cups chestnut flour*
¾   *cup sugar*
¼   *cup walnuts, chopped*
¼   *cup pine nuts*
¼   *cup black raisins, soaked in warm water and squeezed dry*
Leaves of 2 sprigs rosemary
Zest of 1 orange in strips

Preheat the oven to 375°F. Oil a pan and set aside. Combine the flour with the sugar. Gradually whisk in the ½ cup olive oil and then enough water to make a creamy paste. Stir in the walnuts, pine nuts, and raisins until well combined. Transfer to the prepared pan. Sprinkle the rosemary and orange zest on top. Bake in the preheated oven until the top is crisp and dark brown, about 30 minutes.

GUBANA 🥖

Fruit and Nut Cake

Marco Pecîle, Fagagna (Udine), Friuli-Venezia Giulia

For the dough, shape 2½ cups flour into a well on a work surface. Place 2 eggs, 3 tablespoons grappa, and 2 sticks plus 2 tablespoons soft butter in the well and knead into a dough. Set aside. For the filling, soak ¾ cup golden raisins in ½ cup Marsala, then squeeze dry and combine with 1 tablespoon breadcrumbs browned in a little butter,

1¼ cups chopped walnuts, ½ cup chopped blanched almonds, 3 tablespoons chopped candied orange peel, 3 tablespoons chopped candied citron, the grated zest of 1 lemon and 1 orange, and 1 egg yolk. Fold together with 1 egg white beaten to stiff peaks. Roll out the dough and sprinkle the filling evenly all over it. Carefully roll up the dough jelly-roll style, then form the roll into a spiral. Place the roll in a buttered pan and brush with an egg yolk beaten with 1 to 2 tablespoons melted butter. Sprinkle with sugar and bake at 350°F until deep golden, about 40 minutes. In Trieste, Elisabetta Franco makes a presnitz, an Easter dessert that is fairly similar but includes ground cloves, cinnamon, and nutmeg in the filling.

TORTIONATA DI MANDORLE 🍴

Hard-to-Cut Almond Cake

Ristorante Allo Storione, Prata di Pordenone (Pordenone), Friuli-Venezia Giulia

This flat, crumbly cake dates back to the Middle Ages and is as delicious as it is difficult to cut. Chop the almonds, but avoid grinding them to a paste.

SERVES 8

14   *tablespoons (1 stick plus 6 tablespoons) unsalted butter, softened, plus more for buttering pan*
2½   *cups unbleached all-purpose flour*
¾   *cup sugar*
1   *egg yolk*
1   *pinch salt*
1   *cup blanched almonds, chopped*

Preheat the oven to 325°F. Butter a pan and set aside. Form a well in a bowl with the flour and place the softened butter, sugar, egg yolk, and salt in the well. Beat until well combined, then beat in the almonds. Transfer to the prepared pan—the batter should not be higher than ¾ inch. Bake in the preheated oven for 1 hour.

MILLEFOGLIE ●━━
Millefeuille
L'Oste della Bon'Ora, Grottaferrata (Roma), Lazio

T raditionally, this dessert is sprinkled with confectioners' sugar, and then rosettes of lightly sweetened whipped cream are piped on top and a strawberry is placed in the center of each rosette. You can, of course, let your imagination run wild.

SERVES 6 TO 8

DOUGH

- 4 cups unbleached all-purpose flour
- 1 pinch salt
- 1 pound (4 sticks) unsalted butter, chilled

FILLING AND FINISHING

- 6 egg yolks
- ¾ cup sugar
- ⅓ cup unbleached all-purpose flour
- 2 cups whole milk, plus more for thinning cream

Grated zest of ½ lemon

For the dough, combine the flour and salt and add enough water to make a soft dough. Shape into a ball and set aside to rest for 10 minutes. Roll out the dough to a thick rectangle with the long sides about 8 inches long. Place the butter in the center and fold the dough envelope style to enclose it completely. Roll out and fold two more times. Set aside to rest for at least 10 minutes and repeat. Roll out and fold four times total, letting it rest for at least 10 minutes each time.

Preheat the oven to 350°F. Divide the dough into 3 equal pieces, roll them out into thin disks, and bake in the preheated oven until crisp, about 30 minutes.

Meanwhile, for the filling, in a saucepan, briskly whisk the egg yolks and ¾ cup sugar. Whisk in the flour, 2 cups milk, and lemon zest. Cook over medium heat, stirring constantly, until thickened. Set aside to cool.

When you are ready to construct the dish, place one disk of dough on a serving platter. Thin the cream with enough milk to make it spreadable but not runny. Spread about half of the cream on top of the disk, then place a second disk on top. Cover with the remaining cream and place the third disk on top. Decorate as described in the note or according to your own taste.

TORTA DI GRANO SARACENO CON CONFETTURA DI MIRTILLI 🍯
Buckwheat Cake with Lingonberry Jam
Osteria Nerina, Malgolo di Romeno (Trento), Trentino-Alto Adige

At the Eggerhoefe in Rasun Anterselva-Rasen Antholz, a similar buckwheat cake with lingonberry jam incorporates hazelnuts, cocoa powder, and grated Reinette apples in place of almonds. At the restaurant, this is always made with raw milk butter from the Malga.

SERVES 8
- 18 tablespoons (2 sticks plus 2 tablespoons) unsalted butter, melted and cooled, plus more for buttering pan
- Flour for flouring pan
- 1¼ cups sugar
- 6 large eggs, separated
- 1½ cups buckwheat flour
- 1 pinch salt
- Vanilla sugar to taste
- 1¾ cups blanched almonds, ground
- 1½ cups lingonberry jam
- ¼ cup confectioners' sugar

Preheat the oven to 350°F. Butter and flour a springform pan and set aside. Beat the 18 tablespoons butter with about half the sugar (½ cup plus 2 tablespoons) until creamy. Beat in the egg yolks one at a time, beating to incorporate between additions, then beat in the buckwheat flour, salt, vanilla sugar, and almonds. Beat the egg whites to stiff peaks, gradually adding the remaining sugar as you beat them. Fold the egg whites into the batter. Transfer the batter to the prepared pan and bake in the preheated oven until a tester emerges clean, about 45 minutes.

Allow to cool completely, then cut in half horizontally and spread the jam in between the layers. Sift the confectioners' sugar over the assembled cake.

ROCCIATA 🍎
Olive Oil Strudel
Ristorante Il Bacco Felice, Foligno (Perugia), Umbria

The dough for this strudel uses o flour, which is a more coarsely ground flour than oo flour. You can sprinkle a little alchermes (a scarlet-colored spice liqueur) over the finished dessert if you like.

SERVES 8
DOUGH
- ⅔ cup olive oil
- 1 pinch salt
- ¼ cup white wine
- 8 cups o flour

FILLING AND FINISHING
- ¾ cup blanched almonds, ground
- ¾ cup walnuts, ground
- 1¼ cups golden raisins, rehydrated in water and squeezed dry
- 2 pounds apples, peeled, cored, and diced
- ⅓ cup pine nuts
- ¼ cup unsweetened cocoa powder
- ½ cup plus 2 tablespoons olive oil
- 1 tablespoon plus 1 teaspoon ground cinnamon
- 2 tablespoons anise seeds
- Crushed plain dry cookies, if needed
- ½ cup sugar

Preheat the oven to 425°F. Line a baking sheet with parchment and set aside. For the dough, bring 4 cups water to a boil. Add the olive oil, salt, and wine. Cover and simmer for a few minutes, then allow to cool. When the water is almost completely cooled, create a well on the work surface with the flour and add the water mixture in small amounts until you have a soft and elastic dough, similar to a pasta dough. Shape the dough into a ball, cover with a dish towel, and let it rest while you prepare the filling. For the filling, in a bowl combine the almonds, walnuts, raisins, apples, pine nuts, cocoa powder, ½ cup olive oil, cinnamon, and anise seeds and toss to combine.

Roll out the dough to a thin sheet. Scatter the filling evenly over half of the dough. (If your apples are giving off a lot of liquid, scatter some crushed plain dry cookies over the dough under the filling to absorb the juices.) Fold the empty half of the dough over the filled half and seal the edges. Carefully shape into a long rope, then shape the rope into a spiral. Transfer to the prepared pan. Brush the surface with the remaining 2 tablespoons oil and sprinkle on the sugar. Bake in the preheated oven until crisp and golden, about 15 minutes.

SFRATTO 🟤
Pastry Logs with Spiced Walnut Filling
Elena Servi, Pitigliano (Grosseto), Toscana

The name of this dessert literally means "eviction," because the pastry logs were designed to resemble the sticks used to bang on the doors of Jewish homes in the early 1600s when the members of the relatively large Jewish community in Pitigliano were being re-located to a ghetto. Today, *sfratto*—also known as *sfratto dei goym*, or "gentile eviction"—has its own Slow Food Presidium.

For the filling, by hand chop 4 cups walnuts with the grated zest of 1 orange and some freshly grated nutmeg. Place 1¾ cups honey in a saucepan and melt over low heat for 30 minutes. Remove the honey from the heat and stir in the walnut mixture. While the mixture is cooling, make a dough of 5⅔ cups flour, ½ cup white wine, ½ cup extra-virgin olive oil, and 1½ cups sugar. Roll the dough and cut into strips about 8 inches long and 4 to 5 inches wide. Divide the filling equally among the strips of dough and arrange it in the center of the dough. Roll the dough cigar style to enclose the filling and stretch the logs slightly as you do. They should be about 12 inches long and 1 inch or slightly more in diameter. Bake in a preheated 350°F oven until golden, about 30 minutes. Allow to cool before slicing.

CRESCIA FOGLIATA 🌿
Flaky Cylinder Filled with Apple, Pear, Figs, Raisins, and Nuts
Ristorante Il Camino, Matelica (Macerata), Marche

This traditional dessert from the Marche is softer than a strudel because the dough incorporates a leavening agent. The anise liqueur and orange brandy in the filling can be replaced with rum and alchermes.

SERVES 8

FILLING
1   cup sugar
2   pounds apples, peeled, cored, and diced
3   pears, peeled, cored, and diced
1⅓ cups diced dried figs
1¼ cups golden raisins
2   cups walnuts, chopped
1½ cups blanched almonds, chopped
3   tablespoons anise liqueur
2   tablespoons orange brandy
Grated zest of 1 lemon
Grated zest of 1 orange
¼   teaspoon vanilla extract

DOUGH
5⅔ cups unbleached all-purpose flour
4   large eggs, lightly beaten
2   tablespoons anise liqueur
¼   teaspoon vanilla extract
2   tablespoons oil
1½ teaspoons sugar
2   teaspoons baking powder
1   egg yolk, lightly beaten
Butter for pan

Combine all the ingredients for the filling in a bowl, stir to combine, and set aside to rest for a couple of hours.

Preheat the oven to 400°F. For the dough, on a work surface, make a well out of the flour. Place the whole eggs, liqueur, vanilla, oil, and sugar in the center. Knead until you have a soft dough, then knead in the baking powder. Roll the dough out to an even thickness. Spread the filling evenly on the dough, leaving a 1-inch border. Roll up jelly-roll style to make an even cylinder. Brush the outside of the cylinder with the egg yolk, then butter a pan and set the cylinder on the pan. Cook in the preheated oven until golden, about 30 minutes. Allow to cool completely before slicing.

TORTA DI PESCHE
Peach Cake
Ristorante Il Capolinea, Castelnovo ne' Monti (Reggio Emilia), Emilia-Romagna

This cake has a tender texture because of the peaches—despite the fact that it contains no butter or oil. The peaches should be very ripe.

SERVES 8 TO 10

1 cup sugar
3 large eggs, separated
1 cup unbleached all-purpose flour or 00 flour
1 to 3 tablespoons whole milk, if needed
3½ pounds (10 to 12) peaches, peeled, pitted, and sliced
¼ cup raw almonds, chopped
20 amaretto cookies, crushed
1 tablespoon plus 1 teaspoon baking powder

Preheat the oven to 350°F. Whisk the sugar with the egg yolks, then gradually whisk in the flour. Whisk in the milk a little at a time, if necessary, to make a pourable batter. Fold the peaches, almonds, and amaretto cookies into the batter. Whip the egg whites to stiff peaks and gradually fold them into the batter. Sprinkle the baking powder on top and fold that in as well. Transfer to a round cake pan and bake in the preheated oven for 30 minutes.

CERTOSINO
Chocolate Spice Fruitcake
Pasticceria Paolo Atti & Figli, Bologna, Emilia-Romagna

This cake is sometimes known as *panspeziale*. The choices for candied fruit are almost endless—choose among candied oranges, citron, cherries, pears, figs, and apricots. Mostarda is candied fruit in a syrup flavored with mustard seed. Use any type you like (recipes on pages 415 to 416). Like most fruitcakes, this one improves with age—wrap the finished cake in aluminum foil or parchment paper and let it sit for 10 days to enjoy it at its best.

SERVES 12

1 tablespoon unsalted butter
1½ cups blanched almonds
1 cup honey
¾ cup diced candied fruit
2½ cups unbleached all-purpose flour
2 ounces dark chocolate, roughly chopped
⅓ cup pine nuts
½ cup unsweetened cocoa powder
¾ cup mostarda (see note)
¼ teaspoon ground cinnamon
1 tablespoon plus ¾ teaspoon ammonium bicarbonate
¼ cup Marsala
½ cup sugar

Butter a ring pan with the butter and set aside. Chop ½ cup of the almonds and set aside. Place ¾ cup honey in a saucepan and melt over low heat. Stir in half of the candied fruit. Combine the flour with the chocolate and shape into a well on a work surface and place the chopped almonds, pine nuts, cocoa powder, mostarda, cinnamon, ammonium bicarbonate, Marsala, and the honey with the candied fruit in the center. Knead until well combined, then shape into a ring. Transfer to the prepared pan and set aside to rise in a warm place for 3 to 4 hours.

Meanwhile, in a pan melt the sugar and add the remaining almonds, tossing them over low heat so that they are coated in the caramel. When you are ready to bake the cake, preheat the oven to moderate heat, about 350°F. Sprinkle the caramelized almonds and the remaining candied fruit on top and bake until golden, about 40 minutes. Let the cake cool completely. Unmold the cake and heat the remaining ¼ cup honey over low heat. When it is fluid, brush it all over the cake.

TORTA DI CIOCCOLATO AL PEPPERONCINO 🌶

Chocolate Cake with Chili Pepper

Enoteca Guidi, Sansepolcro (Arezzo), Toscana

Chili pepper adds zing to this rich cake. Obviously, you can adjust the amount to your taste. Let the butter soften at room temperature for at least 30 minutes before beginning.

SERVES 6 TO 8

- 9 tablespoons (1 stick plus 1 tablespoon) unsalted butter, softened
- 1 tablespoon unbleached all-purpose flour
- 1 ounce dark (70%) chocolate
- 6 large eggs, separated
- ¾ cup sugar
- ½ teaspoon ground chili pepper
- ¼ cup unsweetened cocoa powder

Preheat oven to 325°F. Butter and flour a 9-inch cake pan with 1 tablespoon butter and 1 tablespoon flour and set aside. Melt the chocolate and the remaining 8 tablespoons butter in the top of a double boiler and set aside to cool slightly. Beat the egg yolks with ½ cup sugar until foamy. Beat the egg whites with the remaining ¼ cup sugar to stiff peaks. Fold the chocolate mixture into the yolks with a spatula. Fold in the chili pepper, then the egg whites. Transfer to the prepared pan and bake at 325°F for 20 minutes, then raise the oven heat to 350°F and bake until a crisp crust has formed on top but the center of the cake remains very soft,

about 10 additional minutes. Invert a platter over the cake, turn both cake and platter, and lift the cake pan to unmold. Sprinkle with cocoa powder and serve.

MATTONE ☕

Coffee, Chocolate, and Hazelnut "Brick"

Ristorante del Belbo da Bardon, San Marzano Oliveto (Asti), Piemonte

This is an icebox cake made with plain tea cookies. It highlights several of Piemonte's favorite products: chocolate, coffee, and hazelnuts. Use any flavor liqueur you like.

SERVES 6 TO 8

- 2 pounds (8 sticks) unsalted butter, softened
- 5 cups sugar
- 5 egg yolks
- 10 ounces dark chocolate, grated (about 3 cups)
- 1 espresso
- 2 tablespoons liqueur (see note)
- 1 pound rectangular or square dry plain tea cookies
- 1 cup hazelnuts, toasted, skinned, and finely chopped

To make the chocolate buttercream, with a whisk or electric mixer, beat the butter, sugar, and egg yolks until light and fluffy. Divide in half. Stir the grated chocolate into one half. In a bowl, combine the espresso and liqueur and dip the cookies in the mixture to soften. On a serving platter, arrange about one sixth of the cookies in a single layer and cover with a layer of about one third of the light buttercream. Top with another layer of cookies and then a layer of the chocolate buttercream. Continue making layers, ending with the chocolate buttercream on top. Sprinkle on the hazelnuts. Refrigerate for about 2 hours, then let rest at room temperature for 5 minutes before serving.

FUGASSA PASQUALE ▦
Sweet Easter Bread
Pasticceria Bolzani, Vicenza, Veneto

This is the Vicenza version of this enriched bread; the version made in Venezia includes cinnamon, ground ginger, cloves, almonds, and grappa in place of the Torcolato, which is a sweet white wine. Another version is made in Padova with orange zest and orange juice.

MAKES 4 OR 5 LOAVES

- 2 tablespoons active dry yeast
- 8 cups unbleached all-purpose flour or 00 flour
- 16 tablespoons (2 sticks) unsalted butter, softened and cut into pieces
- 1¼ cups sugar
- 10 egg yolks
- 3 large eggs
- 1 tablespoon honey
- 1 tablespoon salt
- 2 cups Torcolato wine
- Grated zest of ½ lemon
- Vanilla extract to taste
- Egg white and pearl sugar for finishing

In a large bowl, dissolve the yeast in a small amount of warm water. Stir in 2 cups of the flour and 1 scant cup warm water. Mix to combine and set aside at a warm room temperature (about 85°F) for about 1 hour. Stir in 6 tablespoons butter, ¼ cup sugar, 4 egg yolks, 1 whole egg, and 2 cups flour and knead at length. Cover and set aside to rise until doubled in volume, about 2 hours. Stir in the remaining 1 cup sugar, 6 yolks, 2 whole eggs, the honey, the salt, and the remaining 4 cups flour. Knead until you have a compact dough, then knead in 6 tablespoons butter, the Torcolato, grated lemon zest, and vanilla. Shape into a ball, cover, and set aside to rise for 1 hour. Divide the dough into 4 or 5 equal portions, shape into loaves, and either place them in individual pans or set them on a baking sheet with a generous amount of space between them. Set aside to rise until doubled in volume, at least 3 hours.

Preheat the oven to 350°F. Slash a cross in the top of each bread. Dot the center of each slash with the remaining butter. Brush with egg white and sprinkle with pearl sugar, then bake in the preheated oven until golden, about 1 hour.

MERINGATA ●
Meringue and Whipped Cream Cake
Osteria da Gemma, Roddino (Cuneo), Piemonte

This is delicious and not terribly difficult, but it does require a low, slow baking time. You can use chopped torrone nougat candy in place of the chestnuts if you like. For a decorative touch, hold back a little plain whipped cream and pipe rosettes on top, or garnish with a few whole candied chestnuts.

SERVES 6

- 3 egg whites
- 1 cup sugar
- 2 cups heavy cream or whipping cream
- 12 candied chestnuts, diced

Preheat the oven to 200°F to 225°F. Line a pan with parchment paper and set aside. In a large bowl, whip the egg whites with about half the sugar to very stiff peaks. Whip in the remaining sugar. Pour the whipped egg whites into the prepared pan, smooth gently, and bake in the preheated oven until dry, at least 8 hours. When the meringue is cooked and has cooled, whip the cream to very stiff peaks. Fold the diced candied chestnuts into the cream. Place the meringue on a serving platter and spread the whipped cream thickly on top. Serve immediately.

POLENTA E OSEI
"Polenta with Game Birds"
Pasticceria Cavour, Bergamo, Lombardia

This cake is decorated to mimic the classic savory dish of the same name (recipe on page 260). The windows of pastry shops in Bergamo are full of these confections—as delightful to look at as they are to eat.

SERVES 6

CAKE
- 3 tablespoons unsalted butter, melted (still warm), plus more for buttering pan
- ⅔ cup unbleached all-purpose flour, sifted, plus more for flouring pan
- 2 large eggs
- ⅔ cup sugar
- 4 egg yolks
- ¼ cup potato starch, sifted

BUTTERCREAM
- ¾ cup plus 2 tablespoons sugar
- ¼ cup glucose syrup
- 2 egg whites
- 21 tablespoons (2 sticks plus 5 tablespoons) unsalted butter, softened
- 3 tablespoons 60-proof alcohol
- 2 ounces dark chocolate, melted and cooled

FINISHING AND DECORATION
Vanilla syrup
Yellow food coloring
Sugar
Almond paste
Grated chocolate

To make the cake, preheat the oven to 340°F. Butter and flour a half sphere cake pan and set aside. In the top of a double boiler, whisk the whole eggs with the sugar until the mixture reaches 110°F. Add the yolks one at a time, whisking to combine between additions, then add the flour and potato starch. Whisk in the melted butter. Transfer to the pan and bake in the preheated oven until a tester emerges clean, about 30 minutes. Allow to cool completely.

Meanwhile, make the buttercream. In a saucepan, combine ¾ cup sugar with 1 tablespoon plus 1 teaspoon water and the glucose syrup. Bring to 275°F. Whip the egg whites with the remaining 2 tablespoons sugar. Combine the cooked sugar syrup, butter, alcohol, and melted chocolate. Fold in the egg whites.

When the cake has cooled, cut it into 3 layers. Reassemble the cake layers, brushing vanilla syrup on the layers and filling the layers with some of the buttercream. Frost the outside of the cake with the remaining buttercream. Chill the cake in the refrigerator for 2 hours. Gently brush vanilla syrup on the outside of the cake. Combine a few drops yellow food coloring with about ¼ cup water and some sugar. Sprinkle some of the resulting yellow sugar over the cake, then knead yellow sugar with almond paste. Roll out the almond paste into a thin sheet and drape it over the cake to mimic the polenta. Combine more almond paste with grated chocolate and shape that brown almond paste into a small bird and place the bird on top of the cake. If you are feeling ambitious, you can also make decorative green sage leaves and slices of white pancetta with additional almond paste.

CASSATA 🍴
Classic Sicilian Ricotta Cake
Pasticceria Alba, Palermo, Sicilia

A cassata is a cross between a trifle and a layer cake: it has the softness of the former, but cuts into slices like the latter. Drain your ricotta if it is excessively watery. A classic cassata mold is round with sides that slope gently outward.

SERVES 10 TO 12

CAKE
10 large eggs
2 cups sugar
2½ cups unbleached all-purpose flour or
      00 flour
1½ cups starch

RICOTTA FILLING
2 pounds sheep's milk ricotta
2 cups sugar
¼ teaspoon vanilla extract
1¾ cups dark chocolate chips

ALMOND PASTE
10 cups sugar
⅔ cup glucose syrup
10½ cups almond flour

FINISHING AND DECORATION
Fondant
Mixed chopped candied fruit
Confectioners' sugar
Lemon juice
Candied violets

Preheat the oven to 350°F. Line a round cake pan with parchment. To make the cake, beat the eggs with the sugar. Gradually add the flour and starch, beating to combine between additions. Beat in enough water to make a pourable batter, about ½ cup. Transfer to the prepared pan and bake until a tester emerges clean, about 40 minutes. Cool completely.

To make the filling, in a large bowl combine the ricotta, sugar, and vanilla. Stir to combine, then force through a fine sieve to make completely smooth. Fold in the chocolate chips.

For the almond paste, combine the sugar and glucose syrup in a saucepan with ½ cup water. Bring to a boil, then turn down to medium and gradually add the almond flour, whisking constantly, until you have a dense mixture that has reached a temperature of 115°F. Remove from the heat and set aside to cool for 2 hours. Roll out the almond paste to a little less than ½ inch thick and cut into strips, then cut the strips into rectangles about 1½ inches long. Set aside.

Line the bottom (which will be the top when inverted) of a mold with a disk of cake. (You may need to cut the cake horizontally as well as vertically.) Line the sides of the mold with rectangles of cake. Cover with a layer of almond paste rectangles. Continue alternating layers of cake and almond paste until you have used up both. Transfer the ricotta filling to the center of the mold and smooth the top with a spatula. Crumble any remaining cake and sprinkle the crumbs over the top of the filling. Overturn a serving platter on top of the mold, turn over both mold and platter, and place the trifle—still in the mold—and platter in the refrigerator. Chill for 2 hours.

To finish the trifle, gently lift off the mold. Cover the trifle with a single sheet of fondant and trim it. The fondant should be shiny, smooth, and even. Arrange the chopped candied fruit decoratively on the fondant. Make icing by dissolving confectioners' sugar in lemon juice, then transfer to a pastry bag and use to pipe decorations on the surface. Finally, arrange candied violets on the trifle.

❧{ TARTS & PIES }❧

TORTA DI TAGLIATELLE
Noodle Tart
Antica Trattoria Volano, Ferrara, Emília-Romagna

This short-crust tart filled with alternating layers of thin noodles and sugared almonds is made in the area south of Mantova.

SERVES 6 TO 8

DOUGH
- 10 tablespoons (1 stick plus 2 tablespoons) unsalted butter, softened and cut into pieces, plus more for buttering pan
- 2½ cups unbleached all-purpose flour, plus more for flouring pan
- 2 egg yolks
- ½ cup sugar
- 1 tablespoon Marsala wine

FILLING
- ¾ cup unbleached all-purpose flour or 00 flour
- 1 large egg
- ½ cup sugar
- ¾ cup toasted almonds, ground
- ½ cup bitter almond liqueur

Preheat the oven to 300°F. Butter and flour a pan and set aside. For the dough, shape the flour into a well on the work surface. Place the other ingredients in the center and form a dough, working the dough as little as possible. Roll out to fit the pan you wish to use and set the crust inside the pan.

For the filling, combine the flour and the egg and knead at length until you have a compact pasta dough. Roll out very thin (it helps to let the dough rest briefly) and cut into thin noodles. Combine the sugar and almonds (it's helpful to grind them together) and enough of the liqueur to make a spreadable paste. (Reserve remaining liqueur.) Spread a thin layer of the almond paste on the tart shell and top with a thin layer of the noodles. Continue making alternating layers of almond paste and noodles,

ending with the noodles on top. Bake in the preheated oven until golden, about 40 minutes. Drizzle on any remaining liqueur. Allow to cool completely before serving.

CROSTATA DI FICHI
Fresh Fig Tart
Ristorante Il Gatto & la Volpe, Formia (Latina), Lazio

This can be made with any of the types of figs that grow in Lazio: San Giovanni figs (which ripen in late June), Dottato figs (available in August), and September figs. Use any short crust you like for this tart, including the one in the previous recipe. Either serve this tart immediately or brush a little clear gelatin on top to keep it looking pretty as it sits.

SERVES 4
- 2 cups whole milk
- Zest of ½ lemon, in strips
- 4 egg yolks
- ¾ cup sugar
- ½ cup unbleached all-purpose flour
- ½ cup heavy cream or whipping cream
- 1 blind-baked short-crust tart crust
- 2 pounds fresh figs

Combine the milk and lemon zest in a saucepan and bring to a simmer. In a bowl, whisk the egg yolks with the sugar and flour. When the milk begins to bubble, remove and discard the lemon zest and pour the milk into the egg yolk mixture in a thin stream, whisking constantly. Whisk until combined, then return to the saucepan and cook, whisking constantly, over low heat until thickened. Let the mixture cool, and when it has, whip the cream to stiff peaks and fold into the mixture. Arrange the baked tart crust on a serving platter and spread the cream inside the crust. Peel, trim, and halve the figs and arrange decoratively on top.

PASTIERA 🥧
Ricotta and Wheat Berry Tart
Ristorante La Torre, Massa Lubrense (Napoli), Campania

P astiera, an Easter classic, is perhaps the most famous of the many desserts in the Napoli area. It dates back centuries and has emigrated all over the world with Italians from the area. In the United States, it is often labeled "grain pie." Sometimes Italian gourmet stores sell jars of the cooked wheat berries during the Easter season; if they are not available, simply boil wheat berries in a generous amount of water until tender, then drain and proceed. In place of the wheat berries, you can also use barley—soak overnight and then boil—or rice.

SERVES 6

DOUGH
14 tablespoons (1 stick plus 6 tablespoons) unsalted butter
1 cup sugar
2 large eggs
Grated zest of 1 lemon
4 cups unbleached all-purpose flour

PASTRY CREAM
1½ cups sugar
1 cup unbleached all-purpose flour
8 egg yolks
4 cups whole milk, scalded
Zest of 1 lemon, in strips

FILLING
1 cup whole milk
1 tablespoon unsalted butter
1 cinnamon stick
3 cups cooked wheat berries
2½ cups ricotta
2½ cups sugar
7 large eggs
3 egg yolks
Orange flower water to taste
¼ teaspoon vanilla extract
1¼ cups chopped candied fruit

For the dough, combine the butter and sugar. Beat in the eggs one at a time, then the lemon zest, and finally the flour. Shape into a ball, wrap in plastic, and refrigerate for 1 hour.

For the pastry cream, combine the sugar and flour in a heatproof bowl. Beat in the egg yolks, then whisk in the milk in a thin stream. Add the lemon zest. Cook over low heat, whisking constantly, until thickened. Remove and discard the lemon zest and set aside to cool. (If the pastry cream is lumpy, force through a strainer.)

For the filling, combine the milk, butter, cinnamon stick, and cooked wheat berries in a saucepan. Simmer gently until the wheat berries have absorbed the milk, then remove and discard the cinnamon stick and set the wheat berries aside to cool. Force the ricotta through a sieve, then combine with the sugar, eggs, egg yolks, orange flower water, vanilla, and pastry cream. Fold in the candied fruit and cooled wheat berries.

Preheat the oven to 350°F. Roll out about two thirds of the dough and use it to line a round pan. Pour the wheat berry mixture into the center and smooth with a spatula. Trim the borders of the crust, then roll out the remaining dough. Cut strips about ¾ inch wide with a serrated pastry cutter from the dough and use them to create a lattice top on the pie. Bake in the preheated oven until filling is set and crust is golden, about 40 minutes.

SPONGATA
Double-Crust Tart with Spiced Filling
Pasticceria Spagna, Monticelli d'Ongìna (Piacenza), Emìlia-Romagna

This recipe has been made in the area for centuries, but it is believed to be based on an ancient Jewish spice cake. Traditionally, the dough for *spongata* was formed in a wooden press that imprinted fruits and flowers onto the dough. The finished tart is rather flat, and the dough is wonderfully crisp.

SERVES 8 TO 10

FILLING
- ¾ cup honey
- ¾ cup sugar
- 1 cup dry white wine
- 1½ cups walnuts, chopped
- ¾ cup almonds, chopped
- ⅓ cup pine nuts
- 40 dry amaretto cookies, crushed
- 5 slices bread, toasted very dark and crumbled
- ¼ cup plus 1 tablespoon golden raisins, soaked and squeezed dry
- Freshly ground cloves to taste
- Freshly grated nutmeg to taste
- Ground cinnamon to taste
- Grated zest of 1 orange

DOUGH
- 4¾ cups unbleached all-purpose flour
- ¾ cup sugar, plus more for sprinkling
- 10 tablespoons (1 stick plus 2 tablespoons) unsalted butter, plus more for buttering pan
- 1 tablespoon olive oil
- Whole milk for softening dough
- Dry white wine for softening dough

Preheat the oven to 350°F. Butter a round pan and set aside. For the filling, place the honey in a saucepan and melt over low heat until very liquid. Stirring constantly, add the remaining ingredients. Cook until combined, then keep warm.

For the dough, mix the flour, ¾ cup sugar, 10 tablespoons butter, and oil to a shaggy dough. Add equal amounts milk and wine to make a tender dough and knead briefly. Divide the dough into two equal pieces. Roll out one piece of dough to a disk and use it to line the bottom and sides of the prepared pan. Pour the filling into the pan and smooth the top. Roll out the remaining dough to a disk and use it to cover the filling. Seal and crimp the edges of the two crusts, then bake in the preheated oven until golden. Allow to cool and sprinkle with a little sugar just before serving.

CROSTATA CON CREMA DI LIMONI
Procida Lemon Custard Tart
Trattoria Il Focolare, Isola d'Ischia (Napoli), Campania

Procida lemons are sweeter than standard lemons and have a very thick bumpy rind and a wide ring of pith that is edible and served as a salad. They are sometimes called "bread lemons." Procida is a tiny island in the Gulf of Napoli off the coast of Ischia that is home to about ten thousand people.

SERVES 6

DOUGH
- 2¾ cups unbleached all-purpose flour
- ¾ cup cornstarch
- 12 tablespoons (1½ sticks) unsalted butter, cut into pieces, plus more for buttering pan
- 1 large egg, lightly beaten
- 2 egg yolks, lightly beaten
- ¾ cup plus 2 tablespoons sugar

FILLING

- 6 egg yolks
- ½ cup sugar
- ⅓ cup unbleached all-purpose flour
- 2 cups whole milk
- Zest of 3 Procida lemons (see note)
- ½ cup heavy cream or whipping cream

Make the dough by combining the flour and cornstarch, then shaping them into a well on a work surface. Add the 12 tablespoons butter, egg, egg yolks, and sugar to the center of the well. Briefly knead until well combined, then shape into a ball, wrap in plastic, and refrigerate for 1 hour.

While the dough is chilling, for the filling, beat the egg yolks with the sugar and add the flour a little at a time, beating to combine between additions. In a saucepan combine the milk with the lemon zest. Bring to a boil, then strain out the zest and discard. Whisk in the egg yolk and sugar mixture and cook over medium heat, whisking constantly, until thickened. Set aside to cool. When the lemon mixture has cooled, whip the cream to soft peaks and fold it into the lemon mixture.

Preheat the oven to 300°F. Butter a pan and set aside. Roll out about two thirds of the dough and use it to line the pan. Transfer the lemon mixture to the pan and smooth the top. Roll out the remaining dough and use it to create a lattice top. Bake in the preheated oven until the crust is golden and filling is set, about 30 minutes.

TIMBALLO DI PERE MARTINE 🥧
Martin Sec Pear Tart in a Cornmeal Crust
Osteria dell'Arco, Alba (Cuneo), Piemonte

The secret to the success of this tart is that Martin Sec pears are very firm and give off little liquid as they cook. Dolcetto d'Alba is a dry red wine.

SERVES 6

- 2 cups Dolcetto d'Alba wine
- 1 cup sugar
- 8 Martin Sec pears (about 1 pound), peeled, cored, and quartered
- 8 whole cloves
- 8 tablespoons (1 stick) unsalted butter
- ¾ cup plus 2 tablespoons cornmeal
- ⅔ cup unbleached all-purpose flour or 00 flour
- 3 egg yolks

Combine the wine and ½ cup sugar in a saucepan and whisk to dissolve. Add the pears and the cloves. Bring to a boil, then simmer over medium heat until the pears are tender and easily pierced with the tip of a paring knife but hold their shape, about 1 hour. Set aside to cool.

Preheat the oven to moderate temperature (about 350°F). To make the crust, melt and cool 7 tablespoons butter. Butter a round or rectangular pan with the remaining tablespoon butter. Combine the cornmeal and flour and form into a well on the work surface. Place the egg yolks, remaining ½ cup sugar, and melted butter in the center and knead briskly into a dough. Roll out a little more than half of the dough to a rectangle or disk (depending on the shape of your pan) about ¼ inch thick. Line the buttered pan with the dough. Remove the cooked pears with a slotted spoon (discard the cloves) and place them on the crust. Roll out the remaining dough to make a top crust, put it in place, and seal the edges. Bake, increasing the heat gradually as the tart cooks, until golden, about 1 hour.

PITA 🍎
Apple Tart
Ristorante Bellavista, Ravascletto (Udine),
Friuli-Venezia Giulia

The name of this tart is local dialect for a full bag, presumably because this tart has a double crust.

SERVES 4 TO 6

DOUGH
- 1¾ cups unbleached all-purpose flour or 00 flour
- ¼ cup sugar
- 2 teaspoons baking powder
- 10 tablespoons (1 stick plus 2 tablespoons) unsalted butter, melted and cooled
- 1 tablespoon heavy cream or whipping cream
- 2 tablespoons rum

FILLING
- 6 apples, peeled, cored, and thinly sliced
- ⅓ cup sugar
- ½ cup walnuts, chopped
- ¼ cup plus 1 tablespoon golden raisins
- 1 pinch ground cinnamon
- Grated zest of 1 lemon
- Butter for buttering pan

For the dough, on a work surface shape the flour into a well and place the sugar, baking powder, melted butter, cream, and rum in the center. Knead into a soft dough, shape into a ball, cover with a dish towel, and set aside to rest for 30 minutes.

For the filling, combine the apples with the sugar, walnuts, raisins, cinnamon, and lemon zest and stir to combine. Preheat the oven to 350°F. Butter an 8-inch pan and set aside. Divide the dough into two equal parts and roll into thin disks. Use one disk to line the prepared pan. Transfer the filling to the pan and smooth it evenly. Cover with the second disk of dough and seal the edges. Bake in the preheated oven until golden, about 50 minutes.

CROSTATA DEL DIAVOLO 🎃
Orange Marmalade Tart with Spicy Pepper Preserves
Ristorante Sabbia d'Oro, Belvedere Marittimo (Cosenza), Calabria

Make your own pepper preserves: seed 2 pounds red chili peppers and strip out any white filaments. Seed 4 pounds bell peppers. Dice both types of peppers. Toss the peppers with 2½ cups sugar and let sit at room temperature for 4 to 5 hours. Transfer the peppers and sugar to a saucepan, add water to cover, and cook over low heat for 1 hour and 30 minutes. Add another 2½ cups sugar and 3 tablespoons honey and cook for an additional 2 hours.

SERVES 6 TO 8
- 6 tablespoons unsalted butter, plus more for buttering pan
- ¾ cup sugar
- 2 egg yolks
- 1 egg
- Grated zest of 1 lemon
- 2½ cups unbleached all-purpose flour
- ½ cup orange marmalade
- ¼ cup plus 1 tablespoon pepper preserves
- ¾ cup blanched almonds, ground

Preheat the oven to 350°F. Beat the 6 tablespoons butter and sugar together. Beat in the egg yolks, egg, and lemon zest. Add the flour a little at a time, beating to combine between additions, and beat until you have a smooth and well combined dough. Butter a pan. Roll out about two thirds of the dough and use it to line the pan. Spread the marmalade and the preserves on the crust (in separate layers). Sprinkle on the ground almonds, then roll out the remaining dough, cut into strips, and make a lattice top. Bake in the preheated oven until the crust is golden, about 40 minutes.

ZONCLADA
Traditional Ricotta Tart with Nuts and Cinnamon
Ristorante Il Tirante, Monastier di Treviso (Treviso), Veneto

This ancient tart has a long list of ingredients, but the techniques required to make it are not complicated. In the Treviso area, it dates back to the Middle Ages, and at one time contests were held to determine which of the pastry chefs in the province produced the best version. The municipality of Treviso even established a specific weight and cooking time for *zonclada* and forbade the use of anything but whole milk. Some (presumably permissible) versions include dried apricots and figs. Adele Visentin of Treviso makes a slightly lighter version that omits the nuts and dried fruit in the filling. She sprinkles walnuts on top and then makes a lattice crust and brushes it with a little beaten egg yolk before baking the tart.

SERVES 10

DOUGH
- 9 tablespoons (1 stick plus 1 tablespoon) unsalted butter, plus more for buttering pan
- ¼ cup plus 2 tablespoons sugar
- 1 large egg
- 2 egg yolks
- 1¾ cups unbleached all-purpose flour or 00 flour
- 1 teaspoon honey
- Grated zest of 1 lemon
- 1 pinch salt

FILLING
- 2 large eggs, separated, plus 1 egg yolk
- 1 cup (about 9 ounces) ricotta
- ¾ cup sugar
- 1 pinch ground cinnamon
- Grated zest of 1 lemon
- ½ cup plus 2 tablespoons chopped candied fruit
- ⅓ cup pine nuts
- ¾ cup almonds
- ¾ cup walnuts
- ½ cup plus 2 tablespoons black raisins, soaked in grappa and drained

FINISHING
- 10 amaretto cookies, crushed
- ⅓ cup almonds, ground

Make a dough by mixing together the 9 tablespoons butter, sugar, egg, egg yolks, flour, honey, lemon zest, and salt. Try not to overwork the dough. Shape into a ball, wrap in plastic, and set aside to rest for about 30 minutes.

Meanwhile, for the filling whip the egg whites to stiff peaks. In a bowl, combine the ricotta, sugar, 3 egg yolks, cinnamon, and grated lemon zest. Fold in the whipped egg whites, candied fruit, pine nuts, almonds, walnuts, and raisins.

Preheat the oven to 300°F. Butter a springform pan. Roll out the dough and use it to line the pan. Pour in the filling and smooth the top with a spatula, then sprinkle on the crushed amaretto cookies and ground almonds. Bake until the filling is set and crust is golden, about 40 minutes.

ELVEZIA ▦
Almond Meringue Zabaione Torte
Panificio Freddi, Mantova, Lombardia

Layers of zabaione alternate with almond meringue disks in this elegant torte.

SERVES 6 TO 8

MERINGUES
1¾ cups blanched almonds
8 egg whites
1¼ cups sugar

FILLING
4 egg yolks
¼ cup sugar
2 tablespoons Marsala
18 tablespoons (2 sticks plus 2 tablespoons) unsalted butter, softened
Dark chocolate shavings for sprinkling (optional)

Preheat the oven to 400°F. For the meringues, grind the almonds very fine. Combine the egg whites and sugar and beat to stiff peaks. Set aside 2 to 3 tablespoons ground almonds and fold the rest into the egg whites. Transfer to a pastry bag. Line baking sheets with parchment and pipe three disks of concentric circles of the same size. Bake in the preheated oven until crisp and starting to turn golden, about 20 minutes. Let cool.

For the filling, make a zabaione by whisking the yolks, ¼ cup sugar, and Marsala in the top of a double boiler until thickened. Set aside to cool. Whip the butter until fluffy.

To assemble the torte, place one disk on a serving platter. Spread about half of the butter on the disk, and then spread about half of the zabaione on top. Sprinkle on a thin layer of chocolate shavings, if using. Smooth the top and top with a second disk. Spread with the remaining butter, zabaione, and more chocolate shavings, if using. Top with the third disk. Smooth the outside of the cake with an offset spatula, then press the reserved almonds against the sides.

TORTA SBRISOLONA ❗
Crisp Almond Tart
Hostaria Viola, Fontane di Castiglione delle Stiviere (Mantova), Veneto

This pleasantly sandy tart can't be cut into neat slices. Instead, it is served in attractively craggy shards. Accompany with grappa for dipping. You can sprinkle the pieces with a little confectioners' sugar if you like. Don't grind the almonds—they should be in large pieces.

MAKES THREE 11- OR 12-INCH TARTS

4 cups unbleached all-purpose flour or 00 flour
3 cups finely ground cornmeal
2½ cups sugar
¼ teaspoon vanilla extract
1 pinch salt
2 large eggs
4 egg yolks
21 tablespoons (2 sticks plus 5 tablespoons) unsalted butter, softened and cut into pieces, plus more for buttering pans
1 cup lard, cut into pieces
¾ cup almonds, roughly chopped

In a large bowl, combine the flour, cornmeal, sugar, vanilla, and salt and mix with a wooden spoon. Incorporate the eggs and yolks, the 21 tablespoons butter, and the lard. Stir in the almonds.

Mix by hand just until the ingredients are combined and the mixture has the texture of coarse meal. Set aside to rest in a cool place for 30 minutes.

Preheat the oven to 325°F. Butter three 11- or 12-inch-diameter pans with low sides. Drop clumps of the dough into the pans by hand, dividing it into equal amounts and taking care to cover the surfaces of the pans evenly and not leave any holes. The dough should fill the pans about ¾ inch high. Bake in the preheated oven until crisp and golden, 35 to 40 minutes. Cool before serving.

CROSTATA DI PESCE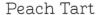
Peach Tart
Ristorante Locanda Alpina, Chiusa di Pesio
(Cuneo), Piemonte

The easiest way to peel peaches is to cut a small x in the base of each, drop them briefly into boiling water, then remove them with a slotted spoon. The peels should lift right off. Don't slice the fruit paper-thin.

SERVES 8 TO 10

1 cup skinned hazelnuts, ground
1 cup unbleached all-purpose flour
¾ cup sugar
10 tablespoons (1 stick plus 2 tablespoons) unsalted butter, softened
2 to 3 tablespoons unsweetened cocoa powder
Ground cinnamon to taste
6 to 8 peaches, peeled, pitted, and sliced

Preheat the oven to 350°F. For the dough, combine the ground hazelnuts, flour, and sugar. Work in the butter. Add the cocoa powder and a pinch of cinnamon and combine thoroughly. Form into a ball, wrap in plastic, and set aside to rest in a cool place for 1 hour.

Preheat the oven to 350°F. Roll out the dough and place it in a pan. Arrange the peach slices in concentric circles on the dough. Bake in the preheated oven for 20 minutes. Allow to cool to room temperature before serving.

'MPANATIGGHIA
Sweet Meat Pies
Dolceria Bonajuto, Modica (Ragusa), Sicilia

A dessert pie that incorporates ground beef is unusual, to say the least. The origins of this pie from the Modica area are most likely Arab, though the name derives from the Spanish word *empanadilla*, and these do indeed resemble small empanadas.

SERVES 6 TO 8

FILLING
1 beef fillet, finely ground
4¼ cups blanched almonds, toasted and ground
5 cups sugar
1 tablespoon honey
1 cup unsweetened cocoa powder
4 ounces dark chocolate from Modica, chopped (about 1⅔ cups)
4 large eggs, separated
Ground cinnamon to taste
Ground cloves to taste
3 egg whites

DOUGH
⅔ cup lard or 8 tablespoons (1 stick) unsalted butter
2½ cups unbleached all-purpose flour or 00 flour
5 egg yolks, lightly beaten
1 teaspoon baking soda

For the filling, place the beef in a saucepan and cook over low heat until it has given up all of its liquid and is dry and cooked through. Combine the beef with the almonds, sugar, honey, cocoa powder, chocolate, 4 egg yolks, cinnamon, and cloves. Add the 7 egg whites. The filling should be moist. Cover and refrigerate for 24 hours.

To make the dough, cut the lard into the flour until it resembles coarse meal. Mix in the egg yolks and the baking soda. Add cold water 1 tablespoon at a time until the mixture forms a soft dough. (Do not overwork the dough—it's fine if there are still streaks of lard in it.) Shape the dough into a ball, wrap in plastic, and set aside to rest at a cool room temperature for 2 to 3 hours.

When you are ready to bake the pies, preheat the oven to 425°F. Roll out the dough and cut into disks or ovals about 4¾ inches in diameter. (Reroll and cut scraps.) Divide the filling evenly among the pieces of dough. Fold each piece of dough in half to form a semicircle and seal the edges. Cut a slash in the top of each pie. Bake in the preheated oven until golden, about 20 minutes.

TORTA CO' BECCHI 🌳
Sweet Spinach Pie
Ristorante Mecenate, Gattaiola di Lucca (Lucca), Toscana

This savory-sweet pie from the Lucca area with a lovely decorative border can be made more savory with a little pepper, or its sweetness can be highlighted with cinnamon, nutmeg, pine nuts, and candied fruit. This recipe comes from the restaurant owner's mother, Maria Antonietta, who learned it in the tiny village of Coselli, where she was relocated during the war. When purchasing or picking the greens for this tart, keep in mind that they will cook down drastically. Maria Antonietta measures by the fistful when squeezing and uses 2 fistfuls of cooked chard and 1 of field greens.

SERVES 8 TO 10

DOUGH
- 1¾ cups unbleached all-purpose flour, plus more for flouring pan
- 9 tablespoons (1 stick plus 1 tablespoon) unsalted butter, softened and cut into pieces, plus more for flouring pan
- 2 large eggs, lightly beaten
- 2 egg yolks
- ⅓ cup sugar
- 1 pinch salt
- Whole milk for moistening dough, if needed

FILLING
- 4 large eggs
- ½ cup blanched, squeezed, and chopped chard
- ¼ cup blanched, squeezed, and chopped field greens or spinach
- Leaves of 1 sprig parsley, minced
- 2 slices bread soaked in milk to soften, squeezed dry, and crumbled
- ½ cup plus 2 tablespoons black raisins
- ¼ cup pine nuts
- ½ cup grated aged sheep's cheese
- ½ cup grated Parmigiano Reggiano
- 1 pinch freshly ground black pepper

To make the dough, shape the 1¾ cups flour into a well on the work surface and place the 9 tablespoons butter and the remaining ingredients in the well. Knead quickly into a dough, adding a few drops of milk if the dough feels dry. Shape into a ball, wrap in plastic, and set aside to rest in a cool, dry place for 30 minutes.

When you are ready to bake the pie, preheat the oven to 350°F. Butter and flour a pan and set aside.

For the filling, beat the eggs in a bowl, then mix in the remaining ingredients.

Roll out the dough to a disk that will cover the bottom and sides of the pan and overhang a bit. Place it in the prepared pan. Pour the filling into the center and smooth with a spatula. To create the rim, make diagonal cuts in the folded dough about 1 inch apart and fold over each section as you go to create a chain of diamonds around the rim. (If you have leftover dough, you can use it to make lattice strips on the top.) Bake in the preheated oven until the filling is set and the crust is golden, about 55 minutes.

TORRONE ALLA VANIGLIA
Vanilla Nougat
Pasticceria Lanfranchi, Cremona, Lombardia

You can vary the number of egg whites you use to make a stiffer or softer nougat. If you want to use pistachios and are making a softer version, boil the pistachios so they will be soft as well. Leave yourself plenty of time to make this—the sugar and the honey have to cook over low heat, and you need to pay close attention and remove them from the heat at just the right time.

SERVES 6 TO 8
5 to 7 egg whites
Wafers or wafer paper to line molds
     (see page 442)
1½ cups honey
2½ cups sugar
Vanilla extract to taste
3½ pounds sweet almonds, shelled and
     blanched
½   cup pistachios (optional)

Beat the egg whites to stiff peaks. Line pans or molds with wafers. Place the honey in the top of a copper double boiler and heat until all the water has evaporated. Gradually fold beaten egg whites into the honey. Cook the sugar into a caramel and stir it into the honey mixture. Stir in the vanilla extract. Stir with a spatula until well combined, then remove from the heat and stir in the almonds and the pistachios, if using. When the mixture is well combined, transfer it to the lined pans or molds. Let the nougat set for at least 30 minutes before unmolding.

GIUGGIULENA
Sesame Candies
Pasticceria Corsino, Palazzolo Acreide
(Siracusa), Sicilia

This candy is a type of nougat sometimes called *cubbàita*. It is found throughout Sicilia and is sometimes cut into diamonds rather than rectangles.

MAKES ABOUT 6
DOZEN PIECES
2   cups sugar
1¼ cups thyme honey
6⅔ cups (about 2 pounds) sesame seeds
3½ cups almonds, toasted and chopped
Zest of 1 orange, minced
1   pinch ground cinnamon

Combine the sugar and honey in a copper pot and place over medium heat. Stir in the sesame seeds, the almonds, orange zest, and cinnamon and cook, stirring, for a few minutes. Pour onto a damp marble work surface and spread into a long rectangle a little less than ½ inch thick. Slice while still warm and allow to cool completely.

CROCCANTE
Hazelnut Brittle
Rosanna Dotta, Novello (Cuneo), Piemonte

Toast and skin about 1⅔ cups hazelnuts. Cut the hazelnuts in half. Melt 1 cup sugar in a copper pot over low heat to make a light caramel. Add the hazelnuts and stir energetically with a wooden spatula over low heat until the hazelnuts are completely coated. Pour the mixture onto an oiled work surface and use an offset spatula to spread it as thinly as possible. Allow to cool for a few minutes, then cut into pieces while still warm. Cool completely and transfer to a tightly sealed glass container, where the candy will keep for a long time.

GATTÒ
Little Nut Candies
Ristorante Paolo Perella, Villasalto (Cagliari), Sardegna

These candies are made using a clever technique—lemons as rolling pins. They softly scent the candy. You can also make these with shelled and peeled hazelnuts or pistachios in place of the almonds. Traditionally, each piece of candy is served on a fresh bay leaf or a lemon leaf, which further impregnates them with a pleasant aroma.

SERVES 10
2½ cups sugar
2 tablespoons honey
4½ cups slivered almonds
2 tablespoons grappa or anise liqueur (optional)
1 tablespoon extra-virgin olive oil
2 to 3 lemons

In a pot, melt the sugar over low heat to make a caramel. Add the honey, almonds, and grappa, if using. Stir until well combined. Brush a marble work surface with the olive oil. Use the lemons, pressing forcefully and rolling them like rolling pins, to spread the caramel mixture to a thickness of a little less than ¼ inch. Allow to cool slightly and cut into diamonds or squares with a sharp knife. Allow to cool completely.

PRALINE DI CASTAGNE
Chestnut Pralines
Ristorante Il Moderno, San Martino al Cimino di Viterbo, Lazio

Originally, the term *praline* referred to a toasted almond covered in caramelized sugar, but the word has expanded to include all sorts of confections. These are a lovely treat at the end of a meal.

SERVES 6 TO 8
2 pounds chestnuts, shelled
6 cups whole milk
1 cup sugar
¼ teaspoon vanilla extract
2 tablespoons rum
7 ounces dark chocolate, chopped (about 1⅔ cups)
2 to 3 tablespoons chestnut flour, if needed
Chopped hazelnuts for decoration

Cook the chestnuts in the milk until tender, then drain. Skin the cooked chestnuts and crush them with a potato masher. Transfer the puree to a bowl and combine with the sugar, vanilla, and rum. Fold in the chocolate. If the mixture seems too soft, add chestnut flour a little at a time until you can roll the mixture into a ball. Pinch off small amounts of the mixture, shape into balls, then roll the balls in chopped hazelnuts to coat.

TARTUFI DI CIOCCOLATO
Chocolate Truffles
Francesca Ronco, Dusino San Michele (Asti), Piemonte

Piemonte is known for fine chocolate confections, many of which feature the justly famous local coffee and hazelnuts. Beat 10 tablespoons (1 stick plus 2 tablespoons) unsalted butter with ¼ cup sugar until light and fluffy, then with a wooden spoon stir in 9 ounces melted dark chocolate (the highest quality you can find, obviously) and 1 teaspoon espresso and a tablespoon or two of water if the mixture is stiff. Stir in 2 beaten egg yolks until no streaks remain. Refrigerate the mixture until firm, at least 30 minutes. Form the mixture into small balls and roll them in chopped hazelnuts. You can also roll them in grated chocolate and/or cocoa powder.

SALAME DEL PAPA ❧
Chocolate Salami "Fit for a Pope"
Osteria La Torre, Cherasco (Cuneo), Piemonte

This is a home-style classic in the Langhe area of Piemonte, where a slice or two is often served to guests along with a small glass of dry Marsala. The name was meant to indicate that it was even better than the snacks usually served to the priests who visited a home. You can substitute liqueur for the rum if you like—orange liqueur is particularly nice. Digestive biscuits work nicely for the dipped and crumbled cookies.

SERVES 10

- ½ cup espresso
- 2 tablespoons Marsala wine
- 2 tablespoons rum
- 1 pound dry plain cookies
- 1⅔ cups hazelnuts, toasted and chopped
- 23 tablespoons (2 sticks plus 7 tablespoons) unsalted butter, softened
- 1¼ cups sugar
- 2 large eggs, lightly beaten
- 3⅔ cups unsweetened cocoa powder

Mix the espresso with the Marsala and rum and dip half of the cookies in the mixture. Crush the other half of the cookies. Grind the chopped hazelnuts in a mortar and pestle. Beat the butter with the sugar. Add the eggs, cocoa powder, hazelnuts, dipped cookies, and crumbled cookies. Stir until well combined. Place the mixture on a piece of parchment paper and shape into a long log like a salami. (You can make smaller salamis if you like and make more than one.) Wrap in the parchment and refrigerate for at least 12 hours before serving.

PASTA REALE ❗
Almond Paste for Cookies and Pastries
Filomena Piazza, Palermo, Sicilia

Sicilia is famous for incredibly lifelike fruits, vegetables, and other items sculpted from almond paste. To make your own, combine 1½ cups water and 4 cups sugar in a pot and place over very low heat. Cook, stirring frequently, until the sugar has dissolved and the mixture forms a syrup, meaning that when you lift the spoon out of the pot and let the syrup drip off of it, it forms a string. Stir in 8⅓ cups almond flour, ¾ cup Maiorca wheat flour (an ancient strain from Sicilia), and ¼ teaspoon vanilla extract and cook, stirring, until the mixture cleans the sides of the pot. Pour the mixture onto a marble work surface and let it cool. When it has cooled, knead by hand until compact and smooth. Once the paste is ready, you can use molds to shape it as you like. Typically, these sculptures are then decorated with food coloring and made shiny with an application of gum arabic.

POMPÌA INTREA 🏺
Candied Pompia Peel
Panificio Francesca Pau, Siniscola (Nuoro), Sardegna

Pompia is a citrus fruit native to Sardegna that has grown wild on the island for at least two centuries. It looks like a cross between a grapefruit and a pumpkin, as its very bumpy rind is divided into ribs. The fruit is dry and acidic, but the peel of pompia is frequently candied and is used in some other sweet preparations as well. Make a hole at the top of each of 6 pompia fruit and remove the fruit sections through the hole, taking care not to break the skin. Blanch the peels for 5 minutes. Drain and dry the peels on a dish towel with the holes facing downward. Make a sugar syrup in a large pot (for 6 pompia, use about

5 cups sugar and 6 cups water). Add the peels with the holes facing up. Cook at a brisk simmer for 3 hours, turning them occasionally. Add ¾ cup honey and cook for an additional 3 hours. The pompia peels should be soft and golden; take care that they do not burn. While the peels are still hot, remove with a slotted spoon and transfer to a glass jar. Pour the cooking liquid, which should be thick, over the peels. Seal tightly and store in a cool, dark place for up to 1½ years.

LIBRETTO DI FICHI SECCHI ◉
Pressed Dried Figs with Chocolate and Almonds
Osteria del Priore, Mosciano Sant'Angelo
(Teramo), Abruzzo

This traditional Christmas dish is made in November and should last until March if stored in a cool, dry place. You will need a wooden or iron press. Sprinkle the inside of the press with flour and place sun-dried white figs that have been cut in half, cut sides up, in it. Make a mixture of sugar, grated dark chocolate, finely chopped raw almonds, grated orange zest, grated lemon zest, and ground cinnamon. You can also include a few drops of vanilla extract. Sprinkle a layer of toasted slivered almonds on top of the figs. Top that with a layer of slices of candied citron. Top that with chopped dark chocolate, and a layer of the sugar mixture you prepared previously. Repeat layers, ending with a layer of figs on top. Firmly screw down the top of the press so that the ingredients are all pressed together and leave for several hours. Remove the pressed figs from the press, sprinkle with a little flour, and wrap in waxed paper. Let rest for at least 20 days before serving.

PANICIELLI 🌿
Zibibbo Grapes Baked in Citron Leaves
Ristorante La Rondinella, Scalea (Cosenza), Calabria

Harvest zibibbo grapes just before they are fully ripe and dry them in the sun. Cover the surface of citron leaves with the dried grapes and fold into little packets. Sometimes the packets are tied with stalks of esparto grass, a plant that is harvested in May. Bake for about 10 minutes, then serve. When you open the leaves, you will find that the grapes have absorbed the taste and scent of the citron leaves. You can use this same technique with other small green grapes.

COTOGNATA 🏺
Quince Paste
Rosella Donato, Imperia, Liguria

Quince paste is enjoyed in Puglia, in Abruzzo (where it is flavored with lemon juice and zest), in the Veneto (where it is made with ground cloves and cinnamon), and elsewhere in Italy. Peel, core, and dice quince, then boil in a pot with a small amount of water and lemon juice. As soon as the quince are soft, before they begin to fall apart, remove from the heat and puree with a food mill. Set aside to cool. Weigh the puree. In a pot, cook the cooled puree over low heat, stirring in 2 cups sugar for every 1 pound puree. Bring to a boil, then cook for 30 minutes, stirring frequently to keep it from sticking. When it is very thick and no longer sticks to the surface of the pot, it is ready. Transfer to ceramic molds or spread ¾ inch thick on a large platter. Allow to dry at room temperature in a cool (not cold or hot) and well-ventilated place. Cut into lozenges and toss the pieces in confectioners' sugar. For long-term storage, layer between wax paper in glass jars, ceramic jars, or wooden boxes.

GENERAL INDEX to the RECIPES

CONVERSION CHARTS

All conversions are approximate.

Liquid Conversions

U.S.	Metric
1 tsp	5 ml
1 tbs	15 ml
2 tbs	30 ml
3 tbs	45 ml
¼ cup	60 ml
⅓ cup	75 ml
⅓ cup + 1 tbs	90 ml
⅓ cup + 2 tbs	100 ml
½ cup	120 ml
⅔ cup	150 ml
¾ cup	180 ml
¾ cup + 2 tbs	200 ml
1 cup	240 ml
1 cup + 2 tbs	275 ml
1¼ cups	300 ml
1⅓ cups	325 ml
1½ cups	350 ml
1⅔ cups	375 ml
1¾ cups	400 ml
1¾ cups + 2 tbs	450 ml
2 cups (1 pint)	475 ml
2½ cups	600 ml
3 cups	720 ml
4 cups (1 quart)	945 ml (1,000 ml is 1 liter)

Weight Conversions

U.S./U.K.	Metric
½ oz	14 g
1 oz	28 g
1 ½ oz	43 g
2 oz	57 g
2 ½ oz	71 g
3 oz	85 g
3 ½ oz	100 g
4 oz	113 g
5 oz	142 g
6 oz	170 g
7 oz	200 g
8 oz	227 g
9 oz	255 g
10 oz	284 g
11 oz	312 g
12 oz	340 g
13 oz	368 g
14 oz	400 g
15 oz	425 g
1 lb	454 g

Oven Temperatures

°F	Gas Mark	°C
250	½	120
275	1	140
300	2	150
325	3	165
350	4	180
375	5	190
400	6	200
425	7	220
450	8	230
475	9	240
500	10	260
550	Broil	290

Originally published in the Italian language as
Le ricette di Osterie d'Italia
Copyright © 2011 Slow Food Editore S.r.l.
via Audisio, 5 - 12042 Bra (Cn) Italy
Phone: + 39 0172 419611
Fax + 39 0172 411218
editorinfo@slowfood.it – http://slowfoodeditore.it

First published in the United States of America in
2017 by Rizzoli International Publications, Inc.
300 Park Avenue South
New York, NY 10010
www.rizzoliusa.com

© 2017 Rizzoli Publications, Inc.

For the original Italian-language edition:
Curators: Bianca Minerdo, Grazia Novellini
Editorial department: Elisa Azzimondi,
Angelo Surrusca

We wish to thank Michela Bunino, Silvia Tropea
Montagnosi, Cecilia Toso, and Luisella Verderi.

For the English-language edition:
Translator: Natalie Danford
Designers: de Vicq Design
Typesetter: Nancy Leonard
Senior editor: Christopher Steighner
Project editor: Sarah Scheffel
Coordinating editor: Jennifer Duardo

2017 2018 2019 2020 / 10 9 8 7 6 5 4 3 2 1

Distributed in the U.S. trade by Random House,
New York

Printed in China

ISBN: 978-0-8478-5998-6

Library of Congress Catalog Control Number:
2017936723

ITALY